中國思想下的
全球化選法規則

陳隆修◆著

獻詞

謹以本書獻給

——查良鑑教授

中國思想下的全球化選法規則
Globalization of Choice of Laws Rules Based on Chinese Philosophy

　　於2009年在台北舉辦的第5屆兩岸國際私法研討會中，趙相林教授及黃進教授倡議兩岸應發展具有中華文化特色的國際私法。後2010年黃進教授與個人於台中共同認為我們民族綿延兩千多年的「王道」精神（the way of heavenly beneficence）或許應為中國式法學之核心基礎思想。中國傳統上兩千多年來的「王道」哲學、「禮運大同」思想、及「不患寡患不均」的至高政策，是與現代聯合國1948人權宣言、1992 Rio宣言、及2002 Johannesburg宣言之理想是一致的，故而21世紀的全球化法學自然應順理成章的以中國「王道」思想及聯合國上述宣言為共同核心之基礎——而這或許亦是黃進教授所主張的「中國法學革命」（Chinese legal revolution）之特色。

　　在*Erie Railroad v. Tompkins*, 304 U.S. 64(1938)中，美國最高法院禁止聯邦法院於依憲法應以州法為依據之範圍內，去適用或創造聯邦判例法。但其仍舊於管轄規則及選法規則上先後創造及適用一個於各州管轄規則及選法規則上最低限度之標準。先前美國最高法院因為沒有正視英國母法對送達境外視為「過度、例外」（見陳隆修，《國際私法管轄權評論》，台北，五南圖書公司，民國75年11月，初版，45～47頁。）之法理，故而對所引發之情形，個人認為minimum contacts於管轄規則上在美國已造成「最大程度之混亂」（minimum contacts cause maximum chaos）；於選法規則上因為忽視所牽連的

實體政策，故構成「最大程度之欺騙」（minimum contacts constitute maximum deception）。

羅馬II的要點14自稱引用最密切關連標準為規避條款，即能同時達成穩定性與個案正義之目標。最重要關連的質與量之間的爭議，是長久以來沒有被完全釐清的基本哲學性問題。在可預見的未來，只要羅馬II大量的使用最密切關連作為規避法則，至少於短期內其自己吹噓的穩定性即不可能達成。於目前的階段，各國還是應將選法規則的重點放於個案正義的追求，只有各國於實質上對個案正義的結果有著大致上同樣的看法時，法律的一致性與穩定性才會真正達成。美國法律協會1994 Complex Litigation Proposal雖未被正式採納通過，但其對「假衝突」的公開引用，卻是美國司法界及學界之共識。由年輕至今個人已分析過甚多之實際案例，一昧仰賴區域選法規則而迴避實質政策分析是無法充份保障個案正義的——這亦是於選法規則上美國可敬的前輩同僚們百多年來留給人類子孫的共同文化遺產。無論台灣、大陸、或歐盟，如果鑑於法院無法一時完全適應於實體政策之分析，個人建議應如美國目前於實務及學理上一般——必須在於確認所牽連之國家之相關法律於實體政策上有重大衝突後，才可適用法院地之選法規則；而最重要關連標準之適用亦必須加入實體政策之衡量。（一如美國第二新編的第六條）。

羅馬公約及規則I於第4條及許多其他條文所採的固定模式之程序首先為推定規則（包括特別及一般推定），在其次以最重要關連為規避法規（或於無法推定時適用），最後則為所牽連的強行法規（羅馬I為法院地、案件事實唯一發生地、及履行地強行法）。這三個步驟中之每一個所牽連的法學概念無

一不是國際私法之爭議風暴中心。第一階段所謂特別推定及一般推定（即特徵性履行之規定），即為英國客觀說長久以來的爭議點或甚至已為判例法所拒絕，尤其是近來大陸法的特徵性履行更是為英美法界普遍所懷疑的概念。而第2階段的最重要關連更是自Westlake主張"the most real connection"以來已經歷超過一百五十年的爭議。美國第2新編一面倒全力使用這概念只是使得池水更加混濁而已，沒有任何有理智的人會說美國選法規則很「平靜」。至於第3階段的強行法概念更是英美法所沒有，而於大陸法之國內法亦為屢有爭議之概念。它的爭議性延續至國際法上自然更加不可控制，羅馬公約7(1)條之經驗即為鐵證。羅馬公約及規則將這三個非常無法控制的概念混在一起使用，而自吹自擂認為可以達到判決的可預測性及法律適用的穩定性，任何有常識的人都會對此加以懷疑。

羅馬II的要點7規定其範圍與條文需與Brussel I及羅馬公約一致，羅馬 I 與II之方法論亦皆大致上相似。皆以某些地域關連點未規劃一些籠統的區域選法規則，而區域性選法規則的阿奇里斯腳踝（heel of Achilles）即在於被地域性關連點所指定國家之法律若於實體上是落後之法律，則自然容易會造成「武斷或基本上不公平之後果」。為了確保個案正義，羅馬 I 與II不得不仰賴以實體政策為基礎的21世紀鬼見愁法學——強行法。

如同恩師Prof. Hartley所說："Law is made for man, not man for the law." 21世紀全球化法學的心與靈魂是在個案正義。誠信原則早於希臘時期已存在，Cicero於公元前則更已對其立下可為今日楷模之定義。CISG (1980) 7(2)條有關公約所未規定之問題，應以其引以為基礎的一般原則為依據之規定，為2004

UNIDROIT Principles的1.6條及歐盟契約法原則1：106條所採納，而U.C.C的s.1-102(1)亦規定該商法應於促進其基本目的及政策下而被解釋及適用，故而個人認為這個規則應是世界契約法全球化之共同核心理念。而CISG的7(1)條又規定「誠信原則」於國際貿易中必須被遵守，相同的規定亦被明示於2004 UNIDROIT Principles之1.7條、歐盟契約法原則1：106條、及美國U.C.C 1-304條。歐盟契約法原則1：201條亦規定誠信原則應被遵守及不可加以限制，其解釋報告A說：「本條文規定一個貫穿本契約法原則的基本原則。」故而以大陸法主觀之誠信原則，做為全球化實體契約法上「引為基礎的一般原則」之共同核心概念，個人以為應該有相當之依據。而相對的客觀上之合理性之標準，不但為英美法於判例法上所常用之標準，亦為2004 UNIDROIT Principles及歐盟契約法原則所遠較誠信原則所更為被大量引用之標準。一般亦經常以客觀之合理性來解釋主觀誠信原則之規定。故而相較於大陸法之誠信原則，判例法之合理性標準無論是於被引用之數量及品質上亦或許應為契約法之共同核心。亦即誠信原則及合理性標準不但應為全球化實體契約法（包含國際契約法及國際私法）上「引為基礎之一般原則」，亦應為全球化實體契約法（包含國際契約法及國際私法）上之警察原則，以對抗實體法及程序法上之可能於個案上之不公平正義。

誠信原則與合理性之標準既然是數千年來人類文明及法律科學的最核心主流價值，自然是21世紀人類國內法及國際私法黑死病——公序良俗、強行法及合理性——的最佳救贖。誠信原則與合理性事實上數千年來亦一直都是包括民法、刑法、訴訟法、親屬法、繼承法、憲法、人權法、國際公法、國際私

法在內，所有法學「引為基礎之一般原則」及「警察原則」。Cardozo說「法學上的概念應受制於自我設限的常識及公平原則的限制」，故恩師Prof. Graveson說「英國國際私法實現正義的概括性目的給予邏輯一致性的政策必要的限制」。這或許就是古老的誠信原則與合理性的現代式說法，更亦就是二千多年來中國文化「人法地，地法天，天法道，道法自然」的自然天道。

在International Shoe Co. v. Washington, 326 U.S. 310, 326中，Black J.引用Holmes J.的話來表達其對自然法概念（natural justice）的適用之可能侵害到州或聯邦立法的憂慮：'I have not yet adequately expressed the more than anxiety that I feel at the ever increasing scope given to the Fourteenth Amendment in cutting down what I believe to be the constitutional rights of the States. As the, decisions now stand, I see hardly any limit but the sky to the invalidating of those rights if they happen to strike a majority of this Court as for any reason undesirable.' Baldwin v. Missouri, 281 U.S. 586, 595, 50 S.Ct. 436, 439, 72 A.L.R. 1303. 但是個人必須認為於追求中國思想下的全球化法學（legal globalization based on Chinese Philosophy）之過程中，或許天空不但不是界限，於某種程度上它可能跨越了時空，而使得二千多年來的「王道」與「禮運大同」哲學與21世紀的全球化法學結合。人是上帝的作品，而法律是人的作品，以人的作品企圖去解決上帝作品所產生的問題，自然有時會有捉襟見肘之時。中世紀時認為誠信原則與合理性是源自上帝，或許於任何時空這些概念皆應作為法學的共同核心基礎──「道常無名」，但是這些法學概念似亦符合我們中國傳統上超乎天地上沛然莫之能禦的「自然道法」。

承蒙東海陳美蘭助教與研究生林郁甄小姐的打字、校稿及編排，本書方得以完成，於此致上真誠的謝意。台灣的學術環境惡劣，自年輕時五南即替個人出書，這是五南楊榮川董事長台灣熱血男子漢對學術的堅持，個人於此表達特別的敬意。個人自認為是與五南一起成長，並於學術上深感榮幸。

　　故東海大學董事長查良鑑博士為中國國際私法界的最前輩，個人亦甚感謝與思念其對個人於中華文化上之啟蒙，故謹以本書呈獻給最敬愛的查董事長：查伯伯，晚輩自當謹記您的叮嚀不能太聰明。

陳隆修

目錄

第一章　美國選法革命於實體政策上之發展　　　　　　　**1**

一、實體法上之政策與羅馬 II　　　　　　　　　　　　　　1

二、Allstate Insurance Co. 449 U.S. 302; 101 S. Ct. 633　　　9

三、Phillips Petroleum Co. 472 U. S. 797; 105 S. Ct. 2965　　16

四、Sun Oil Co. 486 U.S. 717; 108 S. Ct. 2117　　　　　　23

五、Kelly Kearney 39 Cal. 4th 95; 137 P.3d 914; 2006 Cal. LEXIS
　　8362　　　　　　　　　　　　　　　　　　　　　　　36

六、羅馬 II一山寨版的第二新編　　　　　　　　　　　　　44

七、ALI Complex Litigation Proposal　　　　　　　　　　52

第二章　羅馬 II 規則評論　　　　　　　　　　　　　　**59**

一、羅馬 II 的區域選法規則　　　　　　　　　　　　　　59

二、建議　　　　　　　　　　　　　　　　　　　　　　66

三、分割式選法　　　　　　　　　　　　　　　　　　　69

四、契約與非契約行為　　　　　　　　　　　　　　　　80

　(一)侵權行為與其他　　　　　　　　　　　　　　　　80

　(二)外國法之證明　　　　　　　　　　　　　　　　　86

五、羅馬 II 其他規則與實體法規則　　　　　　　　　　　97

第三章　羅馬I規則評論　　　　　　　　　　　　　　　**115**

一、前言　　　　　　　　　　　　　　　　　　　　　　115

二、美國法律協會之建議　　　　　　　　　　　120

　(一)契約成立與默示準據法　　　　　　　　121

　(二)違反履行地法　　　　　　　　　　　　125

三、適當法理論與其範圍　　　　　　　　　　127

四、契約之存在　　　　　　　　　　　　　　131

五、選法自由　　　　　　　　　　　　　　　133

六、不患寡而患不均　　　　　　　　　　　　138

七、以實體法為契約準據法　　　　　　　　　141

八、實體法原則　　　　　　　　　　　　　　147

九、引用之方式與選定準據法　　　　　　　　153

十、合理性標準　　　　　　　　　　　　　　155

十一、默示準據法　　　　　　　　　　　　　168

十二、保險契約　　　　　　　　　　　　　　185

十三、契約自由受限於合理性與誠信原則　　　194

十四、假設準據法與強行實體政策　　　　　　200

　(一)假設推定準據法　　　　　　　　　　　200

　(二)強行法於實體政策上之適用範圍　　　　205

　(三)以法院地之實體政策為強行法之基礎　　213

十五、契約之成立及效力及強行法　　　　　　225

十六、契約法之共同核心政策（誠信原則）　　246

十七、契約違反履行地法　　　　　　　　　　261

　(一)國內法及國際法之共同法則　　　　　　261

　(二)違反履行地法之案例　　　　　　　　　270

十八、契約之成立及效力依實體法規則　　　　283

十九、主觀說與客觀說　　　　　　　　　　　296

二十、實體政策之全球化　　　　　　　　　　302

二十一、一般基本及特別推定與契約基本政策　322

二十二、中國思想下的全球化實體規則　　　　344

二十三、王道與聯合國人權公約　　　　　　　355

一、實體法上之政策與羅馬 II

　　一個重新再崛起的國家法學制度之建立，不能只基於與既有勢力之爭奪利益，本身必須具有著足以開創世界新紀元之最先進法學思想才能領袖群倫。而無可諱言兩岸三地之法學基礎目前皆甚為薄弱，仍必須參考先進國家之法學。歐盟2007年的羅馬 II 規則（Regulation (EC) No 864/2007 of the European Parliament and of the Council of 11 July 2007 on the law applicable to non-contractual obligations (Rome II)）有著濃厚的大陸法風味，但卻為Prof. Symeonides評述為「一個錯失的機會[1]」。他對羅馬 II 規則之評估大致上為負面的[2]：「雖然在法律穩定性及靈活性問題維持一個適度的均衡永遠是困難的，羅馬 II 的錯誤是太重視穩定性，而這樣最後可能證明是不切實際的[3]」。

　　光陰如梭，如果回顧歐洲近三十年來之變化，其實整體上仍大有進步。1978年奧地利國際私法率先引進美式「最重要關連說[4]」，繼而於不當得利與無因管理如英美法般不只單純的以行為地法為依據[5]，隨後瑞士、德國及比利時等國接著變法，歐洲於非契約上之責任變化是相當大。

---

[1]　SYMEON C. SYMEONIDES, *Rome II and Tort Conflicts: A Missed Opportunity* , 56 Am. J. Comp. L. 173 (2008)。

[2]　同上，The author's assessment is by and large negative.

[3]　同上，Although attaining a proper equilibrium between legal certainty and flexibility is always difficult, Rome II errs too much on the side of certainty, which ultimately may prove elusive.

[4]　陳隆修，《比較國際私法》，台北，五南圖書公司，78年10月，初版，頁181～186。

[5]　同上，365～368頁。

尤其是對於廣義的「國家利益[6]或政策的公開承認」，相較於個人年輕時，簡直可說是翻天覆地的變化。在早期所牽連國家相關連法律的內容是禁止被討論的，故而Prof. Cavers稱之為「jurisdiction-selection rules[7]」（區域選法規則）。於機械式的法規下，通常只能依公序良俗、定性及反致等規避技巧去達成法官所要的個案正義。但於羅馬II中，對歐盟之確定政策及歐盟與當事人之相關利益是公開的陳列於宣言之要點中，並以條文來貫徹這些政策與利益。如要點16陳述作為公約基石第4條基本原則為：「與直接損害發生地國家之連接（損害發生地法），可以達到被主張應負責之人與受害人間利益的公平平衡，並且表達現代民事責任的趨勢及無過失責任的制度[8]」。

要點20則為有關第5條產品責任：「於產品責任方面之國際私法規則，應達成的目標為於現代高科技的社會中所應含有的公平分散危險，保障消費者之健康，刺激創意，確保不扭曲之公平競爭及促進貿易[9]」。要點21則為有關第6條之不公平競爭，第6條是本於第4(1)條之損害發生地法：「有關不公平競爭，國際私法的規則應在於保護競爭者、消費者及一般大眾與確保市場的經濟功能可以適當的運作[10]」。因為公平競爭事實上牽涉到公法上之問題，這或許為第6(4)條不允許當事人依第14條自訂準據

---

[6] 陳隆修，《美國國際私法新理論》，台北，五南圖書公司，民國76年1月，初版，頁50～52。

[7] David F. Cavers, A Critique of the Choice-of-Lew Problem, 47 Harv. L. Rev. 173 (1933).

[8] Recital 16

Uniform rules should enhance the foreseeability of court decisions and ensure a reasonable balance between the interests of the person claimed to be liable and the person who has sustained damage. A connection with the country where the direct damage occurred (lex loci damni) strikes a fair balance between the interests of the person claimed to be liable and the person sustaining the damage, and also reflects the modern approach to civil liability and the development of systems of strict liability.

[9] Recital 20

The conflict-of-law rule in matters of product liability should meet the objectives of fairly spreading the risks inherent in a modern high-technology society, protecting consumer's health, stimulating innovation, securing undistorted competition and facilitating trade.

[10] Recital 21

The special rule in Article 6 is not an exception to the general rule in Article 4(1) but rather a clarification of it. In matters of unfair competition, the conflict-of-law rule should protect competitors, consumers and the general public and ensure that the market economy functions properly.

另外對限制競爭之定義則規定於Recital 23。

法之主要原因。要點25則為有關第7條環境損害之規定，該第7條允許受害人選擇損害發生地或行為地為準據法。這個偏向受害人的作法是基於歐盟的環保政策：「有關環境損害，歐盟公約174條規定此方面應加以高度之保護，而且應基於預警原則及事先預防之原則，於根源上之糾正為優先之原則，及污染者應負代價之原則，這些使得偏向受害者有利之原則合理化[11]」。歐盟雖不採納懲罰性賠償，但懲罰性賠償「阻止及預防」（deter and prevent）之政策於此充分表現。要點27則為有關第9條之工業行為，因為這亦牽涉到公法，且各國於此方面之法規亦不同：「因此，本規則假設一個基本規則，亦即工業行為發生地法應被適用，其目的是為了保護僱主及勞工之權利及義務[12]」。但是如果保護勞工又保護僱主，這個政策似乎不知所云。要點31則是有關14條當事人自主非契約準據法時保護弱勢之政策：「當於建立合意之存在時，法院應尊重當事人之意願。應以對當事人之選擇加以某些限制之方式來保護弱勢[13]」。最有趣的是對引起選法革命風暴的道路交通案件，要點34為有關17條於決定被告之責任時應以事實問題的方式來參考行為地之行為及安全規則：「即使是該非契約義務之準據法為其他國家之法律，為了達成當事人間合理的平衡，於合適之情況下，必須考慮到損害行為作成地之行為及安全規則[14]」。另外要點33又

---

[11] Recital 25

Regarding environmental damage, Article 174 of the Treaty, which provides that there should be a high level of protection based on the precautionary principle and the principle that preventive action should be taken, the principle of priority for corrective action at source and the principle that the polluter pays, fully justifies the use of the principle of discriminating in favour of the person sustaining the damage.

[12] Recital 27

The exact concept of industrial action, such as strike action or lock-out, varies from one Member State to another and is governed by each Member State's internal rules. Therefore, this Regulation assumes as a general principle that the law of the country where the industrial action was taken should apply, with the aim of protecting the rights and obligations of workers and employers.
要點28則規定不能傷害工會之地位。

[13] Recital 31

Where establishing the existence of the agreement, the court has to respect the intentions of the parties. Protection should be given to weaker parties by imposing certain conditions on the choice.

[14] Recital 34

In order to strike a reasonable balance between the parties, account must be taken, in so far as appropriate, of the rules of safety and conduct in operation in the country in which the harmful act was committed, even where the non-contractual obligation is governed by the law of another country.

規定：「於根據目前國內法去賠償道路交通事故之受害者時，在事故並非發生於被害者之慣居地時，於計算人身傷害之賠償數額時，繫屬法院應考慮到個別受害者之相關事實情況，這包含傷後照護與醫療追蹤之實際損失與費用[15]」。要點33之規定完全符合民事損害賠償之原則，唯一的問題是—聯合國及歐盟人權公約皆明文規定所有的受害者都應受到有效的救濟，為什麼羅馬II只給予道路事故受害者這樣的基本救濟？

　　雖然理論上這些寬廣的政策性要點於效力之次序上是後於那些明確的條文，但不可否認的條文之最終目的是在於執行要點中所宣示之政策。個人自年輕[16]至今耗費一輩子都在宣揚這一天的來臨，以個人一生懸命之所繫，羅馬II自然遠不及個人之期望。Savigny認為每個「法律關係」應屬於一個「地域[17]」，而同樣之類似觀念又為美國的Story[18]、英國的Dicey[19]、及法國的Pillet[20]所宣揚。由宏觀的歷史進化過程而言，羅馬II的政策宣言得以發生在Savigny的家園所在誠屬不易。羅馬II的政策宣言大致上亦應為世界上大部分的文明國家所接受及推行中，事實上個人年輕時所主張的共同主流核心價值所涵蓋的政策性範圍較羅馬II之政策宣言似乎還更為廣泛。個人足足等了三十多年，政策導向的法學方法論終於光明正大

---

[15]　Recital 33

According to the current national rules on compensation awarded to victims of road traffic accidents, when quantifying damages for personal injury in cases in which the accident takes place in a State other than that of the habitual residence of the victim, the court seised should take into account all the relevant actual circumstances of the specific victim, including in particular the actual losses and costs of after-care and medical attention.

[16]　陳隆修，《美國國際私法新理論》，台北，五南圖書公司，民國76年1月，初版，頁17～30。

[17]　Friedrich Carl von. Savigny (1779-1861), *Private International Law, A Treatise on the Conflict of Laws and the Limits of their Operation in Respect of Place and Time* (1st ed. 1869, 2d ed. 1880), 108 (translated into English by William Guthrie.)

It is [the] diversity of positive laws that makes it necessary to mark off for each... the area of its authority, to fix the limits of different positive laws in respect to one another... When a legal relation presents itself for adjudication, we seek a rule of law to which it is subject, and in accordance with which it is to be decided... [The task is to determine] that legal system to which the legal relation belongs according to its particular nature (where it has its seat).

[18]　Joseph Story, Commentaries on the Conflict of Laws § 4.

[19]　A.V. Dicey, A Digest of the Law of England with Reference to the Conflict of Laws, at xliv (1896). 「The nature of a right acquired under the law of any civilized country must be determined in accordance with the law under which the right is acquired.」

[20]　A. Pillet, Principes de droit international prive 33 (1903).

的於某些範圍上做為選法規則的指引。個人可以作證這些政策早在逾三十多年前就已是各文明國家之基本政策，為何延宕了三十多年歐盟才於其選法規則中公開、正式承認這些政策的合理及合法性？地球於過去三十年有停止運轉嗎？人類過去三十年有停止老化嗎？於滿目瘡痍之廢墟中再次站起的中國，必須以歐盟為殷鑑，無論於國內法或國際法上，應勇於創造、接受新論點，中國有歐盟般的雄厚底子可以延宕三十年嗎？

　　另外羅馬 II 序言中之政策要點所代表的並非某一會員國之政策，其雖然是歐盟的一致性政策，但事實上亦是大部份文明國家之基本政策。Cook認為法院於處理衝突案件之選法問題時，應引用「事實上於處理侵權、契約、物權等完全只牽連到國內案件之同樣方法[21]」。而Currie甚至認為沒有選法規則可能對我們更好，適用法院於處理國內案件時解釋法律之方法即可處理衝突案件：「正如我們根據那個程序去決定法條適用之時間，及於邊緣案件應如何適用，我們也可以同樣的決定於牽連外國因素時它應如何的被適用[22]」。而個人數十年如一日，一向主張應以所牽連部門實體上最先進或最能為大多數所接受之主流共同核心價值、政策、原則、或潮流（trend）為衝突法案件之依據[23]。雖然個人之實體法論述大部份是本著國內法之政策而來，但兩者並不完全一致。三十多年前於歐洲機械式規則、最重要關連規則、及利益說之夾殺下，個人之論述經常會被誤認為「利益說」之分支[24]，但如前述，個人終身所信仰的為「有效正義」，

---

[21] Walter Wheeler Cook, The Logical and Legal Bases of the Conflict of Laws, 20, 21, 43 (1942), "the same method actually used in deciding cases involving purely domestic torts, contracts, property, etc." "The forum, when confronted by a case involving foreign elements, always applies its own law to the case, but in doing so adopts and enforces as its own law a rule of decision identical, or at least highly similar, though not identical, in scope with a rule of decision found in the system in force in another state with which some or all of the foreign elements are connected... The rule thus 'incorporated' into the law of the forum, ...the forum... enforces not a foreign right but a right created by its own law."

[22] Brainerd Currie, Selected Essays on the Conflict of Laws, 183, 184 (1963), "Just as we determine by that process how a statute applies in time, and how it applies to marginal cases, so we may determine how it should be applied to cases involving foreign elements."

[23] 陳隆修，《美國國際私法新理論》，台北，五南圖書公司，民國76年1月，初版，17～30頁。

[24] 陳隆修、許兆慶、林恩瑋、李瑞生四人合著，《國際私法—管轄與選法理論之交錯》，台北，五南圖書公司，2009年3月，初版1刷，252～260頁。

是以能達成最大個案正義為目標之實體政策為核心價值之方法論。故而與Curie將私人利益融入州利益中不同的[25]，個人並不侷限於所牽連之國內法，而是基於個案正義上以相關部門實體上之世界性之發展為依據。經過數十年後，現今對這種論述的流行名詞為「全球化法學」。經過三十多年後，羅馬 II 序言的政策性要點並非基於任何一個會員之國內法規而來，卻是代表歐盟整體相關部門之政策，甚或為全世界大部份文明國家之共同政策或價值。個人認為於此處時間還給個人年輕時之主張一個公道。

有趣的是個人年輕返台前夕曾將當時剛形成之論述寄給故Prof. Reese，前幾年無意中方發現其對個人間接之回應：「有一些作者對第2新編提出批評，他們認為第2新編之選法規則並未給予唯一──或至少主要──價值適當的重視。這就是法院應注意到與案件相關連之州可能被適用之州內法之政策[26]...如果這些作者是對的，那麼很明顯的第2新編便是錯的。新編的立場是這些價值雖然重要，並不是唯一的，並且還有其他價值應被加以考慮。對一些相關價值的堅持，是第2新編之規則可以被合理的認為模糊之主要理由。但可作為答辯的是，一直到在一個個別之情形下有些價值是最後可以被認定為應有著最重要的地位以前，我們可以說價值的平衡程序是不可避免的不穩定。而在許多情形下，這個時間是還未到達[27]」。

---

[25]　一般是認為Curie以透過州利益之方式達成私人利益。見Curie, Selected Essays on the Conflict of Laws, 610, "No place in conflict-of-laws analysis for a calculus of private interests by the time the interstate plane is reached the resolution of conflicting private interests has been achieved; it is subsumed in the statement of the laws of the respective states."
　　對利益說於此方面之批評見陳隆修，《美國國際私法新理論》，台北，五南圖書公司，民國76年1月，初版，53～56頁。

[26]　陳隆修，《美國國際私法新理論》，台北，五南圖書公司，民國76年1月，初版，119頁。

[27]　Willis Reese, The Second Restatement of Conflict of Laws Revisited, 34 Mercer L. Rev. 501, at 518 (1983), "A criticism made of the Restatement Second by a number of writers does not give proper emphasis to what, in their opinion, is the only-or at least the principal-value in choice of law. This is that the court should look to the policies underlying the potentially applicable local law rules of the state having contacts with the case... If these writers are correct, the Restatement Second is plainly wrong. It takes the position that this value, although important, does not stand alone and that there are other values to be considered. This insistence that there are a number of relevant values is a primary reason for what can be justly termed the vagueness of some of the Restatement Second formulations. In defense, it can be said that a balancing of values inevitably will be an uncertain process until it is finally determined which of there values should carry the greatest weight in a given situation. In many instances, such a time has not yet come."

第2新編的模糊不穩定性，一般是認為其第145及188條之最重要關連點之「質」與「量」取捨之困難造成其之不可預測性。「最重要關連點」為一種純地域性主義的選法規則[28]，個人認為其於歐洲如野火燎原般的當者披靡，亦是由於其地域性主義所帶與之直覺性正義感[29]。富有彈性之最重要關連標準，再加上包羅萬象之第6條7個大原則性之價值，第2新編之方法論可謂包山包海，幾乎囊括所有之方法論（包括利益說及實體法論）。這麼大的一個第2新編百貨公司，任何法官都可以在裡面選購到其所要的方法論，第2新編的不穩定自然可預期。第2新編的海納百川，造成它於美國全勝的假象。它的什麼都有，也就是什麼都沒有。

羅馬II序言之政策性要點清楚的說明，在已確定了許多「一個個別之情形下有些價值是最後可以被認定為應有著最重要的地位」，故而「價值的平衡程序是不可避免的不穩定」是過度的消極，並且會積極的造成不符合正義之情形。至少在歐盟羅馬II政策性要點之範圍內，「這個時間還未到達」是不正確的。個人與尊敬的Prof Reese在時光隧道中意見之極端不合，或許時間於三十年後將羅馬II之政策要點推向個人這邊。

然而個人完全沒有喜悅，遲來三十年的正義已不是正義，我們已經

---

[28] 陳隆修，《美國國際私法新理論》，台北，五南圖書公司，民國76年1月，初版，80頁，個人或許為早期率先批評最重要關連標準為具有多個屬地連結因素之區域選擇法規。

[29] 於陳隆修、許兆慶、林恩瑋，《台灣財產法暨經濟法研究叢書（十三）—國際私法：選法理論之回顧與展望》，台灣財產法暨經濟法研究協會發行，2007年1月，初版，177、178頁個人如此評述：「地域性主義與我們根深蒂固的傳統行為模式相符，自然順理成章的成為世人評量公平正義的基準。最重要關連說經常衡量案件中關連點的結集數量，並進而以此做為準據法取捨之依據。故而以與案件事實有最多關連點之地之法做為準據法，自然成為一般人認為合理之解決方案。亦理所當然地被認為既然是表面上合情理之法，無論案件之結果為何應該也是符合公平正義的一種作法。

然而以案件事實情況之關連點的結集做為準據法的依據，如前述是一種半機械式的作法，實務上有可能導致對意外侵權行為之被害人無法給予賠償之情況。因為『地域性主義』的屬性，使得最重要關連說忽視案件所牽連的實體法，導致可能對被害人造成不公平的後果的判例已一再發生。地域性主義固然符合我們傳統的行為模式，因而依據地域性主義而得知判決亦有著表面之合理性。在現代化社會裏，我們對法院判決的結果必須問一個根本問題：即我們要求的是社會上表面上直覺的合理性，還是於做了學術研究後維持當事人間的真正公平正義？歐洲社會對行為地法的堅持及最重要關連說的採納代表前者，美國社會對利益說的狂熱與崇拜或許可以代表後者」。

Dym v. Gordon, 14N.Y.2d 120, 262 N.Y.S. 2d 463, 209 N.E. 2d 792 (1965), 案即為地域性主義造成不幸結果的早期代表，參陳隆修，《美國國際私法新理論》，台北，五南圖書公司，民國76年1月，初版，頁137～143。

浪費了三十年。在Milliken v. Pratt[30]中，Prof. Currie以已婚婦女之訂約能力作了十四種分析[31]，進而發展出個人認為對國際私法有史以來最偉大的貢獻[32]。他很自信的宣佈：「就該爭點而言，有誰能說緬因州或麻薩諸塞州是錯誤的？[33]」已婚婦女沒有訂約能力是違反美國憲法公平保護條款及適當程序條款，並且違反1948年聯合國人權宣言第1及7條之平等保護條款。故而全世界的人都可以說歧視婦女是錯誤的。很奇怪的，在1878年Milliken案的首席法官Gray已經認為已婚婦女完全沒有訂約能力是所有的文明國家所不能接受的觀念[34]，Prof. Currie及當時的美國卻仍對基於Milliken而來之州利益分析樂此不疲。時至今日，全美國的學者及法院無論是屬於哪一教派，仍對「假衝突」之利益分析視為具有憲法一般的效力[35]。尊重已婚婦女的價值在美國那麼不可行嗎？這些時光隧道中的劃痕只是充分證明一件事—所謂有些價值的確認的時間尚未到達經常是極度的不對的。崛起中的中國是沒有如歐盟及美國般虛擲光陰的本錢。數十年如

---

[30]　125 Mass. 374 (1878).

[31]　Brained Currie, Selected Essays on the Conflict of Laws, Chapter 2: "Married Women's Contracts: A Study in Conflict-of-Laws Method."

[32]　S. C .Symeonides, Revolution and Counter-Revolution in American Conflicts Law: Is There a Middle Ground? 46 Ohio St. L.J. 549, 564 (1985), "That this is by now taken for granted, even by critics, and forms the common denominator of all current choice of law methodologies is no reason to deny him the credit rightfully due to him. Even if this were Currie's only contribution to conflicts theory, it would be sufficient to secure him a permanent position in the conflicts 'Hall of Fame.'"

[33]　Brained Currie, Selected Essays on the Conflict of Laws, Chapter 2: "Married Women's Contracts: A Study in Conflict-of-Laws Method.", P.85, "Who can say that Massschusetts for that matter, was wrong? All that happened was that in each state the legislature weighed competing considerations, with differfnt result".

[34]　陳隆修，《美國國際私法新理論》，台北，五南圖書公司，民國76年1月，初版，頁226～228。"But it is not true at the present day that all civilized states recognize the absolute incapacity of married women to make contracts. The tendency of modern legislation is to enlarge their capacity in this respect, and in many states they have nearly or quite the same powers as if unmarried. In Massachusetts, even at the time of the making of the contract in question, a married woman was vested by statute with a very extensive power to carry on business by herself, and to bind herself by contracts with regard to her own property, business and earnings；and, before the bringing of the present action, the power had been extended so as to include the making of all kinds of contracts, with any person but her husband, as if she were unmarried. There is therefore no reason of public policy which should prevent the maintenance of this action. "

[35]　個人對Prof. Currie的尊敬乃是基於其打破區域選法規則之地域性主義而來，詳參陳隆修、許兆慶、林恩瑋，《台灣財產法暨經濟法研究叢書（十三）—國際私法：選法理論之回顧與展望》，台灣財產法暨經濟法研究協會發行，2007年1月，初版，198、199。

一日，個人自始就發現只要透過比較法學的程序，於許多範圍中通常就會輕易的發現主流共同核心價值事實上早已存在。這亦是個人認同劉仁山教授以基礎法學之角度研究國際私法之主要原因。經過歲月的磨鍊，個人更認為辨認主流共同核心價值的必要性，或許於許多其他部門之法學亦一體的應被加以適用。更或許個人用另一種時髦的術語更能被年輕的同僚所能認同-亦即法學全球化之概念正鋪天蓋地的席捲全世界的所有法律制度。

自Babcock v. Jackson[36]後美國法院的選法理論通常是融合各派學說夾雜在一起[37]，大致上可說是本著地域性的關連點來操作政策（或利益）的分析[38]。或許是受到這個影響，傳統上甚少對各州選法規則加以拘束的美國最高法院，亦基於美國憲法第四條1項的充分互信條款及第十四修正案的適當程序條款而給予各州之選法規則一個微量的限制。

二、Allstate Insurance Co. 449 U.S. 302; 101 S. Ct. 633

於Allstate Insurance Co., v. Hague, Personal Representative of Hague's Estete[39]中，被上訴人先生之摩托車於威士康新州被一車子所撞而死亡，其時被上訴人、其死亡之先生、及肇事者皆為威州之居民。雙方車子皆未保險，但死者之三部車皆有向上訴人各投保上限15,000元之保險，於車禍後但於起訴前，被上訴人嫁給一名明尼蘇達州之人，並於該地居住。於同一時間被上訴人被明州指定為死者之遺產管理人，其於明州提起訴訟要求依明州法累積三個保險之給付，共45,000元。上訴人則主張應依威州法，不得累積保險給付額。

---

[36] 12 N.Y. 2d 473, 240 N.Y.S 2d 743, 191 N.E. 2d 279 (1963).

[37] William A. Reppy, Jr., Eclecticism in Choice of Law: Hybrid Method or Mishmash?, 34 MERCER L. REV. 645 (1983).

[38] 陳隆修、許兆慶、林恩瑋，《台灣財產法暨經濟法研究叢書（十三）—國際私法：選法理論之回顧與展望》，台灣財產法暨經濟法研究協會發行，2007年1月，初版，208~220。

[39] 449 U.S. 302; 101 S. Ct. 633; 66 L. Ed. 2d 521; 1981 U.S. LEXIS 52; 49 U.S.L.W. 4071; 1981 Auto. Cas. (CCH) P10,911。本案為各州選法之基準，故各州皆須遵循本案，例如見James A. Meschewski, Choice of Law in Alaska: A Survival Guide for Using the Second Restatement 16 Alaska L. Rev. 1, 32, 33 (1999); Laura B. Bartell, the Peripatetic Debtor: Choice of Law and Choice of Exemptions 22 Bank. Dev. J. 401, 408 (2006)。

　　有趣的是明州地院直接認定適用威州法是「對明州的公序良俗有害的[40]」，而給予對被上訴人有利之快速判決。明州最高法院維持地院之決定，於判決中其依判例法[41]採用Prof. Leflar的「五種考慮因素[42]」，法院認為雖然依前四種考慮因素明州的關連點不足以適用明州法，但第五點較佳法律是有利於明州法的適用[43]。法院強調大部分州是允許累積的，並且允許累積的判決「是較近而且充分的考慮到目前使用車輛的情況」。況且法院發現明州的法律較威州的法律優良，是「因為它所要求與未保險的駕駛人發生事故的費用能較威州的法律透過保險費而更廣泛的分散」。法院又認為「汽車保險契約是自己成為一種類別」，因為保險公司「知道汽車是一種移動的東西，會由一州被開往另一州」。因此法院認為適用明州法，並「沒有武斷及不合理的情形，以至於會違反適當程序條款[44]」。依照「五種考慮因素」的方法論，因為明州的土地關連點不足，只有第五點較佳法律是偏向明州，然而法院仍認為第五點之重要性可以壓倒可預測性、國際秩序、簡化、及審判地的利益這四種考量，故而法院並未忠實的執行Prof. Leflar的五種考慮因素。如果純由法院的論述，我們很可能會誤會法院是在忠誠的執行「實體法方法論」，這或許是個人極為尊敬的Prof. Leflar於生前賜名個人之理論為「multistate theory」之原因。有趣

---

[40] App. C to Pet. For Cert. A-29. "Inimical to the public policy of Minnesota."

[41] Milkovich v. Saari, 295 Minn. 155, 203 N.W. 2d 408 (1973).

[42] R. A. Leflar, Choice-Influencing Considerations in Conflicts Law, 41 N. Y. U. L. Rev. 267 (1966). 並見陳隆修，《美國國際私法新理論》，台北，五南圖書公司，民國76年1月，初版，82~87頁。

[43] 289 N.W. 2d 43 (1978).

[44] 449 U.S. "302, The court emphasized that a majority of States allow stacking and that legal decisions allowing stacking 'are fairly recent and well considered in light of current used of automobiles.' 'In addition, the court found the Minnesota rule superior to Wisconsin's because it requires the cost of accidents with uninsured motorists to be spread more broadly through insurance premiums than does the Wisconsin rule.'...'That contracts of insurance on motor vehicles are in a class by themselves' since an insurance company 'knows the automobile is a movable item which will be driven from state to state.' From this premise the court concluded that application of Minnesota law was 'not so arbitrary and unreasonable as to violate due process.' "（註解省略）

的是如果依該案發生30年後之羅馬 II 規則第18條[45]及第4(2)條[46]，因車禍當
事人共同慣居地及車禍地點皆為威州，故遺孀只能得到15,000元之保險。
歐盟這樣子有達到其要點16「表達現代化民事責任的趨勢及無過失責任
的制度」的政策嗎？如果由歐盟的注重土地關連而言，第4(3)之規避條款
是不能被引用的。一個三十年後才產生的法規仍會產生這樣可笑的結果，
歐盟是應該反省的，而中國是應引以為殷鑑的。就此一著名的權威案例
而言，羅馬 II 的「改良式」新機械式理論，是遠較30年前的美國還不如
的。

　　可惜的是美國最高法院宣稱其只就明州判決的是否違憲性加以審
查，而不碰觸實體法之政策。於Alasla Packers[47]中其曾衡量阿拉斯加與加
州之利益，以決定充分互信條款之問題。但於Nevada v. Hall[48]中，最高
法院已經不再要求去平衡各州之利益。這種作法似乎甚為符合Prof. Cur-
rie之訓示，但個人記得早期甚多前輩同僚[49]對此種作法是有強烈的表達反

---

[45]　Article 18 Direct action against the insurer of the person liable.
　　The person having suffered damage may bring his or her claim directly against the insurer of the person liable to provide compensation if the law applicable to the non-contractual obligation or the law applicable to the insurance contract so provides.

[46]　Article 4 General rule
　　1.Unless otherwise provided for in this Regulation, the law applicable to a non-contractual obligation arising out of a tort/delict shall be the law of the country in which the damage occurs irrespective of the country in which the event giving rise to the damage occurred and irrespective of the country or countries in which the indirect consequences of that event occur.
　　2.However, where the person claimed to be liable and the person sustaining damage both have their habitual residence in the same country at the time when the damage occurs, the law of that country shall apply.
　　3.Where it is clear from all the circumstances of the case that the tort/delict is manifestly more closely more closely connected with a country other than that indicated in paragraphs 1 or 2, the law of that other country shall apply. A manifestly closer connection with another country might be based in particular on a preexisting relationship between the parties, such as a contract, that is closely connected with the tort/delict in question.

[47]　Alaska Packers Assn. v. Industrial Accident Comm'n, 294 U.S. 532 (1935).

[48]　Nevada v. Hall, 440 U.S. 410 (1979).

[49]　F. Juenger, Choice of Law in Interstate Torts, 118 U. Pa. L. Rev. 200, 206-7 (1969), "Ever since conflicts law first developed, courts did precisely what Currie would forbid them to do; no judge has ever been impeached for inventing or applying a choice of law rule that sacrifices forum interests." A. A. Ehrenzweig, A Counter Revolution in Conflicts Law? 80 Harv. L. Rev. 377, 389 (1966): "As far as I can see, all courts and writers who have professed acceptance of Currie's interest language have transformed it by indulging in that very weighing and balancing of interest from which Currie refrained."

對意見的,個人並稱之為「評價之禁忌[50]」。如前述對「諸法皆空自由自在」的歐盟法院,這種禁忌是不存在人間的。但對美國而言,這種禁忌似乎已被大部分之同僚及法院提昇到超越憲法,接近聖經之地位。個人於此引用一般認為建立美國三權分立之Marbury v. Madison中之論述以為參考:「去確認什麼是法律,很明顯的是司法部門的範圍與責任。那些將法律適用到個別案件上的人,於必要之情形下必須闡明與解釋該法律。如果兩個法律彼此衝突,法院必須決定各個法律之適用[51]」。故而兩百多年前美國的先祖們於確立三權分立之架構時,已經黑紙白字的立下不可動搖之明訓:「如果兩個法律彼此衝突,法院必須決定各個法律之適用」。美國最原始、最權威的判例法已經很清楚的規定:法院之責任即在確認相衝突法律之適用範圍,以達成當事人間之權利義務之歸屬[52]。言必稱遵守憲法的「利益說」,很諷刺的反而是違反了其最古老、最權威的憲政判例法。歷經三十年,個人維持對「評價禁忌」之觀點[53]。歐盟法院之無法無天固然違反憲政原則;美國最高法院過分推託,亦是規避職責而沒有主持司法正義,故而亦是違反三權分立原則。

在*Allstate Insurance Co.*中美國聯邦最高法院立下法院選法規則之基本規範:「一州之實體法如果要在符合憲法之規範下被選為準據法,該州必須要有一個重要的關連點,或一群重要的關連點,而產生州利益,以使得其法律之被適用而不會造成武斷或基本上不公平之後果[54]」。這個規則已成為美國適用法院地法之最基本的少量要求。

---

[50] 陳隆修,《美國國際私法新理論》,台北,五南圖書公司,民國76年1月,初版,59~63頁。

[51] Marbury v. Madison 1 Cranch 137, 2 L. Ed. 60 (1803), "It is emphatically the province and duty of the judicial department to say what the law is. Those who apply the rule to particular cases, must of necessity expound and interpret that rule. If two laws conflict with each other, the courts must decide on the operation of each."

[52] Marbury v. Madison 1 Cranch 137, 2 L. Ed. 60 (1803), "The province of the court is solely, to decide on the rights of individuals..."

[53] 陳隆修,《美國國際私法新理論》,台北,五南圖書公司,民國76年1月,初版,59~63頁。

[54] 449 U.S. 302, 312, 313, "For a State's substantive law to be selected in a constitutionally permissible manner, that State must have a significant contact or significant aggregation of contacts, creating state interests, such that choice of its law is neither arbitrary nor fundamentally unfair."

　　於該案中，首先死者每天通車至明州工作，故法院認為州在對通車的
非居民受僱者之安全及福祉有著關心的利益，而同樣的效果亦出現在僱主
上[55]。第二，保險公司始終於明州都有營業；而且保單之範圍是涵蓋整個
美國，故保險公司是明確的有預期死者可能會於威州以外之明州或美國其
他地方發生車禍[56]。第三，被上訴人於訴訟前已移居於明州，並無證據顯
示其移居是為了本訴訟或為了尋找對本訴訟有利之環境[57]。最高法院最後
認為「明尼蘇達跟當事人及事件有著一群重要的關連點，產生州利益，使
得其法律之適用不會產生武斷及基本上不公平之後果。故而明尼蘇達最高
法院之適用明尼蘇達法，並未違反適當程序條款或充分互信條款[58]」。美
國最高法院的作法是本著地域性的關連點去進行州利益之分析。無論是採
狹義Currie式保護本州居民之州利益[59]，或廣義的政策式州利益分析[60]，地
域性關連點與州利益於理論上是沒有關連的。「最重要關連說」與「利益
說」本就是兩個獨立不同之理論。但在紐約法院於Babcock中將它們一起

---

[55] 449 U.S. 302, 314, 316, "The State's interest in its commuting nonresident employees reflects a state concern for the safety and well-being of its work force and the concomitant effect on Minnesota employers." "Employment status is not a sufficiently less important status than residence…"

[56] 449 U.S. 302, 317, 318。

[57] 449 U.S. 302, 318, 319。個人對選購法院之看法較為傳統，見陳隆修、許兆慶、林恩瑋、李瑞生四人合著，《國際私法-管轄與選法理論之交錯》，台北，五南圖書公司，2009年3月，初版1刷，頁213，美國法傳統上亦如大陸法般，對選購法院並不贊同，英國法院傳統上則甚為尊重原告之利益，但較近亦有所改變。見Cheshire and North's, Private International Law, 13th ed. P.345, "At one time great weight was attached to this factor, and if the claimant obtained a substantial advantage from trial in England the courts were unlikely to grant a stay of the English proceedings. The House of Lords in the Spiliada case sought to reduce the weight given to the advantage to the claimant when exercising the discretion to stay. Hence the principle that the mere fact that the claimant has a legitimate personal or juridical advantage in proceedings in England cannot be decisive." The Spiliada [1987] AC 460。又14th ed. P.439, "The concern to reduce the weight to be attached to the advantage to the claimant is a development to be welcomed. Although there has been considerable judicial condemnation of the practice of forum shopping, it appears in the past that the more the claimant had to gain from this practice the more likely he was to be allowed to continue his action in England. The emphasis in the House of Lords is now very much on chauvinism being replaced by judicial comity."

[58] 449 U.S. 302, 320, "Minnesota had a significant aggregation of contacts with the parties and the occurrence, creating state interests, such that application of its law was neither arbitrary nor fundamentally unfair. Accordingly, the choice of Minnesota law by the Minnesota Supreme Court did not violate the Due Process Clause or the Full Faith and Credit Clause."

[59] 陳隆修，《美國國際私法新理論》，台北，五南圖書公司，民國76年1月，初版，50～52頁。

[60] 陳隆修，《美國國際私法新理論》，台北，五南圖書公司，民國76年1月，初版，69~77頁，討論關於加州之比較損害之方式。

使用後，美國所有的法院幾乎都跟著將這兩個涇渭分明的理論混合使用，以便達成他們所要的符合正義之結果。如個人所一再強調─地域性主義只能給予表面上直覺的合理性，要達成當事人間真正的公平正義還是須對實體上之政策加以分析[61]。

　　法院的第3理由是選購法院的哲學性問題，與新理論較無關連。但第一個理由將受僱人之地位提升之居民之地位，則顯然是基於Currie的狹義式利益；第二個理由是基於保險公司之營業地及營業範圍而來，亦似乎與狹義式州利益較有關，而相較之下似乎與實體法之政策分析較少關聯。不似明尼蘇達法院幾乎完全以實體政策之分析來決定適用明州法是「沒有武斷及不合理的情形，以至於會違反適當程序條款」，美國最高法院仍拘泥於狹義式之州利益。無論於法規上是否有做到，羅馬II規則至少於表面上對一些實體上之政策有公開的宣誓效忠。美國最高法院卻仍避開對實體政策之遵從，如此情形下要怎麼決定「法律的適用不會產生武斷及基本上不公平之後果」？要如何決定個案的公平正義及當事人間之權利義務？

　　實體法政策的論述是明州法院判決之基礎，美國最高法院卻避開實體法政策之論述，如此怎麼能客觀的鑑定明州「法律的適用不會產生武斷及基本上不公平之後果」？假設在相反的情況下，威州法是允許保險金額45,000元之累積，而明州法是不得累積只能請求15,000元。如果排除較為先進而為大部份州所接受的累積法則，並且這個法則又是雙方當事人之共同住所地法、保險契約訂定法及車禍發生地法，而採用較為後進且不符合現代社會需求之被害人受僱地之法則，難道美國最高法院及全世界之其他同僚不會認為這是「武斷而且基本上不公平之後果」？一如往常，全世界都知道美國最高法院真正判決之理由，但是一如往常，沒有人去揭發美國最高法院「國王的新衣」。

　　個人三十年前即這麼主張：「交通意外事故案例是國際私法選擇法

---

[61]　陳隆修、許兆慶、林恩瑋，《台灣財產法暨經濟法研究叢書（十三）─國際私法：選法理論之回顧與展望》，台灣財產法暨經濟法研究協會發行，2007年1月，初版，174～178頁。

革新的重點所在。毫無疑問，在工業國家中的共通價值，是給予受害人迅速合理的賠償。當然此項價值未必須以相關州的有關內州法代表[62]」。而如前述羅馬 II 要點16亦宣示：「表達現代民事責任的趨勢及無過失責任的制度」。對於保險制度在意外侵權法上之影響，個人早期已引用當時之學術證據及理論[63]作為論述之基礎[64]。非常可惜的是，做為半世紀前選法革命之麥加，美國最高法院仍受困於「關連點」與「州利益」必須連結之神話幻景，無法依實體法而實際的對「武斷及基本上不公平之後果」給予一個真實性評估的標準。相較於陷入法律邏輯之泥沼，數十年來慣性的用關連點及州利益的障眼法自欺欺人的美國最高法院，台灣最高法院撥雲見日大開大闔的宣示：「按侵權行為法之理想，在給予被害人迅速及合理之賠償，務使其能獲得通常在其住所地可得到之保障及賠償[65]」。請問大陸年輕同僚─中華民族的國際私法在目前沒有能力領導世界嗎？

---

[62] 陳隆修，《美國國際私法新理論》，台北，五南圖書公司，民國76年1月，初版，131頁。

[63] Stig Jorgensen, "The Decline and Fall of the Law of Torts", 18 Am. J. Comp. Law 39 (1970), 53.
J. G. Fleming "The Collateral Source Rule and Loss Allocation in Tort Law," 54 Cal. L. Rev. 1478 (1966), 1548.
J. G. Fleming, Law of Torts, 5th ed., P.11.
Ehrenzweig, "Negligence Without Fault," 54 Cal. L. Rev. 1422 (1966), P.1448.
Guido Calabresi, The Costs of Accidents. Fleming James, Jr., The Law of Torts. Robert E. Keeton and Jeffery O'Connell, Basic Protection for the Tarffic Victim. Walter J. Blum and Harry Kalven, Jr., Public Law Perspectives on a Private Law Problem-Auto Compensation Plans. Warren G. Magnuson (Chairman of the U.S. Senate Committee on Commerce), "Nationwide No-Fault," 44 Miss. L. J. 132 (1973).
F. A. Trindade, "A No-Fault Scheme for Road Accident Victims," [1980] 96 L.Q. Rev. 581.

[64] 陳隆修，《美國國際私法新理論》，台北，五南圖書公司，民國76年1月，初版，129~134，個人並如此寫著：「但作者並不認為依照事實狀況來決定『合理的賠償』，對法院來說有什麼困難。判斷事實上所受的損害，是法院的例行公事。如果在勞工賠償案列中，有關迅速合理的賠償並沒有太大的問題發生，則給予交通事故受害人迅速合理的賠償，也該不致有什麼重大的困難。何況，法院所必須做的，只是依照這項價值選出適當的法律，或以該價值做為限制和指引，以便適用法律選擇法則。法院並不需要真正制訂出國際實體法，來決定給予受害人的賠償金額。因此，或許適用這項含糊的價值並不若習慣法學者所想像的來得艱難。想想，『具有一般知識經驗的人』（reasonable men）以及『預見』（forseeability）等含糊的標準，既然都已常為習慣法系所運用，以『迅速合理』做為選擇適當法的關連因素，對習慣法而言，自不會有任何困難。況且，『迅速合理賠償』的定義，很可能較其他某些傳統的聯繫因素，如『住所』（domicile）或『侵權行為地』（the place of the tort）等的定義，來得精確」。個人並認同加州法院其時之表現可為「迅速合理賠償」之表徵，見In re Paris Air Crash of March 3, 1974, 399F. Supp. 2d 732 (D. C. Calif. 1975)。

[65] 96年度台上字1804號判決。

三、Phillips Petroleum Co. 472 U. S. 797; 105 S. Ct. 2965

　　美國最高法院的將關連點與州利益連結在「武斷及不公平」上，又於 Phillips Petroleum Co. v. Shutts[66]中再次表現出來。於該案中，上訴人石油公司在11個州中承租土地，所取得之瓦斯大部份賣至美國各州。被上訴人因出租土地而有權利金，他們對上訴人提起集體訴訟，要求給付被遲延的權利金之利息。被上訴人居住於全美50州、哥倫比亞特區、及數個外國中。上訴人雖主張肯薩斯州沒有管轄權及其法律不應為所有交易行為之準據法，肯州法院仍判被上訴人應取得利息之給付，而肯州最高法院維持地院之判決。美國最高法院認為當事人有依法給予選擇退出之機會[67]，故肯州法院有管轄權，但肯州並未與所有的集體訴訟成員有著重要的關連點，故不能於所有的交易行為上皆適用肯州法。

　　對於肯州最高法院認為原告之集體希望能適用肯州法[68]，美國最高法院認為原告自然希望適用法院地法，但引用Hague認為這樣可能會鼓勵選

---

[66] 472 U. S. 797; 105 S. Ct. 2965; 86 L. Ed. 2d 628; 1985 U. S. LEXIS 104; 53 U. S. L. W. 4879; 2Fed. R. Serv. 3d (Callaghan) 797; 85 Oil & Gas Rep. 486.

[67] 集體訴訟（class actions）是美國法對人訴訟基礎（presence power）於一事不再理原則前讓步之表徵。Sovereign Camp v. Bolin, 305 U.S. 66 (1938)中規定美國有關集體訴訟之判決被承認之要件為：在同一訴訟因下(1)該集體中沒出席之成員是適當的被代表，並且(2)合理數目的成員受到適當的通知並且有著適當表達之機會。美國的Federal Rule of Civil Procedure Rule 23 (a)(2)規定「集體必須有相同的法律或事實的問題」。Rule 23 (b) (1), (2),為有關強制性的集體訴訟之規定。Rule 23(b)(3)為法院認為於集體訴訟成員間相同的法律或事實上之問題的重要性超越了任何只影響單獨成員之問題，並且欲公平的及有效率的解決紛爭，集體訴訟是較其他可供利用的方法為優良之情形。但是23(c)(2)(B)又規定於(b)(3)之集體訴訟中，應依實際情形在可行之下給予成員最好之通知。包括在透過合理之努力即可辨認之成員應全部受到個別之通知；該通知並且應告知被通知人如果任何成員要求不被列入集體訴訟中，法院會將其排除。故而(b)(3)集體訴訟通常被稱為「得選擇」（"opt-out"）集體訴訟。(b)(1)及(b)(2)訴訟則無此種通知之要求，但即使是於非(b)(3)之訴訟，法院有時基於裁量權仍會要求此種通知。見陳隆修，《2005年海牙法院選擇公約評析》，台北，五南圖書公司，2009年1月，初版1刷，130、261～264頁。於本案中法院陳述："The burdens placed by a State upon an absent class-action plaintiff are not of the same order or magnitude as those it places upon an absent defendant."472 U.S. 797, 808。又再引述以前之判例法如下："In Hansberry v. Lee, 311 U.S. 32, 40-41 (1940). Which explained that a class or representative suit was an exception to the rule that one could not be bound by judgment in personam unless one was made fully a party in the traditional sense. Ibid., citing Pennoyer v. Neff, 95 U.S. 714 (1878). 472 U.S. 797, 808。"

[68] "Plaintiff class members have indicated their desire to have this action determined under the laws of Kansas." 235 Kan., at 211, 222, 679 P. 2d. at 1174, 1181.

購法院[69]。

於有適當的通知及代表下，肯州最高法院認為除非有迫切的理由須去採用其他法律，否則於全國性之集體訴訟中法院地法應被適用[70]。美國最高法院卻認為這是個自我矛盾的鞋帶理論，當原告的請求是與其他州有主要關連點時，而州法院於主張管轄權時，是不可以用假設的管轄權來增加憲法所許可的選用實體法的分量，「它不可以在一個與法院沒有或甚少關連的交易上適用法院地法，以便滿足程序上應有『共同法律問題』之要件[71]」。

於其部份反對意見中，Justice Stevens引用Leflar及 Scole[72]之論述，認為本案應屬於「假衝突[73]」之案件，因為於相關之前判例中並未顯示肯薩斯之法律會與德州及奧克荷馬州之法律會有重大衝突[74]。他又注意到肯州最高法院認為：重要的是這些權利金並非屬於石油公司所有[75]。雖然Stevens大法官本於利益說而認為沒有其他州之利益會受損，但更有趣的是他不自覺的實體論證：「但是同樣的，一個根據憲法上『不公平的驚訝』而來的主張，不能僅是根據無預期性的選擇某法而來—它必須根據適用該法律所產生而有充份證明的無預期的結果而來。因此在沒有任何衝突法規下，單就它們所產生的後果，適當程序條款並沒有被侵犯。這是因為

---

[69] "In most cases the plaintiff shows his obvious wish for forum law by filing there. If plaintiff could choose the substantive rules to be applied to an action... the invitation to forum shopping would be irresistible." 472 U.S. 797, 820。

[70] 235 Kan., at 221-222, 679 P. 2d, at 1181.

[71] "We think that this is something of a 'bootstrap' argument. The Kansas class-action statute, like those of most other jurisdictions, requires that there be 'common issues of law or fact.' But while a State may, for the reasons we have previously stated, assume jurisdiction over the claims of plaintiffs whose principal contacts are with other States, it may not use this assumption of jurisdiction as an added weight in the scale when considering the permissible constitutional limits on choice of substantive law. It may not take a transaction with little or no relationship to the forum and apply the law of the forum in order to satisfy the procedural requirement that there be a 'common question of law.'" 472 U.S. 797, 821。

[72] R. Leflar, American Conflicts Law ＄ 93, p. 188 (3d ed. 1977). See also E. Scoles & P. Hay, Conflict of Laws ＄ 2.6, p. 17 (1982)

[73] 陳隆修，《美國國際私法新理論》，台北，五南圖書公司，民國76年1月，初版，49、50頁。

[74] 472 U.S. 797, 838, 839.

[75] 472 U.S. 797, 829, "As the Kansas court noted: 'What is significant is these gas royalty suspense monies never did nor could belong to Phillips.'"

選法規則上適當程序條款的主張之基礎理論為，必須當事人於有關他們行為的法律後果上，依據他們的正當期待有事先計畫他們的行為及契約上的關係。例如，他們的決定的依據是在於相信某一特別州的法律會被適用[76]」。在本案中肯州最高法院拒絕適用自己之州法，而採納上訴人石油公司於契約上所同意之統一聯邦利率，其認為「衡平原則要求，而契約原則命令，權利人必須得到相同的待遇[77]」。故而Stevens大法官之結論為：「肯州最高法院之適用衡平法之基本原則，它於契約之解釋，它對委員會規則之依據，及它在一般法律條款之解釋上，並沒有違反其他州既有之法律原則，因此不能被定性為對上訴人造成武斷或基本上不公平之後果[78]」。

　　大多數法官如此陳述：「集體訴訟是依據衡平原則而產生，原因是於訴訟中牽涉及太多人之利益而無法集中訴訟，為了幫助法院達成判決之故[79]」。並且又引用學者之著作認為：「由原告之觀點而言，集體訴訟類似一種『由法官所主導之準行政程序[80]』」。法學字典上「衡平」的定義

---

[76] 472 U.S. 797, 837, 838, "Again, however, a constitutional claim of 'unfair surprise' cannot be based merely upon an unexpected choice of a particular State's law – it must rest on a persuasive showing of an unexpected result arrived at by application of that law. Thus, absent any conflict of laws, in terms of the results they produce, the Due Process Clause simply has not been violated. This is because the underlying theory of a choice-of-law due process claim must be that parties plan their conduct and contractual relations based upon their legitimate expectations concerning the subsequent legal consequences of their actions. For example, they might base a decision on the belief that the law of a particular State will govern. But a change in that State's law in the interim between the execution and the performance of the contract would not violate the Due Process Clause."

[77] 472 U.S. 797, 831, "[Equitable] principles require, and contractual principles dictate, that the royalty owners receive the same treatment."

[78] 472 U.S. 797, 842, "The Kansas Supreme Court's application of general principles of equity, its interpretation of the agreements, its reliance on the Commission's regulations, and its construction of general statutory terms contravened no established legal principles of other States and consequently cannot be characterized as either arbitrary or fundamentally unfair to Phillips."

[79] 472 U.S. 797, 808, "The class action was an invention of equity to enable it to proceed to a decree in suits where the number of those interested in the litigation was too great to permit joinder."

[80] 472 U.S. 797, 809, "From the plaintiffs point of view a class action resembles a 'quasi-administrative proceeding, conducted by the judge.' 3B J. Moore & J. Kennedy, Moore's Federal Practice para. 23. 45 [4.-5] (1984); Kaplan, Continuing Work of the Civil Committee: 1966 Amendments to the Federal Rules of Civil Procedure (I), 81 Harv. L. Rev. 356, 398 (1967)."

為：「公平；不偏頗；平等的對待[81]」。肯州法院適用石油公司所同意的
聯邦統一利率自然是公平的。Stevens大法官以當事人的「正當期待」做
為是否違反適當程序條款的標準，事實上個人早期於契約法上亦主張「雙
方當事人的正當期待應被賦予效力[82]」。雖然於28,100個集體成員中，就
只有不到1,000個成員居住於肯州，並有3,400個成員選擇退出，及1,500
個成員無法通知而被排除，如最高法院所說的如果肯州沒有管轄權，則上
訴人於全世界各地可能會遭遇到無數個訴訟[83]。對被上訴人而言，平均之
請求權才只有100美元，如果不集中請求根本就不可行[84]。美國最高法院
駁回肯州最高法院之選法適用，可能迫使原告之集體成員因訴訟之延宕及
費用之增加而提前與被告石油公司和解。

　　於2005年美國國會鑒於「過去十年集體訴訟制度之被濫用」（Sec.
2(a)(2)），故而通過Class Action Fairness Act of 2005，其目的就是為了
避免「集體成員經常於集體訴訟中取得太少或沒有取得利益，甚至有時受
到傷害」（Sec. 2(a)(3)）。對律師於訴訟程序中獲得太多報酬，以至集
體之成員取得太少或無法取得利益，則特別再加規定於2個條文中[85]。由

---

[81] Black's Law Dictionary, 7th ed., P.560, "Fairness; impartiality; evenhanded dealing."

[82] 陳隆修，《美國國際私法新理論》，台北，五南圖書公司，民國76年1月，初版，223、224頁中
個人之部分論述如下：「雙方當事人的正當期待應賦予效力」，此一概括的說法，已將「當事
人意思自主」的價值及該價值的例外情況，均包含於其中。顯然，當事人意思自主的價值，即
為維護當事人間正當的期待。當事人意思自主原則的例外情況，起因於「正當期待」之限制要
件。「正當期待」（justified expectation）是個概括性的措辭，無怪乎Schlesinger教授以它做為
結論。例如契約可能含有詐欺（fraud）；或者契約可能於當事人懷有違反「契約履行地」法的
故意之情況下訂立；或者我們甚至可以說「標準格式契約」（standard form contract）中，交易
能力（bargaining power）較強之一方，可能有以不公平方式獲取交易能力能較弱一方的利益之
意念；或者，一個經驗豐富的商人和一個十四歲的小孩訂立契約，前者於賣後者一部跑車時，
並無所謂「正當期待」的意念存在。R. B. Schlesinger, Formation of Contracts, at 71.

[83] 472 U.S. 797, 801, 805.

[84] 472 U.S. 797, 809, "This lawsuit involves claims averaging about $ 100 per plaintiff; most of the plain-
tiffs would have no realistic day in court if a class action were not available."

[85] 28 USC 1711 note. SEC. 2. FINDINGS AND PURPOSES.
(a) FINDINGS.—Congress finds the following:
(2) Over the past decade, there have been abuses of the class action device that have—
(A) harmed class members with legitimate claims and defendants that have acted responsibly;
(B) adversely affected interstate commerce; and
(C) undermined public respect for our judicial system.
(3) Class members often receive little or no benefit from class actions, and are sometimes harmed, such

於在可能構成集體訴訟之程序中，全世界有如此多之訴訟成員在競爭有限的資源，過份強調地域性原則的關連點，可能會嚴重的影響集體訴訟的有效性及公平性。Prof. Scoles的書上對美國聯邦民事訴訟法Rule 23(b)(1)及(2)之兩種集體訴訟是否符合憲法上最低限度關連點之要求，如此寫著：「與其注意於地域性之原則上，更合理的問題及答案應是，於程序上允許以強制集體訴訟之方式去進行時，是否會對不具名的非居民原告造成明顯的不公平。如果這種不公平是不存在的，那麼那些非居民原告是否與法院地有著最低限度之關連點，則於分析中是幾乎不必考慮的[86]」。個人以為這個論述不但適用於強制集體訴訟之管轄規則上，亦應適用於包含Rule 23 (b)(3)在內之所有之集體訴訟之管轄及選法規則上。正如Hague中之明州最高法院，本案中之肯州最高法院亦務實的以實體法政策之分析來達成判決。個人以前如此寫著：「個人深感覺到無論國際私法的機械式技巧如何的如桎梏般的鎮住我們，於處理國際糾紛時我們回歸實體基本政策的渴望，正如魚蝦回歸大海河川一般的殷切[87]」。非常遺憾的美國最高法院於本案中遵守Hague之表面規則，只是強調與地域性關連點有關之州利益，對肯州法院及Stevens大法官基於分析實體法政策而來之真正「武斷及基本上不公平」之標準視若無睹。

Stevens大法官之所謂「當事人的正當期待」，固然符合個人早期就

---

as where—

(A) counsel are awarded large fees, while leaving class members with coupons or other awards of little or no value.

(b) PURPOSES.—The purposes of this Act are to—

(1) assure fair and prompt recoveries for class members with legitimate claims.

§ 1713. Protection against loss by class members

The court may approve a proposed settlement under which any class member is obligated to pay sums to class counsel that would result in a net loss to the class member only if the court makes a written finding that nonmonetary benefits to the class member substantially outweigh the monetary loss.

[86] Eugene F. Scoles, Peter Hay, Patrick J. Borchers, Symeon C. Symeonides, Conflict of laws, 3rd ed., P.439, "Rather than focusing on territoriality, a more sensible question to ask and answer is whether there is any palpable unfairness to the unnamed, nonresident plaintiffs in allowing the matter to proceed as a mandatory class action. If there is no such unfairness, then whether those nonresident plaintiffs have minimum contacts with the forum ought have little weight in the analysis."

[87] 陳隆修、許兆慶、林恩瑋，《台灣財產法暨經濟法研究叢書（十三）—國際私法：選法理論之回顧與展望》，台灣財產法暨經濟法研究協會發行，2007年1月，初版，199頁。

已主張之主流價值，事實上更符合現代之歐盟契約法原則[88]。其5：101條有關契約之解釋第1項規定即使與文義不和，契約應依雙方之合意解釋之，第3項規定應以有理性之人於相同情況下解釋之[89]。第5：102條規定於解釋契約時應注意誠信原則、慣例、契約之性質與目的、及當事人間之習慣[90]。肯州法院於本案依據衡平原則而來之解釋是完全符合這個大陸法之契約原則。應注意的是5：103條規定：「當契約條款不是個別洽商時，對其條款有疑慮時，其解釋應偏向對供給該條款之一方不利之方向[91]」。這個契約法原則為英美法與大陸法所共同遵守之共同主流核心價值，肯州最高法院依據實體法政策而作成之判決是符合這個價值的，美國最高法院根據土地關連點及州利益分析而作成之判決是明顯的違背這個價

---

[88] 見the Commission of European Contract Law, Principles of European Contract Law, edited by Ole Lando and Hugh Beale (2000).較近之共同參考架構（CFR）請參考Principles, Definitions and Model Rules of European Private Law, Edited by Christian von Bar, Eric Clive and Hans Schulte-Nölke and Hugh Beale, Johnny Herre, Jérôme Huet, Matthias Storme, Stephen Swann, Paul Varul, Anna Veneziano and Fryderyk Zoll及European Contract Law. Materials for a Common Frame of Reference: Terminology, Guiding Principles, Model Rules, Edited by Bénédicte Fauvarque-Cosson and Denis Mazeaud.

[89] ARTICLE 5:101: GENERAL RULES OF INTERPRETATION
(1) A contract is to be interpreted according to the common intention of the parties even if this differs from the literal meaning of the words.
(2) If it is established that one party intended the contract to have a particular meaning, and at the time of the conclusion of the contract the other party could not have been unaware of the first party's intention, the contract is to be interpreted in the way intended by the first party.
(3) If an intention cannot be established according to (1) or (2), the contract is to be interpreted according to the meaning that reasonable persons of the same kind as the parties would give to it in the same circumstances.

[90] ARTICLE 5:102: RELEVANT CIRCUMSTANCES
In interpreting the contract, regard shall be had, in particular, to:
(a) the circumstances in which it was concluded, including the preliminary negotiations;
(b) the conduct of the parties, even subsequent to the conclusion of the contract;
(c) the nature and purpose of the contract;
(d) the interpretation which has already been given to similar clauses by the parties and the practices they have established between themselves;
(e) the meaning commonly given to terms and expressions in the branch of activity concerned and the interpretation similar clauses may already have received;
(f) usages; and
(g) good faith and fair dealing.

[91] ARTICLE 5:103: CONTRA PROFERENTEM RULE
Where there is doubt about the meaning of a contract term not individually negotiated, an interpretation of the term against the party which supplied it is to be preferred.又見共同參考架構（CFR），第5:101、5:102、5:103及5:104條。

值的。故而肯州最高法院是符合憲法適當程序條款的,而美國最高法院的判決於實質結果上是「武斷而基本公平的」,故而它自己本身是違反適當程序條款及充份互信條款的。

　　歐盟契約法原則6:105條規定:「當價格或其他契約條款是由一方所決定,並且該一方之決定是重大不合理時,那麼即使於有任何相反之規定時,一個合理之價格或其他條款應取代之[92]」。故而很明顯的契約法的共同核心原則是,即便於契約條款有規定下,強勢一方所規定的不合理條款是不應被遵守的。美國最高法院已經脫離了現代人類文明的契約法之基本規範。2005年美國國會所通過的集體訴訟公平法案之目的就是為了保護弱勢之集體成員,美國最高法院對於上述之歐盟契約法原則是無法辯稱美國不遵守上述基本的契約法原則的。2005年集體訴訟公平法Sec.2(b)(1)即開宗明義宣示:「本法之目的為(1)對有合法請求權之集體成員給予公平及迅速補償之保障」。美國最高法院迷惑於地域性關連點及州利益之分析,不做實質考量,延宕訴訟,增加弱勢一方之訴訟費用,是不符2005年法案Sec.2(b)(1)要求公平、迅速賠償之規定。很怪的,本案為集體訴訟及選法規則之指標性案例,美國國會對本案之美國最高法院打了一個響亮的大巴掌,美國同僚卻好像不覺得疼痛。地域性關連點與

---

[92] ARTICLE 6:105: UNILATERAL DETERMINATION BY A PARTY
Where the price or any other contractual term is to be determined by one party and that party's determination is grossly unreasonable, then notwithstanding any provision to the contrary, a reasonable price or other term shall be substituted.
又見較近之共同參考架構(CFR)第6:107條及5:105條,
Article 5:105: Preferential Interpretation (modification of article 5:103)
When a contractual rule has been established under the dominant influence of one party, if there is any doubt, the provision must be interpreted in favour of the other party. In particular, terms of the contract will be interpreted against the party which supplied them.
Article 6:107: Unilateral Determination by a Party (completion of article 6:105)
Where the price or any other contractual term is to be unilaterally determined by one party and the determination is grossly unreasonable, then, notwithstanding any provision to the contrary, a reasonable price or any other reasonable term shall be substituted. The same applies when a party who was to fix the price or any other term of the contract, fails to do so.
見European Contract Law Materials for a Common Frame of Reference: Terminology, Guiding Principles, Model Rules, Edited by Bénédicte Fauvarque-Cosson and Denis Mazeaud.

州利益之重要性[93]已很明顯的凌駕於「造成武斷及基本上不公平的後果」[94]上。如前所述，二百多年前於確立美國三權分立時，Marbury v. Madison中美國最高法院其時已明白規定「法院唯一的範圍就是去確定當事人的權利」。現今美國最高法院的過分沉溺於地域性關連點及州利益，不但違反公平正義之原則，亦反諷的自己本身已造成違憲之事實。相較於歐盟法院的無法無天，本案之美國最高法院則顢頇頑固故步自封的漠視其之墨守成規是否會於實際上造成「武斷及基本上不公平」之後果。

四、Sun Oil Co. 486 U.S. 717; 108 S. Ct. 2117

但有趣的是於後續之類似案件中，美國最高法院卻跳過地域性關連點及州利益，而直接以「武斷或不公平」為違反適當程序及充份互信條款之基準。於Sun Oil Co. v. Wortman[95]中，肯薩斯州地院在Phillips Petroleum Co. v. Shutts[96]之判決下再次審理本集體訴訟案，認定在依據其他州之法律下，上訴人應依據聯邦能源委員會（FPC）之利率而付利息。地院又認為Shutts Ⅲ並未禁止肯州5年消滅時效之適用。肯州最高法院維持第一審之判決。美國最高法院亦維持肯州最高法院之判決。即使實體上之準據法為外州法，美國最高法院一向不認為憲法禁止法院地法之消滅時效之適用[97]。因為「充份互信條款並未強迫『一個州在其立法管轄能力相關之事項內，去以他州法來取代本州法[98]』」。「在憲法被通過後的幾十年內州

---

[93] 美國ALI Complex Litigation Proposal第6章選法規則之6.03條是有關當事人沒有有效的約定準據法之情形。該第6.03條仍是本於關連點及利益說而來，但(c)項則多了比較損害利益之加州理論。整個規則則是非常籠統而缺少要點。

[94] 個人認為minimum contacts於管轄規則上在美國已造成「最大程度之混亂」（minimum contacts cause maximum chaos），於選法規則上因為忽視所牽連的實體政策，故構成「最大程度之欺騙」（minimum contacts constitute maximum deception）。

[95] 486 U.S. 717; 108 S. Ct. 2117; 100 L. Ed. 2d 743; 1988 U.S. LEXIS 2723; 56 U.S.L.W. 4601; 101 Oil & Gas Rep.1

[96] 472 U.S. 797, 816-823, 86 L. Ed. 2d 628, 105 S. Ct. 2965 (1985) (Shutts Ⅲ).

[97] Wells v. Simonds Abrasive Co., 345 U.S. 514, 516-518, 97 L. Ed. 1211, 73 S. Ct. 856 (1953); Townsend v. Jemison, 50 U.S. 407, 9 HOW 407, 413-420, 13 L. Ed. 194 (1850); Mcmoyle v. Cohen, 13 Pet. 312, 327-328 (1839).

[98] 486 U.S. 717, 722, "The Full Faith and Credit Clause does not compel "a state to substitute the statutes

之案例顯示，法院毫不遲疑的參考國際法以得到本案問題之提示[99]……」
當時的法官根據國際法的規則，認為於州際案件中適用地院法的消滅時效
是合適的[100]。Erie案之法理是包含聯邦訴訟法在內意圖於聯邦法院及聯邦
法院所在之州法院間達成可預測結果之重大一致性。相對的，於充份互信
條款之規範下，實體程序二分法之目的不在建立統一性，而是在確認對州
立法權能範圍之限制[101]。最高法院認為法院不能脫離在憲法強制規定下，

---

of other states for its own statutes dealing with a subject matter concerning which it is competent to legislate." Pacific Employers Ins. Co. v. Industrial Accident Comm'n, 306 U.S. 493, 501, 83 L. Ed. 940, 59 S. Ct. 629 (1939).

[99] 486 U.S. 717, 724, "The reported state cases in the decades immediately following ratification of the Constitution show that courts looked without hesitation to international law for guidance in resolving the issue underlying this case: which State's law governs the statute of limitations. The state of international law on that subject being as we have described, these early decisions uniformly concluded that the forum's statute of limitations governed even when it was longer than the limitations period of the State whose substantive law governed the merits of the claim."Nash v. Tupper, 1 Cai. 402, 412-413 (N. Y. 1803); Pearsall v. Dwight, 2 Mass. 84, 89-90 (1806); Ruggles v. Keeler, 3 Johns. 263, 267-268 (N. Y. 1808) (Kent, C. J.); Graves v. Graves's Executor, 5 Ky. 207, 208-209 (1810).

[100] 同上，"Obviously, judges writing in the era when the Constitution was framed and ratified thought the use of the forum statute of limitations to be proper in the interstate context. Their implicit understanding that the Full Faith and Credit Clause did not preclude reliance on the international law rule carries great weight." Medbury v. Hopkins, 3 Conn. 472, 473 (1820); cf. McCluny v. Silliman, 3 Pet. 270, 276-277 (1830); Hawkins v. Barney's Lessee, 5 Pet. 457, 466 (1831).

[101] 同上，726, 727, "In the context of our Erie jurisprudence, see Erie R. Co. v. Tompkins, 304 U.S. 64, 82 L. Ed. 1188, 58 S. Ct. 817 (1938), that purpose is to establish (within the limits of applicable federal law, including the prescribed Rules of Federal Procedure) substantial uniformity of predictable outcome between cases tried in a federal court and cases tried in the courts of the State in which the federal court sits. See Guaranty Trust, supra, at 109; Hanna v. Plumer, 380 U.S. 460, 467, 471-474, 14 L. Ed. 2d 8, 85 S. Ct. 1136 (1965). The purpose of the substance procedure dichotomy in the context of the Full Faith and Credit Clause, by contrast, is not to establish uniformity but to delimit spheres of state legislative competence." 歐盟布魯塞爾公約及規則是被稱為「歐洲的充份互信條款」，但相對於美國之「充份互信條款」並不意圖建立一致性，反而是尊重確認各州之立法權，歐盟之意圖消滅英美法是甚為反諷而低級。更有趣的是Erie（見陳隆修、許兆慶、林恩瑋，《台灣財產法暨經濟法研究叢書（十三）—國際私法：選法理論之回顧與展望》，台灣財產法暨經濟法研究協會發行，2007年1月，初版，194頁）案之目的是尊重各州之法律及判決，卻被認為是可以促進統一，歐盟何時才能進化為文明之國家？
事實上亦有美國同僚注意到歐盟以鐵血政策意圖消滅英國判法，進而達到法律之統一，並促成內部市場發達之作法是美國經驗不合的。見George A. Bermann，Rome I: A Comparative View，於Rome I Regulation: The Law Applicable to Contractual Obligations in Europe edited by Franco Ferrari, Stefan Leible, pp. 355, 354:
We may conclude then that a leavening of differences among the contract laws of the States through Restatements of Contracts, combined with a leavening of differences among the conflicts of law rules of the States through Restatements of Conflict of Laws, has struck Americans as the better recipe for coherence than the legal federalization of either the one or the other body of law. It is thought better to leave some "breathing space" both in substantive state contract law and in state conflicts law than to establish a federal law strait-jacket in either.

長久以來所建立的國際私法判例及慣例，因此肯州之適用其消滅時效並未違反充份互信原則[102]。

至於肯州適用自己之消滅時效是否違反適當程序條款，最高法院認為這種作法長久以來並未被質疑，「如果一件事於大眾同意下已被實行二百年，那麼需要很強的證據才能以十四修正案去影響它[103]」。其之結論為：「一個州之利益於規定其法院之負擔及決定一個請求權是否太久而不能被判決，當然足以構成其於立法管轄上以消滅時效之規定來控制其法院所給予之救濟。另外這個法規適用之歷史如美國本身一般的久，上訴人是絕對不會受到不公平的驚訝的。因此，簡單的說，肯州於此之判決是沒有『武斷或不公平』的……因此違反適當程序條款的指控是沒有理由的[104]」。這樣子的論述已擺脫土地關連點及「狹義」州利益之糾纏，而堂堂正正的邁入實體法上之政策分析。事實上最高法院亦引用早期之權威著作以為實體分析之基礎：「對於訴訟上陳舊的請求權所定下的適當時間之限制，在

⋮

There remains one other tempting explanation. The United States, due to its long and incrementally accomplished federalism, is simply less intent than the European Union on pursuing market integration through legislative action. Achievement of a market without internal borders simply is not and has nor for scome Cime been an oveniding political objective. While the orocesses of conscious union-building wirhin the EU are undoubredly plagued virh controversy, rhe subjecr itselfremains a major preoccupat:ion. The United Srates by conrrasr has developed over Cime the sense thar formal unihcation of commercial law is simply noc essential Co the survival of eirher the American tarket or American federalism.

故而由Erie案的經驗顯示，尊重各州之法律及判決是在確保判決的實質統一及預測性。美國二百多年來經驗顯示法律形式上之統一對聯邦內部市場的生存並不重要。於大中華經濟區再次崛起之際，有兩千多年歷史的中華民族應向有二百多年歷史的美國學習，或走向有五十多年鐵血統一經驗的歐盟，答案或許是很清楚的。

[102] 486 U.S. 717, 729.
[103] 486 U.S. 717, 730, "If a thing has been practiced for two hundred years by common consent, it will need a strong case for the Fourteenth Amendment to affect it." Jackman v. Rosenbaum Co., 260 U.S. 22, 31, 67 L. Ed. 107, 43 S. Ct. 9 (1922).
[104] 486 U.S. 717, 730, "State's interest in regulating the workload of its courts and determining when a claim is too stale to be adjudicated certainly suffices to give it legislative jurisdiction to control the remedies available in its courts by imposing statutes of limitations. Moreover, petitioner could in no way have been unfairly surprised by the application to it of a rule that is as old as the Republic. There is, in short, nothing in Kansas action here that is 'arbitrary or unfair,' Shutts Ⅲ, 472 U.S. at 821-822, and the due process challenge is entirely without substance."

考慮自己之利益及便利下，是每個政府於州內政策及規定下所擁有的裁量權[105]」。

　　另外最高法院又引用判例法[106]認為必須違反其他州明確建立之法律，及該違反已經被上訴人呈現於該州法院前，州法院對外州法律之解釋才構成違反充份互信條款及適當程序條款，而肯州法院並未到達這個標準[107]。有趣的是法院引用實體政策之分析來回答反對意見：「部分反對意見似乎假定契約法規定承諾人必須明示接受其義務方能被視為有拘束力。但是一般契約法的規定是，即使當事人並不知情，其仍受習慣或慣例之拘束，並且即使其有相反意圖亦應如此[108]」。法院並引述舊統一商法及第2新編契約法為實體法上之依據[109]。歐盟契約法原則1：105條規定：「(1)經由當事人所同意及他們之間所建立的模式而來之慣例，對當事人有拘束力。(2)除非此種慣例之適用是不合理的，否則一般當事人於相同情形下通常會被認為適用之慣例應對當事人有拘束力[110]」。2004年新版之統一商法1-303(c)條規定如下：「一個『商業習慣』是任何交易之行為或方式，

---

[105] 486 U.S. 717, 726, J. Kent, Commentaries on American Law 462-463 (2d ed. 1832): "The period sufficient to constitute a bar to the litigation of sta[1]e demands, is a question of municipal policy and regulation, and one which belongs to the discretion of every government, consulting its own interest and convenience."

[106] Pennsylvania Fire Ins. Co. v. Gold Issue Mining & Milling Co., 243 U.S. 93, 96, 61 L. Ed. 610, 37 S. Ct. 344 (1917); Western Life Indemnity Co. v. Rupp, 235 U.S. 261, 275, 59 L. Ed. 220, 35 S. Ct. 37 (1914); Louisville & Nashville R. Co. v. Melton, 218 U.S. 36, 51-52, 54 L. Ed. 921, 30 S. Ct. 676 (1910); Banholzer v. New York Life Ins. Co., 178 U.S. 402, 408, 44 L. Ed. 1124, 20 S. Ct. 972 (1900).

[107] 486 U.S. 717, 730, 731。

[108] 486 U.S. 717, 733, "the partial dissent appears to assume that contract law requires promisor to make a conscious assumption of an obligation in order to be bound. It is standard contract law, however, that a party may be bound by a custom or usage even though he is unaware of it, and indeed even if he positively intended the contrary. 參陳隆修，《2005年海牙法院選擇公約評析》，台北，五南圖書公司，2009年1月，初版1刷".

[109] U.C.C. §§ 1-201(3), 1-205(3), and Comment 4, 1 U. L. A. 44, 84, 85 (1976); Restatement (Second) of Contracts § 221, and Comment a (1981).

[110] 見the Commission of European Contract Law, Principles of European Contract Law, edited by Ole Lando and Hugh Beale (2000).
ARTICLE 1:106: USAGES AND PRACTICES
(1) The parties are bound by any usage to which they have agreed and by any practice they have established between themselves.
(2) The parties are bound by a usage which would be considered generally applicable by persons in the same situation as the parties, except where the application of such usage would be unreasonable.

在一個商業、職業、或地方經常性的被遵守，以至在有關爭議中之交易之會被遵守是符合期待的[111]」。至於歐盟契約法原則中合理性之要求，一如英美法之慣例，統一商法中非但有著更詳盡之規定[112]，並且於(d)項中規定慣例可以補充、限制、及解釋契約中之條款[113]。於解釋報告第5段中認為現今雖然推定慣例通常為合理的，但仍應受到法院之監督[114]。「合理之慣例」之拘束性，為契約法上英美法與大陸法長久或自古以來無可爭議的主流共同核心價值。一個案件是否會「造成武斷及基本上不公平之後果」如果不以「合理之慣例」做為衡量之基準，而以土地關連點及州利益做為基準，那麼這種衡量本身就是「武斷及不公平」。

「合理之慣例」本身是一個爭議性較少之古老之世界性主流共同核心價值，本案之主要爭點為消滅時效究竟為實體法或程序法。因為大陸法較

---

[111] U.C.C. 1-303

1-303.COURSE OF PERFORMANCE, COURSE OF DEALING, AND USAGE OF TEADE

(c) A "usage of trade" is any practice or method of dealing having such regularity of observance in a place, vocation, or trade as to justify an expectation that it will be observed with respect to the transaction in question. The existence and scope of such a usage must be proved as facts. If it is established that such a usage is embodied in a trade code or similar record, the interpretation of the record is a question of law.

[112] (e) Except as otherwise provided in subsection (f), the express terms of an agreement and any applicable course of performance, course of dealing, or usage of trade must be construed whenever reasonable as consistent with each other. If such a construction is unreasonable:

(1) express terms prevail over course of performance, course of dealing, and usage of trade;

(2) course of performance prevails over course of dealing and usage of trade; and

(3) course of dealing prevails over usage of trade. 及

(g) Evidence of a relevant usage of trade offered by one party is not admissible unless that party has given the other party notice that the court finds sufficient to prevent unfair surprise to the other party.

[113] (d) A course of performance or course of dealing between the parties or usage of trade in the vocation or trade in which they are engaged or of which they are or should be aware is relevant in ascertaining the meaning of the parties' agreement, may give particular meaning to specific terms of the agreement, and may supplement or qualify the terms of the agreement. A usage of trade applicable in the place in which part of the performance under the agreement is to occur may be so utilized as to that part of the performance.

[114] 5. The policies of the Uniform Commercial Code controlling explicit unconscionable contracts and clauses (Sections 1-304, 2-302) apply to implicit clauses that rest on usage of trade and carry forward the policy underlying the ancient requirement that a custom or usage must be "reasonable." However, the emphasis is shifted. The very fact of commercial acceptance makes out a prima facie case that the usage is reasonable. But the anciently established policing of usage by the courts is continued to the extent necessary to cope with the situation arising if an unconscionable or dishonest practice should become standard.

常偏向前者，而英美法較常偏向後者[115]，故而長久以來無論於實務或學理上各國爭執不斷。有趣的是於本案中美國最高法院對此爭點採實體政策之分析，以決定是否會違反憲法上「武斷或不公平」之標準。美國最高法院引用判例法陳述：早期在憲法通過之初「法院毫不遲疑的參考國際法以得到本案問題之指示」。最高法院並據以作成肯州適用自己之消滅時效為不違憲之依據。如果二百年前的最高法院會引用當時的國際法，那麼現在的最高法院引用的應是二百年前的國際法，還是現今的國際法？答案應是很清楚的。

　　消滅時效過去近二百年來的確為定性及分割問題[116]（dépecagè）中之要角，但現今歐盟羅馬公約第10(1)(d)條明文規定消滅時效為契約準據法之範圍，較近之羅馬I亦於第12(1)(d)條做同樣之規範[117]，而羅馬II則於第15（h）條規定非契約準據法決定消滅時效之適用[118]。以大陸法為主之歐盟，於契約及非契約上之消滅時效以實體上之準據法為依據，自然是可預測的。但於尚未加入歐盟前，英國之Foreign Limitation Periods Act 1984, s.1(1)即規定消滅時效應依外國準據法而定[119]，這自然是對英國兩百

---

[115] 陳隆修，《比較國際私法》，台北，五南圖書公司，78年10月，初版，142～144頁，168～171頁。

[116] 陳隆修，《比較國際私法》，台北，五南圖書公司，78年10月，初版，37～39頁。

[117] Regulation (EC) No 593/2008 of the European Parliament and of the Council of 17 June 2008 on the law applicable to contractual obligations (Rome I).
Article 12 Scope of the law applicable
1. The law applicable to a contract by virtue of this Regulation shall govern in particular:
(d) the various ways of extinguishing obligations, and prescription and limitation of actions.

[118] Article 15 Scope of the law applicable
The law applicable to non-contractual obligations under this Regulation shall govern in particular:
(h) the manner in which an obligation may be extinguished and rules of prescription and limitation, including rules relating to the commencement, interruption and suspension of a period of prescription or limitation.

[119] 1.-(1) Subject to the following provisions of this Act, where in any action or proceedings in a court in England and Wales the law of any other country falls (in accordance with rules of private international law applicable by any such court) to be taken into account in the determination of any matter—
(a) the law of that other country relating to limitation shall apply in respect of that matter for the purposes of the action or proceedings; and
(b) except where that matter falls within subsection (2) below, the law of England and Wales relating to limitation shall not so apply.
(2) A matter falls within this subsection if it is a matter in the determination of which both the law of England and Wales and the law of some other country fall to be taken into account.

年來之國際私法之一大變革。或許對大陸法同僚而言，英國傳統上於此方面之判例過份複雜[120]，但個人一向覺得甚合乎邏輯。無論如何，於無損於個案正義下，此方面法律之統一總算是解套。英國會做如此之讓步，最主要是早期為了加入歐盟所做之準備。但大陸法與英美法長久的隔閡並非短時間就可泯滅於無形。最大的問題可能是大陸法一向視消滅時效為公法，故為強行法規，以至於當事人不得修正時效之期間，而英美法一向允許當事人以契約修正時效之期間。為避免造成不公正之情況[121]，於1984年之the Foreign Limitation Periods Act中，section2 (1).有保留裁量權給予法院去拒絕採用過長或過短的外國消滅時效。另外section2 (2)中又對當事人不知所適用的外國準據法禁止的情況下，而同意延長消滅時效，因而所造成的不適當的困擾，法院得以違反公共政策為由不去適用該準據法。另外對消滅時效的起算、暫停起算、權利人對時效的延遲是否有過失等，皆有詳細規定。而所謂外國法之適用，是排除國際私法而包含其實體法與程序法在內[122]。

　　以實體法政策分析之角度而言，個人認為消滅時效之相關議題上，最主要並不是實體與程序上之區分，而是在於大陸法是否能追隨先進之

---

[120] 陳隆修，《比較國際私法》，台北，五南圖書公司，78年10月，初版，142～144頁。

[121] 陳隆修、許兆慶、林恩瑋，《台灣財產法暨經濟法研究叢書（十三）─國際私法：選法理論之回顧與展望》，台灣財產法暨經濟法研究協會發行，2007年1月，初版，117頁。

[122] 2.—(1) In any case in which the application of section 1 above would to any extent conflict (whether under subsection (2) below or otherwise) with public policy, that section shall not apply to the extent that its application would so conflict.

(2) the application of section 1 above in relation to any action or proceedings shall conflict with public policy to the extent that its application would cause undue hardship to a person who is, or might be made, a party to the action or proceedings.

4.— (1) Subject to subsection (3) below, references in this Act to law of any country (including England and Wales) relating to limitation shall, in relation to any matter, be construed as references to so much of the relevant law of that country as (in any manner) makes provision with respect to a limitation period applicable to the bringing of proceedings in respect of that matter in the courts of that country and shall include—

(a) references to so much of that law as relates to, and to the effect of, the application, extension, reduction or interruption of that period; and

(b) a reference, where under that law there is no limitation period which is so applicable, to the rule that such proceedings may be brought within an indefinite period.

(2) In subsection (1) above "relevant law", in relation to any country, means the procedural and substantive law applicable, apart from any rules of private international law, by the counts of that country.

英美法，同樣的允許當事人修正私人權利義務的期限。法學之進展是無法以意識型態去阻擋的，當羅馬Ⅰ、Ⅱ顢頇頑固的得意於大陸法之多數暴力時，歐盟契約法原則14：601條[123]澆了他們一頭冷水：「(1)當事人得以約定修改時效之規定，特別是於有關縮減或延長期間的限制。(2)但限制的時間不得低於一年，或自14：203條時效開始計算後被延長超過三十年[124]」。故而當事人得延長或縮短時效，改變時效起算時間，或他們可以增加或減少時效暫停計算之理由。歐盟契約法委員會之立法解釋如下：「這些反對意見通常是根據請求權的限制所代表的公共利益而來。但是必須注意的是，請求權的限制最主要是為了保護債務人。而當債務人自己放棄這種保護時，當事人自主應可被視為超越公共利益。並且在反對這種當事人得同意使得限制更為困難的國家裏，通常所採用的限制期間是較為長（10、20、或30年），以至於再度延長時間的確可能造成困難；至少比起我們有較短的一般時效期間的情況會較有困難。因此通常在時間是特別的短的時候，延長時間的約定是會特別的被允許的。於建築物或物品潛在的瑕疵之保證即可能有該種效果，並且給予一個明顯的及實際上重要的例子[125]」。故而無論將時效定性為實體上或程序上之問題，大陸法接受英美

---

[123] 見the Commission of European Contract Law, Principles of European Contract Law, edited by Ole Lando and Hugh Beale, Part Ⅲ.

[124] Article 14:601: Agreements Concerning Prescription

(1) The requirements for prescription may be modified by agreement between the parties, in particular by either shortening or lengthening the periods of prescription.

(2) The period of prescription may not, however, be reduced to less than one year or extended to more than thirty after the time of commencement set out in Article 14:203.

[125] 同上，P.207, "Agreements rendering prescription more difficult are more widely regarded as objectionable than agreements facilitating prescription. These objections are usually based upon the public interest which the prescription of claims is intended to serve. It must, however, be remembered that the prescription of claims predominantly serves to protect the debtor and that, where the debtor renounces such protection, private autonomy may well be seen to prevail over the public interest. Also, the general prescription periods applying in countries objecting to agreements rendering prescription more difficult are comparatively long (ten, twenty, or thirty years) so that a further lengthening may indeed be problematic; much more problematic, at any rate, than where we have a short general prescription period. Widely, therefore, agreements lengthening the period are specifically admitted, where the period is, exceptionally, a short one. Contractual warranties concerning latent defects in buildings or goods can have that effect and provide an obvious and practically important example. Equally, it tends to be accepted that the prohibition does not affect agreements which indirectly render prescription more difficult, such as agreements postponing the due date of a claim, or pacta de non petendo (agreements allowing addi-

法[126]之作法允許當事人以約定去修正時效之相關問題已是既成之國際法。大陸法所謂的公共利益事實上主要亦是在保護弱勢，個人認為契約法上一般的規定，例如前述歐盟契約法5：103條有關非個別洽商條款、6：105條一方所決定之不合理條款、及1：201條之誠信原則條款[127]等皆應被適用於時效修正條款中對弱勢之保護上。U.C.C. s. 2-302雖亦有限制或禁止不公平條款之適用之規定，但個人一向覺得英美法或許較沉溺於資本主義，對弱勢之保護政策不若大陸法之明張旗鼓。尤其個人由年輕至今一向認為英美法之時效雖可被加以修正，但相較之下似乎較為短，如此可能破壞當事人折衝之空間，有鼓勵訴訟之反效果。對主張事緩則圓之中國文化而言，這是一種負面文化及不良之法律。

事實上這種中國文化多少於時效上是反映在法學上的，歐盟契約法原則14：301條規定：「債權人不知或無法合理的知道下列情況時，時效是暫時停止的：(a)債務人之身份；或(b)引起得提起請求之事實，這包含於請求損害賠償之權利時有關損害之種類[128]」。歐盟契約法委員會之立法理由為：「今日這是逐漸被加以承認的。令人不感到意外的是，這種發現標準的興起是與一般傾向較短的時效間有密切關連。更正確的說，最近有個趨勢傾向（i）考慮到債權人對目前有關一系列興起的請求權的無知，而（ii）一方面藉由轉移不知道的標準至合理發現的標準，以降低此方面的考量會遲延了時效的進行。本法規代表了此方面的發展[129]」。英國法亦早

---

tional time for performance)."
[126] 英國Limitation Act 1980, Part I, s. 1(2)即開宗明義的規定，通常時效是可以根據Part II 的相關規定而排除或延長的。
[127] 美國則見U.C.C.的2-302條中亦有類似規定。
[128] Article 14:301: Suspension in Case of Ignorance
The running of the period of prescription is suspended as long as the creditor does not know of, and could not reasonably know of:
(a) the identity of the debtor; or
(b) the facts giving rise to the claim including, in the case of a right to damages, the type of damage.
[129] 見the Commission of European Contract Law, Principles of European Contract Law, edited by Ole Lando and Hugh Beale (2000), Part III, p.175, "This is increasingly recognized today. Not surprisingly, the rise of the discoverability criterion has been closely related to the general tendency towards shorter prescription periods. More precisely, there has been a trend towards (i) taking account of the creditor's ignorance with regard to a growing range of claims while (ii) reducing the inherent potential of this

就有類似的立法，但就立法的時間與技術而言，英國似乎皆較歐盟先進。英國的Limitation Act 1980 s.33(1)給予法院裁量權於相關人身傷害或死亡時，法院得於衡平法則下排除時效之適用[130]。相較於大陸法的死硬，英國法院得依個案之需求，於衡平原則下行使裁量權，而s.33(3),(4),(5)則規定裁量行使之準則[131]。除了合理性之共同點外，英國法似乎較大陸法注重個案之衡平性，並給予繫屬法院裁量權以達成個案正義。個人認為這是中國及全世界本著現今既有的合理性共同核心價值上，無論於國際私法或

---

consideration for delaying the course of prescription by moving from lack of knowledge towards a test of reasonable discoverability. The Principles reflect these developments."

[130] If it appears to the court that it would be equitable to allow an action to proceed having regard to the degree to which—

(a) the provisions of section 11 [F1 or 11A] or 12 of this Act prejudice the plaintiff or any person whom he represents; and

(b) any decision of the court under this subsection would prejudice the defendant or any person whom he represents;

the court may direct that those provisions shall not apply to the action, or shall not apply to any specified cause of action to which the action relates.

[131] (3) In acting under this section the court shall have regard to all the circumstances of the case and in particular to—

(a) the length of, and the reasons for, the delay on the part of the plaintiff;

(b) the extent to which, having regard to the delay, the evidence adduced or likely to be adduced by the plaintiff or the defendant is or is likely to be less cogent than if the action had been brought within the time allowed by section 11 [F4, by section 11A] or (as the case may be) by section 12;

(c) the conduct of the defendant after the cause of action arose, including the extent (if any) to which he responded to requests reasonably made by the plaintiff for information or inspection for the purpose of ascertaining facts which were or might be relevant to the plaintiff's cause of action against the defendant;

(d) the duration of any disability of the plaintiff arising after the date of the accrual of the cause of action;

(e) the extent to which the plaintiff acted promptly and reasonably once he knew whether or not the act or omission of the defendant, to which the injury was attributable, might be capable at that time of giving rise to an action for damages;

(f) the steps, if any, taken by the plaintiff to obtain medical, legal or other expert advice and the nature of any such advice he may have received.

(4) In a case where the person injured died when, because of section 11 [F3 or subsection (4) of section 11A], he could no longer maintain an action and recover damages in respect of the injury, the court shall have regard in particular to the length of, and the reasons for, the delay on the part of the deceased.

(5) In a case under subsection (4) above, or any other case where the time limit, or one of the time limits, depends on the date of knowledge of a person other than the plaintiff, subsection (3) above shall have effect with appropriate modifications, and shall have effect in particular as if references to the plaintiff included references to any person whose date of knowledge is or was relevant in determining a time limit.

國內法之案件於有關消滅時效上所應效法的主流共同核心價值。

　　另外相對於西方社會，中國社會是將訴訟視為不得已的最後手段。鑑於現今全世界法院案件的累積，西方社會縮短時效以致於變相鼓勵訴訟是有必要加以檢討的，個人看不出「事緩則圓」的二千年文化為何無法移植於西方法界。例如個人於西安兩岸研討會中所報告之日本名古屋裁判所平成8（7）1433與7（7）4179號華航名古屋空難判決[132]，日本法院只給予台灣受害人大約日本受害人1/3之賠償額，顯然是違反人權法與衡平原則之野蠻行為。但自上報後個人雖然立即出書已經歷多時，受害人家屬自然無法「合理的發現」這個國際私法上少有（或沒有）的野蠻行為之違反人權公約，故依衡平原則自應排除時效之適用或進行。於瞬息萬變日新月異的現代社會中，任何人都可能成為無辜之受害者。今年的金融海嘯已充份證明對企業的保護只會傷害到社會，「人為財死，鳥為食亡」，企業追逐利潤就如同非洲草原上獅子追逐草食動物。近年來之趨勢為以縮短時效來降低企業責任[133]，特別是產品責任方面最為明顯，對此個人並不認同。個

---

[132] 陳隆修，《2005年海牙法院選擇公約評析》，台北，五南圖書公司，2009年1月，初版1刷，290、291頁。

[133] 於the Commission of European Contact Law, Principles of European Contract Law, edited by Ole Lando and Hugh Beale (2000), Part Ⅲ, p.175,歐盟契約法委員會認為並非所有的請求權皆應受到一致的客觀標準，但非契約之請求與基於違反契約之請求是可能密切相關的。對同一個事實而來之請求權，有些國家認為是侵權行為，而有些國家則認為應屬契約或不當得利。例如基於責任而來之請求，於法國可能是侵權，而於英國可能是屬於契約之保證。又如超過授權範圍之智慧財產權之侵犯，究竟應屬於契約或侵權，各國可能認定不同。歐盟契約法委員會不知所云的無法提出解決之方法。2005年海牙法院選擇公約則充份認知這個問題於國際上的複雜性，其於第2(2)(0)條有關智慧財產權之解釋報告中闡明：「於許多原因上這個規定是很重要的。於有些國家當事人只需申訴事實：法院應去決定適宜的法律上的定性。法院是否選擇契約或侵權可能是根據哪種類別較易建立。於其他國家，當事人自己決定是以契約或侵權起訴。他們可能有好理由去做如此選擇（例如取得較高賠償之機會）。因此不能根據這些偶然的考慮因素來決定一個案件是否包含於公約範圍內」。Explanatory Report by Trevor Hartley and Masato Dogauchi, para. 81, 於Kalfelis v. Schroder, Case 189/87 [1988] ECR 5565中歐盟法院給予侵權或準侵權一個自主性之定義。Source Ltd v. TUV Rheinland Holding A G [1998] QB54即讓英國法院基於Kalfelis而對契約與侵權之關係甚感困擾。Kleinwort Benson Ltd. v. Glasgow City Council, Case C-346/93 [1996] QB57,歐盟法院拒絕處理本案，使得英國法院於契約法與不當得利間甚感困擾（void ab initio）。

個人注意到1999年海牙管轄草約第21條1項有關lis pendens之適用範圍侷限於當事人相同及訴因相同，而當事人所請求之救濟則為無關。"1. When the same parties are engaged in proceedings in courts of different Contracting States and when such proceedings are based on the same causes of action, irrespective of the relief sought, the court second seised shall suspend the proceedings if the court

人認為應實質的擴大法院之裁量範圍，以便於個案中確保衡平原則的被遵守。

　　故而在消滅時效之實體法發展上，英美法與大陸法共同之發展趨勢（trend；或核心價值）應可歸納如下：(1)首先於不違反強行規定下，當事人可以經由約定而修正時效之條件。(2)於「合理發現的標準」下，時效是可以停止進行的；但有關此點個人較為認同英國法的授予法院裁量權，以便於個案中依衡平原則而主持正義。並且個人主張於現代科技社會之都市叢林中，每個人都如非洲草原之草食動物，面對跨國企業之大小獅群惶惶不可終日，法院為上帝於人間主持正義之最後或唯一的地方，法院裁量權之運用應隨著科技發展而擴大。

　　美國最高法院於Sun Oil中大致上跳脫以土地關連點及狹義的州利益做為衡量「武斷或基本上不公平」之依據，轉而以所涉及的實體法之政策分析為衡量之基準，這是令人非常贊許的作法。於契約慣例之拘束力上，法院是引用舊統一商法及第2新編契約法為實體法上之依據，這個分析不

---

first seised has jurisdiction and is expected to render a judgment capable of being recognised under the Convention in the State of the court second seised, unless the latter has exclusive jurisdiction under Article 4 or 12."個人認為國際法實體法之實質統一遙遙無期，故而主張於目前應以一事不再理之訴訟程序解決這個實體法上之技術性差異：「有關判決之承認與執行上，並不只侷限於有關管轄條款之判決，個人還是認為無論是基於契約、侵權或衡平法之請求，只要是有經過適當之送達、為合適之自然法院及給予當事人充分之表達機會（包括應利用原來法院之救濟程序），則該判決或決定皆應有一事不再理之效果。不過如前所述，如果欲追加新訴因，則必須再取得對新訴因之管轄權」。參陳隆修，《2005年海牙法院選擇公約評析》，台北，五南圖書公司，2009年1月，初版1刷，138頁。亦即無論是於訴因禁止反言或爭點禁止反言，如果當事人於程序上有受到公平正義的對待，並且有著充分之機會，則應受到原作成判決法院地訴訟法之拘束，如果原法院為英美法院，當事人無論有無提出抗辯，有關同一事實之請求及抗辯，皆應受到訴因禁反言及爭點禁反言之拘束。如果原作成法院為大陸法院，則可能必須當事人相同、訴之聲明相同、及標的相同之嚴格情形下才受到拘束。亦即基於同一事實而來之契約、侵權、或不當得利（衡平法）之請求與抗辯，是否對後來之案件（無論當事人是否相同）於訴因及爭點禁止反言上有拘束力，應依原作成判決法院之規定為依據。英國創設訴因（cause）及爭點（issue）禁止反言（estoppel）之最主要目的乃在主持公平正義，依原作成判決法院地法當事人才能被給予完全充分保障之機會，公平正義之目的才能被達到，這亦是個人主張以「有效正義」為一事不再理或禁止反言之基礎的主要原因。有關美國一事不再理之發展見Howard M. Erichson, interjuriseictional preclusion, 96 Mich. L. Rev. 945, (1998); Robert B. Quigley, an examination of res judicata principles precluding infringement 30. claims arising from the approved purchase of a copyright at a bankruptcy sale, 37 Creighton L. Rev. 1029 (2004); Randy D. Gordon, only one kick at the cat: a contextual rubric for evaluating res judicata and collateral estoppel in international commercial arbitration, 18 Fla. J. Int'lL. 549 (2006).

但與新統一商法1-303條吻合，並且與大陸法之歐盟契約法原則1:105條一致。通常如果英美法與大陸法一致，除非有強而有利之理由可以徹底加以反駁，否則即應構成國際社會之主流共同核心價值。於本案之主要爭點消滅時效之問題上，已如前述目前國際社會（包含英美法及大陸法）中已存在兩個共同之趨勢（或核心價值），這不可爭辯的亦就是目前已存在之事實上（de facto）之國際法。兩百年前將消滅時效性定性為程序法之「國際法」，事實上並未得到大陸法之認同，只能說是英美法所認定之「國際法」。而前述之兩個實體法上之趨勢（或核心價值）是共同為大陸法及英美法所認可的，故自然為真正的國際法，而其中之第2個趨勢（或價值）是直接應適用於本案複雜之集體訴訟中的。法院可以跳脫土地關連點與狹義州利益的桎梏自然是可喜，但憲法剛通過時「法院毫不遲疑的參考國際法以得到本案問題之指示」，為什麼現今的美國最高法院拘泥於評價的禁忌，而不敢對現在真正的、事實上之國際法加以參考，「以得到本案問題的指示」？本案之個案正義並未受到傷害，但是法院引用二百年前先祖們其時之「國際法」（？）為「武斷或不公平」之依據，而不以現時之真正國際法於實體法上之共識為依據，這種作法本身就是「武斷及不公平」，故而非常反諷的可能違反適當程序條款及充分互信條款。

　　無論於國際案件或國內案件上，為避免造成「武斷及基本上不公平的後果」，實體政策的分析不但是必要的，而且通常應做為主要之基準。這種實體政策分析之方法論幾乎可適用於國際及國內法之大部分之公、私法之範疇內。無論於國際或國內案件，採用實體政策之分析，通常皆可促進相關領域之發展。對於法學較為落後之國家，採用實體政策分析之方法論，對國家整體法學之發展更是明顯的助益[134]。故而今年4月個人於武漢國際法研究所與年輕同僚座談時，一再不怕惹人煩的提醒這些熱情的國際

---

[134] 例如台灣引進英美法不方便法院對訴訟法之影響，參陳隆修，《國際私法管轄權評論》，台北，五南圖書公司，民國75年11月，初版，168～173頁。又如台北地院監字第84號民事裁定引用1989年聯合國兒童權利公約之「兒童最佳利益」，對台灣親屬、國私、及人權法之深遠影響，另參陳隆修、許兆慶、林恩瑋、李瑞生四人合著，《國際私法—管轄與選法理論之交錯》，台北，五南圖書公司，2009年3月，初版1刷，152～160頁。

法同僚：「你們知道自己的責任嗎？」

五、Kelly Kearney 39 Cal. 4th 95; 137 P.3d 914; 2006 Cal. LEXIS 8362

　　加州的「比較損害利益[135]」與Leflar的「較佳法律[136]」是美國新理論中與實體政策分析較有直接關連的兩種理論。實體政策分析方法論為Prof. Leflar所賜名為"multistate theory"，並被他太過客氣而且不吝指教的認為超過較佳法律之範圍。實體方法論與比較損害利益之區別，個人認為實體方法論之重點即在評量實體政策之內容，而比較損害利益則基於利益說對評價之禁忌[137]基本上是採迴避及尊重之自我矛盾之作法。加州法院較近於Kelly Kearney[138]中，為了避免對實體政策加以評價而所採取的折衷方式，或許於方法論上是超越紐約法院的將關連點與利益混合之作法[139]。加州四十年來基於比較損害所做的一系列判決[140]是令人讚賞。於本案中被

---

[135] 陳隆修，《美國國際私法新理論》，台北，五南圖書公司，民國76年1月，初版，69～77頁。

[136] 陳隆修，《美國國際私法新理論》，台北，五南圖書公司，民國76年1月，初版，82～87頁。

[137] 陳隆修，《美國國際私法新理論》，台北，五南圖書公司，民國76年1月，初版，59～63頁。

[138] Kelly Kearney v. Salomon Smith Barney, Inc., 39 Cal. 4th 95; 137 P.3d 914; 45 Cal. Rptr. 3d 730; 2006 Cal. LEXIS 8362; 153 Lab. Cas. (CCH) P60, 240; 2006 Cal. Daily Op. Service 6326; 2006 Daily Journal DAR 9206.

[139] 陳隆修、許兆慶、林恩瑋，《台灣財產法暨經濟法研究叢書（十三）—國際私法：選法理論之回顧與展望》，台灣財產法暨經濟法研究協會發行，2007年1月，初版，208～220頁。

[140] Reich v. Purcell (1967) 67 Cal. 2d 551 [63 Cal. Rptr. 31, 432 P 2d 727]; Hurtado v. Superior Court (1974) 11 Cal. 3d 574 [114 Cal. Rptr. 106, 522 P. 2d 666]; Bernhard v. Harrah's Club (1976) 16 Cal. 3d 313 [128 Cal. Rptr. 215, 546 P. 2d 719]; Offshore Rental Co. v. Continental Oil Co. (1978) 22 Cal. 3d 157 [148 Cal. Rptr. 867, 583 P.2d 721]。早期個人對Bernhard案之分析維持原來之見解，陳隆修，《美國國際私法新理論》，台北，五南圖書公司，民國76年1月，初版，179~181頁。另外於Offshore Rental中，原告加州公司之一職員於被告公司位於路易西安那之土地上受傷。於訴訟前被告公司已經對該受傷之職員給予損害賠償。原告依加州法主張僱主得向對重要員工加以傷害之人請求損害賠償，而路州並無此種法律。加州法院認為即使有這樣的舊法，沒有任何加州法院對此爭點有直接判決，並且直接的陳述該法規為「於聯邦的法律中為陳舊且個別」的條文。" has…exhibited little concern in applying section 49 to the employer employee relationship: despite the provisions of the antique statute, no California court has heretofore squarely held that California law provides an action for harm to business employees, and no California court has recently considered the issue at all. If…section 49 does provide an action for harm to key corporate employees, …the section constitutes a law 'archaic and isolated in the context of the laws of the federal union.' "(Offshore Rental, 22 Cal. 3d at p.168.)因此路州有著較強且更現實的利益，其法律如果不被適用路州之利益會受到較大傷害，故而路州法應被適用為準據法。"[w]e do not believe that California's interests in application of its law to the present case are so compelling as to prevent an accommodation to the

告SSB是個大型的全國性仲介公司，其於加州有許多辦公室並廣泛的營業，其於喬治亞州的員工經常性的於未取得加州客戶的同意下，或告知客戶下，將對話加以錄音。依喬治亞州法這是合法的行為，但卻違反了加州的法律。有幾個加州的客戶於加州提起訴訟，要求被告停止錄音及損害賠償。地院及高院適用喬州法，並拒絕原告之請求。最高法院依據比較損害分析而加以折衷，命令被告停止錄音，但拒絕原告損害賠償之請求。「雖然加州法律明示允許違反632條（637.2條a款）之損害賠償之請求，但是我們合理的相信對因秘密電話錄音而造成侵犯隱私所應給予的金錢價值的估量是困難的，並且這種潛在的金錢損害賠償的嚇阻性價值並不能影響到過去已發生的行為。在這種情形下，我們認為對於過去表面上依據他州法律所做行為之損害賠償請求之拒絕—並且在我們宣佈於此情形下那一州之法律應適用前—並不會嚴重的傷害加州之利益[141]」。因此加州法律雖大致上適用，並且原告可以請求禁止命令以要求被告於將來遵循加州法律，但對於被告過去行為之潛在金錢上之賠償責任加州最高法院適用喬州法，因此被告過去錄音之行為被解除損害賠償責任。

---

stronger, more current interest of Louisiana. We conclude therefore that Louisiana's interest would be the more impaired if its law were not applied, and consequently that Louisiana law governs the present case." (Id. At p. 169.)很明顯加州法院以加州法律為「陳舊且非為一般所共同接受」的評價來做為比較損害利益之基礎，這不是實體政策的分析嗎？「評價禁忌」突然被遺忘了嗎？

Prof. Currie「利益分析」之最主要的基礎即為認定在三權分立之下，法院應對各州之法律政策完全尊重（陳隆修，《美國國際私法新理論》，台北，五南圖書公司，民國76年1月，初版，56~59），絕對禁止法院對各州法律政策之是否合宜或優劣加以斷論。如前所述，「評價禁忌」於美國目前似乎超乎憲法的拘束力，而被哄抬至近乎聖經的位階，前述三個美國最高法院於選法規則的三部曲（被稱為"trilogy"）中，亦於表面上對這個「天條」必恭必敬。如果按照評價禁忌的首要基本守則，一個州之法律是否為"archaic and isolated"，完全與法院於處理案件無關，法院只能忠誠的執行法律，法院是司法單位，沒有能力及權力去質疑法律的過時及沒有被其他州所接受。加州法院於本案是徹底的違反「利益分析」教派不得評價州政策的教條，亦觸犯了美國近四十年來所有各門各派的天條大忌（除了較佳法律學派外）。

[141] 39 Cal. 4th 95, 131, "At the same time, although California law expressly authorizes the recovery of damages for violations of section 632 (§ 637.2, subd. (a)), we believe that it is appropriate to recognize that ascribing a monetary value to the invasion of privacy resulting from the secret recording of a telephone conversation is difficult in any event, and that the deterrent value of such a potential monetary recovery cannot affect conduct that already has occurred. Under these circumstances, we conclude that denying the recovery of damages for conduct that was undertaken in the past in ostensible reliance on the law of another state—and prior to our clarification of which state's law applies in this context—will not seriously impair California's interest."

　　無論是否同意加州法院之折衷式判決，法院賴以為比較損害利益之論述是極度奇怪的。每一個法院都知道非財產上的侵權行為於損害賠償上之「金錢價值的估量是困難的」，「金錢價值的估量」幾乎是每一個侵權、契約、及衡平訴訟的重心，但沒有一個法院敢據此而拒絕給予受害人應有的合理損害賠償─全世界的法院都不敢，除了本審的加州法院以外。

　　法院據以為比較損害賠償利益的第2個理由為：「這種潛在的金錢損害賠償嚇阻性價值並不能影響到過去已發生的行為」。全世界的每一個被害人、每個國會、及每個法院都知道事後的金錢損害賠償「並不能影響到過去已發生的行為」，但幾乎每個受害人都會要求損害賠償，每個國會都會立法給予被害人損害賠償，而每個法院亦都會依法給予被害人合理的損害賠償。事實上不只於民事訴訟上損害賠償「不能影響到過去已發生之行為」，於刑事訴訟上刑罰之量刑亦「不能影響過去已發生之行為」。加州法院這個論述是在挑戰包含中國法制史在內的全人類有史以來所有的民刑訴訟制度；相信絕大部分有理智的人都不會認為加州法院荒謬的論述可以構成對人類司法制度史上的任何威脅。

　　加州法院的判決素來令個人相當程度的感到佩服[142]，但本案引為判決基礎的兩個論述卻幼稚到令人啼笑皆非。這或許是法院太執著於「利益分析」中所堅持的評價禁忌之故。比較損害利益之所以能傲視於美國，乃是其號稱能解決全美國各門各派所公認無法解決之「真衝突」困難案件。於真衝突中法院「應評價及比較各個區域於適用其法律之性質及力道上的利益，『以決定那一州之政策如果屈服於其他州之政策其利益會受到比較大之傷害』……並且最後以『其法律如果沒被適用其利益會較受到損害之州之法律』為依據」。但是比較損害分析之另一目的為：「因為這個方法論的目的之一為『所有政治實體的基本意旨的最大程度的達成』……因此於本案例上是可以適當的對加州法的適用加以節制，以便對過去合理的於喬州依據該州法而行為的人加以保護免得該行為受到金錢上損害賠償之請求

---

[142] 陳隆修，《美國國際私法新理論》，台北，五南圖書公司，民國76年1月，初版，220～229頁。

之喬州合理之利益加以包容[143]」。故而很明顯的加州法院避免去評價相衝突的政策，而盡力去折衷兩個衝突的政策。事實上加州法院知道依據最高法院之判決，加州法院是可以依憲法而引用加州法為準據法的，因為於跨國性的行為中，對於本州內之行為許多州皆可立法保護居民的利益[144]。

　　正如法院引用最高法院之判決認為：「至少大致上而言，一個於其他州營業之外州公司是被要求去遵守其所選擇去營業的地方及州之法律[145]」。並且加州法院自己於Bernhard案中亦要求外州酒店之所有人應遵守加州法[146]。數十年如一日，個人屢屢於著作中強調契約之履行通常不得違反履行地法之基本國際私法觀念[147]，並且於去年將此觀念提昇為國際及國內法共通之主流共同核心價值[148]。事實上這個國際法上之觀念於美國並不完全陌生，美國新編202條第2項亦規定：「當依履行地法該契約之履行是不合法時，該契約通常是會被拒絕執行[149]」。而英國甚早於此方面即有明確之判例，有關不得違背契約履行地法的標準案例為Ralli Bros. v. Compania Naviera Sota y Aznar[150]，一船東與一托運人約定載貨從加爾

[143] 39 Cal. 4th 95, 100, 101, "Although we conclude that the comparative impairment analysis supports the application of California law in this context, we further conclude that because one of the goals of that analysis is 'the maximum attainment of underlying purpose by all governmental entities' (Offshore Renal, 22 Cal. 3d 157, 166, italics added), it is appropriate in this instance to apply California law in a restrained manner that accommodates Georgia's reasonable interest in protecting persons who in the past might have undertaken actions in Georgia in reasonable reliance on Georgia law from being subjected to monetary liability for such actions."

[144] Watson v. Employers Liability Corp. (1954) 348 U.S. 66, 72 [99 L. Ed. 74, 75 S. Ct. 166]
"As a consequence of the modern practice of conducting widespread business activities throughout the entire United States, this Court has in a series of cases held that more states than one may seize hold of local activities which part of multistate transactions and may regulate to protect interests of its own people, even though other phases of the same transactions might justify regulatory legislation in other states."

[145] 39 Cal. 4th 95, 126, "An out-of-state company that does business in another state is required, at least as a general matter, to comply with the laws of a state and locality in which it has chosen to do business. (See, e.g., Watson v. Employers Liability Assurance Corp., supra, 348 U.S. 66, 72.)"

[146] Bernhard, 16 Cal. 3d 313, 322-323.

[147] 陳隆修，《國際私法契約評論》，台北，五南圖書公司，民國75年2月，初版，80～85頁。

[148] 陳隆修，《2005年海牙法院選擇公約評析》，台北，五南圖書公司，2009年1月，初版1刷，92～95頁。

[149] Second Restatement, s.202(2): "When performance is illegal in the place of performance, the contract will usually be denied enforcement."

[150] [1920] 2K. B. 287 (C.A.).

各答到巴塞隆納，價格為一頓50鎊，運費於巴塞隆納交付。在契約訂定後，但在船尚未到達巴塞隆納，西班牙政府規定運費超過每噸10鎊以上為非法，雖準據法為英國法，但英法院判船東不得請求超過每噸10鎊以上的運費。Scrutton, L. J.認為當一個契約之履行地於外國時，除了有特殊情況下，當事人已默認契約之條款必須符合履行地之法律[151]。

　　大陸法的歐盟對這個合乎商業習慣的國際法並不是有著十分清楚的概念，於1980的羅馬公約第7條第1項只是模糊的規定違反有密切關聯國家的強行法規（即刻適用法）時，該強行法得被適用[152]。因為這個條款的模糊性，故為英、德等國際私法先進國家所罷簽。於去年的羅馬Ⅰ規則第9條第3項中，歐盟終於規定契約違反履行地的強行法規（即刻適用法），該強行法規「得」被給予效力[153]。事實上歐盟對這個規則還是不十分了解，不是「得」被給予效力，而是「通常」應被給予效力才是。如早期個人所主張的：「只要契約履行地的法律不是違反世界上大部分文明國家所共同接受的公共政策，則違反契約履行地法律的契約應為無效（或者至少不應被強制執行）[154]」，經過二十多年後，個人於去年闡明「人類文明的公理」應理所當然的包含聯合國1948年人權宣言、1966年聯合國人權宣言、1950年歐盟人權公約、2000年歐盟基本權利憲章、其他文明國家之憲法人權條款，及契約法上共通之基本原則在內[155]。

---

[151] 同上，p.394.

[152] CONVENTION ON THE LAW APPLICABLE TO CONTRACTUAL OBLIGATIONS
Article 7
Mandatory rules
1. When applying under this Convention the law of a country, effect may be given to the mandatory rules of the law of another country with which the situation has a close connection, if and in so far as, under the law of the latter country, those rules must be applied whatever the law applicable to the contract. In considering whether to give effect to these mandatory rules, regard shall be had to their nature and purpose and to the consequences of their application or non-application.

[153] 3. Effect may be given to the overriding mandatory provisions of the law of the country where the obligations arising out of the contract have to be or have been performed, in so far as those overriding mandatory provisions render the performance of the contract unlawful. In considering whether to give effect to those provisions, regard shall be had to their nature and purpose and to the consequences of their application or non-application.

[154] 陳隆修，《國際私法契約評論》，台北，五南圖書公司，民國75年2月，初版，80、81頁。

[155] 陳隆修，《2005年海牙法院選擇公約評析》，台北，五南圖書公司，2009年1月，初版1刷，94、95頁。

撤開複雜的國際法，於常識上被告公司真的無辜？美國National Association of Securities Dealers （NASD）給予會員的通告明文：「公司應被要求獨自去認定州法律的被遵守。每個案件中最好的方法就是由會員公司去告知他們的登記人員及客戶，他們的電話已被錄音[156]」。所有的人都知道在羅馬要遵守羅馬人的規矩，沒有一個大公司的法律事務所會冒著被告的危險而不去警告公司不要違反當地的法規。

加州法院引為結論的兩個論述不但無厘頭的奇怪，亦違反了契約通常不得違反履行地法的國際法及慣例，更違反了商業常識。個人一向尊重的加州法院於這個判決中，造成了大草原中的羊群保護獅子的怪異現象。會造成這種令人瞠目結舌的怪異論述及違反國際私法上基本原則的極端現象，最主要就是美國自最高法院以降，幾乎所有的法院都嚴格的遵守Currie的「假衝突」及「評價禁忌[157]」的理論。由實體政策分析的觀點而論，擅自妨礙秘密偷錄電話交談會有那麼難以評價嗎？如前述履行契約履行地法被遵守的先決要件為「不能違反人類文明的公理」，禁止私自錄音的法律是否違反文明的公理？聯合國1948年人權宣言第12條規定：「沒有任何人可以武斷的被干擾到他的隱私、家庭、住家或通訊，亦不可被攻擊其人格及名聲。每個人皆應享有法律的保護以對抗這種干擾及攻擊[158]」。另

---

[156] "The question of which state law applies when a conversation occurs between a person in a one-party statute state and a person in a two-party statute state is an open issue that depends on the individual laws of each state and the individual facts. Firms would be required to independently determine that state laws are satisfied. The best practice in each case would be for member firms to notify their registered persons and customers that their telephone calls are being tape recorded."(NASD Notice to Members 98-52, p.394)"

[157] 例如於Thomas v. Washington Gas Light Co., 488 U.S. 261, 100 S.Ct. 2647, 65 L. Ed. 2d 757 (1980) 中，即認為充份互信條款並未要求最高法院去「平衡」利益："the Full Faith and Credit Clause did not allot to this Court the task of 'balancing' interests where the 'public Acts, Records and Judicial proceedings' of a state were involved. It simply directed that they be given...'Full Faith and Credit'...Id. at 296, 100 S.Ct. at 2668 (Rehnquist, J., dissenting).

[158] Universal Declaration of Human Rights
Article 12
No one shall be subjected to arbitrary interference with his privacy, home or correspondence, nor to attacks upon his honour and reputation. Everyone has right to the protection of the law against such interference or attacks.

外有此規定的尚有歐盟1950年基本自由及人權公約第8條[159]，歐盟2000年
基本權利憲章除第7條祕密通訊外更有第8條個人資料保護的詳細規定[160]，
及聯合國1966年公民及政治權利公約第17條[161]。因為這是現代社會相當基
本的條款，故而許多國家的憲法[162]及刑法[163]亦皆有規定。被告之行為不但
已違反加州之民刑法，亦違反了美國之憲法。美國開國之先祖們於立國時
便於憲法之序言宣佈：「為保障我們自己及我們的後代有著自由的福報，

---

[159] Convention for the Protection of Human Rights and Fundamental Freedoms
Article 8- Right to respect for private and family life
1. Everyone has the right to respect for his private and family life, his home and his correspondence.
2. There shall be no interference by a public authority with the exercise of this right except such as is in accordance with the law and is necessary in a democratic society in the interests of national security, public safety or the economic well-being of the country, for the prevention of disorder or crime, for the protection of health or morals, or for the protection of the rights and freedoms of others.
[160] CHARTER OF FUNDAMENTAL RIGHTS OF THE EUROPEAN UNION
Article 7
Respect for private and family life
Everyone has the right to respect for his or her private and family life, home and communications.
Article 8
Protection of personal data
1. Everyone has the right to the protection of personal data concerning him or her.
2. Such data must be processed fairly for specified purposes and on the basis of the consent of the person concerned or some other legitimate basis laid down by law. Everyone has the right of access to data which has been collected concerning him or her, and the right to have it rectified.
3. Compliance with these rules shall be subject to control by an independent authority.
[161] International Covenant on Civil and Political Rights
Article 17
1. No one shall be subjected to arbitrary or unlawful interference with his privacy, family, or correspondence, nor to unlawful attacks on his honour and reputation.
2. Everyone has the right to the protection of the law against such interference or attacks.
[162] 例如台灣憲法12條：：「人民有秘密通訊之自由」。
[163] 例如台灣刑法315之1及315之2條：
第315條之1（窺視竊聽竊錄罪）
有下列行為之一者，處三年以下有期徒刑、拘役或三萬元以下罰金：
一、無故利用工具或設備窺視、竊聽他人非公開之活動、言論、談話或身體隱私部位者。
二、無故以錄音、照相、錄影或電磁紀錄竊錄他人非公開之活動、言論、談話或身體隱私部位者。
第315條之2（便利窺視竊聽竊錄罪）
Ⅰ意圖營利供給場所、工具或設備，便利他人為前條第一項之行為者，處五年以下有期徒刑、拘役或科或併科五萬元以下罰金。
Ⅱ意圖散布、播送、販賣而有前條第二款之行為者，亦同。
Ⅲ製造、散布、播送或販賣前二項或前條第二款竊錄之內容者，依第一項之規定處斷。
Ⅳ前三項之未遂犯罰之。

因此制定及建立美國聯邦的本憲法[164]」。

本案中加州法院之論述不但語無倫次，偏離國際私法既有的理論基礎與慣例，違反近代所有人權公約的明文規定，更令人不可接受的是加州之判決及喬州之法律皆違反了它們自己的憲法，辜負了美國先祖們以犧牲生命所換來給予他們後代子孫「自由的福報」。這種泯滅良知的作風應該不只是「評價禁忌」所能單獨造成。個人認為或許亦根源於整個法學理論的以「利益」為導向，故而迷失了正義的方向。

如前述個人主張人權法之終極目標雖全世界應為一致，但現實的人權標準應根據社會及經濟發展的階梯為依據。台灣及大陸雖位於階梯之中下層，但本案中如果錄音的為台灣或大陸之公司，可想而之違反人權公約及憲法條款的指控一定排山倒海而來。加州[165]及喬州於本案中迷惑於商業利益及評價禁忌，故而對不得違反契約履行地法及保護通信秘密之自由，這兩個人類文明中之主流共同價值加以忽視。可嘆的是美國社會正是位於階

---

[164] We the People of the United States, in Order to form a more perfect Union, establish Justice, insure domestic Tranquility, provide for the common defence, promote the general Welfare, and secure the Blessings of Liberty to ourselves and our Posterity, do ordain and establish this Constitution for the United States of America.

[165] 加州法院以折衷之方式來避免其判決之溯及既往，39 Cal. 4th 95, 130, 131, "In light of our decision, of course, out-of-state companies that do business in California now are on notice that, with regard to future conduct, they are subject to California law with regard to the recording of telephone conversations made to or received from California, and that the full range of civil sanctions afforded by California law may be imposed for future violations."

有趣的是三十年前個人於創立實體政策分析主張共同價值之確認時，亦面對同樣的問題：「另一項強而有利的辯詞是，如果我們支持這種價值，則法院的判決將產生溯及既往的效力，而違反了被告應有的權利。這是很好的見解，但是在沒有現行國際法來審理目前發生的國際案件之情況下，這項價值溯及既往的功能，便不列為重要考慮因素。最重要的是這項辯詞，會造成對兩種西方法律制度的創立根據，提出挑戰。無論是大陸法系或習慣法系，社會上所發生的爭執，往往只有在沒有明確的法律規範時，才循訴訟途徑解決。因此，無論我們是否願意，法院的判決都會溯及既往。在沒有人提出較妥善的建議，來彌補這兩種西方法律制度的根本弊端以前，我們無從對它做任何處置。作者不但認為而且建議，西方國家應該接受中國傳統的『政府的教育功能』（the educational function of government）—這正是中共目前以強硬的方式在實施著。無怪乎這一世界上人口最多的地區，能夠在沒有法學家的情形下持續超過二十年。然而這是一項相當艱難的法理學上的爭點（jurisprudential issue），對我們而言，可以將其視為一件法律衝突法上的小問題」。

陳隆修，《美國國際私法新理論》，台北，五南圖書公司，民國76年1月，初版，132，133頁，並見183頁的註11，經過30年，個人完全認同其時對儒家理論及中國社會之見解。政府的教育功能必須本於統一的人類文明的公理上。

梯理論中之最上層的。二十七、八年前時,台灣其時之所得或許低於現在
之大陸,故而其時國際契約準據法常為外國法,個人當時經常以契約不得
違反履行地法台灣法為依據,於國際商業糾紛中替台灣商人解套。故而個
人正式提出這個論述較歐盟早二十多年,其時之論述亦較歐盟今日之論述
完整。個人甚至認為對「履行地法必須符合人類文明的公理」之論述,及
主張「契約通常不得違反履行地法應同時為國際法及國內法」之論述,或
許可能較英美法現今於此方面之論述先進。

　　國際私法固然為一國際性之法學,於公平正義原則下全世界應遵守
相同之法則。但於第三世界發展之困苦過程中,我們有第一世界難以體會
之辛酸,這亦是中國式國際私法發展中應注意之處。個人認為或許藉由實
體政策的分析,我們能保障階梯理論中之實際人權,促進國內及國際法上
之實質發展,並可撥雲見日的以如虹之氣勢帶領全世界走出國際法上的泥
沼。

六、羅馬 II —山寨版的第二新編

　　歐盟目前所立之法規幾乎都是本於歐盟公約65條建立內部市場的目
的而設立,2007年的864/2007號羅馬 II 規則亦是如此。其要點6規定:
「為了內部市場的適當功能,須要判決結果可預測性的改進,法律適用的
穩定性,及判決的自由流通性,故於國際私法的法規上,無論訴訟是於那
一個國家之法院被提起,各國應指定相同國家之法律。」[166]羅馬 II 正如其
他歐盟之法規,重點是在法律的可預測性及穩定性,故而在這前提下各國
之岐異性應被消滅,而應適用相同之法律。有趣的是如前述美國最高法院
於Sun Oil[167]中引述Erie[168]而要求聯邦法院採納所在地之州法律之「目的為

---

[166] "The proper functioning of the internal market creates a need, in order to improve the predictability of the outcome of litigation, certainty as to the law applicable and the free movement of judgments, for the conflict-of-law rules in the Member States to designate the same national law irrespective of the country of the court in which an action is brought."

[167] 486 U.S. 717,726,727.

[168] Erie Railroad v. Tompkins, 304 U.S. 64(1938)。見陳隆修、許兆慶、林恩瑋,《台灣財產法暨經濟

建立可預測結果的實質統一」，而充份互信條款「相對的並不是在建立統
一性，而是在確認州的立法權限。」故於該案中美國最高法院於憲法之規
定下「是在確認州的立法權限」，而尊重各州法律之被適用的目的是「為
建立可預測結果的實質統一」。在這種充份互信各州法律之架構下，沒有
人會懷疑美國內部市場的功能受到阻礙。歐盟應認真的反省其與美國經驗
背道而馳的作法。如果地球真的是一個村，個人認為中國式國際私法應採
取有二百多年的美國經驗，而非只有數十年的歐盟經驗。

　　羅馬Ⅱ的強調可預測性及穩定性，被Prof. Symeonides引述Prof Cav-
ers之論述[169]而批評如下：「如果美國經驗有值得借鏡之處，那就是它提醒
了我們一個制度如果太過死硬－正如同美國過去傳統的制度－最後一定
無法達成它所欲造成的可預測性，因為在一個民主社會中沒有任何制度
可以作成『機械式的判決』，並且當其如此作時法官會不遵守它。」[170]而
Prof Weintraub亦如此批評：「反諷的是羅馬Ⅱ的規則如果能給予充份的
彈性，它反而較能成功的給予合理的預測性。[171]」

　　但是美國的制度又合理嗎？除了於「假衝突」之共識上，美國似乎
亦不見得有章法，而所謂「利益上之假衝突」本身就充滿了歧異。個人
認為羅馬Ⅱ處處充滿了1971年第2新編的影子。首先前述之政策性要點可
謂類似第2新編第6條2項之7個基本的指導性原則[172]；而羅馬Ⅱ第4條的基

法研究叢書（十三）—國際私法：選法理論之回顧與展望》，台灣財產法暨經濟法研究協會發行，2007年1月，初版,194頁。

[169] David F. Cavers, Restatement of the Law of Conflict of Laws, 44 Yale L. J. 1478, 1482(1935).

[170] Symeon C.Symeonides* Rome Ⅱ and Tort Conflicts: A Missed Opportunity 56 Am. J. Comp. L. 173, 180 (2008), "If the American experience has something to offer, it is a reminder that a system that is too rigid – as the traditional American system was – ultimately fails to deliver the promised predictability because in a democratic society no system can mechanize judgment and, to the extent it attempts to do so, judges will ignore it."

[171] Russell J. Weintraub, Rome Ⅱ and the Tension Between Predictability and Flexibility, 19 Riv. Dir. Int' le priv. e process. 561 (2005), "ironically Rome Ⅱ is more likely to succeed in providing reasonable foreseeability if its rules provide sufficient flexibility."

[172] 陳隆修，《美國國際私法新理論》，台北，五南圖書公司，民國76年1月，初版，79頁。

(1) A court, subject to constitutional restrictions, will follow a statutory directive of its own state on choice of law.

(2) When there is no such directive, the factors relevant to the choice of the applicable rule of law include:

本規定則類似第2新編第145條於侵權行為法上最重要關連點之規定（或於契約法上188條最重要關連點之規定）；最後羅馬Ⅱ有關產品責任（5條）、不公平競爭（6條）、環境損害（7條）、侵害智慧財產（8條）、及工業行為（9條）之規定，則有些類似第2新編146~149、151、152、154及155條於有關個別類型之侵權行為上之規定（或於契約法上189至197條之規定）。

　　自1969年第2新編通過後至今已四十年整，歐洲的第2新編影子版終於正式上路。個人之前曾如此寫著：「例如最重要關連說，先產於美國，傳至歐洲，再由我國及日本做後面之接棒者。[173]」並認為實體法論之精髓為「法學上沒有理論之不同，只有進化腳步的不同。[174]」或許於羅馬Ⅱ與第2新編之順序關連上，以上之論述於某些方面是正確的。事實上經過四十年的歲月，第2新編之理論架構雖然依舊，但鮮少人討論到整個時代重心之改變。於Babcock v. Jackson[175]這個現代選法革命的始祖案例中，紐約法院只是討論到最重要關連與利益說而已，到較近之一些案例則增加了一些論述，其中包含了第6條2項的一些基本原則在內[176]。如果美國法院都需要時間才能夠將最重要關連與第6(2)條之基本政策結合運用，則歐盟法院可能需要更久的時間才能將宣言中的政策性要點與最密切關連結合運用。

(a) the need of the interstate and international systems,

(b) the relevant policies of the forum,

(c) the relevant policies of other interested states and the relative interests of those states in the determination of the particular issue,

(d) the protection of the justified expectations,

(e) the basic policies underlying the particular field of law,

(f) certainty, predictability and uniformity of result, and

(g) ease in the determination and application of the law to be applied.

[173] 陳隆修、許兆慶、林恩瑋、李瑞生四人合著，《國際私法-管轄與選法理論之交錯》，台北，五南圖書公司，2009年3月，初版1刷，259頁。

[174] 同上，260頁。

[175] 12 N.Y. 2d 473, 240 N.Y.S. 2d 743, 191 N.E. 2d 279 (1963)。

[176] 陳隆修、許兆慶、林恩瑋，《台灣財產法暨經濟法研究叢書（十三）─國際私法：選法理論之回顧與展望》，台灣財產法暨經濟法研究協會發行，2007年1月，初版，208~220頁中所討論之紐約案例，經常引用「合理的期待」（第6條2項d款）。

　　嚴格的說第2新編是所謂的「三層架構」（「three‑tier struc-
ture」[177]）。如果由下而上，或中後至前，第一層應為如第1新編般大至
上有著特定地域性連結點的個別類型侵權行為[178]。但與第1新編最大不同
之處乃在第2新編此處的地域連結因素並非機械式的適用，而是可被推翻
的。第2層則是Babcock案所引用的最重要關連點，於侵權行為是規定於
第145條[179]中（契約為第188條[180]）。最重要關連標準是60、70年代美國
選法革命僅次於州利益之暴風中心，亦是後來奧地利、瑞士、德國等大
陸法國家及許多國際公約採用之準則。第3層則為第6條2項之7個基本原
則，而如前述這7個寬廣的原則是包含利益說及實體法論在內包羅萬象之
萬應靈藥原則。經過時間的洗鍊許多美國法院已由原始的第145、188條
最重要關連標準，進化到連帶使用第1層的特殊規則及第6條2項之基本原

---

[177] James A. Meschewski, CHOICE OF LAW IN ALASKA: A SURVIVAL GUIDE FOR USING THE SECOND RESTATEMENT, 16 Alaska L. Rev.1 (1999).

[178] 第146～149條、151、152、154及155條，契約則為189～197條。

[179] (1) The rights and liabilities of the parties with respect to an issue in tort are detemined by the local law of the state which, with respect to that issue, has the most significant relationship to the occurrence and the parties under the principles stated in §6.
　　(2) Contacts to be taken into account in applying the principles of §6 to determine the law applicable to an issue include:
　　　　(a) the place where the injury occurred,
　　　　(b) the place where the conduct causing the injury occurred,
　　　　(c) the domicile, residence, nationality, place of incorporation and place of business of the parties, and
　　　　(d) the place where the relationship, if any, between the parties is centered.
　　These contacts are to be evaluated according to their relative importance with respect to the particular issue.

[180] (1) The rights and duties of the parties with respect to an issue in contract are determined by the local law of the state which, with respect to that issue, has the most significant relationship to the transaction and the parties under the principles stated in §6.
　　(2) In the absence of an effective choice of law by the parties (see 187), the contacts to be taken into account in applying the principles of §6 to determine the law applicable to an issue include:
　　　　(a) the place of contracting,
　　　　(b) the place of negotiation of the contract,
　　　　(c) the place of performance,
　　　　(d) the location of the subject matter of the contract, and
　　　　(e) the domicil, residence, nationality, place of incorporation and place of business of the parties.
　　These contacts are to be evaluated according to their relative importance with respect to the particular issue.
　　(3) If the place of negotiating the contract and the place of performance are in the same state, the local law of this state will usually be applied, except as otherwise provided in 189-199 and 203.

則[181]。

　　事實上如果繼續遵循Babcock v. Jackson只採用最重要關連標準的地域性規則原始作法，第2新編之方法論或許較為可預測，但如果採納第2新編完整的3層式方法論，則整個方法論變得包山包海無從預測。Prof. Sterk擺明著說：「一個法院可以幾乎於任何選法規則的案件中達到任何結果並且於第2新編中得到對其結果之一些支持。[182]」Prof. Smith亦給予同樣意見的說：「這個新編是所有可以想像出來的選法理論的奇怪組合，所有的理論都混在一起，內容變得幾乎無法解讀。[183]」這個現象同時也可以解釋前述有些大陸法學者，或許基於大陸法慣性的對最重關連地域性主義之迷戀，及對於利益說之厭惡，故意以操縱的方式去解讀法院判決的表面統計，以達到宣揚第2新編之目的[184]。於第2新編剛完成時Prof. Ehrenz-

---

[181] Collins v. Trius, Inc., 663 A.2d 570, 572-73 (Me. 1995)，引用6、145及146條；Cosme v. Whitin Mach. Works, Inc., 632 N.E.2d 832, 834-836 (Mass. 1994)，引用6、145及146條；Bates v. Superior Court, 749 P.2d 1367, 1367-72 (Ariz. 1988)，引用6、145及146條。146條為人身傷害依損害發生地法，"In an action for a personal injury, the local law of the state where the injury occurred determines the rights and liabilities of the parties unless, with respect to the particular issue, some other state has a more significant relationship under the principles stated in 6 to the occurrence and the parties, in which event the local law of the other state will be applied."

[182] Stewart E. Sterk, The Marginal Relevance of Choice of Law Theory, 142 U. Pa. L. Rev. 949,974 (1994)," a court can reach virtually any result in any choice of law case and find some support for the result in the Second Restatement".

[183] Gregory E. Smith, Choice of Law in the United States, 38 Hastings L.J. 1041, 1170 (1987), "The Restatement is a curious montage of virtually every choice of law theory imaginable, all brought together in one, almost undecipherable text."

[184] Symeon C. Symeonides, Choice of Law in the American Courts in 1999: One More Year, 48 Am. J. Comp. L. 143 (2000)；又參考其著作
Symeonides, Symeon C. (1996), Choice of Law in the American Courts in 1995: A Year in Review, 44 Am. J. Comp.L.181.
Symeonides, Symeon C. (1997), Choice of Law in the American Courts in 1996: Tenth Annual Survey, 45 Am. J. Comp.L.447.
Symeonides, Symeon C. (1997), The Judicial Acceptance of the Second Conflicts Restatement: A Mixed Blessing, 56 Md. L. Rev. 1248.
Symeonides, Symeon C. (1998), Choice of Law in the American Courts in 1997, 46 Am. J. Comp.L.233.
Symeonides, Symeon C. (1999), Choice of Law in the American Courts in 1998: Twelfth Annual Survey, 47 Am. J. Comp.L.327.
Symeonides, Symeon C. (2000), The Need for a Third Restatement (And a Proposal for a Tort Conflicts), 75 Ind. L. J. 437.
Symeonides, Symeon C. (2001), Choice of Law in the American Courts in 2000: As the Century Turns, 49 Am. J. Comp. L.1..
Symeonides, Symeon C. (2002), Choice of Law in the American Courts in 2001: Fifteenth Annual Sur-

weig即鐵口直斷第2新編的未來：「許多新的個別條文將會不可避免增加
它原來版本既有的混亂。[185]」但持平而論，「混亂」並非美國各種選法規
則的專利權，自Babcock後「混亂」、「嘈雜」、「進步」是全世界國際
私法的代名詞。自美國選法革命後，全世界的同僚都知道法官通常先有
答案後再找理由。Prof. Reese自己亦承認於作成選法決定之過程法院順序
之相反是一種常態（「common phenomenon」）[186]，而第2新編的包山包
海自然更是法院可以隱藏其判決真正理由的最佳工具。Prof. Borcher除了
感嘆第2新編的精神分裂（「schizophrenic」）外，更直言：「第2新編
的被引用通常只不過是用來遮掩司法的直覺而已。[187]」有關選法規則的混
亂與司法的直覺，個人於年輕時便已有同樣的論述[188]。現今年輕一代的同
僚亦有同樣的觀點：「由於在國際私法的案件上去適用第2新編所包含的
這麼多的因素，而衡量這些因素的指示又這麼的少，法院因此可以『倒
轉』他們決定而不會被發現。亦即法院可以利用第2新編的模糊性，而首
先選定法院『覺得』正確的結果（而不必從事任何真正的選法規則的分
析），然後再試圖以指出一組關連點與所要的區域之關係並稱他們為『最

---

vey, 50 Am. J. Comp. L. 1.

Symeonides, Symeon C. (2003), Choice of Law in the American Courts in 2002: Sixteenth Annual Survey, 51 Am. J. Comp.L.9.

Symeonides, Symeon C. (2004), Choice of Law in the American Courts in 2003: Seventeenth Annual Survey, 52 Am. J. Comp.L.9.

[185] Albert A. Ehrenzweig, The Second Conflicts Restatement: Last Appeal for its Withdrawal, 113 U. Pa. L. Rev. 1230, 1231-1236(1965), "Many new specific provisions will inevitably add to the confusion created by the original version."

[186] Willis L.M. Reese, Conflict of Laws, 33 Am. J. Comp. L. 332, 334-37 (1985).

[187] Patrick J. Borchers, Courts and the Second Conflicts Restatement: Some Observations and an Empirical Note, 56 Md. L. Rev. 1232, 1233, 1240 (1997),"citation to the Second Restatement is often little more than a veil hiding judicial intuition"

[188] 於「美國國際私法新理論」16、17頁中個人早期引用Willis Reese，"American Trends in Private International Law", 33 Vand. L. Rev. 717, 737 (1980), 而作出下列觀點：然而美國近代法律衝突漫無法規的情況，已被廣泛地承認。「導致判決結果的主因是贊成原告受償的一種偏見或是法院想在類似案例中適用他們的本地法的傾向？」有以上疑惑的法學專家絕不僅是Reese教授一人。美國法學院的法律衝突教授盡力地在尋找法院判決的理論基礎，以便向滿懷困惑的學生解釋。當作者在密西根法學院從事研究時，James Martin教授經常作一項有趣的試驗。在他教學生們近代法律選擇理論前，Martin教授會叫他們憑直覺（intuition）對手邊的案例想一個最理想的判決結果，雖然學生們均不具備國際私法學的知識或未受過訓練，但幾乎全體學生所作的判決結果均有利於原告受償。Martin教授認為這是一種大膽的直覺。

重要』，來合理化它所選擇之結果。」[189]

　　以上之論述雖然言詞激烈，但與個人30年前之論述卻幾乎完全一致[190]。羅馬 II 於架構上與第2新編類似，故而上面之論述自然於羅馬 II 亦大致上適用。但嚴格上而言，於邏輯上羅馬 II 還是在架構上略有不同之處。第2新編的前述3層規則架構於適用之次序上並無一定之順位，而有些或許多法院是混合著使用。更有些年輕的同僚已不耐煩三層架構的疊床架屋，建議州法院以第6條之基本原則為依據，再直接適用第1層的個別規則；而於沒有個別規則可適用時，才可於第6條基本原則的指導下適用最重要關連標準[191]。這固然是見仁見智的創意，但個人以為這真正反應了對第2新編包山包海三層式架構的焦慮與不安。而羅馬 II 序言之政策性要點，一般可能會認為於適用次序上會後於正式規則中之第4條的一般性規則及5、6、7、8及9條之個別規則。至於第4、5、10、11及12條中之最密切關連標準，則為要點14定性為「規避條款」[192]，故於理論上適用之次序

---

[189] James A. Meschewski, Choice of Law in Alaska: A Survival Guide for Using the Second Restatement 16 Alaska L. Rev. 1, 19 (1999), "Because conflict of law cases applying the Second Restatement contain so many factors and minimal direction on how to weigh these factors, court are able to work backwards in their decisions without being detected. That is, courts may take advantage of the Second Restatement's ambiguity by first selecting the outcome of the case that feels correct to the court (without engaging in any genuine choice-of-law analysis), and then attempting to justify its selected result by pointing to a set of contacts connected to the desired jurisdiction and labeling them as the most significant"

[190] 陳隆修，《美國國際私法新理論》，台北，五南圖書公司，民國76年1月，初版，第1、2章。

[191] James A. Meschewski, Choice of Law In Alaska: A Survival Guide for Using The Second Restatement 16 Alaska L. Rev. 1, 35, 36(1999), "To avoid further ambiguity and confusion, Alaska courts should regroup and announce a new, more analytically sound methodology for interpreting the Second Restatement. While this is easier said than done, Alaska courts should abandon their current approach, in which the courts inconsistently apply the various tiers of the second Restatement, and adopt a new method that employs one of two distinct analyses. The particular type of analysis used by the court in a given instance should depend on whether one of the Second Restatement's presumptive sections applies to the specific set of facts before the court. If a presumptive section is triggered, the court should advance directly from the presumptive section to a Section 6 analysis. If a presumptive section is not triggered, the court should interpret the Section 6 factors in light of the considerations listed in the applicable general area of law section."

[192] "The Regulation provides for the connecting factors which are the most appropriate to achieve these objectives. Therefore, this Regulation provides for a general rule but also for specific rules and, in certain provisions, for an 'escape clause' which allows a departure from these rules where it is clear from all the circumstances of the case that the tort/delict is manifestly more closely connected with another country. This set of rules thus creates a flexible framework of conflict-of-law rules. Equally, it enables

應為條文主要內容之後。而第4條之一般性規則已明文規定於沒有其他個別規則適用時才可適用。故而羅馬II在立法技術層級之適用上，似乎較第2新編來的明確，或者如Prof. Weintraub所謂較沒有「給予彈性」，故而不看好其之「合理的預測性」。

　　但是於探討第2新編與羅馬II之異同性時，個人認為重點不應放在表面上立法技術順序上之差別，重點應是大陸法於傳統上是偏向法律原則適用之條理上，而英美法則是偏向最後個案之結果上。個人以前對一些國家於最重要關連標準立法技術之歧異上即做出以下之結論：「無論美、英、德、奧、瑞等五國對最重要關連說的採納方式，是以一般通用原則的適用方式，或是以特殊例外原則的適用方式，事實上於大方向上並無巨大的不同。對於最重要關連說之採納是否有所不同，不應以表面立法技術之理論差異為基準，而應以各國法院於實務案件上對個別案例之處理為依據，在同樣的案例上，有些法院可能仍偏向採用行為地法等傳統的『法域選擇法』（Jurisdiction selecting rules），而有些法院可能偏向採用較有彈性的最重要關連說。故而於理論上採用何種方式立法，或採用何種方式之最重要關連說，並不如研究法院於實務上之做法重要，這也充分證明最重要關連說受詬病之『無法狀態』（nonrule）之另一面。[193]」個人相信即使英美法與大陸法之立法一致，法院於適用之結果還是會有不同的重點。例如羅馬公約的最重要關連說[194]與英國契約法的適當法[195]是理論上大致類似的，但英國於加入歐盟後對歐盟之作法卻仍有岐異。

　　倒是歐盟應注意的是第2新編6(1)條規定選法規則應在憲法規範下進行，於30年前美國最高法院的確是竭盡所能的不願處理選法規則的，但自*Allstate Insurance Co. V. Hague*[196]及其後之一系列判決後，美國憲法已

the court seised to treat individual cases in an appropriate manner.
[193] 陳隆修、許兆慶、林恩瑋，《台灣財產法暨經濟法研究叢書（十三）—國際私法：選法理論之回顧與展望》，台灣財產法暨經濟法研究協會發行，2007年1月，初版，167頁。
[194] 第4條。
[195] 陳隆修，《國際私法契約評論》，台北，五南圖書公司，民國75年2月，初版，21～65頁。
[196] 449 U.S. 302 (1981).

正式踏入選法規則的水深火熱中。如前所述，美國最高法院雖然遮遮掩掩的表面上以地域關連點及州利益為最低之選法規則之限制，但於第一線面對有正當請求權的當事人，各州法院仍不可避免的以實體政策之分析為判決之依據，而這個實體政策分析的結果或甚至方法論本身，自然難免成為最高法院衡量案件之結果是否為「武斷或基本上不公平」之標準。再加以近四十年來「假衝突」之認定已幾乎成為美國選法規則上之共識，而無論認同「假衝突」之方法論與否。羅馬 II 似乎對此點並沒有加以應有之重視與論述。羅馬 II 似乎仍本著60年代美國選法革命時期之最重要關連說而立法：歐盟似乎怪異的對60年代的美國最重要關連說有著固執性的偏好，對美國近年來法院於實務之發展視而不見。對羅馬 II 的閉門造車，個人認為這個本著過時理論的過時立法，正如第1新編一般，它一出生就已過時。

七、ALI Complex Litigation Proposal

　　歐盟及大陸法系國家會極端的排斥「利益分析」，與雙手熱情的擁抱完全基於地域關連之「最重要關連」是個人30年前已預見的現實。而「實體政策分析」是個人本於大陸法之偏重法學原則所創之方法論，雖然年輕時或許為英美前輩同僚所欣賞，但個人以為不受判例法拘束之大陸法系未來接受之程度會比想像中容易。對羅馬 II 之偏重於60年代之最重要關連標準，而忽視美國最高法院及各州法院近二十多年來之實務發展，自然令人感到遺憾。如果歐盟能夠接受當時具有高度爭議性之最重要關連，那麼對美國法律協會（American Law Institute ("ALI")）於1994年所建議的「複數訴訟提議」（ALI Complex Litigation Proposal）[197]更應加以

---

[197] § 3.01 Standard for Consolidation
　　(a) Actions commenced in two or more United States District Courts may be transferred and consolidated if:
　　　　(1) they involve one or more common questions of fact, and
　　　　(2) transfer and consolidation will promote the just, efficient, and fair conduct of the actions.
　　(b) Factors to be considered in deciding whether the standard set forth in subsection (a) is met include

參考。雖然同樣的具有高度爭議性，但至少這或許較60年代的「三層架構」能代表美國法律協會近來之「共識」（或一如往常的「具有爭議的共識」）。

於6.01條[198]集體侵權行為選法規則上，法律協會即於(a)項開宗明義的

---

(1) the extent to which transfer and consolidation will reduce duplicative litigation, the relative costs of individual and consolidated litigation, the likelihood of inconsistent adjudications, and the comparative burdens on the judiciary, and

　(2) whether transfer and consolidation can be accomplished in a way that is fair to the parties and does

In considering those factors, account may be taken of matters such as

a. the number of parties and actions involved;

b. the geographic dispersion of the actions;

c. the existence and significance of local concerns;

d. the subject matter of the dispute;

e. the amount in controversy;

f. the significance and number of common issues involved, including whether multiple laws will have to be applied to those issues;

g. the likelihood of additional related actions being commenced in the future;

h. the wishes of the parties; and

i. the stages to which the actions already commenced have progressed.

§ 5.01 Removal Jurisdiction

(a) Except as otherwise provided by Act of Congress, the Complex Litigation Panel may order the removal to federal court and consolidation of one or more civil actions pending in one or more state courts, if the removed actions arise from the same transaction, occurrence, or series of transactions or occurrences as an action pending in the federal court, and share a common question of fact with that action.... the Complex Litigation Panel should consider factors such as

a. the amount in controversy for the claims to be removed;

b. the number and size of the actions involved;

c. the number of jurisdictions in which the state cases are lodged;

d. any special reasons to avoid inconsistency;

e. the presence of any special local community or state regulatory interests;

f. whether removal and consolidation will result in a change in the applicable law that will cause undue unfairness to the parties; and

g. the possibility of facilitating informal cooperation or coordination with the state courts in which the cases are lodged.

[198] § 6.01 Mass Torts

(a) Except as provided in § 6.04 through § 6.06, in actions consolidated under § 5.01 in which the parties assert the application of laws that are in material conflict, the transferee court shall choose the law governing the rights, liabilities, and defenses of the parties with respect to a tort claim by applying the criteria set forth in the following subsections with the objective of applying, to the extent feasible, a single state's law to all similar tort claims being asserted against a defendant.

(b) In determining the governing law under subsection (a), the court shall consider the following factors for purposes of identifying each state having a policy that would be furthered by the application of its laws:

(1) the place or places of injury;

(2) the pace or places of the conduct causing the injury; and

要求下列各項選法規則的適用須於「當事人所主張應適用的法律是有重大的衝突」情形才適用。亦即歐盟及全世界之大陸法系必須注意的是美國現今的共識是－選法規則只有於真衝突之情形下才適用。這很明顯的是Prof. Currie「利益分析」[199]的壓倒性全面大勝。當美國法律協會選擇放棄其60年代之「三層架構」時，任何以表面上判決之統計數字來鼓吹創始人自己已棄守的理論的作為，都是提襟見肘的行為。我們只能驚嘆於歐裔美國人對歐洲地域性主義至死不渝的文化及血液上之偏執。

抛開歐裔美國人瘋狂性的偏執，法律學會很聰明（或狡猾）的使用

---

(3) the primary places of business or habitual residences of the plaintiffs and defendants.

(c) If, in analyzing the factors set forth in subsection (b), the court finds that only one state has a policy that would be furthered by the application of its law, that state's law shall govern. If more than one state has a policy that would be furthered by the application of its law, the court shall choose the applicable law from among the laws of the interested states under the following rules:

  (1) If the place of injury and the place of the conduct causing the injury are in the same state, that's state's law governs.

  (2) If subsection (c)(1) does not apply but all the plaintiffs habitually reside or their primary places of business in the same state, and a defendant has its primary place of business or habitually resides in that state that state's law governs the claims with the respect to that defendant. Plaintiffs shall be considered as sharing a common habitual residence or primary place of business if they are located in states whose laws are not in material conflict.

  (3) If neither subsection (c)(1) nor (c)(2) applies, but all of the plaintiffs habitually reside or have their primary places of business in the same state, and that state also is the place of injury, then that state's law governs. Plaintiffs shall be considered as sharing a common habitual residence or primary place of business if they are located in states whose laws are not in material conflict.

  (4) In all other cases, the law of the state were the conduct causing the injury occurred governs. When conduct occurred in more than one state, the court shall choose the law of the conduct state that has the most significant relationship to the occurrence.

(d) When necessary to avoid unfair surprise or arbitrary results, the transferee court may choose the applicable law on the basis of additional factors that reflect the regulatory policies and legitimate interests of a particular state not otherwise identified under subsection (b), or it may depart from the order of preferences for selecting the governing law prescribed by subsection (c).

(e) If the court determines that the application of a single state's law to all elements of the claims pending against a defendant would be inappropriate, it may divide the actions into subgroups of claims, issues, or parties to foster consolidated treatment under § 3.01, and allow more that one state's law to be applied. The court also may determine that only certain claims or issues involving one or more of the parties should be governed by the law chosen by the application of the rules in subsection (c), and that other claims or parties should be remanded to the transferor courts for individual treatment under the laws normally applicable in those courts, in either instance, the court may exercise its authority under § 3.06 (c) to sever, transfer, or remand issues or claims for treatment consistent with its determination.

[199] 陳隆修，《美國國際私法新理論》，台北，五南圖書公司，民國76年1月，初版，49、50頁。

「衝突」字眼，而不使用爭議性的「利益衝突」。個人雖無法提出統計數目之證據，但個人相信Currie式狹義的利益（較近被稱為屬人法式理論）通常是無法為許多美國同僚及法院所完全接受的[200]。前述加州法院的利益分析則毫無疑問的有著濃厚的實體法政策分析之比例在內。個人認為包含最高法院在內的大部份美國法院都不由自主的接受Currie的魔咒（或詛咒？），認為州之利益乃在於保護居民，但另一方面又不由自主的受到良心的呼喚，不時以實體法之政策分析來主持個案的正義。美國法律協會很明顯的避開了「利益」之名詞。於上個世紀個人充份見證了歐洲人的地域性情結及美國人的狹義州利益情結，個人期望於本世紀在個案正義的旗幟號召下，能打破上世紀的兩個大魔咒。

　　於辨別各州政策是否有真衝突之情形時，6.01條(b)項採用下列關連點以決定相關連之州之政策：損害發生地、行為地、及當事人之慣居地或營業地。但應注意的是這些關連點之「目的是用來辨認各州是否法律被適用後其政策會被促進之考慮因素。」換言之，法院之重點不應在地域性關連，而在相關州之實體政策。(b)項之條文明顯的降低地域關連的重要性及排除「州利益」名詞之適用，而將其重點放在州實體法政策之促進－這個作法似乎橫跨於實體法論及加州之比較損害利益之間。

　　(c)項規定如果只有一州之政策會被促進，則該州法應被適用；但如果許多州之政策會被促進，則應根據下列次序決定適用之法律：(1)損害發生地與行為地為同一州之法；(2)所有原告之慣居地或主要營業在同一州，而該州又為一被告之慣居地或營業地，則對該被告該州之法應為準據法；(3)所有原告之慣居地或主要營業地在同一州，而該州又為損害發生地，則該州法應為準據法；(4)以行為地法為依據，若有數個行為地，則以與事件最有關連地為依據。於(2)、(3)款時原告之慣居地或主要營業地法並無重大衝突時，視為在同一州。換言之，在州政策有真衝突時，法律學會並不採加州之比較損害政策之作法，而是恢復機械式土地關連之排列

---

[200] 陳隆修，《美國國際私法新理論》，台北，五南圖書公司，民國76年1月，初版，50～52頁。

組合。經過第1新編的陣痛，或許全世界沒有民族會比美國人更了解機械式土地關連之缺點。故於(d)項中再小心翼翼的規定為了避免不公平的驚奇及武斷的結果，除了可以不遵循(c)項的次序外，其他非(b)項所為認之個別州的政策或利益可被引為做為選擇準據法之依據。

　　故而很明顯的*Babcock v. Jackson*後所引為判決依據的最重要關連及州利益，於美國法律協會較近之提議中已被貶至較不重要之地位，而以相關州之政策為主。但其於州政策假衝突之情況下雖採用Prof. Currie之方法論，但於州政策真衝突之形下，並不取採用加州的比較損害方法，反而回復土地關連點的機械式排列，這或許可以視為一種機械式的最重要關連。然後再以(d)項的州政策或利益做為避免不公平或武斷後果的最後規避技巧。但若(b)項中的州政策有真衝突時，似乎只能以規避(c)項的次序以達成個案正義[201]。

---

[201] 對Andreas F. Lowenfeld, Mass Tort and the Conflict of Laws: The Airline Disaster, 1989 U.ILL.L.REV. 157, 173(1989)，於評述複數侵權行為時承認，如果採用實體法上之立法對衝突法的教授而言是一種認輸之告白，個人認為這應是最好之解決方案："It may be thought to be an admission of defeat for a conflict-of-laws professor to tell a conflict of laws symposium that the only way to solve the assigned problem is to adopt substantive legislation."

而Russell J. Weintraub, Methods for Resolving Conflict-of-Laws Problems in Mass Tort Litigation, 1989. U.ILL.L.REV. 129, 133(1989)，更警告於建立此方面之選法規則應甚為謹慎："Mass tort litigation is not already so unwieldy that nothing can make it worse. We can make anything worse if we put our minds to it."

Linda Mullenix, Federalizing Choice of Law for Mass-Tort Litigation, 70 Tex. L. Rev. 1623, 1630(1992)，對the ALI Complex Litigation Project，特別是選法規則，批評如下：

In the larger sense, then, the ALI Complex Litigation Project as a whole reflects a failure of political will. On a smaller scale, with regard to its various proposals for procedural reform, the Project also reflects a failure of creative thinking in its general approach of harnessing existing, often problematic rules to complex mass-tort litigation. And this is nowhere more evident than in the Project's provisions for determining applicable law.

In federalizing applicable-law rules, the Institute's proposals are troubling because they subvert basic Erie doctrine in garden-variety diversity cases, blithely endorse vertical forum shopping, and inadequately justify a federalized regime in mass-tort cases. It is not enough to simply keep repeating that mass-tort cases are bigger and more complicated and therefore justify overriding all pre-existing rules and doctrines in the interest of sound judicial administration. While stating that the objectivce of the choice-of-law proposals is to curb judicaial discretion, in reality the proposed multifactor approaches encourage creative judicial deductive reasoning from the judge's choice of applicable law to the factors supporting that choice. And if it is true that a purpose of multifactor choice-of-law schemes is to reduce unbridled jucicial discretion, then perhaps what we ought to do, if we choose a modified Restatement route, is to take the judge out of the decisional process altogether and have applicable law determined by computer. If ever an area of law was susceptible to decision-tree analysis, then surely it would be

　　法律協會的這個提議除了證明美國於「州政策假衝突」方法論之共識外，另外又證明了美國不可自拔的陷於「評價禁忌」[202]的迷思中。在州政策真衝突之情形下，它所提出的解決方案是幼稚而可笑的，故而不得不仰賴憲法上「不公平或武斷」的標準作為最後規避手段，但個人於此必須再重覆第2新編之前報告人Prof. Reese回覆個人理論之論述：「新編之立場是這個價值（即實體政策分析），雖然重要，並不是唯一的，並且還有存在其他許多價值應被考慮。[203]」但是在法律學會的這個提議中，第6條2項

---

multifactor choice-of-law rules.

Perhaps the most disturbing aspect of the ALI choice-of-law proposals is that they will not meaningfully assist in determining law in truly dispersed mass-tort litigation. For the hard cases, the reformers have proposed virtually useless rules. Although the provisions and commentary sound perfectly plausible and reasoned (albeit reflection the proposers' own conflicts preferences), the proposed rules will not work for truly massive tort cases.

ALI於假衝突上的認定的確是表達了於此方面美國大部份（或所有）同儕的共識，但是正如利益說於真衝突（困難；hard）的案件上一般，其迴避了案件所牽連的實體政策的評價（評價禁忌），故對困難案件而言，其所提議的規則是「於實際上無用的規則」。

Richard L. Marcus, They Can't Do That, Can They?: Tort Reform Via Rule 23, 80 Cornell L. Rev. 858, 859(1995)，對於集體訴訟在聯邦法院無法迴避州落伍的不合時宜法規，集體成員尚未發病前之請求權，及成員無法受到通知或選擇退出之困難，對侵權行為法之改革所造成之障礙陳述如下：

This fact makes it evident that the class action has landed like a 600-pound gorilla in the arena of tort reform, where there has of late been increasing interest in replacing tort litigation with scheduled benefits like those provided in these class action settlements. One reaction to using class actions to accomplish this reform might be: "They can't do that, can they?"

⋮

Turning to the question whether Rule 23 can be employed to effectuate tort reform of this sort, Part III considers three grounds for categorically rejecting such power--Erie's limitations on the law-making power of the federal courts, the problem of unmatured claims, and the challenge of giving notice. It concludes that these serious obstacles probably do not absolutely preclude an undertaking of this sort, provided there is a genuine opportunity to opt out.

但即使有這麼多的困難，個人同意其結論：「集體訴訟可能是隻鳳凰，而非恐龍」。

"Perhaps the class action is, after all, a Phoenix rather than a dinosaur," (Cornell L. Rev. 907)

在多數人爭奪有限的資源時，集體訴訟不但是21世紀平民大衛對抗企業哥利亞巨人的彈弓，更是21世紀法學的先驅。無論於選法規則或管轄規則上，20世紀曾引以為傲的法學邏輯，應在21世紀的現實中加以退讓。故而憲法上最低限度的要求，無論在對人訴訟管轄之要求或選法規則上之最低標準，皆應在給予成員迅速及合理（公平）的賠償之基本概括性目的下退讓。這亦是中國式法學「道法自然」的真諦，「天行健，君子以自強不息」。

[202] 陳隆修，《美國國際私法新理論》，台北，五南圖書公司，民國76年1月，初版，59～63頁。

[203] "It takes the position that this value, although important, dose not stand alone and that there are other values to be considered." Willis Reese, The Second Restatement of Conflict of Laws Revisited, 34 Mercer L. Rev. 501, at 518 (1983). 又見陳隆修、許兆慶、林恩瑋、李瑞生四人合著，《國際私法—管轄與選法理論之交錯》，台北，五南圖書公司，2009年3月，初版1刷，252～260頁。

的州際制度的需要、判決的預期性、及易於適用的法律等其他價值都消失不見了，只剩下個人所堅持的「政策」因素。個人認為在與尊敬的Prof. Reese的爭辯中，或許時間已透過美國法律學會自己的提案給予實體法方法論一個公道。

一、羅馬 II 的區域選法規則

　　美國法律學會雖然於真衝突之解決方案甚為可笑，但其能站在確認「政策假衝突」之立場還是遠較歐盟高明的。羅馬 II 序言中雖然揭櫫了許多實體政策，但法院要將這些政策落實至具體個案中是需要長久的時間。羅馬 II 的規則雖是號稱要實現這些基本政策，但是近70億人口的行為是不可能完全符合這些機械式的規定。近30年來個人一向主張：「我們為何要設計一套選擇法法則來表示那些『趨勢』，或者價值、或原則、或政策？實現它們最重的方式應該是讓它們能為自己說話：亦即將它們視為牽連因素或指導方針，以便從有關的內州法中選出最能符合它們的法律。[1]」以羅馬 II 最基本、最代表性的第4條一般性規則之適用次序而言，首先其第1項是適用損害發生地法（不考慮間接的後果發生地法）。第2項則規定若行為人與被害人於損害發生時有共同慣居地，則該慣居地法優先於損害發生地法。但第3項規定若有一國家與該侵權行為有更密切關連時，該國法應被適用。「與其他國家有著更密切關連是可以特別的存在於當事人間事先存在的關係，例如契約，而這關系是與系爭的侵權行為有著更密切關連的。[2]」

---

[1]　陳隆修，《美國國際私法新理論》，台北，五南圖書公司，民國76年1月，初版，67頁。

[2]　Article 4
General rule
1. Unless otherwise provided for in this Regulation, the law applicable to a non-contractual obligation arising out of a tort/delict shall be the law of the country in which the damage occurs irrespective of the country in which the event giving rise to the damage occurred and irrespective of the country or countries in which the indirect consequences of that event occur.

　　雖然於序言中之政策性宣言講的冠冕堂皇，但這個最重要及最具有代表性的第4條基本原則卻完全看不出要點16的「民事責任於現代的趨勢及無過失責任制度的發展。」不要忘記第2新編第6條的基本原則是直接做為最重要關連及個別類型侵權行為之基石準則的。面對三十多年前的第2新編，歐盟應該感到羞愧而無地自容。

　　第1項的損害發生地是國際法上長久以來公認的地域連繫因素，而第2項的共同慣居地法是自美國選法革命以來經常被引用的地域連繫因素。這個連繫因素的產生，或許不只是緣起於最重要關連標準，可能亦起因於各州有保護居民之利益而來。紐約法院早期著名的 *Neumeier v. Kuehner*[3] 的三法則之第1個即為當事人之共同居住地。1999年德國國際私法修正後之侵權行為條款40(2)條[4]亦採此美國式作法。無論這些土地關連點是多麼的符合一般社會直覺上的合理性，個人認為這都構成Prof. Cavers所謂的「jurisdiction selecting rules」[5]（區域選法規則）。因為無論這些土地關連點是多麼符合一般直覺上的合理性，如果該些關連點所指向的國家的法律是不符合時代的需求或現代的法學趨勢，則非常可能造成不公平正義的結果。[6]羅馬 II 的許多規則都有著德國法的影子，個人以前於評論德國法

---

2. However, where the person claimed to be liable and the person sustaining damage both have their habitual residence in the same country at the time when the damage occurs, the law of that country shall apply.

3. Where it is clear from all the circumstances of the case that the tort/delict is manifestly more closely connected with a country other than that indicated in paragraphs 1 or 2, the law of that other country shall apply. A manifestly closer connection with another country might be based in particular on a preexisting relationship between the parties, such as a contract, that is closely connected with the tort/delict in question.

[3]　286 N.E. 2d 454 (1972)，見陳隆修，《美國國際私法新理論》，台北，五南圖書公司，民國76年1月，初版，147～151頁。

[4]　EGBGB，art 4(2)，(2) If the person liable to provide compensation and the injured person had their habitual residence in the same state at the time the act took place, the law of that state shall be applied. In the case of enterprises, associations, or legal persons the place of their principal administration, or, in the case of a branch of its location, shall be the equivalent of habitual residence.

[5]　David F. Cavers, A Critique of the Choice-of-Law Problem, 47 Harv. L. Rev. 173 (1933).

[6]　陳隆修、許兆慶、林恩瑋，《台灣財產法暨經濟法研究叢書（十三）—國際私法：選法理論之回顧與展望》，台灣財產法暨經濟法研究協會發行，2007年1月，初版，176～178頁。

的採納美式共同慣居地法時[7]，即曾以顛倒Babcock v. Jackson[8]及英國著名的*Boys v. Chaplin*[9]的事實的方式來舉證共同屬人法的不一定能保證個案的公平正義性。於同篇論文中又對其時紐約法院剛作成之*Elson v. Defren and Avis Rent-A-Car*[10]，說明即使紐約法院亦不見得遵守自己於Neumeier中之共同居住地法則：「因為Babcock v. Jackson[11]已經創造出一種『利益說』的規則，亦即對解決特殊爭點有著最大利益的州之法律應被適用。並且紐約法院於本案及其他案件中一再重申：由與相衝突的法律的目的有關的事實或關連點的評量，去決定較大的利益[12]。依照這個方式重要的關連點通常是當事人的住所地或侵權行為地[13]。於有關行為的規則相衝突的情況，紐約法院通常採用侵權行為地法，因為該地對控制發生於其境內之行為有著最大之利益[14]。如果是損害分配的規則相衝突的情況，Neumeier v. Kuehner的三個原則應被適用。而本案系爭之問題，則是有關損害之分配。因此艾比士（被告）主張依Neumeier的第一個原則，當事人的共同住所地法紐約法應被適用[15]。紐約法院承認依損害分配的原則去分析，紐約法應被適用，但於本案該車從未於紐約被使用過，如若於嚴格的執行紐約法的情況下，艾比士（被告）則不必負起責任，這樣會挫敗了紐約及艾得荷法律的目的。因此，紐約法院採用艾得荷法。」[16]事實上於該案中紐約法院可能主要是依據實體政策之分析[17]，故而個人認為本案是共同住所地法於實體政策分析之個案正義下讓步之一個表徵。盲目遵循共同慣居地

---

[7]　同上，192頁。

[8]　12 N.Y. 2d. 473

[9]　[1971] A.C. 356; [1969] 3 W.L.R. 322。

[10]　726 N.Y.S. 2d 407; 2001 N.Y. App. Div. Lexis 6269.

[11]　12 N.Y.2d 473, 481, 240 N.Y.S. 2d 743, 191 N.E. 2d 279.

[12]　Schultz v. Boy Scouts of America, Inc., 65 N.Y.2d 189, 197, 491 N.Y.S.2d 90, 480 N.E. 2d 679.

[13]　Miller v. Miller, 22 N.Y.2d 12, 15-16, 290 N.Y.S. 2d 734, 237 N.E. 2d 877.

[14]　Cooney v. Osgood Machinery, Inc., 81 N.Y. 2d 66, 72, 595 N.Y.S.2d 919, 612 N.E.2d 277.

[15]　Paduls v. Lialarn Props. Corp., 84 N.Y. 2d 519, 620 N.Y.S. 2d 310, 644 N.E. 2d 1001; Cooney v. Osgood Machinery, Inc., 81 N.Y. 2d 66, 595 N.Y.S. 2d 919, 612 N.E. 2d 277.

[16]　陳隆修、許兆慶、林恩瑋，《台灣財產法暨經濟法研究叢書（十三）—國際私法：選法理論之回顧與展望》，台灣財產法暨經濟法研究協會發行，2007年1月，初版，217頁。

[17]　同上，216頁，Matter of Allstate v. Stolarz, 81 N.Y. 2d 219, 223, 597 N.Y.S. 2d 904, 613 N.E.2d 936; Portanova v. Trump Taj Mahal Assoc., 270 A.D.2d 757, 759-60, 704 N.Y.S.2d 380.

法的德國及歐盟應該認真的思考將實體政策分析置於共同慣居地的區域選法規則之上。

　　最近三十多年來共同屬人法所造成之最惡名昭彰的案件或許應屬曾締造全世界選法革命的紐約法院。於Schultz v. Boy Scouts of America[18]中，一紐澤西慈善機構之員工，於該慈善機構所主辦之夏令營中，於紐約對一兒童進行性侵，該兒童住所於紐澤西之父母於紐約對該慈善機構提起訴訟。因為紐澤西有著慈善機構免責法規（「charitable immunity law」），紐約上訴法院採當事人之共同住所地法原則，故依紐澤西法拒絕給予損害賠償。紐約法院判決之結果自然違反1948年聯合國人權宣言第8條：「對於法律或憲法所給予保障的基本權利所受的侵犯，每個人針對該行為得請求有管轄權之國家法院之有效救濟。」同樣的權利亦規定於1966年聯合國公民及政治權利公約2(a)、(b)條，1950年歐盟基本自由及人權保護公約第6條及13條，及2000年歐盟基本權利憲章47條。另外令人不可置信的是慈善機構免責法是很顯然的違反了各種人權公約所宣示的平等權。例如1948年聯合國人權宣言的第7條規定：「所有的人於法律前是平等的，並且享有不受任何歧視而法律上公平保護之權利。」同樣的平等權亦規定於1966年聯合國公民及政治權利公約26條，1950年歐盟基本自由及人權保護公約14條反歧視條款，及2000年歐盟基本權利憲章20條平等條款及21條反歧視條款。此外個人亦認為慈善機構免責條款不但是過時的法律，而且可能違反美國憲法14修正案中的適當程序條款及公平保護條款。故而紐約法院於此案充份證明了損害發生地法或共同慣居地法等區域選法規則，如若沒有以實質政策分析做為「武斷或不公平」之標準，會有可能造成不符公平正義之結果。特別是如果對相關之實質政策不加以應有之評價，則過時或違反人權之政策可能會對當事人造成重大之不公平之結果。

　　羅馬Ⅱ第4條3項的「明顯的更密切關連」的法律為要點14所認為是

---

[18]　480 N.E.2d 679 (N.Y. 1985)。

一般規則及特殊規則的規避條款，故而第4條之損害發生地法及共同慣居
地法可能不得不以「更密切關連地法」為規避條款。但首先所謂「更密切
關連」是注重關連（connection）的質（quality）還是量（quantity）？
第2新編145及188條的第2項之最後都陳述：「這些關連點應根據他們對
特定爭點的相關重要性來衡量他們。」故而第2新編可能於理論上是較為
注重關連點的質。Prof. Reese自己於著作中亦一再強調the most significant contact是質的標準，而非量的標準[19]。但於最原始的Babcock v. Jack-
son案就可見識到法院對於「量」的採用較為自在，在許多法院的運用下
皆成為the most significant contact。因為對於「質」的評估可能較客觀上
的「量」為困難，故而許多法院的傾向是可理解的。個人以前是如此評述
的：「「center of gravity」的方式，亦即是「grouping of contacts」，
這種方法論於美國契約法之判例較常見[20]，並且因為是半機械式理論故亦
可能導致不公平的判決[21]。這種方法論的重點在於以關連點的數量為重要
的依據，故而有失機械式之嫌，其之最大詬病為無法找到適當的準據法。
當然如果案件沒有壓倒性的關連點的集結時，自然亦成問題。[22]」於質無
法確認時，轉而以量為依據是自然之反應。但於有些情況下質的優勢是很
明顯的[23]，例如於故意侵權行為上，因為行為地與公法上之公共政策有相
關的關係，行為地於質上之考量自然應特別加重。

　　除了質與量的固有爭執為羅馬Ⅱ所沒有解決外，更重要的是「關
連」與「利益」間之連帶問題。剛開始之Babcock v. Jackson雖然將「最
重要關連」與「利益」分開使用，但隨著時間的演進許多法院於衡量最
重要關連點時常以「利益」為依據[24]。於制定1995年之新侵權行為法時[25]

[19] W. Reese , "Choice of Law: Rules vs. Approach", 57 Cornell L. Rev. 315 (1972); "American Trends in Private International Law", 33 Vand L. Rev. 717 (1980).
[20] Auten v. Auten, 308 N. Y. 155 (1954).
[21] Rubin v. Irving Trust Co., 305 N. Y. 288 (1953).
[22] 陳隆修、許兆慶、林恩瑋，《台灣財產法暨經濟法研究叢書（十三）—國際私法：選法理論之回顧與展望》，台灣財產法暨經濟法研究協會發行，2007年1月，初版，170，171頁。
[23] 同上，171～172頁。
[24] Gutierrez v. Collins, 583 S.W. 2d 312 (Tex. 1979，同上，208，220頁。
[25] 見英國於侵權行為之立法Private International Law (Miscellaneous Provisions) Act 1995 Part Ⅲ。

英國其時的[26]「Law Commissions明白的拒絕適用『利益說』[27]做為英國之選法規則,而Cheshire & North[28]則公開的呼應此說法。Cheshire & North認為判例於此方面雖然有法官提起這種理論,但有關政府政策的考量與政府的利益是個繁複的方法論,如果判例法真要採納則不可能僅止於此。Dicey & Morris則有不同的看法,他們認為Law Commissions的拒絕『利益說』只是適用於一般侵權行為選法的規則而已,並不必然的排除『利益說』於特殊規則的第十二條做為應用上的考慮因素。」[29]個人認為Prof. Currie狹義的詮釋州利益方式,的確於早期嚇走了包括許多美國同僚在內的全世界其他同僚。但如果仿效美國法律協會於複數訴訟之提議中,以「政策」來取代「州利益」,則實在很難看出世界上會有這麼多的反對聲浪。尤其於注重法律原則排列組合的大陸法國家,法律政策的次序排列與評價本就是司法日常功能的一部份。故而如果以「政策」取代「利益」,則於最重要關連的考量上再加以政策為基礎,不但是美國現代法院每日在進行的司法事實,亦較容易為驚弓之鳥的大陸法系所接受。

於英美法上一般會同意美國版的「最重要關連標準」是英國契約法上「適當法」(「proper law doctrine」)[30]的侵權行為版本,或許更正確的說法應是客觀說(objective tet)[31]的適當法理論。亦即是150年前Westlake所主張的做為準據法的國家應與該交易行為有著「最真實的關係」[32]。近數十年來以德語系國家為首,歐陸國家陸續幾乎全面性的採用最重要關連標準。故而個人以前如此評述:「現今歐洲國際私法,無論以最重要關連說為一般適用通則或特殊例外規定,都是混合機械式傳統區域

---

[26] 陳隆修、許兆慶、林恩瑋,《台灣財產法暨經濟法研究叢書(十三)—國際私法:選法理論之回顧與展望》,台灣財產法暨經濟法研究協會發行,2007年1月,初版,151頁。

[27] Law Com Working Paper No 87 (1984), paras 4.36-4.45.

[28] Cheshire and North's Private International Law, 13th ed., P.639.

[29] Dicey and Morris, the Conflict of Law, 13th ed., P.1554.

[30] 陳隆修,《國際私法契約評論》,台北,五南圖書公司,民國75年2月,初版,21～65頁。

[31] 同上,22、23頁。

[32] 即適當法的國家應與契約"has the most teal connection." John Westlake, A Treatise on Private International Law 237 (London, William Maxwell & Son 2d ed. 1880) (1858).

選擇法規與最重要關連說兩種理論的產物。他們都企圖達到機械式理論的穩定性與最重要關連說的彈性，亦是極力避免前者的死硬性（hard and fast）與後者的不可預測性。任何受過適度法律訓練的國際私法學生，都可看出這是一種一廂情願的美夢。最合理、最客觀的說法應是，這種混合機械式理論與彈性理論的做法，雖可保有兩者的優點，但自然不可避免的亦繼承兩者的缺點。亦即這種歐洲式混合做法，在宣稱其優點之餘，連帶的也有傳統機械式法域選擇法規的死硬，及最重要關連說的不可捉摸性（elusive）。[33]」

　　因為被「利益」一詞所震懾，歐洲人通常對美國法院以「利益」之名行政策分析之實可能並不十分完全體會，故而可能對美國理論之引用有著過度不正當的期望與作法。個人雖主張應偏重實體政策之分析，但不得不屈就歐陸的迷戀區域選擇法則情結，故而務實的建議歐陸應將最重要關連標準視為一種「規避法則」（escaping device）。收起對「實體法論」於學術良心上的自信與自傲，個人低聲下氣十分不情願而無可奈何的建議：「德語系國家既然沒有美國判例法的靈活，又對傳統機械式行為地法之優點仍抱以厚望，勉強湊合成一個混合式的方法論。這個自欺欺人的混合方法論，保有原始的兩個理論的優缺點。或許德語系國家的思潮應加以修正，而不必有如此遮遮掩掩的做法。或許他們應仍正大光明的保有傳統的行為地法理論，至於最重要關連說則保留做為反致、定性、公序良俗外，另一種規避傳統死硬機械式法規的『規避技巧』之一。雖然這種逆向建議看起來似乎違反國際私法的潮流，但相信在法院的實務運作上並無多大區別。這種歐洲國際私法的『正名』運動，只是意圖幫助歐洲人去名正言順的採用他們心儀的行為地法理論而已。……個人這看似偏激的理論，相信很多人會同意於法院實務操作上，與歐洲式的混合理論相差不多。『正名』之重要性乃在釐清歐洲人的迷惑，幫助他們了解美國理論表面上的震

---

[33] 陳隆修、許兆慶、林恩瑋，《台灣財產法暨經濟法研究叢書（十三）—國際私法：選法理論之回顧與展望》，台灣財產法暨經濟法研究協會發行，2007年1月，初版，169頁。

憾性與不可抗拒性。

　　事實上『最重要關連說』一詞，無論在歐洲或美國被真正有效的定義出來，它可能比『公共政策』一詞還模糊、混淆。故而從大陸法之觀點，它應該較合適做『規避技巧』之工具之一。」[34]現今如前述羅馬 II 要點14已明言：「本法則有規定一般性之通則，及特別的規則，並且於某些規則中還有『規避條款』，以便於所有的情形下可以清楚的顯示該侵權行為是重大的與其他國家有著密切的關連時，可以脫離那些規則的適用。」[35]

二、建議

　　回顧當年波濤洶湧驚天駭地的選法革命，如今只有「最重要關連」被歐盟保留為「規避條款」，或許令人有點不勝唏噓。個人於此再次坦白的評論，這是美國理論於歐盟的全面性大敗。因為地域性關連選法規則於傳統上已有公序良俗及定性做為規避技巧，多一個模糊的最重要關連規避技巧實在是無關大局。對於羅馬 II 現今的法學方法論，個人雖早已預言，但對預言的實現個人並無任何喜悅。個人早期有鑑於歐盟的故步自封沉迷於土地關連，無法利用大陸法所嫻熟的法律原理的分析，只好出此無可奈何的下下策。以最重要關連做為地域性關連選法規則之規避法規，是無法具體的施行實體政策分析的大陸法唯一的出路，而且是非常落伍而原始的出路。做為一個國際法上比較法的學生，個人誠心的認為歐盟應向選法規則的麥加美國虔誠的膜拜。個人再次重申－地域性關連點只能給予直覺上之合理性，只有透過實體政策分析才能避免「武斷或不公平」的後果。美國理論於歐盟全面性的大敗，就是公平正義的理念於歐盟的全面性大敗。

　　挾著對羅馬 II 法學方法論預測成功之便，基於美國法律協會於複數訴

---

[34]　同上，169、170頁。

[35]　Recital 14, "this Regulation provides for a general rule but also for specific rules and, in certain provisions, for an'escape clause' which allows a departure from these rules where it is clear from all the circumstances of the case that the tort/delict is manifestly more closely connected with another country."

訟之方法論及歐盟之方法論，除了上次於管轄規則之建議外[36]，個人於此再次務實的對大陸及台灣之選法規則提出這個基礎性之建議：**以慣常適用的地域關連點為條文之依據，而最重要關連標準應為規避法則；但是選法規則條文必須於先確認相關連國家所應適用的政策有重大衝突後才適用，而關連點的考量必須加入政策因素的考量在內。**

於管轄規則之建議，是個人參考近20年來美國最高法院於*Burnham v. Superior Court.*[37]與英國最高法院於*Spiliada Maritime Corpn v. Consulex Ltd*[38]中，公開承認對境外被告送達裁量權行使的規範，根據兩國判例法百多年來累積之豐富經驗所做出之建議。個人自認為這個建議或許於實務上是最切合實際，於理論上或許為最先進，或許可與實體法論並列皆為個人畢生得意之作。

但是目前這個於選法規則之建議，前半段顯然是基於歐盟大陸法之方法論，而後半段顯然是基於美國在「假衝突」之共識及法院於政策分析之實務上作法而來。這個混合式的建議融合了大陸法系之現代方法論及美國法院之實務方法論。前者是旨在安撫大陸法注重地域性關連點的直覺上合理性，後者則意圖在前者這種過時的「區域選法規則」中以「實體政策分析」來避免於個案中所可能造成之「武斷或基本上不公平之後果」。

於Ali Complex Litigation Proposal中6.01條選法規則之次序是(1)先為辨認是否有政策上之重大衝突[39]；(2)於有政策上之真衝突時，再以區域

---

[36] 陳隆修、許兆慶、林恩瑋、李瑞生四人合著，《國際私法-管轄與選法理論之交錯》，台北，五南圖書公司，2009年3月，初版1刷，序言，及248頁中，個人對大陸及台灣於管轄規則之建言如下：「於民商管轄規則上，歐盟Council Regulation No. 44/2001、1999海牙草約、美國各州送達境外被告之長手法規及英國送達境外被告之R.S.C. Order 11, rule 1 (1)（即1998 C.P.R.s.6.20），與大陸法各國國內管轄規則相去並不遠，故個人建議於行使民商管轄權時：各國仍以國內管轄規則為基礎（英美則仍為所在理論）。但訴訟之通知若於境內已適當的被送達，或被告承認法院之管轄權時，法院應以『不方便法院』原則為拒絕或停止訴訟裁量之依據（例如訴因與法院地沒有合理關連時）；而若法院欲送達通知至境外時，首先必須認知此為一種例外之過度管轄，其判決有可能不為外國法院所承認，應以『方便法院』原則來確認法院是否為合適、自然之管轄法院（例如為了公平正義之目的或訴因與法院地有強烈之牽連時）。」

[37] 495 U.S.604(1990).

[38] [1987]AC 460.

[39] S.6.01(a),(b).

關連之排序次序為依據[40]，(3)最後為避免武斷或不公平之後果，前述之區域關連次序得不被遵守，更重要的是其他非(b)項之個別州的政策或利益得被引為選法的依據[41]。故而事實上依第2層s.6.01(c)中之區域關連所決定之準據法，不但其適用之次序可被推翻，於個案正義之需求下，非(b)項中之其他州之政策及合法利益亦可被引為適用準據法之依據。故而依(c)項之地域關連所作成之準據法，不但適用之次序可隨時被推翻，其準據法亦可為其他非(b)項之州政策所取代。很明顯的美國法律協會於訴訟選法規則之提議，於假衝突之確認上固然是完全以實體政策分析為依據，即使於政策上有真衝突之情形，(c)項中以地域性關連點為依據之準據法仍可被(d)項中之非(b)項州之政策所取代，故而美國法律協會這個提議實質上可能大部份還是以實體政策分析為主要之依據的。於遭受個人以實體法方法論對其攻擊後，尊敬的Prof. Reese如老獅王保護地盤的以下列答辯做為結論：「第2新編有些方法論可以合理的被稱為模糊，主要的理由就是於有許多相關七價值的存在這個堅持。於答辯上，它可以說一直到最後終於決定這些價值中那個價值應於一個特殊的情形中有著最重要的份量，於價值的平衡中不可避免的會是個不確定的程序。於許多情形下，這個時間尚未到來。」[42]這個時間是否到來，個人以為Prof. Reese自己的美國法律協會於複數訴訟之選法提議中講的很清楚。

　　無論是歐盟羅馬Ⅱ序言中之政策要點，或美國法律協會於複數訴訟中之選法提議，不可否認的是許多實體政策已成為選法規則之基礎。但是很明顯的是選法理論較為落後之歐盟，似乎尚無法於實務上落實這些已被確認的實體政策。相對之下美國法律協會之方法論則高明許多。個人亦十

---

[40]　S.6.01(c).

[41]　S.6.01(d).

[42]　Willis Reese, The Second Restatement of Conflict of Laws Revisited, 34 Mercer L. Rev. 501, at 518 (1983), "This insistence that there are a number of relevant values is a primary reason for what can be justly termed the vagueness of some of the Restatement Second formulations. In defense, it can be said that a balancing of values inevitably will be an uncertain process until it is finally determined which of these values should carry the greatest weight in a given situation. In many instances, such a time has not yet come."

分高興法律協會的避開實體政策的「評價禁忌」。事實上對所牽連的「實體政策的分析」，是個國內案件經常每日在實施的方法論，假衝突、真衝突、或評價禁忌都不是那麼機械的步驟或重要。實體政策分析方法論的時間並非現在才到來，自有現代法律學開始它早已存在於每個國家的每個法律部門中。個人「發現」實體政策分析時是於「最重要關連」橫掃歐洲如日中天時。

三、分割式選法

　　另外讓個人十分驚訝的是羅馬Ⅱ的拒絕採用分割式的選法規則[43]（dépeçage；issue by issue；picking and choosing）。所謂分開式（或分割式）選法規則，即是於同一件案中所包含之不同爭點（issues），「得」交付不同之選法規則處理。例如羅馬Ⅱ 4(1)條即規定：「因侵權行為而引起的非契約上責任應依損害發生地之國之法律。」而第2新編的第145條（侵權）及188條（契約）的第1項則是如此規定：「有關當事人於侵權行為（或188條於契約）中之一爭點之權利義務，是由於有關該爭點上，與該行為（或188條為交易）與當事人依據第6條之原則是最有重大關連之州之當地法為依據。」羅馬Ⅱ會讓個人感到訝異之處，乃在羅馬Ⅰ第3(1)條是允許當事人採分割原則去選定準據法的：「經由他們的選擇，當事人得選擇適用於契約之全部或只是一部份之準據法。」[44]事實上於1980年的羅馬公約3(1)條即有完全一樣的規定，很明顯的羅馬Ⅰ是承襲自1980年的羅馬公約。而且根據羅馬公約的官方報告，這個「分割原則」（severability）並非限於明示選法：「有關之專家並且強調這個分割原則應非只限於明示選擇法律之情形。[45]」同一個國家對同一個這麼重

---

[43] 陳隆修，《比較國際私法》，台北，五南圖書公司，78年10月，初版，37～39頁。

[44] art . 3 (1), "By their choice the parties can select the law applicable to the whole or to part only of the contract."

[45] Report on the Convention on the law applicable to contractual obligations by Mario Giuliano, and Paul Lagarde, Official Journal C 282, 31/10/1980，於第3條之解釋報告："The experts concerned also emphasized that severability should not be limited to cases of express choice of law."

要的法學方法論，於幾乎同一時間所推動的兩個極重要的基本法規會有如此截然不同的作法，這是令人跌破眼鏡的。

　　事實上英國判例法於美國選法革命之前就一向採用dépeçage，對英國法而言這本就是天經地義符合公平正義之務實作法。最佳的證明就是於Private International Law (Miscellaneous Provisions) Act 1995 Part Ⅲ之新國際私法侵權行為之立法上[46]，於第十條取消判例法之適用時就明文規定包括過去於相關爭點準據法之適用：判例法之規則，在他們有關：(a)為了決定侵權行為是否得以起訴，須法院地法及其他國家之法皆同時得以起訴；或(b)為了決定案件所引起的爭點，或其中之一爭點，而（作為上述(a)款之例外）允許一單一國家的法律被適用，在他們被適用於侵權行為之請求權方面，於此被撤銷適用，但此不包含本法案下面所規定之第十三條。」[47]英國新侵權行為1995年之立法自然仍沿續這個「選擇問題方式」之判例法傳統。其第12條規定：「(1)如若在比較所有情況下看來－(a)一般原則下所應適用為準據法之國家與構成侵權行為之因素的關連性；及(b)其他國家與構成侵權行為之因素的關連性，該其他國家的法律是更明顯的適合當準據法去決定案件中所有的爭點，或其中之爭點，則一般原則應被取代，而該其他國家的法律應做為準據法去決定案件中所引起的所有爭點或個別爭點。(2)為了本條文之目的，與一個國家及侵權行為之連結有關之因素應特別包括，與當事人有關之因素，構成該系爭侵權行為之任何情況之因素，或這些情況所造成的任何影響或後果之因素。」[48]

---

[46]　見陳隆修、許兆慶、林恩瑋，《台灣財產法暨經濟法研究叢書（十三）－國際私法：選法理論之回顧與展望》，台灣財產法暨經濟法研究協會發行，2007年1月，初版，141～163頁。

[47]　10.The rules of the common law, in so far as they-

(a) require actionability under both the law of the forum and the law of another country for the purpose of determining whether a tort or delict is actionable; or

(b) allow (as an exception from the rules falling within paragraph (a) above) for the law of a single country to be applied for the purpose of determining the issues, or any of the issues, arising in the case in question,

are hereby abolished so far as they apply to any claim in tort or delict which is not excluded from the operation of this Part by section 13 below.

[48]　12－(1) If it appears, in all the circumstances, from a comparison of－

(a) the significance of the factors which connect a tort or delict with the country whose law would be

　　一九九五之新法對於「侵權行為」（tort）或「有關侵權行為之爭點」（issues in tort）並未下定義。第九條第二項規定：「為了國際私法之目的去定性基於請求權而來的爭點是否與侵權行為的爭點有關，應由法院地決定。」[49]依法院地法去決定「爭點」之相關議題，自然是一種務實之作法[50]。而且基於英國法院對於「分割問題」（「dismemberment」）長久累積下來的判例，相信歐盟或美國應有相當多借鏡之處。例如於有關其他國家與構成侵權行為因素之關連性，使得其法律成為爭點之合適準據法之相關判例，個人以前即曾大致上加以敘述。[51]有關當事人之因素可能包含當事人在社交上完全與身體所在的實際地理脫節的情況，例如在領海或領空之船[52]或飛機內；或當事人有相同的僱主[53]；或之前當事人已有契約關係存在[54]；或當事人為親屬關係；或當事人有相同的住所或慣居地[55]等。構成侵權行為情況的因素可能包括例如當一架飛機於飛航過數個國家時，而墜毀於一個國家[56]；或者一物品於運送當中，而被運送人於某一國家毀損時[57]；或者被害人於旅行當中，在一個與請求權的發生無甚關連的國家遭受到一個有瑕疵的產品的傷害。至於這些情況所造成的影響或後果的因

---

the applicable law under the general rule; and
(b) the significance of any factors connecting the tort or delict with another country,
that it is substantially more appropriate for the applicable law for determining the issues arising in the case, or any of those issues, to be the law of the other country, the general rule is displaced and the applicable law for determining those issues or that issue (as the case may be) is the law of that other country.

(2) The factors that may be taken into account as connecting a tort or delict with a country for the purposes of this section include, in particular, factors relating to the parties, to any of the events which constitute the tort or delict in question or to any of the circumstances or consequences of those events.

[49] (2) The characterization for the purposes of private international law of issues arising in a claim as issues relating to tort or delict is a matter for the courts of the forum.

[50] 陳隆修，《比較國際私法》，台北，五南圖書公司，78年10月，初版，6～9頁。

[51] 陳隆修、許兆慶、林恩瑋，《台灣財產法暨經濟法研究叢書（十三）—國際私法：選法理論之回顧與展望》，台灣財產法暨經濟法研究協會發行，2007年1月，初版，148～149頁。

[52] Mackinnon v. Iberia Shipping Co., 1995 S.C.20.

[53] M'Elroy v. M'Allister, 1949 S.C. 110.

[54] Johnson v. Coventry Churchill International Ltd. [1992] 3 AE.R.14.

[55] Boys v. Chaplin [1971] A.C.356.

[56] Kilberg v. Northeast Airlines Inc., 9N.Y.2d34, 391 F.Supp. 31(S.D.N.Y.1975).

[57] C－51/97 Reeunion europeenne S.A. v. Spliethoff's Beverachtingskantoor B.V. [1998] E.C.R.I.－6511.

素可能包括，對人身或物品所造成的傷害在一個國家（第十一條所指定應適用之國家），但是金錢上或非金錢上的損失卻發生於另一個國家，例如被害人之慣居地[58]，或所有人之公司成立地等[59]；或者當人身傷害是在一個國家（第十一條所指定應適用之國家），而被告的行為卻發生於另一個國家時[60]。

　　事實上英國Private International Law (Miscellaneous Provisions) Act 1995第12條的替代條款（displacement）之性質與羅馬Ⅱ 4 (3)條規避條款之性質類似。但因為英國立法遵循判例法採分割問題之方式，故而其豐沛的判例法自然較羅馬Ⅱ能避免對個案造成「武斷及基本上不公平之後果」。大陸法通常對分割之方式加以極端激烈之反對，一般反對之理由乃在避免破壞案件之整體性及避免法官之可能操縱結果。個人以為分割之方式不但是國際法之問題，亦是國內法每日經常所不可避免之問題。無論國內法或國際法，法律邏輯一致性之要求應在個案正義之基本目的下讓步，法院之最基本之目的乃在避免造成「武斷或基本上不公的後果」。

　　美國學界或法院於實務上[61]一般皆與英國一致，採取分割方式之選法規則，第2新編如前述自然亦是採此方法論[62]。第2新編145、188條之相關評論如下：「法院長久以來便承認他們沒有必要依一州之州內法去決定所有之爭點……如果依兩個或更多潛在有利益之州之州內法該爭點應被不同的解決，則該爭點應受到單獨的考慮。」[63]

　　事實上歐盟議會的修正提議中是有採納分割式選法的，其第4條的結尾規定如下：「繫屬法院於解決選法適用問題時，若於有必要時，可

---

[58]　Vile v. Von Wendt (1979) 103 D.L.R. (3d) 356 (Ont.).

[59]　Skyrotors Ltd. V. Carriere Technical Industries (1979) 103 C.L.R. (3d) 356 (Ont.).

[60]　Lubbe v. Cape plc [1999] I.L.Pr. 113 (C.A.).

[61]　例如NL Indus. V. Commercial Union Ins. Co., 65 F. 3d 314 (3d Cir. 1995)

[62]　Restatement (Second) of Conflict of Laws ss. 145(2), 146-49, 151-52, 154-55, 188(2), 189-97.

[63]　"the courts have long recognized that they are not bound to decide all issues under the local law of a single state ... Each issue is to receive separate consideration if it is one which would be resolved differently under the local law rule of two or more of the potentially interested states." Restatement (Second) of Conflict of Laws, 145 cmt. D, 188 cmt. d.

將各個特定爭點交付不同之分析。[64]」很可惜的這個歷經英美法院多年所累積的經驗與智慧最後並未為歐盟所接受。相反的，歐盟更於第15條對非契約義務準據法的適用範圍加以擴大為：(a)應負責任之人及責任之範圍；(b)責任之豁免、限制、及分割；(c)損害之存在、性質及估量與請求的救濟[65]；(d)於程序法之允許範圍內，法院得採取之步驟以防止或終止傷害或損害，或確保賠償之規定；(e)損害賠償之請求得否移轉或繼承；(f)人身傷害是否可以要求損害賠償；(g)對其他人行為之責任（如對受僱員工）；(h)時效之問題[66]。準據法適用範圍之擴大固然展現大陸法期望法律

---

[64] "In resolving the question of the applicable law, the court seised shall, where necessary, subject each specific issue of the dispute to separate analysis." Eur. Parl. Final A6-0211/2005,(June 27, 2005) 19/46.

[65] 見the Explanatory Memorandum

(a) "The conditions and extent of liability, including the determination of persons who are liable for acts performed by them"; the expression "conditions... of liability" refers to intrinsic factors of liability. The following questions are particularly concerned: nature of liability (strict or fault-based); the definition of fault, including the question whether an omission can constitute a fault; the causal link between the event giving rise to the damage and the damage; the persons potentially liable; etc. "Extent of liability" refers to the limitations laid down by law on liability, including the maximum extent of that liability and the contribution to be made by each of the persons liable for the damage which is to be compensated for. The expression also includes division of liability between joint perpetrators.

(b) "The grounds for exemption from liability, any limitation of liability and any division of liability": these are extrinsic factors of liability. The grounds for release from liability include force majeure; necessity; third-party fault and fault by the victim. The concept also includes the inadmissibility of actions between spouses and the exclusion of the perpetrator's liability in relation to certain categories of persons.

(c) "The existence and kinds of damage for which compensation may be due": this is to determine the damage for which compensation may be due, such as personal injury, damage to property, moral damage and environmental damage, and financial loss or loss of an opportunity.

有關損害之估量，請參考羅馬 I 相關之註解，應限於法律之規定較妥。

[66] Article 15

Scope of the law applicable

The law applicable to non-contractual obligations under this Regulation shall govern in particular:

(a) the basis and extent of liability, including the determination of persons who may be held liable for acts performed by them;

(b) the grounds for exemption from liability, any limitation of liability and any division of liability;

(c) the existence, the nature and the assessment of damage or the remedy claimed;

(d) within the limits of powers conferred on the court by its procedural law, the measures which a court may take to prevent or terminate injury or damage or to ensure the provision of compensation;

(e) the question whether a right to claim damages or a remedy may be transferred, including by inheritance;

(f) persons entitled to compensation for damage sustained personally;

(g) liability for the acts of another person;

(h) the manner in which an obligation may be extinguished and rules of prescription and limitation, in-

適用一致性之企圖，但反諷的是適用範圍愈大，愈不容易達到法律一致之目標。例如前述於消滅時效上英國雖配合大陸法將其視為實體法，但於衡平規則上仍有保留性之規定；(f)款為人身傷害之問題，可能牽涉及各國憲法基本人權之堅持；(c)及(d)款為損害之實際估量、性質與執行之問題，這些問題通常於英美法是屬於程序上之問題[67]，而會依繫屬法院地法為依據[68]。個人認為羅馬II不應將這些問題過份簡單的歸諸法系之不同，而應紮實的正視這些問題於個案上有時是與造成「武斷或不公平的後果」有直接牽連的。

　　羅馬II的強調拒絕分割式選法規則之適用是有點奇怪的，因為至少無論如何第16條法院地的強行法規[69]及第26條法院地的公序良俗的適用，是

---

cluding rules relating to the commencement, interruption and suspension of a period of prescription or limitation.

[67] 陳隆修，《比較國際私法》，台北，五南圖書公司，78年10月，初版，155～157頁。

[68] Mc Millan v. Canadian Northern Ry. Co. [1923] A. C. 120 (P. C.).; Phrantzes v. Argenti [1960] 2 Q. B. 19 35.; Baschet v. London Illustrated Standard [1900] 1 ch. 73.; Warner Brothers Pictures Incorporated v. Nelson [1937] 1 K. B. 209.; Phrantzes v. Argenti [1960] 2 Q. B. 19.

[69] 有趣的是或許亦是因為羅馬公約在強行法上所造成的困擾，羅馬II如同羅馬I一般，就只有在第二級的「超越性強行法規」（如同第16條）上才使用強行法之名詞，而基於基本第一段的強行法（如第14(2)、(3)條）上則使用「當事人不可以約定違反」之名詞。
羅馬規則強行法的概念，一般是認為受到ECJ於Joined Cases C-369/96 and C-376/96 [1999] ECR I-8453，Arblade 案之影響，見Paras. 30,31,
"30
as regards the second question referred in each of the two cases, concerning the classification of the provisions at issue as public-order legislation under Belgian law, that term must be understood as applying to national provisions compliance with which has been deemed to be so crucial for the protection of the political, social or economic order in the Member State concerned as to require compliance therewith by all persons present on the national territory of that Member State and all legal relationships within that State.
31
The fact that national rules are categorised as public-order legislation does not mean that they are exempt from compliance with the provisions of the Treaty; if it did, the primacy and uniform application of Community law would be undermined. The considerations underlying such national legislation can be taken into account by Community law only in terms of the exceptions co Community freedoms expressly provided for by the Treaty and, where appropriate, on the ground that they constitute overriding reasons relating to the public interest."
而the Explanatory Memorandum from the Commission, accompanying the Proposal For Rome II，PP.24,25中則認為超越性強行法是各國法院甚至不必適用其選法規則及於實際上去評估應適用之準據法是否會違反法院地之價值，而直接去適用其自己之規則："What is specific about them is that the courts do not even apply their own conflict rules to determine the law applicable to a given situation and to evaluate in practical terms whether its content would be repugnant to the values of the forum, but they apply their own rules as a matter of course."

21世紀全球化法學的心與靈魂是在個案正義（the heart and soul of twenty-first century legal globalization lies in individual justice），「公共利益」是不見得能永遠與私人利益結合的。如Cheshire and North, 14thed.,p739中所說的 "This definition brings out the protectionist nature of mandatory provisions. The danger of defining what overriding mandatory provisions are protecting is that may restrict the use of the concept. In particular, the definition will exclude provisions which aim to protect purely private interests."

在Arblade (Joined Cases C-369/96 and C-376/96)案中，雖然the EC Treaty要求人、服務、貨物、資本之自由流通（第4條），但歐盟最高法院仍允許會員國對於外國機構短暫派於本國內之工人加以最低工資及提供社會工作文件之規定，以保護工人。

1. Articles 59 of the EC Treaty (now, after amendment, Article 49 EC) and 60 of the EC Treaty (now Article 50 EC) do not preclude the imposition by a Member State on an undertaking established in another Member Stare, and temporarily carrying out work in the first State, of an obligation to pay the workers deployed by it the minimum remuneration fixed by the collective labour agreement applicable in the first Member State, provided that the provisions in question are sufficiently precise and accessible that they do not render it impossible or excessively difficult in practice for such an employer to determine the obligations with which he is required to comply.
4. Articles 59 and 60 of the Treaty do not preclude the imposition by a Member State on an undertaking established in another Member Stare, and temporarily carrying out work in the first State, of an obligation to keep social and labour documents available, throughout the period of activity within the territory of the first Member State, on site or in an accessible and clearly identified place within the territory of that State, where such a measure is necessary in order to enable it effectively to monitor compliance with legislation of that State which is justified by the need to safeguard the social protection of workers.

這個論述成為歐盟以「公共利益」為強行基礎之依據，但個人還是認為21世紀的全球化法學應以個案為基礎－而這自然包含強行法規在內。又如後述，個人又深信中華民族幾千年來盛行的「王道」「不患寡患不均」之文化是與聯合國人權公約相通的，於此案事實上是亦可由中國「王道」文化及人權公約為解決之基礎的。聯合國1966年經濟、社會及文化權利公約第7條規定：

Article 7
The States Parties to the present Covenant recognize one right of everyone to the enjoyment of just and favorable conditions of work which ensure, in particular:
(a) Remuneration which provides all workers, as a minimum, with
　　(i) Fair wages and equal remuneration for work of equal value without distinction of any kind, in particular women being guaranteed conditions of work not inferior to those enjoyed by men, with equal pay for equal work;
　　(ii) A decent living for themselves and their families in accordance with the provisions of the present Covenant;
(b) Safe and healthy working conditions;
(c) Equal opportunity for everyone to be promoted in his employment to an appropriate higher level, subject to no considerations other than those of seniority and competence;
(d) Rest, leisure and reasonable limitation of working hours and periodic holidays with pay, as well as remuneration for public holidays.

而歐盟自己2000年的基本權利憲章第31條及第36條亦規定：
Article 31
Fair and just working conditions
1. Every worker has the right to working conditions which respect his or her health, safety and dignity.
2. Every worker has the right to limitation of maximum working hours, to daily and weekly rest periods and to an annual period of paid leave.

目前國際公約普遍承認之原則[70]：但是個人最為震驚，最感到荒謬的是第4條3項中之更密切關連例外條款。該條款明文規定當事人先前既存之關係，例如契約，可做為明顯的更密切關連之依據，而又如前述羅馬公約及羅馬I規則署名「自由選擇」之第3條1項，皆明文規定允許當事人所選擇之準據法得適用於契約之全部或一部。而且如前述羅馬公約之解釋報告還更進一步闡明：「強調這個分割原則應非只限於明示選擇法律之情形。」故而大陸法之歐盟於契約法上是採英美法之分割式選法規則，但歐盟精神分裂之症狀乃在於非契約責任上其卻拒絕（至少於表面上）分割式選法規則之適用。無論依英美法或大陸法侵權行為、不當得利、或無因管理（後兩者於英美法通常為衡平法）之行為若與契約有重大牽連，則其準據法經常為該契約之準據法[71]。故而契約準據法之適用既然是本著分割式選法規則而來，則與契約有關連之侵權行為、無因管理、及不當得利準據法之適用上，自然不可避免的經常亦會本著分割式選法規則而來。

　　這種分割式選法規則之適用亦可能發生於第14條當事人得自由選定非契約準據法之情形，因為非契約準據法之約定一經同意就已轉換成約定之契約準據法，而應適用全世界於此方面共同適用之分割式選法規則。歐盟委員會於草案中對第4條3項之解釋報告中認為應適用同一法律之理由為「經由依同一法律去適用在他們所有之關係上，這種方法可以尊重當事人之合法之期待及符合依正義原則處理事情之需要。由一個更為技術上之層面而言，這種事實上的後果就是，同一個關係於契約上可能依某會員國

Article 36

Access to services of general economic interest

The Union recognises and respects access to services of general economic interest as provided for in national laws and practices, in accordance with the Treaty establishing the European Community, in order to promote the social and territorial cohesion of the Union.

而又如後述歐盟契約法原則自己又闡述人權公約應為最強行之規定，任何違反這些規定之一定是無效。故而強行法以中國「王道」文化及人權公約為基礎是全球化法學順理成章之自然道法。黃進教授於2011年9月於台北兩岸國際私法年會中曾明確的對個人表達中國法學必須具有特色—「王道」文化與人權公約結合而來的21世紀全球化法學或許就是中國法學革命的特色。

[70] Symeon C. Symeonides認為第8(2)、14、17、18、19、20條及要點33皆構成例外，Rome II and Tort Conflicts: A Missed Opportunity 56 Am. J. Comp. L. 173, 185, 186 (2008).

[71] 陳隆修，《比較國際私法》，台北，五南圖書公司，78年10月，初版，365～368頁。

之法律而侵權行為依其他會員國之法律，這種現象可被緩和。[72]」事實上於國際私法上歐盟較近一些會員國亦有類似之規定[73]。但無論歐盟各大陸法系是如何的排斥分割式選法規則，「經由同一法律去適用在當事人之所有關係上」之願望是於理論上及實務上皆為天方夜譚。如前述非契約關係於現代社會中是經常與契約有著重大之牽連，而無論於英美法或大陸法於此情形下是通常以契約準據法為依據的。又在契約準據法之適用上，無論英美法或大陸法皆一致的採用分割式選法規則，故而非契約準據法之適用自然亦會採用分割式選法規則——歐盟大陸法系「經由同一法律去適用在當事人之所有關係上」之論述是個可笑的神話。

台灣最高法院96年台上1804號判決，對香港女學生搭台灣同學機車於台灣車禍死亡之案件中，認定「按侵權行為法之理想，在給予被害人迅速及合理之賠償」，並採「分割」式選法規則「用以追求個案具體之妥當性」。故依台灣法侵權行為地法去決定被上訴人之侵權行為損害賠償責任；而被害人父母（上訴人）是否得向被上訴人請求被害人之扶養義務部份，則依扶養義務人之本國法香港法為依據。

首先對於本案之具體結果，個人以前如此論述：「共同核心觀念或主流價值的維護，無論於國際或國內案件上各國不應退讓；但這些觀念或價值之適用於具體個案之事實上，應尊重承審法院之認定。[74]」故而於此僅就法院之方法論評述。個人一再重覆許多英美判例法是經歷時間千錘百鍊

---

[72] Commission of the European Communities, Proposal for a Regulation of the European Parliament and the Council on the Law Applicable to Non-Contractual Obligations, (COM 427)(2003) final, 2003/0168(C)(D), Explanatory Report, 13,"By having the same law apply to all their relationships, this solution respects the parties' legitimate expectations and meets the need for sound administration of justice. On a more technical level, it me ans that the consequences of the fact that one and the same relationship may be covered by the law of contract i n one Member State and the law of tort/ delict in another can be mitigated."

[73] 例如瑞士國際私法 Art. 133 (3), "...when the tortuous act constitutes a violation of a pre- existing legal relationship between the tortfeasor and the injured party, claims founded on this act are governed by the law applicable to that legal relationship."及最近之比利時國際私法 Art. 100, "an obligation resulting from an injurious event having a close connection with a pre-existing legal relationship between the parties is governed by the law applicable to that relationship."

[74] 陳隆修，《2005年海牙法院選擇公約評析》，台北，五南圖書公司，2009年1月，初版1刷，27頁。

而形成，所有「武斷或不公平」的判例都會為時代所淘汰，去蕪存菁所存的判例法是等同大自然演進的一環，除非有迫切而明顯的相反理由，我們應該遵循這些人類共同祖先生活智慧的結晶。分割式選法規則是英美法院所累積下來的寶貴經驗，大陸法系對此方法論加以排斥抗拒之行為是可笑而反動的。通常於法學上之進化順序為英美法，歐洲大陸法，日本法，台灣法，很明顯的台灣最高法院於本案中打破了這個法學的食物鏈。

　　本案中令個人最為感動的並非於分割規則之適用，因為個人認為這是理所當然之程序。最高法院於本案中表明「追求個案具體之妥當性」，及「侵權行為法之理想，在給予被害人迅速及合理之賠償」，這不折不扣的是實體政策分析之代言案例。請問於本案中法院有討論到政策之「假衝突」、「真衝突」，及香港與台灣之實體政策之「不能評價」（「evaluate」）嗎？個人於此再次重申－實體政策分析是所有法系的法官於所有的民刑國內、國際案件所每日進行之例行演練。當美國同僚無謂的自陷於「評價禁忌」的泥淖中，本案中可敬的台灣大陸法系法官如魚得水般的自在的操演著實體政策分析。藉著這個政策方法論，個人真誠的認為中華民族的法學方法或許於此案件上已經越過美國，而至少於這一點上或許已躍居法學食物鏈之頂端。但如果兩岸之法院要全面性的如美國法院一般，經常以例行公事般的於具體個案上實施實體政策分析，可能還要一段非常遙遠的路。歐盟於第4(3)條中採用契約準據法做為基於同一事實而來之非契約關係之準據法，於無因管理或不當得利上英美法或許與大陸法於一般案件上會有共同之作法。但侵權行為法之基本政策乃在給予被害人迅速及合理之賠償，而契約法之基本政策乃在保障當事人正常之期待，這兩個法學部門之政策於實際運用上之結果有時是會不一致的，故而第4(3)條適用於侵權行為時是應加以保留的。雖然是基於同一事實，但侵權行為法或契約法之基本政策是不一致的，不能硬性的皆以契約準據法做為侵權行為之準據法。如近三十年前個人即以英國著名的 *Sayers v. Internatienal Drilling*

Co. N. V.[75]案，討論契約準據法與侵權行為法之政策有衝突時，不合適以契約條款作為侵權行為之抗辯的情形[76]。本著名案例因個人已一再加以討論[77]，故於此不再贅述，另外於*Siegleman v. Cunard White Star Ltd.*[78]與*Fricke v. Isbrandtsen Co.*[79]中，亦已討論過附合契約的準據法不能作為人身傷害之準據法之問題[80]。另外又於*Levy v. Daniels U-Drive Auto Renting Co.*[81]中，討論及契約條款是否得作為侵權行為訴因之問題[82]。在理想中基於同一事實的案件裏，契約行為與侵權行為皆以同一準據法為依據自然甚好，但法律邏輯一致性的要求還是應在個案正義的基本目的前讓步[83]。故

---

[75] [1971] 3 All E. R. 163; [1971] 1W. L. R. 1176。

[76] 陳隆修，《美國國際私法新理論》，台北，五南圖書公司，民國76年1月，初版，242～244頁。

[77] 陳隆修、許兆慶、林恩瑋，《台灣財產法暨經濟法研究叢書（十三）—國際私法：選法理論之回顧與展望》，台灣財產法暨經濟法研究協會發行，2007年1月，初版，161～163頁。

[78] 221 F. 2d 189 (2d Cir 1955)。

[79] 151 F. Supp. 465 (S.D.N.Y. 1957)。

[80] 陳隆修，《美國國際私法新理論》，台北，五南圖書公司，民國76年1月，初版，242～243頁。

[81] 108 Conn. 333, 143 A. 163 (1928)。

[82] 陳隆修，《美國國際私法新理論》，台北，五南圖書公司，民國76年1月，初版，247、248頁。

[83] 但極度有趣的是Explanatory Memorandum, p11 ,於論及第3(1)條時，當損害是發生於不同國家時，這些國家之法律是皆被適用的：The place or places where indirect damage, if any, was sustained are not relevant for determining the applicable law. In the event of a traffic accident, for example, the place of the direct damage is the place where the collision occurs, irrespective of financial or non-material damage sustained in another country. In a Brussels Convention case the Court of Justice held that the "place where the harmful event occurred" does not include the place where the victim suffered financial damage following upon initial damage arising and suffered by him in another Contracting State.
The rule entails, where damage is sustained in several countries, that the laws of all the countries concerned will have to be applied on a distributive basis, applying what is known as "Mosaikbetrachtung" in German law.
Case C-364/93 Marinari v Lloyds Bank [1995] ECRI-2719
這種德國同僚所謂的「馬賽克法則」"Mosaikbetrachtung" (mosaic principle)，英國判例法上在類似訂約前責任之案件中亦加以適用，Morin v Bonhams & Brooks Ltd [2003] EWCA Civ 1802, [2004] 1 Lloyd's Rep 702. 另外於租賃飛機之案件中，有關飛機維修之損害賠償（於柬埔寨）及租金之請求（柬埔寨外之銀行戶頭）亦適用此原則，Protea Leasing Ltd v Royal Air Cambodge [2002] 2 All ER 224。
「馬賽克法則」對於跨國企業之損害賠償之請求是十分精準的，但對於弱勢之請求者是不利的，見台灣最高法院99台上2001號生活費用之請求案件，台灣法院所鐵血執行的即為「馬賽克法則」（台灣、大陸及德國法）。事實上於96台上1804號判決中，個人不但建議台灣最高法院「分割選法規則」之適用，更直接建議意外侵權行為法之全球化共同核心為「給予被害人迅速及合理的賠償」。這兩個建議皆為判決主文所採用，最高法院更令個人眼眶泛紅的表示法院「追求個案具體妥當性」之決心。
無論是德式的「馬賽克法則」或英美的「分割式法則」，皆必須謹記—「法學上的概念是受制於自我設限的常識及公平原則的限制」，以及「邏輯並非判例法的最高價值，英國國際私法實

而羅馬 II 第4(3)條於契約與侵權行為準據法認定之關連性上應特別小心，應以是否會於個案當事人間「造成武斷或基本上不公平的後果」為裁量權行使之依據，尤其是關連性之認定上自然應以實體政策分析為依據。個人於此必須再次提醒歐盟：契約當事人間之平衡性為契約法上強行之超越性考量，這是與訴訟法上當事人立足點平等（或武器平等）一般，皆為21世紀全球化法學之共同核心政策。

四、契約與非契約行為

(一)侵權行為與其他

　　如前述基於同一事實而來之請求，有時於某些國家可同時構成契約及非契約之請求，或於一個國家只能為契約上之請求，而於其他國家可能只為非契約之請求。例如某些基於產品責任而來之請求權，於法國是屬於侵權行為，而於英國可能是屬於契約之保證[84]。這種情形於超過智慧財產權授權契約範圍而來之請求權亦常發生。個人認為這不應只是單純的選法規則的歧異而已，更是牽涉及各國訴訟制度之問題。通常於英美法系只要是基於相同事實而得請求之救濟（即同一訴因），即有禁止反言之效力。而大陸法國家一事不再理之要件則較為嚴格，通常會要求當事人、標的、及訴的聲明皆相同。但是即使於英美法系間，對訴因禁止反言及爭點禁反言間認定亦皆不同。故而個人以前如此論述[85]：「於承認其他訂約國判決上Brussels Convention希望：『判決的承認能夠有如同作成判決國家所給予的判決的權力與效力的結果[86]。』歐盟法院於*Hoffmann v.*

現正義的概括性目的給予邏輯一致性的政策必要的限制」，而這亦就是中國是法學之「道法自然」。

[84] 於Case C-26/91 Jacob Handte GmbH v TMCS [1993] E.C.R. I-3967中，即使沒有牽連到消費者傷害之問題，歐盟法院採納法國最高法院侵權行為之見解，而非契約之見解。

[85] 陳隆修，《2005年海牙法院選擇公約評析》，台北，五南圖書公司，2009年1月，初版1刷，139頁。

[86] 571.Jenard Report, p.43, "Recognition must have the result of conferring on judgments the authority and effectiveness accorded to them in the State in which they were given."

*Krieg*中又重申『根據公約第26條所被承認之外國判決須原則上如同於作成判決國家之國內一般的於被請求執行國家有一樣的效力[87]。』同樣的美國聯邦憲法第4條第1項亦規定各州對其他州之判決應給予充分互信[88]。而The Judiciary Act 1790又加以解釋the judicial Proceedings（司法判決）應被給予『同樣的充分互信如同……那些州法院所有之法律或慣例……而該些州為判決作成地[89]。』故而第二新編評論：『於憲法之限制下，作成判決之州之當地法決定該判決是否，並且於什麼程度上，於當事人間，或他們的關係人間，在另外一個請求或訴因時所牽連的爭點的最後終局的效果。[90]』故而於歐盟及美國等聯邦或邦聯，無論於有關訴因禁止反言或爭點禁止反言上，各國或各州於理論上應予他國或他州之判決，如同於作成判決之原來之國或州之同樣一事不再理或排除之效力。」

　　故而個人認為「有關判決之承認與執行上，並不只侷限於有關管轄條款之判決，個人還是認為無論是基於契約、侵權或衡平法之請求，只要是有經過適當之送達、為合適之自然法院及給予當事人充分之表達機會（包括應利用原來法院之救濟程序），則該判決或決定皆應有一事不再理之效果。」[91]而於外國判決之承認上，個人則務實的建議：「除非能證明

---

[87] 572.Case 145/86 [1988] E.C.R. 645, "A foreign judgment which has been recognized by virtue of Article 26 of the Convention must in principle have the same effects in the State in which enforcement is sought as it does in the State in which the judgment was given."

[88] Article IV
Section 1. Full Faith and Credit shall be given in each State to the public Acts, Records, and judicial Proceedings of every other State.

[89] 28 U.S.C.A. § 1738, "the same full faith and credit as .... have by law or usage in the courts of such State .... from which they are taken."

[90] Second Restatement, Conflict of Laws, s. 95, comment (g)(1971), "the local law of the State where the judgment was rendered determines, subject to constitutional limitations, whether, and to what extent the judgment is conclusive as to the issues involved in a later suit between the parties, or their privies, upon a different claim or cause of action." 於Faunteroy v. Lum, 210 U.S. 230, Mississippi 仍然承認Missouri的判決，雖然該判決之訴因（賭博）於Mississippi是不合法的。於Baker v. General Motors, 522 U.S. 222,233, 美國最高法院即表示公共政策不能違反充分互信。但Second Restatement, s.103規定：" A judgment rendered in one State of the United States need not be recognized or enforced in a sister State if such recognition or enforcement is not required by the national policy of full faith and credit because it would involve an improper interference with important interests of the sister State." 英國Foreign Judgments Act 1933, art 4 (1)(a)(v)仍有公共政策條款。

[91] 陳隆修，《2005年海牙法院選擇公約評析》，台北，五南圖書公司，2009年1月，初版1刷，138頁，但如果欲追加訴因，則必須再取得對新訴因之管轄。

判決作成地法給予該判決不同之排除效力，否則原來判決之排除效力應被推定為與被申請承認地法院給予類似判決同樣之效力。」[92]這樣務實的建議下，則英美法院的判決通常應被認定為只要基於同一事實而得請求之救濟，無論是有關契約或侵權行為請求權之決定於大陸法系皆應有一事不再理之既判力。反過來，即使是基於同一事實而得請求之救濟，大陸法法院所作之判決之效力，於英美法院之承認上通常應被認定為只能具有大陸法法院於判決中所直接認定之侵權行為法或契約法上之效力，而對於沒有認定之其他法域上有關契約或侵權行為之請求並沒有禁止反言之排除效果。但是個人雖然於契約法與侵權行為法世界性的糾纏中給予務實的建議，個人還是以 *Adams v. Cape Industries plc*[93]為例，主張於一事不再理或禁止反言之問題上，仍應以實體政策分析為依據[94]才能避免「武斷或不公平」之後果。於全世界訴訟法及實體法上皆有甚大差異下，羅馬 II 企圖以第4(3)條之簡單規定，來解決世界性契約法、侵權法、及訴訟法盤根錯節之糾纏，個人認為歐盟野心太大，而努力太少。

　　另外德國國際私法新法42條規定，於引起非契約責任之事件發生後，於不影響第三人權利下，當事人得自由選擇應適用之準據法。[95]羅馬

---

[92]　陳隆修，《2005年海牙法院選擇公約評析》，台北，五南圖書公司，2009年1月，初版1刷，141頁。舉證責任之不同可能使得於兩個訴訟程序中之爭點變得不同，因此使得禁止反言不適用，Cobb v. Pozzi, 363 F.3d 89, 113 (2d Cir. 2003)。美國的Restatement (Second) of Judgments §28 (4)(1982)亦同樣規定如下"Relitigation of the issue in a subsequent action between the parties is not precluded... the party against whom preclusion is sought had a significantly heavier burden of persuasion with respect to the issue in the initial action than in the subsequent action... or the adversary has a significantly heavier burden than he had in the first action."無論是被主張禁止反言之當事人於前個訴訟中被要求較法院地更嚴格的舉證責任，或其相對人於法院地被要求較前個訴訟更為嚴格的舉證責任，只要符合公平正義之標準，或不會改變案件之結果，不能因外國程序或法院之不同而不承認外國判決。這亦是個人一再強調現今之一事不再理原則，不能以避免不一致的判決及司法資源的浪費為基礎理由之故，而應以Prof. Graveson的「有效正義」為基礎理論。避免各國技術法規之不同，而積極的注重實體上個案案件之正義，才是實體法論之精神。

[93]　588. [1990] Ch. 433.

[94]　陳隆修，《2005年海牙法院選擇公約評析》，台北，五南圖書公司，2009年1月，初版1刷，141、142頁。

[95]　EGBGB, Article 42
　　Party Autonomy
　　After the event giving rise to a non-contractual obligation has occurred, the parties may choose the law that shall apply to the obligation; rights of third parties remain unaffected.

II 則於第14條中有類似而更詳細之規定。第1項規定(a)於引起損害發生之事件發生後之約定；或(b)所有當事人之目的乃在從事商業行為時，於引起損害發生之事件發生前，所自由洽商之約定，有關於上述兩個約定當事人得選擇非契約責任所應適用之法律，但該選擇不能妨害第三人之權利，並且必須為明示或依案件情形顯示出合理的確定性。第2項規定當造成損害時之行為之所有要素皆集中於一個國家，而該國之法律並未被選為準據法時，當事人之選法並不能違背該國之強行法規。第3項規定當造成損害時之行為之所有要素皆集中於會員國內時，當事人之選法不能違背歐盟之相關強行法規[96]。

　　羅馬 II 14(3)條有關歐盟強行法規為羅馬 I 3(4)條之翻版。而羅馬 II 第14條2項之規定很明顯的是羅馬 I 第3條有關選法自由中，第3項當案件事實皆集中於一國時，當事人所選之法律不能違背該國強行規定之翻版條文。[97]而羅馬 I 第3(3)條是沿續羅馬公約3(3)條之規定。羅馬 II 第14條1項後段之「選法應該明示或由案件之情形可以顯示出合理之確定性」，很

---

[96] Article 14

Freedom of choice

1. The parties may agree to submit non-contractual obligations to the law of their choice:

(a) by an agreement entered into after the event giving rise to the damage occurred; or

(b) where all the parties are pursuing a commercial activity, also by an agreement freely negotiated before the event giving risee to the damage occurred.

The choice shall be expressed or demonstrated with reasonable certainty by the circumstances of the case and shall not prejudice the rights of third parties.

2. Where all the elements relevant to the situation at the time when the event giving rise to the damage occurs are located in a country other than the country whose law has been chosen, the choice of the parties shall not prejudice the application of provisions of the law of that other country which cannot be derogated from by agreement.

3. Where all the elements relevant to the situation at the time when the event giving rise to the damage occurs are located in one or more of the Member States, the parties' choice of the law applicable other than that of a Member State shall not prejudice the application of provisions of Community law, where appropriate as implemented in the Member State of the forum, which cannot be derogated from by agreement.

4.

[97] 3. Where all other elements relevant to the situation at the time of the choice are located in a country other than the country whose law has been chosen, the choice of the parties shall not prejudice the application of provisions of the law of that other country which cannot be derogated from by agreement.

明顯的可以看出是羅馬I第3條第1項於當事人選法規定之翻版。而羅馬I第3(1)條這個當事人於契約選法自由之規則是完全沿續羅馬公約第3(1)條之規定。羅馬I規則及羅馬公約3(1)條這個規定是有關當事人於選法時，不但可採用明示之方亦可採用默示選擇準據法之方式。無論明示或默示選擇準據法，這些都是判例法上所允許的當事人自主契約準據法之方式。[98]故而很明顯的羅馬II第14條即是在規定當事人得將「非契約義務」以「契約」（「agreement」）之方式而「洽商」（「negotiate」）約定準據法，亦即透過約定準據法之方式將該「非契約義務」依新約定（包括明示或默示）之新契約之準據法處理。故而羅馬II 14條當事人自由約定準據法之規定，事實上就是羅馬I規則有關契約準據法之規定。

　　既然歐盟自羅馬公約至羅馬I規則，已累積有近30年之判例與豐富經驗，個人覺得羅馬II 14條之簡陋規定似乎是畫蛇添足。有關14 (1)(a)條須事後才允許自由選擇之規定，羅馬I的3(2)、(3)及(4)、5、6、7、8、9、10、13及21條，為有關改變準據法、契約發生地之強行法、運送契約、消費契約、保險契約、僱傭契約、法院地及履行地之強行法、契約之存在、效力及同意、訂約能力、及法院地之公共政策等規定，個人認為羅馬I這些規定遠較羅馬II之14 (1)(a)及(b)條詳盡及合理，且更能保障弱勢。故而相較於羅馬I，個人認為羅馬II 14條是個粗糙而可能於適用上會對弱勢一方（如受僱者、消費者、或小商人），造成個案不公平正義之後果之不良規定。羅馬II 14條將來於適用上必須仰賴羅馬I之規則以為補救。這亦是個人以前於評述其時德國新國際私法時，對該德國42條懶得理會之故[99]。更重要的是德國42條與歐盟羅馬II 14條之規定，反面而言是否代表著一個重要的法學理念：在沒有法律明文允許下，當事人不得擅自將非契約義務之關係經由合意而改變成契約關係？如果這個反面假設是錯

---

[98] 陳隆修，《國際私法契約評論》，台北，五南圖書公司，民國75年2月，初版，54～65頁。個人於57頁中認為只要當事人沒有明定準據法，法院即可依個案之特殊事實而推定準據法。

[99] 陳隆修、許兆慶、林恩瑋，《台灣財產法暨經濟法研究叢書（十三）—國際私法：選法理論之回顧與展望》，台灣財產法暨經濟法研究協會發行，2007年1月，初版，178～193頁。

誤的，當事人得自由將非契約關係經由合意而轉變成契約關係，那麼德國
42條與羅馬 II　14條不但是畫蛇添足，更由於他們的簡陋及不完備可能會
於個案上對弱勢造成不公平正義的情形。

　　一般而言，現今無論於民法或訴訟法上，通常世界各國都會於許多
法域內允許當事人自己同意選定準據法去處理他們之間之權利義務關係。
自然各國之授權範圍可能不太一致，但通常如果各國會允許仲裁之事項，
則會允許當事人自定準據法。故而如若於有關親屬繼承之身份、能力問
題，及牽涉及公法之事項，一般而言各國是不會授權給當事人自行解決。
除了這些涉及重大公共政策之事項外，通常經由當事人之合意，契約即
可成立而有效的解決當事人間之紛爭。歐盟自己的契約法原則[100]第2章有
關契約之成立，即於2:101條開宗明義的規定：「(1)於下列情形下契約
就已成立：(a)當事人有意被合法的拘束，並且(b)他們已達成足夠的協
議，而不要求其他的條件。(2)契約不需要以書面之方式去訂立或證明，
於形式上亦不需要任何其他之要求。契約得以包含人證之所有其他方法
去證明之[101]。」當事人之「意思」及「足夠的協議」分別規定於2:102[102]及
2:103[103]條。可見歐盟自己之契約法在實體上是認同非契約關係得經由當
事人之同意而更具體的轉換成契約關係的。

---

[100] 見the Commission of European Contract Law, Principles of European Contract Law, edited by Ole Lando and Hugh Beale (2000).

[101] Article 2:101: Conditions for the Conclusion of a Contract
(1) A contract is concluded if:
　(a) the parties intend to be legally bound, and
　(b) they reach a sufficient agreement
　without any further requirement.
(2) A contract need not be concluded or evidenced in writing nor is it subject to any other requirement as to form. The contract may be proved by any means, including witnesses.

[102] Article 2:102: Intention
The intention of a party to be legally bound by contract is to be determined from the party's statements or conduct as they were reasonably understood by the other party.

[103] Article 2:103: Sufficient Agreement
(1) There is sufficient agreement if the terms:
　(a) have been sufficiently defined by the parties so that the contract can be enforced, or
　(b) can be determined under these Principles.
(2) However, if one of the parties refuses to conclude a contract unless the parties have agreed on some specific matter, there is no contract unless agreement on that matter has been reached.

(二)外國法之證明

　　尤其值得羅馬 II 注意的是，歐盟契約法原則於第1章第1條宣示其適用範圍後，即緊接著公開的揭櫫契約自由原則於1:102條如下：「(1)在誠信及公平交易原則與本契約原則所建立之強行法規之規定下，當事人得自由訂定契約及決定其內容。(2)除非本契約原則另有規定，當事人得排除本契約原則之適用，或違反本契約規則，或改變其效力。[104]」有關強行法規則規定於1:103條[105]。

　　另外更要的是當事人自由選法之問題，不只是選法規則之問題而已，更牽涉到有些國家於訴訟程序中經常如德、法一般，在允許當事人「自由處分他們的權利」（「free disposition of their rights」）[106]下，透過不主張外國法準據法之方式而去適用法院地法。這個較近為許多大陸法所採用之方式，早已為英美視為理所當然之必要訴訟方式[107]。

　　在主要大陸法中，或許德國與英國法之差異較大。英國法將外國法視

---

[104] Article 1:102: Freedom of Contract

　　(1) Parties are free to enter into a contract and to determine its contents, subject to the requirements of good faith and fair dealing, and the mandatory rules established by these Principles.

　　(2) The parties may exclude the application of any of the Principles or derogate from or vary their effects, except as otherwise provided by these Principles.

[105] Article 1:103: Mandatory Law

　　(1) Where the law otherwise applicable so allows, the parties may choose to have their contract governed by the Principles, with the effect that national mandatory rules are not applicable.

　　(2) Effect should nevertheless be given to those mandatory rules of national, supranational and international law which, according to the relevant rules of private international law, are applicable irrespective of the law governing the contract.

[106] "En une matiere ou les parties ont la libre disposition de leurs droits." See also Courde cassation, Civ. 4 Oct. 1989, Rev.crit.dr.int.pr. 1990.316, note P. Lagarde. 有關德、法、及瑞士相關法律引自 Trevor C. Hartley, Pleading and Proof of Foreign Law: The Major European Systems Compared, 45 Int'l & Comp. L.Q. 271 (1996)。

[107] 陳隆修，《比較國際私法》，台北，五南圖書公司，78年10月，初版，157～160頁。見 P M North, JJ Fawcett, Cheshire and North's Private International Law, 14thed.pp.111,112 "The esrablished rule is that knowledge of foreign law, even of the law obtaining in some other part of the common law world, is not to be imputed to an English judge. Even though the foreign law is notorious, it has been said that the court cannot take judicial notice of it. Unless the foreign law with which a case may be connected is pleaded by the party relying thereon, it is assumed that it is the same as English law. The onus of proving that it is different, and of proving what it is, lies on the party who pleads the difference. If there is no such plea, or if the diference is not satisfactorily proved, the court must give a decision according to English law, even though the case may be connected solely with some foreign country, and the law of that foreign country is applicable according to English choice of law rules.

為事實（「fact」），而德國法將外國法視為法律（「law」）[108]。法院應依職權去確認外國法[109]，其有裁量權去選擇確認外國法之方法[110]，並得請求當事人之協助。如果是於德國選法規則允許之範圍內，通常最主要是於契約與侵權之範圍內，德國法院會允許當事人雙方同意選擇德國法為準據法。如果準據法本應為外國法，而當事人只主張德國法，德國法院通常會將此視為當事人默示選擇德國法為準據法[111]。除非德國下級法院沒有履行其依德國法去適用外國法之職責，否則只有關於德國法之問題才能上訴到最高民事法院[112]，外國法律之問題則不行。

　　法國最高法院（「the Cour de cassation」）於幾經修改其立場後，於1988在Rebouh and Schule[113]兩個案件中決定法院應依職權（ex officio）去認定外國法是否應被適用。如果法院未遵循此原則[114]，其判決會於上訴中被駁回。但很快的於1990年的Coveco中[115]法國最高法院又接著補充，如果當事人未主張外國法之適用，判決不能因適用法院地法而被主張有瑕疵。但是這個補充規則必須適用於外國法不會因國際公約而應被適用[116]，及案件是適用於「當事人得自由的處分他們的權利」之法律範

---

[108] Jan Kropholler, Internationales Privatrecht (2nd edn, 1994), p.519; Christian von Bar, Internationales Privatrecht, Vol.1: Allgemeine Lehren (1987), note 372; Reinhold Geimer, Internationales Zivilproze β recht (1987), note 2136; Peter Arens, Prozessuale Probleme bei der Anwendung auslandischen Rechts im deutschen Zivilprozeb, Festschrift fur Imre Zajtay (1982), p.7 at p.8; Lorenz Fastrich, "Revisibilitat der Ermittlung auslandischen Rechts" (1987) 97 Z.Z.P. 423, 427.

[109] Bundesgerichtshof, judgment of 21.02.1962, B.G.H.Z. 36, 348, 353; Bundesgerichtshof, judgment of 30.03.1976, N.J.W. 1976, 1581, 1582.

[110] Bundesgerichtshof, judgments of 23.12.1981, N.J.W. 1961, 410; 10.07.1975, N.J.W. 1975, 2142, 2143; 30.03.1976, N.J.W. 1976, W.M. 1987, 25.26。

[111] Bundesgerichtshof, judgment of 18.01.1988, N.J.W. 1988, 1592.

[112] Zivilproze β ordnung, 2.549(1).

[113] Civ. 11 and 18 Oct. 1988, Clunet 1989.349, note Alexandre; J.C.P. 1989.11.21327, note Courbe; Rev. crit.dr.int.pr. 1989.368; B. Ancel and U. Lequette, Grands arrest de la jurisprudence francaise de droit international prive (2nd edn, 1992), Nos 70 and 71.

[114] "Le juge droit trancher le litige conformement aux regles de droit qui lui sont applicables."

[115] Civ. 4 Dec. 1990, Clunet 1991.371, note Bureau; Rev.crit.dr.int.pr. 1991.558, note Niboyet-Hoegy; Ancel and Lequette, at No.72.

[116] 但是事實上截至目前為止，大部份的公約，甚至包括管轄公約在內，皆儘量不去碰觸各國之程序法規。例如羅馬Ⅰ第1(3)條即規定。

　　3. This Regulation shall not apply to evidence and procedure, without prejudice to Article 18. 同樣的羅馬公約第1(2)(h)亦有相同的規定。

圍。所謂「當事人得自由的處分他們的權利」的範圍，可能會包含大部份的一般選法規則的範圍[117]，例如契約、侵權、及物權（包含夫妻財產及繼承），而身份及行為能力問題則不包含在內。於外國法之證明上法國最高法院亦改變其立場。於1993年之Amerford[118]案件中，最高法院認為在有關當事人得自由處分權利之案件，主張外國法之適用會造成與法國法之適用有不同結果之一方，必須以外國法內容之證明來建立此差異；否則法國法會以法院地法而被適用。有趣的是不同於德國法及其他許多大陸法，外國法通常應被視為事實般的去證明，故而外國法之問題只能被上訴到高等法院，而不能上訴到最高法院[119]。

瑞士1987年聯邦國際私法16(1)條雖然如台灣民訴法般規定法院應依職權適用外國法，並且得請求當事人之協助，但於當事人得自由處分之權利上，外國法之舉證責任在於當事人；若當事人沒有盡到舉證責任則依16(2)條應適用法院地法。於1987年新法之前，一般將外國法視為有關事實之問題。另外於瑞士國際私法允許當事人自主選法之情形，若當事人於訴訟程序中同意不適用外國法，則瑞士法院地法自然會適用[120]。

於美國方面其早期尚未獨立時即採納英國式意見，將外國法視為「事實」[121]（「fact」），後又為Chief Justice Marshall所引用而正式為美國法[122]。這個觀點同樣的適用於外國法及外州法[123]，故而希望引用非法院地法的當事人須依證據規則而去主張及證明外國法。後來有些州之判例法終於給予外州法司法承認（「judicial notice」），但並不包含外國法在內[124]。通常如果牽涉到外國法，而該法並未被充份證明，則常會被推定

---

[117] Lagarde, Rev.crit.dr.int.pr. 1994.332.337.

[118] Ch.com. 16 Nov. 1993, Rev.crit.dr.int.pr. 1994.332, note Lagarde; Clunet 1994.98, note Donnier.

[119] Compagnie algerienne de Credit et de Banque v. Chemouny, Civ. 2 Mar. 1960, Rev.crit.dr.int.pr. 1960.97.

[120] 見Hartley, 45 Int'l & Comp. L.Q. 271, 277.(1996).

[121] Mostyn v. Fabrigas, [1774] 1 Cowp. 161, 174.

[122] Church v. Hubbart, 6 U.S. (2 Cranch) 187, 236, 2 L.Ed. 249 (1804).

[123] Cox v. Morrow, 14 Ark. 603, 610 (1854).

[124] Choate v. Ransom, 74 Nev. 100, 323 P.2d 700 (1958); Prudential Insurance Co. of America v. O'Grady, 97 Ariz. 9,396 P.2d 246 (1964); National Transportation Co. v. J.E. Faltin Motor Transportation Co.,

為與法院地法一致[125]；或於外國法未被主張或證明時，當事人被推定為默示選定法院地法[126]。但是於默示選法上，由於美國契約法上過去於此方面並未完全遵循英國母法，故而個人認為是有盲點存在。

　　個人早期如此論述[127]：「當事人雖得在『當事人自主』之大原則下選定準據法，但此『當事人自主』原則是否為絕對呢？亦即當事人是否得選擇一與該交易行為或當事人完全沒有關係之國家以其法律為準據法？英國國際私法一向比歐洲大陸在許多方面都較為開放，並且於此方面似乎較美國為開放。但此問題並不是簡簡單單地就可以回答，因為此問題牽涉到甚多因素，例如脫避法律（evasion of the law）與誠信原則（good faith）等令人頭痛的法律問題。由著名的Vita Food Products[128]看來似乎英國法院容許當事人選擇一個和契約或當事人不相干的國家的法律為準據法，但事實上有學者謹慎的將Vita Food判例限制於當商業習慣或傳統都與被選定的國家有關係才可選擇此不相干國家的法律為準據法。」個人於年輕時大陸法系於此方面一般而言相當保守，但後來於羅馬公約中因對強行法規有著甚多規定，故歐盟態度已較為開放，並在羅馬I中允許以非國家之法律做為依據[129]，歐盟同僚並且風水輪流轉的大肆批評美國法。美國法於第2新編187(2)條中規定被選定之法若與當事人或交易沒有重要關係且沒有合適的理由時，當事人之選法可以無效[130]；而舊統一商法105條亦規定選擇法律必須有合理之理由[131]。但美國2004年之新統一商法1-301條(c)項(2)款已經於國際契約中不再要求被選定準據法之國與該交易須有關連，而於1-302條(b)項之註解(2)規定當事人得以法律原則或跨國性規則為準據

---

　　109 N.H. 446, 255 A.2d 606 (1969).

[125] Restatement, First, Conflict of Laws §§ 621-22 (1934). 於Louknitsky v. Louknitsky, 123 Cal. App.2d 406,266 P.2d 910 (1954)中，加州之共有財產制度被推定為與中國法一致。

[126] Beverly Hills National Bank and Trust Co.v.Compania De Navegacione Almirante S.A., Panama, 437 F.2d 301, 307 (9th Cir. 1971), cert,. denied 402 U.S. 996, 91 S.Ct. 2173, 29 L.Ed. 2d 161 (1971)。

[127] 陳隆修，《國際私法契約評論》，台北，五南圖書公司，民國75年2月，初版，27，28頁。

[128] Vita Food Products Inc. v. Unus Shipping Co., [1939] A.C. 277 (P.C.).

[129] Recital 13。

[130] 陳隆修，《國際私法契約評論》，台北，五南圖書公司，民國75年2月，初版，113～120頁。

[131] 同上。

法。美國以前對契約選法自由有如此的限制，自然會阻礙於訴訟法上當事人沒主張或證明外國法時以法院地法為依據之發展。故而個人甚早就批評統一商法對「當事人訂約自由加以不合理的限制」[132]。再一次個人二十多年前之先見之明總算於美國實現，希望這個改變有助於當事人於訴訟程序上自由適用準據法。

今日有些州採納[133]Uniform Interstate and International Procedure Act，無論是主張外州法或外國法，它要求主張之一方當事人必須給予合理之通知[134]；外國法之問題須由法院解決，而非由陪審團解決[135]；法院得不受證據法之拘束，或即使當事人沒有提供證據，亦得考慮任何相關資料[136]；而更重要的是法院所認定之外國法問題，得以法律問題般的被加以上訴而審核[137]。這已和英國母法視外國法為事實之作法脫離，而接近大陸法。

於聯邦法上Federal Rule of Civil Procedure 44.1條是根據Uniform Interstate and International Procedure Act而來，因此於內容上是與後者之4.01～4.03條之內容相似。44.1條規定：「當事人意圖主張外國法之問題時，必須以訴狀或書面給予通知。無論是否符合聯邦證據法，或當事人是否有提供，法院於認定外國法時，得考慮任何相關資料或來源，這包含證言在內。法院之認定須被視為於法律問題之決定。[138]」為了避免不公平的驚訝，「通知」必須以「書面」及為「合理的」[139]。新規則給予法院

---

[132] 陳隆修，《國際私法契約評論》，台北，五南圖書公司，民國75年2月，初版，120頁。

[133] 但有些州採納較早期的Uniform Judicial Notice of Foreign Law Act.

[134] 134 4.01條。

[135] 4.03條。

[136] 4.02條。

[137] 4.03條，"subject to review on appeal as a ruling on a question of law"。

[138] Rule 44.1. Determining Foreign Law

A party who intends to raise an issue about a foreign country's law must give notice by a pleading or other writing. In determining foreign law, the court may consider any relevant material or source, including testimony, whether or not submitted by a party or admissible under the Federal Rules of Evidence. The court's determination must be treated as a ruling on a question of law.

[139] 其解釋報告對「合理性」有下列規定："The liberal provisions for amendment of the pleadings afford help if the pleadings are used as the medium of giving notice of the foreign law; but it seems best to permit a written notice to be given outside of and later than the pleadings, provided the notice is

權力去獨立審核外國法[140]。另外由於「司法承認」之觀念不是非常明確，例如是否有裁量權及當事人於協助法院之義務之程度上，其範圍並非十分明確，故而本規則於適用外國法上避免使用「司法承認」[141]。當事人若沒有提起外國法之適用，則可推定他們同意外國法之不被加以適用[142]，於此情形下法院地法通常會被適用[143]。另外44.1條中雖未提及，但解釋報告中認為外國法的確認是法院的職責，而非陪審團之功能。最重要的是解釋報告認為外國法之確認為法律問題，而非事實問題，故而上訴審之審核不能狹隘的依52(a)條之規定，而限於「明顯的錯誤」（「clearly erroneous」）[144]。

　　美國法較近之仿效德語系國家，將外國法之適用視為法律問題，而非英美法原來之視為事實問題，這對於上訴之審核及法官之獨立調查權上自然放寬甚多。但個人於法律技術層面上必須提醒美國同僚一個基本法學架構之問題。個人早期於評述英國法時曾如此論述[145]：「由於外國法被視為案件之事實，故不能由以前之判例來引申及確定同一外國法律，以適用於以後之案件。以前判例所確定之外國法，只能於以後之案件中做為證據，

---

reasonable...The stage which the case has reached at the time of the notice, the reason proffered by the party for his failure to give earlier notice, and the importance to the case as a whole of the issue of foreign law sought to be raised, are among the factors which the court should consider in deciding a question of the reasonableness of a notice."

[140] 解釋報告："it may engage in its own research and consider any relevant material thus found."

[141] 解釋報告："The new rule refrains from imposing an obligation on the court to take 'judicial notice' of foreign law because this would put an extreme burden on the court in many cases; and it avoids use of the concept of 'judicial notice' in any form because of the uncertain meaning of that concept s applied to foreign law."

[142] Carey v. Bahama Cruise Lines, 864 F.2d 201 (1st Cir.1988); Nikimiha Securities Ltd. V. Trend Group, Ltd., 646 F.Supp. 1211 (E.D.Pa.1986); Howard Fuel v. Lloyd's Underwriters, 588 F.Supp.1103. (S.D.N.Y.1984); Clarkson Co. Ltd. V. Shaheen, 660 F.2d 506 (2d Cir.1981), cert. denied 455 U.S. 990, 102 S.Ct. 1614, 71 L.Ed.2d 850 (1982); Geiger v. Keilani, 270 F.Supp. 761 (E.D.Mich.1967); Michael v. S.S. Thanasis, 311 F.Supp. 170 (N.D.Cal.1970); Jetco Electronic Industries Inc. v. Gardiner, 325 F.Supp. 80 (S.D.Tex.1971)

[143] Vishipco Line v. Chase Manhattan Bank, N.A., 660 F.2d 854 (2d Cir.1981) cert. denied 459 U.S. 976, 103 S.Ct. 313, 74 L.Ed.2d 291 (1982); Restatement, Second, Conflict of Laws § 136, cmnt. (h), Rep. Note (1971).

[144] 144 Cf. Uniform Judical Notice of Foreign Law Act s.3; Note, 72 Harv L Rev 318 (1958).

[145] 陳隆修，《比較國際私法》，台北，五南圖書公司，78年10月，初版，158頁。

以證明該外國法[146]。此自與處理英國內國法之情形不同。於國際案件中，對外國法之證明實甚為困難，我國雖非採英美法系統，但作者亦贊同我國採類似如此之謹慎作法。」美國無論於此方面之法律如何的採納大陸法，其司法架構仍不脫英國判例法之架構－亦即於法律問題之認定上，前判例是拘束後判例的。故而天真的美國同僚如果將所適用之外國法視為法律，則該外國法之適用自然會拘束後來之類似案件。這種問題於大陸法是不會造成大問題，但美國法院如果忠誠的遵循判例法的基本規則下卻會造成大問題。

　　於大部份之國家基於法律理由去上訴，通常較基於事實之理由容易；而於所有的國家，通常最高審之上訴只能基於法律而來。美國這種融合大陸法及英美法之作風於法律邏輯上是不通的，但其動機是可以體會的。對這種違背判例法架構及傳統之作風，美國似乎應再特別立法加以補救。畢竟於國際法上視外國法為法律之國家，通常視其為一種「特別的法律」而不允許其問題被上訴到最高審[147]；而將外國法視為事實的國家，亦將其視為一種「特別的事實」[148]而與一般事實不同[149]，上訴審較易推翻第一審認定的外國法律事實。[150]

---

[146] 英國Civil Evidence Act 1972, s.4(2).

[147] 陳隆修，《比較國際私法》，台北，五南圖書公司，78年10月，初版，158頁，「但許多德、法、義學者認為最高法院只為法律審，外國法律雖被視為『法律』，但最高法院只應處理本國法之問題，對外國法無法處理。故對外國法若有爭議，不可上訴於最高法院，此見解似乎過份謹慎。」

[148] 見著名之英國判例法 Parkasho v. Singh [1968] P.223,250, "although a question of fact, is a question of fact of a peculiar kind".

[149] Trevor C. Hartley,
Pleading and Proof of Foreign Law: the Major European Systems Compared,
45 Int'l & Comp. L.Q. 271,272 (1996), "It might be thought that a comparative analysis should begin with the division between those systems that regard foreign law as fact and those that regard it as law. Though it may appear fundamental, this distinction is actually of only limited importance, since few countries in either camp accept the full consequences of their official position. Moreover, even if a country regards foreign law as law, it will not necessarily treat it on a par with forum law: it is law, but law of a different kind. Countries in the foreign-law-as-fact camp, on the other hand, may regard foreign law as 'fact of a peculiar kind', not to be treated in the same way as normal fact. The result is that there may be little difference in practice between the attitudes of the two camps to particular issues."

[150] Cheshire and North, 14thed., p.113說明其為「特別的事實」如下：Foreign law is, therefore, treated as a question of fact but it is "a question of fact of a peculiar kind". To describe it as one of fact is no doubt apposite, in the sense that the applicable law must be ascertained according to the evidence of

　　有關英國法於此方面之變動並不大，故早期個人如此評述[151]：「與大陸法之將外國法視為法律之不同，英美法將外國法視為事實（fact）[152]。故若當事人欲主張外國法時，其必須如同主張其他事實一般，自動提出，否則英國法院處理此涉外案件時，將會如同其處理國內案件一般。……

　　外國法之舉證責任雖是在於主張外國法之一方當事人，但是由於外國法之證明相當困難，故於該當事人無法完全證明外國法之情況下，英國法院則採用英國法律[153]。」法院地法於此情況下被適用，無論是基於假設外國法與法院地法一致或當事人被認為默示之同意[154]，於學理上都有些問題。但個人認為這是務實之作法，與學理上之邏輯並無大關連。英國法院於實務上證明外國法之作法，個人已有論述故於此不再贅述[155]。但與美國法改變傳統判例法作風不同的是，英國法仍舊遵循判例法之傳統。英國法院傳統上不能參考證人所提供以外之法律來源，亦不能獨立進行外國法之研究[156]。至於上訴至最高法院只能是基於與大眾有重要影響的法律問題[157]，而一般認為只能基於英國法而上訴。較近於Attorney General of

---

witnesses, yet there can be no doubt that what is involved is at bottom a question of law. This has been recognised by the courts. The rule, for instance, in a purely domestic case is that an appellate court will disturb a finding of fact by the trial judge only with the greatest reluctance, but this is not so when the "fact" that has been found in the court below is the relevant rule of a foreign legal system. In such a case the role of the appellate court has been described in terms of a "duty... to examine the evidence of foreign law which was before the justices and to decide for ourselves whether that evidence justifies the conclusion to which they came". Nevertheless, the courts have concluded that a mistake as to foreign law is to be regarded as a mistake of fact.
Parkasho v Singh [1968] P 233 at 250。
又於Parkasho v Singh, at254, Sir Jocelyn Simon P接著又說明："Foreign law is, it is true, regarded in English courts as a question of fact; and appellate courts are slow to interfere with trial courts on questions of fact; but that only applies with particular force as regards the assessment of relative veracity and the judgment of matters of degree. Where the inference of fact depends on the consideration of written material, an appellate court is at no particular disadvantage compared to a trial court and will regard itself as freer to review the decision of the trial court.

[151] 陳隆修，《比較國際私法》，台北，五南圖書公司，78年10月，初版，157，160頁。
[152] Fremoult v. Dedire (1718) 1 P. Wm. S. 429.
[153] Lloyd v. Guibert (1865) L. R. 1 Q. B. 115, 129.
[154] Eugent F. Scoles, Peter Hay, Patrick J. Borchers, Symeon C. Symeonides, Conflict of laws, 3rd ed. , P.539。
[155] 陳隆修，《比較國際私法》，台北，五南圖書公司，78年10月，初版，157~160頁。
[156] Bumper Corpn v. Comr of Police of Metropolis [1991] 1 W.L.R. 1362 (CA).
[157] Administration of Justice Act 1960, s. 1(2).

New Zealand v. Oriz[158]中，英國最高法院於判決中卻負起對紐西蘭法律解釋之責任。恩師Prof. Hartley認為英國最高法院會對法國法或美國法有不一樣之態度[159]，個人完全認同此觀點。對於類似本案但更為積極的觀點，個人年輕時就如此寫著：「但若案件之準據法為大英帝國協會員國之法律時，如若案情需要，即使當事人不主張外國法，法院亦可主動去確認外國法。[160]」儘管恩師正確的認為紐西蘭法是外國法，故而英國最高法院（House of Lords）仍是處理外國法[161]。但事實上至今很多大英國協會員國之最高法院仍是「Privy Council」，而雖然於行政上機構不同，但英國最高法院與大英國協最高法院之成員完全一致，並且判決互為參考。加以英國法與國協會員國之法律通常相似，解釋之方式亦幾乎一致，故而英國最高法院自然有信心於正義的需求下去處理紐西蘭法律。個人並不以為英國最高法院會常態性的去處理非國協之法律。

　　對於當事人沒有主張或舉證外國法的事實時即依英國法院地法的規則（「default rule」），Prof Fentiman充滿自豪的如此下結論：「為什麼許多衝突案件只是牽涉到管轄權問題的理由之一是，事實上許多當事人於管轄問題解決後，即直接解決他們間之歧異。但另一個理由是如若糾紛之解決程序超越管轄權之階段，則該糾紛會以國內法，而非衝突法，案件之方式解決。這卻正是因為英國法允許當事人去擺脫他們的糾紛所引起的選法問題的結果。因此選法規則問題的相對不重要性，部份原因可能直接歸於英國有關於法律主張及證明的規則……更明顯的是，這樣看起來好像是此種主張及證明的方式之目的，並不是在外國法之適用，而是在外國法適用之避免。[162]」對於現今這個當事人未證明外國法時即適用法院地法這

---

[158] [1984] A.C.1.

[159] Hartley, 45 Int'1 & Comp. L.Q. 271, 285 (1996)。

[160] 陳隆修，《比較國際私法》，台北，五南圖書公司，78年10月，初版，157頁。

[161] Hartley, 45 Int'l & Comp. L.Q. 271, 285 (1996)。

[162] Richard Fentiman., Foreign Law In English Courts, L.Q.R. 142,156 (1992),
"This is not, however, to deny the significance of the English approach to foreign law in the conflicts process. Indeed, its importance is precisely that it helps to ensure that the majority of conflicts disputes do concern jurisdiction not choice of law, thereby contributing to the distinctive shape of English pri-

個世界性通用作法，個人早於許多大陸法尚未採此作法時即謹慎的建議：
「既然於國際案件中外國法甚難舉證，作者亦主張於無法證明外國法時，
我國法院似亦可採用我國法，由於我國法院職責與英美法院不同，或許法
院應取得雙方當事人之同意較好。」[163]正如過去三十年來之經驗所顯示－
個人之建議經常為時間所背書，如果有不正確之處，那通常是個人早期之
建議太過謹慎而保守。個人之經驗顯示人類文明進化之速度超乎我們的預
期。

　　但即使於嚴格遵守當事人主義之英國法院，於有些少許例外情況下上
述之default rule可能亦不適用，法院還是會堅持外國法之證明。最明顯的
情況即為與未成年兒童之利益有關之情形[164]；另外有關身份問題，例如是
否有重婚之情形[165]；及有關事實無爭議之判決（「summary judgment」）
不適用同意法院地法之假設[166]。現今幾乎全世界的訴訟制度多少都本於不
同程度上的當事人進行主義。於當事人之能力不對稱之下，個人現今於此
再建議：或許於當事人能力不對稱下，法院依職權調查外國法之功能應加

vate international law. One reason why many conflicts cases involve nothing more that a jurisdictional dispute is, indeed, that many litigants simply settle their differences once the question of jurisdiction is resolved. But another is that such disputes as do proceed beyond the jurisdictional stage sometimes do so as domestic, not conflicts, cases. This, however, is precisely because English law permits the parties to dispense with any choice of law questions their dispute might beg. In part, therefore, the relative lack of importance of choice of law issues might be directly attributable to the English rules concerning pleading and proof.
In the end such reflections help justify the English approach to foreign law and explain its importance. But they also lead to an intriguing paradox. It begins to look as if a hidden consequence of the English rules on pleading foreign law is to marginalize those concerning its proof, by giving litigants a choice whether to refer to foreign law at all. More starkly still, it seems as though the purpose of this approach to pleading and proof is not so much the application of foreign law as its avoidance."
[163] 陳隆修，《比較國際私法》，台北，五南圖書公司，78年10月，初版，160頁。台灣民訴283條：「外國法為法院所不知者，當事人有舉證責任。但法院得依職權調查之」
[164] 陳隆修、許兆慶、林恩瑋、李瑞生四人合著，《國際私法─管轄與選法理論之交錯》，台北，五南圖書公司，2009年3月，初版1刷，140～143頁。
[165] R. v. Nagib, [1917] 1 K.B. 359。
[166] National Shipping Corporation v. Arab, [1971] Lloyd's Rep. 363,366 (CA), Buckley LJ, "The submissions which have been put forward - with great clarity - on behalf of the plaintiffs depend upon the presumption - which is one undoubtedly recognized by our law - that the law of a foreign country is the same as English law except where evidence is adduced to show that it is different. But it does not seem to me that it would be satisfactory that the plaintiffs should obtain summary judgment in a case in which foreign law is clearly involved upon the basis of that presumption." 又見Fentiman, L.Q.R. 142(1992)。

強，而最高法院亦可適度的審查外國法律之適用。根據個人年輕執業時之經驗，外交部相關單位調查外國法之進度是極度緩慢而推托；相對之下昂貴的跨國性事務所是遠較迅速而詳盡。故而嚴守表面上中立的當事人主義之規則，於實際上對弱勢一方是極不中立且為不公平之規則。[167]

故而羅馬 II 14條允許當事人於非契約義務上去選定應適用之法律，是重覆歐盟契約法原則及共同參考架構[168]有關訂定契約自由之規定。但第14條規定之問題不在於其累贅重覆之性質，而在於其相較於歐盟契約法或共同參考架構之相對規則皆太過於簡陋，這是任何讀者將註釋中之條文逐條比較即可發現之簡單事實。

另外羅馬 II 14(1)(a)及(b)條兩款之目的似乎在保護弱勢，但如前述相對於羅馬公約及羅馬I規則之整體所有條款，(a)、(b)兩款很明顯的不足，無法充份保護弱勢。該14條應該直接依據羅馬I規則較能給予弱勢充份之保護。事實上如若相較於歐盟契約法規則或共同參考架構，該(a)、

---

[167] 有關當事人「立足點平等」之規定，見英國Civil Procedure Rules 1998，
Rule 1：
(1) These Rules are a new procedural code with the overriding objective of enabling the court to deal with cases justly.
(2) Dealing with cases justly includes, so far as practicable-
    (a) ensuring that the parties are on an equal footing;
    (b) saving expense;
    (c) dealing with the case in ways which are proportionate-
        (i) to the amount of money involved;
        (ii) to the importance of the case;
        (iii) to the complexity of the issues; and
        (iv) to the financial position of each party;
    (d) ensuring that it is dealt with expeditiously and fairly; and
    (e) allotting to it an appropriate share of the court's resources, while taking into account the need to allot resources.
又見歐盟人權法院對當事人「武器平等」之闡述，
Dombo Beheer v. Netherlands ECtHR Ser.A. 274 at para.33 (1993)：
"equality of arms implies that each party must be afforded a reasonable opportunity to present his case-including his evidence-under conditions which do not place him at substantial disadvantage vis-a-vis his opponent".
[168] European Contract Law
Materials for a Common Frame of Reference; Terminology, Guiding Principles, Model Rules
Edited by Benedicte Fauvarque-Cosson and Denis Mazeaud, articles 0-101, 0-102, 0103, 2:201, 2:202, 及2:203。

(b)兩款更是原始而不充足。例如共同參考架構之01-201條、0-301條及0-302條有關契約訂立時應遵守公平、誠信原則，4:101條契約無效條款，4:207條及4:208條對弱勢之保護，4:411條違反歐盟會員國基本法律之契約無效，5:105及6:107條契約由單方決定時應保護弱勢，及6:102條契約應默示包含衡平條款等。上述這些共同參考架構條文之列舉只是代表一小部份之歐盟契約法基本原則，相較之下羅馬 II 14(1)(a)及(b)條之粗糙規則不能只用「原始」兩字足以形容，讀者可以自行加以全盤詳細比較。歐盟好像是一個發育過快的恐龍，手腳腦袋好像完全沒有考慮要相互配合，希望再次崛起的中華民族以此為殷鑒。這種自以為聰明的創見，由於過度的極端簡陋與粗糙，可能會於許多個案上造成不符合公平正義之結果。14條之論述應加上於合適之處適用羅馬I規則或歐盟契約法原則之補充規定。

最後如上所述，幾乎全世界現今皆允許當事人於得自由處分之權利上，以default rule去適用法院地法－這亦是早期個人所推薦之作法。關於default rule雖然世界各國尚有一些不同之作法，但不可否認的是於訴訟法上全世界大致上是有一個基本上之主流共同核心價值之存在。對這個於訴訟實務上甚為重要之主流核心價值，羅馬 II 14條似乎完全無視其之存在。羅馬 II 之企圖心很強，但似乎努力不足。

五、羅馬 II 其他規則與實體法規則

羅馬 II 規則於第3條中規定，無論準據法是否為會員國之法律皆應適用[169]。較為特出的為其第7條為了貫徹歐盟公約174條對於環境保護的高標準[170]，故與第4條基本條款不同的，給予被害人選擇損害發生地法或行為

---

[169] Article 3
Universal application
Any law specified by this Regulation shall be applied whether or not it is the law of a Member State.

[170] 見recital 25:Regarding environmental damage, Article 174 of the Treaty, which provides that there should be a high level of protection based on the precautionary principle and the principle that preventive action should be taken, the principle of priority for corrective action at source and the principle that

地法之權利[171]。這自然是對請求權人較有利之作法，亦是與歐盟實體政策較能配合的歐域選擇法規。但整體而言羅馬 II 之規則通常都是以經由關連點排列式之區域選擇法規為依據。於第5條之產品責任，第10條的不當得利，第11條的無因管理，及第12條的訂立契約前之義務，皆附加最密切關連標準做為最後之規避條款。另外第6條有關不公平競爭及限制自由競爭之規定，及第8條有關侵犯智慧財產權之規定，皆不允許當事人違背其條文規定，而依第14條去選定準據法。這可能是歐盟認定這兩個條文之規定與歐盟之重大政策有關，故為不屬於「當事人得自由處分權利」之範圍。事實上除了第4條之基本原則外，個人認為於這些個別的非契約義務，歐盟與其利用一些地域關連點來規劃這些籠統的區域選法規則，倒不如制定一些實質性的規則。因為區域性選法規則的阿奇里斯腳踝（heel of Achilles）即在於被地域性關連點所指定國家之法律若於實體上是落後之法律，則自然容易會造成「武斷或基本上不公平之後果」。[172]

例如羅馬 II 10條1項不當得利之規定如下：「包括錯誤的取得付款在內的不當得利所引起的非契約義務，是有關例如因契約或侵權行為等所既存之關係，而這些關係與不當得利有密切關連，則應由這些關係的準據法

---

the polluter pays, fully justifies the use of the principle of discriminating in favour of the person sustaining the damage.

又見Explanatory Memorandum, p.19, "The basic connection to the law of the place where the damage was sustained is in conformity with recent objectives of environmental protection policy, which tends to support strict liability. The solution is also conducive to a policy of prevention, obliging operators established in countries with a low level of protection to abide by the higher levels of protection in neighbouring countries, which removes the incentive for an operator to opt for low-protection countries. The rule thus contributes to raising the general level of environmental protection."

[171] Article 7
Environmental damage
The law applicable to a non-contractual obligation arising out of environmental damage or damage sustained by persons or property as a result of such damage shall be the law determined pursuant to Article 4(1), unless the person seeking compensation for damage chooses to base his or her claim on the law of the country in which the event giving rise to the damage occurred.

[172] 陳隆修、許兆慶、林恩瑋，《台灣財產法暨經濟法研究叢書（十三）—國際私法：選法理論之回顧與展望》，台灣財產法暨經濟法研究協會發行，2007年1月，初版，174、175頁。

為依據。[173]」如前述這個規定為英美法判例法所既有之規定[174]，而如今亦已為甚多大陸法國家所採納[175]。既然這個規定於國際法已大致上有一個共同主流核心價值，新崛起之歐盟應挾著其於法律科技及高經濟發展之優勢，大開大闔的直接以實體法之共同核心原則為依據，徹底拋開區域選法規則阿奇里斯腳踝所揮之不去的永遠夢魘。

　　事實上歐盟契約法共同參考架構即已本著原有之歐盟契約法原則[176]，

---

[173] Article 10

Unjust enrichment

1. If a non-contractual obligation arising out of unjust enrichment, including payment of amounts wrongly received, concerns a relationship existing between the parties, such as one arising out of a contract or a tort/delict, that is closely connected with that unjust enrichment, it shall be governed by the law that governs that relationship.

[174] 雖然不似第11條之無因管理與第12條之訂約前責任，英國法並無直接相關連之法學概念，但對於第10條之不當得利英美法是有著相對之法學概念，只是英美法於不當得利上之法學邏輯可能不會與大陸法一致，

美國的the American Law Institute, Restatement (Second) of Conflict of Laws §221 (1971) 規定如下：

§221. Restitution

(1) In actions for restitution, the rights and liabilities of the parties with respect to the particular issue are determined by the local law of the state which, with respect to that issue, has the most significant relationship to the occurrence and the parties under the principles stated in §6.

(2) Contacts to be taken into account in applying the principles of §6 to determine the law applicable to an issue include:

(a) the place where a relationship between the parties was centered, provided that the receipt of enrichment was substantially related to the relationship,

(b) the place where the benefit or enrichment was received,

(c) the place where the act conferring the benefit or enrichment was done,

 (d) the domicil, residence, nationality, place of incorporation and place of business of the parties, and

(e) the place where a physical thing, such as land or a chattel, which was substantially related to the enrichment, was situated at the time of the enrichment. These contacts are to be evaluated according to their relative importance with respect to the particular issue.

最主要的是其comment (a)認為本條文之範圍為有關契約或侵權行為以外不當得利之請求，或許英國法於國際案件上亦應如此定性。"a. Scope of section. The rule of this Section applies to claims, which are based neither on contract nor on tort, to recover for unjust enrichment."

另外對於利益發生地的確認上之困難，Cheshire and North, 14thed., p.830說明其困難如下："If money is paid into a branch in Country A to be transferred to an account in a branch of the same bank in Country B does the benefit accrue where the immediate benefit occurred (A) or in the country of ultimate enrichment (B)? What money is paid mistakenly into bank accounts in a number different countries? Rather than applying a series of different laws it would be batter to apply the escape clause under Article 10(4). "

[175] 陳隆修，《比較國際私法》，台北，五南圖書公司，78年10月，初版，365～368頁。

[176] Article 4:115 & 15:104。

而規定因契約無效所引起之不當得利。4:503條規定:「(1)於契約無效後,只要當事人同時歸還其之所取得,當事人之一方得請求歸還依契約或契約無效之部份所供給之東西。(2)無效之原因發生於契約正被履行中時,於適當的考慮契約之性質與目的下,恢復原狀之請求只得基於當事人保有他們所取得的東西是不公平之情形。(3)10:201條有關暫時停止履行之權利,於合適之情形下得適用在所有之情況。[177]」第4:504條接著又規定:「當事人於訂約時對無效之原因完全知悉,或應該去知悉這個原因時,得被剝奪這個恢復請求權[178]。」4:505條規定:「恢復請求權及其請求之內容必須遵循10:312條之規定。[179]」10:312條第4項是有關合理期限內之通知、由司法程序去終止、及時效之規定。另外同樣的關於契約終止後之恢復請求權則規定於10:312條[180]。第10:313條規定歸還請求權原則

---

[177] European Contract Law

Materials for a Common Frame of Reference: Terminology, Guiding Principles, Model Rules

Produced by

Association Henri Capitant des Amis de la

Culture Juridique Francaise and Societe de Legislation Comparee

Edited by

Benedicte Fauvarque-Cosson and Denis Mazeaud

Article 4:503: Right to Restitution (modification of articles 4:115 & 15:104)

(1) (modification of article 4:115) As a consequence of invalidation, either party may claim restitution of whatever it has supplied under the contract or the invalid part of the contract, provided it makes concurrent restitution of whatever it has received.

(2) (addition) When the cause of invalidity arises during the performance, there is restitution only if it seems unjust for the parties to keep what they have already received with due regard to the nature and purpose of the contract.

(3) (addition) In all cases, the provisions of article 10:201 concerning the right to suspend performance, apply with appropriate adaptations.

10:201條是有關同時履行之抗辯權。

[178] Article 4:504: Loss of Right to Restitution (addition)

They party who contracted in full knowledge of the cause of the invalidity or ought to have known of such cause may be deprived of its right to restitution.

[179] Article 4:505: Restitution Regime (restatement of article 6:211 DCFR)

The claim for restitution and its subject matter are subject to the rules of article 10:312.

[180] Article 10:312: Right to Restitution (addition)

(1) As a result of termination, each party is entitled to ask for the return of what it supplied under the contract, so long as it simultaneously returns what it received.

(2) When the cause of termination arises in the course of performance, restitution will take place only if it seems unfair, having regard to the nature and the purpose of the contract, for the parties to keep what they have already received

(3) The provisions of article 10:201 concerning the right to suspend performance apply to all cases.

上是請求返回同種類之物，但若不能時，得請求相同價值之合理金額[181]。
共同參考架構不但是集歐盟各國契約法之大成，並且亦為Unidroit Prin-
ciples of International Commercial Contracts所參考及引用，個人認為歐
盟應將類似這方面之實體規則擴及侵權及其他相關方面之國際法上。如果
中華民族之經濟發展及法律科技發展之階梯及於歐盟現今之一半，則個人
真誠的認為就可以拋棄區域性選法規則，而直接訴諸實體規則，帶領全世
界走出國際法上目前的泥淖。

　　另外一個更明顯的例子即為羅馬 II 12條有關訂約前之責任[182]。於國
際法上這方面之責任過去並未被廣泛之討論，一般可能會是依各法院地法
而去定性應適用之範圍及法律。歐盟既然以崛起之姿興起開天闢地之雄心
壯志，實在不應眈溺於舊有過時傳統上之區域選法規則，而應認清其於經
濟及法律發展上之優勢，直接訴諸於其既有之實體法規則。羅馬 II 12條
規定：「1、無論契約是否於實際上被訂定，於契約訂定前之行為所引起
之非契約義務之準據法，應為該契約之準據法或如若該契約成立時之準據
法。2、如果準據法不能依第1項而定，其應為：(a)不論有關引起損害發
生事件之國家，及不論該事件所引起間接後果之國家或一些國家，損害發
生地國家之法律；或(b)當引起損害之事件發生時當事人之慣居地於同一

　　(4) The claim for restitution and its subject matter are subject to the rules of articles 10:303-10:307.
[181] Article 10:313: Subject matter of Restitution (addition)
　　(1) After breach of the contract, and insofar as it is possible, the principle is that of restitution in kind.
　　(2) When restitution in kind is impossible, the party which supplied the performance without receiving
　　　　any consideration may obtain a reasonable sum corresponding to the value to the other party of the
　　　　performance.
[182] Cheshire and North, 14thed., p.833，認為第12條應包含訂立契約誠信之義務，這是包含契約未成
　　立及契約已成立之情形。"These two situations reflect the two different types of pre-contractual li-
　　ability under the substantive law. First, there is pre-contractual liability where no contract ensues. This
　　includes duties in negotiation of a contract. For example, under Italian law there is a requirement to act
　　in good faith during the negotiation of a contract. There is no such requirement or cause of action under
　　English law but there may be liability in tort under Hedley Byrne v Heller for negligent misstatements
　　made during the course of negotiations or liability in tort for fraudulent misrepresentation. Secondly,
　　there is pre-contractual liability where a Contract ensues. In most countries, once a contract ensues
　　there is no need for pre-contractual liability. Nonetheless, most countries have dories of disclosure. Un-
　　der English law there can be an action to avoid (ie rescind) an insurance contract on the basis of non-
　　disclosure prior to entering the contract."[1964] AC 465.

個國家，該國之法律；或(c)由案件之所有之情況清楚的顯示，訂定契約前之行為所引起之非契約義務，是明顯的與非(a)及(b)款所指定國家之其他國家有著更密切關連時，該其他國家之法律。[183]」

　　首先有關12條1項末段句子所謂「契約如果成立時之準據法」[184]（putative proper law），於傳統上是個令人困擾的觀念。雖然羅馬公約8(1)條及羅馬I 10(1)條皆採納這個英國傳統判例法上之觀念，故而於契約之存在、成立、成效上，似乎除了美國外，主要國家間似乎已有共同核心價值之存在，但這個「推定準據法」是有邏輯上之問題。這個「推定準據法」是以當事人所宣稱之契約中所指定之法律為依據，或是以如若當事人沒有指定法律或管轄法院時應為準據法之法律為依據？羅馬公約是以前者為依據，如此一來當事人可以授權給自己將不合法之契約變為合法，自然於邏輯上會有問題，但其帶來之穩定性自然亦可能為商業界所歡迎。另外更重要的是當事人的同意（「consent」）究竟是事實還是法律上之問題？如果是前者自然應依法院地法，如若是後者自然適用選法規則。個人認為或許以實體法之規則來解決這些問題是較為合適。[185]

　　歐盟共同參考架構[186]略為修正了歐盟契約法原則，將訂約前之洽商規

---

[183] Article 12

Culpa in contrahendo

1. The law applicable to a non-contractual obligation arising out of dealings prior to the conclusion of a contract, regardless of whether the contract was actually concluded or not, shall be the law that applies to the contract or that would have been applicable to it had it been entered into.

2. Where the law applicable cannot be determined on the basis of paragraph 1, it shall be:

  (a) the law of the country in which the damage occurs, irrespective of the country in which the event giving rise to the damage occurred and irrespective of the country or countries in which the indirect consequences of that event occurred; or

  (b) where the parties have their habitual residence in the same country at the time when the event giving rise to the damage occurs, the law of that country; or

  (c) where it is clear from all the circumstances of the case that the non-contractual obligation arising out of dealings prior to the conclusion of a contract is manifestly more closely connected with a country other than that indicated in points (a) and (b), the law of that other country.

[184] 陳隆修，《國際私法契約評論》，台北，五南圖書公司，民國75年2月，初版，97～100頁。

[185] 陳隆修，《2005年海牙法院選擇公約評析》，台北，五南圖書公司，2009年1月，初版1刷，79～97、121、122頁。

[186] European Contract Law

Materials for a Common Frame of Reference: Terminology, Guiding Principles, Model Rules

Produced by

定於2:101條如下：「(1)當事人之行為如若符合誠信及公平交易之規定下，得自由的去提起、繼續、及終止訂約前之洽商。只有於一方之行為違反誠信及公平交易原則或有過失之情形下，訂約前之洽商無法達成才會產生責任。(2)一方當事人若沒有意願去訂立一個契約，但卻進入或要求訂約前之洽商，這即為不遵守依誠信及公平交易原則去洽商之規定。(3)當一方當事人沒有合法的理由而去終止訂約前之洽商，而他方卻合法的相信契約會被訂定時，該行為違反了誠信及公平交易原則。[187]」第2:102條規定：「(1)原則上，契約當事人自己應查清楚契約訂立之條件。(2)於訂約前之洽商中，每個當事人皆有義務去忠實的回答被提出之問題，並且應透露任何可能影響到契約訂立之資訊。(3)有關契約客體的內容有著特別技術上能力之一方當事人，對有關他方的資訊有著更重大的責任。(4)除非一方當事人有著合法的理由去相信資訊是正確的，否則沒有遵守上述幾項有關資訊責任之規定，或給予不正確的資訊，應負起責任。[188]」原來的契

Association Henri Capitant des Amis de la
Culture Juridique Francaise
And
Societe de Legislation Comparee
Edited by
Benedicte Fauvarque-Cosson and Denis Mazeaud

[187] Article 2:101: Duty to Negotiate in Good Faith and Fair Dealing
(replacing article 2:301: Negotiations Contrary to Good Faith)
(1) Parties are free to initiate, continue and break off pre-contractual negotiations, provided they act in accordance with the requirements of good faith and fair dealing. The failure of precontractual negotiations can only give rise to liability if it is the consequence of a fault or actions contrary to good faith and fair dealing of either party.
(2) A party who enters into or pursues pre-contractual negotiations without the intention of concluding a contract, does not respect the requirement to negotiate in accordance with good faith and fair dealing.
(3) A party who breaks off pre-contractual negotiations for no legitimate reason, while the other party could legitimately believe that a contract would be concluded, acts contrary to the requirements of good faith and fair dealing.
第3項為原契約法原則2:301條之(1)、(2)及(3)項所沒有。所謂「合法」似乎應修改為「合理」（"reasonable"）較為妥當。

[188] Article 2:102: Duty of Information (addition)
(1) In principle, each of the parties to a contract must inform itself of the conditions of the conclusion of the contract.
(2) During pre-contractual negotiations, each of the parties is obliged to answer with loyalty any questions put to it, and to reveal any information that may influence the conclusion of the contract.

約法原則2:302條為共同參考架構移到2:103條如下：「無論契約是否事後有訂定，於洽商過程中一方所洽予之秘密資訊，他方有義務不去暴露該資訊或為自己之目的去使用它。對於違反該義務之救濟得包含損害之賠償，及他方當事人所取得利益之返還。[189]」

　　羅馬Ⅱ 12條自以為天衣無縫之規則事實上是充滿了國際法及契約法上最艱困之問題──即契約之成立、存在、及效力之問題。例如契約是否應有對價（「consideration」）[190]，沉默與契約之成立[191]，新要約與契約之成立[192]，相衝突的不同組標準格式條約[193]，錯誤、詐欺、及脅迫對契約成立之影響[194]，誠信及公平交易[195]，公共政策與個案正義[196]，法院地之強行法規[197]及不得違反履行地法[198]等問題。這些問題歐盟於羅馬公約上與英、美判例法間是有甚多歧異存在的。另外前述「契約成立時之準據法」與當事人之「同意」，亦是長久以來之問題。羅馬Ⅱ 12條之企圖心太大，而努力又太小。正如前面所提及於有關契約「成立」或「存在」之問題，個人一向主張以實體政策為解決之方案。於羅馬Ⅱ 12條個人亦認為歐盟應配合自己於實體法發展上之絕對壓倒性先進優勢，而直接以契約法

---

(3) A party which has a particular technical competence regarding the subject matter of the contract bears a more onerous duty of information as regards the other party.

(4) A party who fails to comply with its duty of information, as defined in the preceding paragraphs, or who supplies inaccurate information shall be held liable unless such party had legitimate reasons to believe such information was accurate.

[189] Article 2:103: Duty of Confidentiality
(restatement of article 2:302: Breach of Confidentiality)
If confidential information is given by one party in the course of negotiations, the other party is under a duty not to disclose that information or use it for its own purposes whether or not a contract is subsequently concluded. The remedy for breach of this duty may include compensation for losses suffered and restitution of the benefit received by the other party.

[190] 陳隆修，《2005年海牙法院選擇公約評析》，台北，五南圖書公司，2009年1月，初版1刷，71、72頁。

[191] 191 同上，72～74頁。

[192] 同上，74、75頁。

[193] 同上，75、76頁。

[194] 同上，79～82頁。

[195] 同上，84～87頁。

[196] 同上，87～90頁。

[197] 同上，91～99頁。

[198] 同上，99～102頁。

原則或共同參考架構之相關實體規則為依據。如此一來不但於個案正義上會比充滿不穩定因素的12條較有保障，更或許判決一致性之目標亦較易達成。

　　有趣的是訂約前責任不但歐盟共同參考架構有規定，美國統一商法亦有類似規定U.C.C. 1-303(b)條規定：「一個『交易的過程』是有關當事人間過去交易中之一個特定交易之一系列行為，而在解釋他們的表達與其他行為上可相當程度的被認為是建立一個共同理解的基礎。[199]」(d)項中又規定「交易過程」與確認當事人之意思是有關的，得對協議中的個別條款給予獨特之解釋，或限制協議中之條款[200]。(e)項中接著規定協議中之明示條款與履行之過程、交易之過程、或貿易習慣必須合理的被解釋為彼此相互協調。如果這種解釋為不合理時，(1)明示條款優先於履行過程、交易過程、及貿易習慣；(2)履行過程優先於交易過程及貿易習慣；及(3)交易過程優先於貿易習慣[201]。而U.C.C. 1-201(b)(3)條規定：「『協議』應與『契約』不同，指的是當事人間於言詞或得默示之其他情形在有關事實上之議價，這包含1-303條所規定的履行過程、交易過程、及貿易習慣。[202]」

---

[199] 1-303. Course of Performance, Course of Dealing, and Usage of Trade

(b) A "course of dealing" is a sequence of conduct concerning previous transactions between the parties to a particular transaction that is fairly to be regarded as establishing a common basis of understanding for interpreting their expressions and other conduct.

其之解釋報告2如下：

2. "Course of dealing," as defined in subsection (b), is restricted, literally, to a sequence of conduct between the parties previous to the agreement. A sequence of conduct after or under the agreement, however, is a "course of performance." "Course of dealing" may enter the agreement either by explicit provisions of the agreement or by tacit recognition.

[200] (d) A course of performance or course of dealing between the parties or usage of trade in the vocation or trade in which they are engaged or of which they are or should be aware is relevant in ascertaining the meaning of the parties' agreement, may give particular meaning to specific terms of the agreement, and may supplement or qualify the terms of the agreement.

[201] (e) Except as otherwise provided in subsection (f), the express terms of an agreement and any applicable course of performance, course of dealing, or usage of trade must be construed whenever reasonable as consistent with each other. If such a construction is unreasonable:

(1) express terms prevail over course of performance, couse of dealing, and usage of trade;

(2) course of performance prevails over course of dealing and usage of trade; and

(3) course of dealing prevails over usage of trade.

[202] (3) "Agreement", as distinguished from "contract", means the bargain of the parties in fact, as found

　　無論歐盟或美國於商業契約上有關訂立契約前之交易過程，皆是被賦予一定之法律效力，尤其是聯合國2004年的國際商業契約法原則2.1.15及2.1.16條[203]亦採此規定，故而是有著一定的主流共同核心價值。又大致上可能美國統一商法所謂之「合理」，於歐盟共同參考架構可能稱之為「誠信及公平交易原則」。但正如於所有法學上之其他爭點一般，自然各國法系間仍還是會有所不同。如共同參考架構2:102(3)條要求有著特別技術能力之一方對有關他方之資訊應有著更重大之責任，個人懷疑本著資本主義架構而來之英美法會對此規定能如大陸法般的全盤接受。個人向來主張羊群不應保護獅羣，改自然較傾向歐盟這個具有社會主義色彩之規則。但依實體法論一貫之觀點，各國於訂約前責任在實體規定上之不同[204]，並非

---

in their language or inferred from other circumstances, including course of performance, course of dealing, or usage of trade as provided in Section 1-303.

[203] Unidroit Principles of International Commercial Contracts 2004
Article 2.1.15
(Negotiations in bad faith)
(1) A party is free to negotiate and is not liable for failure to reach an agreement.
(2) However, a party who negotiates or breaks off negotiations in bad faith is liable for the losses caused to the other party.
(3) It is bad faith, in particular, for a party to enter into or continue negotiations when intending not to reach an agreement with the other party.
Article 2.1.16
(Duty of confidentiality)
Where information is given as confidential by one party in the course of negotiations, the other party is under a duty not to disclose that information or to use it improperly for its own purposes, whether or not a contract is subsequently concluded. Where appropriate, the remedy for breach of that duty may include compensation based on the benefit received by the other party.

[204] 例如德國BGB 311條第3項即增加對非契約當事人（第3人）之訂約前義務如下：
Section 311
Obligations created by legal transaction and obligations similar to legal transactions
(1) In order to create an obligation by legal transaction and to alter the contents of an obligation, a contract between the parties is necessary, unless otherwise provided by statute.
(2) An obligation with duties under section 241 (2) also comes into existence by
1. the commencement of contract negotiations
2. the initiation of a contract where one party, with regard to a potential contractual relationship, gives the other party the possibility of affecting his rights, legal interests and other interests, or entrusts these to him, or
3. similar business contacts.
(3) An obligation with duties under section 241 (1) may also come into existence in relation to persons who are not themselves intended to be parties to the contract. Such an obligation comes into existence in particular if the third party, by laying claim to being given a particularly high degree of

操縱選法規則即可解決。根本解決之道還是應務實而紮根的對這些不同的
實體規則，在比較法及社會學之基礎上加以實體政策之評量。個人對於羅
馬 II 12條忽略了歐盟於此方面所累積之實體政策上之發展而感覺可惜，
更對羅馬 II 於此方面放棄了跟英美法在比較法學上互相切磋之進展而失
望。[205]

　　另外於侵權行為上有些美國同僚贊同有關行為規範的規則（「con-
duct-regulation rules」）應依侵權行為地法，因為該地政府對其境內之
行為之規定有著最大利益[206]；而有關損害分配之規則（「loss-allocation
or loss-distribution rules」）自然理所當然的依被害人之住所地法[207]。

---

trust, substantially influences the pre-contract negotiations or the entering into of the contract.
其註釋中說明第3項之第3人應為有取得利益之第3人。241條是有關義務人之責任範圍。個人以
為此有關第3人責任之問題，應以2004年聯合國契約法原則3.11條為依據：

Article 3.11 (Third persons)

(1) Where fraud, threat, gross disparity or a party's mistake is imputable to, or is know or ought to be
    known by, a third person for whose acts the other party is responsible, the contract may be avoided
    under the same conditions as if the behaviour or knowledge had been that of the party itself.

(2) Where fraud, threat or gross disparity is imputable to a third person for whose acts the other party is
    not responsible, the contract may be avoided if that party knew or ought to have known of the fraud,
    threat or disparity, or has not at the time of avoidance reasonable acted in reliance on the contract.

[205] Cheshire and North, 14thed., p.806表達了英國亦拒絕這種對特別侵權行為給予特殊規則之選法
理論："The introduction of specific rules for special torts follows the model adopted in a number of
European civil law jurisdictions and in relation to contract choice of law under the Rome Convention
but rejected in England under its choice of law rules in tort on the ground that any special rule might be
difficult to put into statutory language and would make the position more complex. In the United Kingdom, the case for having in the Regulation some of these specific rules was not thought to have been
made out. The European Parliament was also unconvinced and unsuccessfully sought the deletion of
some of these rules." 又見Law Commission Working Paper No 87 (1984), Paras 5.1-5.70.
又如第8條相關智慧財產的侵權行為，是採波恩公約及巴黎公約中舉世承認之「地域原則」，見
Explanatory Memorandum, p.20, "The treatment of intellectual property was one of the questions that
came in for intense debate during the Commission's consultations. Many contributions recalled the existence of the universally recognised principle of the lex loci protectionis, meaning the law of the country
in which protection is claimed on which e.g. the Bern Convention for the Protection of Literary and Ar-
tistic Works of 1886 and the Paris Convention for the Protection of Industrial Property of 1883 are built.
This rule, also known as the "territorial principle", enables each country to apply its own law to an infringement of an intellectual property right which is in force in its territory: counterfeiting an industrial
property right is governed by the law of the country in which the patent was issued or the trade mark or
model was registered; in copyright cases the courts apply the law of the country where the violation was
committed. This solution confirms that the rights held in each country are independent."

[206] Cooney v. Osgood Mach., 81 NY. 2d 66,72.

[207] Padula v. Lilarn Props. Corp., 84 NY.2d 519, 522.

這種二分法事實上自Babcock v. Jackson[208]以來紐約法院即開始有此觀念（雖然沒有明示），但個人認為如同前述之共同慣居地法則，這只不過是另一種形式的區域選法規則。更何況大部份之侵權行為法其實即使有所偏重，但大部份還是兼俱上述之兩種功能。對於紐約法院這種二分法，個人以前即批評[209]：「『有關損害分配的規則依住所地法，而有關行為標準的規則依侵權行為地法』，這個英美法看起來甚合理的趨勢，作者依實體法方法論的觀點，認為是個機械式的法域選擇法規，有可能在少數個案造成不公平正義的結果，因而向來有保留之意見。本案如果依當事人的共同住所地法紐約法，則很明顯的無辜的被害人不能取得適當的賠償，故而紐約法院於此拒絕去執行這個看似合理的法域選擇法規。紐約法院的判決，使得個人於此方面之主張不辯自明——亦即任何看似完美的法域選擇方法論，因為忽視了實體法的內容，故而可能於個案造成不公平與正義的判決。」故對美國句僚這種基於區域選法規則而對羅馬 II 所作之批評，個人似乎無法加以認同。

　　羅馬 II 要點14認為規則中所引用的連結因素是最能同時達成法律穩定性及個案正義之最合適規定[210]。但是這是事實上的客觀陳述，還是一廂情願的幻想？行為及安全規則不但為羅馬 II 所再三強調，亦為60年代引起全世界選法革命之核心案件[211]，故而於此以道路交通安全事故為檢驗要點14之基本目的之案例。於交通案件中首先當事人如若有共同慣居地，依第4條2項應以該慣居地法優先適用。於無共同慣居地時，一般自然依第4條1項通則規定以損害發生地法為準據法。再來即為選法規則的規避條款，即為第4條3項的明顯的更密切關連國家之法律。但第17條又

---

[208] 191 N.E. 2d 279 (N.Y. 1963)。

[209] 陳隆修、許兆慶、林恩瑋，《台灣財產法暨經濟法研究叢書（十三）—國際私法：選法理論之回顧與展望》，台灣財產法暨經濟法研究協會發行，2007年1月，初版，218頁，於評析Elson v. Defren and Avis Rent-A-Car, 726 N.Y.S.2d 407; 2001 N.Y.App. Div. Lexis 6269案所作之結論。

[210] Recital 14, "The requirement of legal certainty and the need to do justice in individual cases are essential elements of an area of justice. This Regulation provides for the connecting factors which are the most appropriate to achieve these objectives."

[211] 陳隆修，《美國國際私法新理論》，台北，五南圖書公司，民國76年1月，初版，134～167頁。

規定：「於評估被主張應負責之人之行為時，應於合適之情形下及以事實之方式，來對引起責任事件發生時之地當時的行為與安全之規則加以考慮。[212]」另外有趣的是要點33又小心翼翼的補充解釋：「當事故發生於不是被害人之慣居地時，於根據道路交通事故現行之國內損害賠償法規，去評估被害人之人身傷害損害賠償時，繫屬法院應考慮到個別被害人所有之相關實際情形，尤其特別包括實際之損失與傷後之照顧及醫療之費用。[213]」

第17條[214]及要點33雖然皆加以「應該」（"shall" on "should"）「考慮」（「take into account」）之命令語句，但「考慮」之表達字眼很明顯的是給予法院裁量之空間。另外17條還加以須要在「合適之情形下」，故而更不是命令式之硬性法規。因為17條及要點33皆非為強制性規定，故而個人將其列為第4條中之3項法規之後。又序言中所列之要點在理論上之位階應後於正式規則，故而要點33似乎於適用順位上後於第17條。但是第15條(c)款又規定準據法應適用於損害之評估上，故而要點33或許是15條(c)款之例外。第17條與要點33事實上類似紐約法院所倡導的「行為標準的規則依行為地法，損害賠償的標準的規則依住所地法」，但歐盟很明顯的對這個二分法不十分具有信心，故而給予法院大陸法少有的裁量權。

另外更有趣的是草案的解釋報告對17條的適用規定如下：「考慮到

---

[212] Article 17 Rules of safety and conduct
In assessing the conduct of the person claimed to be liable, account shall be taken, as a matter of fact and in so far as is appropriate, of the rules of safety and conduct which were in force at the place and time of the event giving rise to the liability.

[213] Recital 33, "According to the current national rules on compensation awarded to victims of road traffic accidents, when quantifying damages for personal injury in cases in which the accident takes place in a State other than that of the habitual residence of the victim, the court seised should take into account all the relevant actual circumstances of the specific victim, including in particular the actual losses and costs of after-care and medical attention."

[214] 見草案之解釋報告Explanatory Memorandum, p.25, "This article is based on the corresponding articles of the Hague Conventions on traffic accidents (Article 7) and product liability (Article 9). There are equivalent principles in the conflict systems of virtually all the Member States, either in express statutory provisions or in the decided cases.

外國法並非如適用外國法一般：法院只應依選法規則去適用應適用之法律，但它應以事實之觀點去考慮到其他法律，例如為了評量損害賠償之目的去認定過失之嚴重性或行為人之善意或惡意。[215]」首先這段話產生於大陸法系是有邏輯上之缺陷的－大陸法系於理論上是不採懲罰性賠償的[216]。第二它對17條行為之標準依行為地法之基本規則加以過份的限制，行為地法只能依事實而被加以參考，而非以準據法之地位加以適用。

　　故而就以最通常的車禍案件而言，應適用法規的排列次序就有五層－更何況法院適用選法之次序並無一定的規則。加以在最密切關連、第17條及要點33之適用上，法院都被賦予英美法式之裁量權，故而任何人都會合理的推斷要點14所自豪的穩定性是不太可能達成的。事實上拋開道路安全案件不論，羅馬II的大量使用最密切關連為規避法則，就已注定其會有著美國式不穩定之傾向。個人年輕時著名的R.J.Traynor法官即對第2新編提出一個當時膾炙人口的質疑：「你要如何將2斗的馬毛與明日互相衡量？[217]」最重要關連的質與量之間的爭議[218]，是長久以來沒有被完全釐清的基本哲學性問題。在可預見的未來，只要羅馬II大量的使用最密切關連作為規避法則，至少於短期內其自己吹噓的穩定性即不可能達成。於目前的階段，各國還是應將選法規則的重點放於個案正義的追求，只有各國於實質上對個案正義的結果有著大致上同樣的看法時，法律的一致性與穩定性才會真正達成。

　　於同一案件中不同的爭點得適用不同的選法規則，是法院於近代五光十色瞬息萬變的大千世界中，賴以主持正義的必要法律技巧。羅馬II的拒

---

[215] Explanatory Report, art. 13, "taking account of foreign law is not the same thing as applying it: the court will apply only the law that is applicable under the conflict rule, but it must take account of another law as a point of fact, for example when assessing the seriousness of the fault or the author's good or bad faith for the purposes of the measure of damages."

[216] 陳隆修，《2005年海牙法院選擇公約評析》，台北，五南圖書公司，2009年1月，初版1刷，299、300頁。

[217] "Can you weigh a bushel of horsefeathers against next Thursday?"
The Disinterested Third State, 28 Law & Contemp. Probs. 754 (1963).

[218] 陳隆修、許兆慶、林恩瑋，《台灣財產法暨經濟法研究叢書（十三）—國際私法：選法理論之回顧與展望》，台灣財產法暨經濟法研究協會發行，2007年1月，初版，170～172頁。

絕公開承認分割技巧，不但與時代脫節，更與羅馬公約及羅馬I規則不一致。更奇怪的是如英美法一般羅馬II於第4、10、11、12及14條皆大量的引用契約準據法為非契約義務之準據法，而於契約法上羅馬I規則是採納分割技巧的，故而剩下來唯一的合理問題是－到底是羅馬I還是羅馬II有精神分裂症狀？

　　羅馬II上述之問題個人認為並非為其最大之問題。羅馬II序言中之要點雖然揭櫫了許多重要之實體政策，但或許除了第7及18（對保險人之直接訴訟）條外，這些實體政策並無法於個案中完全發揮應有之作用。由年輕至今個人已分析過甚多之實際案例，一昧仰賴區域選法規則而迴避實質政策分析是無法充份保障個案正義的──這亦是於選法規則上美國可敬的前輩同僚們百多年來留給人類子孫的共同文化遺產。無論台灣、大陸、或歐盟，如果鑑於法院無法一時完全適應於實體政策之分析，個人建議應如美國目前於實務及學理上一般──**必須在於確認所牽連之國家之相關法律於實體政策上有重大衝突後，才可適用法院地之選法規則；而最重要關連標準之適用亦必須加入實體政策之衡量（一如美國第二新編的第六條）。**

　　最後必須一提的是羅馬II於－(2)(g)條中排除侵犯隱私權及包含誹謗在內之人身權之適用[219]，這個立法精神與英國或許有些相似。在英國Private International Law Act 1995中與其他侵權行為皆適用新法不同的是，第13條規定有關妨害名譽引起之爭點[220]，仍是適用傳統判例法Phillips v. Eyre[221]中的雙重法規[222]。但相對的通常只要案件之事實發生於英國，第13

---

[219] (g) non-contractual obligations arising out of violations of privacy and rights relating to personality, including defamation.

[220] 13.(1) Nothing in this Part applies to affect the determination of issues arising in any defamation claim.
(2) For the purposes of this section "defamation claim" means -
    (a) any claim under the law of any part of the United Kingdom for libel or slander or for slander of title, slander of title, slander of goods or other malicious falsehood and any claim under the law of Scotland for verbal injury; and
    (b) any claim under the law of any other country corresponding to or otherwise in the nature of a claim mentioned in paragraph (a) above.

[221] (1870) L R 6 Q B1, 10B & S 1004, 40L J Q B28.

[222] 陳隆修，《比較國際私法》，台北，五南圖書公司，78年10月，初版，372～374頁。

條即不適用，英國法通常即為準據法。[223]有關妨害名譽方面之侵權行為法固然是在保護被人之名譽，但尚牽涉到保障被告言論自由之問題。言論自由不但為各國憲法所明文保障，亦為所有的人權公約所保障的基本權利，例如1948年聯合國人權宣言19條[224]。及歐盟1950年基本自由及人權保護公約第10條[225]皆有明文規定。但是除了妨害名譽外，其他故意侵權行為（「intentional tort」）所侵犯的權利亦經常為各種人權公約所保障，例如1948年聯合國人權宣言12條所保障之穩私權，第3及22條之人身權，第17條之財產權，及第23條之工作權等。故而個人以前曾如此論述[226]：「英國將有關誹謗方面之侵權行為特別舉出來，而與一般侵權行為適用之準據法不同，此固然為一甚至比美國還先進之措施，除了應加以讚許外，更令人尊崇。但個人一向自年輕時即主張於國際私法上故意侵權行為與意外侵權行為（accidental tort）應分別處理，前者經常牽涉到行為地的公共政策及刑法，而後者則可能是偶發性的（fortuitous）。故而包括誹謗行為在內之故意侵權行為，應特別注重行為地的公共政策與刑事政策。不只於所應適用的準據法，甚至於管轄權的基礎亦應與行為地有最大關連方是[227]。而且既然是於各國之侵權行為皆分別有一訴因存在，所謂『行為

---

[223] Metall und Rohstoff A.G. v. Donaldson, Lufkin & Jenrette Inc. [1990] Q.B. 391 (C.A.).

[224] Article 19

Everyone has the right to freedom of opinion and expression; this right includes freedom to hold opinions without interference and to seek, receive and impart information and ideas through any media and regardless of frontiers.

[225] Article 10 Freedom of expression

1. Everyone has the right to freedom of expression. This right shall include freedom to hold opinions and to receive and impart information and ideas without interference by public authority and regardless of frontiers. This article shall not prevent States from requiring the licensing of broadcasting, television or cinema enterprises.

2. The exercise of these freedoms, since it carries with it duties and responsibilities, may be subject to such formalities, conditions, restrictions or penalties as are prescribed by law and are necessary in a democratic society, in the interests of national security, territorial integrity or the protection of the reputation or rights of others, for preventing the disclosure of information received in confidence, or for maintaining the authority and impartiality of the judiciary.

[226] 陳隆修、許兆慶、林恩瑋，《台灣財產法暨經濟法研究叢書（十三）—國際私法：選法理論之回顧與展望》，台灣財產法暨經濟法研究協會發行，2007年1月，初版，156頁。

[227] 布魯塞爾公約5(3)條規定損害發生地法院有管轄權，故於C-68193 Shevill v. Presse Alliance S.A. [1995] E.C.R.I -41中，歐盟法院認定：損害發生地應為該刊物被分送且原告主張名譽受損之地，但該地之法院只能對當地所發生損害有管轄權而已。於有關誹謗之判例法上，英國法傳統上以

地」則不妨廣義的包括被告的實際行為地及原告之損害發生地，以令被告對其有意之行為負完全責任。」

故而個人於此對台灣、大陸、及羅馬Ⅱ再次重申個人數十年來之一貫看法。意外侵權行為應與故意侵權行為分開，前者之共同核心價值乃在給予被害人迅速合理之賠償，而於後者之情形，通常會與行為地或損害發生地的強烈公共政策或刑法有關[228]。在處理故意侵權行為時，於憲法及各種人權公約之限制範圍內，通常應盡量尊重行為地或損害發生地之公共政策。尤其是羅馬Ⅱ14條當事人自主準據法之規定，應在尊重行為地、損害發生地、及法院地之強烈公共政策下才能被執行。

該誹謗性文章被發表之地為行為地，Bata v. Bata [1948] W.N.366。當同一文章於數個國家發表時，與上述歐盟法院見解相同的，每一個國家的發表行為構成一新訴因，從而該國家之法律則變得相關。見陳隆修、許兆慶、林恩瑋，《台灣財產法暨經濟法研究叢書（十三）—國際私法：選法理論之回顧與展望》，台灣財產法暨經濟法研究協會發行，2007年1月，初版，153～157頁。

[228] Recital 32認為懲罰性賠償是有關各國之公共政策及超越性強行法之問題。(32) Considerations of public interest justify giving the courts of the Member States the possibility, in exceptional circumstances, of applying exceptions based on public policy and overtrading mandatory provisions. In particular, the application of a provision of the law designated by this Regulation which would have the effect of causing noncompensatory exemplary or punitive damages of an excessive nature to be awarded may, depending on the circumstances of the case and the legal order of the Member State of the court seised, be regarded as being contrary to the public Policy (ordre public) of the forum.
又於評釋第14條選法自由之限制時（委員會之條文與最終版不同），Explanatory Memorandum, p.23，認為國內公共政策與強行法應與第16條之超越強行法及第26條之國際性公共政策不同：
In this Article the concept of "mandatory rules", unlike the overriding mandatory rules referred to in Article 12, refers to a country's rules of internal public policy. These are rules from which the parties cannot derogate by contract, particularly those designed to protect weaker parties. But internal public policy rules are not necessarily mandatory in an interactional context. They must be distinguished from the rules of interactional public policy of the forum referred to in Article 22 and from the overriding mandatory rules referred to in Article 12.
於Kuwait Airways Corpn v Iraqi Airways Co (Nos 4 and 5), [2002] 2 AC 883, HL中，英國最高法院再次重申已明顯的被建立之國際法規則亦是英國之公共政策，而應被給予效力。於該案中，在1990年伊拉克侵科威特後，請求人科威特航空之飛機即依伊拉克法為被告伊拉克航空所佔有。英國三級法院皆盼請求人得要求飛機之返還及損害賠償。英國最高法院認為於重大的違反國際法之情況下，並不需要與英國有關連即可適用公共政策之否定效力，因為這並非本於英國國內性質之英國公共政策。故伊拉克之沒收法規是被英國法院所不承認，而直接適用侵權行為地伊拉克之侵權行為法。

一、前言

　　羅馬 I 號規則大致上沿著Convention on the Law Applicable to Contractual Obligations 1980 (80/934/EEC)（羅馬公約）之架構而來，經過幾乎30年，其增加條款中較為重要或繁複的為3(1)條自由選法規則之放寬，4(1)條個別契約準據法之推定，6(4)(b)、(c)、(d)、及(e)條排除於一般消費契約選法規則上之適用，5(2)條增加對旅客運送之選法規則，8條於個別僱傭契約中再加上更密切關連法律之強行法規對受僱者之保護，另外與44/2001號民商管轄與判決承認規則相呼應的增加了7條保險契約選法規則條款，最後增加16條於有多數債務人時以原債權準據法來決定他們間法律關係之規定。故而羅馬 I 雖是用來取代羅馬公約，但其主要的架構仍是幾乎原封不動本著羅馬公約而來。對於新增的一些較為繁複的規則，事實上歐盟是可以訂定一些較為紮實的實體規則以取代他們。無論是羅馬公約、羅馬 I 規則、或羅馬 II 規則，都不離歐洲近三十年來的立法基本趨勢——」rule-plus-exception」的方法論。亦即基本上是以地域關連點為硬性選法規則的連結因素，再以最密切關連標準為規避性之例外規則。故而羅馬公約於三十年前飽受爭議之處，如今於羅馬 I 規則亦似乎有同樣之爭議[1]。個人認為對羅馬公約及羅馬 I 規則最好的評語來自Prof.

---

[1]　相較於早期美國同僚形容美國選法革命為「陰暗的沼澤」見陳隆修，《美國國際私法新理論》，台北，五南圖書公司，民國76年1月，初版，4頁。有些歐洲同僚形容羅馬I為「迷宮」、「叢林」、或「地獄」。見Urs Peter Gruber, Insurance Contracts:
Heiss, a leading expert on international private law for insurance contracts, called the new rules on insurance contracts "another recent failure of the European lawgiver." Many scholars have especially

Juenger早期對羅馬公約之評語：「傾向諷刺的人可以說公約試圖去成文法化兩個法學趨勢，第一個趨勢當事人自主並不需要立法，而第二個趨勢司法的裁量是無法條文化的。[2]」暫時不論羅馬公約及羅馬Ⅰ之技術性規則，單就由羅馬Ⅰ序言中之要點而言，其政策性之宣言較羅馬Ⅱ似乎相對性的較少。這或許是羅馬公約早已有解釋報告[3]，官方立場已在解釋報告中表明之故。或許其較為基本的政策性要點為要點11及23。要點11重申當事人選法之自由為有關契約義務上選法規則之基石[4]。要點23規定：「有關與被視為較弱勢之當事人所訂立之契約，這些當事人應受到比一般通常原則對他們的利益較為有利之選法規則之保護。[5]」這兩個基本政策自然為英美法與大陸法共通之價值，但於實際上之執行程度可能不盡一致。

　　正如歐盟於其他方面之規則一般，羅馬公約及羅馬Ⅰ之最基本政策似乎仍是在為了促進內部市場功能之目的，而去達成法律之統一。羅馬Ⅰ的

---

criticised the complexity of the rules by comparing them with a labyrinth or a jungle. Leible und Lehmann have even gone one step further asserting that the existing rules on insurance contracts constitute the "hell" of international private law.

但相較下有些美國同僚認為這些詞句更合適美國法，見George A. Bermann, Rome I: A Comparative View：

Perhaps Rome I is, as has been suggested, in many ways a "labyrinth". The law of conflicts of law in contract in the United States is assuredly not a labyrinth, since labyrinths presuppose walls and boundaries. I do not regard it as in any sense a "jungle", either, as has been suggested, because jungles connote confusion, and by American standards the Rome I Regulation sows very little confusion. Nor is it the 'swamp," to which U.S. conflicts law itself has so often been likened. It is certainly doubtful that the United States law of conflicts in matters of contract leaves for the Rome I Regulation any room in the "hell" to which the Regulation has itself hyperbolically in this conference been likened.載於Rome I Regulation: The Law Applicable to Contractual Obligations in Europe edited by Franco Ferrari, Stefan Leible, pp. 110, 111, 358.（註解省略）

[2]　Friedrich K. Juenger, Contract Conflicts. The EEC Convention on the Law Applicable to Contractual Obligation: A Comparative Study. Edited by P.M. North, P.306, "the cynic might say that the Convention tries to codify two approaches, the first of which ,party autonomy, needs no codification and the second, judicial choice, cannot be codified". Prof. F. A. Mann亦認為這是對羅馬公約的最好的評論，Book Reviews, Vol. 32 I.C.L.Q. 265 (1983)。

[3]　Report on the Convention on the law applicable to contractual obligations by Mario Giuliano, and Paul Lagarde, O.J.C 282, 31/10/1980,以下簡稱Giuliano Report或解釋報告。

[4]　(11) The parties' freedom to choose the applicable law should be one of the cornerstones of the system of conflict-of-law rules in matters of contractual obligations.

[5]　(22) As regards contracts concluded with parties regarded as being weaker, those parties should be protected by conflict-of-law rules that are more favourable to their interests than the general rules.

序言明文該規則是特別根據歐盟公約61(c)條之67(5)條而來[6]，而該兩條款之目的是為了執行歐盟公約65條而來。65條(b)款之規定是為了促進會員國間國際私法及管轄權法律適用之相容性，而此點於序言之要點2又再次被強調[7]。歐盟公約3(1)(h)條所規定協調法律以建立共同市場，及65條為了增進內部市場功能的目的以協調法律，又被重申於開宗明義的要點1[8]。要點6又補充說明：「為了增進訴訟結果的可預測性，法律結果的穩定性，及判決的自由流動，無論訴訟是於那一國之法院被提起，內部市場的適當功能需要各會員國之選法規則去指定同一國家之法律[9]。」而做為羅馬 I 法源的羅馬公約的序言更是直接挑明：「歐盟公約的訂約國，急於繼續歐體已經完成部份之國際私法範圍內之工作，特別是有關已完成之管轄權及執行判決之範圍，希望能建立有關契約義務準據法之統一法規[10]」。

當全世界的共識是就只有在個案正義充份受到保障下，社會才能在法治的基礎上完全的發展。歐盟卻反其道而行，念茲在茲的是內部市場功能之促進，以此為國家之最高目標。進而認為在促進內部市場的需求下，法律之穩定性及預測性是有絕對的必要性，故而各國國際私法必須被加以統一。如個人所一再重申，沒有人可以懷疑美國內部市場功能的旺盛，但美

---

[6] Having regard to the Treaty cstablishing the European Community, and in particular Article 61(C) and the second indent of Article 67(5)thereof.

[7] (2) According to Article 65, point (b) of the Treaty, these measures are to include those promoting the compatibility of the rules applicable in the Member States concerning the conflict of laws and of jurisdiction.

[8] (1) The Community has set itself the objective of maintaining and developing an area of freedom, security and justice. For the progressive establishment of such an area, the Community is to adopt measures relating to judicial cooperation in civil matters with a cross-border impact to the extent necessary for the proper functioning of the internal market.

[9] (6) The proper functioning of the internal market creates a need, in order to improve the predictability of the outcome of litigation, certainty as to the law applicable and the free movement of judgments, for the conflict-of-law rules in the Member States to designate the same national law irrespective of the country of the court in which an action is brought.

[10] PREAMBLE
THE HIGH CONTRACTING PARTIES to the Treaty establishing the European Economic Community, ANXIOUS to continue to the field of private international law the work of unification of law which has already been done within the Community, in particular in the field of jurisdiction and enforcement of judgments, WISHING to establish uniform rules concerning the law applicable to contractual obligations,於羅馬公約之前，歐體已於布魯塞爾公約建立管轄權及承認判決之規則。

國各州的國際私法的百家爭鳴是已為多數所公認的－包括美國同僚在內亦可能承認其法律之混亂。美國各州的國際私法通常不但不會受到消滅，而且在充份互信條款的保障下是受到充份尊重的。很難想像根據美國憲法商業條款而立的法律，可以去侵犯憲法適當程序條款中所保障之個人權利。歐盟將市場功能、法律穩定性、及法律之統一視為神聖不可分割的合體，是一種病態的野蠻作法，完全漠視近代文明中各種人權公約及憲法保障基本人權之要求。

但是如果單就羅馬公約而言，因為其有著一些英國法之概念，亦有英國同僚認為因為其大致上與英國法有相似之處，故而贊同羅馬公約之引進英國。Prof. North就認為：「最後，實施羅馬公約的後果是，英國於契約之選法規則上將會有一個清楚、穩定的成文法基礎。那些長期運作良好的規則將不會有重大的改變，但於歐體內有關服務及貨物自由供給的重要部門之法律，在整個歐體內將會有著重大協調的利益存在。[11]」羅馬公約是否與英國傳統判例法大致上相似是個主觀上認定之問題，如果粗糙的由基本架構而言自然是相似，但如果加以嚴格的要求自然會不一樣[12]。於相當程度之爭議下，英國通過the Contracts (Applicable Law) Act 1990以引進羅馬公約。

羅馬公約及羅馬Ⅰ中所主要引用的強行法規（「mandatory rule」）及特徵性履行（「characteristic performance」）的觀念是英美法所沒有的。即使是英美法所慣常遵守的當事人自主原則（「party autono-my」），亦為歐盟用其他名詞而被加以條文化，這或許會使得英國法感覺陌生。Prof. Mann對1989年瑞士國際私法的評語個人以為亦可適用於

---

[11]　P.M.North, Contract Conflicts. The EEC Convention on the Law Applicable to Contractual Obligations: A Comparative Study. Edited by P.M.North, P.23, "At the end of the day, the result of implementation of the Rome Convention in England will be that the choice of law rules in contract are put on a clear, firm, statutory basis. There will be no great substantial change in the rules which have worked well for a long period, but there will be the benefit of substantial harmonization throughout the EEC in an area of law of real significance for the free provision of goods and services within the Community."

[12]　陳隆修，《國際私法契約評論》，台北，五南圖書公司，民國75年2月，初版，21～65頁個人早期評述英國判例法。

羅馬公約及羅馬 I 上：「雖然偶而會有錯誤，但在同時會有許多人會對令人印象深刻的判例法系統的消失而感到遺憾，因為這些判例法是構成司法技巧的最大成就之一，並且相較於成文法可能在許多方面是更好的法律，有著更大的穩定性、預測性、及靈活性，因為某些（但不可能是全部）方面之國際私法，如果成文法超過了大致上導引性的指示，是特別的不合適成文法的限制。[13]。」或許本著同樣的理由，其對羅馬公約支持者批評：「他們所說的都不能除去公約是基於錯誤考慮下所提議的後果的結論，將會可能侵害我們目前的法律，並且應被拒絕－為避免引起對全世界之不穩定及刺激應愈早愈好。[14]」雖然根據羅馬 I 要點45，於羅馬 I 通過時英國其時尚未加入，但加入與否之決定權是操之在政客手中，政客考量之重點乃在自以為可能存在之經濟利益，故而最後決定已加入羅馬 I 規則的是商業利益團體，非學界同僚，而這個答案應是很清楚的[15]。但於學術上欲解決對羅馬公約及羅馬 I 之爭執，美國作法或許應被加以參考。

---

[13] F.A.Mann, Book Reviews, Vol.38 I.C.L.Q.,P.716(1989), "In the meantime there will be many who will regret the disappearance of an impressive body of judge-made law which, not-withstanding occasional mishaps, constitutes one of the greatest achievements of judicial skill and may in many respects have provided better law, greater certainty and predictability and also flexibility than statutory texts, for several (by no means all) aspects of the conflict of laws are singularly unsuited to the constraint which statutes, if they exceed the most general indications, necessarily impose."

[14] F.A.Mann, Book Reviews, Vol.32,I.C.L.Q.,p.266(1983),"With due respect to the intellectual effort which the contributors to this volume have made and which no-one will hesitate to acknowledge, nothing said by them is apt to eliminate the conclusion that the Convention results from a misconceived initiative, would be likely to corrupt our present law and should be rejected – the sooner the better if insecurity and irritation all over the world are to be avoided."

[15] 見英國法務部 Minister of Justice, Romel – Should the UK opt in? Consultation Paper CP05/08, Published on 2 April 2008, Executive Summary, "Choice of law in contract is an issue affecting all UK businesses that enter into or advise on cross-border transactions as well as UK consumers buying goods or services from abroad. The scale of this economic activity is immense. The UK's financial markets alone deal with billions of pounds worth of international transactions on a daily basis. This business extends beyond the City of London, with Edinburgh and Glasgow (taken together) being among the ten largest European centres in several financial markets. Sound choice of law rules help to give traders, investors and consumers confidence in the legal effect of their contracts and underpin their value." www.justice.gov.uk

二、美國法律協會之建議

於選法規則之適用上，如前所述美國學界及法院許多（或絕大部份）同僚認同於處理衝突案件時，首先必須去認定所牽連之各州法律是否於政策上有真正之衝突。美國法律協會（「ALI」）在其1994 Complex Litigation Proposal中順應美國潮流，無論於侵權行為或契約採納這種美國式共識。另外更值得注意的是，ALI又遮遮掩掩於假衝突之情形下，對加州的比較損害加以認可。但是於各州之政策有真衝突時，ALI卻迴避去比較各州相衝突政策之損害－而這點卻是加州方法論重點之所在。

有關當事人之選法，6.02條規定：(a)在依3.01條集中或依5.01條移轉之訴訟中，當事人所主張應適用的法律有重大衝突時，當事人有關契約請求之權利、義務、及抗辯應依當事人於契約中所指定之法律，除非法院認定(1)依6.03條之規定原來應為準據法之州法認定詐欺、脅迫、不當影響、或錯誤，該條款為無效，或(2)依6.03條之規定原來應為準據法之州法於基本法規之目的上，是與當事人所選定之法有重大衝突。(b)於合適之情形下，受移轉之法院得決定將訴訟分成次集團之請求或當事人，並得適用不只一州之法律[16]。

6.02條(a)項(2)款類似早期第2新編187(2)(b)條之規定，其規定：

---

[16]　§ 6.02 Mass Contracts: Law Chosen by the Parties

(a) In actions consolidated under § 3.01 or removed under § 5.01, in which the parties assert the application of laws that are in material conflict, the rigts, liabilities, and defenses of the parties with respect to a contract claim shall be governed by the law designated by the parties in the contract, unless the court finds either

(1) that the clause is invalid for reasons of misinterpretation, duress, undue influence or mistake, as defined under state law that otherwise would be applicable under § 6.03,or

(2) that the law chosen by the parties is in material conflict with fundamental regulatory objectives of the state law that otherwise would be applicable under § 6.03.

(b) In appropriate cases, the transferee court may determine that the actions should be divided into subgroups of claims or parties, allowing more than one state's law to be applied. The court may determine that only some of the claims involving some of the parties should be governed by the law chosen by the parties to apply to their respective contracts and that other claims or parties should be governed by different laws selected under § 6.03. In that event, the transferee court may retain all the claims treating them under the appropriately designated laws, or may exercise its authority under § 3.06 (c) to sever, transfer, or remand the claims to the transferor courts for individual treatment consistent with its determination.

「被選定之準據法違反他州之重大政策，而該州對該特定爭執問題之決定較被選定為準據法之州有著更重大利益，並且該州之法依188條在當事人沒有有效的選定準據法時應為準據法。[17]」羅馬 I 之相對條款是以大陸法所慣用之強行法規之方式，表達於3(3)條及9條。

另外更有趣的是6.02(a)(1)條有關詐欺脅迫、錯誤等問題，這是通常被認為有關契約存在（「exsistence」）或成立（「formation」）之問題，英國法早期即似「假定契約存在時之準據法」（「putative proper law」；「推定準據法」）為依據[18]，而羅馬公約8條及羅馬 I 10條亦皆引用此作法。無論是於(1)款或(2)款中，現今美國法律協會亦採用此同一作法[19]，國際私法於此問題在實質上已被統一－除了2005年海牙選擇法院公約第5條仍堅持以被選定法院地法為依據外[20]。 以被選定法院為唯一有專屬管轄法院，並且再火上加油硬性機械式的以該地法為條款成立之準據法，這不但是藐視弱勢一方人權之史無前例之野蠻作法，並且已為個人一再指控歷歷的證明這亦是違反英、美、及歐盟國內判例法之國際恐怖行為。美國法律協會6.02(a)(1)及(2)條之規定只不過再次證實了個人對法律先進國家血淋淋的殘暴行為之指控。更可惡的是這些法律先進國家食髓知味明目張膽的背叛保護弱勢國家多年的漢堡規則，於United Nation Convention on Contract For the International Carriage of Goods Wholly on Partly by Sea（2008）第66、67條中得寸進尺的再作了侵犯第3世界人權之主張。

(一)契約成立與默示準據法

如個人去年於論文中之結論指出，「有關契約之存在（成立）與效

---

[17] 有關此條之評語，請見陳隆修，《國際私法契約評論》，台北，五南圖書公司，民國75年2月，初版，112～119頁。

[18] 有關此方面見陳隆修，《國際私法契約評論》，台北，五南圖書公司，民國75年2月，初版，97～100頁。

[19] 事實上，U.C.C. 1-301條(f)項亦採同一理論。

[20] 見陳隆修，《2005年海牙法院選擇公約評析》，台北，五南圖書公司，2009年1月，初版1刷，79～84頁。

力之問題，例如前述之當之沉默、契約無對價、錯誤、詐欺、脅迫、合併
條款、額外附加條款、其他有關當事人間之同意及合法性等問題，英國傳
統判例法及較近之羅馬公約第8條第1項皆採納假設契約成立時應為契約
之準據法為依據（「putative proper law」）[21]。」儘管「推定準據法」並
不是一個簡單的概念，個人去年主張以實體契約原則之共同核心價值取代
它[22]。但無論如何於國際法上它先由英國所接受，再由歐盟羅馬公約所公
開引用，現今連國際法自成一格的美國亦於法律協會之6.02(a)(1)、(2)條
中採納[23]，至少在它還沒被實體契約共同核心原則推翻以前，仍不折不扣
的是國際法中少有的共同主流核心價值。美國與歐盟於2005年海牙公約
及2008年鹿特丹規則之表現，充份證明這些法律先進國家於國內及國際
場合邏輯上的不一致。這些滿口人權的法律先進國家，事實上是踐踏弱勢
國家人權的最凶殘怪獸，是人類有史以來最大的國際詐騙集團。這亦是個
人一再期盼中國式國際私法能以禮運大同篇為最高宗旨之理由。個人期盼
他日於中華民族真正崛起後，年輕同僚能本著人溺己溺之人本精神，不以
短期的商業利益為藉口，去侵犯弱勢民族的基本訴訟權、平等權、財產
權、適當程序權、及最基本的生存發展權。個人希望兩岸年輕同僚於創造
法律理論時，能牢牢謹記我們遠祖告誡過「天道好還」。

　　ALI在契約選法規則創新之處在於6.02(a)條規定，應於當事人所主
張應適用的法律有重大衝突時當事人之選法才適用。這與2004年U.C.C.
1-301(c)條及第2新編187(1)條之規定並不一樣。雖然於此處或許作用並
非十分明顯，但對於選法規則的以實體政策分析為導向，個人自然十分認
同，並且建議中國式國際私法對此點應非常的加以注意。

　　於當事人沒有有效的選定準據法時，6.03條規定：(a)除非6.02條有規
定，否則當事人所主張應適用之法有重大衝突時，被移轉之法院應依下列

---

[21]　陳隆修，《2005年海牙法院選擇公約評析》，台北，五南圖書公司，2009年1月，初版1刷，95、96頁。
[22]　同上96～98頁。
[23]　新版的U.C.C.亦於1-301條(f)款中採此理論。

之規定而選擇準據法，而於對同一當事人之相同或類似契約所主請求應以適用同一州之法律為目的。(b)於決定(a)項所規定之準據法時，為了確認各州是否於其法律被適用時是否有政策會被促進，應考慮下列因素：(1)訂約訂定地；(2)契約履行地；(3)契約標的所在地；及(4)原告及被告之主要營業地或慣居地。(c)如果於分析(b)項之因素時，法院認定就只有一州之政策會因其法律之適用而被促進，該州法應被適用。如果不止一州之政策會因其法律之適用而被促進，法院應適用共同的當事人之主要營業地法，除非法院認定該地法會與履行地法或他方契約當事人之慣居地法之規定目的有著重大之衝突。在此情形下，法院應在該些州法之合法範圍內適用這些州法。(d)如果法院決定對類似契約之共同當事人所主張之所有請求皆適用一州之法是不合適的，它可將訴訟分成請求、爭執、或當事人之次團體，根據3.01條使其得以被集中處理，並允許一州以上之法律得以被適用。[24]

---

[24]　§ 6.03 Mass Contracts: Law Governing in the Absence of Effective Party Choice

(a) Except as provided in § 6.02, in actions consolidated under § 3.01 or removed under § 5.01, in which the parties assert the application of laws that are in material conflict, the transferee court shall chose the law governing the rights, liabilities, and defenses of the parties with respect to a contract claim by applying the criteria set forth in the following subsections with the objective of applying a single state's law to every claim being asserted under the same or similar contracts with a common party.

(b) In determining the governing law under subsection (a), the court shall consider the following factors for purposes of identifying each state having a policy that would be furthered by the application of its law:

   (1) the place or places of contracting;

   (2) the place or places of performance;

   (3) the location of the subject matter of the contract; and

   (4) the primary places of business or habitual residences of the plaintiffs and defendants.

(c) If, in analyzing the factors set forth in subsection (b), THE COURT FINDS THAT ONLY ONE STATE HAS A POLICY THAT WOULD BE FURTHERED BY THE APPLICATION OF ITS LAW, THAT STATE'S LAW SHALL GOVERN. If more than one state has a policy that would be furthered by the application of its law, ther court shall apply the law of the state in which the common contracting party has its primary place of business, unless the court finds that law is in material conflict with the regulatory objectives of the state law in the place of performance or where the other contracting parties habitually reside. In that event, the court shall apply those state laws to the contracts legitimately within their scope.

(d) If the court determines that the application of a single states law to all the claims being asserted under similar contracts with a common party would be inappropriate, it may divide the actions into subgroups of claims, issues, or parties to foster consolidated treatment under § 3.01, and allow

　　於沒有有效的約定準據法時，6.03(a)條仍舊是規定只有(b)項中所規定之所牽連之州法有重大衝突時，選法規則才會被啟動。個人之所以大幅的評述ALI的複數訴訟選法規則，最主要乃是在提醒國際法的同僚實體政策分析的方法論已為ALI所正式採納。若以利益說之立場而言，或許於假州利益衝突上已被採納（但ALI所採納的為政策分析而非利益分析）；若以實體法論而言，至少已正式進入實體政策分析之階段，至於實體政策評價的公開被接受，個人可能還需要耐心的等待－除非兩岸的年輕同僚能儘早促其發生。

　　另外有趣的是無論於U.C.C.、第2新編187、188條、複數訴訟的提議、甚或美國的判例法，幾乎絕大部的同僚皆忽略了美國於契約法上並未大張旗鼓的採英國式之默示準據法方法論。個人自年輕時就認為世界各國並沒有必要去承受這種英國歷史上之負擔[25]。個人早期即如此評述[26]：「前面雖然敘述了許多當事人於沒有明定準據法時尋找準據法之連結因素，但大部份英國學者認為法院在替當事人推定準據法時應先尋找當事人默示的意思（implied intention, tacit intention, inferred intention），亦即他們認為當事人選定準據法之方式，除了明示外，尚有默示的方式。換言之，法院應先探求當事人明示的意思（expressed intention），然後再求默示的意思，若兩者皆無則再替當事人推定他們的意思（presumed intention）。這種先求當事人的明示準據法，若沒有再求默示的準據法，最後於前兩者皆無的情況下，再替當事人推定一個準據法的理論並不見得為所有的英國學者所贊同，如恩師Graveson教授即為其中最著名者[27]。美國並

---

more than one state's law to be applied. The court also may determine that only certain claims involving one or more of the parties should be governed by the law chosen by the application of the rules in subsection (3), and that other claims or parties should be remanded to the transferor courts for individual treatment under the laws normally applicable there. In either instance, the transferee court may retain all the claims, treating them under the appropriately designated law, or it may exercise its authority under § 3.06 (3) to sever, transfer, or remanded the claims to the transferor courts for individual treatment there consistent with its determination.

[25] 陳隆修，《國際私法契約評論》，台北，五南圖書公司，民國75年2月，初版，56頁。
[26] 陳隆修，《國際私法契約評論》，台北，五南圖書公司，民國75年2月，初版，54、55頁。
[27] R.H. Graveson, Conflict of Laws, 7th ed, pp. 413～432.

未採取這種三步驟程序，於美國只要當事人沒有明定準據法，則法院皆以客觀原則去替當事人尋找準據法。主張要三步驟的人最大的困難大概是如何去劃分第二步驟與第三步驟，亦即何謂當事人默示的意思與何種情況下才算法院替當事人推定的準據法。一般說來契約中若有較有影響力的連結因素或由其他特殊情況得知當事人有選定某法律為依據時，法院因而推定的準據法謂之『默示的意思表示』。可是主張三步驟的學者對於何種情況下能判定當事人有默示意思並不能解釋情楚。」

　　羅馬公約及羅馬Ⅰ[28]雖皆於3(1)條中對當事人之默示選法有給以大致上之定義，但其定義流於過份形式化及機械性，並不見得為大部份英國同僚所能接受。如果公平的論斷，英國司法制度是以當事人為重心，對於此方面學術邏輯的困擾並不會影響司法的運作與正義的結果。慣於接受司法傳統的英國法對此傳統論點雖然甘之如飴，但美國很顯然的無法承受這個英國歷史上的包袱。英國判例法為美國判例法之母法，兩國於文化上又可謂是同文同種，如果連美國都不願十分公開的世襲這個英國傳統，大陸法的歐盟卻自以為高明的挑起這個歷史上的負擔。個人真誠的認為中國式國際私法若無謂的承襲這個過去人類文明進展所帶來的包袱，則不能被稱為崛起中民族的開創性法學。

(二)違反履行地法

　　另外於所牽連州之政策有真衝突時，6.03(c)條是以共同契約當事人之主要營業地法為依據，但該法若與契約履行地法或他方當事人之慣居法有重大衝突時，則後者之法得在其合法範圍內得被適用。類似之規定羅馬

---

[28] 英國已於2008年12月22日加入羅馬Ⅰ規則，見COMMISSION DECISION of 22 December 2008 on the request from the United Kingdom to accept Regulation (EC) No 593/2008 of the European Parliament and the Council on the law applicable to contractual obligations (Rome I), OJL 10/22,15.1.2009. Ministry of Justice, Rome I-Should the UK Opt in? Response to Consultation CP05/08CP(R), January 2009, available at: http://www.justice.gov.uk/docs/rome-i-consultation-govt-response.pdf. "78% ... of respondents felt the Regulation was now... as good as or better than the Rome Convention. As the UK currently applies the Convention, there would be a continuing advantage to British business in applying uniform choice of law rules, ensuring a consistent approach across as wide an area of Europe as possible. Aligning UK law to that in the rest of the EU would achieve this and in turn should lead to a reduction in both legal and transaction costs." (Para 21).

公約規定於7（1)條，這個以大陸法強行法規概念之方式，並不見得為英國同僚所接受，加以其裁量權行使之標準無法確定，故英、德並未簽訂這個爭議性條款。羅馬Ｉ9(3)條則改頭換面的以違反履行地之強行法規得被拒絕執行之規定取代之。

　　個人年輕執業時即見識了跨國公司於台灣予取予求巧取豪奪，再加上跨國律師事務所及本土律師事務所為其後盾，跨國公司於第3世界的台灣成為貨真價實的東方不敗。故而個人年輕時即主張「只要契約履行地的法律不是違反世界上大部份文明國家所共同接受的公共政策，則違反履行地法律的契約應為無效（或者至少不應被強制執行）」[29]。

　　無論跨國公司的法律技術如何高超，財力如何雄厚，其祖國如何霸道，到羅馬應遵守羅馬人之規矩。履行地國人民之生命、身體、財產、及工作權應受到保障，當地之環保法、稅法及金融法規亦應受到尊重。個人這個主張是根據英國判例法而來[30]，但因判例法中所牽涉之履行地法與契約準據法經常為同一個法律，故違反履行地法不能被執行到底是一種國際法，或是純粹基於國內法而不能被執行（「frustration」），仍是個無法決定的重要法律問題。雖然許多英國同僚認為這個法則應屬於國內契約法中不能履行之問題[31]，基於台灣成長的經驗，個人於去年主張「契約違反履行地法不可被強制執行這個法規，應可構成國內契約法及國際私法之共通規則，而同時適用於國際及國內案件。[32]」但基於經驗，個人年輕時更

---

[29]　陳隆修，《國際私法契約評論》，台北，五南圖書公司，民國75年2月，初版，80、81頁。

[30]　Ralli Bros. v. Compania Naviera Sota y Aznar, [1920] 2K. B. 287 (C. A.).

[31]　"Whether the Ralli Bros principle survives the Rome Convention will only arise for decision in a case where (a) English law is the lex fori; (b) the law applicable to the contract is the law of State A; (c) performance is to take place in State B, where it is illegal; and (d) the rule relating to supervening illegality under the law of State A is sufficiently different from English law so as to require performance. Such a combination of factors would undoubtedly be very rare, and is no doubt the reason why the issue whether the rule in Ralli Bros is a rule of domestic law or a rule of the conflict of laws has not arisen for decision in more than 80 years since it was decided and in more than 60 years since the issue was raised in academic writing. If it does arise, it is suggested that the better view is that it is a rule of the domestic law of contract."Dicey and Morris, the Conflict of Laws, 14th ed., p.1597.

[32]　陳隆修，《2005年海牙法院選擇公約評析》，台北，五南圖書公司，2009年1月，初版1刷，92～95頁。

主張履行地法應符合「人類文明的公理」才可被遵守，以應付這些大小流氓國家似是而非之掠奪性殖民地主義。去年更進一步闡明所謂「文明的公理」應包含聯合國人權公約及基本的契約法原則[33]（如歐盟契約法原則及聯合國2004年商業契約法原則）。個人之主張不但早於ALI 6.03條及羅馬 I 9(3)條[34]，並且明確的不給予法院裁量迴避之空間。與英國法不同的是個人認為這個天經地義的規則可同時適用於國內及國際案件，故亦應同時構成國內法及國際法。另外個人又基於經驗，主張這個規則應受限於「文明的公理」，亦即應受限於各種人權公約、憲法、及基本契約法之原則。個人年輕時之主張，現已為羅馬 I 9(3)條所緩慢的接受中。個人誠摯的想像不出中國式的國際私法，會有何務實的理由去拒絕個人現今更為成熟之主張？

三、適當法理論與其範圍

如果不是為了經濟上的利益不得不加入歐盟，英國於國際契約法上之「適當法理論」（「the proper law doctrine」）經歷國際貿易實務長久以來的磨鍊，事實上通常是較羅馬公約或羅馬 I 靈活而完備的。Cheshire & North如此敘述：「這個理論的主要特點如下。於幾乎沒有限制下，當事人得選定其準據法。如果當事人並沒有明示這個選擇，並且法院無法由其之默示而得知這種選擇，則客觀之標準會被適用。這是為了定位契約，以便尋找與交易最有密切關連的法律制度。因此做為適當法基礎的兩個理

---

[33] 同上。

[34] Jonathan Harris, Mandatory Rules and Public Policy under the Rome I Regulation, 於Rome I Regulation: The Law Applicable to Contractual Obligations in Europe edited by Franco Ferrari, Stefan Leible, p.269: "Of all the issues arising in the negotiation of the Rome I Regulation, none has proved more problematic than the revision of the provisions relating to mandatory rules.
Much of this debate centred around the effects of applying third state's mandatory rules, and, in particular, whether any perceived benefits, both practical and doctrinal, in applying such rules could be said to outweigh any uncertainty that might ensue. Subsequently, the text of the Regulation was revised and the third state mandatory rule provisions were substantially narrowed in scope; indeed, they were narrowed to such an extent that the ensuing provision in Article 9(3) of the final Rome I Regulation may be considered nor significantly different to the pre-Rome Convention position in the United Kingdom."

論為，確認當事人意思的主觀說，及為了定位契約的客觀說。至於個別的爭執點可以引用特別的規則。通常準據法是相關的，但當考慮有些爭執點時，法院應不只是引用準據法而已。因此，例如，當爭執點是合法性的問題時，法院不但應考慮到依準據法之合法性而已，亦應考慮到依履行地之合法性。個別性質的契約是會有特別的規則的，例如保險契約。這些規則不是有著特別的規定以確認準據法，就是完全脫離準據法。[35]」故而如Prof. North所說的，羅馬公約（羅馬 I）與英國法適當法理論於大致上之架構是相似的。

　　首先羅馬公約及羅馬 I 只適用於民商契約，而於第1條排除自然人之身份及能力，有關親屬及扶養義務，夫妻財產、遺囑及繼承，票據及可流通證券之義務，仲裁及選擇法院條款，公司及非法人組織之相關問題，對於第3人代理人是否可以拘束本人及分行與總部之問題，信託相關問題，訂約前責任，及某些歐盟有特別規定之保險契約，及程序及證據規則。至於準契約責任因為公約10(1)(e)條及規則12(1)(e)條皆有規定契約準據法之適用範圍包括契約無效之後果，這種將準契約（quasi - contract）責任視為契約責任為大陸法之作法，故英國選擇不簽訂公約10(1)(e)條。而且於管轄權上英國判例法並不將恢復原狀（「restitution」）請求權視為契約上之問題[36]。但羅馬 II 對這些傳統上英美法視為衡平法之問題已有特別規定，英國並已加入羅馬 II，或許羅馬 I 不再需要處理這些衡平法之問

[35]　P M North, JJ Fawcett, Cheshire and North's Private International Law, 13th ed., pp.534, 535, "The key features of the doctrine were as follows. The parties could choose the proper law, with very little restriction on this right. If the parties did not express a choice, and one could not be inferred by the courts, an objectie test was applied. This sought to localize the contract by looking for the system of law with which the transaction was most closely connected. The twin theories which underlay the proper law were therefore the subjective theory, which looked to the intentions of the parties, and the objective theory, which sought to localise the contract. Special rules were adopted for particular issues. The proper law was usually relevant, but the court was required to go beyond the proper law when considering certain issues. Thus, for example, with the issue of illegality the courts were concerned not only with illegality by the proper law but also with illegality by the law of the place of performance. There were also special rules for particular contrats, such as insurance contracts. These rules either made special provision for ascertaining the proper law or departed from the proper law altogether."這個論述於14th ed., pp.666,667中再次被重述。

[36]　Kleinwort Benson Ltd v Glasgow City Council [1999] 1 AC 153, HL.

題。

　公約第18條特別規定這些規則之解釋與適用必須注意到其國際性之特質，以取得統一之解釋與適用[37]。或許是歐盟法院統一之功能太優良，羅馬Ⅰ並無此規定。基於同一事實而來之請求，有些國家是定性為契約，而有些則定性為侵權。歐盟法院對於契約上之定性問題，自然有著自主性之獨立解釋，並且其之解釋是一貫的配合1968之布魯塞爾管轄公約之發展。

　於Jakob Handte & Co GmbH v Traitements Mecano-Chimiques des Surfaces SA.[38]中，原告法國公司從一瑞士公司處購得一德國公司之機器，而該機器由德國公司之法國關係企業所裝置。後因該機器不符合標準，原告於法國告該德國公司及其法國關係企業。歐盟法院認定：「當一個次購買人由一個中間賣者處買得貨品後，以貨品未符合規定而對製造人提告時，應注意的是次購買人與製造人間並無契約關係存在，因為後者並未對前者承擔任何契約義務。[39]」法院又接著解釋：「尤其特別是當在有關國際性連鎖契約時，當事人契約上之責任可能於個別契約上皆不一致，故而次購買人對其直接出賣人可以執行之契約上權利，與製造人及第一個購買人間所承受的關係並不見得一致。[40]」故而歐盟法院認為於此並不符合布魯塞爾公約5(1)條契約特別管轄之規定，一般認為應可適用5(3)條侵權行為之特別規定。或許因為本案並未牽涉及消費者，故而法院

---

[37] Article 18
Unifomrm interpretation
In the interpretation and application of the preceding uniform rules, regard shall be had to their international character and to the desirability of achieving uniformity in their interpretation and application.
[38] Case C-26/91, [1992] ECR I-3967.
[39] Para. 16, "Where a sub-buyer of goods purchased from an intermediate seller brings an action against the manufacturer for damage on the ground that the goods are not in conformity, it must be observed that there is no contractual relationship between the sub-buyer and the manufacturer because the latter has not undertaken any contractual obligation towards the former."
[40] Para 17, "Furthermore, particularly where there is a chain of international contracts, the parties' contractual obligations may vary from contract to contract, so that the contractual rights which the sub-buyer can enforce against his immediate seller will not necessarily be the same as those which the manufacturer will have accepted in his relationship with the first buyer."

會做如此決定。如若次購買人是基於產品責任，而對製造人提出人身傷害或財產損害之請求，或許會有更清楚的判決。於Reunion Europeenne SA v Spliethoffs Bevrachtingskantoor BV[41]中，提單是由澳大利亞公司所作成，海上運送人為一荷蘭公司，受貨人於運送契約完成後發現遭受損害，即依據提單而對海上運送人提起訴訟。歐盟法院認為提單並未顯示受貨人與運送人間有何自由訂定之契約關係，因此本案並不在布魯塞爾公約5(1)條契約之特別管轄範圍內。但本案應在5(3)條侵權行為之特別管轄範圍內。於SPRL Arcado v SA Haviland[42]中，歐盟法院還是重申「有關契約之問題」，不應依個別會員國之法律而解釋[43]，應依公約之目的而有獨立之定義[44]。於本案中兩個請求權之一為有關商業代理契約之代理酬金之請求，這自然屬於契約之範圍[45]。另一請求為有關不當的過早終止契約之損害賠償，被告對此請求主張應屬於準侵權行為之範圍。但歐盟法院認為該請求是基於沒有給予合理之通知而終止契約，因此是沒有履行契約責任，故為有關契約之問題[46]。法院引用羅馬公約第10條，認為沒有履行契約義務之後果是依據契約準據法而決定，故而本訴訟之性質應屬於契約之範圍[47]。

---

[41]　Case C-51/97 [1999] I L Pr 205.

[42]　Case 9/87 [1988] ECR 1539

[43]　Para. 10, As the Court held in its judgment of 22 March 1983 in Case 34/82 (Martin Peters Bauunter-mebmung GmbH v Zuid Nederlandse Aannemers Vereniging [1983] ECR 987) the concept of 'matters relating to a contract' serves as a criterion to define the scope of one of the rules of special jurisdiction available to the plaintiff. Having regard to the objective and the general scheme of the Convention, it is important that, in order to ensure as far as possible the equality and uniformity of the rights and obliga-tions arising out of the Convention for the Contracting States and the persons concerned, that concept should not be interpreted simply as referring to the national law of one or other of the States concerned.

[44]　Para.11.

[45]　Para.12.

[46]　Para. 13, The same view must be taken of a claim for compensation for the wrongful repudiation of such an agreement as the basis for such compensation is the failure to comply with a contractual obliga-tion.

[47]　Para. 15, In addition, Article 10 of the Convention on the Law applicable to Contractual Obligations of 19 June 1980 (Official Journal 1980, L 266, p.1) confirms the contractual nature of judicial proceedings such as those in point inasmuch as it provides that the law applicable to a contract governs the conse-quences of a total or partial failure to comply with obligations arising under it and consequently the contractual liability of the party responsible for such breach.

四、契約之存在

於Effer SpA v Hans-Joachim Kantner[48]中，歐盟法院認為即使當事人之爭執是為有關契約之成立與否，布魯塞爾公約5(1)條契約履行地之特別管轄權仍可引用。法院認定：「因此依公約的條文，並且特別是第2章7段的規定，於公約5(1)條所規定的案件中，各國法院於決定有關契約之問題時，是包括契約本身各個組成部份之是否存在，因為欲使得訴訟發生地之各國法院去決定依公約其是否有管轄權這是不可避免的。如果不是如此，公約5(1)條會被剝奪其法律效果，因為否則會造成，只要一方當事人主張契約不存在即足以產生挫敗這個條文的規則的效果。相反的，在尊重公約的目的及精神下，這些規則須要被解釋為當法院必須去決定依契約所引起的紛爭時，在考慮相關當事人所提供的切確及有關之證據後，得以在自動檢驗其自身管轄權存否之主要先決條件下，確認契約之存在與否。[49]」如去年個人為了反對2005年海牙法院選擇公約所代表的新掠奪式殖民主義，一再強調有關契約之存在（existence）或成立（formation）與效力（Vatidity）之問題，例如當事人之沈默、契約無對價、標準格式契約、錯誤、詐欺、脅迫、合併條款、額外附加條款、相衝突條款、其他有關當事人間之同意及合法性之問題，於目前國際法上是以假設契約成立時應為契約準據法為依據（putative proper law[50]）。這個理論截至目前為

---

[48] Case 38/81 [1982] ECR 825.

[49] Para.7, It follows from the provisions of the Convention, and in particular from those in Section 7 of Title Ⅱ, that, in the cases provided for in Article 5(1) of the Convention, the national court's jurisdiction to determine questions relating to a contract includes the power to consider the existence of the constituent parts of the contract itself, since that is indispensable in order to enable the national court in which proceedings are brought to examine whether it has jurisdiction under the Convention. If that were not the case, Article 5(1) of the Convention would be in danger of being deprived of its legal effect, since it would be accepted that, in order to defeat the rule contained in that provision it is sufficient for one of the parties to claim that the contract does not exist. On the contrary, respect for the aims and spirit of the Convention demands that that provision should be construed as meaning that the court called upon to decide a dispute arising out of a contract may examine, of its own motion even ,the essential preconditions for its jurisdiction, having regard to conclusive and relevant evidence adduced by the party concerned, establishing the existence or the inexistence of the contract.

[50] 陳隆修，《2005年海牙法院選擇公約評析》，台北，五南圖書公司，2009年1月，初版1刷，70～98頁。

止，仍是世界的主流價值－雖然個人認為其時代性之任務已可由更具體的
契約法實體原則來取代。這個putative proper law doctrine已為新版美國
U.C.C. 1-301 (f)條及美國法律協會於複數訴訟之建議的6.02條所接受，
稍早於1980為羅馬公約8條（羅馬 I 10條）所引用，更為英國判例法所
長久引用[51]。對這個英美、歐盟所共同接受的主流共通核心價值，2005年
海牙法院選擇公約第5條卻獨排眾議的堅持於這個問題上以被選定法院地
法為依據，充份的顯示2005年海牙公約傲慢的新殖民地主義心態。另外
2005年海牙公約的第5條又硬性的規定於此問題上，被選定的法院為唯一
專屬管轄法院，這亦是違反了英[52]、美[53]判例法法院地有管轄權去認定這個
問題之傳統作法[54]。亦違反了聯合國紐約仲裁公約第2條第3項依法院地法
去決定自己管轄權之規定（competence - compentence）[55]。更違反了歐
盟法院[56]於本案Effer v. Kantner中白紙黑字的結論：「即使是當事人間對
請求權所依據的契約的存在有爭議，原告仍可根據1968年9月27日民商管
轄權與判決執行公約5(1)條至履行地法院主張管轄權。[57]」這些法律及經

---

[51] 陳隆修，《國際私法契約評論》，台北，五南圖書公司，民國75年2月，初版，97～100頁。

[52] The Sennar (No. 2) [1985] 1 W L R 490, at 500.

[53] The Bremen v. Zapata Off – Shore Co., 407 U.S.1 (1972).

[54] 陳隆修，《2005年海牙法院選擇公約評析》，台北，五南圖書公司，2009年1月，初版1刷，
18～57頁。

[55] 陳隆修，《2005年海牙法院選擇公約評析》，台北，五南圖書公司，2009年1月，初版1刷，6～
10頁。

[56] 於Kleinwort Benson Ltd v Glasgow City Council [1999] 1 AC 153案，因為歐盟法院認為這是大英
國協內部案件，故而拒絕審理，使得英國最高法院於審理此案時，對大陸法之觀念顯得無所適
從。大多數法官認為依布塞爾公約5(1)條，只有根據契約而來的義務，法院才能有著契約履
行管轄權。於本案中雙方當事人於事後皆承認契約自始無效(void ab initio)，本案之請求權是要
求返還基於該號稱之契約而已給付之金錢。大部份法官認為雙方既已承認契約自始無效，因此
並無適用5(1)條契約義務之餘地；該請求是基於不當得利之概念，而非契約義務，因此超出5(1)
條之範圍。少部份法官則認為這種嚴格的解釋會使得即使以契約不存在為抗辯時，契約不履行
之損害賠償之請求仍會符合5(1)條；而基於契約不存在之成功抗辯而來之附加的不當得利之請
求，則不屬於 (5)1條之範圍。這樣會造成對同一糾紛之分割。個人認為英國加入大陸法之歐盟
後，法學邏輯上之困擾並非短期可以解決，專注於實體法論是惟一之出路。

[57] The plaintiff may invoke the jurisdiction of the courts of the place of performance in accordance with
Article 5(1) of the Convention of 27 September 1968 on Jurisdiction and the Enforcement of Judgments
in Civil and Commercial Matters even when the existence of the contract on which the claim is based is
in dispute between the parties.但有趣的邏輯是：如果契約不成立，則契約之履行地在哪裡？但於
Franceco Benincasa v. Dentalkit Srl Case C-269/95 [1997] 中歐盟法院認為被指定法院有專屬管轄
權，paragraph 332, "The answer to the national court's third question must therefore be that the courts

濟上先進整國家不但不會自慚於他們在2005年海牙法院選擇公約之無理
霸道行為，更於2008年聯合國鹿特丹規則66、67條中撤銷漢堡規則行之
多年對弱勢保護之規定，這已不是對第三世界侵門踏戶之暴行而已，更是
基本上藐視第三世界於人權法及國際私法上之缺乏專業知識。

五、選法自由

羅馬 I 規則第1條1項規定本規則適用於有關於民商契約義務上牽涉
及衝突法之問題[58]。與公約第1條第1項之用語「契約義務牽涉及選擇不同
國家之法律」[59]略有不同。這或許是因為規則之政策要點13允許當事人引
用國際公約或契約法規則之故。公約的解釋報告說明：「這些情形包含對
一個國家整內部社會制度而言是牽連到一個或數個外國因素之情形（例
如，訂約一方或所有的當事人是外國人或慣居於外國的事實，契約是於
外國訂定的事實，當事人一方或多方之義務必須於外國履行之事實等），
因此造成數個國家之法律制度得主張適用之結果。[60]」美國舊版之統一商

---

of a Contracting State which have been designated in a jurisdiction clause validly concluded under the first paragraph of Article 17 of the Convention also have exclusive jurisdiction where the action seeks in particular a declaration that the contract containing that clause is void."但歐盟這個判決仍就受限於「先繫屬優先原則」，而與2005年海牙公約並不相同。另[2009]EUECJ C-185/07 Allianz SpA v. West Tankers Inc.亦引用紐約公約 II (3)條，而認定繫屬法院應有權力去決定仲裁條款之效力及存在。而於選法規則上英國法院一向務實認定應以英國法院地法為依據。Dicey, Morris and Collins, p.517, "Accordingly, and as a matter of the common law principles of the conflict of laws, the law which governs the contract will also generally govern the jurisdiction agreement. This means, as will be seen below, that this law governs the construction and interpretation of the agreement; it will also, in principle at least, govern the original validity of the agreement. Difficulty arises in cases in which it is necessary to take a preliminary decision as to whether there is a jurisdiction clause in a contract in order to help identify the law which governs that contract. It has been held, and appears to be correct, that this preliminary assessment has to be undertaken by reference to English domestic law principles." Mackender v Feldia AG [1967] 2 Q.B. 590, 602; The Iran Vojdan [1984] 2 Lloyd's Rep. 380; The Frank Pais [1986] 1 Lloyd's Rep. 529. 見陳隆修，《2005年海牙法院選擇公約評析》，台北，五南圖書公司，2009年1月，初版1刷，99、100頁。

[58] 1.This Regulation shall apply, in situations involving a conflict of laws, to contractual obligations in civil and commercial matters.

[59] 1.The rules of this Convention shall apply to contractual obligations in any situation involving a choice between the laws of different countries.

[60] Giuliano Report, p.11, "These are situations which involve one or more elements foreign to the internal social system of a country (for example, the fact that one or all of the parties to the contract are foreign nationals or persons habitually resident abroad, the fact that the contract was made abroad, the fact that

法1-105(1)條規定當事人所約定之準據法之州（或國家）須與該交易有合理關係，為個人早期批評為：「對當事人訂約之自由加以不合理之限制」。[61]2004年修正版1-301(c)條則明定當事人所指定準據法之州（或國家）不須與該交易有關連。這個新規定表面上合乎個人早期之建議，但事實上仍未完全符合個人早期之建議－非常奇怪的是，個人早期之許多建議歐盟及美國經常歷經二十多年後只能履行一半。修正版之U.C.C.1-301條將交易分為國內交易與國際交易[62]，前者只能適用各州法，而後者得適用各州法或外國法。國內交易如果想擺脫不合適的州法，或許只能依據1-302(a)條而指定國際性組織之規則或原則，但這仍是無法選定其他國家之法律為準據法。

U.C.C.1-301條C項(1)款規定：「無論交易與被指定的州是否有關連，國內交易之當事人對於任何或所有他們的權利義務約定以本州或他州法律為依據是有效的」[63]。因為本款規定「任何或所有的權利義務」，故而U.C.C.本條是很明顯的採納英美法慣用的分割原則。但是對不能選定外國準據法之限制，個人是不以為然的。於批評其舊法要求須有「合理關係」的書中，早期個人之陳述[64]還是可以適用於1-301(c)條上：「當事人雖得在『當事人自主』之大原則下選定準據法，但此『當事人自主』原則是否為絕對呢？亦即當事人是否得選擇一與該交易行為或當事人完全沒有關係之國家以其法律為準據法？英國國際私法一向比歐洲大陸在許多方面都較為開放，並且於此方面似乎較美國為開放。但此問題並不是簡簡

---

one or more of the obligations of the parties are to be performed in a foreign country, etc.), thereby giving the legal systems of several countries claims to apply."

[61]　陳隆修，《國際私法契約評論》，台北，五南圖書公司，民國75年2月，初版，120頁。

[62]　所謂國際交易是指與美國以外國家有合理關係的交易，而非國際交易即國內交易，見1-301條(a)項：In this Section:

(1) "Domestic transaction" means a transaction other than an international transaction.

(2) "International transaction" means a transaction that bears a reasonable relation to a country other than the United States.

[63]　(1)an agreement by parties to a domestic transaction that any or all of their rights and obligations are to be determined by the law of this State or of another State is effective, whether or not the transaction bears a relation to the State designated; and

[64]　陳隆修，《國際私法契約評論》，台北，五南圖書公司，民國75年2月，初版，27～30頁。

單單就可以回答，因為此問題牽涉到甚多因素，例如脫避法律（evasion of the law）與誠信原則（good faith）等令人頭痛的法律問題。由著名的 Vita Food Products[65] 看來似乎英國法院容許當事人選擇一個和契約或當事人不相干的國家的法律為準據法，但事實上有學者謹慎的將 Vita Food 判例限制於當商業習慣或傳統都與被選定的國家有關係才可選擇此不相干國家的法律為準據法。較為謹慎的說法是英國法院雖然不一定准許不相干國家的法律為準據法，但也不一定不准許它。……但亦有甚多學者認為英國法若被選為準據法，英國法與該契約並不一定要有牽連。其原因或許由於自古以來英國海上貿易發達，許多商業習慣皆以英國為主，並且英國長久以來享有崇高司法名譽，故許多契約雖與英國無關，但皆以英國法為準據法。從事國際貿易的人都深知此為許多種類國際貿易之傳統。尤其是英國常為貿易糾紛之仲裁地，而依英國法律只要仲裁地於英國，就算契約與英國無關，英國法院仍有權力引用英國法為準據法[66]，何況依英美之慣例，只要當事人不舉證外國法，則外國法被推定與法院地法相同。」

　　事實上四十多年前於台灣經濟起飛時，個人即親身見證台灣高雄拆船業間船隻買賣契約是以英國法為準據法之英文格式簽訂的，當事人皆為台灣人，而船亦在高雄。管轄法院是被指定為英國法院，個人懷疑台灣當時之法院及相關海商法是否有能力處理這方面之糾紛。至少於海商、保險、及其他行之有年之國際商業貿易上，美國 U.C.C. 1-301(c)(1) 條對國內交易僅能指定國內各州法之要求是太過狹隘[67]。或許中國式國際私法應記取

---

[65]　The Vita Food Produts Inc. v. Unus Shipping Co. Ltd. [1939] A.C. 277 (P.C.).

[66]　Swisse Arlantizve Societe d Armement Maritime S. A. v. N. V. Rotterdamsche Kolen Cen trale [1967] 1 A. C. 361.

[67]　事實上第2新編187條有關當事人選法規則2項b款的註釋中，亦表明在當事人於訂約國之法律可能甚為不完備時，故選定一個較為發達的法律制度是有著「合理的基礎」，例如於海上運送契約中當事人應得以較著名及較發達之法律為準據法。Comment(f), "The parties to a multistate contract may have a reasonable basis for choosing a state with which the contract has no substantial relationship. For example, when contracting in countries whose legal systems are strange to them as well as relatively immature, the parties should be able to choose a law on the ground that they know it well and that it is sufficiently developed. For only in this way can they be sure of knowing accurately the extent of their rights and duties under the contract. So parties to a contract for the transportation of goods by sea between two countries with relatively undeveloped legal systems should be permitted to submit

台灣經驗，至少於法律尚未完備前，暫時保留彈性空間。

1-301(c)(2)條對國際交易則規定如下：「無論交易與被指定的州或國家是否有關連，國際交易之當事人對於任何或所有他們的權利義務約定以本州、他州、或其他國家之法律為依據是有效的。[68]」無論是國內交易或國際交易都應該適用此款，以確保當事人自主的合法自由。1-301條c款除了採用英美法慣用的分割問題的方法論外，亦保有美國於契約選法規則的傳統－不大肆公開的採用英國式默示準據法的傳統包袱。這亦是美國法律協會於複數訴訟建議6-02條及第2新編187條之作法。第2新編187條之comment(a)雖有提及於充份證據下，法院得尊重當事人意思，但187條仍遵循美國式傳統－亦即至少於條文上不若羅馬 I 規則及公約般的公開主張默示準據法。並且於Comment (a)中表明當事人之選法通常是明示的，而且這才是保證當事人自主最佳之方式[69]，更有趣的是對當事人意思之推定[70]（「presumed intention」）居然擺明不採用「主觀說」之論點[71]。如果公開表明不會完全去尊重當事人之主觀意願，事實上就法律邏輯而言就幾乎等於不會完全去採納當事人之默示選法。而U.C.C.1-301條的comment則完全不提默示準據法：「1-301(d)條規定，除了有關消費交易之特殊規定，在缺乏有效的指定契約準據法時，法院應採用法院地的一般選法原則。[72]」

羅馬 I 及公約的第2條規定，無論契約是否與訂約國有任何關連，這些規則有著世界性的適用。尤其是根據第2條之規定，訂約當事人並不須

---

their contract to some well-known and highly elaborated commercial law."

[68] (2)an agreement by parties to an international transaction that any or all of their rights and obligations are to be determined by the law of this State or of another State or country is effective, whether or not the transaction bears a relation to the State or country designated.

[69] "When the parties have made such a choice, they will usually refer expressly to the state of the chosen law in their contract, and this is the best way of insuring that their desires will be given effect."

[70] 陳隆修，《國際私法契約評論》，台北，五南圖書公司，民國75年2月，初版，56、57頁。

[71] "It does not suffice to demonstrate that the parties, if they had thought about the matter, would have wished to have the law of a particular state applied."

[72] "Section 1-301(d) provides that, in the absence of an effective contractual designation, the forum should apply the forum's general choice of law principles, subject to certain special rules in consumer transactions."

要於訂約國有著住所或居所，可適用於第3國之國民、住民、或居民。[73]

因羅馬 I 1(3)條及公約1(2)(h)條皆規定證據及程序規則被排除在適用範圍內，故而如若當事人不舉證應適用之準據法，各國法院是否得依據各國之程序規則而自動適用法院地法？Cheshire & North認為公約之目的會因此而被當事人迴避，因此不應如此解讀[74]。恩師Prof. Hartley則認為：「雖然訂約國並無法律義務依職權去自動適用外國法，但有人會認為不如此作公約的目的會受到破壞。可是公約最重要的目的卻是在於給予當事人自由去選定準據法。因為這是為了當事人之利益的緣故，如果當事人皆不想要適用外國法，而法院卻去適用外國法，那麼這將會是非常奇怪的。因此本文建議，於當事人已選定準據法或可能已選定準據法之情形下，羅馬公約的精神並不要求依職權自動去適用外國法。[75]」個人認同這個論述，因為在沒有違反強烈的公共政策下，尊重當事人的自由會是較符合契約法的傳統原則。於當事人沒有適當的證明外國法時，法院通常是引用法院地法為依據的。這種作法的理由之一就是於當事人沒有舉證外國法時，即可被視為默示選定法院地法為準據法。[76]

對於羅馬公約3(3)條及7(1)條（規則3(3)條及9(3)條）牽涉及強行法規時，Prof. Hartley認為這可能會關係到契約之合法性之問題，故應如英

---

[73] Giuliano Report, P.9,"From the very beginning of its work the Group has professed itself to be in favour of uniform rules which would apply not only to the nationals of Member States and to persons domiciled or resident within the community but also to the nationals of third States and to persons domiciled or resident therein."

[74] P M North, JJ Fawcett, Cheshire and North's Private International Law, 13th ed., p.545, "However, the purpose of the Convention is not going to be met if the English courts allow the parties to side-step the uniform rules contained therein by a simple omission to plead and prove foreign law. It would therefore be better if this sort of case was regarded as coming within the Convention."

[75] Trevor C. Hartley*, Pleading and Proof of Foreign Law: the Major European Systems Compared, 45 I. C. L. Q. 271, 291 (1996), "Though there is no legal obligation on contracting States to apply foreign law ex officio, it might be thought that failure to do so could undermine the objectives of the Convention. The most important objective, however, is to give the parties freedom to choose the governing law. Since this is meant to be for the benefit of the parties, it would seem perverse for a court to apply foreign law when neither of them wanted it to do so. It is suggested, therefore, that the spirit of the Rome Convention does not require ex officio application of foreign law in those cases in which the parties chose, or could have chosen, the applicable law."

[76] 陳隆修，《國際私法契約評論》，台北，五南圖書公司，民國75年2月，初版，50～53頁，當事人之指定仲裁地或管轄法院，是可以強烈的推定當事人有意以該地法為契約之準據法。

國法院般於此情形下自動依職權去適用應適用之法律。[77]原則上個人雖認同，但是對「強行法規」之定義可能應嚴格的限定於人權公約、憲法、及契約法之基本原則所允許之規範內。

公約5及6條對消費契約及僱傭契約（規則6及8條，另外新增之5條之旅客運送，及7條之保險契約）中，為了保護弱勢一方被迫去簽訂對其不利之選法條款，皆有著特別的規定。但Prof. Hartley卻認為：「但是，一但訴訟程序已開始，其經濟上之弱勢地位並不能阻止其去主張外國法；故而沒有理由去要求法院依職權去主動適用外國法。[78]」或許是其於南非之成長背景，恩師是英國法律學生中可說是非常不冷血之一位。對這個論述其非常不英國式的（於美國或許亦沒有）於註解中認為，如果消費者或受僱者因無知而沒有主張外國法，法院或許應對其加以解釋，並且給予其選擇修正其主張之機會[79]。

六、不患寡而患不均

英國是資本主義的母國，其法律制度的建立自然是深受資本主義laissez-faire之影響[80]。相較於大陸法的積極介入私人行為，英國法傳統上似乎較為不願意介入私人行為，以避免妨礙市場的自然機能。但是這樣的法律經濟學於十年前的亞洲金融風暴，已經充份證明是個過時不符合現代社會需求的不公不義之理論。無視於亞洲人其時的哀鴻遍野，西方同僚沒有「人溺己溺」之「王道法學」基礎，不肯對基於自由經濟而來之資本主義法學加以修正，終於在今年的世界金融風暴中飽受十年前亞洲人所受之痛

---

[77] Hartley, 45 I. C. L. Q. 291 (1996)。

[78] Id, "However, once litigation has begun, his economically weak position would hardly prevent him from pleading foreign law; so there is no rreason why the court should be require to apply foreign law ex officio."

[79] Id, note 102, "However, where the consumer or employee fails to plead foreign law due to ignorance, it might be desirable for the court to explain the position to him and to give him the opportunity to amend his pleadings if he so wishes."

[80] Victoria時期的英國法官即對Jeremy Bentham的功利思潮甚為尊重，見R. H. Graveson, Lectures on the Conflict of Laws and International Contracts (1951), pp 6-8.

苦。或許中國式的法學在認清「天道好還」之基礎上，對本著資本主義而來的整個法律架構必須加以適度修正。對於經濟上弱勢之一方，自當本著「不患寡而患不均」「扶弱抑強」的祖訓加以扶助。更如前述，於外國法之適用時，外國法之主張固然不易，外國法之證明更是困難。昂貴的跨國性事務所證明外國法的效率是通常遠超過外交部的，這自然對弱勢不利，而對強勢絕對有利。不只於羅馬公約或規則I之適用上，個人如前述已主張若準據法為外國法時，法院對其之主張及證明應依裁量權而對弱勢加以主動之扶助。

　　不只應侷限於國際私法上，個人以為整體中國式之法學皆應認知基於資本主義架構而來法律制度，已透過全球性的金融災難而證明不符合現代的人類文明。例如美國2004年的修正版U.C.C. 1-301條即對舊版的1-105條加以修正，區分消費契約與非消費契約，以對弱勢的消費族群加以保護[81]。美國這個法學方法論的修正自然是為時甚晚，但這至少代表著現代資本主義法學最後堡壘的開始棄守，這是中國式法學所應注意之處。

　　羅馬I規則及羅馬公約的主要條款為第3條有關選法自由，及第4條推定準據法之規定。規則第3條(1)項規定：「契約以當事人所選定之法為依據。該選擇必須為明示或由案件之情形或契約的條款清楚的顯示出來。經由其選擇當事人得將所選之法律適用至契約之全部或只有一部份上。[82]」與舊法公約3(1)條相較，舊法對默示選法只須由契約款或案件的事實中顯示出「合理的確定」[83]即可，而規則中之新法則要求必須「清楚

---

[81] U.C.C., S. 1-301, comment, With respect to the power to select governing law, the draft affords greater party autonomy than former Section 1-105, but with important safeguards protecting consumer interests and fundamental policies.
Section 1-301 addresses contractual designation of governing law somewhat differently than does former Section 1-105. Former law allowed the parties to any transaction to designate a jurisdiction whose law governs if the transaction bears a "reasonable relation" to that jurisdiction. Section 1-301 deviates from this approach by providing different rules for transactions involving a consumer than for non-consumer transactions, such as "business to business" transactions.

[82] 1.A contract shall be governed by the law chosen by the parties. The choice shall be made expressly or clearly demonstrated by the terms of the contract or the circumstances of the case. By their choice the parties can select the law applicable to the whole or to part only of the contract.

[83] 1.A contract shall be governed by the law chosen by the parties. The choice must be expressed or dem-

的」顯示才可，可見歐盟亦發現默示準據法之法學技巧於現今之國際商務中並非是一個完美的理論，必須加以更嚴格的規範。這個法學發展亦符合早期個人之主張之模式，二十多年前個人即進一步的主張於當事人沒有明示準據法時，即應將默示準據法與推定準據法之步驟合在一起[84]。羅馬 I 只是將公約於默示選法上之要求加以更嚴格的規定，這或許並非基本上撥亂返治之道。

由公約與規則的3(1)與4(1)條的用語而論，似乎準據法於契約訂定之時即應被加以確認，故而「浮動準據法」（a floating applicable law）之觀念是不為歐盟所接受的。亦即給予他方權利於將來在數個法律中選擇一個準據法是無效的。英國判例法傳統上亦作同樣的規定[85]。不過應注意的是公約及規則的3(2)條皆允許當事人於訂約後，更改依本條文先前所約定之準據法，或更改根據其他條文而來所約定之準據法[86]。這是本著當事人自主原則而來之權利，故而此項更改可以明示或默示[87]。但不能危害及

---

onstrated with reasonable certainty by the terms of the contract or the circumstances of the case. By their choice the parties can select the law applicable to the whole or a part only of the contract.

[84] 陳隆修，《國際私法契約評論》，台北，五南圖書公司，民國75年2月，初版，54～58頁。

[85] Dubai Electricty Co v Islamic Republic of Iran Shipping Lines. The Iran Vojdan [1984] 2 Lloyd's Rep 380 at 385: Cantieri Navali Riuniti SpA v NV Omne Justitia, The Stolt Marmaro [1985] 2 Lloyd's Rep 428 at 435; cf Astro Venturoso Compania Naviera v Hellenic Shipyards SA, The Mariannina [1983] 1 Lloyd's Rep 12 at 15.於Armar Shipping Co Ltd v Caisse Algerienne d'Assurance [1981] 1 W.L.R. 207 (CA)中，上訴法院認為準據法不能溯及既往的依訂約時或甚至履行時尚未發生的事情而決定；或準據法得依一方行為之後果而改變。於The Iran Vojdan [1984] 2 Lloyd's Rep. 380中，提單中給予運送人權利去選擇德里蘭法院時依伊朗法，漢堡法院時依德國法，及倫敦法院時依英國法，依德國法法院選擇條款是無效的，而英國法院認定整個選法是無效的。於陳隆修，《國際私法契約評論》，台北，五南圖書公司，民國75年2月，初版，32、33頁中，個人主張當事人若同意於中國起訴依中國法，在他國起訴依他國法之條款似應被尊重，因為於雙方皆同意下這樣的條款似乎應受尊重。法院所應禁止的是一方過份強勢完全主導選法條款及法院選擇條款，而非於市場機能下雙方之公平、自由選擇權，法院之強制主導功能應在當事人間之公平性，而非其自由權。於the Star Texas [1993] 1 Lloyd's Rep. 445 (CA)中，被告得以選擇在北京或倫敦之浮動仲裁條款是被認為有效的。同樣的，個人認為重點應在當事人間之公平性，而非其自由選擇權。

[86] 羅馬I，第3條2項：The parties may at any time agree to subject the contract to a law other than that which previously governed it, whether as a result of an earlier choice made under this Article or of other provisions of this Regulation. Any change in the law to be applied that is made after the conclusion of the contract shall not prejudice its formal validity under Article 11 or adversely affect the rights of third parties.

[87] 公約的解釋報告認為準據法的改變應與最初的選法適用同樣的規則，見Report on the Convention on the law applicable to contractual obligations by Mario Giuliano, and Paul Lagarde, Official Journal C 282, 31/10/1980, P.22, "As to the way in which the choice of law can be changed, it is quite natural

已經符合之11條形式要件之效力，及第3人之權利。另外公約的解釋報告認為訴訟程序中準據法的選定或改變，應只能依各國之相關訴訟程序法規[88]。

七、以實體法為契約準據法

由羅馬公約3(3)條中特別規定一國之法律而論，3(1)條似乎是不允許當事人指定國際貿易傳統上所接受之原則（lex mercatoria）做為準據法。即使於傳統上英國法院一般向來是較為傾向尊重當事人之自由，英國判例法於此問題還是採迴避之態度。英國法院遲疑之原因，可能主要是相較於英國判例法，lex mercatoria有時可能較為不清楚及沒有完備的規範。但於仲裁方面聯合國1985年模範公約第28條規定依當事人自主法律之規則，若當事人沒有自主時則由仲裁庭決定應適用之國際私法，但如果於當事人明示允許下仲裁庭得以公平正義原則決定案件之紛爭，但在所有之情形下仲裁庭應考慮契約條款及應適用之貿易習慣[89]。這個規定亦為英國1996年之the Arbitration Act Section 46採納如下：(1)仲裁庭處理糾紛時──(a)應依當事人所選定適用於糾紛之實體之法律，或(b)如果當事人同意，應依當事人所同意或仲裁庭所決定之其他考量……(3)如果沒有這

---

that this change should be subject to the same rules as the initial choice."

[88] Id, "If the choice of law is made or changed in the course of proceedings the question arises as to the limits within which the choice or change can be effective. However, the question falls within the ambit of the national law of procedure, and can be settled only in accordance with that law."

[89] UNCITRAL Model law on International Commercial Arbitration 1985
Article 28
(1) The arbitral tribunal shall decide the dispute in accordance with such rules of law as are chosen by the parties as applicable to the substance of the dispute. Any designation of the law or legal system of a given State shall be construed, unless otherwise expressed, as directly referring to the substantive law of that State and not to its conflict of laws rules.
(2) Failing any designation by the parties, the arbitral tribunal shall apply the law determined by the conflict of laws rules which it considers applicable.
(3) The arbitral tribunal shall decide ex aequo et bono or as amiable compositeur only if the parties have expressly authorized it to do so.
(4) In all cases, the arbitral tribunal shall decide in accordance with the terms of the contract and shall take into account the usages of the trade applicable to the transaction.

種選擇或同意，或者該糾紛不在其同意或選擇範圍內，仲裁庭應採用其認為合適之國際私法規則所決定之法律。[90]」如同模範法規，第46條第1項a中當事人所選定的法律制度得為某國之法律制度或國際法，但所選擇的法律必須為實體法而非國際私法之規則[91]。而第46條第1項b款亦如同模範法規一般，除了允許當事人自主去選定某國之法律制度外，亦允許當事人去選定一個不屬於任何國家之法律原則，或者一般商業習慣之傳統慣例與規則（lex mercatoria）。又如模範法於當事人明示允許仲裁庭得以公平正義原則（「ex aequo et bono」 or 「amiable compositeur」）處理紛爭，英國現今亦允許仲裁庭於當事人同意下，依公平正義原則（equity and fairness）處理紛爭[92]。

這個以國際通認的契約法原則，lex mercatoria 或ex aequo et bono為仲裁之依據，亦已為國際上主要之仲裁機構ICC[93]及LCIA[94]等所接受[95]。故而Dicey & Morris如此評論：「這個潮流是『仲裁去地方化』發展的另一面，這方面的發展認為法庭地選法規則的強行適用是對當事人自主原則加以不必要的束縛[96]。」於Channel Tunnel Group Ltd. v. Balfour Beatty Construction Ltd.[97]中，當事人約定建造橫跨英吉利海峽鐵路，契約中有加入準據法條款，要求契約之解釋必須符合英國與法國共有之原則，若於

---

[90]　(1)The arbitral tribunal shall decide the dispute-
　　(a) in accordance with the law chosen by the parties as applicable to the substance of the dispute, or
　　(b) if the parties so agree, in accordance with such other considerations as are agreed by them or determined by the tribunal
　　(3) If or to the extent that there is no such choice or agreement, the tribunal shall apply the law determined by the conflict of laws rules which it considers applicable.
[91]　同前註，Section 46(2)，For the purpose the choice of the laws of a country shall be understood to refer to the substantive laws of that country and not its conflict of laws rules.
[92]　The Report of the Departmental Advisory Committee on Arbitration Law (1997) 13 Arb. Int. 275, 310。
[93]　International Chamber of Commerce Court of Arbitration (ICC) rules, art. 17(1)。
[94]　London Court of Internation Arbitration (LCIA) rules, art 22.3.
[95]　見陳隆修，《2005年海牙法院選擇公約評析》，台北，五南圖書公司，2009年1月，初版1刷，55～57頁。
[96]　Dicey and Morris, the Conflict of Laws, 14th ed. P. 730, "The trend was another aspect of the development of 'delocalised arbitration', which saw the mandatory application of the choice of law rules of the forum as an unnecessary fetter on party autonomy."
[97]　[1993] A.C. 334.

沒有共同原則時，則適用各國或國際間仲裁庭所適用之國際貿易法基本原則。

　　於大西洋對岸美洲的the Inter - American Convention on the Law Applicable to International Contracts of 1994雖然參考羅馬公約而來，但其條文[98]隱含著允許當事人去選擇以lex mercatoria為依據。但是最明顯的應為新修U.C.C. 1-302條，其(a)項規定：「除非於(b)項或本法其他地方有另外規定，本法中條文之效力得依約定而改變之。[99]」其註釋(2)敘述如下：「當事人經由約定以改變統一商法條文的效力，得說明用以為依據而取代被更改的條文之規則。或著另外的，當事人得說明他們的關係應以被公眾所認可的機構之規則或適用於商業交易的原則為依據，以更改這些條文的效力。這些機構的規則或原則得包括，例如，UNCITRAL或Unidroit等跨國性機構所提倡之規則（例如Unidroit Principles of International commercial Contracts），或著一些非法律規則，例如貿易規則。[100]」

---

[98] INTER-AMERICAN CONVENTION ON THE LAW APPLICABLE TO INTERNATIONAL CONTRACTS

Article 3

The provisions of this Convention shall be applied, with necessary and possible adaptations, to the new modalities of contracts used as a consequence of the development of international trade.

Article 9

If the parties have not selected the applicable law, or if their selection proves ineffective, the contract shall be governed by the law of the State with which it has the closest ties.

The Court will take into account all objective and subjective elements of the contract to determine the law of the State with which it has the closest ties. It shall also take into account the general principles of international commercial law recognized by international organizations.

Nevertheless, if a part of the contract were separable from the rest and if it had a closer tie with another State, the law of the State could, exceptionally, apply to that part of the contract.

Article 10

In addition to the provisions in the foregoing articles, the guidelines, customs, and principles of international commercial law as well as commercial usage and practices generally accepted shall apply in order to discharge the requirements of justice and equity in the particular case.

[99] (a) Except at otherwise provided in subsection (b) or elsewhere in [the Uniform Commercial Code], the effect of provisions of [the Uniform Commercial Code] may be varied by agreement.

[100] 2.An agreement that varies the effect of provisions of the Uniform Commercial Code may do so by stating the rules that will govern in lieu of the provisions varied. Alternatively, the parties may vary the effect of such provisions by stating that their relationship will be governed by recognized bodies of rules or principles applicable to commercial transactions. Such bodies of rules or rules or principles may include, for example, those that are promulgated by intergovernmental authorities such as UNCITRAL or Unidroit (see, e.g., Unidroit Principles of International Commercial Contracts), or non-legal codes such as trade codes.

　　或許有鑑於時代之趨勢，區盟委員會提議第3條第2項如下：「當事人亦得選定歐盟或國際上公認之實體契約法原則或規則為準據法。但是應依據這些原則或規則而解決之相關問題，若於原則或規則中並未規定，則應由其所引為基礎的基本法理為依據，或於沒有這些原則下，應依本規則所規定於沒有選法時應適用之法律為依據。[101]」以歐盟或國際上承認之實體契約法原則為國際契約之準據法，是一種非常務實而且於大部份情形下可能亦是非常符合公平正義的作法。事實上於評析2005年海牙法院選擇公約時，對於一些棘手而相關契約存在及效力之問題，例如合併條款、額外附加條款、當事人之沈默、錯誤、詐欺、脅迫、契約沒有對價、不同標準格式之衝突條款、當事人間慣例之拘束及其他有關當事人是否同意之問題，個人即主張得以歐盟契約法原則為依據[102]。並且於個人以英美相關之國際法上之實務案例為分析時，經常發現歐盟契約法原則中之提議會較傳統上所盛行之國際私法的選法規則能主持正義。對英國法、羅馬公約及羅馬 I 以putative proper law來解決契約成立及效力之問題，個人即如此評述：「若該應適用之putative proper law之相關國內契約法於沒有妥善之規定或甚至沒有規定時，公平正義之解決方案是無法達成的。而國際契約包羅萬象，經常每一個國家的國內法對根據其他法系而來之契約是無法應付的，例如英美法院是經常無法理解於大陸法中時效之利益是不得拋棄的，及違約金之規定於大陸法之契約是甚為天經地義之條款而非為不法條款。[103]」

　　歐盟契約法委員會亦很明顯的同意這個論述，其對歐盟契約法原則如

---

[101] 2.The parties may also choose as the applicable law the principles and rules of the substantive law of contract recognized internationally or in the Community.

　　However, questions relating to matters governed by such principles or rules which are not expressly settled by them shall be governed by the general principles underlying them or, failing such principles, in accordance with the law applicable in the absence of a choice under this Regulation.

[102] 陳隆修，《2005年海牙法院選擇公約評析》，台北，五南圖書公司，2009年1月，初版1刷，70～98頁。

[103] 陳隆修，《2005年海牙法院選擇公約評析》，台北，五南圖書公司，2009年1月，初版1刷，97頁。

此介紹：「這些原則是被用來反映契約法問題的解決方案的共同核心。這其中有些問題已經對各國法院及立法者逐漸造成困擾。這些原則是有意的被造成較為先進的。於這多各國法所涵蓋的爭點的範圍內，相較於傳統的法律思想這些原則提供了較為令人滿意的答案。例如這些原則中有關契約履行的保證及環境的改變使得於平衡之情況下契約之履行變成一種過份況重之負擔，這些難題是重覆的發生且大部份國家的法律並無規定。這些原則因此可以幫助相關的歐洲的法院及立法機構，以促使歐盟契約法有成效的發展。[104]」歐盟契約法原則所代表的法理不但擴及中歐及東歐，而且又為UNIDROIT Principles of International Commercial Contracts 2004所大量引為參考之基礎。以UNIDROIT Principles of International Commercial Contracts 2004與歐盟契約法原則相似的程度，或許Prof. Schlesinger所夢想的契約法「共同核心」（「common core」）[105]已達成。

　　Prof. Schlesinger於契約法上「共同核心」之遠見，是個人年輕時以博士論文創造「主流價值」時於契約上主要之依據。當時引用其論述如下：「就我們所研究的所有法律體系而言，契約法的概念是一致的。就其範圍而言，契約法的範疇或許不可能被所有法律體系以相同的法律訂立出來，但就其核心（core）而言，契約的意義所到之處皆同。在我們研究的所有法系中，依『契約』此一文字之中心意義言，其構成契約之第一要

---

[104] The Commission of European Contract Law, Principles of European Contract Law, edited by Ole Lando and Hugh Beale (2000), Introduction, (1)(D), "The Principles are intended to reflect the common core of solutions to problems of contract law.
Some of these have proved increasingly troublesome for national courts and legislators. The Principles are also intended to be progressive. On many issues covered by national law they may be found to offer a more satisfactory answer than that which is reached by traditional legal thinking. For example, their provisions relating to the assurance of performance and to the grant of relief where a change of circumstances renders performance of the contract excessively onerous deal in a balanced way with recurrent difficulties on which most national laws are silent. The Principles are thus available for the assistance of European courts and legislatures concerned to ensure the fruitful development of contract law on a Union-wide basis. Even beyond the borders of the European Union, the Principles may serve as an inspiration for the Central and Eastern European legislators who are in the course of reforming their laws of contract to meet the needs of a market economy."

[105] R.B. Schlesinger, Formation of Contracts, p.17，見陳隆修，《美國國際私法新理論》，台北，五南圖書公司，民國76年1月，初版，24、25頁。

件，均係指協議或合意（agreement）的存在，亦即兩人的當事人間一致同意的明白表示（manifestations of mutual assent）。契約事實上是否為雙方當事人所共同約定，我們依其明示（manifestations）而視其契約係雙方共同一致之約定。在所有法系裡，『同意』（assent）均可以文字或其他方式表。協議（agreement）是否可視為契約，有賴於法律的規定。倘法律認定協議係契約，則可循司法救濟（judicial relief）要求強制契約之履行；所有的法系均以不同的方式，試圖制定『救濟』的形式及要件，目的在使雙方當事人的正當期待能得到公正的救濟。[106]」於堅持「我們必須承認有事實上普遍性的衝突法（de facto universal conflicts law）的存在[107]」下，個人其時主張尊重交易能力相等之當事人訂立一合法契約之誠意」為有關契約法之主流價值[108]。個人其時即堅信於契約、侵權、親屬、及繼承等主要方面之法律，全世界大致上是有共通的主流價值存在的，並應直接以這些既存的主流價值為國際案件之依據。經過三十年這些當時被視為有爭議或不明顯的價值在許多方面已陸續突顯出來。其中最為明顯的自然是聯合國1989 Convention on the Rights of the Child的公開再次追認兒童最佳利益的普世價值[109]。這些個人早期所謂的主流價值，或者現在可直接稱為「全球化法學」。

---

[106] R. B. Schlesingger, Formation of Contracts, p.71，"The notion of 'contract' is common to all legal systems under consideration. At its fringes, the field of 'contract' may not be asked out in an identical manner in all legal systems; but as to its core, the meaning of the term is the same everywhere. In all legal systems under consideration, the first requirement of a 'contract', in the core meaning of the word, is the existence of an agreement, i.e., of manifestations of mutual assent on the part of two or more persons. Whether or not they are promissory in nature, these manifestations as a rule must be referable to each other. In all legal systems under consideration, assent may be manifested by words or in other ways. Whether an agreement is recognized as a contract, depends on rules of law. If it is so recognized, it will be enforced by judicial relief; all legal systems under consideration seek in various ways, so to fashion the form and conditions of such relief that the justified expectation of the parties are given effect." 見陳隆修，《美國國際私法新理論》，台北，五南圖書公司，民國76年1月，初版，219頁。

[107] 陳隆修，《美國國際私法新理論》，台北，五南圖書公司，民國76年1月，初版，219頁。

[108] 陳隆修，《美國國際私法新理論》，台北，五南圖書公司，民國76年1月，初版，224頁。

[109] 陳隆修、許兆慶、林恩瑋、李瑞生四人合著，《國際私法-管轄與選法理論之交錯》，台北，五南圖書公司，2009年3月，初版1刷，154～160頁中個人公開譴責台灣違背1989年公約31條保障兒童休息、休閒、遊戲、及娛樂之權利，至今仍未得到應有之回應。個人對這種野蠻的社會風俗甚為反對，這可能是所有東北亞之問題與罪惡。

八、實體法原則

　　於契約方面最為突顯的自然是軟性的歐盟契約法規則及2004 Unidroit Principles of International Commercial Contracts 之成立。前者是引用硬性的the United Nations Convention on Contracts for the International Sale of Goods of 1980 (CISG)，而後者是引用前者，故而兩個軟性原則有著相似性。三十年前或許由於個人無法精準的闡釋主流價值的概念，恩師Prof. Hartley以沈重的心情告之甚多資深同僚無法接受實體法論，有位望重士林「前輩」的認為個人「是瘋狂的，應被送回台灣」。但個人三十多年來從未對實體法論有過絲毫的懷疑。現今於多年後這兩個軟性原則遠較硬性的CISG完備，或許以他們的相似度亦可於大致上構成契約法上的共同核心主流價值。歐盟契約法委員會將歐盟契約法原則設定之目的是同時可以適用於國內及國際案件[110]上，自認為是現代版之lex mercatoria[111]，並且希望被引用為全世界貿易之準據法[112]。歐盟契約法原則於國際私法上最大的優點，可能是在其自己號稱能融和大陸法與英美法於法律哲學上之不同[113]。

　　對於歐盟契約法原則上述之功能，例如做為國際貿易契約之基本原則、當事人所約定之準據法、做為被約定適用的一般法律原則或lex mercatoria、當事人未約定準據法時得作為被適用之法律、解釋或補充國際上

---

[110] Lando and Beale, Introduction (3), "But while the Principles will be found particularly useful in international trade transactions within Europe, they are not confined to such transactions and may be applied equally to purely domestic contracts."

[111] Id, Introduction 2 (C).

[112] Id, Introduction (2) (B)，The Principles will be useful for parties who are living or carrying on business in different States and who wish their contractual relations to be governed by a set of neutral rules not based on any one national legal system but drawing on the best solutions offered by the laws of jurisdictions within (and sometimes outside) Europe. They can declare that the contract is to be governed by the Principles of European Contract Law.

[113] Introduction (1) (E)，One of the major benefits offered by the Principles is to provide a bridge between the civil law and the common law by providing rules designed to reconcile their differing legal philosophies. 於有些技術性之規則，例如前述之時效問題，歐盟契約法原則的確是有建設性之功能。但個人以為英國契約法本著過時的資本主義，較為偏向自由放任原則，這一點似乎並未為歐盟契約法委員加以徹底的研究。如果對自由經濟所造成的不公不義不加以剖析，則註定無法成為契約法上長久的主流價值。

之統一法規、及解釋或補充國內法，UNIDROIT Principles（2004）的序言中對其目的皆有著同樣的規定[114]。故而歐盟委員會對羅馬 I 第3(2)條提議得以實體契約法原則為契約準據法，乃是一種順應潮流務實之作法。至於其所加上「若於原則或規則中並未規定，則應由其所之引為基礎的基本法理為依據」，或再其次由應為準據法之法為依據。或許於較早之CISG中會有此現象，以歐盟契約法原則之完備，或許較一般國家之契約法為完備，可能會發生這些狀況的情形或許會較以一般國家之法律為準據法之情況少。

　　歐盟委員會於羅馬 I 第3(2)條有關於原則或規則中沒有規定之提議，與CISG第7(2)條中之規定類似[115]。CISG於訂立時國際間尚有冷戰存在，有些第3世界形成一個不結盟之組織，而中國其時尚不是the International Commission for International Trade Law（UNCITRAL）之完全會員，故而各國意見岐異[116]。例如西方國家認為契約不必以書面，而社會主義國家則強烈要求（12、29、96條）；西方國家支持習慣之效力，而社會主義國家與第3世界則反對（7(1)、9(2)、25條）；有關買方於交貨後應於合理期間內通知貨品之瑕疵及未為通知之後果，工業化國家與發展中國家有著不同之看法（16、68條）；對於價格的確認是否為買賣契約成立之先決要件，西方國家又與社會主義國家及第3世界有不同的看法（28、55

---

[114] Unidroit Principles of International Commercial Contracts 2004
Preamble (Purpose of the Principles)
These Principles set forth general rules for international commercial contracts.
They shall be applied when the parties have agreed that their contract be governed by them.
They may be applied when the parties have agreed that their contract be governed by general principles of law, the lex mercatoria or the like.
The may be applied when the parties have not chosen any law to govern their contract.
They may be used to interpret or supplement international uniform law instruments.
They may be used to interpret or supplement domestic law.

[115] (2) Question concerning matters governed by this Convention which are not expressly settled in it are to be settled in conformity with the general principles on which it is based or, in the absence of such principles, in conformity with the law applicable by virtue of the rules of private international law. UNCITRAL於2007已公開認可2004 UNIDROIT principles，並認為該7 (2)條可由2004 UNIROIT principles 來加以補充解釋。

[116] Michale Joachim Bonell* The CISG, European Contract Law and the Development of a World Contract Law 56 Am. J. Comp. L. 1, 2, 3 (2008)。

條）；最後回教國家又對欠款之課徵利息加以強烈之反對[117]。這些問題個人以為真正構成美國選法規則上所謂「政策的真衝突」。CISG並未解決這些真衝突，通常其於主要規則後會再加上一個同樣寬廣的例外規則，亦即其基本上是於個案上給予訂約國兩個選擇，視情形而做決定。**於CISG這種號稱國際統一的貿易法規上，在第一世界與第三世界上述的真衝突中，選法規則是故意模糊的，真正決勝點是在於管轄法院的確認，以便適用法院地的法律原則。這亦是海牙2005年法院選擇公約對三世界而言特別重要之處。**

但Prof. Bonell仍認為：「整體而言於國際買賣契約上，CISG無疑的提供一個最有價值及相當創新的法律制度。[118]」首先相對於相關部門的國內法，它對契約法的基本重要部份加以規範，如契約成立與解釋、契約履行的暫停、契約違背的預期、及損害賠償及不履行契約之理由；另外它又規定了一些其時大部份國內法所沒有之法規[119]。International Institute for the Unification of Private law （UNIDROIT）基於CISG之經驗重新再建立（retate）國際契約法，因此訂立了非拘束性的軟性UNIDROIT principles[120]。UNIDROIT principles並不侷限於買賣契約，而是及於所有之商業契約。該原則不但為蘇聯及一些大陸法系國家所引用，英美法系國家如

---

[117] Gyula Eorsy, A Propos the 1980 Vienna Convention on Contracts for the Internationa Sale of Goods, in 31 Am. J. Comp. L. 333 et seq. (1983).

[118] Bonell, 56 Am. J. Comp. L. 4 (2008)。"Still, on the whole there can be no doubt that the CISG provides a most valuable and fairly innovative normative regime for international sales contracts."

[119] 同上，"There are also several provisions which were virtually unknown at the time to most, if not all, traditional domestic sales laws: mention may be made of the substantially unitary approach to the different cases of non-performance by both seller and buyer and to the respective remedies; the seller's right to cure defects in its performance not only up to the date of delivery but even thereafter, provided that it can do so without unreasonable delay and without causing the buyer unreasonable inconvenience, and the passing of the risk of loss of, the goods which was separated from the passing of 'property rights' in the goods and instead linked to their 'delivery,' etc."

[120] 該原則已於UNCITRAL 2007年40次大會被認可，Report of the United Nations Commission on International Trade Law on the work of its fortieth session, Vienna, 25 June – 12 July 2007 (A/62/17 Part I), PP 209-13.第3版的新增原則正在進行中，其中包含合法性，多數債權人與債務人，正當理由下結束長期契約等。

澳洲[121]、紐西蘭[122]、及英國[123]等，亦於一些基本契約上之特定問題有引用該原則之趨勢。

但是CISG及UNIDROIT principles都是侷限於買賣或商業契約上，即使是歐盟契約法原則或修正中之共同參考架構（CFR）亦都會被質疑是否只可適用於商業對商業或商業對消費者之契約上。但如同去年個人對2005年海牙選擇法院公約之質疑一般，小生意人並未充份具有保護自己之能力，或許這樣嚴格區分並非通常是恰當的[124]。但是無疑的歐盟的the Directive of the 1999 on Certain Aspects of the Sale of Consumer Goods and Associated Guarantees[125]及 the 1993 Directive on Unfair Terms in Consumer Contracts[126]對弱勢之消費者給予其應有之保護。例如賣方對產品之品質與履行應依廣告或包裝而負責[127]；買方對不履行契約所行使之救濟權並不須通知賣方[128]；買方雖通常應證明貨品於交貨時之瑕疵，但於六個月內之明顯瑕疵推定於交貨時即已存在[129]；最後之賣方如果因同一連鎖契約中之前賣方或製造人之行為或過失，而對消費者應負起契約不履行之責任時，得對前賣方或製造人提起救濟[130]；及於賣方或製造人提供超過應適用之國內法給予消費者之救濟時，這種契約上之保證於內容及形式皆須

---

[121] Hughes Aircraft Systems International v. Airservices Australia, in 146 Australian Law Reports (1998), 1 (per Finn J); GEC Marconi Pty Ltd. V. BHP Information Technology Pty Ltd. And Others), in 128 Federal Court Reports (2003) 1 (per Finn J).

[122] Hideo Yoshimoto v. Canterbury Golf International Limited, in [2001] 1 New Zealand Law Reports, 253 (per Thomas J).

[123] Proforce Recruit Limited v. The Rugby Group Limited, in [2006] EWCA Civ 69 (per Arden L J); The Square Mile Partnership Ltd v. Fitzmaurice McCall Ltd (per Arden L J), in [2006] EWCA Civ 1690). Michael Joachim Bonell, The UNIDROIT Principles and CISG Sources of Inspiration for English Courts?, Uniform L. Rev. 305 (2006).

[124] Bonell, 56 Am. J. Comp. L. 1, 18 (2008)., 對於原則中之「警察條款」，其評論如下：''These provisions reject the widespread belief that business people are always professionals who have equal experience and who always act fairly.''

[125] Council Directive 1999/44/EC, 1999 O.J. (L 171) 12 (EC)（以下稱Consumer Sales Directive）。

[126] Council Directive 93/13/EEC, 1993 O.J. (L 095) 29 (EC)（以下稱Unfair Terms Directive）。

[127] Consumer Sales Directive art. 2(2)(d).

[128] Consumer Sales Directive art. 5(2).

[129] Consumer Sales Directive art. 5(3).

[130] Consumer Sales Directive art. 4, 交予國內法去決定請求之對象及範圍。

符合規定[131]。歐盟的Comsumer Sales Directive及Unfair Term Directive或許於許多方面是世界上有關消費者保護最優良法律之一，它們不但應為歐盟羅馬Ⅰ第3 (4)及9條之強行法，而且或許應為全世界國際貿易上之強行法[132]。

　　無論是主要之貿易者或中小企業可能於許多不同情形下會選擇去避開國內法，而寧願去依據一個較為中立的跨國性法律制度[133]。International Chamber of Commerce （ICC）或International Trade Center （ITC）/ UNCTAD/WTO等國際性紛爭解決機構，於實務上已經以法律原則做為契約準據法（或與其他國內法、商業原則、或習慣相互配合為準據法）。如果羅馬Ⅰ 3(1)條不能公開的支持當事人得自由選定國際上認可之法律原則做為準據法時，那麼有可能同一事件於仲裁庭或法院所採用之準據法會不同。歐盟一向將法律之統一視為最高目標，但依1985UNCITRAL Model Law on the International Commercial Arbitration 第16(3)條當事人對仲裁庭管轄權之認定得請求法院救濟，有些國家（如英國）於特定情形下當事人亦得請求法院救濟，如此一來仲裁庭與法院所適用之準據法於理論上是有可能不一致的。

　　歐盟委員會對羅馬Ⅰ第3(2)條提議之解釋報告認為以UNIDROIT principles、歐盟契約法原則、或歐盟將來有可能的其他法律為準據法，可以同時排除不精確的lex mercatoria或國際上尚未認可的私人法典的適用[134]。歐盟委員會3(2)條之第2句又小心翼翼的加上於這些原則沒有規定

---

[131] Consumer Sales Directive art. 6.

[132] Bonell, 56 Am. J. Comp. 6. 1, 16 (2008), "Likewise, the idea of a specifically European lex mercatoria, as opposed to the international lex mercatoria or lex mercatoria tout court, seems rather awkward." KlausPeter Berger, European Private Law, Lex Mercatoria and Globalisation, in Towards a European Civil Code, 3rd ed. 43 at 55 (Arthur K. Harkamp et al. eds., 2004,) "There is no such thing as a 'European' lex mercatoria!(⋯) The lex mercatoria is not a regional but a truly global law.".

[133] Eckart Brodermann, The Growing Importance of the UNIDROIT Principles in Europe – A Review in Light of Market Needs, the Role of Law and the 2005 Rome I Proposal, Uniform L. Rev. 749, at 751 (2006).

[134] "the ⋯ words used would authorize the choice of the UNIDROIT Principles, the Principles of European Contract Law, or a possible future optional Community instrument, while excluding the lex mercatoria, which is not precise enough, or private codifications not adequately recognized by the international community ...."

時應以其所依據之基本法理為準據，或於再沒有之情形下則以羅馬 I 所規定之準據法為依據。事實上個人認同Prof. Bonell之意見，UNIDROIT principles及歐盟契約法原則的內容之品質及一致性於許多方面是超越許多國家之法律內容的[135]。個人去年以歐盟及英美之判例法來解析當事人選擇法院條款之成立與效力之問題時，發現英、美法院對這個國際私法之重要議題事實上是以實體法之內容來保護弱勢及主持正義（而歐盟則企圖以詳盡的形式要件來證明契約之成立）。只是大陸法及英國法認為契約之成立應依putative proper law之問題，美國同僚卻直接了當的視為契約效力之問題。另外更有趣的現象是－「歐盟法院認為形式要件的確認是事實問題，而2005年海牙公約的解釋報告似乎認為同意之確認是事實問題。[136]」至少於管轄條款之成立及效力問題，個人對歐盟及英美之實務案例曾以歐盟契約法原則加以評析[137]，個人其時非常訝異其效果之順利－如熱刀劃過奶油般的順利。不同於只能適用於商務契約的UNIDROIT principles，歐盟契約法原則對條款之成立及效力遠較國際私法的選法規則有著更詳盡規定，而且充滿著「誠信」、「合理」等彈性標準，故而遠較死硬的國際法選法規則能保護弱勢及主持公平正義。出書後經過一年之反覆思量，當時雖非常謹慎的以選法規則搭配歐盟契約法原則，以解析歐盟及英美案例，但顯然充滿彈性的歐盟契約法原則之適用性是遠超過死硬、粗糙的選法條款。直接適用歐盟契約法原則不但於保護弱勢主持正義上會有較好的效果，相對於混亂的選法規則，歐盟契約法原則於一致性（或法律統一性）之優勢上似乎是無庸致疑的。故而個人認為歐盟委員會3(2)條第2句之但

---

[135] Bonell, 56 Am. J. Comp. L. 1, 23, 24 (2008), 其引用Vischer 對於UNIDROIT principles之評語如下：''a codification of high quality and homogeneity in contents which in many respects even surpasses the quality of traditional national legal orders.''
Frank Vischer, The Relevance of the UNIDROIT Principles for Judges and Arbitrators in Disputes Arising out of International Contracts, 1 The Eur. J. of L. Reform 203, 211 (1998/1999).

[136] 陳隆修，《2005年海牙法院選擇公約評析》，台北，五南圖書公司，2009年1月，初版1刷，122頁。

[137] 陳隆修，《2005年海牙法院選擇公約評析》，台北，五南圖書公司，2009年1月，初版1刷，5～123頁。

書預備規則是多慮的,似乎並無明顯的需要。

九、引用之方式與選定準據法

但是因為擔心選定法律原則為準據法會較選定一個國家之國內法不穩定及無法預測,非常令人遺憾的歐盟委員會這個提議沒有被接受。或許於不得已之情形下為了配合時代潮流,羅馬 I 序言之要點13規定如下:「本規則並不禁止當事人以引用之方式將非國家組織之法律或國際公約加入契約。[138]」羅馬 I 沒有公開的接受歐盟委員會的建議,而以隱晦的語氣規定要點13。美國法律協會第2新編187條第1項的comment (c)對這種引用的方式特別解釋如下:「本項之規則是規定有關以引用之方式而加入契約,並且這並不是一個選法的規則。當事人通常是有權利去決定契約所約定之條款。他們得規定契約之條款。另外,他們得引用外面的資料以加入契約,尤其是得引用有些外國法之條款。於此種情形下,法院應適用被指定州法律之應適用條款,以便執行當事人之意思。[139]」英國法學對此種引用之方式早就有更清楚的判例[140],Cheshire & North如此寫著:「應仔細的分開明示會選擇準據法與於程序上完全不同的將一外國法之某些國內法條文引用進契約中,而使得這些條文變成契約條款,在判例法之規則下將他們是很重要的。[141]」依據Cheshire & North羅馬公約第3條只是有關準據

---

[138] (13) This Regulation does not preclude parties from incorporating by reference into their contract a non-State body of law or an international convention.

[139] "The rule of this Subsection is a rule providing for incorporation by reference and is not a rule of choice of law. The parties, generally speaking, have power to determine the terms of their contractual engagements. They may spell out these terms in the contract. In the alternative, they may incorporate into the contract by reference extrinsic material which may, among other things, be the provisions of some foreign law. In such instances, the forum will apply the applicable provisions of the law of the designated state in order to effectuate the intentions of the parties."

[140] The Stolt Sydness [1997] 1 Lloyd's Rep 273.

[141] P M North, JJ Fawcett, Cheshire and North's Private International Law, 13th ed., P.561, "Under the common law rules it was important to distinguish carefully the express selection of the proper law from the quite different process of the incorporation in the contract of certain domestic provisions of a foreign law, which thereupon became terms of the contract. The same distinction must be drawn under the Convention, for Article 3 is only concerned with selection of the applicable law." 又見14th ed., p.701。

法的選定[142]，故而與外國法條文的引用（incorporation）之規定是不一樣的。因為羅馬Ⅰ第3條於此方面之規定是與羅馬公約第3條相似的，故而依同樣的邏輯羅馬Ⅰ第3條亦應只是有關選擇準據法之規定，而非外國法條文之引用。以羅馬公約3(3)條及羅馬Ⅰ3(3)條前半段用語是有關選定一國之法律，而後半段是不得違反「一國之規則」（公約「rule of the law of that country」，規則「provision of the law of that other country」）而論，這個英美法式的區別應是正確的推論。對英國判例法而言，外國法條文的引用與準據法的適用是有著嚴格的區別，早期判例法上此類條款是以有關海上運送較多[143]。於實務上對這兩者適用之區別，個人早期曾經仔細的舉例加以特別的解釋[144]。外國法的被引用可以逐字全條被納入之方式，或以簡單的方式提及某方面之權利義務依該些條文亦可。

　　歐盟對於法律之解釋一向依據自主獨立之方式，或者歐盟法院對於外國法條文的被引用不願受英國判例法之拘束，而直接訴諸公約及規則3(1)

---

[142] 同上。又「引用」之方式通常必須以大黑字體明白的充分表示，見Shamil Bank of Bahrain v Beximco Pharmaceuticals Ltd [2004] EWCA Civ 19 at [48]-[52], [2004] 1 WLR 1784.

[143] 例如於海牙規則（Hague Rules），英國的Carriage of Goods By Sea Act 1924，或美國的Carriage of Goods By Sea Act 1936。

[144] 陳隆修，《國際私法契約評論》，台北，五南圖書公司，民國75年2月，初版，31，32頁，「當事人將某一外國法加入契約中做為契約之一部份（incorporation of foreign law）。例如美商銀行將美金貸款與臺電，契約於紐約簽訂，並請中央銀行於紐約做保證人。此時保證契約雖指明以紐約法為準據法，但該契約中之條款又明定中銀依據中國民法七四六條放棄中國民法七四五條先訴抗辯權之權利，或只籠統的申明中銀放棄中國民法上一切有關先訴抗辯權之權利時，則此自無不可。所應注意的是就算契約雖有訂定準據法，但他國法律則因被契約中之條款明白地引用，故已成為契約之一部份，在此種情形下就算於契約期間該他國法律雖有變更，但他國舊法律被契約引用之部份於契約中仍不應變更，蓋該部份之舊法律已成為契約中之條款。例如設中國民法修正後，有關先訴抗辯權部份已被修改，但該契約條款有關舊法律方面仍舊不應。又此借貸契約準據法雖為紐約法，但契約既明定中國民法七四五條，則有關此方面法律之解釋自應依中國法，而非依美國法。另外應注意的是此契約條款引用之他國法律與契約準據法不同的是前者為死的法律，後者為活的法律。亦即前者一經契約條款引用即為契約一部份，無論該他國法律如何變更永不更改，而後者只要準據法之國家變更法律，該準據法亦變更。換句話說，被引用為契約條款一部份之他國法律應永遠為被引用時之法律，而契約之準據法則隨著其本國法之修正而跟著。如於F. & W. Jabbour v. Custodion of Israeli Absentee Property中，一個契約之訂定地與契約之履行地皆為巴勒斯坦，巴勒斯坦之法律為準據法，英國法院判決由於『起訴時』巴勒斯坦已由以色列佔領，巴勒斯坦人原來的政權已瓦解，巴勒斯坦的新法律為以色列法，故契約之準據法為巴勒斯坦之以色列法。」[1954] 1 W. L. R. 139; [1954] 1 All E. R. 145 at p.157.又於Re Halbert Wagg & Co Leds Claim [1956] Ch. 323, 契約之準據法為德國法，當事人之義務由於契約訂定時與契約履行時中間法律有變更，故當事人之義務亦變更。

後段有關分割適用之規定亦有可能。但是或許更有可能的是，於國際商業發展的迫切需求下及為了避免與仲裁庭所適用之準據法發生衝突，歐盟法院可能將第3條當事人自由選法之權利儘量擴及國際上所認可的實體法原則，例如歐盟契約法原則及UNIDROIT principles.

十、合理性標準

歐盟委員會於羅馬 I 第3(2)條第2句不放心的附加上提議，在該些實體法原則沒有規定下則依該些原則所引為基礎之基本法理為依據。什麼是英美法與大陸法共同於契約法上「引為基礎之基本法理」？或許最為基本之法理於大陸法應是「誠實信用原則」[145]（「good faith test」），而於英美法則是「善意而合法」[146]（bona fide and legal）的要求。這些「誠信」及「善意而合法」之基本的要求，無論於英美法或大陸法於愈困難愈模糊而法律適用有困難之中間地帶，愈經常會被引為法條適用基礎之基本法理。例如UNIDROIT principles籌備會之主席Prof. Bonell很自豪的認為[147]：「另外而且更重要的，相對於CISG及其他國際性規則，他們對有關契約實質效力之問題完全並未加以處理，UNIDROIT principles卻有提供許多不同的契約或其個別條款上之『警察』條款以同時對抗程序上及實質上之不公平。下列的條款就足以說明這個情形，如標準格式中的突襲條款、過分的不平等、免責條款、及懲罰條款等。」

如果對Prof. Bonell所自豪的契約實質效力上之警察條款加以分析，

---

[145] 台灣民法148(2)條：「行使權利，履行義務，應依誠實及信用方法。」

[146] The Vita Food Products Inc. v. Unus shipping Co. Ltd. [1939] All E. R. 513, p.521，Lord Wright: "where there is an express statement by the parties of their intention to select the law of the contract, it is difficult to see what qualifications are possible, provided the intention expressed is bona fide and legal, and provided there is no reason for avoiding the choice on the ground of public policy."

[147] Bonell, 56 Am. J. Comp. L. 1, 18 (2008), "Moreover and most significantly, in contrast to the CISG and other international instruments which do not deal at all with questions concerning the substantive validity of contracts, the UNIDROIT Principles provide a variety of means for 'policing' the contract or its individual terms against both procedural and substantive unfairness. Suffice it to mention the provisions on surprising clauses contained in standard terms, gross disparity, exemption clauses, and penalty clauses."

則或許UNIDROIT principles所「引為基礎之基本法理」就會清楚浮現。
其2.1.20條第1項規定：「除非明白的為他方當事人所接受，標準格式契
約中帶有使得他方無法合理預測之性質的條款是無效的。[148]」3.10條規
定：「如果於訂約時，契約或契約條款給予一方當事人過分的利益，他方
當事人得要求該契約或條款為無效。於所有之考慮因素中應特別考慮，
(a)該一方當事人由他方當事人處取得不公平的利益是由於他方當事人之
無法獨立、經濟上之困難、或急迫之需要，或由於其輕率、無知、沒有經
驗、或缺乏議價之技巧，及(b)契約之性質與目的。(2)在得要求契約無效
之他方當事人之請求下，法院得修正契約或該條款使其符合公平交易中之
合理商業標準。(3)於受到無效通知之一方當事人之請求下，法院亦得修
正契約或該條款，但是該一方當事人必須於接受這個通知後即刻通知他方
當事人其之請求，並且必須於他方當事人合理的依賴該通知而有作為之
前。3.13(2)條之規定於此適用。[149]」7.1.6條規定：「於考慮契約之目的
下，一條款限制或排除一方當事人不履行之責任，或允許一方當事人去施
行與他方當事人合理之預期重大不同之履行時，如果因此會造成重大不公
平時不得主張該條款有效。[150]」7.4.13條規定。「(1)當契約規定一方當事

---

[148] Article 2.1.20 (Surprising terms)
  (1) No term contained in standard terms which is of such a character that the other party could not reasonably have expected it, is effective unless it has been expressly accepted by that party. 事實上個人認為標準格式契約中，對弱勢之保護應以「顯失公平」為依據，而不應以「可預測性」為依據。3.10條之目的與本條之目的並不完全相同。

[149] Article 3.10 (Gross disparity)
  (1) A party may avoid the contract or an individual term of it if, at the time of the conclusion of the contract, the contract or term unjustifiably gave the other party an excessive advantage. Regard is to be had, among other factors, to
    (a) the fact that the other party has taken unfair advantage of the first party's dependence, economic distress or urgent needs, or of its improvidence, ignorance, inexperience or lack of bargaining skill, and
    (b) the nature and purpose of the contract.
  (2) Upon the request of the party entitled to avoidance, a court may adapt the contract or term in order to make it accord with reasonable commercial standards of fair dealing.
  (3) A court may also adapt the contract or term upon the request of the party receiving notice of avoidance, provided that that party informs the other party of its request promptly after receiving such notice and before the other party has reasonably acted in reliance on it. The provisions of Article 3.13(2) apply accordingly.

[150] Article 7.1.6 (Exemption clauses)

人未履行義務時，為了此種未履行應給付受損之一方一定之金額，無論其
實際所受之損害為何受損之一方仍得取得該一定之金額。(2)但是相對於
由於不履行而引起之損害及其他之情形，該約定之一定金額是非常的超過
時，即使有相反的約定，該金額仍得被縮減至一定合理的數額。[151]」

　　這4個條款是Prof. Bonell很自豪的認為得於契約實質效力之問題上，
用以同時對抗程序上及實質上不公平的警察條款。我們可以發現於這4個
條款中同時出現的標準為對「合理性」的要求。或許如果更嚴苛一點而
言，於3.10條中它並非是最主要的標準，但於這4個條款中「合理性」之
標準為他們共通使用之標準則無可置疑。除了這4個有關商業契約實質效
力上極為重要之警察條款外，事實上整個UNIDROIT principles無論是於
重要的基本條文或者較為不是基本的條文中，「合理性」之要求經常被
引用為條文中各種測試（test）之標準。例如1.8條不一致行為之標準，
1.9條當事人間及國際貿易慣例之標準，2.1.12條書面承諾中包含額外附
加條款之效力，2.1.14條契約中空白條款之效力，2.1.18條契約更改或終
止之例外，2.1.20條標準格式契約效力之限制，2.2.5條無權代理之效力，
2.2.7條代理人與本人有利益衝突時之規定，2.2.8條代理人之指定次代
理，2.2.9條本人追認無權代理之效力，3.5條錯誤的效力（引用3次），
3.8條詐欺之效力，脅迫之效力，3.10條第3人之錯誤、詐欺、脅迫、及交
易能力不平等之效力，3.13條宣佈無效之權利之喪失，3.15條宣佈無效之
合理期限，3.16條部份無效之規定，4.1條契約之解釋，4.2條行為及意思
表達之解釋，4.8條契約條款缺失之補充，5.1.2條默示條款之定義，5.1.3

A clause which limits or excludes one party's liability for non-performance or which permits one party to render performance substantially different from what the other party reasonably expected may not be invoked if it would be grossly unfair to do so, having regard to the purpose of the contract.

[151] Article 7.4.13 (Agreed payment for non-performance)

(1) Where the contract provides that a party who does not perform is to pay a specified sum to the aggrieved party for such non-performance, the aggrieved party is entitled to that sum irrespective of its actual harm.

(2) However, notwithstanding any agreement to the contrary the specified sum may be reduced to a reasonable amount where it is grossly excessive in relation to the harm resulting from the non-performance and to the other circumstances.

條當事人之合作義務，5.1.4條當事人盡力履行之義務，5.1.6條義務履行之品質的標準，5.1.7條產品價格之決定（引用「4」次），5.1.8條無期限契約的終止，5.2.5條授予第3人權利之終止，6.1.1條履行義務之時間，6.1.12條數個債務之清償次序，6.1.16條無法取得公家許可時之終止契約之時效（2次），6.1.17條無法取得公家許可時契約之效力，6.2.2條契約之履行對不利之一方造成困難，6.2.3條契約履行對不利之一方造成困難之後果（2次），7.1.5條受損之一方給予他方延長之期限（3次），7.1.7條不可抗拒之困難（3次），7.2.2條非金錢債務之履行為不合法或不合理（3次），7.2.5條受損之一方得改變請求，7.3.1條受損一方終止契約之要件，7.3.2條終止契約之期限，7.3.4條要求如期履行之保證（2次），7.3.6條恢復原狀之請求，7.4.3條損害之確認，7.4.4條損害之可預測性，7.4.5條受損一方替代交易之損失（2次），7.4.6條受損一方依市價之求償權及其他之損害請求權，7.4.8條受損一方減少損害之義務（2次），8.4條被作為抵銷之義務之通知，9.1.12條權利轉讓之適當證據。故而除了第10章有關消滅時效沒有規定，第9章權利義務之轉讓及第8章抵銷各只有一條規定外，UNIDROIT principles之各章皆大量倚賴「合理性」之要求做為條文之標準。於5.1.7條有關商業契約之中心點「價格」上，更是不可思議的連續引用4次。另外於契約實務上可能容易引起爭議的困難部份則引用3次，例如3.5條錯誤的效力，7.1.5條受損之一方給予他方延長履行期限之情形，7.1.7條因不可抗拒之困難而不履行之情形，及7.2.2條非金錢債務之履行為不合法、不可能、或負擔過重之情形。該7.2.2條即為羅馬公約飽受爭議的第7條(1)項及現今之羅馬Ⅰ第9條，而對此個人二十多年前主張於人權法及契約法原則之規範下契約不得違反履行地法。

　　有關第10章消滅時效、第9章轉讓、及第8章抵銷之規定，早期英美法皆視為程序法或與程序法有關之事項。例如時效於英國加入歐盟前是視為程序法的[152]；而權利之轉讓與於訴訟程序上何者得為合適當事人有關，

---

[152] 見陳隆修，《比較國際私法》，台北，五南圖書公司，78年10月，初版，142～144頁。

故自然與程序法有關[153]；抵銷只是將兩個於實質上獨立之訴訟合併為一訴訟而已，傳統上英美法自然視其為程序法之問題[154]。故而其他有關契約義務於實質上之是否成立及其之效力與範圍，愈是基本或愈有爭議之部份，「合理性」之測試標準愈是被倚為重心。

對Prof. Bonell自豪的4個條款，或許個人可以擴張解釋如下：**有關契約的成立與否及其實質效力，UNIDROIT principles不但經常是以「合理性」的標準做為警察條款，以同時對抗契約或其條款於程序上及實質上之不公平，並且許多條款是引用其為基礎之基本法理**。如前述無論是於錯誤、詐欺、脅迫、當事人能力不平等、標準格式契約、慣例、空白條款、額外附加條款、及違反履行地法等，有關契約於基本上成立與否及效力之問題，經常於關鍵性之問題上採用合理性之標準。UNIDROIT principles中亦經常採用大陸法慣用之誠信原則及比例原則，但其被引用之次數遠低於合理性標準之被引用次數。若以實體法論之觀點而言，合理性、誠信原則、及比例原則所代表的皆為契約法之共同核心，這些基本原則差異性並不是甚大。

歐盟委員會羅馬 I 3(2)第2句之提議及CISG 7(2)條之規定亦被規定

Huber v. Steiner　　　　　　　　(1835) 2 Bing. N. C. 202.
British Linene Co. V. Drummond　(1830) 10 B. & C. 903.
Harris v. Ouine　　　　　　　　(1869) L. R. 4 Q. B. 653.

[153] 同前註，144~148頁，「即使原告依法院地之程序法為一合適之當事人，其自然仍須依系爭法律關係之準據法（lex causae）為有權利之人方可。但又即使其為有權利之人，法院地法或準據法有時會規定其不得以自己之名義起訴，而須以他人之名義起訴，或不得單獨以自己之名義起訴，而須共同與他人提起訴訟。此情形，一般以債權（choses in action）之轉讓最常發生，而依英國法債權不得轉讓（須另以契約為之）。英法院對於此方面之法規是否為程序法抑實體法，似尚無絕對之看法。但一般英國學者皆贊同將之定性為實體法，認為承認及引用此方面之外國法規，將不會增加英國法院程序上之困難。」O'Callaghan v. thomond (1810) 3 Taunt. 82.

[154] 陳隆修，《比較國際私法》，台北，五南圖書公司，78年10月，初版，154、155頁，「抵銷之法律行為依大陸法一般為實體上之問題，然依英美法一般為程序上之問題。因為英美法認為抵銷實質上為兩個訴訟，只是將其併合為一訴訟而已，被請求申請抵銷之程序若依英國法被拒絕，其只須再提起另一獨立訴訟。故英國法院認為抵銷係法院給予當事人便利，以避免重覆訴訟，而與原訴訟無關，故為一程序上之問題。一請求權是否可經由反訴而被提起，亦基於同樣地理由而被認為程序上之問題，由法院地法決定。」Marfarline v. Norris (1862) 2 B. & S. 783; Holmes v. Kidd (1858) 3 H. & N. 891; South African Republic v. Companie FrancoBelge du Chemin de Fer du Nord [1897] 2 ch. 487 (C.A.).

於歐盟契約法原則1：106條2項[155]，應注意的是CISG第7條1項亦為歐盟契約法原則1：106條1項所引用。CISG 7(1)條規定：「於解釋本公約時，應注意到其國際性質，及其適用時促進統一性之需求，及國際貿易上誠信原則之遵守。[156]」故而CISG 7(1)條所明文強調的是統一性及誠信原則，而歐盟契約法原則1：106(1)條所強調的除了統一性及穩定性外，亦是誠信及公平交易原則[157]。歐盟契約法原則於1：201條對誠信原則之強制性規定如下：「(1)訂約當事人應遵守誠實信用及公平交易原則。(2)當事人不得排除或限制此責任。[158]」其解釋之註(1)說明如下：「於所有之會員國，誠信及公平交易原則是被認可的，或至少於契約行為上看起來是以準則之方式而被適用。但是於各法律制度中對該原則深入之強度及廣泛性是有著相當大的差異。於光譜的一端所代表的制度是該原則改革了契約法（及其他部份的法律）並且增加了該制度獨特的特徵（德國）。於另一端我們發現有些制度並不承認當事人必須遵守誠信原則之基本義務，但卻於許多案例中以明確之規則去達成許多其他制度經由誠信原則所達成的結果（英國及愛爾蘭）。[159]」對於英國沒有「誠信原則」的明文規定，但是於判例

---

[155] (2) Issues within the scope of these Principles but not expressly settled by them are so far as possible to be settled in accordance with the ideas underlying the Principles. Failing this, the legal system applicable by virtue of the rules of private international law is to be applied.有趣的是1985 UNCITRAL Model Law on International Commercial Arbitration 於2006的增訂條文中，亦將CISG 第7條納入如下： Article 2 A. International origin and general principles (As adopted by the Commission at its thirty-ninth,ression, in 2006)
(I) In the interpretation of this Law, regard is to be had to its international origin and to the need to promote unifonnity in its application and the obsewance of good faith.
(2) Questions concerning matters governed by this Law which are not expressly settled in it are to be settled in conformity with the general Principles on which this Law is based.

[156] (1) In the interpretation of this Convention, regard is to be had to its international character and to the need to promote uniformity in its application and the observance of good faith in international trade.

[157] (1) These Principles should be interpreted and developed in accordance with their purposes. In particular, regard should be had to the need to promote good faith and fair dealing, certainty in contractual relationships and uniformity of application.

[158] **Article 1:201: Good Faith and Fair Dealing**
(1) Each party must act in accordance with good faith and fair dealing.
(2) The parties may not exclude or limit this duty.

[159] The commission of European Contract Law, Principles of European Contract Law, edited by Ole Landoand Hugh Beale (2000), pp.116, 117, "the principle of good faith and fair dealing is recognized, or at least appears to be acted on as a guideline for contractual behaviour, in all Member States. There

法上卻有類似之主張，個人二十多年於討論規避法律時即有類似之論述，當時即引用著名之Vita Food[160]而作如此之論述：「英國沒有禁止規避法律之判例，但正如成文法國家的誠信原則（good faith test），英美法亦有要求契約必須合理（reasonableness test）的規定，故於Vita Food中，Lord Wright認為當事人所選定的準據法必須是有誠意的（bona fide and legal）。」個人認為誠信原則、合理性、誠意且合法、及比例原則，這些都是契約法上各國所經常「引以為基礎的基本法理」，或許它們皆是各國契約法上的共同核心。但是無可置疑的，各國或甚至同一國家間不同的法院，引用這些共同核心的強度與廣泛度是可能不一致的。

「合理性」既然為UNIDROIT principles所最常引用，而「誠信原則」又不為英國判例法所明示引用，故而以「合理性」之要求做為這個契約法的共同核心之「代表」或許爭議性較少。合理性及不合理性亦為歐盟契約法則所大量引用。對在最初的9章中歐盟契約法委員會為了顯示出合理性及不合理性之大量的被引用，於1：302條之註釋中特別逐條標示出

is, however, a considerable difference between the legal systems as to how extensive and how powerful the penetration of the principle has been. At the one end of the spectrum figures a system where the principle has revolutionized the contract law (and other parts of the law as well) and added a special feature to the style of that system (GERMANY). At the other end we find systems which do not recognize a general obligation of the parties to conform to good faith, but which in many cases by specific rules reach the results which the other systems have reached by the principle of good faith (ENGLAND and IRELAND)" 另外在其note (3)中引用數個判例法以解釋此現象: "the judgment of Bingham L.J. in Interfoto Picture Library Ltd. v. Stilletto Visual Programmes Ltd. [1989] Q.B. 433 (C.A.); but contrast Walford v. Miles [1992] 2 A.C. 208(H.L.). For example, the courts have on occasion limited the right of a party who is the victim of s slight breach of contract to terminate the contract on that ground when the real motive appears to be to escape a bad bargain: see Hoenig v. Isaacs [1952] 2 All E.R. 176 (C.A.), and Hong Kong Fir Shipping Co Ltd. v. Kawasaki Kisen Kaisha Ltd. [1962] 2 Q.B. 26 (C.A.). Conversely, the victim of a wrongful repudiation is not permitted to ignore the repudiation, complete his own performance and claim the contract price from the repudiating party, unless the victim has a legitimate interest in doing so: see Attica Sea Carriers Corp. v. Ferrostaal Poseidon Bulk Reederei Gmbh [1976] 1 Lloyd's Rep. 250 (C.A.). There are many examples of the courts interpreting the terms of a contract in such a way as to prevent one party using a clause in circumstances in which it was probably not intended to apply. The clearest examples of this occur in relation to clauses excluding or limiting liability...but other terms have been construed similarly: see for example Carr v. JA Beriman Pty Ltd. (1953) 27 A. L. J. R. 273 (High Court of Australia), where it was held that an architect under a construction contract could not exercise a power to order work to be omitted simply in order to give the same work to another contractor who was prepared to do it for less"

[160] [1939] 1A 11 E.R. 513 at p.521.

其之一再被重覆引用[161]。正如Unidroit principles之8、9、及10章一般，歐盟契約法原則的新增後8章中除了於15、16章外，大多於早期英國法中與程序上之規則有些關連，故合理性之規定甚少[162]。15章為契約合法性之規定，15：103及15：104條皆有合理性之要求；16章為契約條件之規定，16：102條中有著誠信及公平交易原則之要求。歐盟契約法委員會認為於認定合理性時，包含契約之性質及目的在內之一切相關因素皆應被加以考慮；個案的情形應被加以考慮；尤其是每種貿易或職業之習慣或行為皆應被加以考慮[163]。「合理性」之標準對歐盟契約法原則既然這麼重要，其於1：302條中則加以明文規定如下：「於這些原則下，合理性應被認定為依據有誠信的人之行為及當事人會認為合理之相同情況下之標準。特別是，於評量合理性時應考慮及所牽連之契約之性質及目的，案件之情

---

[161] A. The terms 'reasonable' and 'unreasonable' in the Principles
　　(i) 'Reasonable'
　　　In these Principles the term reasonable is used to express various requirements for example:
　　　What may one expect a party to know or to take into account? Articles 1:303(4), 2:102, 2:202(3), 3:201(3), 3:206, 3:209(3), 6:111(2)(a), 8:103(2), 8:108(1) and 9:503.
　　　How long may a party wait to act? Article 2:206(2) and (3), 3:203, 7:109(2), 7:102(3), 8:106(3), 8:105(2), 8:108(3), 9:303(2) and (3) and 9:506.
　　　How long may the parties take to reach agreement? Article 6:111(3).
　　　How long should the notice be? Articles 4:113(1) and (2), 6:109 and 8:104(3).
　　　Is a price or a term equitable? Articles 4:105(3), 4:115, 6:104, 6:105, 6:106(2), 7:110(2)(a) and (b), 9:101(2)(a), 9:506 and 9:509(2).
　　　Which efforts can one expect a party to make? Article 7:110(1), 9:102(2)(d) and 9:505(1).
　　　Is there a proportionate relationship between value and effort? Article 7:110(3).
　　　Is there a proportionate relationship between the seriousness of the non-performance and the remedy exercised? Article 9:201(1).
　　　How great is the likelihood of a future contingency? Article 1:303(2), 8:105(1) and 9:501(2)(b).
　　　See also Article 6:108.
　　(ii) 'Unreasonable'
　　　The term unreasonable is used:
　　　To explain how great a nuisance a party must suffer from the other party's behaviour: Article 7:103.
　　　What constitutes an unconscionable usage or an unreasonable term: Articles 1:105(2), 6:105, and 6:106(2).
　　　Whether there is a proportionate relationship between value and cost (unreasonably expensive): Article 7:110(1).
　　　What constitutes an unreasonable omission? Article 9:303(3)(b).
　　　What makes the burden upon the party too great: Article 9:101(2)(b) and 9:102(2)(b).
[162] 第10～17章之規定，見Principles of European Contract Lqaw (Part Ⅲ), prepared by The commission on European Contract Law, edited by Ole Lando, Eric Clive, Andre Prum and Reinhard Zimmermann
[163] Lando and Beale, p.127, Comment B.

形，貿易或職業之習慣及行為。[164]」用「誠實信用」來解釋合理性是可以
被接受的，但用「合理」來解釋「合理性」只能顯示「合理性」的不可或
缺。

　　雖然不用誠信原則，但英國的Unfair Contract Terms Act 1977中大量
的引用「合理性的要求」（the requirements of reasonableness）及「公
平及合理」（fair and reasonable）做為標準（test），故而其於schedule
2中特別規定「合理性適用之準則」如下：「特別是有關6(3)、7(3)及
(4)、20、及21條之目的下之問題，下列因素是應有關連的－(a)當事人間
相較下其議價能力，（於所有之其他考慮中）應尤其考慮顧客需求之替代
方法是否可以達成；(b)是否顧客曾經受到誘導而同意訂立條款，或於接
受該條款前其有著機會去於不同條款下與他人訂立相同契約；(c)是否顧
客知道或應合理的知道該條款之存在及範圍（於許多事情中尤其應考慮到
該行業之慣例及當事人間訂約前之行為）；(d)當條款排除或限制若條件
未被履行之相關責任時，應考慮於訂約時對該條件之履行視為合乎實際之
期待是否為合理；(e)是否該產品之生產、處理、或修改符合顧客之特別
指示。[165]」無論是歐盟契約法原則1：302條，或英國及蘇格蘭於1977 Un-

---

[164] Article 1:302: Reasonableness

Under these Principles reasonableness is to be judged by what persons acting in good faith and in the
same situation as the parties would consider to be reasonable. In particular, in assessing what is reasonable the nature and purpose of the contract, the circumstances of the case and the usages and practices
of the trades or professions involved should be taken into account.

[165] SCHEDULE 2

"Guidelines" for Application of Reasonableness Test

A

The matters to which regard is to be had in particular for the purposes of sections 6(3), 7(3) and (4),
20and 21 are any of the following which appear to be relevant –

(a) the strength of the bargaining positions of the parties relative to each other, taking into account
(among other things) alternative means by which the customer's requirements could have been met;

(b) whether the customer received an inducement to agree to the term, or in accepting it had an opportunity of entering into a similar contract with other persons, but without having a similar term;

(c) whether the customer knew or ought reasonably to have known of the existence and the extent of the
term (having regard, among other things, to any custom of the trade and any previous course of dealing between the parties);

(d) where the term excludes or restricts any relevant liability if some condition was not complied with,
whether it was reasonable at the time of the contract expect that compliance with that condition
would be practicable;

fair contract Term Acts對「合理性要求」之標準，這三個文明法系對「合理性」之規定或解釋都須以「合理」為「引為基礎的基本法理」。故而若於國際上所認可的實體契約法規則及原則沒有規定時（gap），以「合理性」做為該些實體契約法「引為基礎的基本法理」，於許多情形下或許應是可被接受的。

　　大陸法所偏重的誠信原則及英美法所偏重的合理性標準，無可置疑的皆為實質的契約法之共同核心，而屬於英美法的美國自然是較偏重合理性之要求。例如第2新編187(2)(a)中即規定若「被選定之州與當事人或交易沒有重大關係並且當事人之選擇並無其他合理之基礎」時，該選法即不能被適用。2004年修正版之U.C.C.自然亦常引用合理性之標準，但其亦有引用誠信原則做為標準，例如1-304條及1-302(b)條。依照前述之其他國際慣例，U.C.C.自然不能免俗的以「合理」來解釋「合理性」，1-302(b)

(e) whether the goods were manufactured, processed or adapted to the special order of the customer.

對1977 Unfair contract Terms Act大陸法的蘇格蘭之修正案Part II對合理性之標準規定如下：

24 The "reasonableness" test

(1) In determining for the purposes of this Part of this Act whether it was fair and reasonable to incorporate a term in a contract, regard shall be had only to the circumstances which were, or ought reasonably to have been, known to or in the contemplation of the parties to the contract at the time the contract was made.

(2) In determining for the purposes of section 20 or 21 of this Act whether it was fair and reasonable to incorporate a term in a contract, regard shall be had in particular to the matters specified in Schedule 2 to this Act; but this subsection shall not prevent a court or arbiter from holding, in accordance with any rule of law, that a term which purports to exclude or restrict any relevant liability is not a term of the contract.

[F1(2A) In determining for the purposes of this Part of this Act whether it is fair and reasonable to allow reliance on a provision of a notice (not being a notice having contractual effect), regard shall be had to all the circumstances obtaining when the liability arose or (but for the provision) would have arisen.]

(3) Where a term in a contract [F2or a provision of a notice] purports to restrict liability to a specified sum of money, and the question arises for the purposes of this Part of this Act whether it was fair and reasonable to incorporate the term in the contract [F2or whether it is fair and reasonable to allow reliance on the provision], then, without prejudice to subsection (2) above [F2in the case of a term in a contract], regard shall be had in particular to –

(a) the resources which the party seeking to rely on that term [F2or provision] could expect to be available to him for the purpose of meeting the liability should it arise;

(b) how far it was open to that party to cover himself by insurance.

(4) The onus of proving that it was fair and reasonable to incorporate a term in a contract [F3or that it is fair and reasonable to allow reliance on a provision of a notice] shall lie on the party so contending.

規定：「統一商法所規定之誠信、勤奮、合理性、及應注意性之義務不能依協議而被拋棄。當事人得依協議而決定這些義務被履行之標準，但這些標準不能明顯的不合理。當本法要求一行為於一合理時間內被實施時，當事人得經由協議而決定該時間，但該時間不能明顯的不合理。[166]」但更為有趣的是U.C.C.雖然1-304條採用大陸法式之誠信原則，但無論是於第1條總則或第2條買賣，其於定義性條文中對誠信原則的解釋都是本著合理性而來。1-201(b)（20）條規定：「除了第5條之另外規定外，『誠信原則』即為於實際上之誠實及遵守公平交易之合理商業標準。[167]」故而以目前國際上之立法例而言，無論是誠信原則或合理性之要求，通常以「合理性」為基本之法理似乎是較能廣泛的被接受。

「誠信原則」顧名思義似乎是一個較為主觀之標準而「合理性之要求」由表面上而言似乎是個較為客觀之標準，這情形或許如早期英國於推定契約準據法之主觀說及客觀說一般。主觀說表面上較能尊重當事人訂定合法契約之意願，似較能維護契約之本質；但客觀說較為注重客觀上交易行為之事實情況，法官較為容易推定準據法[168]。個人早期是認為法院可能會以客觀之事實來推定當事人主觀之意識[169]，「誠信原則」與「合理性」亦可能是契約法共同核心之一體兩面。

---

[166] (b) The obligations of good faith, diligence, reasonableness, and care prescribed by [the Uniform Commercial Code] may not be disclaimed by agreement. The parties, by agreement, may determine the standards by which the performance of those obligations is to be measured if those standards are not manifestly unreasonable. Whenever [the Uniform Commercial Code] requires an action to be taken within a reasonable time, a time that is not manifestly unreasonable may be fixed by agreement.

[167] (20) "Good faith," except as otherwise provided in Article 5, means honesty in fact and the observance of reasonable commercial standards of fair dealing. 而2-103 (1) (b)亦大致上遵循此一定義：(j) "Good faith" means honesty in fact and the observance of reasonable commercial standards of fair dealing.

[168] 陳隆修，《國際私法契約評論》，台北，五南圖書公司，民國75年2月，初版，23頁。歐盟契約法原則1:201條comment E認為誠信原則是「心中之誠實與公平，這些是主觀之概念。」Lando and Beale, p.115, "'Good faith' means honesty and fairness in mind, which are subjective concepts."另外comment A對「誠信與公平交易」原則之可以成為歐盟契約法原則「引為基礎之基本法理」陳述如下：「本條文之規定為一貫穿整個契約法原則之基本原則。當事人之契約責任於成立、履行、及執行上誠信及公平交易原則是應被遵守的，同樣的當事人在行使契約上權利時亦應遵守此原則。"This Article sets forth a basic principle running through the Principles. Good faith and fair dealing are required in the formation, performance and enforcement of the partie's duties under a contract, and equally in the exercise of a party's rights under the contract" p.113。

[169] 同上，24頁。

　　個人認為「誠信原則」、「合理性」、甚至「比例原則」不但通常可為契約法於實體上及國際私之共同核心，而且或許亦應為憲法及刑法等其他法共同核心價值[170]。這些概念不但於各種法學上是可被引為基礎的基

---

[170] 事實上在管轄權上亦是以「合理性」為基礎，見the American Law Institute之Restatement (Second) of Conflict of Laws §24 (1988 Revision)。

　　§24. Principle Underlying Judicial Jurisdiction Over Persons

(1) A state has power to exercise judicial jurisdiction over a person if the person's relationship to the state is such as to make the exercise of such jurisdiction reasonable.

(2) The relationships which are sufficient to support an exercise of judicial jurisdiction over a person are stated in §§27-52. 又見Restatement of the Law, Third, Foreign Relations Law of the United States, §403(1987)

　　§403 Limitations on Jurisdiction to Prescribe

(1) Even when one of the bases for jurisdiction under §402 is present, a state may not exercise jurisdiction to prescribe law with respect to a person or activity having connections with another state when the exercise of such jurisdiction is unreasonable.

(2) Whether exercise of jurisdiction over a person or activity is unreasonable is determined by evaluating all relevant factors, including, where appropriate:

　　(a) the link of the activity to the territory of the regulating state, i.e., the extent to which the activity takes place within the territory, or has substantial, direct, and foreseeable effect upon or in the territory;

　　(b) the connections, such as nationality, residence, or economic activity, between the regulating state and the person principally responsible for the activity to be regulated, or between that state and those whom the regulation is designed to protect;

　　(c) the character of the activity to be regulated, the importance of regulation to the regulating state, the extent to which other states regulate such activities, and the degree to which the desirability of such regulation is generally accepted;

　　(d) the existence of justified expectations that might be protected or hurt by the regulation;

　　(e) the importance of the regulation to the international political, legal, or economic system;

　　(f) the extent to which the regulation is consistent with the traditions of the international system;

　　(g) the extent to which another state may have an interest in regulating the activity; and

　　(h) the likelihood of conflict with regulation by another state.

(3) When it would not be unreasonable for each of two states to exercise jurisdiction over a person or activity, but the prescriptions by the two states are in conflict, each state has an obligation to evaluate its own as well as the other state's interest in exercising jurisdiction, in light of all the relevant factors, Subsection (2); a state should defer to the other state if that state's interest is clearly greater.

Restatement (Third) of Foreign Relations Law of the United States S 421 (1987)

　　§421 Jurisdiction To Adjudicate

(1) A state may exercise jurisdiction through its courts to adjudicate with respect to a person or thing if the relationship of the state to the person or thing is such as to make the exercise of jurisdiction reasonable.

(2) In general, a state's exercise of jurisdiction to adjudicate with respect to a person or thing is reasonable if, at the time jurisdiction is asserted:

　　(a) the person or thing is present in the territory to the state, other than transitorily;

　　(b) the person, if a natural person, is domiciled in the state;

　　(c) tbe person, if a natural persoo, is resident in the state;

　　(d) the person, if a natural person, is a national of the state;

　　(e) the person, if a corporation or comparable juridical person, is organtzed pursuant to the law of

本法理，而且是程序法及實體法上對抗不公平的警察概念。如若對於案件事實基本上之誠信、合理、或比例之認知無法協調，那麼很可能採用任何實體法上或選法規則上之原則皆無法協調於這方面基本上之歧異。於此種基本觀念之大歧異下，歐盟委員會羅馬後3(2)條第2句之提議、CISG 7(2)條、及歐盟契約法原則1：106(2)條皆以選法規則所指定之國家（或制度）之法律為依據，個人並不以為這些法律可以於這種情形下解決這些歧異。有趣的是羅馬 I 序言要點14規定，設若歐盟有通過實體契約法規則，這些規則可以允許當事人去選為準據法[171]。

雖然對於誠信原則或合理性，各個不同之法律制度都試圖給予其精準之定義，但似乎至目前為止尚未完全成功。一百五十多年前Lord Granworth謂：「所謂住所，我們指家，即永久之家，假如你不懂你自己永久之家，那麼我覺得沒有任何其他之外國作者或外國語言之解釋，可以有效的幫助你了解這一點。」[172]或許同樣的：「假如你不懂誠信原則或合理性

---

the state;

   (f) a ship, aircraft or other vehicle to which the adjudication relates is registered under the laws of the state;

   (g) the person, whether natural or juridical, has consented to the exercise of jurisdiction;

   (h) the person, whether natural or juridical, regularly carries on business in the state;

   (i) the person, whether natural or juridical, had carried on activity in the state, but only in respect of such activity;

   (j) the person, whether natural or juridical, bad carried on outside the state an activity having a substantial, direct, and foreseeable effect within the state, but oily in respect of such activity; or

   (k) the thing that is the subject of adjudication is owned, possessed, or used in the state, but only in respect of a claim reasonably connected with that thing.

(3) A defense of lack of jurisdiction is generally waived by any appearance by or on behalf of a person or thing (whether as plaintiff, defendant, or third party), if the appearance is for a purpose that does not include a challenge to the exercise of jurisdiction.

另外ALI /UNIDROIT Principles of Transnational Civil Procedure (2004)第3條之註釋亦如此論述：P-3A The term "reasonable" is used throughout the Principles and signifies "proportional," "significant." "not excessive," or "fair," according to the context. It can also mean the opposite of arbitrary. The concept of reasonableness also precludes hyper-technical legal argument and leaves a range of discretion to the court to avoid severe, excessive, or unreasonable application of procedural norms.

[171] (14) Should the Community adopt, in an appropriate legal instrument, rules of substantive contract law, including standard terms and conditions, such instrument may provide that the parties may choose to apply those rules.

[172] "by domicile, we mean home, the permanent home, and if you do not understand your permanent home, I am afraid that no illustration drawn from foreign writers or foreign languages will very much help you to it". Whicker v. Hume (1858) 7 H. L. C. 124, 160.

基本上之大致意義，那麼我覺得沒有任何其他之外國作者或外國語言之解釋，可以有效的幫助你了解這一點。」

十一、默示準據法

　　至於當事人之選法自由，羅馬Ⅰ及羅馬公約皆允許當事人以默示之方式去選法。公約3(1)條規定：「該選擇必須為明示或由案件之情形或契約之條款可以顯示出合理之確定。」羅馬Ⅰ 3(1)條卻進一步的要求：「該選擇必須為明示或由案件之情形或契約之條款可以清楚的顯示。」雖然英國法務部之報告認為公約之立場於此點並非完全清楚，但其認同羅馬Ⅰ新條文的除去「不確定的因素」[173]。該法務部之報告似乎更為不清楚。新條文要求「清楚的顯示」比起公約要求「合理之確定」，似乎不僅是除去「不確定的因素」而已，更似乎有著較為嚴格之要求。如前述個人認為歐盟不應僅只於對默示選法有著更嚴格之要求而已，應如美國般將默示選法之地位降至幾乎不存在之地位。

　　在英國一般認為於當事人沒有明示準據法時，並且不能由案件之情形認定當事人默示之意思時，契約應由與交易有著最密切及真實關係之制度之法律為依據[174]。於當事人沒有明示選法時，通常是由契約的性質、

---

[173] Ministry of Justice
Romel – Should the UK opt in?
Consultation Paper CP05/08, para. 45,
It is now deemed sufficient if the choice is clearly demonstrated by the parties by reference to the terms of the contract or the circumstances of the case. Clarity as regards the additional flexibility available to parties is useful and reflects commercial practice in some instances. The current position under the Convention is not entirely clear on this point. The position under UK law, deriving from the Convention, is satisfactory in that Article 3 merely requires that a choice be demonstrated with "reasonable certainty". However this clarity is not reflected in all language versions. In particular, the French version of the Convention appears to require a higher level of certainty of choice; it refers to "de facon certaine". The removal of this element of uncertainty from the new text is therefore welcome.
www.dfpni.gov.uk

[174] Compagnie Tunisienne de Navigation SA v Compagnie d' Armement Maritime SA [1971] A.C. 572; Coast Lines Ltd v Hudig & Veder Chartering NV [1972] 2 Q. B. 34 (CA); Monterosso Shipping Ltd v International Transport Workers Federation [1982] I.C.R. 675 (CA); X AG v A Bank [1983] 2 All E.R. 464; Amin Rasheed Shipping Corp v Kuwait Insurance Co [1984] A.C. 50, 61.
Dicey and Morris, the Conflict of Laws, 14th ed., p.1539, "When the intention of the parties to a con-

條款及案件的一般情形來認定其默示之意思[175]。但如個人於年輕時即一再強調：「主張要有三步驟的人最大的困難大概是如何去劃分第二步驟與第三步驟，亦即何謂當事人默示的意思與何種情況下才算是法院替當事人推定的準據法。[176]」隨著時間的推展，較近有些案件很明白的顯示出這種混亂。於 Armadora Occidental SA v Horace Mann Insurance Co[177]中第一審的 Kerr J.即認為該準據法之確認是依第 2 步驟，上訴審雖維持原議，但卻認為是依第 3 步驟而來。而於 Amin Rasheed Shipping Corp v Kuwait Insurance Co[178]中，對於相同的結果 Lord Wilberforce 認為是第 3 步驟，而其他大法官卻認為應屬第 2 步驟。

　　較近版本的 Dicey and Morris 將這種困境解釋的很清楚：「尋找默示之意思與尋找與契約有最密切與真實關連之法律制度間的界限是很精細的，並且經常是模糊不清的。於理論上，在缺乏明示選法的第一個測試的情形下，法院應該考慮是否當事人之意思有其他之指標可做為第二個測試，並且只有在沒有這種指標時才能繼續考慮第三個階段，亦即契約與前一個法律制度有著最密切而真實的關連[179]。但事實上於採用第二或第三測試時皆可達成同樣的結果，法院並且經常直接由第一階段移到第三階段。

---

tract with regard to the law governing it was not expressed and could not be inferred from the circumstances, the contract was governed by the system of law with which the transaction had its closest and most real connection."

[175] Whitworth Street Estates (Manchester) Ltd v James Miller and Partners Ltd [1970] A.C. 583; Amin Rasheed Shipping Corp v Kuwait Insurance Co [1984] A.C. 50; The Stolt Marmaro [1985] 2Lloyd's Rep. 428 (CA); The Komninos S [1991] 1 Lloyd's Rep. 370 (CA). 見 Dicey and Morris, 同上, "When there was no express selection of the governing law, an intention with regard to the law to govern the contract could be inferred from the terms and nature of the contract and from the general circumstances of the case."

[176] 陳隆修，《國際私法契約評論》，台北，五南圖書公司，民國 75 年 2 月，初版，54、55 頁。

[177] [1977] 1 W.L.R. 520

[178] [1984] A.C. 50。Cheshire and North, 14thed., 於 p.704,除了於註 320 中說："There was much confusion at common law over the meaning of intention, and between the intentions of the parties and objective factors";另外又一針見血的宣示："The upshot is that it may be harder to draw an inference of intention under the Convention than it was under the common law rules."

[179] Amin Rasheed Shipping corp v Kuwait Insurance Co [1984] A.C. 50, 61, per Lord Diplock; Whitworth Street Estates (Manchester) Ltd v James Miller and Partners Ltd [1970] A.C. 583, 611, per Viscount Dilhorne; coast Lines Ltd v Hudig & Veder Chartering NV [1972] 2 Q.B. 34, 46, per Megaw L.J.; akai Pty Ltd v People's Insurance Co Ltd (1996) 188 C.L.R. 418, 440-442.

這大部份是由於默示之意思與密切關連之測試彼此相互融和，及由於以前在客觀的密切關連測試尚未完全建立時，默示之意思於事實上是一種客觀的測試，其不是被用來引導出當事人真正之意思，而只是在於賦予一種不曾存在之當事人之意思。於第二種測試中案件周遭的情形是被考慮用來確認當事人之真正的意思，所謂真正的意思是假如若其時被問及時他們所會表達的意思；於第三階段，案件周遭的情形是被考慮用來客觀的決定那一個法律制度與交易有著最密切而真實的關係，並且這情形是不論當事人意思的，而且這個程序是有關法律規則的適用，而非法律解釋的程序。[180]」

個人早期年輕氣盛，對默示準據法與推定準據法間精緻之區別甚感不耐，故而曾加以揣測這三步驟之起因或許是基於歷史傳統而來：「依作者之見，所謂當事人有默示之意思表示，不外是案件之事實上有著強烈的影響法官決定準據法的考慮因素而已。所謂第二步驟與第三步驟之區別只不過是前者有著明顯而有力的影響法官決定準據法的事實因素，而後者則缺少能直接有力的幫助法官決定準據法的事實因素而已。故依作者之見，硬是要區別第二與第三步驟之實益不是很大。作者猜想或許這三步驟之來由是由於早期當事人不能自定準據法，而法院又採主觀說，故法院尋找準據法之重點乃放在當事人訂約時之默示意思表示，當事人沒有默示時再替當事人推定其意思。時至今日當事人已可自主準據法，但由於英國法界傳統之

---

[180] Dicey and Morrie, pp. 1539, 1540, "But the line between the search for the inferred intention and the search for the system of law with which the contract had its closest and most real connection was a fine one which was frequently blurred. In theory, in the absence of an express choice as the first test, the court had to consider as a second test whether there were any other indications of the parties' intention, and only if there was no such indication go on to consider the third stage, namely with what system of law the contract had its closet and most real connection. But in practice the same result could be reached by the application of the second or third tests, and frequently the courts moved straight from the first stage to the third stage. This was largely because the tests of inferred intention and close connection merged into each other, and because before the objective close connection test became fully established the test of inferred intention was in truth an objective test designed not to elicit actual intention but to impute an intention which had not been formed. In the second test the surrounding circumstances were considered in order to ascertain the parties' actual intention, in the sense of what they would have said if asked at the time; at the third stage, the surrounding circumstances were considered to determine, objectively and irrespective of the parties' intention, with which system of law the transaction had its closest and most real connection, and that process involved the application of a rule of law, not a process of construction." The Komninos S [1991] 1 Lloyd's Rep. 370, 374 (CA), per Bingham L.J.

保守作風，故將原來之兩個步驟前加上一個明示的意思表示，而將兩個步驟傳統性的保留下來。事實上既然當事人已可自主，則當事人默示之意思表示自應除去，而將最後推定當事人的意思的步驟加以擴大方是。[181]」

在羅馬公約第3條的解釋報告[182]中，有關於早期會員國法、德、義、比利時、荷蘭、及盧森堡在此方面之法規，各國就只有承認訂約自由之規定，並無默示選法之規定。例如其時法國民法2312條第1項即僅只規定：「具有國際性質之契約及其所引發之義務，應以當事人所意圖選法之法律為依據。[183]」其他國家亦通常只有選法自由之規定或判例而已。而該報告有關意大利之法規是如此評論的：「根據大部份學者之理論及最高法院之一貫判決，契約準據法主要是依據當事人明示之意思而決定；就只有於當事人沒有選法時契約準據法才會由上述條款所規定之連繫因素決定。[184]」故而於該報告中有關其時意大利法是要求當事人之意思表示是以明示為之的。報告中承認默示選法的國家就只有英國法系統之國家，其敘述如下：「依英國法（及相同情況之蘇格蘭法及愛爾蘭法），在當事人沒有明示選擇他們契約之準據法時，法院會考慮是否由契約之條款可以發現當事人默示應適用之選法。[185]」故而至少由羅馬公約之解釋報告可以推定默示選法並非歐盟訂公約前之共識。

---

[181] 陳隆修，《國際私法契約評論》，台北，五南圖書公司，民國75年2月，初版, 56頁。

[182] Report on the convention on the law applicable to contractual obligations by Mario Giuliano, Official Journal C 282, 31/10/ 1980.

[183] Id, "In French law the rule conferring this power (or 'autonomie de la volonte' as it is called) upon the parties is founded on case law dating back to the judgment delivered on 5 December 1910 by the court of Cassation in American Trading Company v. Quebec Steamship Company Limited. The French draft law of 1967 to supplement the Civil Code in matters of private international law merely confirms the state of French law in this matter by providing in the first paragraph of Article 2312; 'Contracts of an international character and the obligations arising from them shall be subject to the law under which the parties intended to place themselves."

[184] Id, "According to the respondant view of theorists and consistent decisions by the Court of Cassation, the law applicable to the contract must be determined primarily on the basis of the express will of the parties; only in default of such a nomination will the law of the contract be determined by the connecting factors stipulated in the above mentioned provisions"

[185] Id, p.19，"Under English law (and the situation is similar in Scots law and Irish law), in the case where the parties have not expressly chosen the law to govern their contract, the court will consider whether the parties' choice of law to be applied can be inferred from the terms of the contract."

　　仲裁條款、管轄條款、及選法條款或許可被認為國際契約中最重要
之三個條款，而且通常這三個基本條款是相互牽連的。有趣的是於仲裁條
款上聯合國紐約公約第2條1及2項是規定須以書面為之[186]，同樣的1985之
模範公約第7條2項亦規定須以書面為之[187]。於管轄條款上歐盟布魯塞爾公
約之修正版布魯塞爾規則（No 44/2001 Regulation）第23條第1、2項[188]，

---

[186] Article II
1. Each Contracting State shall recognize an agreement in writing under which the parties undertake to submit to arbitration all or any differences which have arisen or which may arise between them in respect of a defined legal relationship, whether contractual or not, concerning a subject matter capable of settlement by arbitration.
2. The term "agreement in writing" shall include an arbitral clause in a contract or an arbitration agreement, signed by the parties or contained in an exchange of letters or telegrams.
英國Arbitration Act 1996第5條對書面要求更是詳細規定如下：
5.(1) The provisions of this Part apply only where the arbitration agreement is in writing, and any other agreement between the parties as to any matter is effective for the purposes of this Part only if in writing.
The expressions "agreement", "agree" and "agreed" shall be construed accordingly.
(2) There is an agreement in writing-
(a) if the agreement is made in writing (whether or not it is signed by the parties),
(b) if the agreement is made by exchange of communications in writing, or
(c) if the agreement is evidenced in writing.
(3) Where parties agree otherwise than in writing by reference to terms which are in writing, they make an agreement in writing.
(4) An agreement is evidenced in writing if an agreement made otherwise than in writing is recorded by one of the parties, or by a third party, with the authority of the parties to the agreement.
(5) An exchange of written submissions in arbitral or legal proceedings in which the existence of an agreement otherwise than in writing is alleged by one party against another party and not denied by the other party in his response constitutes as between those parties an agreement in writing to the effect alleged.
(6) References in this Part to anything being written or in writing include its being recorded by any means.
[187] (2) The arbitration agreement shall be in writing. An agreement is in writing if it is contained in a document signed by the parties or in an exchange of letters, telex, telegrams or other means of telecommunication which provide a record of the agreement, or in an exchange of statements of claim and defence in which the existence of an agreement is alleged by one party and not denied by another. The reference in a contract to a document containing an arbitration clause constitutes an arbitration agreement provided that the contract is in writing and the reference is such as to make that clause part of the contract.
[188] Article 23
1. If the parties, one or more of whom is domiciled in a Member State, have agreed that a court or the courts of a Member State are to have jurisdiction to settle any disputes which have arisen or which may arise in connection with a particular legal relationship, that court or those courts shall have jurisdiction. Such jurisdiction shall be exclusive unless the parties have agreed otherwise. Such an agreement conferring jurisdiction shall be either:
(a) in writing or evidenced in writing; or
(b) in a form which accords with practices which the parties have established between themselves; or

由於企圖以透過形式要件之方式來確認當事人訂約之意願，從而確認契約之存在，故對條款形式要件之要求及當事人間之習慣與貿易慣例有著詳細的規定[189]。歐盟法院並且認為這是自主化之規則，應為歐盟統一之規則與解釋，任何會員國之規定與第23條發生衝突則應為無效[190]。另外2005年海牙選擇法院公約第3條C項亦對專屬管轄條款形式要件之要求有著明確之規定[191]。較近2008年的 United Nations Convention on Contracts for the International Carriage of Goods Wholly or Partly by Sea （鹿特規則）第67條1項(a)款對專屬管轄條款之成立要件（包含實質及形式要件）亦有著規定[192]。

故如果通常與選法條款並列的管轄條款及仲裁條款，皆以明確的形式要件的要求來確認當事人間訂立該些條款的意思，而選法條款卻得以模糊而不確定的默示意思來推定當事人之選法，這似乎是於法學邏輯上不甚一致之作法。如Dicey and Morris所謂：「事實上於採用第二或第三測試時皆可達成同樣的結果，法院並且經常直接由第一階段移到第三階段。」由當事人之觀點而言，重點是在適用他們所主張之法律，而非選法測試的過程。Dicey and Morris既然認為「默示之意思與密切關連之測試彼此相互

[c) in international trade or commerce, in a form which accords with a usage of which the parties are or ought to have been aware and which in such trade or commerce is widely known to, and regularly observed by, parties to contracts of the type involved in the particular trade or commerce concerned.

2. Any communication by electronic means which provides a durable record of the agreement shall be equivalent to 'writing'.

[189] 個人認為契約之成立與存在仍應依契約法之實體原則而定，不能完全以形式要件之規定取代之。陳隆修，《2005年海牙法院選擇公約評析》，台北，五南圖書公司，2009年1月，初版1刷，68頁。

[190] Case 25/79 Sanicentral GmbH v Collin [1979] E.C.R. 3423, Case 150/80 Elefanten Schuh GmbH v Jacqmain [1981] E.C.R. 1671.

[191] c) an exclusive choice of court agreement must be concluded or documented –
i) in writing; or
ii) by any other means of communication which renders information accessible so as to be usable for subsequent reference;

[192] (a) Is contained in a volume contract that clearly states the names and addresses of the parties and either (i) is individually negotiated or (ii) contains a prominent statement that there is an exclusive choice of court agreement and specifies the sections of the volume contract containing that agreement. 另外對於非契約當事人是否應受管轄條款之拘束，則於2項(b)款規定形式要件如下：(b)That agreement is contained in the transport document or electronic transport record.

融和」，則或許可以如早期個人所建議，直接將兩種測試合而為一。亦即如美國於實務上一般，如若當事人沒有明示選法則通常以「最重要關連」之法律來決定該爭點之準據法[193]。個人認為歐盟應如美國一般，即使沒有公開的否認默示意思之存在，亦應儘量於實務上降低其重要性。歐盟羅馬公約及規則的第3條皆明文鼓吹當事人之默示選法，而默示選法卻是個不確定的概念，這與歐盟一向強調法律穩定性之作法是背道而馳的。

　　個人認為中國式的國際私法似乎沒有必要背負英國判例法進化過程中之歷史包袱，而或許應將當事人自主原則限定在只適用於明示選法之情形。另外美國第2新編第6條2項d款雖有規定應尊重「合理期待之保護」，但188條及一般法院於操作上，似乎過於偏重與案件有關連之客觀事實，而對當事人於主觀上之默示意思較為忽略。除了受限於契約法的基本原則外，第一階段的當事人明示選法於現今之社會是通常會被接受的。但是於融合第二階段及第三階段而替當事人推定準據法時，個人認為當事人主觀之意願仍應被加以考慮，亦即主觀說之測試及客觀說之測試皆應被加以考慮。契約中之條款通常是可被用來詮釋訂約時當事人之主觀意思，故於此階段中仍應被加以考慮。例如包括美國在內的世界各國，對於管轄條款與仲裁條款的重要性，幾乎都給予壓倒性之考慮。

　　羅馬公約及規則第3(1)條對默示準據法，是規定應由案件之事實或契約條款所清楚的顯示出來。雖然羅馬公約只是要求「顯示出合理之確定」，不若規則I般的嚴格，但其解釋報告仍然舉甚多例子說明如下：「當事人之選法通常為明示，但公約認可法院得在考慮所有的事實下，即使當事人沒有於契約中明白的規定，仍有可能認定當事人已做一個真正的法律選擇。例如即使沒有明白的表示，契約可能是用一種通常是以某特定之法律制度為依據之標準格式，並且可能達到此種選法之效果，如Lloyds的海商保險契約。於其他情形，當情況顯示當事人並未有意的改變政策並且選法條款是被忽略時，當事人過去的交易是依據包含明示選法的契約而

---

[193] Second Restatement, s. 188.

來時，得促使法院無疑的認定爭議中之契約是依過去的選法而定。於某些情形下特定法院之選擇可以充份確認當事人以法院地法為契約依據之意思，但這種情形一定須考慮到契約之其他條款及案件之所有情形。同樣的雖然於沒有明示選法之情形，契約中有參考加入法國民法之特定條文時，法院可能認定當事人是故意選定法國法。其他可能促使法院認定當事人已經有著真實的選定法律之事情可能包括，相同當事人間相關交易之明示選法，或糾紛應交付仲裁時有指定仲裁地並且有顯示仲裁者應適用當地法之情形。[194]」

對羅馬公約解釋報告中所舉的默示選法的例子及情形，Dicey and Morris很清楚的寫著：「這些例子明顯的是受到公約之前的英國判例法之啟發。[195]」例如於Amin Rasheed shipping corp v Kuwait Insurance Co[196]中，一於杜拜營業之賴比瑞亞公司，向一科威特保險公司投保一貨船，該保單是根據Lloyd's的海商保險的標準格式而來。依英國法契約準據法為英國法時，法院有裁量權將訴訟之通知送達國外之被告[197]，故賴比瑞亞公司要求將通知送達給科威特公司。雖然契約中沒有明示準據法，但法院認

---

[194] Giuliano and Lagarde Report, The choice of law by the parties will often be express but the Convention recognizes the possibility that the Court may, in the light of all the facts, find that the parties have made a real choice of law although this is not expressly stated in the contract. For example, the contract may be in a standard form which is known to be governed by a particular system of law even though there is no express statement to this effect, such as a Lloyd's policy of marine insurance. In other cases a previous course of dealing between the parties under contracts containing an express choice of law may leave the court in no doubt that the contract in question is to be governed by the law previously chosen where the choice of law clause has been omitted in circumstances which do not indicate a deliberate change of policy by the parties. In some cases the choice of a particular forum may show in no uncertain manner that the parties intend the contract to be governed by the law of that forum, but this must always be subject to the other terms of the contract and all the circumstances of the case. Similarly references in a contract to specific Articles of the French Civil Code may leave the court in no doubt that the parties have deliberately chosen French law, although there is no expressly stated choice of law. Other matters that may impel the court to the conclusion that a real choice of law has been made might include an express choice of law in related transactions between the same parties, or the choice of a place where disputes are to be settled by arbitration in circumstances indicating that the arbitrator should apply the law of that place.

[195] Dicey and Morris, the Conflict of Laws, 14th ed., p.1573, "the examples are plainly inspired by the English case-law prior to the Convention."

[196] [1984] A.C. 50.

[197] 陳隆修，《國際私法管轄權評論》，台北，五南圖書公司，民國75年11月，初版，51頁。

為當事人之意思是以英國海商保險法為其權利及義務之依據。至今已有甚多判例認定，依羅馬公約於倫敦市場經由經紀人所定之再保險契約是默示以英國法為依據[198]。

至於相同當事人間過去的交易或相關連的交易皆有明示選法，而本次交易卻疏忽而未選法，故而本次交易以過去交易或相關交易之準據法為依據是通常合理的[199]。但是Cheshire and North認為[200]：「英國法院於相同情況下，在判例法上是使用默示意思之語詞。但是，他們亦會由那些純粹的客觀因素去推論默示之意思，例如當事人的居所[201]或契約內容主體之性質與所在[202]，可是依公約這些因素是不合適去推論當事人默示的真正意思。」

至於在不同當事人間之相關契約，英國判例法一般亦採用相同之原則。例如無論是以明示或默示，如若傭船契約之準據法為英國法，法院可能推論提單之準據法亦是被默示為相同之法律[203]。另外於一契約中依一特

---

[198] Gan Insurance Co Ltd v Tai Ping Insurance Co Ltd [1999] I.L.Pr. 729 (CA); Tiernan v Magen Insurance Co Ltd [2000] I.L.Pr. 517; Ace Insurance SA-NV v Zurich Insurance Co [2000] 2 Lloyd's Rep. 423, affirmed [2001] EWCA Civ. 173, [2001] 1 Lloyd's Rep. 618; Tryg Baltica International (UK) Ltd v Boston Cia de Seguros [2004] EWHC 1186 (Comm.)

[199] Re United Railways of Havana, etc. Warehouse Ltd [1960] Ch. 52, 94 (CA), affirmed. [1961] A.C. 1007; The Evia Luck [1986] 2 Lloyd's Rep. 165, 172-173.

[200] North and Fawcett, Private International Law, 13th ed., p.563, "The English courts under the common law rules used the language of inferred intent in similar circumstances. However, they also inferred an intent from the sort of purely objective factors, such as the residence of the parties or the nature and location of the subject of the contract, from which it would be inappropriate to infer an actual intention under the Convention." 又見14thed. P.702中 "The English courts, under the common law rules, used the language of inferred intent in similar circumstances. They also inferred an intern from purely objective factors, such as the residence of the parties or the nature and location of the subject of the subject of the contract. This approach has continued to be used in relation to the Rome Convention. In American Motorists Insurance Co (Amico) v Cellstar Corp the Court of Appeal inferred a choice of Texas law from the fact that a company from its base in Texas chose on behalf of its whole group of companies to negotiate world-wide cover in Texas with insurers also based in Texas. Whatever the position was at common law, it is submitted that it is inappropriate to infer an actual intention as required under the Convention from objective factors."
[2003] EWCA Civ 206, [2003] IL Pr 22.

[201] Jacobs v Credit Lyonnais (1884) 12 QBD 589.

[202] Lloyd v Guibert (1865) LR 1 QB 115 at 122-123.

[203] The Adriatic [1931] P.241; The Njegos [1936] P. 90; The San Nicholas [1976] 1 Lloyd's Rep. 8 (CA); The Freights Queen [1977] 2 Lloyd's Rep. 140; The Elli 2 [1985] 1 Lloyd's Rep. 107 (CA); The Delfini [1988] 2 Lloyd's Rep. 599, affirmed [1990] 1 Lloyd's Rep. 252 (CA).

定準據法時，對該契約義務之保證英國法院亦可能推論當事人默示以同一法律為依據，這種情形以保證人與被保證人間有關連時更有可能[204]。

另外如所謂的qui eligit indicem eligit ius，許多與英國無關的契約有關會指定英國法院為管轄法院，英國法院此時通常會認為這亦是默示選定英國法為準據法。羅馬公約之解釋報告要求：「於當事人沒有選擇法律的清楚意思下，本條文不允許法院以默示推論當事人有可能選擇法律。這種情形應以第4條為依據。[205]」英國法院認為於仲裁條款之情形當事人若沒有指定仲裁地，則通常無法推論其默示之意思。若即使其有指定仲裁地，但除了依據國際仲裁機構（如ICC）之規定外並無規定選任仲裁者之辦法，此時默示英國法為準據法之推論則較為薄弱[206]。若清楚的指定仲裁地及仲裁者是於該地營業或該國人，則英國法院通常會推定該地法可能默示之選法[207]，如於仲裁者是倫敦之海商仲裁者或保險代理人之情形等。

一個非常有趣的問題是，依公約及規則Ⅰ 3(1)條當事人之明示或默示選法於被確認後，除了違反公序良俗（公約16條、規則21條）、強行法

---

[204] Broken Hill Pty Co Ltd v Xenakis [1982] 2 Lloyd's Rep. 304; Mitsubishi Corp v Alafonzos [1988]1 Lloyd's Rep. 191; Wahda Bank v Arab Bank Plc [1996] 1 Lloyd's Rep. 470 (CA); Turkiye Is Bankasi AS v Bank of China [1993] 1 Lloyd's Rep. 132; Bank of Baroda v Vysya Bank [1994] 2 Lloyd's Rep. 87; Bank of Credit and Commerce Hong Kong v Sonali Bank [1995] 1 Lloyd's Rep. 227 and contrast Attock Cement Co Ltd v Romanian Bank for Foreign Trade [1989] 1 W.L.R. 1147 (CA) Armadora Occidental SA v Horace Mann Insurance Co [1977] 1 W.L.R. 520, affirmed [1977] 1 W.L.R.1098 (CA).於陳隆修，《比較國際私法》，台北，五南圖書公司，78年10月，初版，362頁中，個人於評述奧地法國際私法45條時如此論述：「本條文明定從債務之準據法應依該主債務之準據法而來，尤其特別明白指出保證債務之準據法應依原來之主債務之準據法。此點由大陸法之眼光而言，從債務本即應隨著主債務，故為一天經地義之規定。但依英美法而言，契約本應有對價，故如保證契約無對價，或其他之從債務無對價，則此契約或從債務根本不成立。故依英美法而言，保證契約或其他欲成立之從債務既然有對價，自然應為一獨立之契約或獨立之債之關係，而應依一般準據法推定原則獨立地被加以考慮其準據法，不過自然地原來之債之關係於推定保證契約或從債務之準據法時應會被加以適當地考慮。」

[205] Giuliano and Lagarde Report, "This Article does not permit the court to infer a choice of law that the parties might have made where they had no clear intention of making a choice. Such a situation is governed by Article 4."

[206] Atlantic Underwriting Agencies Ltd v Compagnie di Assicurazione di Milano [1979] 2 Lloyd's Rep. 240; Steel Authority of India v Hind Metals Inc [1984] 1 Lloyd's Rep. 405.

[207] NV Kwik Hoo Tong Handel Maatschappij v James Finlay & Co Ltd [1927] A.C. 604; The Njegos [1936] P. 90, 100; NV "Vulcaan" v A/S J. Ludwig Mowinckels Rederi [1938] 2 All E.R. 152, 156 (HL); The Mariannina [1983] 1 Lloyd's Rep. 12 (CA).

規（公約3(3)、7條及規則3(3)、9條）、及運送、消費者、保險與僱傭等相關基本規定外，當事人之明示或默示選法通常皆應被法院所尊重。在尊重當事人自主之旗幟下[208]，通常各國法院應尊重當事人透過明示或默示之方式所作的法律選擇。亦即在基本契約法原則及強行法規沒有被違反時，各國法院應會尊重當事人明示或默示之選法，而幾乎沒有裁量權行使之空間。公約及規則3(1)條之起頭句子即毫無通容的規定「契約應以當事人選定之法律為依據」，第2句則加上當事人之選法包含明示及默示選法在內。故而在基本契約法原則及強行法規之範疇內，歐盟秉持大陸法之架構，在3(1)條並不想給予各國法院裁量權之意圖是昭然若揭的。

　　但是個人以為歐盟於此方面真正的窘境在於當事人之默示選法是一種英國式之概念，而英國法於傳統上是給予法院大量的裁量權以便於不同的個案中達成正義的結果。相對於較為偏向達成正確結果的英國法，大陸法一般相較，可能是較為注重適用正確的法律。故而一般國際上的同僚許多人應是會承認在國際私法上相對於英美法，大陸法表面上是較不傾向給予法院裁量的空間。公約及規則3(1)條有關默示選法之規定即為典型大陸法之表達方式－表面上是不給予法院裁量之空間的。但問題是默示選法是一種典型的英國法學傳統－而什麼時候英美法會在面對爭議性紛爭時不給予法院裁量權去面對以後不可預測的紛爭？公約與規則3(1)條尷尬之處在於條文中是不給予法院裁量權的，公約的解釋報告並且要求當事人必須有「清楚的意思」（clear intention）才能被視為默示選法，但如前述解釋報告中所舉的每一個默示選法的例子，都充滿英國風味的保留甚大的彈性空間。如果解釋報告所引用的例子皆忠於英國原味的預留彈性空間，而3(1)條之文句卻沒有給予法院裁量之空間，顯而易見的大陸法的歐盟在引進英國式默示選法規則時是欠缺考慮而無法適應的。歐盟在法律的統一上又再次證明其有時「太多資源給予太多聰明的人做了太快的決定。[209]」歐

盟好像愛麗絲夢遊記中的愛麗絲，迷失在英國默示選法幻境中不知如何自處。

或許累積了近三十年的經驗，羅馬 I 序言的要點12規定當事人的指定專屬管轄法院是決定當事人是否有「清楚的顯示」選定準據法的因素之一[210]。要點12事實上與公約的解釋報告完全一致。於解釋報告中所記載的默示選法之所有因素中，選定管轄法院事實上是較為穩定的因素[211]，或許要點12是被用以證明歐盟採彈性默示選法之決心。如果是如此則似乎於3(1)條之主文中，公開採用彈性認定默示選法或許較為妥適。或許Compagnie Tunisienne de Navigation SA v Compagnie d'Armement Maritime SA[212]案能充份的顯示於默示選法的過程中，法院需有裁量權以便達成正

---

a far-reaching research project involving hundreds of scholars from all over Europe and aiming at the preparation of a draft 'academic' CFR covering the entire field of European contract law, the European Commission suddenly decided drastically to restrict the scope of the "political" CFR and to reduce it to the review – important as it may be – of the consumer acquis. This erratic course is not exactly what one would expect from an institution committed to the principles of transparency, proportionality, and subsidiarity." Michael Joachim Bonell

The CISG, European Contract Law and the Development of a World Contract Law 56 Am. J. Comp. L. 1, 15 (2008). 而Prof. Muir Watt則引用Pierre Legrand, Book Review, 58 Cambridge L.J. 439, 442 (1999) 做出如此結論："The construction of the European legal system requires long-term reflection on its political, social, and cultural dimensions; it is not an agenda for 'clever minds in a hurry.'"

Horatia Muir Watt

Experiences from Europe; Legal Diversity and the Internal Market 39 Tex. Int'l L.J. 429, 459 (2004).做為一個中國國際法的學生，個人覺得「太少的資源使得很多聰明的人不容易做決定」。法律科學是一種極度牽連民族文化的高科技，不盡早研發對後代子孫的傷害可能會大於自然科技的落後。

[210] (12) An agreement between the parties to confer on one or more courts or tribunals of a Member State exclusive jurisdiction to determine disputes under the contract should be one of the factors to be taken into account in determining whether a choice of law has been clearly demonstrated.

[211] 陳隆修，《國際私法契約評論》，台北，五南圖書公司，民國75年2月，初版，53頁，「早期的國際私法發展史是偏重管轄權，一般法院常以法院地法為準據法(事實上至今於親屬法上仍是如此)。故當事人如願將糾紛交付該地法院解決，則可推定當事人有意思以該法院地法為準據法。」

[212] [1972] A.C. 572. 於案中Lord Wilberforce認為："that the selection of a certain place for arbitration … is an indication that the parties intended the law of that place to govern is a sound general rule", p. 596。而Lord Diplock亦認為仲裁條款通常顯示當事人選擇準據法之意思，並且"should be so construed unless there are compelling indications to the contrary in the other terms of the contract or the surrounding circumstances of the transaction."P.609。但Lord Diplock又特別強調於國際期貨市場(commodity market)同一批貨在交到最後之買主手中時該批貨不知已被買賣了多少次，因此從商業上的便利來著眼，凡有關於供給、交貨、運輸、裝載、責任之履行等等複雜的法律關係應越簡單越好，故這些有關同一批貨的多次買賣應以同一準據法來決定其中之法律關係較為符合實際上的需要。在此時這些有關同一批貨之買賣應以同一地為仲裁地，並且仲裁地應為推定準據

確的結果。於該案中法國船東答應替突尼西亞公司從一突尼西亞港口載石油至另一突尼西亞港口，契約是在巴黎透過經紀人商討（negotiate）而簽訂的，運費是以法郎在巴黎簽訂的，而突尼西亞又是使用法國法，契約中規定貨物必須由該法國船東所控制租用（charter）的船舶來運送，契約中又規定準據法為運送貨物之船旗國法，及規定契約糾紛之仲裁地為倫敦，後由於該船東之船（掛法國旗）全部太小不能載貨，只能僱用一瑞典船，一挪威船，一保加利亞船，一法國船及二利比亞船載貨，此時準據法的選定已變為沒有意義，故英國法院推定準據法為法國法。雖然仲裁地為英國，法院仍認為法國法應為準據法，此契約雖以英文及英國格式簽訂，但於海商契約中此乃為一種標準格式，故英國法院不認此為強有力之連結因素。換言之，由仲裁地的指定雖可以推定當事人有意以仲裁地法為準據法，但在當事人有明示或其他證據強烈顯示當事人有意以其他法律為準據法時，則此種推定可以被推翻。

另外個人認為解釋報告中對默示意思之推論最為有問題的是，於沒有明示選法之情形，契約中若有參考加入（references）法國民法之特定條款則得用以確認當事人之有意選定法國法為準據法。如前述於台北之貸款保證契約中常有指定外國法為準據法[213]，但皆會要求保證人依台灣民法746條放棄745條先訴抗辯權。設若強勢的外商銀行沒有指定準據法時，此時台灣法院若遵循歐盟之規則以台灣法為準據法，該外商之商會及母國政府所發出排山倒海之壓力是可預見的。外國法條文的參考加入雖可作為推論準據法之依據[214]，但如前述外國法條文的引用（incorporation）可能只有契約條款簡述之效果，而與選定準據法無關[215]。於實務上對外國法條

　　法的強烈因素，如此國際商業的進行才能穩定。P.609,見前註，52頁。另外對被告得以選擇在倫敦或北京仲裁之條款，英國法院並不認為得以確認當事人默示之意思。The Star Texas [1993] 2 Lloyd's Rep. 445 (CA)."

[213] 陳隆修，《國際私法契約評論》，台北，五南圖書公司，民國75年2月，初版，31、32頁。

[214] Amin Rasheed Shipping Corp v Kuwait Insurance Co [1984] A.C. 50, 69, per Lord Wilberforce.

[215] Dicey and Morris, 14thed. P. 1572, "In such a case the incorporation of the foreign statute would only have effect as a matter of contract. Where there is no express choice of law, the reference to the foreign statute may be neither a choice of the foreign law nor an indication that the parties intended foreign law

文的引用以海上運送較多，此時被引用之外國法條文則變成當事人所同意
之契約條款[216]。契約中外國法條文的被引用為契約條款與外國法的被引用
為準據法，基本上不同之處在於前者被視為契約條款之一部份[217]，故應為
死的固定條款，而於後者被引用之準據法應隨著外國法之改變而變更之活
法律。因此當外國法條文被引用為契約條款時，即使該外國法條文被修改
或廢除，該舊外國法條文仍構成契約之一部份[218]。當外國法被引用為準據
法時，於契約有效期間外國法之改變修正或解除契約之義務時，對當事人
是有拘束力的[219]。

　　故而無論於學理上或實務上，外國法條文的被引為（incorporation）
契約條款之一部份及契約中有參考加入（reference）外國法條文以使得
該外國法成為默示準據法，這兩者於判例法上之適用結果是不相同的。
除了Diey and Morris認為：「於沒有明示選法之情形，參考加入外國
條文可能既不是選擇外國法，亦不是當事人意圖外國法做為準據法之表
示。[220]」Cheshire and North亦小心翼翼的於註釋中加上：「除了選擇法
國準據法外，這亦可能牽涉到以參考加入之方式而引用該法律。[221]」契約

---

to govern." Vita Food Products Inc v Unus Shipping Co Ltd [1939] A.C. 277, 286 (PC); The Stolt Sydness [1997] 1 Lloyd's Rep. 273, 282.

[216] 陳隆修，《國際私法契約評論》，台北，五南圖書公司，民國75年2月，初版，31、32頁，例如引用美國以前的Harter Act，或採納海牙規則(Hague Rules)的英國Carriage of Goods By Sea Act 1971，或美國Carriage of Goods By Sea Act 1936，例如Stafford Allen & Sons Ltd v Pacific Steam Navigation Co [1956] 1 W.L.R. 629 (CA); Adamastos Shipping Co Ltd v Anglo-Saxon Petroleum Co Ltd [1959] A.C. 133.判例法認為當事人引用國際公約或外國法條文時，必須清楚的顯示出可合適被引用為契約條款的條文，只是大致上提及適用Sharia法律之原則是不夠的。Shamil Bank of Bahrain EC v Beximco Pharmaceuticals Ltd [2004] EWCA Civ. 19, [2004] 1 W.L.R. 1784.

[217] Dobell & Co v The SS Rossmore Co Ltd [1895] 2 Q.B. 408, 412, "reading into it as if they were written into it the words"。英國判例法認為當外國法條文於英國契約中被引用時，因為法院是在解釋英國契約之條款，而非於適用外國法，故並不受限於外國法專家所提供之證據。Stafford Allen & Sons Ltd v Pacific Steam Navigation Co [1956] 1 W.L.R. 629, 636 (CA).但如前註書，9、10、31、及32頁所述，外國法之專門術語或法律之解釋，基本上仍是應依該外國法。

[218] 陳隆修，《國際私法契約評論》，台北，五南圖書公司，民國75年2月，初版，31、32頁，Vita Food Products Inc v Unus Shipping Co Ltd [1939] A.C. 277(PC).

[219] Re Helbert Wagg & Co Ltd [1956] Ch. 323, 342; Rossano v Manufacturers' Life Ins Co [1963] 2 Q.B. 352.又如於Barcelo v Electrolytic Zinc Co of Australasia Ltd (1932) 48 C.L.R. 391中利率之降低；於R. v International Trustee, etc. [1937] A.C. 500中以黃金價格為本位之條款被溯及既往的宣佈無效。

[220] Dicey and Morris, the Conflict of Laws, 14th ed., p.1572.

[221] PM North, JJ Fawcett, Cheshire and North's Private International Law, 13th ed., P. 562, note 20, "In-

中牽涉到外國法之特定條文到底是以引用（incorporation）之方式，或是以參考加入（reference）之式，兩者之效力是不一致的。前者於英國傳統判例法上是有著明確的判決，而後者又為羅馬公約解釋報告中白紙黑字的規定。

問題是於過去及現在法院皆無法立下一個確定絕對標準[222]，以區分契約中外國法特定條文的被引用或參考加入。雖然這種區別是應由個案之特別情形加以單獨考量，並且或許於被用來做為默示選法之考量時其範圍應較為廣，但個人自第一次看到羅馬公約於此點的解釋報告即直覺的認為這是歐盟於採用英國默示準據法過程中之失誤。這種法律邏輯上的混亂於實務上可能對訴訟當事人造成截然不同之後果，並於實質上會對公平正義之追求有著巨大的影響。個人認為契約中外國法特定條文的被加入，只是推論當事人默示意思之參考證據之一，於許多或有些情況下並不具有絕對之影響力，並且無論是否構成默示選法之主要因素，該特定外國法條文已成為當事人契約中不可變更之固定條款。

由外國法特定條文的引用可見歐盟於採納默示意思推論在理論上之紊亂與無所適從，或許根本解決之道還是應將當事人自主之意思限定於明示之意思表示，而將第2階段的默示選法與第3階段的推定選法順理成章的合而為一。更有趣的是英國於契約法之選法3階段理論，於邏輯上雖然無法劃清界限，但基於悠久的判例法習慣，於實務上並無大困難。但自歐盟採用英國式默示選法理論後，英國法於此方面反而似乎有點陷入「剪不斷理還亂」之困境。個人認為英國判例法於進化過程中之歷史包袱不應由全

---

stead of a choice of French law this may involve an incorporation by reference.".本論述又再次重申於14thed. P.702中。

[222] Dicey and Morris, P. 1573, 對此寫著："It has been held that the circumstances which may be taken into account when deciding whether or not the parties have made an implied choice of law under Art.3 range more widely than the considerations ordinarily applicable to the implication of a term into a written agreement."

Aeolian Shipping SA v ISS Machinery Services Ltd [2001] EWCA Civ. 1162, [2001] 2 Lloyd's Rep 641, [16]; Samcrete Egypt Engineers and Contractors SAE v Land Rover Exports Ltd [2002] EWCA Civ. 2019, [2002] C.L.C. 533, [28]."

世界之其他地區（包含大中華經濟地區）所背負，甚至英國本身亦不應背負其歷史包袱。Dicey and Morris這麼寫著：「公約解釋報告如同判例法般將最密切關連與默示意思之標準同樣的做區分。如同前面之見證，英國於此方面之區別是混淆的。默示意思與最密切關連之標準是彼此相互融合的，並且以前在客觀的密切關連標準完全建立之前，默示意思之標準只是於事實上做為一種客觀的標準，它不是用來探求當事人之真意，而只是用來假設一個未存在過之意思。」因此其認為羅馬公約第3條之默示選法及第4條的最密切關連標準會有同樣區別上之問題[223]。Cheshire and North同樣的認為[224]：「於判例法之案例中，雖然經常用到默示意思之語辭，但有關法院是否在尋找當事人真正或實際之意思這一點上則非常不清楚[225]。有可能依公約去推論當事人默示之意思是比依判例法之規則更為困難的。」而對於英國判例法Cheshire and North更是一針見血的挑明：「判例法上對於意思的定義，及當事人之間的意思與客觀的因素是有著甚大的混亂。」國際契約法本身就可能是國際法中最複雜中的部份，於當事人自主之大纛下英國傳統判例法於此方面之混亂是可諒解的。個人一向認為判例法經過歷史的演進及歲月的淬鍊，故而「學術理論之創作最好不要逆天而行與判例法相抗衡[226]」，但判例法於此方面是混亂而不十分明確的。現代科技日新月異的進步已不容許判例法好整以暇從容的發展，加上歐盟大陸

---

[223] Dicey and Morris, p.1573, "The Report draws the same distinction as the common law did between the test of inferred intention, and of closest connection. It has already been seen that in England the distinction was blurred. The tests of inferred intention and close connection merged into each other, and before the objective close connection test became fully established the test of inferred intention was in truth an objective test designed not to elicit actual intention but to impute an intention which had not been formed. There will be the same difficulty in distinguishing between inferred intention to choose the applicable law under Rule 203 and the test of closest connection under Rule 204."

[224] Cheshire and North, pp.562, 563, "In the common law cases, although the language of inferred intent was often used it was by no means clear that the courts were looking for a real or actual intention on the parties' part. The upshot is that it may be harder to draw an inference of intention under the Convention than it was under the common law rules." "There was much confusion at common law over the meaning of intention, and between the intentions of the parties and objective factors."。又見14thed. pp.703,704.

[225] In Coast Lines Ltd v Hudig and Veder Chartering NV [1972] 2 QB 34, p.50.

[226] 陳隆修，《2005年海牙法院選擇公約評析》，台北，五南圖書公司，2009年1月，初版1刷，94頁。

法魯莽而粗糙的企圖融和英國判例法，國際法於默示選法上的紊亂是可預期的。選法條款是與仲裁及管轄條款並列，於當事人自主之原則下這三個條款是通常應受尊重的，但有鑑於其重要性，對這三個重要的基本條款皆應限制於明示之意思表示。當事人間若可能有默示的意思存在，則可被融和入第3階段做為推定契約準據法的因素之一或成為其中之最密切關連之最絕對因素。將第2階段的默示選法與第3階段的推定最密切關連之法律合而為同一階段之「建議」，事實上如前述Dicey and Morris之評論，只是一種將英國判例法上之實際作法誠實的公開承認而已。這種作法亦符合美國法院於實務上經常採2階段之作法。但與第2新編188條2項「最重要關連」之偏向客觀標準[227]，及羅馬公約及規則第4條的完全採用客觀標準不同的是，將第2階段的默示選法與第3階段的最密切關連標準融合之作法，是明顯的融合主觀標準與客觀標準。時至今日，一般通常會承認當事人默示之意思經常為法院所加以推論而來，個人早期就認為法院經常會以契約客觀之事實來推定當事人主觀之意識，故這種爭論於實務上並無多大益處[228]。個人於此問題上維持25年前之意見：「事實上現今似乎已沒有必要如此麻煩的分成三個步驟，只要當事人沒有明定準據法，法院就應兼採主觀說與客觀說，依各個案件特殊之事實來推定準據法。Tunisenne中仲裁地（兼法院地與契約形式的來源國）之法律不被採納為準據法，可做為通常應被考慮為當事人有默示選定之準據法不一定會被法院尊重之證據，故強調學理之機械性適用常會造成國際私法為困難法學之錯誤形象。[229]」

---

[227] 陳隆修，《國際私法契約評論》，台北，五南圖書公司，民國75年2月，初版，118頁，「一八八條與第二新編於侵權行為一樣，是採用『最有牽連關係』說。事實上此說與英國流行的客觀說近似，可是觀之英國經長久以來的演進，至今尚無完全排除『主觀』說之定論，一八八條之缺點乃在於太注重客觀之事實，而完全忽略了當事人於訂約時之主觀意思。於侵權行為中，當事人之主觀意思對於準據法之推定並不重要，但於契約行為時就不然了。尤其是其名雖為『最有牽連關係』說，但法院實際上運用起來常常無法推定那一牽連點為最有牽連關係，常常是看那一州有著最多的牽連點（grouping of contacts），而以該州之法為準據法。第二新編國際私法的發言人Reese教授雖謂牽連點的質（quality）重於量（quantity），但他對法院的實際現象卻似乎始終無法解釋的很清楚。」

[228] 陳隆修，《國際私法契約評論》，台北，五南圖書公司，民國75年2月，初版，24頁。

[229] 同前註，57、58頁。

十二、保險契約

　　另外這個敘述為解釋報告所陳述並廣為接受認為沒有爭議之部份：「即使沒有明白的表示，契約可能是用一種通常以某特定之法律制度為依據之標準格式，並且可能達到此種選法之效果，如Lloyd's的海商保險契約。」羅馬規則 I 第7條雖有保險契約之規定，但公約並沒有這個新增之規定。個人將解釋報告這句論述留在最後評述，乃在顯示兩個冷酷的事實：1.傳統上英國判例法扶持英國跨國企業之資本主義精神；2.包括歐盟在內世界上大部份地區都無意識的接受以英國利益為主軸之英國判例法。個人於此只是簡單的提出一個合理的問題：請問這些全世界最具歷史及經驗的英國跨國保險企業為何不簡單明瞭的明示以英國法為準據法?很明顯的這些跨國保險企業憑藉著母國於法律科技的優勢，於全世界各地混水摸魚掠取商業利益。英國法院以司法正義之名做為英國跨國企業獲取商業利益的後盾，這是「掠奪式新殖民主義」之標準司法正義。除了給予保險公司「正當合理期待」之保護外，全世界保險法之重要政策是在保護被保險人或保單持有人而非保險公司[230]。肩負著扶弱抑強義務的解釋報告於此完全被英國判例法的指鹿為馬混淆了。經過28年羅馬 I 第7條的規則展現了保護弱勢的保險法政策，亦不啻宣示了過去歐盟於此問題上被掠奪式新殖民主義法學所誤導的謬誤。

　　羅馬 I 7條1項規定本條文排除再保險之適用。第2項第1段規定除了人壽險外，有關歐盟所規定範圍內的大數量危險是由企業直接投保的保險，是以當事人依第3條所約定之法律為依據。第2段規定：「於當事人沒有選定準據法之情形，保險契約應以保險人慣居地國家之法律為依據。當由案件之所有情況清楚的顯示契約是明顯的與另一國家有著更密切關連

---

[230] 羅馬I的要點32規定保單持有人應受到適當程度之保護：(32) Owing to the particular nature of contracts of carriage and insurance contracts, specific provisions should ensure an adequate level of protection of passengers and policy holders. Therefore, Article 6 should not apply in the context of those particular contracts.

時，該另一國家之法律應被適用。」[231]企業直接投保的大數量危險之保險契約一般是被認為與通常的保險契約有區分的，因為企業是被認為較具有議價能力，故這種保險契約之選法是一般較會被賦予效力的。美國第2新編193條有關火災、保全、或傷害保險契約之comment e即認為：「當被保險人有著較強的議價立場（參考192條評論h），並且尤其是在於有著當一個或更多被保險的危險是主要位於被選法的州的額外因素時，這種選法條款是更有可能被賦予效力。[232]」192條是有關人壽保險，其comment h如此敘述：「相較於一般人之人壽保險，集體人壽保險契約中之選法條款是較可能被給予效力。這是由於取得主要保險契約之組織或個人通常相較於單獨的被保險人是有著較強的議價立場，因此選法條款比較不會有著當事人『無法議價』的性質。[233]」

　　第2新編193條之註釋e認為對當事人之選法法院是有裁量權的，而其裁量之重要因素為危險是否位於被選法之州。雖然羅馬Ⅰ7(2)條是排除人壽險，但相對下第2新編192條註釋h是較該7(2)條優良。註釋h認為於集體人壽保險時每個被保險人有著相同的保險及權利是較為妥當的。因此於僱主安排其受僱者接受集體人壽保險時，若缺乏有效之選法條款之情形，個別受僱者對保險人之權利，通常並不以受僱者之住所及取得保單地法為依據，而是以主保險契約中相關爭點之準據法為依據。而這通常是僱主之

---

[231] 2. An insurance contract covering a large risk as defined in Article 5(d) of the First Council Directive 73/239/EEC of 24 July 1973 on the coordination of laws, regulations and administrative provisions relating to the taking-up and pursuit of the business of direct insurance other than life assurance shall be governed by the law chosen by the parties in accordance with Article 3 of this Regulation.
To the extent that the applicable law has not been chosen by the parties, the insurance contract shall be governed by the law of the country where the insurer has his habitual residence. Where it is clear from all the circumstances of the case that the contract is manifestly more closely connected with another country, the law of that other country shall apply.
EEC Directive 73/239(1973) art. 5(d) 中有規定人數或營業數量。

[232] "Effect is more likely to be given such choice-of-law provision in a situation where the insured enjoys a relatively strong bargaining position (compare s 192, Comment h), and particularly where in addition one or more of the insured risks is principally located in the state of the chosen law."

[233] "Choice-of-law provisions contained in group life insurance policies are more likely to be given effect than in the case of ordinary life insurance. This is because the organization or individual which procures the master policy will usually have a stronger bargaining position than an individual insured with the result that the choice-of-law provision is less likely to have a 'take-it-or-leave-it' character."

主要營業地之州法[234]。雖然有著7(4)條的限制條款[235]及最密切關連條款，但7(2)條2段的規定於沒有選法條款時以保險人之慣居地法為依據，相較於美國是充滿英國資本主義風味而令人感到不安。

　　對於非有關7(2)條大數量危險之範圍，7(3)條第1段將當事人之選法限制於：(a)訂約時危險所在地之會員國法[236]；(b)保單持有人之慣居地法；(c)於人壽保險時保單持有人之國籍法；(d)保險契約涵蓋之危險只限於某一會員國所發生之事情而該會員國又非為危險之所在地，該會員國之法律；(e)本段所規定之契約保單持有人是從事一商業或工業行為或自由職業時，而有關該些行為之保險契約涵蓋兩個或更多危險並且這些危險是位於不同會員國時，相關會員國之法律或保單持有人之慣居地法。7(3)條第2段規定於前段(a)、(b)、或(e)款之情形時，相關會員國之法律可給予當事人更大之選法自由。7(3)條第3段規定當事人未依本第3項之規定而選

---

[234] h. group life insurance. In the case of group life insurance, rights against the insurer are usually governed by the law which governs the master policy. This is because it is desirable that each individual insured should enjoy the same privileges and protection. So where an employer arranges for group life insurance for its employees, the rights of a particular employee against the insurer will usually be determined, in the absence of an effective choice-of-law clause and at least as to most issues, not by the local law of the state where the employee was domiciled and received his certificate but rather by the law governing the master policy with respect to that issue. This will usually be the state where the employer has his principal place of business.

[235] 第7(4)條是有關強制保險契約，許多歐洲同僚，包含Max Planck Institute 在內，認為應直接以規定之國家之法律為依據。見Urs Peter Gruber, ,insurance Contracts, 於Rome I Regulation: The Law Applicable to Contractual Obligations in Europe edited by Franco Ferrari, Stefan Leible, p.124 : "Article 7 (4) contains a rather complicated rule for Compulsory insurance contracts. As has been pointed out by other writers, the existing rule could easily be replaced by a much simpler rule. Compulsory insurance contracts should simply be subject to the law of the country which prescribes the legal obligation to insure.
Article 7 (4) only applies if－at least with regard to contracts on mass risks－the risk is located within the EU. As there is no reason for a differentiation between contracts on mass risks situated within or outside the EU, the new rule should be extended to all contracts.

[236] 對於7(1)條規定除了大數量危險外，本條文只適用於歐盟內之危險，甚多歐洲同僚，包含Max Planck Institute 在內，對此皆加以批評，認為保險持有人皆應受到相同之保護（特別是中小企業）。見Urs Peter Gruber, Insurance Contracts, pp.123,124: "The differentiation between risks located inside and outside the EU already existed in the old law. It lacks a convincing explanation and has been heavily (and rightly) criticised in scholarly writing. There is no reason why the protection of the policy-holder should be different and－especially with regard to contracts on mass risks not concluded by a consumer, but by a small or medium-sized enterprise-weaker if the risk is situated outside the EU."

法時，應依訂約時危險所在地會員國之法律[237]。美國第2新編192條規定。於人壽保險契約時，若被保險人自己申請保險契約時，在申請時其並未有效的選定準據法，以其申請保單時之住所地法做為其權利之依據，除非在有關特定之爭點上，依據第6條之原則其他州對當事人及交易有著更重大關連，於此情形下該其他州法應為依據[238]。至於人壽保險中被保人非為申請人時，第2新編認為並不適用本規則，因為沒有其他確定之規則，於當事人沒有有效選法之情形下，只能以188條之規則為依據[239]。第2新編193條規定火災、保全或傷害保險契約之效力及契約中之權利，依於保單有效期間當事人所理解應為被保之危險之主要所在地之法律為依據，除非於有關特定之爭點上，其他州依據第6條之原則對當事人及交易有著更重要關連，於此情形下該其他州之法應為依據[240]。至於船、卡車、飛機、及火車

---

[237] 3.In the case of an insurance contract other than a contract falling within paragraph 2,only the following laws may be chosen by the parties in accordance with Article 3:
(a) the law of any Member State where the risk is situated at the time of conclusion of the contract;
(b) the law of the country where the policy holder has his habitual residence;
(c) in the case of life assurance, the law of the Member State of which the policy holder is a national;
(d) for insurance contracts covering risks limited to events occurring in one Member State other than the Member State where the risk is situated, the law of that Member State.
(e) where the policy holder of a contract falling under this paragraph pursues a commercial or industrial activity or a liberal profession and the insurance contract covers two or more risks which relate to those activities and are situated in different Member States, the law of any of the Member State concerned or the law of the country of habitual residence of the policy holder.
Where, in the cases set out in points (a), (b) or (e), the Member States referred to grant greater freedom of choice of the law applicable to the insurance contract, the parties may take advantage of that freedom.
To the extent that the law applicable has not been chosen by the parties in accordance with this paragraph, such a contract shall be governed by the law of the Member State in which the risk is situated at the time of conclusion of the contract.

[238] 192 Life Insurance Contracts
The validity of a life insurance contract issued to the insured upon his application and the rights created thereby are determined, in the absence of an effective choice of law by the insured in his application, by the local law of the state where the insured was domiciled at the time the policy was applied for, unless, with respect to the particular issue, some other state has a more significant relationship under the principles stated in s.6 to the transaction and the parties, in which event the local law of the other state will be applied.

[239] Second Restatement, conflict of Laws, s. 192, comment a, "The rule does not apply to life insurance issued upon the life of someone other than the applicant; as to such insurance, no more definite rule can be stated, in the absence of an effective choice of law by the parties, than that stated in s.188"

[240] S193 Contracts of Fire, Surety or Casualty Insurance
The validity of a contract of fire, surety or casualty insurance and the rights created thereby are deter-

等物被保險時，因為該些物經常於州際間移動，故沒有被保險的主要危險所在地。於此情形下，危險之所在地對於準據法的決定並沒有大的影響力。第2新編認為於此情形下應依第188條之規則去決定準據法[241]。

　　個人之所以於此評述保險契約，乃是保險契約有著社會安全之性質，對比之下甚能發現各個國家國際法之屬性。基於資本主義英國法院為了保護英國跨國保險公司之商業利益，於保險契約上竭盡所能的以默示英國準據法為國際法之基本原則，或在沒有其他密切關連國家時以保險人之營業地法為準據法，[242]而歐盟亦半推半就的採此原則（至少於羅馬公約）。眾所周知美國衝突法是以美國居民間之州際衝突為主，故而通常衝突法之發展是受到憲法之限制（但管轄法則就甚為歧視外人），以確保選法之結果對美國居民不會造成「武斷及基本上不公平」[243]之後果。故而歐盟應該很冷靜的想一想，第2新編192條註釋a中對於人壽險之申請者不是被保人及193條之火災、保全、或傷害保險中，可能會不承認當事人自定準據法的。於2009年的世界金融危機中，全世界見證了跨國企業於保險及金融業務上之貪婪，美國、英國及歐盟皆受創甚重，全世界還要執迷不悟的追隨英國法院犧牲弱勢而保護跨國企業於保險及金融方面之利益嗎？

　　193條的註釋e如此解釋：「正如同於人壽保險契約中之選法條款不會被給予效力之同樣理由，於火災、保全、或傷害保險契約之選法條款所指定之州法，如果相較於原來所應適用之準據法是給予被保險人較少之

---

mined by the local law of the state which the parties understood was to be the principal location of the insured risk during the term of the policy, unless with respect to the particular issue, some other state has a more significant relationship under the principles stated in s.6 to the transaction and the parties, in which event the local law of the other state will be applied.

[241] Second Restatement, Conflict of Laws, s.193, comment a.

[242] 陳隆修，《國際私法契約評論》，台北，五南圖書公司，民國75年2月，初版，46、47頁，「在當事人沒有指定準據法的情形下，並且沒有其他國家的法律制度與該保險契約有著密切牽連的情況下，英國一般以保險人的營業地法為準據法。若保險人有數個營業地，則以其總公司所在地法為準據法。在保險契約中，契約訂定地是經常很難決定的，因為經常保險公司之代理人須將保險契約寄回公司由公司批准，而且於人壽保險契約時常須保險費繳了後契約方生效。契約履行地的決定亦甚困難，因為經常要保人有權可以選擇數個地方為給付保險金額的地方。」
Greer v. Poole (1880) 5 Q. B. D. 272;
Pick v. Manufacturers Life Insurance Co. [1958] 2 Lloyds Rep. 93.

[243] Allstate Insurance Co. v. Hague, 449 U.S. 302, 313 (1981).

保護，是通常不會被給予效力的。[244]」192條的註釋c認為人壽保險是與強烈的公共政策有關，於大部份州皆有著廣泛之規定，被保險人之住所地對相關爭點有著顯著之利益。「同樣的人壽保險的一個主要立法目的是在於保護個別被保險人及其受益人，而法院則以透過他們選法規則之方法企圖可以幫助這個目的之達成。至少於通常情形下，法院以要求被保人應受到所地法之保護之方式而達到這個目的。[245]」註釋e再次重申選法條款若給予被保險人其原應適用之準據法較少之保護時，該選法條款不會被給予效力，而該原應適用之法律通常即應為被保險人之住所地法。被選定法律於此情形下之不會被尊重理由之一即為人壽保險契約通常是由保險人單方擬定，而被保險人並無選擇之餘地。註釋e認為當事人若可以「明示」選法（非「默示」選法），而「明示」選擇非本州之其他州之法律時應為不一樣。「於此種情形，被保險人行使一個自由之選擇，並且只要合乎187條規則之要求則該選法應受到尊重。該些要求之一即為被選定適用之州法不能違背他州之基本政策，而該州於決定一特定爭點上較被選定之州有著實質上更重大的利益，並且依188條於當事人未有效選法時該州法應為準據法。[246]」而後者之州通常即為被保險人之州，而給予被保險人較其自己州

---

[244] e. Choice of law by the parties. Effect will frequently not be given to a choice-of-law provision in a contract of fire, surety or casualty insurance which designates a state whose local law gives the insured less protection than he would receive under the otherwise applicable law for the same reasons that effect is not given to such a provision in a life insurance contract (see ?192, Comment e).

[245] "Likewise, a major purpose of life insurance legislation is to protect the individual insured and his beneficiaries, and the courts have sought to assist in the achievement of this purpose by means of their choice-of-law rules. They have done so by requiring that, at least as a general rule, the insured should receive the protection accorded him by the local law of his domicile."其comment d又解釋於軍人或供及年金之契約等，住所可能有時並不是絕對因素；另外新住所可能決定離婚是否會自動撤銷妻子為受益人之身份。

[246] "The situation is different when the insured at the time he applies for the insurance is given a choice between having the contract governed by the local law of the state of his domicile or of some other state and expressly chooses in his application the local law of the other state. In such a situation, the insured exercises a free choice and the chosen law should be applied provided that the requirements of the rule of s187 are satisfied. One of these requirements is that application of the law of the chosen state must not be contrary to a fundamental policy of a state which has a materially greater interest than the chosenstate in the determination of the particular issue and which, under the rule of s188, would be the state of the applicable law in the absence of an effective choice of law by the parties. This latter state would usually be that where the insured was domiciled at the time the policy was applied for. Since life insurance is a matter of intense public concern and since the major purpose of legislation in this area is to

法更少的保護即可能會違背該州之基本政策。類似此種基本政策之強行適用羅馬 I 規定於7條4項。其a款規定保險契約之訂立須依會員國所加諸責任之特別規定。而危險所在地會員國法與加諸訂保險契約責任之會員國法彼此衝突時，後者優先。B款規定會員國得不遵守2、3項之規定，而要求保險契約依加諸訂立保險契約責任之會員國法[247]。

　　羅馬 I 7條5項規定第3項3款及第4項之情形，若契約涵蓋不止位於一會員國之危險，該契約應被視為由數個契約構成，而一契約只與一會員國有關[248]。第2新編193條註解f亦規定一個保險契約涵蓋位於數個州之危險時，通常法院應視其為有關數個契約，而每個契約只投保一個危險[249]。例如一個保單保險位於3個州之不同房子。

　　相較於羅馬公約之解釋報告，羅馬 I 第7條是大部份針對歐盟而立法，故明顯的與美國第2新編較為吻合並似乎較為公平。但仍可預見的會

---

protect the individual insured and his beneficiaries, it might well be repugnant to a fundamental policy of the state of the otherwise applicable law to give the insured less protection than this state would accord him under its own local law."

以下為拒絕給予選法條款效力之判決：

New York Life Ins. Co. v. Cravens, 178 U.S. 389 (1900); New England Life Ins. Co. v. Olin, 114 F.2d 131 (7th Cir. 1940), cert. den. 312 U.S. 686 (1941); Great Southern Life Ins. Co. v. Burwell, 12 F.2d 244 (5th Cir. 1926), cert. den. 271 U.S. 683 (1926); Albro v. Manhattan Life Ins. Co.,119 Fed. 629 (D.Mass. 1902), aff'd 127 Fed. 281 (1st Cir. 1904), cert. den. 194 U.S. 633 (1904); Mutual Life Ins. Co. v. Mullen, 107 Md. 457, 69 A. 385 (1908); Harwood v. Security Mut. Life Ins. Co., 263 Mass. 341, 161 N.E. 589 (1927); Dolan v. Mutual Reserve Fund Life Ass'n, 173 Mass. 197, 53 N.E. 398 (1899); Pietri v. Seguenot, 96 Mo. App. 258, 69 S.W. 1055 (1902); N.Y. Life Ins. Co. v. Block, 6 Ohio Cir. Dec. 166 (1893); Keatley v. Travelers' Ins. Co., 187 Pa. 197, 40 A. 808 (1898).

[247] 4.The following additional rules shall apply to insurance contracts covering risks for which a Member State imposes an obligation to take out insurance;

(a) the insurance contract shall not satisfy the obligation to take out insurance unless it complies with the specific provisions relating to that insurance laid down by the member state that imposes the obligation. Where the law of the Member State in which the risk is situated and the law of the Member State imposing the obligation to take out insurance contradict each other, the latter shall prevail;

(b) by way of derogation from paragraphs 2 and 3, A Member State may lay down that the insurance contract shall be governed by the law of the Member State that imposes the obligation to take out insurance.

[248] 5. For the purposes of paragraph 3, third subparagraph, and paragraph 4, where the contract covers risks situated in more than one Member State, the contract shall be considered as constituting several contracts each relating to only one Member State.

[249] "If so, the single policy will usually incorporate the special statutory forms of the several states involved. Presumably, the courts would be inclined to treat such a case, at least with respect to most issues, as if it involved three policies, each insuring an individual risk."

產生許多問題，如192條中被保險人之不誠實是否阻止其請求之權利；人壽保險之借貸問題[250]；未付保險金而遭沒收時被保人有何對抗之保障；及年金給付保險與意外及健康殘廢保險是否適用與人壽保險相同之選法規則[251]。另外193條中被保人之不誠實是否阻止損害請求權；危險是否涵蓋於保單中；被保人之請求權是否只限於實際損害；因投保之危險而遭受訴訟時得否請求訴訟費用；保險人是否得因被保人未立即通知意外之發生而解除責任；及於保單作成後主要之危險所在地卻移至他州之情形[252]。無論是第2新編的192、193條及羅馬Ⅰ要點33皆公開的承認於保險契約中保護保單持有人之共同核心價值，以這兩個經濟體之巨大實力對於以上這些實質上之問題，是有能力規劃出詳盡之實體法規則。但如單就選法規則而言，後進之羅馬Ⅰ第7條過分繁瑣，不如早期第2新編192及193條之簡潔。更重要的是192及193條充份的展示保護保單持有人、被保人、及受益人之決心，其公開的宣誓保險契約之大拇指規則是後進的羅馬Ⅰ所應效法的：有關保險契約之選法規則，無論是包含於契約中、法律之適用上、或被保人是否有自由選擇下之同意，應在於對被保人有利下才能被給予效力[253]。（亦即應給予其較原來應適用之法律較大之保障）

個人於此不厭其煩的評述保險契約之選法規則，是在證明保險契約之共同核心價值乃在保護保單持有人、被保人、及受益人。而前述英國判例法以保險契約之標準格式來推定保險契約準據法應被「默示」為保險人之

---

[250] S.192, comment f, "The law selected by application of the rule of this Section determines the validity of the loan and the rights created thereby. If, however, the insurer should make the insured a loan on terms different from those stated in the original contract, the loan would be a new and separate agreement governed by its own proper law, namely by the local law of the state which, with respect to the particular issue, has the most significant relationship to the loan – as distinguished from the original contract – and the parties."

[251] S.192, comment L 認為這兩種保險應適用192條。

[252] 如若保險人可以合理的預見該危險之移轉至他州時，以該州法為依據對其並非不公平。
Clay v. Sun Insurance Office, Ltd., 363 U.S. 207 (1960), 377 U.S. 179 (1964).

[253] "On the other hand, a choice-of-law provision, whether contained in the contract or in the application and whether or not freely agreed to by the insured, may be given effect if to do so would be to the advantage of the insured. None of the policy considerations discussed above stand in the way of giving the insured greater protection than he would receive under the otherwise applicable law." 見s.192有關人壽保險之comment e。

住所地法（主要營業地法），是違反現代人類文明於保險法之主流核心價值之作法。英國或許是世界上於保險法上最具歷史與最有經驗之國家，對保險法實體法上之共同核心價值自然是最了解的國家。但為什麼於國際契約法上會作出這種違反人類契約法上基本政策之判例?於國際上聲名卓越之英國法院於此顯然選擇維護英國跨國保險公司之商業利益，而放棄對弱勢主持正義之崇高理想。英國法院這種為本國跨國公司之商業利益而放棄保護弱勢人權之作法，雖然於程度及力道上較為微弱，於基本上仍與美國法院以「不方便法院」為理由替美國跨國公司賺取血錢之資本主義作風一致[254]。尊敬的Lord Denning氣勢磅礴的宣示英國法院會對來英國「選購法院」的外國人給予符合公平正義的待遇[255]，但要符合Lord Denning這段膾炙人口的宣示，或許英國法院應該拋棄自Jeremy Bentham以來對資本主義追逐利益（the dogma of laissez - faire）自由放任）的忠誠與擁護，而改以禮運大同篇的王道精神為主軸，積極的維護弱勢者於個案中之正義。

　　羅馬Ⅰ新增的第7條充份的證明羅馬公約解釋報告引用英國判例法之錯誤。羅馬公約與羅馬Ⅰ於此處之不同，不但證明羅馬公約的大謬誤，及英國判例法中之殖民主義掠奪式法學之不正義，更再一次證明辨識實體法中之主流核心共同價值之必要性。個人誠摯的認為可能於許多方面或許實體法方法論於維護個案正義上，其法學方法論之優越性是超過利益說及最重要關連說。

　　另外年輕的同僚必須注意到國際私法之高科技性，很清楚的時間於此

---

[254] 陳隆修，《2005年海牙法院選擇公約評析》，台北，五南圖書公司，2009年1月，初版1刷，294頁，雖然美國最高法院於Overmyer Co. v. Frick Co., 405 U.S. 174 (1972)中要求當事人必須有著「substantially equal bargaining power」。實務上許多有經驗的律師應該都會同意，於國際訴訟上法院地的決定經常幾乎等同案件輸贏的決定，這種情形對弱勢之一方更為明顯。例如美國法院近年來幾乎一面倒的傾向以不方便法院去拒絕接受外國原告所提起的外國訴因之訴訟，以保護美國跨國公司於有關侵權行為之集體訴訟中不受到美國鉅額損害賠償之請求。但近年來實務案例上證明，遭受到以不方便法院為由而被拒絕審理之外國被告，幾乎大部分都因費用過高或賠償額太少而無法於其他國家再提訴訟或只好接受少額之和解金。Walter W. Heiser, Forum non conveniens and choice of law; The impact of applying foreign law in transnational tort actions, 51 Wayne L. Rev. 1161, 1163 (2005)。

[255] The Atlantic Star, [1973] 1 Q.B. 364, 381-82 (C.A.), per. Lord Denning.

已證明羅馬公約的解釋報告是被英國判例法所誤導。崛起中的大中華經濟圈必須注意到先進國家經常以透過判例法習慣或貿易習慣之既成事實來維護其商業利益，例如以標準格式之使用造成默示同意保險人住所地法為準據法之慣例，即為對弱勢及第3世界不公平之習慣。於國際私法[256]上這種憑藉經濟強權所造成之既成事實，要求弱勢及第3世界必須遵守之情況甚多。這種要求弱勢無異議的接受強權所造成之習慣，即使於專注於國內案件之實體法[257]亦所在多有。**不爭的事實是大中華經濟區亦已是世界上主要之經濟力量，隨著崛起的經濟力量，大中華經濟區之法院自然依同樣的法律邏輯，不但可以拒絕歐美法院所造成之「貿易習慣」，進而可以主張對我們有商業利益之「習慣法」。**但個人認為我們的法院應不同於英國及美國法院之追逐商業利益，應以王道精神為法院判決之依據。對於弱勢及第3世界，中華民族之法院或許應本著「人溺己溺」之精神，扶弱抑強於個案中主持正義。而非憑藉著再次崛起的經濟力量，壓迫第三世界，造成對自己民族有利之商業習慣法。滄海桑田「天道好還」，中國式國際商業習慣法的建立，除了消極的要符合「合理性」訴求外，更要積極的實現「禮運大同篇」之祖訓。

十三、契約自由受限於合理性與誠信原則

公約及規則3(1)條最後之一句允許當事人所選擇之法律適用於契約

---

[256] 例如歐盟布魯塞爾規則Council Regulation (EC) No 44/2001第23條1項C款對管轄條形式要件即規定：(c) in international trade or commerce, in a form which accords with a usage of which the parties are or ought to have been aware and which in such trade or commerce is widely known to, and regularly observed by, parties to contracts of the type involved in the particular trade or commerce concerned.

[257] 例如歐盟契約法原則1:105條，但該1:105條為實體法原則，較專注於歐盟間之國內案件，故而有「合理性」之限制。

Article 1:105 Usages and Practices

(1) The parties are bound by any usage to which they have agreed and by any practice they have established between themselves.

(2) The parties are bound by a usage which would be considered generally applicable by persons in the same situation as the parties, except where the application of such usage would be unreasonable. The UNIDROIT Principles 2004, art. 1.9 追隨歐盟契約法原則1:105條，對習慣的「合理性」亦有規定。

之全部或一部，亦即接受分割式之選法（decpecage；pick and choose；issue by issue；severability）。這種作法是早期英國法院允許當事人明示選擇法律之判例法下[258]，當事人選法自由法律哲學沿續表現。公約的解釋報告亦認為分割方法論是直接與選法自由連接，因此要禁止它是很困難的。但是如同當事人於默示選法時，如果這些默示之意思有衝突時（conflicting inferences），則就不能符合「合理的確定」或「清楚的顯示」之要件。同樣的分割選法必須於邏輯上是一致的，於適用不同的法律時是不能有相衝突之情形。例如同一契約中不同的條文雖可適用不同的法律，但若於因不履行而中止契約上，賣方與買方所適用的法律不同，則可能會產生衝突情形而皆不能適用，此時必須依公約或規則之第4條規定而去推定準據法[259]。

不但於法理上分割適用是尊重當事人自主原則，於實務上亦經常可能是符合經濟邏輯的，例如一個共同投資契約可能於實際上包含數個獨立部份之契約。而且於事實上爭論契約中不同之議題是否得交付不同之準據法是沒有意義的，於形式要件、能力及契約履行之合法等議題上，各國法院是經常不以契約主要準據法為依據的。[260]解釋報告認為分割選法不應限制於明示選法，而應包含默示選法在內[261]。另外當事人之分割選法可能只是針對某一特定部份，故不能被據此而推論該分割之選法應被引用為整個契

---

[258] Gienar v Meyer (1796) 2 Hy Bl 603.

[259] Report on the Convention on the law applicable to contractual obligations by Mario Giuliano and Paul Lagarde. Official Journal C 282, 31/10/1980, "severability is directly linked with the principle of freedom of contract and so would be difficult to prohibit. Nevertheless when the contract is severable the choice must be logically consistent, i.e. it must relate to elements in the contract which can be governed by different laws without giving rise to contradictions."

[260] R.H.Graveson, Conflict of Laws, 7th ed., p.400, "The law of contracts is based broadly on a wide measure of liberty of the individual to make what agreements he pleases. While it can be said that principles are well settled as to what law governs the separate parts of the contract, full effect can only be given to the will of the parties by applying to the most important aspects of their agreement, such as essential validity and discharge, a system of law that they themselves may have selected, known as the 'proper law.' Other aspects, such as form, capacity and legality, ie generally outside the limits allowed by law to the completely free will of parties, and are governed to some extent by different choice of law rules."

[261] "The experts concerned also emphasized that severability should not be limited to cases of express choice of law."

約之準據法,解釋報告認為於此情形應適用第4條[262]。個人認為解釋報告於此所採之法律邏輯,與於默示選法時引用法國民法條文做為契約條款時得以法國法為契約準據法完全不同,這或許是歐盟引用英國判例法之另一盲點。

公約及規則3(2)條規定,於不影響形式要件(公約9條、規則11條)及第3人權利下,無論以前應適用之準據法是當事人以前根據本條文所選定,或公約或規則其他條文所規定,當事人得於任何時間同意改變以前應適用之準據法。這個規定亦是根據契約自由原則而來,故而訂約後改變準據法之規定亦應適用原來第1個選擇時之規則。於訴訟程序中之改變應適用之法律,解釋報告則認為應以法院地之程序法為依據。但本項規定準據法之變更不能影響到契約形式要件之效力及第3人之權利。

羅馬Ⅰ規則3(3)條規定:「於選定法律時所有與案件情形相關之其他因素皆位於非被選定法律之國家時,當事人之選法不能違反該國不能經由約定而被違背之法律規定之適用。」條文表面之文字似乎與公約3(3)條[263]不一樣的是規則3(3)條之所有案件情形之因素是包括當事人之選定管轄條款在內。亦即不似公約3(3)條,當事人欲規避規則3(3)條之適用,只須於契約中加入選定非該欲被規避國家之法院為指定管轄法院,即可達到規避該欲被規避國家之法律。但其要點15卻依舊重申「無論有無伴隨管轄條款本條文應被加以適用」,故仍與公約一致。[264]公約的解釋報告敘述英國同僚認為,只要當事人的選擇是合理的、符合誠信的、可以保障應被保護的利益,則應受到尊重。除了違反非被選定法律之強行法規外,選法自由

---

[262] "The Group did not adopt the idea that the judge can use a partial choice of law as the basis for a presumption in favour of one law invoked to govern the contract in its entirety. Such an idea might be conducive to error in situations in which the parties had reached agreement on the choice of law solely on a specific point. Recourse must be had to Article 4 in the case of partial choice."

[263] 3.The effect that the parties have chosen a foreign law, whether or not accompanied by the choice of a foreign tribunal, shall not, where all the other elements relevant to the situation at the time of the choice are connected with one country only, prejudice the application of rules of the law of that country which cannot be derogated from by contract, hereinafter called "mandatory rules".

[264] "This rule should apply whether or not the choice of law was accompanied by a choice of court or tribunal."

不應受違背。他們舉了甚多與外國無關，但當事人之選定該外國法是完全合理之例子[265]。

　　如前述於2004年U.C.C.1-301(c)(2)條中國際契約之當事人是可以選定不相關國家之法律，但於第(1)款中國內契約之當事人卻必須被限於選擇各州之法律。如個人早期所述[266]，只要於商業習慣或傳統與被選定之國家有關，英國法院通常會允許當事人選定不相干國家之法律為準據法[267]。於R. v. International Trustee for the Protection of Bondholders A.G.中Lord Atkin對契約準據法說明如下：「有關契約適當法的問題，引導英國法院的法律原則現在已經完全是被確定了。當事人意圖適用的法律應即為該法律。他們的意思應以契約所表達之意思為依據，如果他們有意思的話，那他們的意思應為定論。[268]」The Vita Food Products Inc. v. Unus Shipping Co. Ltd.是英國尊重當事人選法自由之著名案例[269]，Lord Wright於該案中對契約自由所下的限制條件為所有教科書必須探討之論述：「……很難看出會有可能之限制，假如當事人所表達之意思是誠信[270]及合

---

[265] Giuliano and Lagarde Report, "and on the other the concern of other experts, notably the United Kingdom experts, that such a correcting factor would be too great an obstacle to the freedom of the parties in situations in which their choice appeared justified, made in good faith, and capable of serving interests worthy of protection. In particular these experts emphasized that departures from the principle of the parties' freedom of choice should be authorized only in exceptional circumstances, such as the application of the mandatory rules of a law other than that chosen by the parties; they also gave several examples of cases in which the choice of a foreign law by the parties was fully justified, although there was apparently no other foreign element in the situation."

[266] 陳隆修，《國際私法契約評論》，台北，五南圖書公司，民國75年2月，初版，27、28頁。

[267] R.H.Graveson, Conflict of Laws, 7th ed. P.412，記載就只有於不方便法院及被選定法院之特殊情形下，才有己知的兩個選法不被尊重的案例："In only two reported cases, so far as we know, has the court refused to uphold an express choice of applicable law, in the particular instance because of the doctrine of forum non conveniens and the special circumstances of the chosen jurisdiction." The Athenee (1922) 11 L1.L.Rep. 6 (C.A.) The Fehmarn [1958] 1 W.L.R. 159.

[268] "The legal principles which are to guide an English court on the question of the proper law of a contract are now well settled. It is the law which the parties intended to apply. Their intention will be ascertained by the intention expressed in the contract, if any, which will be conclusive." [1937] A.C. 500, 529。又見Mount Albert Borough Council v. Australasian Temperance and General Mutual Life Assurance Society Ltd. [1938] A.C. 224.之論述又為The Assunzione [1954] P.150, 175, Singleton L.J.所引用。

[269] 陳隆修，《國際私法契約評論》，台北，五南圖書公司，民國75年2月，初版，26、27頁。

[270] Black's Law Dictionary 7th ed., p.168,對"bona fide"的解釋是符合「誠信」的("good faith")；沒有詐欺或欺騙。

法的，及假如沒有理由因為公共政策而使得該選擇為無效。[271]」

或許是基於上個世紀50年代對自由經濟之信任，最尊敬的恩師Prof. Graveson對Lord Wright限制條件之不確定性評述如下：「相對於美國有些州或法國的fraude a la loi[272]，英國並沒有規避法律的一般性理論，但是我們仍然不能分隔動機與誠信原則。於考慮當事人明示選擇準據法所被給予的寬廣自由時一個這方面的決定性因素是，除非被證明為相反的，他們所作的任何選擇須被推定為符合誠信及合法的。例如自動的適用合理性之標準（這是判例法等同大陸法之誠信原則），會降低明示選法的層次到於沒有明示選法時被考慮的其他因素，而使得當事人選擇的自由變得無效。[273]」Prof. Graveson之信念可能應是基於上世紀自由經濟之理念，而

---

[271] "...it is difficult to see what qualifications are possible, provided the intention expressed is bona fide and legal, and provided there is no reason for avoiding the choice on the ground of public policy", [1939] 1 All E.R. 513, 521.對於其合法性限制於邏輯上之錯誤，恩師睿智的指出其於實際上之必要性。R.H. Graveson, Conflict of Laws, 7th ed., p.412.

"The second of Lord Wright's qualifying factors, the need for the choice to be 'legal', probably means legal when tested by the rules of the proper law governing legality of contracts. Here, as in many places in this subject, one has to assume legality in order to discover the proper law by which legality will be tested. It is a manifest logical error but a practical necessity."

[272] R.H. Graveson, "The Doctrine of Evasion of the Law in England and America" (1937) 19 Journal Comp.Leg. 21 et seq.; "Comparative Aspects of the General Principles of Private International Law," 2 Recueil des Cours de l' Academie (1963), Chap. 4. On tax avoidance, see Re Weston's Settlements [1969] 1 Ch. 234.但澳洲有判例當事人所選的準據法不被尊重，見Golden Acres Ltd v. Queensland Estates Ltd. [1969] St. R. Qd. 378; Queensland Estates Ltd. v. Collas [1971] St R. Qd. 75，其所以不被尊重乃是因規避法院地之法或與契約沒有牽連。於陳隆修，《國際私法契約論評》，台北，五南圖書公司，民國75年2月，初版，28頁，一般說來大陸法系國家，尤其是法國，向來主張不允許有脫避法律的行為（faude a la loi）。但英國基於傳統上民主政治之開放，法院一般認為國家只要制定了法律，人民即有權利做法律所不明文禁止之行為，縱然該行為之目的是在規避法律，只要其不違反法律國家無權干涉，要防止這種規避行為，應由立法上著手（legislation）。英國法院一般都相當自制，而不願以司法干涉立法，故英國判例上幾乎沒有禁止規避法律（evasion of the law）的行為。又見陳隆修，《2005年海牙法院選擇公約評析》，台北，五南圖書公司，2009年1月，初版1刷，165、166頁，個人認為政治性議題及重大政策的改變，於三權分立下應交由國會處理，法院於此方面是沒有judicial power。於此方面英國判例法於1986 the Family Law Act s.46(及其前身1971 Act與1973 Act)通過前，費盡判例法技巧的以Indyka v. Indyka [1969] 1 AC 33 等一系列案件以達成公正之判決，應為人類近代司法史上楷模，見陳隆修，《美國國際私法新理論》，台北，五南圖書公司，民國76年1月，初版，204～206頁，又見陳隆修、許兆慶、林恩瑋、李瑞生四人合著，《國際私法—管轄與選法理論之交錯》，台北，五南圖書公司，2009年3月，初版1刷，225～227頁。又見2005年海牙選擇法院公約19、20條禁止規避法律之規定。

[273] R.H. Graveson, Conflict of Laws, 7th ed. Pp.411, 412, "There is no general doctrine of evasion of the law in England corresponding to that found in certain American states or to the French fraude a la loi, yet one cannot separate the ideas of good faith and motive. A decisive consideration in this matter is that

本世紀初經濟理念之重點應可能是在於環保及加強對企業之監督。但即使於上世紀之自由經濟氛圍，當事人選法自由應受到判例法「合理性」及大陸法「誠信原則」之限制則為不爭的事實。至於「合理性」或「誠信原則」所適用之強度及廣泛程度可能會因法院及個案不同而有所差異。例如於「合理性」及「誠信原則」之限制下，有時輪船公司[274]或保險公司[275]於正義之需求下是應受到保護，而非通常一般所謂之弱勢應受到保護。

　　如前述個人認為契約及其條款皆應受到客觀合理性及主觀誠信原則之限制。亦即實體契約法及契約選法規則皆應以合理性及誠信原則為法學之基本原則，並且合理性及誠信原則亦應作為警察原則，以對抗契約或其條款於程序上或實體上之不公平。除了過分注重西方貿易利益而藐視人權的2005年海牙選擇法院公約外，人類近代文明的法學發展似乎甚少有這麼極端狂熱的支持管轄條款效力及拒絕選法自由的先例[276]。

　　於仲裁條款之成立及效力上，紐約公約第2條3項已規定繫屬法院得認定該條款為「無效」、「不能適用」、或「不能被履行」[277]。相同的規

---

in view of the wide freedom given to the parties to choose expressly the proper law, any choice they make must be presumed bona fide and legal until the contrary is shown. To apply automatically the test of reasonableness, for example (as the common law equivalent of the civilian good faith), would nullify the freedom of choice of the parties by reducing their express choice to the legal level of all other factors which are taken into consideration in the absence of express choice."恩師這個論述與後來英國法院於管轄條款效力之認定上大致上相配合，陳隆修、許兆慶、林恩瑋、李瑞生四人合著，《國際私法—管轄與選法理論之交錯》，台北，五南圖書公司，2009年3月，初版1刷，199~201頁。

[274] 陳隆修，《2005年海牙法院選擇公約評析》，台北，五南圖書公司，2009年1月，初版1刷，80、89頁，於Dimskal Shipping Co., SA v. International Transport Workers Federation, [1992] 2 A.C. 152中，一賴比瑞亞船公司之船停於瑞典港口時，船員工會威脅除非船公司多付船員薪資及捐贈大筆捐款給予工會之福利基金，否則會將船公司列入黑名單中。船公司同意這些條件，一旦明定該「契約」以英國法為準據法，雖然依瑞典法該工會之經濟脅迫（economic duress）並非為非法行為，但英國法為若契約成立時契約之準據法，故契約存在與否及脅迫之效果應依英國法而定。英國最高法院判經濟上之脅迫，構成契約得被撤銷之後果（voidable）。

[275] 同前註，79、89頁，Mackender v. Feldia, [1967] 2 Q.B.590 (CA)個人並不認同英國上訴法院於此案中尊重基於不誠實行為而來管轄條款之效力。

[276] 同前註，51頁。

[277] 3.The court of a Contracting State, when seized of an action in a matter in respect of which the parties have made an agreement within the meaning of this article, shall, at the request of one of the parties, refer the parties to arbitration, unless it finds that the said agreement is null and void, inoperative or incapable of being performed.

定亦重覆於1985之模範公約第8條1項[278]。於管轄條款之成立及效力上，在The Sennar （No.2）[279]中英國最高法院認為個案正義應優先於管轄條款之效力。在The Bremen v. Zapata Off-shore Co.[280]中，美國最高法院認為管轄條款必須為「合理且公平」（reasonable and fair），並且不可以對他方造成「壓迫或不平」（oppressive or unfair）之情形。歐盟法院亦於West Tantker[281]中表示應遵守紐約公約2(3)條，於仲裁條款之適用上應保障人民「應享有之司法保護」之憲政人權。**一切的契約及契約中的條款不但皆應以「合理性」及「誠信原則」為基礎，並且其成立、存在、及效力亦應受到這兩個原則之限制，以避免造成「武斷及基本上不公平之後果」**。[282]既然仲裁條款及管轄條款之成立、存在、及效力皆應以這兩個原則為基礎，並受到這兩個原則之限制，與這兩個條款並列的選法條款自然亦應本於相同之基礎及限制。

十四、假設準據法與強行實體政策

(一)假設推定準據法

羅馬Ⅰ要點23即宣示對弱勢一方之訂約者於選法規則上應加以保護。另外於5(2)條之旅客運送、6條消費者契約、及7(3)、(4)條相關之保險契約上亦皆有強制性之限制。這些規定都是符合Prof. Graveson所謂的「自動適用合理性之標準」，亦證明21世紀法學文明進展的趨勢是與20

---

[278] (1) A court before which an action is brought in a matter which is the subject of an arbitration agreement shall, if a party so requests not later than when submitting his first statement on the substance of the dispute, refer the parties to arbitration unless it finds that the agreement is null and void, inoperative or incapable of being performed.

[279] [1985] 1 WLR 490, p.500，見陳隆修、許兆慶、林恩瑋、李瑞生四人合著，《國際私法-管轄與選法理論之交錯》，台北，五南圖書公司，2009年3月，初版1刷，199～201頁。

[280] 407 U.S. 1(1972)，見陳隆修，《2005年海牙法院選擇公約評析》，台北，五南圖書公司，2009年1月，初版1刷，18、19頁。

[281] Allianz SpA, generali Assicurazioni Generali SpA. V. West Tankers Inc.., [2009] EUECJ C-185/07.

[282] Allstate Insurance co. v. Hague, 449 U.S. 302, 313 (1981)，以地域性之關連點及州利益作為憲法適當程序條款的標準，個人以為不如以英美法及大陸法所共同接受的「合理性」及「誠信原則」為共同核心主流標準。

世紀不同的，我們現在的重心是在監督企業，而不是在無條件的扶助企業的利益。

　　美國第2新編187條對當事人選法之自由亦加以限制。第1項規定於當事人得以明示條款而協議解決之爭點，當事人所選定之州法應被加以適用。第2項規定「即使雙方當事人無法以其契約中之明示規定，解決某特定爭點，其為處理其契約上的權利義務所選擇的州法律，仍應予以適用，除非：

　　(a)制定該被選擇法律（chosen law）的州與當事人或該交易行為並無實質關係（substantial relationship）存在，且沒有任何足以做為當事人選擇該州法律的合理依據存在；或者

　　(b)適用被選擇法律將與另一州的基本政策相違背，而政策被抵觸的州，對於特定爭點較制定被選擇法律的州有更顯著的利益，且依第一八八條規定，倘若當事人間並無有效的選擇法律存在時，該州（政策被牴觸者）的法律將是準據法。」亦即187條對於當事人不能以協議解決之爭點所同意之準據法，就只有於符合2項a款或b款之情形時才不會被適用。

　　所謂當事人「不能以協議解決之爭點」，其註釋b敘述如下：「正如其他的契約條款，如果於訂約時當事人一方之同意是經由不適當之方法取得，例如不實的表達、脅迫、不當的影響、或錯誤，則選法條款不會被給予效力。這種同意是否於事實上經由不適當之方法或錯誤而取得，應由繫屬法院依自己之法律原則而決定。繫屬法院可能考慮的一個因素是選法條款是否包含於一個『附合』契約中，亦即該契約是由強勢一方所單方制定，並且使得弱勢一方沒有真正討價該條款之機會，因此是呈現出一種『接受或拒絕』之基礎。這種契約是通常以印刷之形式而被準備的，並且通常至少他們有些條文是以極端小字的方式而被印刷。通常的例子就是各種票券及保險單。這種契約所包含的選法條款常是會被尊重的。但是繫屬法院會小心的檢視這些契約，並且於對被迫去遵守契約之一方造成重大不

公平時，會拒絕去適用他們所包含之任何選法條款。[283]」

　　首先包括選法條款在內之「任何其他契約條款」，如果當事人一方之同意是以不適當之方法而被取得，則第2新編之註釋b認為不應給予該條款效力。註釋b特別強調於當事人議價能力不相當之附合契約中，選法條款不得對弱勢一方造成實質不公平。所謂任何其他契約條款」自然包含選擇法院條款在內。**個人於此再次重述：2005年海牙法院選擇公約中之選法條款及管轄條款之規定，對弱勢及以不當方法取得他方同意之不公平情形，並沒有給予足夠之限制或保障之規定。註釋b規定：「這種同意是否於事實上經由不適當之方法或錯誤取得，應由繫屬法院依自己之法律原則而決定。」這與2005年海牙公約以被指定法院地法去決定該管轄條款之效力（亦即選法條款）不同[284]，而被指定法院為有絕對專屬管轄[285]亦與187條註釋b保護弱勢之政策違背。美國第2新編187條之規定及精神與2005年海牙公約之規定截然不同，這是岳不群法則適用之另一個現象。**

　　註釋b事實上是有關契約或其條款之成立、存在、及效力。羅馬Ｉ3(5)條規定：「當事人所選擇應適用法律之同意之存在及效力，應依10、11、及13條之規定。[286]」第11條為形式要件，13條為行為能力之相關規定。而相當於註釋b之範圍羅馬Ｉ規定於10(1)條：「契約或契約任何條款

---

[283] Restatement of the Law, Second, Conflict of Laws (1988 Revisions), s.187, Comment b, "Impropriety or mistake. A choice-of-law provision, like any other contractual provision, will not be given effect if the consent of one of the parties to its inclusion in the contract was obtained by improper means, such as by misrepresentation, duress, or undue influence, or by mistake. Whether such consent was in fact obtained by improper means or by mistake will be determined by the forum in accordance with its own legal principles. A factor which the forum may consider is whether the choice-of-law provision is contained in an 'adhesion' contract, namely one that is drafted unilaterally by the dominant party and then presented on a 'take-it-or-leave-it' basis to the weaker party who has no real opportunity to bargain about its terms. Such contracts are usually prepared in printed form, and frequently at least some of their provisions are in extremely small print. Common examples are tickets of various kinds and insurance policies. Choice-of-law provisions contained in such contracts are usually respected. Nevertheless, the forum will scrutinize such contracts with care and will refuse to apply any choice-of-law provision they may contain if to do so would result in substantial injustice to the adherent."

[284] 5(1)、6(a)、及9(a)條。

[285] 5(1)、6(a)、9(a)、及3(d)條。

[286] 5. The existence and validity of the consent of the parties as to the choice of the applicable law shall be determined in accordance with the provisions of Articles 10, 11 and 13.羅馬公約相同規則為3(4)條。

之存在及效力，應依契約或條款如若有效時，依本規則應為準據法之法律為依據。[287]」對於契約之成立、存在、及效力之基本問題，如果於根本上契約不成立時則自然沒有準據法之適用問題。對於此循環性之基本問題，英國傳統判例法上是以假定契約成立時契約之準據法來決定契約是否成立之問題[288]（「putative proper law doctrine」）。羅馬公約及規則亦採此種理論。但是所謂putative proper law doctrine並不是一個簡單的概念，是以當事人所宣稱契約中所指定之法律為依據，或是以如若當事人沒有指定法律或管轄法院時應為準據法之法律為依據？羅馬公約及規則是以前者為依據，如此一來當事人可以授權給自己將不合法之契約變為合法，自然於邏輯上會有問題，但其帶來之穩定性自然亦可能為商界所歡迎。[289]

有趣的是註釋b之論述：「這種同意是否於事實上經由不適當之方法或錯誤而取得，應由繫屬法院依自己之法律原則而決定。」這個論述不但與2005年海牙公約依被指定法院地法不同，亦與羅馬公約及規則的假設推定之準據法不同。187條3項規定：「除非有相反的意思表示，否則應指被選定法律之州之實體法。[290]」繫屬法院之法律原則是否包含選法規則在內，答案似乎應是不包含在內，而且至少是包含實體法在內，或應以實體法為主軸。美國第2新編187條註釋b的以法院地實體法做為契約或其條款成立、存在、及效力之依據，與個人主張應放棄令人感到困惑或有爭議性的putative proper law doctrine，而以實體法為依據之理論大致上相吻合：「的確，相關契約之存在及效力問題，例如前述之合併條款、額外

---

[287] 1.The existence and validity of a contract, or of any term of a contract, shall be determined by the law which would govern it under this Regulation if the contract or term were valid.同樣的條款規定於羅馬公約8(1)條。

[288] 陳隆修，《國際私法契約論》，台北，五南圖書公司，民國75年2月，初版，97～100頁。

[289] 陳隆修，《2005年海牙法院選擇公約評析》，台北，五南圖書公司，2009年1月，初版1刷，79~84、96頁，見Mackender v. Feldia [1967] 2 Q.B.590 (CA) 案之分析。

[290] (3) In the absence of a contrary indication of intention, the reference is to the local law of the state of the chosen law.又見comment h., "When they choose the state which is to furnish the law governing the validity of their contract, the parties almost certainly have the local law, 'rather than the law', of that state in mind (compare s.186, Comment b). To apply the law of the chosen state would introduce the uncertainties of choice of law into the proceedings and would serve to defeat the basic objectives, namely those of certainty and predictability, which the choice-of-law provision was designed to achieve."

附加條款、當事人沉默、錯誤、詐欺、脅迫、契約沒有對價、不同標準格式之衝突條款、當事人間慣例之拘束性及其他有關當事人是否同意之問題，若該應適用之putative proper law之相關國內契約法於沒有妥善之規定或甚至沒有規定時，公平正義之解決方案是無法達成的。而國際契約包羅萬象，經常每一個國家的國內法對根據其他法系而來之契約是無法應付的，例如英美法院是經常無法理解於大陸法中時效之利益是不得拋棄的，及違約金之規定於大陸法之契約是甚為天經地義之條款而非為不法條款。故而雖然putative proper law doctrine是現今國際社會於契約及其條款之成立及效力所最能被共同接受之國際私法規則，但個人認為其時代性之任務已結束，應由更為先進、更為具體之歐盟契約法規則來取代其過去之功能」[291]。

假設推定準據法之理論，過去於英國判例法上是個「令人困惑」的觀念，例如於Mackender v. Fedia[292]案所顯示的；而羅馬規則所採納的，卻是於邏輯上有缺陷（典型的「bootstraps doctrine」），並且太過於對弱勢不利之理論。羅馬公約及規則所採納的假設推定準據法理論是依契約中所指定之準據法，這種作法於契約之成立、存在、或效力有爭議下，對強勢一方是有著指定應適用法律之絕對優勢。歐盟這種對弱勢不利之作法，不但與第2新編187條之精神不合，亦與自己於羅馬Ⅰ要點23保護弱勢之宣示不合，個人再次懷疑歐盟羅馬公約8(1)條及規則10(1)條於未經全盤的思慮下，又錯誤的引用判例法之「putative proper law doctrine」。即使於20世紀，全世界文明國家契約法的核心觀念都是在保護弱勢，而不是在保護強勢，這與大陸法於契約法上之傳統精神不合。

個人於此再次重申－**有關契約成立、存在、及效力等重大影響當事**

---

[291] 陳隆修，《2005年海牙法院選擇公約評析》，台北，五南圖書公司，2009年1月，初版1刷，97頁。

[292] [1967] 2 Q.B.590 (CA)，P.603中，Diplock L.J.認為客觀上契約會成立時之準據法是個「令人困惑」的觀念。有關契約存在或效力準據法有各種提案：法院地法、當事人宣稱所選之法、及於當事人沒有明示選法時應為準據法之法。陳隆修，《2005年海牙法院選擇公約評析》，台北，五南圖書公司，2009年1月，初版1刷，70頁。

人權利義務之基本問題，應放棄「**putative proper law doctrine**」，而
直接以實體契約法原則為依據。個人曾經以歐盟契約法原則對美、英、及
歐盟之判例加以解析，其結果是如熱刀畫過奶油般的順利[293]。美國第2新
編187條之註釋b主張「由繫屬法院依自己之法律原則而決定」，故自然
亦是支持個人前述之實體法論。但在於實體法方法論之旗幟下，個人通常
是認為法院地之國內實體法，於有些情形下是沒有跨國性的實體法原則先
進。故而在有關契約條款成立、存在、及效力之問題，個人於去年之案例
分析中是以歐盟契約法原則為依據[294]。

(二)強行法於實體政策上之適用範圍

第2新編187條之註釋e認為：「契約法之主要目的是在保護當事人
之正當期待，並且使得他們可以準確的預測他們於契約中之權利義務為
何。[295]」並又認為當事人自主是最能達到這個目的，而且最能達成穩定性
及可預測性之結果。註釋e與個人早期主張「保護當事人的正當期待」應
作為契約法之主流價值[296]是一致的。但是又如註釋d所述，於有關當事人

---

[293] 同前註，70～98頁。
[294] 歐盟契約法原則1:101條第4項即開宗明義的規定本原則得適用於準據法沒規定之情形。
(4) These Principles may provide a solution to the issue raised where the system or rules of law applicable do not do so.
其註釋法有著解釋如下：
"F. The filling of Gaps
Even if the contract is subject to a specific national legal system, because of the parties' choice of law or by virtue of the objective connecting factors of the conflict of laws, the Principles may perform a function. Paragraph (4) envisages the case where a national legal system does not contain a rule for the solution of a specific issue. In such a case the court or arbitral tribunal is invited to use the Principles as a source of law from which to fill the gap. Such recourse to the Principles is in line with the practice of many courts to use foreign decisions or legal writings if confronted with a novel problem. A set or rules elaborated on the basis of a careful and comprehensive comparative study of the legal systems of all the Member States may carry at least the same persuasive authority as cases or writings from an individual country." 見the Commission of European Contract Law, Principles of European Contract Law, edited by Ole Lando and Hugh Beale (2000), p.97。
[295] "Prime objectives of contract law are to protect the justified expectations of the parties and to make it possible for them to foretell with accuracy what will be their rights and liabilities under the contract. These objectives may best be attained in multistate transactions by letting the parties choose the law to govern the validity of the contract and the rights created thereby. In this way, certainty and predictability of result are most likely to be secured."
[296] 陳隆修，《美國國際私法新理論》，台北，五南圖書公司，民國76年1月，初版，222～224頁。

之能力、形式要件及實質效力等問題上，並非為當事人得以明示協議所可以解決之問題[297]。

羅馬 I 3(3)條規定於案件事實只與一國有關時，當事人選法之適用不得違反該國不能被當事人以協議而違背之法律條款之適用。公約之3(3)條更直接命名這些不得被違背之法律為「強行法規」。「強行法規」是一種大陸法之概念，為傳統判例法所沒有的。歐盟契約法原則1：103條1項規定於本應適用法律之允許下，當事人得自主選擇歐盟契約法原則為契約之依據。第2項規定：「但是如果根據相關的國際私法規則，無論契約準據法為何這些法規皆應被加以適用，這些國際法、跨國法、及各國法之強行法規應被加以適用。[298]」對於第2新編187條所謂的「基本政策」或英國法學所經常引用的「超越性因素」（「overriding consideration」），歐盟契約法原則1：103條則以強行法規解釋如下，「根據第2項無論契約準據法為何必須適用之各國強行法，法院或仲裁者必須給予其效力，這就是所謂的直接適用規則……見羅馬公約7(1)及(2)條……這些就是表達立法國家的基本公共政策的規則，並且在當契約與該國有著密切關連時該規則應被給予效力。[299]」

個人認為強行法規的概念是有點奇怪，因為所有被通過的法律自然

---

[297] "the rule of this Subsection applies when it is sought to have the chosen law determine issues which the parties could not have determined by explicit agreement directed to the particular issue. Examples of such questions are those involving capacity, formalities and substantial validity." 見陳隆修，《國際私法契約評論》，台北，五南圖書公司，民國75年2月，初版，11～20頁，另外法院地的公共政策及契約履行的方式亦經常與所指定之準據法無關。

[298] Article 1:103: Mandatory Law
   (1) Where the law otherwise applicable so allows, the parties may choose to have their contract governed by the Principles, with the effect that national mandatory rules are not applicable.
   (2) Effect should nevertheless be given to those mandatory rules of national, supranational and international law which, according to the relevant rules of private international law, are applicable irrespective of the law governing the contract.

[299] Lando and Beale, pp. 100, 101, "under pargraph (2) a court or an arbitrator must give effect to national rules which are mandatory irrespective of which law governs the contract, the so-called directly applicable rules (regles d'application immediate), see article 7(1) and (2) of the Rome Convention on the Law Applicable to Contractual Obligations (hereinafter the rome convention). These are rules which are expressive of a fundamental public policy of the enacting country and to which effect should be given when the contract has a close connection to this country." 並見Notes 1中各大陸法國家強行法之名詞。"

是應被執行的，只是法律被執行的範圍是經常有爭議而已。大陸法認為判例法沒有強行法是不進步的表徵，是一種莫名其妙的概念。因為如果「強行法規」真的存在，那麼根據三權分立之原則法院是不應該具備「重大政策」的立法功能，故判例法上自然是不應該有著建立「強行法規」之判例存在[300]。所謂的「強行法規」如果存在的話，自然只能透過國會而去立法。或許英國最著名的「overriding statutory law」（超越性成文法）是 the Unfair Contract Terms Act 1977, s. 27(2)：「當於下列情形存在時（一個或兩個），即使有任何契約條款規定應適用或宣稱應適用英國以外其他國家之法律時，本法仍應被適用：(a)對法院、仲裁者、或裁決者而言，該契約條款之被訂定最主要或完全是為了幫助主張訂定條款之一方去規避本法之適用；或(b)於訂立契約時當事人之一方是居於消費者之地位，並且當時其慣居於英國，及無論是經由自己或透過他人代理，訂立契約所必要之主要步驟是於當地所作成。[301]」根據 the 1977 Act s. 26(3)，」許多種類之國際買賣契約並不包含；而且 s.27(2)只包含明示選法，而應不包含仲裁及管轄條款在內之默示選法。於當事人沒有選法而客觀上應適用之準據法為外國法時，the 1997 Act s.27(2)之限制」法院應無法適用。故 Cheshire and North 認為第27(2)條並不是無論契約準據法為何，其限制條款皆適用，因此羅馬公約7(2)條必須尊重法院地之強行法規之規定於此不適用[302]，但最尊敬的 Prof Hartley 對此對卻有不同意見。這些望重仕

---

[300] 陳隆修，《2005年海牙法院選擇公約評析》，台北，五南圖書公司，2009年1月，初版1刷，165、166頁。

[301] (2) this Act has effect notwithstanding any contract term which applies or purports to apply the law of some country outside the United Kingdom, where (either or both) –
(a) the term appears to the court, or arbitrator or arbiter to have been imposed wholly or mainly for the purpose of enabling the party imposing it to evade the operation of this Act., or
(b) in the making of the contract one of the parties dealt as consumer, and he was then habitually resident in the United Kingdom, and the essential steps necessary for the making of the contract were taken there, whether by him or by others on his behalf.

[302] Cheshire and North, 13th ed., pp.580,581, "Section 27(2) overrides the parties' freedom to choose a foreign law to govern the contract. Article 7(2) will apply therefore to case coming within this section. However, section 27(2) is only concerned with the situation where there has been a choice by the parties. In cases where there has been no such choice and the objective applicable law is foreign it seems that the Act's controls on exemption clauses will not apply., it cannot be said that the controls

林資深前輩同僚於此方面之爭執，或許於某些程度上證明個人觀點－正如

---

on exemption clauses in the Act apply irrespective of the law that otherwise applies to the contract. Article 7(2) will accordingly not operate in this situation. However, the controls on exemption clauses contained in the Act would, of course, be applicable if the governing law under the Convention was English law." 恩師Prof. Hartley對此論述完全不認同："The opposite view is taken by the editors of Cheshire and North, who argue that, as the provisions apply only when there has been a choice of law in favour of a country other than the United Kingdom, they do not apply irrespective of the law otherwise applicable to the contract', as required by Article 7(2). This seems clearly wrong in thecase of Section 27(2)(b), since the operation of that provision is not limited to cases where there has been a choice of law: although Section 27(2) says that the Act has effect 'not-withstanding' a choice-of-law clause, this does not mean that the Act does not have effect if there is no choice-of-law clause. Admittedly, Article 27(2) (a) is, by its very nature, capable of operating only if there is a choice-of-law clause, but this is no reason why it cannot be regarded as covered by Article 7(2). All that Article 7(2) requires is that the provision should be mandatory in a given situation: why should the 'situation' not be defined as one in which the clause was imposed by the supplier for the purpose of allowing him to evade the Act, and the Act would have been applicable if there had been no choice-of-law clause?"
Trevor C. Hartley, Mandatory Rules in International Contracts: the Common Law Approach (1997) 266 Hague Recueil 341, p.382, note 85; (1979) 4ELR 236。這個問題已由公約7(2)條被延伸至規則I 9(2)條，故仍是個既存之問題。如果由英國法嚴謹之傳統，Cheshire and North是正確的；但由比較法較為重視基本政策之精神，顯然歐盟法專家Prof. Hartley的詮釋大陸法之羅馬公約較為正確。故而歸根究底答案應依據一個問題－到底羅馬公約是傳統的英國法，還是以大陸法為主的比較法?答案似乎是很清楚的。無論是英國法或大陸法，國內法或國際法，個人以為這類兩難之問題到處都有，企圖以法律邏輯來解決這些技術性法規，不但過於深奧，而且有可能於個案上有失正義。個人反對以籠統的法律邏輯來解決這些抽象的技術條文，應以實體上之契約原則就個案來確保契約「基本政策」或「超越性因素」的強制執行，以確保個案正義。
對於這些最尊敬的前輩同僚各據立場各有所本之論述，個人衷心佩服，亦皆認同其論述。或許正義不應該是對或錯之絕對式天秤，這種西方哲學或許太過簡化。或許正義應是不絕對之陰陽或許應是太極式－陰中有陽，陽中有陰之圓融式正義。
Cheshire and North, 14thed., 於p.733,734中再次重申前論述。又英國為引進歐盟之保護消費者法（Council Directive (EEC) No 93/13 OJ 1993 L 95/29）通過Unfair Terms in Consumer Contracts Regulations 1999 (SI 1999/2083, amended by SI 2001/1186, replacing SI 1994/3159)，而其Regulations 9則較s.27(2)為簡單與靈活：These Regulations shall apply notwithstanding any contract term which applies or purports to apply the law of a non-Member State, if the contract has a close connection which the territory of the Member States.
Cheshire and North, 14thed., 於p.734,735：Regulation 9 can be seen to be similar in impact to section 27(2) in that overriding effect is given to the substantive law and the choice of the foreign law is not struck out. Moreover, it is only concerned with the situation where there has been a choice by the parties. It is, however, a wider provision than section 27(2) in that there is no limitation in relation to "incarnational supply contracts" and the close connection required is not limited to a specified set of circumstances as happens under section 27(2)(b).What is more, the requisite close connection can be with the territory of the Member States of the European Community and not just with the United Kingdom. There is, though, uncertainty over the meaning of "a close connection", which is not defined. There is also uncertainty in the situation where the parties choose the law of another Member State to govern. The Law Commissions have proposed that the laws of other Member States should be applied if they would be applicable by virtue of existing rules of private international law as long as the consumer is afforded the protections contemplated by the Directive.有趣的是依1999年規則管轄條款亦可能構成不公平條款，Standard Bank London Ltd v Apostolakis (No 2) [2002] CLC 939。

所有於其他方面之法律一般，強行法規（如果其存在的話－重點應是在其適用之範圍，而或許不是在於得否被當事人之協議所違反。

英國the 1977 Act s.27(2)之目的是在於防止當事人於契約與英國有密切關連時，以約定選擇外國法之方式去避開the 1977Act之適用。Prof. Hartley認為s. 27(2)(a)可能是英國法上唯一的規避法律條款[303]。但如若s.27(2)只適用於當事人有選法之情形，the Employment Rights Act 1996 s.204 (1)則有著完全超越性之效果（「complete overriding effect」）。S.204(1)不但超越當事人之選法，並且超越了當事人沒有選法時客觀上應適用之外國準據法。S.204(1)規定：「為了本法之目的，有關任何人僱傭契約之準據法（除了本法外）是否為英國法或英國部份區域之法律並不並重要。[304]」但s.196(1)將s.204(1)之適用範圍限制於受僱人經常性的工作於英國，或僱傭契約之準據法為英國法[305]。因此the 1996 Act s.204(1)及s.196 (1)是完全符合歐盟契約法1：103註釋有關強行法之要件：1.當事人之協議所不能違背（無論準據法為何）；2.立法國家之基本公共政策；3.該國與契約有著密切關連。故而s.204(1)及s.196(1)之超越性及其適用範圍是有著較明確之規定。

有時法條中並無明文其超越性，其超越性須由判例法解釋之，但其適用範圍卻於條文中有明示規定。於Boissevain v. Weil[306]中，一英國人於戰時無可奈何的住於摩洛哥，其向住於摩洛哥之一荷蘭人借法郎，（法郎

---

[303] Trevor C. Hartley, Mandatory Rules in International Contracts: The Common Law Approach (1997) 266 Hague Recueil 341, p.381, "probably the onlye example in English law of fraude a la loi".

[304] (1) For the purposes of this Act it is immaterial whether the law which (apart from the Act) governs any person's employment is the law of the United Kingdom, or of a part of the United Kingdom, or not.

[305] (1) Sections 1 to 7 and sections 86 to 91 do not apply in relation to employment during any period when the employee is engaged in work wholly or mainly outside Great Britain unless –

    (a) the employee ordinarily works in Great Britain and the work outside Great Britain is for the same employer, or

    (b) the law which governs his contract of employment is the law of England and Wales or the law of Scotland.

    (2) The provisions to which this subsection applies do not apply to employment where under the employee's contract of employment he ordinarily works outside Great Britain.

[306] [1949] 1 KB 482, [1949] 1 All ER 146, CA; affd [1950] AC 327, [1950] 1 All ER 728.見陳隆修，《國際私法契約評論》，台北，五南圖書公司，民國75年2月，初版，74、75頁。

為摩洛哥所用貨幣），並答應等到英國法律許可，他馬上會在倫敦以英鎊償還。英國法院判此契約違反英國戰時緊急法規而無效，該法規規定任何商業行為須以英鎊為貨幣。法院認定此緊急法規無論居住於何地之英國人皆應遵守。Lord Radcliffe，認為無論借貸契約之準據法為何，the Emergency Powers （Defence） Act 1939, s. 3(1)[307]皆應被加以適用，故該法律被解釋為有著完全之超越性。另外於Chiron Corpn v Organon Teknika （No 2）[308]中，牽涉及section 44 of the Patent Act 1977[309]中所規定於專利所有人濫用其專利權之情形時，則其契約條款或條件為無效，例如要求客戶或被授權人必須取得其他產品，做為供給專利產品或取得使用專利許可之條件。因此根據s.44(1)該些契約條款為無效，故被告主張以s.44(3)為侵權行為之抗辯。上訴法院認為無論契約準據法是否為英國法，只要有關英國專利之契約或授權，s.44(1)皆應被加以適用。S.44(1)的立法意旨是在防止取得英國專利的人去濫用其權利，故契約準據法為何並無關係，重點是在於與英國專利有關連之契約之效力。

但是所謂的強行法規最困難之地方在於，經常條文本身並沒有明示其超越性或其適用之範圍，故而法院[310]於個案中要解釋其是否適用是相當困難的。於Sayers v. International Drilling co. N. V.[311]中原告是英國人，

---

[307] Defence (Finance) Regulations 1939, reg 2, as amended.

[308] [1993] FSR 567, CA.

[309] Repealed by Competition Act 1998.

[310] 如於English v Donnelly 1958 SC 494及Irish Shipping Ltd v Commercial Union Assurance Co plc [1991] 2 QB 206, [1989] 3 All ER 853中，蘇格蘭法院及英格蘭法院皆給予相關法規適度之超越性效力，而拒絕給予當事人明示選法條款效力。

[311] [1971] 3 All E.R. 163; [1971] 1 W.L.R. 1176. Salman和Stamp兩位法官將案例的審查，偏限於一個問題，即決定契約的適當法(proper law)，從而決定荷蘭法須適用於本案。Prof. North如此評論："this approach is unfortunate because, as we have seen, the effect of an exemption clause on tortuous liability raises issues of tort law as well as the question of the validity of the contractual exemption clause". P.M. North, "Contract As A Tort Defence in the Conflict of Laws", (1977) 26 I.C.L.Q. 914, p.924. Lord Denning M.R.認為原告之請求是基於侵權行為，而被告之抗辯卻基於契約。他認為整個爭點之適當法應為荷蘭法："We cannot apply two systems of law, one for the claim in tort, and the other for the defence in contract. We must apply one system of law by which to decide both claim and defence. To decide it I would ask this question: What is the proper law by which to determine the issues in this case? And I would answer it by saying: it is the system of law with which the issues have the closest connection."
Prof. North對此評論如下："It assumes that the test for determining the proper law of a tort and a con-

他和一家荷蘭公司，即本案之被告，訂立僱傭契約，他受僱在被告的鑽油臺工作。原告被送到奈及利亞領海內的鑽油臺工作。由於他的工作同伴之過失，導致原告受傷害。契約上有一項規定，即除了契約明定者外，其他類似本案的傷害，均不得請求賠償。就國際性契約而言，系爭條款依荷蘭法是有效的約定，依英國內國法則為無效的約定——此乃基於一九四八年人身傷害修正法（Personal Injuries Law Reform Act 1948）。原告就所受之傷害要求賠償。英國高等法院一致判決，原告不能因所受之人身傷害據以要求賠償。本案於個人唸大學時雖為一飽受爭議、討論之案件，但於英國國會通過Private International Law （Miscellaneous Provisions）Act 1995 Part Ⅲ後，這個案件之爭議性終於塵埃落定。其第14條4項規定無論選法規則為何法院地應仍適用之法律並不受影響[312]（即強行規則之適用），故而Dicey and Morris認為the Law Reform （Personal Injuries）Act 1948 s. 1(3)可能於現今會被加以重新解釋[313]。

---

tract are the same - some form of 'grouping of contracts' test." 同上，p.924.

Lawrence Collins, "Exemption Clauses, Employment Contracts and the Conflict of Laws", (1972) 20 I.C.L.Q. 320. In ibid., p.334, Collins quotes Professor Kahn-Freund's statement: "Whenever a technical legal argument becomes intellectually and academically very attractive there is an (admittedly rebuttable but nevertheless strong) presumption that something is wrong with the law." See Kahn-Freund, "Delictual Libaility and the Conflict of Laws" [1968] Ⅱ 124 Hague Rec. 391. 本案例之討論，見陳隆修，《美國國際私法新理論》，台北，五南圖書公司，民國76年1月，初版，244~247頁；陳隆修、許兆慶、林恩瑋，《台灣財產法暨經濟法研究叢書（十三）—國際私法：選法理論之回顧與展望》，台灣財產法暨經濟法研究協會發行，2007年1月，初版，159~163頁。

[312] (3) Without prejudice to the generality of subsection (2) above, nothing in this Part –
　　(a) authorizes the application of the law of a country outside the forum as the applicable law for determining issues arising in any claim in so far as to do so –
　　　(i) would conflict with principles of public policy; or
　　　(ii) would give effect to such a penal, revenue or other public law as would not otherwise be enforceable under the law of the forum; or
　(4) This Part has effect without prejudice to the operation of any rule of law which either has effect notwith standing the rules of private international law applicable in the particular circumstances or modifies the rules of private international law that would otherwise be so applicable.

[313] "It is also possible that, today, if the matter were argued, a provision such as that contained in section 1(3) of the Law Reform (Personal Injuries) Act 1948, which limits the effect of certain exclusion clauses in contracts of employment, would be regarded as a mandatory rule if the employee sued his employer in tort for negligence and the law applicable to the tort and to the contract regarded an exclusion clause in his contract of employment as an effective defense, in contradiction of the terms of the 1948 Act." Dicey and Morris, the Conflict of Laws, 13th ed., P.1559

　　故於早期以實體法之觀點，同時評論傳統國際私法之技巧及當時最為新潮的最重要關連方法論後[314]，經過20年個人仍舊維持原議的再次評述：「Sayers一案如果重新再來，即可能依據第十四條第四項解釋為可以適用一九四八年法案第一條第三項，亦即該第一條第三項之強行規定適用於契約準據法為外國法之侵權行為上。此案荒謬之處在於不但英國內國法不允許僱主逃避責任，即使準據法荷蘭法之內國法亦作同樣規定，只是准許僱主於國際場合特別加以規避而已。於兩國內國法皆有一致的政策時，法院還作相反的判決，由實體法之觀點而論實在是匪夷所思。如作者於年輕時所寫的，於勞工的損害賠償的範疇（workman's compensation）裏，『產品的成本必須包含勞工的血汗』已是全世界文明國家於此方面實體法的共識，勞工必須得到『迅速及合理』（swift and proper）的賠償是個必然的鐵律。英國司法界因為不能體認實體法於國際私法的重要性，故而須遲至一九九五年法案後方能有正確的作法，然而遲來的正義對被害原告已是一種不正義。

　　Salman和Stamp兩位法官過分浸淫於傳統國際私法技巧的缺點固然已飽受質疑，但有歷史性聲譽的Denning M. R.所採用的最密切關連作法難道有達成符合公平正義的判決？個人從年輕時就認為最重要關連說不見得能達成公平正義的判決，經過歲月的證明，Sayers一案或許能充分解釋個人之論點。其實不須一九九五年十四條第四項之規定，只要能充份尊重英、荷兩國內國法之規定，Sayers一案之結果就會不同，法學之進展亦不會浪費如此久之時間，更重要的是對被害人不公正的情況就可避免，英國一九九五年法案雖正式引進最重要關連說，但如果不能承認實體法於國際私法的重要性，個案的公平正義性恐怕無法充份的得到保證。或許經過二十年無情歲月的考驗，時間在Sayers一案還給作者的實體法論一個遲來的公道？」[315]

---

[314] 陳隆修，《美國國際私法新理論》，台北，五南圖書公司，民國76年1月，初版，244～247頁。
[315] 陳隆修、許兆慶、林恩瑋，《台灣財產法暨經濟法研究叢書（十三）—國際私法：選法理論之回顧與展望》，台灣財產法暨經濟法研究協會發行，2007年1月，初版，162，163頁。

　　時間應是所有學術理論最客觀、最無情的終極試鍊。個人以為著名的Sayers案已經充份的替個人於羅馬 I 及羅馬 II 規則中所提出的最為微小、謙卑的建議背書－**亦即最重要關連的考量，不能只基於地域性之關連點，必須對相關連之實體政策加以考量**。同樣的對於大陸法認為理所當然，但對於英國、美國法界卻感到困擾而陌生的「強行法規」，基於同樣的法律邏輯Sayers案或許亦可以給予我們指示－亦即所謂的「強行法規」之重點不應是在於當事人之得否違背其規定，而是在於該法規所牽連的實體政策適用範圍之探討。無論是於國內法或國際法，通常立法者對於法規之超越性及其適用範圍是經常沒有明示規定的。尤其是對於國內公共政策[316]是否得適用於國際案件之困難情形下，法院只能就所牽連之實質政策是否應涵蓋該具體個案而決定。一旦根據實質政策而決定法規之適用範圍，自然當事人得否依協議而違背該法規之問題應可通常迎刃而解。

(三)以法院地之實體政策為強行法之基礎

　　這個以實體法來決定「強行法」[317]之適用範圍之作法亦是受到美國第

---

[316] 羅馬公約7(2)及16條；規則 I 9(2)及21條；英國1995 Act, s.14(3), (4).

[317] 對於羅馬公約與規則中強行法的「正面效力」與公共政策的「負面效力」之區分，普遍為一般同僚所接受，但個人並未十分注重。英美法之前亦未有著明確的強行法之概念。

Jonathan Harris, Mandatory Rules and Public Policy under the Rome I Regulation, p.297, 298, "The basic difference under the Rome Convention and Rome I Regulation is clear: mandatory rules are positive legal provisions designed to apply to certain factual situations. Their application is additional to the law otherwise applicable; and does not involve any direct criticism of the contents of the governing law. By contrast, public policy is an inherently negative process, involving the discretionary disapplication of the governing law in whole or in part, on the basis that its application is repugnant to the norms of the court seised. But when it comes to applying that distinction in English law, matters are greatly complicated by the fact that English law did not draw this distinction before the advent of the Rome Convention. Instead, all cases involving deviation from the governing law were considered under the heading of public policy. The concept of mandatory rules was not used. The doctrine of public policy was employed to encompass both the application of overriding rules of law and the disapplication of the foreign law. It also dealt with the consequences of illegality by another law. Any attempt to analyse what the common law doctrine of public policy stood for, and how it translates into the Rome Convention and Rome I Regulation's approach which distinguishes between the application of mandatory rules and the disapplication of foreign law on public policy grounds, is acutely difficult."

又見Note-Article 7(1) of the European Contracts Convention: Codifying the Practice of Applying Foreign Mandatory Rules, 114 Harvard Law Review 2001, 2462, 2474, "Article 16 clearly contemplates the negative function of public policy - that is, the application of a particular legal norm of a relevant foreign law may give rise to a public policy objection. Thus, a forum may object to the application of a provision of a foreign lex causae if the outcome is problematic on public policy grounds. However,

2新編所支持的。187條2項是有關當事人選法自由之限制[318]，其註釋g對於2(b)款中有關有著實質上更重大利益之非被選定州之基本政策如此論述：「法院應適用自己之法律原則以決定一個已存在之政策是否符合本條文基本性之規定，及於決定該特定爭點時，是否其他州比起被選定之州有著實質上更重要的利益。[319]」解釋報告又認為所謂的「基本」政策，一定要是一個重大的政策。例如除了遺囑外，形式要件[320]通常是不會被認為是重大政策[321]。同樣的已即將過時的法律是不會被認為會形成重大政策，例如已婚婦女之訂約能力[322]，或者於契約法一般認為不會構成重大政策，例如約因之要求[323]。「另一方面而言，一個基本政策可能是包含於一個法條中，而該法條使得一種或多種契約成為不合法之契約，或該條文是被設計用以保護個人來對抗較強議價能力一方之壓迫性之措施。有關個別被

---

article 16 does not appear to contemplate the positive function of public policy - that is, the forum's enforcement of a foreign state's law because of a public policy that favors supporting certain foreign states' legal rules. Thus, it is unclear whether a forum may suggest the application of a foreign mandatory rule on public policy grounds."

[318] 有關187(2)(a)條規定於沒有重大關連或「合理之基礎」時，於當事人所不能以明示條款解決之問題時，當事人所選定之準據法不能被加以適用。但comment f認為當事人甚少，或不曾，於沒有好理由下去選定一個法律，故2(a)條款之適用機會甚少"The forum will not, for example, apply a foreign law which has been chosen by the parties in the spirit of adventure or to provide mental exercise for the judge. Situations of this sort do not arise in practice. Contracts are entered into for serious purposes and rarely, if ever, will the parties choose a law without good reason for doing so."

[319] Comment g, "The forum will apply its own legal principles in determining whether a given policy is a fundamental one within the meaning of the present rule and whether the other state has a materially greater interest than the state of the chosen law in the determination of the particular issue. The parties' power to choose the applicable law is subject to least restriction in situations where the significant contacts are so widely dispersed that determination of the state of the applicable law without regard to the parties' choice would present real difficulties." 但解釋報告又小心翼翼的提醒："The forum will not refrain from applying the chosen law merely because this would lead to a different result than would be obtained under the local law of the state of the otherwise applicable law."

[320] 羅馬I為促進日益增加的遠距離訂約，相對於羅馬公約的第9條，於第11(2)條中增加了當事人或代理人任何一方慣居地法，以放寬形式要件之要求。有關放寬形式要件之要求，個人早期於《美國國際私法新理論》，台北，五南圖書公司，民國76年1月，初版，235～238頁中已有論述。

[321] 陳隆修，《美國國際私法新理論》，台北，五南圖書公司，民國76年1月，初版，235～238頁。
見Unidroit Commercial Contracts 2004 art. 1.2,
Article 1.2 (No form required)
Nothing in these Principles requires a contract, statement or any other act to be made in or evidenced by a particular form. It may be proved by any means, including witnesses.

[322] 同上，226～230頁。

[323] 同上，232～235頁。

保險人對抗保險公司之權利之相關條文即為這方面之例子（見192、193條）。[324]」故而對於有關美國法之「基本政策」（即為類似大陸法之「強行法規」），187條之解釋報告認為「法院應適用自己之法律原則」。另外對於契約形式要件之要求及約因的重要性，由於並不符合「保護當事人正當期待」的主流核心價值，如同解釋報告一般，個人早期亦主張於通常情形下應減低其重要性。另外對於已婚婦女之訂約能力，個人早期較解釋報告有著更強烈之反對意見[325]，認為任何限制已婚或未婚成年婦女行為能力之法律不但違憲，亦為違反聯合國人權公約之野蠻行為。另外有關於保險契約中對於保護保單持有人或被保險人之強制性應為普世核心價值前面已有論述。

故而相較於羅馬公約及羅馬 I 無奈的以區域選法規則做為強行法規辨識之依據，第2新編187條之註釋公開的以「法院地之法律原則」及實體契約法之共同核心主流價值做為「基本政策」（強行法規）辨識之依據。正如於有些大陸法及歐盟近幾十年來於國私方面之立法一般[326]，羅馬公約

---

[324] "To be 'fundamental,' a policy must in any event be a substantial one. Except perhaps in the case of contracts relating to wills, a policy of this sort will rarely be found in a requirement, such as the statute of frauds, that relates to formalities (see Illustration 6). Nor is such policy likely to be represented by a rule tending to become obsolete, such as a rule concerned with the capacity of married women (see Illustration 7), or by general rules of contract law, such as those concerned with the need for consideration (see Illustration 8). On the other hand, a fundamental policy may be embodied in a statute which makes one or more kinds of contracts illegal or which is designed to protect a person against the oppressive use of superior bargaining power. Statutes involving the rights of an individual insured as against an insurance company are an example of this sort (see s.192-193)."

[325] Prof. Currie自信滿滿之宣示："Who can say that Maine, or Massachusetts for that matter, was wrong? All that happened was that in each state the legislature weighed competing considerations, with different results". Brainerd Currie, Selected Essays on the Conflict of Laws, Chapter Two: "Married Women's Contracts: A Study in Conflict-of-Laws Method", p.85.這個評論是其對 Milliken v. Pratt, 125 Mass. 374 (1878)，所作之論述。而更為重要的是—這個案例為尊敬的Prof. Currie所賴以建立其轟動武林驚動萬教之利益方法論之案例，而本句論述即為其方法論最根本之基石。個人以為Prof. Currie的方法論可能會成為近代人類史上影響力最大之方法論。但經過三十年個人還是維持原議，陳隆修，《美國國際私法新理論》，台北，五南圖書公司，民國76年1月，初版，226~230頁。個人真誠的認為Prof. Currie的論述違反聯合國及歐盟所有人權公約中平等權、訴訟權及財產權之規定，更是違反包括美國憲法在內之全世界文明國家憲法上之適當程序條款。Prof. Currie之論述或許充份證明我們人類有時可能會犯下如此明顯無知的錯誤及野蠻、自私的心態—即使睿智的Prof. Currie亦無法逃過人性的弱點。全世界法律學的各種學科—包括國際私法在內—經常必須勇敢的面對所牽連政策加以謹慎的評價。

[326] 陳隆修、許兆慶、林恩瑋，《台灣財產法暨經濟法研究叢書（十三）—國際私法：選法理論之

及羅馬 I 於強行法規之立法，可能於出生時即開始過時。

　　第2新編國際私法90條規定：「當外國訴因之執行會違反法院地之強烈公共政策時，該訴訟不得被審理。[327]」有關這方面之既有案例包含賭博及妨礙公平競爭之案例[328]。所謂法院地之強烈基本政策應被加以嚴格之解釋，其註釋C引用Judge Cardozo之論述，認為就只有於符合下列情形下法院才能拒絕審理該訴訟：「會違反一些正義的基本原則，一些盛行的道德觀念，一些根深柢固共同利益的傳統。[329]」Cardozo法官的這個論述應為美國「基本政策」、英國「超越性考量」、及歐盟「強行法規」的共同核心價值。

　　同樣的在2004年版的U.C.C. s.1-301(f)中亦規定當事人之選法，不能違反(d)項中於沒有選法時本應適用法律之州或國家之基本政策[330]。這個(f)項很明顯的是第2新編187(2)條之複製版，其comment 6甚至同樣而更詳細的再次引用Judge Cardozo於Loucks案中膾炙人口的論述，以作為各

回顧與展望》，台灣財產法暨經濟法研究協會發行，2007年1月，初版，133頁，有關德國、奧地利船舶清償次序之國際私法。

[327] S.90 Action Contrary to Public Policy
No action will be entertained on a foreign cause of action the enforcement of which is contrary to the strong public policy of the forum.

[328] Ciampittiello v. ciampittiello, 134 conn. 51, 54 A.2d 669 (1947) (gambling); cerniglia v. C. D. Farms, Inc., 203 So.2d 1 (Fla.Sup.Ct.1967)(contract against competition); Dorado Beach Hotel Corp. v. Jernigan, 202 So. 2d 830 (Fla.D.C.App.1967)(gambling).

[329] b. A mere difference between the local law rules of the two state will not render the enforcement of a claim created in one state contrary to the public policy of the other.
c. Rule has narrow application. Actions should rarely be dismissed because of the rule of this Section. To come within the scope of the present rule, the local policy must be sufficiently strong to outweigh a state's natural desire to open the doors of its courts to suits involving foreign facts. A court should not refuse to entertain such a suit unless to do so, in the words of Judge Cardozo, "would violate some fundamental principle of justice, some prevalent conception of morals, some deep-seated tradition of the common weal." Loucks v. Standard Oil Co. of New York, 224 N.Y. 99, 111, 120 N.E. 198, 202 (1918). 另外判例法認為就只有於法院地與該交易或當事人有合理關係時，法院才能拒絕依外國法而來之合法抗辯。
Home Insurance Co. v. Dick, 281 U.S. 297 (1930); Holzer v. deutsche Reichsbahn-Gesellschaft, 277 N.Y. 474, 144 N.E. 2d 798 (1938). Contra: Fox v. Postal Tel. Cable Co., 138 Wis. 648, 120 N.W. 399 (1909). Cf. Aboitzy v. Price, 99 F.Supp. 602 (D.Utah 1951).

[330] (f) An agreement otherwise effective under subsection (c) is not effective to the extent that application of the law of the State or country designated would be contrary to a fundamental policy of the state or country whose law would govern in the absence of agreement under subsection (d). 另外(g)項中亦有特別條款之規定。

州法院拒絕適用他州法之試金石[331]（「touchstone」）。而U.C.C.s. 1-301
條(f)項之comment 6對所謂之」fundamental policy」所加以之解釋亦幾
乎為第2新編187(2)條註釋之翻版：「依據基本政策理論，一個法院不能
只因被指定法律之適用，會造成與依本法應適用法律之國家或州法所取得
之結果不同，而拒絕適用該被指定之法律。而於實際上，這個不同一定要
是與該管轄地區之公共政策相違背，而且該種違背是如此重大，以至於它
可以正當的超越現代商事法所引為基礎之穩定性及可預測性，以及一般司
法經濟性之顧慮。[332]」同樣的comment 6亦舉形式要件及約因為通常不會
被視為符合有關基本政策之要求為例子。**於近二、三十年來個人年輕時所
賴以建立實體法論之案例論述，有些已為英國立法（Sayers案）或美國
法律協會及U.C.C.所證實引用，或許包含國際私法在內之中國式法學可
對實體法方法論嘗試著加以嚴格之檢視。這或許可被視為21世紀全球化
法學之共同核心。**

　　有趣的是註釋6用以解釋不得違背本應為準據法州之重大公共政策之

---

[331] "Our own scheme of legislation may be different. We may even have no legislation on the subject. That
is not enough to show that public policy forbids us to enforce the foreign right. A right of action is property. If a foreign statute gives the right, the mere fact that we do not give a like right is no reason for
refusing to help the plaintiff in getting what belongs to him. We are not so provincial as to say that every solution of a problem is wrong because we deal with it otherwise at home. Similarity of legislation
has indeed this importance; its presence shows beyond question that the foreign statute does not offend
the local policy. But its absence does not prove the contrary. It is not to be exalted into an indispensable
condition. The misleading word 'comity' has been responsible for much of the trouble. It has been fertile in suggesting a discretion unregulated by general principles.
The courts are not free to refuse to enforce a foreign right at the pleasure of the judges, to suit the individual notion of expediency or fairness. They do not close their doors, unless help would violate some
fundamental principle of justice, some prevalent conception of good morals, some deep-rooted tradition
of the common weal."
Loucks v. Standard Oil Co. of New York, 120 N.E. 198, 201, 202 (1918).

[332] "Under the fundamental policy doctrine, a court should not refrain from applying the designated law
merely because application of that law would lead to a result different than would be obtained under
the local law of the State or country whose law would otherwise govern. Rather, the difference must be
contrary to a public policy of that jurisdiction that is so substantial that it justifies overriding the concerns for certainty and predictability underlying modern commercial law as well as concerns for judicial
economy generally. Thus, application of the designated law will rarely be found to be contrary to a fundamental policy of the State or country whose law would otherwise govern when the difference between
the two concerns a requirement, such as a statute of frauds, that relates to formalities, or general rules of
contract law, such as those concerned with the need for consideration."

標準並非為第2新編之「法院應適用自己之法律原則」，而是「現代商事法所引為基礎之穩定性及可預測性，以及一般司法經濟性之顧慮」。或許統一商法於本質上是個商事法規，故而其較為偏重商業上之穩定性及訴訟上之經濟性。雖然它不是以法院地之法律原則為依據，但其偏向商業上實際之穩定性及經濟性，明顯的並不屬於任何選法規則。即使是於有關商業法規，個人仍不認同其對於基本政策（強行法規）之確認是以穩定及經濟性為主，但不可否認的是comment 6對「基本政策」之確認是以實質之功能性為主。人雖亦一向偏向實質上之功能性，但並非以商業利益為主軸，而是以個案正義為主軸。

但是更有趣的是comment 9中敘述，關於s.1-301沒有處理而交由其他法律處理之問題時：「首先，當適用當事人所指定非法院地之其他管轄區域之法律時，若適用該法會違反法院地之基本政策，即使其不會違反於契約沒有指定時應為準據法之州或國家之基本政策時，法院仍會偶而拒絕適用該法。適用這個學說的標準主要是有關主權的概念，非商事法之概念，因此是應由承審法院去決定。第2，在決定對於當事人協議以一特定州或國家之法律為他們關係之依據是否應給予效力時，基於須要，法院一定要去處理與該協議之基本效力有關之一些爭點。例如這些爭點可能是有關訂約能力及是否有脅迫之情形。本條文沒有處理這些爭點。[333]」至於統一商法範圍外所規定之問題，則交由法院地的選法規則處理。故而如第2

---

[333] "Among the issues this section does not address, and leaves to other law, three in particular deserve mention. First, a forum will occasionally decline to apply the law of a different jurisdiction selected by the parties when application of that law would be contrary to a fundamental policy of the forum jurisdiction, even if it would not be contrary to a fundamental policy of the State or country whose law would govern in the absence of contractual designation. Standards for application of this doctrine relate primarily to concepts of sovereignty rather than commercial law and are thus left to the courts. Second, in determining whether to give effect to the parties' agreement that the law of a particular State or country will govern their relationship, courts must, of necessity, address some issues as to the basic validity of that agreement. These issues might relate, for example, to capacity to contract and absence of duress. This section does not address these issues. Third, this section leaves to other choice of law principles of the forum the issues of whether, and to what extent, the forum will apply the same law to the non-UCC aspects of a transaction that it applies to the aspects of the transaction governed by the Uniform Commercial Code."

新編187條之註釋一般，comment 9認為法院地之基本政策應「超越」被選定之法律及本應為準據法之基本政策。這個結論及作法固為實體法論所樂見，但其基礎卻是本於主權之憲政概念，而非本於實體契約法之基本原則。正如英國國際私法於許多方面一樣，comment 9雖然務實，但法學邏輯及概念大大有改進之絕對必要。

第2點有關選法條款基本效力之問題，個人近年來一再論述這是與仲裁條款及管轄條款之效力應一併大致上視為邏輯上相似之問題。選法條款之成立與效力英國傳統判例法上是以假設契約成立時契約之準據法為依據[334]，羅馬公約[335]及規則[336]亦採此假設推定準據法理論。個人認為傳統上這是個符合邏輯之合理作法，並據此而對2005年海牙選擇法院公約大肆撻伐[337]。但是個人亦認為假設推定準據法理論已經超過其時代之功能，而應由實體契約法原則取而代之。U.C.C. s.1-301 comment 9所具體陳述的於事實上不但與實體法論吻合，而且更為美國同僚所所忽略的是其所隱含的兩個法律哲學，是與2005年海牙選擇法院公約完全背道而馳的基本法律邏輯－繫屬法院是可以超越管轄條款而處理契約成立與效力之問題；及法院地法可以超越選法條款而處理其之成立與效力之問題。

有關選法條款之成立及效力問題，一如於管轄條款之成立及效力之問題[338]，美國法院似乎完全跳過假設推定準據法之法律邏輯，而直接交由繫屬「法院一定要去處理與該協議之基本效力有關之一些爭點。」所謂的法院地法自然可能包含其選法規則在內，但以美國法院之慣常作風可能會於許多情形下以法院地的法律原則為依據。U.C.C.雖然為一商業法規，其重點自然是在促進商業之發展，但對於契約之成立與效力之一些基本要求仍是有規定，而且這些規定通常即應是符合羅馬公約及規則對「強行法規」

---

[334] 陳隆修，《國際私法契約評論》，台北，五南圖書公司，民國75年2月，初版，97～100頁。

[335] 第8條。

[336] 第10條。

[337] 陳隆修，《2005年海牙法院選擇公約評析》，台北，五南圖書公司，2009年1月，初版1刷，70～120頁。

[338] 同前註、46頁。

之要求。

　　首先U.C.C. s.1-302(b)即規定：「本統一商法所規定的誠信、勤奮、合理性、及小心謹慎之義務不能經由協議而拋棄。如果所訂之標準並非明顯的不合理，當事人得協議訂定衡量履行這些義務之標準。當本法要求一個行為必須於一段合理期間被作成時，當事人得協議約定一段並非明顯不合理之期間。」[339]S. 2-302(1)規定：「如果根據法律法院認為契約或其條款於訂定時是違背良心，法院得拒絕執行該契約，或於除去該違背良心條款外得執行剩餘之契約，或得限制任何違背良心條款之適用以避免任何違背良心之結果。[340]」S.1-304規定：「於本統一商法範圍內之每一契約或責任在其被履行或執行時皆應被加以誠實信用之義務。[341]」s.1-302(g)規定：「一方當事人所提供貿易上之一個相關慣例之證據，除非該當事人已經給予他方當事人通知，並且法院認為該通知足以防止對他方當事人造成不公平驚訝之情形，該證據不應被允許。[342]」統一商法雖為一商事法規，但上述契約法的「基本政策」、「超越性考量」、或「強行法規」為近代所有文明國家契約法上之主流核心共同價值，即使於以促進商業發展為主軸之商事法規亦應受到這些共同核心政策之規範。

　　除了上述一般契約法基本政策之強行規定外，如同其他的契約法U.C.C.自然仍有著許多較為明確之規定，例如s.1-301(g)就有著超越性基

---

[339] (b) The obligations of good faith, diligence, reasonableness, and care prescribed by [the Uniform Commercial code] may not be disclaimed by agreement. The parties, by agreement, may determine the standards by which the performance of those obligations is to be measured if those standards are not manifestly unreasonable. Whenever [the Uniform Commercial Code] requires an action to be taken within a reasonable time, a time that is not manifestly unreasonable may be fixed by agreement.

[340] SECTION 2-302. UNCONSCIONABLE CONTRACT OR TERM
(1) If the court as a matter of law finds the contract or any term of the contract to have been unconscionable at the time it was made, the court may refuse to enforce the contract, or it may enforce the remainder of the contract without the unconscionable term, or it may so limit the application of any unconscionable term as to avoid any unconscionable result.

[341] 1-304. OBLIGATION OF GOOD FAITH
Every contract or duty within [the Uniform Commercial Code] imposes an obligation of good faith in its performance and enforcement.

[342] (g) Evidence of a relevant usage of trade offered by one party is not admissible unless that party has given the other party notice that the court finds sufficient to prevent unfair surprise to the other party.

本政策之許多強行規定。其中s.2A-105為有關規定有權狀物品之準據法；s.2A-106更是直接與羅馬Ⅰ第6條有關之條款，其限制消費者租賃契約中當事人選擇法律及管轄法院之契約自由權利[343]；s.4-102範圍甚廣大致上是有關票據、債券、投資證券、及銀行責任之規定；s.5-116有關信用狀之選法自由，但對選法及管轄條款之方式有著強行規定；s.6-103為對批發出賣人加以限制以保障買受人之規定；s.8-110為有關投資證券之強行規定；ss.9-301~9-307為有關有擔保交易之成立與次序。

　　Unidroit Principles of International commercial Contracts 2004雖然亦為一商業規則，但或許因是參考歐盟契約法原則而來，如Prof. Bonell所說最重要的相對於沒有處理有關契約實質效力問題的CISG及其他國際性規則，the UNIDROIT Principles提供許多方法做為警察條款，以同時對抗契約或其條款中於程序上或實質上之不公平[344]。他所謂的「警察」條

---

[343] § 2A-106. LIMITATION ON POWER OF PARTIES TO CONSUMER LEASE TO CHOOSE APPLICABLE LAW AND JUDICIAL FORUM

(1) If the law chosen by the parties to a consumer lease is that of a jurisdiction other than a jurisdiction in which the lessee resides at the time the lease agreement becomes enforceable or within 300 days thereafter or in which the goods are to be used, the choice is not enforceable.

(2) If the judicial forum chosen by the parties to a consumer lease is a forum that would not otherwise have jurisdiction over the lessee, the choice is not enforceable.

有趣的是其註釋引用美國最高法院之判例，認為非消費租賃之管轄條款只是「表面上乍見」有效而已。這與2005年海牙法院選擇公約對管轄條款效力之鐵血作風顯顯不合，岳不群現象於此再次不辯自明。"This section has no effect on choice of forum clauses in leases that are not consumer leases; such clauses are, as a matter of current law, 'prima facie valid'. The Bremen v. Zapata Off-Shore Co., 407 U.S. 1, 10 (1972)"。同樣的第1項對選法規則亦有限制，這與2005年海牙法院選擇公約的以被指定法院地法亦不同，這自然亦是岳不群法則超越性基本政策上之強行法規之表現。至少U.C.C.s. 2A-106中，岳不群法則是「所有超越性基本政策之強行法規中之最強行法規」。雖然2005年海牙法院選擇公約並不適用於消費者契約，但對於小生意人應加以保護為契約法中核心價值，2005年公約與這個核心價值相去甚遠。本條款以下之註釋亦應適用於一般非消費責任契約上，因為其「真實性危險」亦存在："There is a real danger that a lessor may induce a consumer lessee to agree that the applicable law will be a jurisdiction that has little effective consumer protection, or to agree that the applicable forum will be a forum that is inconvenient for the lessee in the event of litigation. As a result, this section invalidates these choice of law or forum clauses, except where the law chosen is that of the state of the consumer's residence or where the goods will be kept, or the forum chosen is one that otherwise would have jurisdiction over the lessee."

[344] Michael Joachim Bonell, The CISG, European Contract Law and the Development of a World Contract Law, 56 Am. J. comp. L.1, 18 (2008), "Moreover and most significantly, in contrast to the CISG and other international instruments which do not deal at all with questions concerning the substantive validity of contracts, the UNIDROIT Principles provide a variety of means for policing the contract or its individual terms against both procedural and substantive unfairness."

款自然是有關契約法上基本政策之超越性強行規定。第1‧1條雖然對當事人自主有著規定[345]，但整個規則中更充斥著許多強行規定。

　　1.4條規定：「強行規定，無論是國家性的、國際性的、或超國家性來源的，根據相關國際私法的規則應被加以適用，本規則不會限制其適用。[346]」1.7條規定：「(1)每個當事人之行為必須符合國際貿易上誠實信用及公平交易之準則。(2)當事人不得排除或限制這個責任。[347]」1.8條規定：「一方當事人不能於明知之情形下有著不一致的行為，致使他方當事人合理的依賴該行為而有著損害。[348]」1.9條規定：「(1)當事人應受到慣例之拘束，而這些慣例是當事人所同意及他們之間所建立之行為。(2)特別種類貿易當事人間所廣為知道及遵守的國際貿易慣例對當事人有拘束力，但於適用這些慣例會不合理時則除外。[349]」2.1.15條規定：「(1)當事人得自由協商，並且對不能達成協議的失敗不必負責。(2)但是惡意的協商或中止協商的一方當事人，對造成他方當事人之損失應負責。(3)特別是一方當事人於不想與他方當事人達成協議時，仍進入或繼續協商則構成惡意之情形。」[350]

---

[345] ARTICLE 1.1 (Freedom of contract)
　　The parties are free to enter into a contract and to determine its content.
[346] ARTICLE 1.4 (Mandatory rules)
　　Nothing in these Principles shall restrict the application of mandatory rules, whether of national, international or supranational origin, which are applicable in accordance with the relevant rules of private international law.
[347] ARTICLE 1.7 (Good faith and fair dealing)
　　(1) Each party must act in accordance with good faith and fair dealing in international trade.
　　(2) The parties may not exclude or limit this duty.
[348] ARTICLE 1.8 (Inconsistent Behaviour)
　　A party cannot act inconsistently with an understanding it has caused the other party to have and upon which that other party reasonably has acted in reliance to its detriment.
[349] ARTICLE 1.9 (Usages and practices)
　　(1) The parties are bound by any usage to which they have agreed and by any practices which they have established between themselves.
　　(2) The parties are bound by a usage that is widely known to and regularly observed in international trade by parties in the particular trade concerned except where the application of such a usage would be unreasonable.
[350] ARTICLE 2.1.15(Negotiations in bad faith)
　　(1) A party is free to negotiate and is not liable for failure to reach an agreement.
　　(2) However, a part who negotiates or breaks off negotiations in bad faith is liable for the losses caused

　　第三章總共有20條，是有關契約訂立時無法履行、錯誤、詐欺、協迫、不平等、對第三人之效力、承認、喪失撤銷權、通知、時效、溯及既往之撤銷、損害賠償、及單方之意思表達等。有關契約無法履行、錯誤、詐欺、脅迫、及當事人間之重大不平等情形，各文明國家之相關法律莫不視其為與超越性基本政策有關之強行法規，通常是不可能坐視當事人以協議而去對他方造成違背良心（U.C.C.s. 2-302(1)「Unconscionable」）之結果，故UNIROIT Principles 2004亦於art.3.19中規定本章之規定為強行法規：「除了相關僅是於協議上之拘束力，剛開始之無法履行、或錯誤外，本章之條款是具有強制性的。」[351]

　　第三章的強制性法規主要是有關契約或其條款之效力[352]，本章於此方面之規定自然即使沒有3.19條之規定[353]亦屬於一般實體契約法上超越性基本政策之強行規定，任何違背這些強行規定的私人協議皆可能構成「違背良心」之契約或條款而不被強制執行（U.C.C.s. 2-302(1)「Unconscionable」）。但是United Nations Convention on Contracts for the Interna-

---

to the other party.
(3) It is bad faith, in particular, for a party to enter into or continue negotiations when intending not to reach an agreement with the other party.
這個條文即為羅馬Ⅱ規則12條訂約前責任，2.1.16條亦同屬訂約前責任。個人認為羅馬12條應以實體法為依據。
ARTICLE 2.1.16 (Duty of confidentiality)
Where information is given as confidential by one party in the course of negotiations, the other party is under a duty not to disclose that information or to use it improperly for its own purposes, whether or not a contract is subsequently concluded. Where appropriate, the remedy for breach of that duty may include compensation based on the benefit received by the other party.
[351] ARTICLE 3.19(Mandatory character of the provisions)
The provisions of this Chapter are mandatory, except insofar as they relate to the binding force of mere agreement, initial impossibility or mistake.
[352] 排除能力、道德性、及合法性之問題，這與歐盟契約法原則一樣，見art. 3.1。但事實上個人覺得即使於這些方面亦有著共同核心價值。
[353] 3.19條之排除僅是協議上之拘束力、剛開始之無法履行、或錯誤，其官方解釋報告說明如此規定是給當事人引用特別國內法之空間，例如對價或訴因；或一開始之不能即為無效；或不能因一方之錯誤而主張無效。"On the other hand, the provisions of this Chapter relating to the binding force of mere agreement, to initial impossibility or to mistake are not mandatory. Thus the parties may well reintroduce special requirements of domestic law, such as consideration or cause; they may likewise agree that their contract shall be invalid in case of initial impossibility, or that mistake by one of them is not a ground for avoidance."

tional Carriage of Goods Wholly or Partly by Sea 2008, art. 67中除了對形式要求之執著外（art.67(1)(a)），是完全給予強勢之一方超越性之權力，當事人管轄條款之效力超越了這些契約法上有關契約或條款效力於基本政策上之強行規定。而2005年海牙法院選擇公約更是賦予強勢當事人以協議指定管轄法院，並幾乎完全以法院地法為協議條款效力之依據，故2005年公約亦賦予強勢一方權力去超越所有契約法上有關契約及條款效力於基本政策之強行規定。或者我們們可以很安全的下結論認為（it is safe to conclude）-2008年鹿特丹規則67條及2005年海牙法院選擇公約是不折不扣可以超越過所有超越性基本政策之強行法規之最基本之政策及最強行之法規。對這個駭人聽聞的結論個人完全無法認同。除了聯合國人權公約（及大部份之歐盟人權公約）外，或許不應該輕易的有著強行法中之超強行法存在。Court of justice 與court of promoting commerce 是不同的，法院是三權分立下主持憲政及人權正義之機構，而不是推廣跨國企業商務之機構。個人認為鹿特丹規則67條及2005年海牙公約可能有時會造成U.C.C.s. 2-302(1)所規定契約或其條款會造成「違背良心」（「Unconscionable」）之情形，故而於該種情形下不能被加以強制執行。美國U.C.C.s. 2-302(1)所謂的「違背良心」，用中國白話表達就是黑心。鹿特丹規則67條及2005年海牙公約就是黑心的先進國家透過黑心公約對第三世界弱勢人民所加以的黑心強行作為。這些先進國家可以直視第三世界人民的眼睛，然後宣稱這兩個公約沒有違反第二新編187條、U.C.C.的基本政策、UNIDROIT Principles 2004的強行規定嗎？[354]

---

[354] 英國訴訟法上採當事人主義，又因傳統上英美法並無強行法之概念，故自加入歐盟後，英國同僚對於當事人沒有主張強行法之情形下，法院是否應主動適用強行法屢有爭執。於Pro Swing Inc. v. Elta Golf Inc., 2006 Can. Sup. Ct. LEXIS 52; 2006 SCC 52; [2006] S.C.J. No. 52, para. 59, Deschamps J.代表大多數法官認為，即使被告未提出公共政策之抗辯，加拿大法院是加拿大憲法價值的守護者，有關公共政策之爭點有時應自動被提起。個人認為加拿大最高法院這個論述或許應同樣的適用於強行政策上：

Elta Golf did not raise a public policy derence. However, public policy and respect of law go hand in hand. Courts are the guardians of Canadian constitutional values. They are sometimes bound to raise, *proprio motu*, issues relationg to public policy, An obvious example of values a court could raise *proprio motu* can be found in *United States v. Burns*, [2001] 1 S.C.R. 283, 2001 SCC 7. In that case, the

十五、契約之成立及效力及強行法

　　事實上正如所有國家之契約法，UNIDROIT Principles 2004所規定的強行規則還有甚多，最主要的問題還是在於確認個別強行規則的適用範圍。例如有關契約之效力雖是規定於第三章，但第三章事實上亦牽涉到契約同意之成立（formation）及存在（existence）之問題。羅馬公約（8條）及規則（10條）對契約之存在及效力之問題是以假定契約存在時之準據法為依據。美國法院於管轄條款之成立或存在之問題，經常是直接以有關條款之效力問題而加以處理[355]。事實上不只於管轄條款上，第二新編187條及U.C.C.s. 1-301似乎同樣的對契約或其條款之成立或存在之問題，亦一併以契約或條款之效力問題處理。例如U.C.C.s. 1-301就認為脅迫是有關「法院所必須處理的『協議的基本效力』的一些問題」[356]。如前述新編187條是以「法院地之法律原則」去決定基本政策之成立[357]，而U.C.C.s. 1-301亦認為即使沒有違背被指定法律或本應適用為準據法之基本政策，法院仍可以基於法院地之基本政策為理由而不去適用被指定之法律[358]。故而若依歐盟及英國之法律邏輯，美國不但於有關契約或其條款之

Court took Canada's international commitments and constitutional values into consideration in deciding to confirm a direction to the Minister to make a surrender subject to assurances that the death penalty would not be imposed. Public policy and constitutional requirements may also be at stake when the rights of unrepresented third parties are potentially affected by an order. In the case at bar, over and above the concerns articulated by the Court of Appeal and the defences raised by Elta, there are, in my view, concerns with respect to parts of the contempt order inasmuch as is requires the disclosure of personal information that may *prima facie* be protected from disclosure.

[355] 陳隆修，《2005年海牙法院選擇公約評析》，台北，五南圖書公司，2009年1月，初版1刷，18～55頁。

[356] 例如U.C.C.s. 1-301, comment 9, "in determining whether to give effect to the parties' agreement that the law of a particular State or country will govern their relationship, courts must, of necessity, address some issues as to the basic validity of that agreement. These issues might relate, for example, to capacity to contract and absence of duress."

[357] Restatement of the Law, second, Conflict of Laws, s. 187, comment g, "The forum will apply its own legal principles in determining whether a given policy is a fundamental one within the meaning of the present rule and whether the other state has a materially greater interest than the state of the chosen law in the determination of the particular issue."

[358] U.C.C.s. 1-301, comment 9, "a forum will occasionally decline to apply the law of a different jurisdiction selected by the parties when application of that law would be contrary to a fundamental policy of the forum jurisdiction, even if it would not be contrary to a fundamental policy of the state or country whose law would govern in the absence of contractual designation."

成立及效力之問題上，不採「putative proper law doctrine」，而且是將契約或其條款之成立存在之問題上，以契約效力之問題處理。

　　「假設推定準據法理論」於英國傳統判例法上是個「令人困惑的概念」，而歐盟的引用此「令人困惑的理論」雖減少了困惑，卻陷入了「不可自拔的鞋帶困境」之法律邏輯上的困境。如前述第二新編187條認為當事人於契約上之同意，是經由錯誤、詐欺、脅迫、或不正當的影響等不適當的方法而取得，則正如所有之其他契約條款一般，選法條款是不會被給予效力的。而這個同意是否於事實上是以不當的方法取得，則由繫屬法院「依其自己之法律原則而決定[359]」有關契約及其條款之成立及效力（包含「同意」）之問題，重點不應是在於解決方案的法律邏輯，而應是在如第187條comment b於評論附合契約時所論述：「法院會小心的審核這些契約，並且在他們可能包含的選法條款如果會造成對被要求遵守者重大不公平時，會拒絕加以適用。」[360]故而重點不是在要求法律邏輯之一致性，而是在平衡當事人間之公平正義。

　　個人再次重申去年之論述：「契約之存在有問題時，應以當事人所約定之準據法為依據，或還是以如若沒有約定準據法或管轄法院時應為準據法之法律為依據？美國聯邦法院完全無視（或無知？）於這個長久以來困擾國際私法界之問題，以堆土機之氣魄勢如破竹輾壓過這個歷史上國際私法無法克服的邏輯。美國國際私法界繼其選法革命以來，又再一次石破天驚的將歷史上揮之不去的鬼魂留於往日的灰燼中[361]。」

　　美國同僚或許不管歐洲同僚的注重法律邏輯性，但司法正義之大姆

---

[359] S. 187, comment b, "A choice-of-law provision, like any other contractual provision, will not be given effect if the consent of one of the parties to its inclusion in the contract was obtained by improper means, such as by misrepresentation, duress, or undue influence, or by mistake. Whether such consent was in fact obtained by improper means or by mistake will be determined by the forum in accordance with its own legal principles."

[360] S. 187, comment b, "the forum will scrutinize such contracts with care and will refuse to apply any choice-of-law provision they may contain if to do so would result in substantial injustice to the adherent."

[361] 陳隆修，《2005年海牙法院選擇公約評析》，台北，五南圖書公司，2009年1月，初版1刷，86頁。

指規則為當事人間之公平正義，而非法律邏輯。當事人之「同意」問題為有關契約或其條款之成立及效力問題之核心問題。對於布魯塞爾公約（Brussels Convention）第17條歐盟法院於Elefanten Schuh GmbH v. Jacqmain[362]中說明「第17條管轄條款形式要件之目的是為了『確保法律之穩定性及當事人有給予同意』。將第17條形式要件之要求給予自主、獨立性之解釋以達法律之一致性，這或許是可以理解的。但如果當事人間是否有『同意』亦完全由形式要件上來解釋[363]，則未免過於牽強[364]。」「企圖以形式要件之要求（即使公約於此之規定甚為優質）去解決管轄條款上所可能產生之所有爭執，自然會有問題。於Berghofer v. ASA SA 中歐盟法院雖然承認第17條是用來確認當事人清楚而準確的表達同意[365]之意思，但其又承認：『當事人事後並沒提起任何異議，以抗議口頭協議之適用，因此已構成違反誠信之行為[366]。』」故而形式要件之要求「無論其如何的優質」仍就不能完全決定當事人是否「同意」之問題，經常仍需回歸大陸法的誠信及英美法的合理性標準，亦即回歸Lord Wright 於the Vita Food中所說的當事人「所表達的意思必須是誠信而合法的[367]。」個人認為歐盟契約法原則2：301條所規定的洽商違反誠信原則之第2及第3項或許

---

[362] Case 150/80[1981] E.C.R. 1671, PARA. 25, "Article 17 is thus intended to lay down itself the formal requirements which agreements conferring jurisdiction must meet; the purpose is to ensure legal certainty and that the parties have given their consent." 歐盟法院一再重申會員國之法律不得補充或凌駕第17條之規定，Case 25/79 Sanicental GmbH v Collin [1979] E.C.R. 3423.

[363] Case 24/76 Estasis Salotti v Ruewa [1976] E.C.R. 1831, para 7.

[364] 陳隆修，《2005年海牙法院選擇公約評析》，台北，五南圖書公司，2009年1月，初版1刷，119頁

[365] Case 221/84 Berghofer v ASA SA [1985] E.C.R. 2699, para. 13, "According to settled case-law (judgment of 14 December 1976 in Case 24/76, Salotti v RUWA, [1976] ECR 1831; judgment of 14 December 1976 in Case 258/76, Segoura v Bonakdarian, [1976] ECR 1851; judgment of 6 May 1980 in Case 784/79, Porta-Leasing v Prestige International, [1980] ECR 1517; judgment of 19 June 1984 in Case 71/83, Tilly Russ v Haven en Vervoerbedrijf Nova [1984] ECR 2417), the requirements set out in Article 17 governing the validity of jurisdiction clauses must be strictly construed since the purpose of Article 17 is to ensure that the parties have actually consented to such a clause and that their consent is clearly and precisely demonstrated. "

[366] 同上，para 15. "It would therefore be a breach of good faith for a party who did not raise any objection subsequently to contest the application of the oral agreement."

[367] "...it is difficult to see what qualifications are possible, provided the intention expressed is bona fide and legal, and provided there is no reason for avoiding the choice on the ground of public policy ", per Lord Wright [1939]1 All E.R. 513, 521.

亦應適用於該案件，亦即繼續洽商而無訂約之意思即為違反誠信原則[368]。
而本2：301條亦為UNIDROIT Principles 2004的第2.1.15條所引用，這
個條款自然亦應屬於超越性基本政策的強行條款。事實上該案亦應符合
UNIDROIT Principles 2004第1.7條誠信條款、第1.8條不一致行為、及第
1.9條當事人間已建立之習慣等條文，而這些條文自然亦屬於超越性基本
政策之強行法規。

於Mainschiffahrts-Genossenschaft eG v. Les Gravieres Rhenanes
SARL.中，歐盟法院認為：「當系爭契約是由繫屬國法院去決定是否屬於
國際貿易或商業之範圍，而且當事人所經營的國際貿易或商業部門是否有
這種習慣，並且他們知道或被推定為應該知道這個習慣，法院仍應顯示作
成決定所需要的客觀證據[369]。」因此第17條有關形式要件的要求是否已被
滿足，通常為一事實之認定（a question of fact），而與會員國之某一法
律無關[370]。而同樣在管轄條款之形式要件上，2005年海牙法院選擇公約之
解釋報告亦同樣的規定，任何會員國有關形式要件之要求不得加諸於公約
之管轄條款上[371]。其本著公約一貫維護強勢之主旨，認為「同意」之存在

---

[368] Article 2:301: Negotiations Contrary to Good Faith
(1) A party is free to negotiate and is not liable for failure to reach an agreement.
(2) However, a party which has negotiated or broken off negotiations contrary to good faith and fair dealing is liable for the losses caused to the other party.
(3) It is contrary to good faith and fair dealing, in particular, for a party to enter into or continue negotiations with no real intention of reaching an agreement with the other party.

[369] Case C-106/95[1997]E.C.R. I-911, para 21, "Whilst it is for the national court to determine whether the contract in question comes under the head of international trade or commerce and to find whether there was a practice in the branch of international trade or commere in which the parties are operating and whether they were aware or are presumed to have been aware of that practice, the Court should nevertheless indicate the objective evidence which is needed in order to make such a determination."

[370] 同上，para. 23, "Next, whether a practice exists must not be determined by reference to the law of one of the Contracting Parties, Furthermore, whether such a practice exists should not be determined in relation to international trade or commerce in general, but to the branch of trade or commerce in which the parties to the contract are operating. There is a practice in the branch of trade or conduct is generally and regularly followed by operators in that branch when concluding contracts of a particular type. " 陳隆修，《2005年海牙法院選擇公約評析》，台北，五南圖書公司，2009年1月，初版1刷，120‧121頁。

[371] Hartley and Dogauchi Report, para. 110, "Paragraph(c)deals with formal requirements. These are both necessary and sufficient under the Convention; a choice of court agreement is not covered by the Convention if it does not comply with them, but , if it does, no further requirements of a formal nature may

應由被指定法院地法決定[372]。但其又認定「同意」是一種基本事實上之要件[373]，而以類似羅馬公約8(2)條（規則10(2)條）之案例[374]，認為於該種情形下公約並不適用，亦即如果於「正常標準」下該同意不存在則繫屬法院即不必再適用外國法。故而有趣的是歐盟法院認為形式要件的確認是事實問題，而2005年海牙公約的解釋報告認為同意之基本要件之「正常標準」是事實問題。無論是契約形式要件或當事人之同意，都直接關係到契約之成立、存在、與效力，各國於實體法上皆有著明文規定，故而可能既是事實上之問題，亦是法律上之問題。如果暫時排除強行法規之考慮因素，單就選法規則而言，其可能牽涉的為契約準據法、法院地法、被指定法院地法、putative proper law、及他們的選法規則。而契約準據法又可能與契約條款之準據法不同。

故而於此五花八門、眼花撩亂之混亂情形下，個人認為[375]：「歐盟契約法規則有關契約成立最基本之開宗明義條款，雖然是大而化之的入門條款，但或許是返璞歸真、正本清源的最佳辦法。第2：101條規定：『(1)於沒有其他更多條件下，一個契約已訂定如果(a)當事人有意於法律上受拘束，並且(b)他們已達成充分的協議。(2)一個契約並不需要以書面被訂定或證明，並且不需要受到任何其他於形式上之要求。包含證人在內，契約得以任何方法被證明。[376]』第2：102條規定：『當事人於法律上願受契

---

be imposed under national law. ”

[372] 同上，para. 94。

[373] 同上，para. 95 ”However, the Convention as a whole comes into operation only if there is a choice of court agreement, and this assumes that the basic factual requirements of consent exist. If, by any normal standards, these do not exist, a court would be entitled to assume that the Convention is not applicable, without having to consider foreign law.”

[374] 同上，para. 96。

[375] 陳隆修，《2005年海牙法院選擇公約評析》，台北，五南圖書公司，2009年1月，初版1刷，122頁。

[376] Article 2:101:Conditions for the Conclusion of a Contract
　(1)A contract is concluded if :
　　(a) the parties intend to be legally bound, and (b)they reach a sufficient agreement without any further requirement.
　(2) A contract need not be concluded or evidenced in writing nor is it subject to any other requirement as to form. The contract may be proved by any means, including witnesses.
　UNIDROIT Principles 2004 第1.2條與本條第2項之規定一致。

約拘束之意思，應從他方當事人能從其言詞或行為合理的了解為判斷之依據[377]。』」

　　形式要件與當事人之同意固然是有關契約及其條款之存在與效力之重要因素，但是契約法或許應是所有法律部份門最複雜之部門，故形式要件與同意之法規雖經常是被視為有關基本政策之強行法規，但自然仍有許多契約法上經常發生之問題並非單純的依這方面之法規即可解決。例如去年為了證明2005年海牙選擇法院公約於法學邏輯上的缺陷與不公義性，個人曾舉美國、英國及歐盟案例，以討論有關契約法中誠信原則、詐欺、錯誤、脅迫、併入條款、標準格式契約、訴訟有牽涉到第三人、額外附加條款相互衝突、非契約當事人之權利[378]、沒有對價及當事人議價能力不平等種種問題，並非為當事人所指定之法院地法（2005年公約）或假設推定準據法（羅馬公約8條）所能完全解決之問題[379]。有關契約或其條款之存在及效力之問題經常牽涉及有關基本政策之強行法規，故而無論依據何種理論下之選法規則所選定之外國準據法，於若違背這些規定之情形下，是通常不能被加以適用的。這是因為契約或其條款之存在與效力之基本問題，經常是與當事人間之公平正義有關，法院經常需要認定案件之事實是否有違背良心（unconscionable[380]）之情形。這亦是第2新編187(2)(b)條文及U.C.C.s. 2-302(1) comment 9以「法院地之法律原則」為衡量基本政策之標準之重要理由。而個人一生懸命於實體法論，早期即以契約法之「共同核心」[381]，去年進一步以歐盟契約法原則，本文則再佐以

---

[377] Article 2:102: Intention
The intention of a party to be legally bound by contract is to be determined from the party's statements or conduct as they were reasonably understood by the other party.
UNIDROIT Principles 2004第2.1.1條有關契約之成立規定只要當事人之行為足以顯示協議達成，契約即為成立。
ARTICLE 2.1.1(Manner of formation)
A contract may be concluded either by the acceptance of an offer or by conduct of the parties that is sufficient to show agreement.

[378] Hartley and Dogauchi Report, para. 97，則將此問題交由各國法律去決定。

[379] U.C.C.s. 2-302(1)。

[380] U.C.C.s. 2-302(1)。

[381] 陳隆修，《美國國際私法新理論》，台北，五南圖書公司，民國76年1月，初版，218～226頁。

UNIDROIT Principles 2004為衡量這些基本政策之標準。而這些「共同核心」或「基本政策」或許即廣為現今所謂之全球化法學之基礎。

第2新編及U.C.C.雖然於極重要或最重要的「基本政策」上，突破選法規則的桎梏，可以超越選法規則而不受其拘束，但案件的爭點經常就是在確認什麼是「基本政策」？什麼是「超越性考量」？什麼是「強行法規」？實體法的方法論就是一切以「契約共同核心[382]」、歐盟契約法原則[383]、及UNIDROIT Principles 2004為所有契約法爭點（包括基本政策）之衡量標準。因為如前述「超越性考量」、「基本政策」、及「強行法規」如果存在的話，重點是在其適用之範圍。

對於有關誠信原則詐欺、錯誤、脅迫、併入條款、標準格式契約、訴訟有牽涉到第三人、額外附加條款相互衝突、非契約當事人之權利[384]、沒有對價及當事人議價能力不平等種種問題，無論是否為構成有關基本政策之強行法規範圍內之問題，個人真誠的認為只能透過共同契約法的核心價值（如UNIDROIT Principles 2004、歐盟契約法原則、或甚至短命的歐盟共同參考架構），才能取得大多數人所能同意之公平正義的結果。或許推翻美國選法理論是個人之天命，於批評2005年海牙選擇法院公約時，個人又例行性的對美國盛行之選法理論提出個人認為一針見血的質疑[385]：「海牙會議之會員國幾乎遍及世界上大多數主要國家，事實上可能沒有一國之國內法會完全對上述問題皆有符合國際社會期望之完全規定，更遑論於瞬息萬變之國際案件。於實質上國際私法對許多問題完全尚未有共識。個人一輩子都在問一個問題，於此個人鄭重的再次重問一次：Professor Currie的「state interest[386]」、Professor Reese的「the most significant

---

[382] 同前註，218~226頁。

[383] 陳隆修，《2005年海牙法院選擇公約評析》，台北，五南圖書公司，2009年1月，初版1刷，55～110頁。

[384] Hartley and Dogauchi Report, para. 97, 則將此問題交由各國法律去決定。

[385] 陳隆修，《2005年海牙法院選擇公約評析》，台北，五南圖書公司，2009年1月，初版1刷，77頁

[386] Brainerd Currie, Selected Essays on the Conflict Laws.

relationship[387]」及Professor Leflar的「five considerations[388]」對上述問題之解決有何關連？以個人之觀點，至少歐盟契約法的規則於此方面較引起上世紀國際私法革命（revolution）的美國新理論（methodologies），更能給予一個可較為全世界接受的實體上確實方案—尤其是個人認為這些規則通常較能確保個案的實質正義。事實上每個個案都隱藏著數個珍貴的人性尊嚴與價值在內，於滾滾紅塵世界要大刀闊斧、一針見血的提出一個方法論解決全世界人類私事上之糾紛，或許壯志凌雲、氣吞河嶽，但個人真誠的以為只有一步一腳印，針對個案提出該相關領域內大多數人類具有共識之主流核心共同價值，方能兼顧全世界判決之一致性與個案之正義的終極目標。」

　　無疑的早期原始的「共同核心價值」，及較近相對上較為完備的歐盟契約法原則與UNIDROIT Principles 2004，仍會有許多爭點之解決辦法是目前尚未有共識。但如果實體契約法或商業契約法對某些爭點尚未有主流上之共識，「最重要關連點」或「州利益」之強調是在對尋求真正公平正義的解決方案沒有助益的。而求助於傳統選法規則技巧的運用，例如假設推定準據法（「putative proper law」）於契約成立及效力問題上之運用，對於這些契約法上實質爭點之合理解決亦是沒有助益的。任何有理性的人應皆會承認，無論國際契約法或國內契約法上實質上之爭點，惟有本於誠信原則及合理性之標準，於實體上給予符合公平正義之解決方法，才能得到世界上大部份同僚的認同，有關該爭點於法律上的一致性亦才能真正被達到。Prof. Perillo於評論UNIDROIT Principles 2004時認為該原則是：「傾向全球化法律思想的一個重要步驟[389]。」而Prof. Bonell則完

---

[387] 第二新編(Second Restatement)中Williams Reese的「最重要關連」(the most significant relationship)標準，參閱"Conflict of Laws and the Restatement Second", 28 Law & Contemp. Prod. 679(1963), "Choice of Law : Rles or Approach", 57 Cornell L. Rev. 315(1972).

[388] R.A. Leflar, American Conflict of Laws; "Choice of Law: A Well-watered Plateau", Spring 41 Law & Contemp. Prob. 10(1977).

[389] Joseph M. Perillo, UNIDROIT Principles of International Commercial Contracts: The Black Letter Text and a Review, 43 Fordham L. Rev. 281, 282(1994), "a significant step towards the globalization of legal thinking".

全認同這個論述，認為UNIDROIT Principles 2004：「可能，而且事實上亦的確是，成為一個真正的世界性契約法發展的重大的貢獻[390]。」無論是「全球性法律思想」或「真正的世界性契約法」，個人在美國理論排山倒海的席捲全世界時，於三十年前便獨排眾議的主張「契約法的主流共同核心價值」，今日見證了的歐盟契約法原則、歐盟共同參考架構、及UNIDROIT Principles 2004的產生，一路步履蹣跚踽踽獨行的一生懸念於實體法論之不可被取代性。

　　個人於此再次對兩岸的年輕同僚重申-「全球化法律思想」或「真正的世界性法律」不只存在於契約法，事實上於親屬、繼承、信託、侵權、不當得利、訂約前責任，甚至刑法、民刑訴訟法、憲法、及人權法等皆早已有著「主流共同核心價值」之存在。而這些「主流共同核心價值」於今日卻經常被標籤為「強行法規」、「超越性考量」、及「基本政策」。事實上這些「強行法規」或「基本政策」之爭點所在不在其是否存在，而是在其適用之範圍。例如維護未成年人之最佳利益為全世界所公認之超越性基本政策[391]，有關此方面之規定自然為強行法規中之真正超強行法規。而台灣民法1084(1)條規定「子女應孝敬父母」，亦為基督教、回教、佛教、儒教、及或著許多非洲部落所共有之核心價值，這個共同主流核心價值自然是當事人不能以協議而違背之強行法規，但其適用之範圍及強度則遠不及前者。於著名的台上1804號判決，台灣法院雖依台灣法允許被害人之父母取得侵權之賠償，卻不允許其香港父母依台灣法取得被害子女之扶養費（於扶養費之取得依香港法）[392]。

[390] MICHAEL JOACHIM BONELL, The CISG, European Contract Law and the Development of a World Contract Law 56Am. J.Comp.L. 1, 18(2008), "may, and actually do, make a significant contribution to the development of a veritable world contract law. "

[391] 見陳隆修、許兆慶、林恩瑋、李瑞生四人合著，《國際私法-管轄與選法理論之交錯》，台北，五南圖書公司，2009年3月，初版1刷，154~160頁。1989年聯合國兒童權利公約("Convention on the Rights of the Child 1989")，及1961、1980, and 1996 Hague Conventions，另外參考歐盟Council Regulations No. 1347 / 2000 and No. 2201/2003之相關規定。

[392] 陳隆修，《2005年海牙法院選擇公約評析》，台北，五南圖書公司，2009年1月，初版1刷，152頁。

　　故而所有被通過之法律，其最終之目的都是被用以執行的[393]，只是其被執行之範圍經常會有爭議而已。同樣的所謂的「超越性考量」、「基本政策」、或「強行法規」的問題，經常不是他們的存在是否有共識，甚或不是當事人得否以協議而違反（例如侵權涉及契約時），重點應是他們於相關實體法上之適用範圍，而選法規則的操弄通常是無法達成這個目的。羅馬公約與規則除了3(3)條有關強行法規之規定外[394]，公約第7條及規則第9條亦有強行法規之規定。公約第7條規定：「(1)於依本公約適用一國之法律時，如若其他國家與案件之情形有著一個密切的關連，並且如果依後者國家之法律，無論契約準據法為何皆應被加以適用，則該國之強行法規得被給予效力。於考慮是否給予這些強行法規效力時，應注意及他們的性質及目的與他們被適用或不被適用之後果。

　　(2)當無論契約本應適用之法律為何，法院地法皆為強行法規之情形時，本公約並不禁止該法院地法規之適用。[395]」

　　公約7(2)條之規定，規則Ⅰ亦規定於9(2)條[396]。這個有關「法院地強

---

[393] Trevor C. Hartley, Mandatory Rules in International Contracts: the Common Law Approach (1997)266 Hague Recueil341, 381, 382, 其認為英國的the Unfair Contract Terms Act 1977, ss. 26, 27(1)為negatively mandatory rules, 亦即契約之準據法縱使有規定，法院仍應拒絕適用。
S. 27 Choice of law clauses (1) Where the [F1 law applicable to] a contract is the law of any part of the United Kingdom only by choice of the parties[and apart from that choice would be the law of some country outside the United Kingdom]sections 2 to 7 and 16 to 21 of this Act do not operate as part [F1 of the law applicable to the contract].

[394] 羅馬規則Ⅰ多增加3(4)條禁止對歐盟強行法之規避法條款
4. Where all other elements relevant to the situation at the time of the choice are located in one or more Member States, the parties' choice of applicable law other than that of a Member State shall not prejudice the application of provisions of Community law, where appropriate as implemented in the Member State of the forum, which cannot be derogated from by agreement.

[395] Article 7 Mandatory rules
1. When applying under this Convention the law of a country, effect may be given to the mandatory rules of the law of another country with which the situation has a close connection, if and in so far as, under the law of the latter country, those rules must be applied whatever the law applicable to the contract. In considering whether to give effect to these mandatory rules, regard shall be had to their nature and purpose and to the consequences of their application or non-application.
2. Nothing in this Convention shall restrict the application of the rules of the law of the forum in a situation where they are mandatory irrespective of the law otherwise applicable to the contract.

[396] 2. Nothing in this Regulation shall restrict the application of the overriding mandatory provisions of the law of the forum.

行法」之規定，事實上個人認為可能於本質上類似英國於加入歐盟前有關
公共政策之規定，而公共政策於公約16條及規則Ⅰ第21條[397]已有規定。歐
盟契約法委員會亦將公共政策與法院地強行法列為同一級數之強行法：
「公約暗示的區分『普通』強行法，見3(3)、5(2)、6(1)條，與所謂的
『直接適用法』，無論契約準據法為何皆應被適用，見第7條，及『國際
公共政策』之規則，見第16條。第2及3類之法規代表著立法國家之強烈
公共政策。如果當事人或仲裁者之選定本歐盟契約法原則是依選法規則而
來，則仲裁者不需去適用第一種類國家之強行規則。但是他或她則必須去
適用本規則之強行規則。如果本選擇只是透過引用之方式，見1：101頁
註2(b)，他或她則必須適用契約準據法國之強行法規[398]。」Cheshire and
North亦將羅馬公約的強行法規分為兩類：「第一，有一種基本寬廣的強
行法之種類，於此種情形只要顯示出強行法之定義被滿足就可以，例如被
認為其法律應被適用國家之相關法律不能為契約所違背……。第二，另一
種更為狹窄之超越性強行法。於有關這種法規，不能僅是滿足上述強行法
之定義即可，亦應依據相關國家之相關法規，該法規為強行法並且超越了
準據法。[399]」對於這兩種強行法Cheshire and North 所下之結論為：「根

---

[397] Article 21
Public policy of the forum
The application of a provision of the law of any country specified by this Regulation may be refused
only if such application is manifestly incompatible with the public policy (ordre public) of the forum.

[398] The Commission of European Contract Law, Principles of European Contract Law, edited by Ole Lando
and Hugh Beale (2000), P. 102, note 3, "3.Ordinary mandatory rules and mandatory rules carried by a
strong public policy
In spite of the fact that the Rome Convention does not bind arbitrators, some of the principles on the
application of mandatory provisions embodied in the Rome Convention will probably be applied by arbitrators.
The Covention impliedly makes a distinction between 'ordinary'mandatory rules, see arts. 3(3),5(2) and
6(1), the so-called 'directly applicable rules', which are applicable irrespective of which law governs
the contract, see art. 7, and the rules of 'international public policy', see art. 16. The rules of the second
and third category express a strong public policy of the enacting state.
If the parties' or the arbitrators' choice of the Principles is a choice of law, an arbitrator need not apply
national mandatory rules of law of the first category. He or she must, however, apply the mandatory
rules of the Principles. If this choice is only an incorporation, see note 2(b) to Article 1:101, he or she
must apply the mandatory rules of the national law applicable to the contract. The same holds true of a
court which applies the Principles by virtue of an incorporation. "

[399] P M North, JJ Fawcett, Cheshire and North's Private International Law, 13th ed. , 578,

據所適用條文之不同，公約上之強行規定所應給予之效力亦應不同。於有關3(3)、5(2)、及6(1)條，公約所給予的強行法效力應該只能超越當事人選擇準據法之自由。至於依據7(1)、7(2)、及9(6)條而來之強行法，公約所給予之效力是更為強。這種強行法是可以超越依公約所應適用法律之所有之法規（包括於當事人沒有選擇時應被適用法律之規則）。[400]」

公約及規則3(3)條是有關當事人選法自由之限制，公約5(2)條及規則6(2)條是有關消費者慣居地法強行保護消費者之法規，公約6(1)條及規則8(1)條是有關對受僱人給予保護之強行法規。規則Ⅰ新增了第5條運送契約，而第2項對旅客運送契約選法自由之限制亦似應屬於第1類較為寬廣之強行法。至於保險契約公約的解釋報告認為屬於服務契約，故適用消費者契約之規定[401]，這顯然不足。規則Ⅰ第7(3)條對非大危險保險契約選法自由之限制，或許應屬於第一類寬廣之強行法；而7(4)條有關會員國對所有保險契約之強制規定，因為超越了所有之相關規則，或許應被視為第二類更為狹窄之超越性強行法。

公約所規定的第二類更為狹窄之超越性強行法除了第7條外，另外尚

"First, there is the basic wide type of mandatory rule, where all that has to be shown is that the definition of a mandatory rules is satisfied, is under the law of the country with whose rule one is concerned the rule cannot be derogated from by contract. Articles 3(3), 5(2), and 6(1) are all concerned with this basic wide type of mandatory rule. Second, there are the narrower overriding mandatory rules. With these, it must not only be shown that the rule is a mandatory one, within the above definition, but also that under the law of the country with whose rules you are concerned the mandatory rule overrides the applicable law. Articles 7(1), 7(2) and 9(6) all require this additional element."或許是配合前述羅馬Ⅰ之Recital 37對超越性強行法與一般契約所不能違背的法律之新解釋，其於較近之14thed.,731中說明羅馬Ⅰ中，第9條是以「超越性的強行法」之名詞，而對於「契約所不能違背的法律」則基本上不用強行法之名詞。"Using the same expression for two very different concepts causes confusion and the Rome I Regulation addresses this by using the term 'overriding' mandatory rules when this term is being used in the Article 7 sense and by not using the term 'mandatory' at all when referring to provisions that cannot be derogated from by agreement.

[400] 同上，P.578, "the effect given to a mandatory rule under the Convention differs depending on the provision in question. With Article 3(3), 5(5), and 6(1), the effect given to the mandatory rule under the Convention is merely to override the parties' freedom to choose the applicable law. With mandatory rules under Articles 7(1), 7(2), and 9(6) the effect given to the rule under the Convention is much greater. The mandatory rule is able to override all of the rules on the applicable law under the Convention (including the rules on the applicable law in the absence of choice)."

[401] Giuliano and Lagarde Report, "The rule also applies to the supply of services, such as insurance, as well as supply of goods"

有9(6)條有關不動產所在地法有關不動產權利及其使用之權利之契約形式
要件之強行法。公約9(6)條為規則所規定於11(5)條，而9(6)之「使用權」
被11(5)條改為「不動產之租賃」[402]

　　因為英美法並沒有所謂「強行法」之概念，故而英國加入羅馬公約
時，所謂「強行法」之概念便引起英國學界之爭論及困擾。由於公約7(1)
條之不穩定性[403]，故而德國、盧森堡、葡萄牙、愛爾蘭、及英國皆行使公
約給予之保留權而拒絕加入7(1)條。正如公約的解釋報告所陳述：「事實
上，法官必須給予裁量權，尤其是於2個不同的國家之相對立強行法，皆
同時宣稱適用於一個相同情形之案件時，此時必須於他們的之間做一個選
擇。」[404]裁量權是英美法法官所習慣被授予的權利，個人並不以為7(1)條
的問題是在本於裁量權而來的不穩定性。真正的問題是在於「強行法規」
的定義本身。如前述歐盟契約法委員會將強行法分為「普通強行法」及
立法國家之「強烈公共政策」（直接適用法）。而羅馬 I 則為了區分這
兩個強度不同的規則，於「當事人不能以約定來違背之規則」上，避免使
用「強行法」之名詞，這種作法是與羅馬公約不同的；在羅馬 I 的第9條
則使用了「超越性的強行法」之名詞（公約第7條僅使用「強行法」之名
詞）。個人認為或許是剪不斷理還亂掩耳盜鈴的心虛表現，或許所有法律
（包括強行法）的重點是在其於個案被執行的強度及範圍，而不是其被冠

---

[402] 5 Notwithstanding paragraphs 1 to 4, a contract the subject matter of which is a right in rem in immovable property or a tenancy of immovable property shall be subject to the requirements of form of the law of the county where the property is situated if by that law:

(a) Those requirements are imposed irrespective of the country where the contract is concluded and irrespective of the law governing the contract; and

(b) Those requirements cannot be derogated from by agreement.

[403] Giuliano and Lagarde Report, "To complete the comments on Article 7(1) it only remains to emphasize that the words 'effect may be given' impose on the court the extremely delicate task of combining the mandatory provisions with the law normally applicable to the contract in the particular situation in question. The novelty of this provision, and the fear of the uncertainty to which it could give rise, have led some delegations to ask that a reservation may be entered on Article 7(1) (see Article 22(1)(a))."

[404] Giuliano and Lagarde Report, "In fact, the judge must be given a power of discretion, in particular in the case where contradictory mandatory rules of two different countries both purport simultaneously to be applicable to one and the same situation, and where a choice must necessarily be made between them."

予之名稱為何。

　　當事人得否以協議而違背之概念只是所謂之「強行法」之部份核心概念，非為全部。例如，許多國家的法律或許會認為產品責任與智慧財產權之問題上，侵權行為之請求與契約條款之抗辯無關[405]；另外許多歐盟的會員國亦認為法院地之公平交易法應超越契約準據法之適用[406]。故而公約7(1)條不但為規則9(3)條所取代，規則9(1)條並且對引起爭議性的強行法規試圖解釋如下：「1.超越性強行法規是為一個國家為了維護其公共利益而視該法規之被遵守為重要之事情，例如有關其政治、社會及經濟制度，無論依本規則契約本應適用之準據法為何，這些法規重要的程度為任何情形，只要符合他們的範圍皆應被加以適用。」[407]

　　9(1)條對強行法之定義似乎只限制於歐盟契約法委員會所謂的「立法國家之強烈公共政策」，亦即公約7條之「直接適用法」及16條之「國際公共政策」。換言之並不包含「普通強行法」或「基本強行法」（公約3(3)、5(2)及6(1)條），而只是包含所謂的較為「狹窄之超越性強行法」（公約7及16條）。亦即9(1)條之定義可能只適用於規則9(2)條法院地強行法、11(5)條有關不動產物權契約之形式要件，及或許7(4)條對保險契約之強制責任。9(1)條之定義對規則中3(3)、6(2)、8(1)、5(2)及7(3)條等普通或基本強行法（羅馬Ⅰ所使用之名詞為「當事人不能以約定來違背之法律」），並不十分合適，這些規則並未具有超越應適用準據法之強度。

　　或許公約7(1)條所引起之糾紛及抗議，迫使規則Ⅰ取消這個規定，而

[405] 陳隆修，《2005年海牙法院選擇公約評析》，台北，五南圖書公司，2009年1月，初版1刷，137、138頁。

[406] Giuliano and Lagarde Report, "The concern of certain delegations to safeguard the rules of the law of the forum (notable rules on cartels, competition and restrictive practices, consumer protection and certain rules concerning carriage) which are mandatory in the situation whatever the law applicable to the contract may be."

[407] Article 9
Overriding mandatory provisions
1. Overriding mandatory provisions are provisions the respect for which is regarded as crucial by a country for safeguarding its public interests, such as its political, social or economic organization, to such an extent that they are applicable to any situation falling within their scope, irrespective of the law otherwise applicable to the contract under this Regulation.

以9(1)條強行法之定義取代之。但是這個定義條文之目的及功能為何？它真能釐清有關強行法之混亂？

　　首先，無論是否故意，它似乎漏掉了第一層「普通」或「基本」強行法。第二，於第二層之「立法國家之強烈公共政策」上，9(2)條法院地之強行法與21條法院地之公共政策是應幾乎被劃上等號的；11(5)條是與國際上公認之「不動產禁忌」[408]有相當關連之條文；而7(4)條如前述基於社會安全各國對個人保險皆有著強行之規定。因此9(1)條所規定的定義之適用範圍原本就是一般其他國家無法與法院地及其他相關國家有爭議的範圍，故而9(1)條之目的與功能到底為何？反而因為9(1)條之定義可能會使不在其規定範圍內之第一層之「基本」或「普通」強行法之功能與適用產生不必要之困擾。9(1)條又是典型的歐盟式的太多資源使得太多聰明的人作了太快的決定。

　　太多資源、太多聰明人、太快決定的歐盟徵狀一開始便出現在公約7(1)條。有代表團提議強行法之性質與目的應以「國際上承認之標準」為依據（例如其他國家亦有著相同之法律存在或該法規執行著普遍被承認之利益）。公約之解釋報告如此反駁著：「但是，其他專家指出這些國際標準並不存在，並且因此會造成法院之困難。而且這個方法會觸及所給予外國法律制度尊重之敏感問題。為了這些理由，本委員會雖然沒有不贊成這個想法，卻並不採納這個提出之建議。」[409]

　　首先，這些「國際標準並不存在」是真的嗎?甚至在羅馬公約成立之前，年輕時個人之博士論文便引用一些歐美實體契約法前輩同僚[410]之先知

---

[408] 陳隆修，《比較國際私法》，台北，五南圖書公司，78年10月，初版，320、321頁。

[409] Giuliano and Lagarde Report, "One delegation had suggested that this should be defined by saying that the nature and purpose of the provisions in question should be established according to internationally recognized criteria (for example, similar laws existing in other countries or which serve a generally recognized interest). However, other experts pointed out that these international criteria did not exist and that consequently difficulties would be created for the court. Moreover this formula would touch upon the delicate matter of the credit to be given to foreign legal systems. For these reasons the Group, while not disapproving this idea, did not adopt this drafting proposal."

[410] R.B. Schlesinger, Formation of contracts; G. H. Treitel, An Outline of the Law of Contract; John D. Calamari and Joseph M. Perrillo, Contracts.

灼見，主張契約法「共同核心價值」之存在[411]。枉費有著鋪天蓋地的資源，羅馬公約白白的浪費前輩同僚的心血智慧，是個不懂得珍惜我們人類前輩同僚智慧資源的不環保公約。更荒謬的是第7條之解釋報告一開始便公開承認強行法共同原則之存在於會員國間：「委員會於上次會期便重申第7條僅是包含在經濟體內會員國之法律既已存在之原則。經由當事人之選法或經由一個附隨的連繫因素應適用於契約之法規，各國法院可於某些情形下不去適用這些法規而去適用強行法規之原則，已經幾年來同時於法學著作及我們某些會員國與其他地方的實務上被承認著。」[412]

　　這是怎麼一回事？一開始便開宗明義信誓旦旦的宣稱強行法「在經濟體內會員國之法律既已存在之原則」，及「某些情形下」「適用強行法規之原則」「已經幾年來」「於某些會員國與其他地方的實務上被承認著。」短短幾百個字後之結尾卻是「這些國際標準並不存在」。羅馬公約是怎麼了？太多資源、太漫不經心、太快下決定。

　　我們如果忽略羅馬公約解釋報告的精神分裂式頭尾不對稱，國際標準真的不存在[413]？時間經常還給實體方法論一個公道。前述2004U.C.C.、

---

[411] 陳隆修，《美國國際私法新理論》，台北，五南圖書公司，民國76年1月，初版，218～226頁。

[412] Giuliano and Lagrarde Report, "The Group reiterated at its last meeting that Article 7 merely embodies principles which already exist in the laws of the Member States of the Community.
The principle that national courts can give effect under certain conditions to mandatory provisions other than those applicable to the contract by virtue of the choice of the parties or by virtue of a subsidiary connection factor, has been recognized for several years both in legal writings and in practice in certain of our countries and elsewhere."

[413] 見德國Max Planck Institute for Foreign Private and Private International Law, Comments on the European Commission's Green Paper on the Conversion of the Rome Convention of 1980 on the Law Applicable to Contractual Obligations into a Community Instrument and its Modernisation, at 82, "The 'giving effect' to a foreign internationally mandatory rule is easier for a court if the purposes pursued by the rule are recognized on the international level and are also to be found in the legal systems of its own state and other countries or international conventions. Internationally recognized purposes are, for instance, restrictions on exporting art objects based on the protection of the national cultural heritage or prohibitions on forming cartels or abusing positions of market strength for the protection of competition. Internationally mandatory rules that are singular and unprecedented in other legal systems are likely to be refused by a court, even if there is a considerably close connection to the country which has adopted the internationally mandatory rule. The Tribunal de Commerce in Mons, Belgium, recently decided a case in which a corporation situated in Belgium concluded an agreement concerning an exclusive distributorship for Tunisia with a company that was registered in Tunisia. Under Tunisian competition law, exclusive distribution agreements were prohibited. The Belgian court had to decide under

2000年歐盟契約法原則、較近的歐盟共同參考架構、及2004UNIDROIT Principles都是國際契約法上之重要指標，而且彼此互相參考援引，故而都有著大致上之共同核心價值存在。尤其是有關基本政策上之強行法規，更是彼此相差不遠。近三十年來，羅馬公約及規則 I 於強行法規上之混亂無章，就是於強行法規上過份強調選法規則而不注重實體契約法上之共同核心價值所致。事實上所有被通過的法律都是被用來執行的基本政策，一直強調所謂「強行法」的選法規則，而不承認契約法之共同核心就是羅馬公約及規則 I 之阿奇里斯腳踝。於所有法律之共同核心觀念下，所有被通過之法律（包含契約法）都是應被加以執行之強行規定，但其被強行之範圍及程度應視個案之情形而定。

　　所謂的強行法規（如果其存在的話）被歐盟分為：(1)「基本」或「普通」強行法，其超越當事人之自由選法（即當事人不能以協議違背）；(2)「直接適用法」或「立法國家之強烈公共政策」，其不但包括第一個要件，並且超越所有應適用之法律（包含於沒有選法下本應適用之法律）。於共同核心契約法之觀念下，「強行法」是個令人可疑的名詞，而歐盟又將強行法分為兩個不同強度之強行法更是奇怪。例如僱佣及消費契約是於公約及規則中被列為第一級之普通強行法。或許於通常案件中他們的確是屬於普通強行法，但於某些情況下他們亦可能屬於「立法國家之強烈公共政策」。例如僱傭契約中任何牽涉到未或年之工作契約，或又例如於消費契約中涉及人體健康之著名三氯氰胺毒奶粉案例。

---

art. 7(1) Rome Convention whether to give effect to the Tunisian rule of non-exclusivity in the Belgian proceeding and with respect to a contract which apparently was subject to Belgian law. The Court rejected the application of the Tunisian statute because - inter alia - the prohibition of exclusive distribution agreements seemed to be a singular feature of Tunisian law, unparalleled in other jurisdictions." Tribunal de Commerce de Mons 2.11.2000, Rev. dr. com. Belge 2001, 617.

德國同僚雖承認有國際層級之強行法之存在，但第一世界的同僚普遍的輕忽了第三世界反跨國企業獨佔之掠奪性行為。這亦是個人強烈的主張「不患寡患不均」的王道法學之緣故，或許這更亦可能是黃進教授主張「中國式法學之特色」。如後述「王道」法學才是結合聯合國宣言的真正國際強行法。

　　所謂的強行法本身就是一個可疑的概念，而歐盟又自以為天衣無縫的設計了一個兩階段的強行法概念更是加深了其不可測性。歐盟契約法委員會於引用法國法以證明歐盟契約法原則之強行法（指的應僅是普通強行法）不可被當事人之協議違背後[414]，即坦誠承認下面之混亂情形：「如果一契約之準據法為某一國家之法律，而當事人之選擇於條款中引用歐盟契約法原則，該國之強行法應為契約之依據。但是當事人於此情形下得否排除歐盟契約法原則之強行法，則得依情形而定。這樣的操作可能是一種規避（規避法律），因此會違反法院地國家的公共政策。見1：201條誠信原則之註解。」[415]歐盟契約法委員會承認於強行法之適用上是沒有固定的答案，這自然遠較羅馬公約及規則的操弄選法規則以企圖達到機械式答案為優良。但將當事人之協議以規避法律處理之有兩個問題。首先，英國法（尤其判例法）並不熱衷於發展「規避法律」原則[416]，個人亦認為至少於判例法上，「規避法律」之作法可能有時會違反三權分立的憲法上最不可被超越之強行法。因為規避法律不是一種「國際標準」，並不符合共同核心價值，故而它並不合適做為解決強行法的標準。第二，這個論述沒有涵蓋到「立法國家之強烈公共政策」。

　　很顯然的歐盟契約法委員會對「強行法」這個大陸法作繭自縛所造成的莫須有法學怪獸亦不知所措。或許大陸法應該勇敢的面對這個無法控制之怪獸─它之所以不能被控制或許是因為基本上它就不存在。但是遠較

---

[414] The Commission of European Contract Law, Principles of European Contract Law, edited by Ole Lando and Hugh Beale(2000), P.102, "The mandatory provisions of the Principles cannot be excluded by parties who have chosen to have their contract governed by them. This is in harmony with FRENCH law where it has been held that parties who have agreed to have their contract governed by a treaty which is not ipso jure applicable to the contract may not exclude the mandatory provisions of the treaty, see Cass. Com. 4 February 1992, Revue critique de droit international privé 1992 495 with the note by Paul Lagarde."

[415] 同上，P.102, "If the parties choose to incorporate the Principles in a contract which is governed by a national law, the mandatory rules of that law will govern the contract. Whether in such a case the parties may exclude the mandatory provisions of the Principles will depend on the circumstances. Such a manoeuvre may be an evasion (fraude à la loi)which is contrary to the ordre public of the forum country. See notes to Article 1:201 on the good faith principle"

[416] 陳隆修，《國際私法契約評論》，台北，五南圖書公司，民國75年2月，初版，28、29頁。

依賴選法規則的羅馬公約及規則高明的是，歐盟契約法委員會雖無法提供答案，但至少能回歸至契約法之基本原則-誠信原則。其1：201條規定：「(1)當事人之行為必須符合誠實信用及公平交易原則。(2)當事人不能排除或限制此責任。」[417]

如其註釋所說，誠信原則是整個契約法原則的基礎原則。於契約成立、及當事人之責任與權利之履行皆應遵照誠信原則，許多個別條款中皆有著誠信原則的特別規定。[418]例如訂約前之責任（2：301條）；洽商時不得透露他方之秘密（2：302條）；不得因為他方之依賴、經濟困境、或其他弱點而取得不公平之利益（4：109條）；於決定默示條款時誠信原則為重要的考慮因素（6：102條）；債務人有權於履行期限前補救其有瑕疵之履行（8：104條）；契約之履行為不合理時債務人得拒絕履行（9：102條）。其中4：109條規定因為一方之依賴、經濟困難、急迫、欠缺考慮、無知、無經驗、或無議價能力，而使得他方取得非常不公平或過多的利益時，契約得被撤銷。[419]這個舉世共同的核心價值就是2005海牙法院選擇公約及鹿特丹規則67條對第三世界弱勢人民所侵犯的不可被侵犯的訴訟權、財產權、及平等權於民法上之依據。

於去年個人即以英國Dimskal Shipping Co.[420]案為例子，說明4：109

---

[417] Article 1:201: Good Faith and Fair Dealing
(1) Each party must act in accordance with good faith and fair dealing.
(2) The parties may not exclude or limit this duty.
[418] Lando and Beale, Comment A, P.113.
[419] ARTICLE 4:109: EXCESSIVE BENEFIT OR UNFAIR ADVANTAGE
(1) A part may avoid a contract if, at the time of the conclusion of the contract:
  (a) it was dependent on or had a relationship of trust with the other party, was in economic distress or had urgent needs, was improvident, ignorant, inexperienced or lacking in bargaining skill, and
  (b) the other party knew or ought to have known of this and, given the circumstances and purpose of the contract, took advantage of the first party's situation in a way which was grossly unfair or took an excessive benefit.
(2) Upon the request of the party entitled to avoidance, a court may if it is appropriate adapt the contract in order to bring it into accordance with what might have been agreed had the requirements of good faith and fair dealing been followed.
(3) A court may similarly adapt the contract upon the request of a party receiving notice of avoidance for excessive benefit or unfair advantage, provided that this party informs the party which gave the notice promptly after receiving it and before that party has acted in reliance on it.
[420] 陳隆修，《2005年海牙法院選擇公約評析》，台北，五南圖書公司，2009年1月，初版1刷，80

條為契約法之共同核心價值。另外有關該案的經濟脅迫（economic duress），個人又再舉同樣應為所謂「強行法」的4：108條以為共同核心的說明，4：108條規定：「他方當事人行為所造成之急迫而且嚴重的威脅，導致當事人的簽訂契約，如果該行為符合下列要件該當事人得撤銷契約：(a)該行為本身是非法的，或(b)以該行為為手段去取得契約的簽訂是非法的，但前述當事人如果於該情形下有其他合理的選擇則不可行使撤銷權。[421]」故而不但歐盟契約法原則1：201條及其註釋所舉之其他有關誠信原則之條文皆毫無疑問的應屬所謂「強行法」之範圍，另外還有甚多其他條文亦應超越當事人之協議或原應適用之準據法。除了脅迫外，個人又舉例[422]以說明歐盟契約法原則於錯誤（4：103條）及詐欺（4：107條）上之條文亦可為契約法於國際糾紛中之共同核心（即所謂強行法）。

　　另外1：201條註釋B中認為1：105條之慣例[423]及1：302條之合理性，是伴隨著誠信原則以執行歐盟於商業交易中合理、公平、及正派之標準。「它補充契約法原則中條款之不足，並且於嚴格的遵守這些原則的條款會造成明顯的不公平的結果時，得被優先適用。[424]」有關當事人間之慣例，

頁於Dimskal Shipping Co., SA v. International Transport Workers Federation,【1992】2 A.C. 152中，賴比瑞亞船公司之船停於瑞典港口時，船員工會威脅除非船公司多付船員薪資及捐贈大筆捐款給予工會之福利基金，否則會將船公司列入黑名單中。船公司同意這些條件，並且明定該「契約」以英國法為準據法，雖然依瑞典法該工會之經濟脅迫（economic duress）並非為非法行為，但英國法為若契約成立時契約之準據法，故契約之存在與否及脅迫之效果應依英國法而定。英國最高法院判經濟上之脅迫，構成契約得被撤銷之後果（voidable）。

[421] ARTICLE 4:108: THREATS

A party may avoid a contract when it has been led to conclude it by the other party's imminent and serious threat of an act:

　(a) which is wrongful in itself, or

　(b) which it is wrongful to use as a means to obtain the conclusion of the contract, unless in the circumstances the first party had a reasonable alternative.

[422] 陳隆修，《2005年海牙法院選擇公約評析》，台北，五南圖書公司，2009年1月，初版1刷，80、81頁。

[423] ARTICLE 1:105: USAGES AND PRACTICES

　(1) The parties are bound by any usage to which they have agreed and by any practice they have established between themselves.

　(2) The parties are bound by a usage which would be considered generally applicable by persons in the same situation as the parties, except where the application of such usage would be unreasonable.

[424] Lando and Beale, P.113

"The concept is, however, broader than any of these specific applications. It applies generally as a com-

個人去年亦舉例做為契約共同核心價值之參考。[425]

　　至於「合理性」之要求，歐盟契約法原則中有著一系列之條款[426]是圍繞著1：302條合理性條款。如前述，於2004 UNIDROIT Principles及歐盟契約法原則中，合理性條款的引用數量皆甚為龐大，遠超過誠信條款。如果將所有合理性及誠信原則之條款相加，那麼幾乎許多2004 UNIDROIT Principles及歐盟契約法原則之條款，皆屬於當事人不得違背或超越應適用準據法之強行法。如果幾乎整部契約法原則都是強行法，那麼強行法是什麼意涵？更有趣的是如若契約法中充斥著強行法，那麼依照羅馬公約及規則自己對強行法的法律邏輯－羅馬公約及規則幾乎很少適用的餘地。如果按照他們自己的法律邏輯，大陸法的羅馬公約及規則自己作繭自縛的創了一個莫須有的強行法，很有可能把自玩完。或許專注於契約法的實體共同核心是他們唯一的救贖。

　　除了有關基本的合理性及誠信條款外，另外許多一般契約法的規定亦是當事人不得違背或是可以超越應適用之準據法的強行法。如1：202條：「每個當事人對他方當事人應負起促成契約生效之合作責任。」[427]對於去年所討論之美國聯邦選擇法院條款之一系列案件[428]，個人以為4：110條於非個別洽商條款應可適用：「(1)當一契約條款並不是單獨商討而成，如果該條款造成當事人間契約權利及義務的重大不平衡，使得一方甚為不利，並且違反誠實信用及公平交易原則的要件，則該一方當事人得撤銷該條款，但須考慮該契約履行之性質，契約之所有之其他條款，及契約

---

panion to Article 1:104 on Usages. Its purpose is to enforce community standards of decency, fairness and reasonableness in commercial transactions, see Article 1:108 on Reasonableness. It supplements the provisions of the Principles, and it may take precedence over other provisions of these Principles when a strict adherence to them would lead to a manifestly unjust result."（應為1:105條及1:302條）。

[425] 陳隆修，《2005年海牙法院選擇公約評析》，台北，五南圖書公司，2009年1月，初版1刷，73頁。

[426] Lando and Beale, PP. 126, 127頁。

[427] Article 1:202: Duty to Co-operate
Each party owes to the other a duty to co-operate in order to give full effect to the contract.

[428] 陳隆修，《2005年海牙法院選擇公約評析》，台北，五南圖書公司，2009年1月，初版1刷，18～55頁。

訂定時之情形。(2)本條文於下列情形並不適用：(a)解釋契約主要範圍之條款，但該條款必須是明白而可令人了解之語言；或於(b)當事人一方義務之價值相對於他方當事人義務之價值之合適性」。[429]另外6：105條亦有著強烈的公共政策屬性：「當價格或任何其他契約條款是由一方當事人所決定，並且該當事人之決定是十分不合理，那麼即使有著相反的約定條款，一個合理的價格或其他條款應用以取代之。」[430]

十六、契約法之共同核心政策（誠信原則）

歐盟契約法原則之「強行法」自然不只前面所引述。基本上每個法律條款之被通過都須經過一定之繁雜固定法律程序，他們皆代表著該立法國家之基本政策，至於什麼情形下那個政策應超越另一個政策，於許多情形下是沒有規定的，無論是否有違三權分立原則，法院不得不依特定情形於個案中決定某個基本政策應超越另一個基本政策。這種評價禁忌是Prof. Currie所誓死反對並進而引為利益說之基礎，但卻是大陸法所引為法學架構之基礎的法律邏輯之表現。

因為每個實體法之條款都是被用來加以強制執行的，故而很少實體法

---

[429] Article 4:110: Unfair Terms not Individually Negotiated

(1) A party may avoid a term which has not been individually negotiated if, contrary to the requirements of good faith and fair dealing, it causes a significant imbalance in the parties' rights and obligations arising under the contract to the detriment of that party, taking into account the nature of the performance to be rendered under the contract, all the other terms of the contract and the circumstances at the time the contract was concluded.

(2) This Article des not apply to:

(a) a term which defines the main subject matter of the contract, provided the term is in plain and intelligible language; or to

(b) the adequacy in value of one party's obligations compared to the value of the obligations of the other party.

本條款為EC Council Directive 93/13 on Unfair Terms in Consumer Contracts(1993)的延伸，其將該1993年指令延至私人及商業契約。故而1993年指令之Annex所附帶的條款對4:110條亦可能可以適用。但與1993年指令直接認為不公平條款沒有拘束力不同的是，4:110條給予當事人撤銷之權利。

[430] ARTICLE 6:105: UNILATERAL DETERMINATION BY A PARTY

Where the price or any other contractual term is to be determined by one party and that party's determination is grossly unreasonable, then notwithstanding any provision to the contrary, a reasonable price or other term shall be substituted.

會如2004 UNIDROIT Principles 第3.19條般的將有關效力的第三章的大部份皆列為強行法。但這並不表示第三章以外之其他部份不是可為強行之法規。例Prof. Bonell所舉的警察條款的例子[431]arts. 2.1.20, 3.10, 7.1.16, & 7.4.13中，就有三條不是屬於第三章。另外較明顯有1.7條誠信原則不得被排除或限制；1.8條當事人不得有不一致的表現；1.9條習慣對當事人之拘束力；2.1.15條訂約前責任；2.1.16條保密之責任；2.1.19條標準格式契約；2.1.20 條禁止不公平之突襲條款；2.1.22 條雙方標準格式之不同；4.8條替當事人決定條款；5.1.2條默示責任；5.1.3條當事人合作之義務；5.1.4 條履行特定結果或最佳結果之責任。5.1.7條不合理價格的強制規範；7.1.7條不可抗拒之情形；7.2.2契約無法履行；7.3.6條恢復原狀之請求；7.4.3條損害之確認；及7.4.13條違約金之限制。以上這些條款只是由表面上大陸法之觀點較具強行性而已，事實上2004 UNIDROIT Principles與歐盟契約法原則相互援引，他們所列的條款大部份皆應屬世界性契約法的共同核心，幾乎每個條款於不同的個案中皆可能屬於強行性的主流共同核心基本政策。例如4.6條規定契約條件不清楚時，其解釋應對提供條件一方不利[432]；又5.1.7條2項規定當價格是由一方所決定，而該決定是明顯的不合理時，即使有相反的規定，合理的價格應取代之。[433]這種保護弱勢的規定，很難想像會有文明世界的法律會完全沒有爭議的拒絕去適用他們。[434]而對這種保護弱勢的實體法其同核心條款，羅馬公約及規則 I 的選法規則、最重要關連說、及利益說如何能徹底的去執行這些實體法的共同核心政策？

更重要的是個人一再強調-這些共同核心基本政策通常是舉世認同

---

[431] M. J. Bonell, 56 Am. J. Comp. L. 1, 18 (2008)

[432] ARTICLE 4.6 (Contra proferentem rule)
If contract terms supplied by one party are unclear, an interpretation against that party is preferred.

[433] (2) Where the price is to be determined by one party and that determination is manifestly unreasonable, a reasonable price shall be substituted notwithstanding any contract term to the contrary.

[434] 英美法較為傾向資本主義的自由放任原則，力道上可能較為薄弱，見 Lando and Beale, pp.118, 270。

的，差別是在具體個案適用程度上之認同。[435]而羅馬公約及規則 I 之選法規則、最重要關連說、及利益說的適用，對這些實體法上之共同核心基本政策認同程度之差異性於實質上之公平解決是沒有助益的，而且混淆了一些本就甚為困難之實體法上之真正問題。

　　同樣的美國的U.C.C.雖然是個商業法規，但與2004 UNIDROIT Principles一般，其所規定的條文皆是美國有關商業行為的基本政策。至於這些基本政策得否為當事人以協議背離，或超越本應適用之準據法，即使於條文中有大致上之規定，亦可能視個案之情形而加以決定。1-302(a)及(c)條雖基本上規定當事人通常可協議變更U.C.C.法則之規定，但是對有違背公平正義之協議還是不會被允許的。例如1-302(b)條即規定：「本法所規定的誠信、勤勞、合理、及注意義務是不能以協議而被放棄。如果所訂定的標準不是明顯的不合理，當事人得經由協議而決定這些義務被履行的衡量標準。當本法規定一行為應於一合理期間內被履行時，當事人得協議訂定一個不是明顯不合理之期間。」[436]1-303(g)規定：「一方當事人所提供相關貿易習慣的證據，除非法院認定該一方所給予他方之通知是充份而不會構成對他方之不公平驚奇，才能被允許。」[437]1-304條規定：「本法所規定之契約或責任之履行或執行，皆應符合誠實信用原則。」[438]

---

[435] 陳隆修，《2005年海牙法院選擇公約評析》，台北，五南圖書公司，2009年1月，初版1刷，27頁

[436] 1-302. VARIATION BY AGREEMENT
(a) Except as otherwise provided in subsection(b)or elsewhere in [the Uniform Commercial Code], the effect of provisions of [the Uniform Commercial Code] may be varied by agreement.
(b) The obligations of good faith, diligence, reasonableness, and care prescribed by [the Uniform Commercial Code] may not be disclaimed by agreement. The parties, by agreement, may determine the standards by which the performance of those obligations is to be measured if those standards are not manifestly unreasonable. Whenever [the Uniform Commercial Code] requires an action to be taken within a reasonable time, a time that is not manifestly unreasonable may be fixed by agreement.
(c) The presence in certain provisions of [the Uniform Commercial Code] of the phrase "unless otherwise agreed", or words of similar import, dose not imply that the effect of other provisions may not be varied by agreement under this section.

[437] (g) Evidence of a relevant usage of trade offered by one party is not admissible unless that party has given the other party notice that the court finds sufficient to prevent unfair surprise to the other party. 其comment(9)是如此解釋: "9. Subsection(g)is intended to insure that this Act's liberal recognition of the needs of commerce in regard to usage of trade shall not be made into an instrument of abuse."

[438] 1-304. OBLIGATION OF GOOD FAITH

2-302(1)條規定：「如果法院認為於法律上訂約時契約或其他條款是違背良心時，法院得拒絕執行該契約，或其得執行除去違背良心條款後剩餘部份之契約，或其得限制任何違背良心條款之適用，以避免產生任何違背良心之結果。」[439]另外1-301條g項中更是挑明了許多屬於實體法上基本政策之條款，其中亦免不了有著限制當事人選擇法律及法院之規定。（例如2A-106條）[440]

　　上述條款可能為大陸法所較能接受之強烈公共政策或強行法，但事實上其他每個條款亦皆是美國法界所能接受之共同核心觀念，每個條款皆有其應適用之目的及個別情況，於合適之情形下自然亦有著超越性之強行性質。如1-302條之comment 1就以2-201條及9-602條來舉例說明個別條款對契約自由限制的不同程度之明示性：「契約自由原則是於本法中在其他部份受到個別例外之限制，並且亦受到本條所規定的基本例外之限制。這些個別例外的限制之明示程度是不一致的」[441]。2-302條之comment 1 評述：「本條款使得法院可以明示的方式以此做為警察條款以對抗契約或條款的違背良心，而不必企圖以扭曲文詞的方式、操縱要約與承諾之規則的方式、或認定契約條款違反公共政策或契約主要目的之方式來達到這個結

Every contract or duty within [the Uniform Commercial Code] imposes an obligation of good faith in its performance and enforcement.

[439] (1) If the court as a matter of law finds the contract or any term of the contract to have been unconscionable at the time it was made, the court may refuse to enforce the contract, or it may enforce the remainder of the contract without the unconscionable term, or it may so limit the application of any unconscionable term as to avoid any unconscionable result.

[440] 2A-106. Limitation on Power of Parties to Consumer Lease to Choose Applicable Law and Judicial Forum.

(1) If the law chosen by the parties to a consumer lease is that of a jurisdiction other than a jurisdiction in which the lessee resides at the time the lease agreement becomes enforceable or within 30days thereafter or in which the goods are to be used, the choice is not enforceable.

(2) If the judicial forum chosen by the parties to consumer lease is a forum that would not otherwise have jurisdiction over the lessee, the choice is not enforceable.

[441] "This principle of freedom of contract is subject to specific exceptions found elsewhere in the Uniform Commercial Code and to the general exception stated here. The specific exceptions vary in explicitness: the statute of frauds found in Section 2-201, for example, does not explicitly preclude oral waiver of the requirement of a writing, but a fair reading denies enforcement to such a waiver as part of the 'contract' made unenforceable; Section 9-602, on the other hand, is a quite explicit limitation on freedom of contract. "

果。」[442]而1-304之comment 1更是明文誠信原則貫穿整個U.C.C.：「本條文規定了一個貫穿整個統一商法的基本原則。這個原則即為於商業交易中所有協議及責任之履行及執行誠信原則是應被遵守的。當這個責任是於本法中之某些條款所明示規定，本誠信責任是比起這些明示條款之情形更為寬廣，而應如本條文所規定般的普遍適用於本統一商法所規範的每個契約或責任之履行或執行。[443]」

故而如歐盟契約法原則及2004 UNIDROIT Principles一般，U.C.C.亦認為一些契約法之共同核心基本政策（如誠信原則與合理性要求等）是貫穿整個契約法的，而這些共同核心基本政策是當事人不能以協議違反或應超越本應適用之準據法的。如果這些基本政策是貫穿整部商業契約法或一般契約法，那麼唯一自然合理的邏輯就是一整部契約法都屬於基本政策，亦即整部契約法都屬於強行法。在大陸法此種「強行法」的奇怪意涵下，有關「強行法」的真正重點自然只能是在其於個別案件適用情形[444]。務實的美國U.C.C.與其他世界性契約法原則不同的是，其公開的承

---

[442] "1. This section makes it possible for a court to police explicitly against the contracts or terms which the court finds to be unconscionable instead of attempting to achieve the result by an adverse construction of language, by manipulation of the rules of offer and acceptance, or by a determination that the term is contrary to public policy or to the dominant purpose of the contract. The section allows a court to pass directly on the unconscionability of the contract or a particular term of the contract and to make a conclusion of law as to its unconscionability."

[443] "1. The section sets forth a basic principle running throughout the Uniform Commercial Code. The principle is that in commercial transactions good faith is required in the performance and enforcement of all agreements or duties. While this duty explicitly stated in some provisions of the Uniform Commercial Code, the applicability of the duty is broader than merely these situations and applies generally, as stated in this section, to the performance or enforcement of every contract or duty within this Act."

[444] 於Ingmar GB Ltd v Eaton Leonard Technologies Inc Case C-381/98 [2000] ECR I-9305 中，一英國公司替一美國加州公司於英國及愛爾蘭作為代理，契約準據法以加州法為依據。對於代理費用之請求上，歐盟法院認為Council Directive 86/653/EEC of 18 December 1986 on the Coordination of the Laws of the Member States Relating to Self-Employed Agents之17至18條即使在有選法條款下亦適用於外國商人：

"24 The purpose of the regime established in Articles 11 to 19 of the Directive is thus to protect, for all commercial agents, freedom of establishment and the operation of undistorted competition in the internal market. Those provisions must therefore be observed throughout the Community if those Treaty objectives are to be attained.

25 It must therefore be held that it is essential for the Community legal order that a principal established in a non-member country, whose commercial agent carries on his activity within the Community, cannot evade those provisions by the simple expedient of a choice-of-law clause. The purpose served by

認這些條款對契約自由原則限制的明示性之不同。個人認為這就是表達著
基本政策（強行法）的適用性之不同。

羅馬公約7(1)條之規定於剛開始即被德、英等國家所拒絕，於近三十
年後該引人爭議的7(1)條更於羅馬 I 中被取消。無可爭議的這代表著歐盟
企圖以選法規則來規範「強行法」之一大失敗。「強行法」如果存在的
話，應只限於學術上所討論之一個模糊的概念，於國際法上企圖以選法
規則對其加以規範之嘗試可能於目前之階段會是一個災難。歐盟契約法
原則4：110條規定非個別洽商之條款於違反誠信原則時得被撤銷，這個
條款是將the EC Council Directive 93/13 on Unfair Terms in Consumer
Contracts（1993）延伸至私人及商業契約上。但與1993 Directive不同的
是，其並未有不公平條款表列之附錄，因為歐盟契約法委員會認為：「與
指令不同的，本原則並不包含認定為不公平條款的表列。於職業人士間之
契約，契約條款的表列是其本身就是不公平的，因為商業契約的多樣性，
使得表列是被一般認為不可能的。[445]」4：110條只是眾多基本政策（強
行法）中之一部分（或一小部分）[446]，如果連表列本身都是不公平、不可
能，那麼整個世界性的基本政策（或強行法）又如何能明確的規範？

---

the provisions in question requires that they be applied where the situation is closely connected with the
Community, in particular where the commercial agent carries on his activity in the territory of a Member State, irrespective of the law by which the parties intended the contract to be governed.
26 In the light of those considerations, the answer to the question must be that Articles 17 and 18 of the
Directive, which guarantee certain rights to commercial agents after termination of agency contracts,
must be applied where the commercial agent carried on his activity in a Member State although the
principal is established in a non-member country and a clause of the contract stipulates that the contract
is to be governed by the law of that country.

[445] Comment B, "*B. No Black List*
Unlike the Directive, the Principles contain no list of clauses deemed to be unfair. In contracts between
professionals, a listing of contract terms as being *per se* unfair, because of the diversity of commercial
contracts, is generally held to be all but impossible."

[446] Lando and Beale, p. 269, 即對4：109及4：110條適用範圍之區別如下：
"E. *Unfair Terms and Grossly Unfair Advantage*
Articles 4:109 and 4:110 at first sight have something in common. However, they deal with different
situations. Article 4:109 deals with the case where A takes advantage of B's difficult position. The provision covers both the situation where the price or the other essentials of the contract, or the general
conditions are excessive in one way or another. Article 4:110 deals with what mainly are general conditions, and not with the price. It covers a very frequent situation, where one of the parties has drafted the
contract terms in advance."

　　有趣的是在羅馬公約7(1)條對於強行法加以規範之企圖失敗後，歐盟契約法原則1：103(2)條[447]及2004 UNIDROIT Principles 1.4條[448]仍舊規定依據相關之國際私法規則，國家性、國際性、及跨國性之強行法仍應（得）被適用。1：103條是「應」被適用，1.4條較為聰明的改為「不禁止」被適用。於羅馬公約7(1)條之「相關國際私法規則」慘遭淘汰之不可避免命運後，「相關國際私法規則」於此方面之選法規則應幾乎已不存在，或許經由羅馬公約之經驗，同樣的這兩個跨國性契約法原則會由羅馬Ⅰ學到教訓。但1：103條與1.4條皆為跨國性實體契約法原則中之實體規則，他們的引用羅馬公約7(1)條[449]或許代表著實體法與選法規則融合的具體案例（雖然為失敗的案例），另一個更具體且有著突破性成功的例子為2004 UNIDROIT Principles第7.2.2(a)條及羅馬Ⅰ 9(3)條的契約不可違反履行地法規則[450]，7.2.2(a)條及9(3)條或許可代表著實體法契約法與契約選法規則共同的採納契約不可違反履行地法之規則。從而7.2.2(a)條及9(3)條不但代表著個人所主張的契約不得違反履行地法既是實體法亦是國際法之論述[451]是正確的，亦代表著實體法與國際私法融合之趨勢[452]。

---

[447] (2) Effect should nevertheless be given to those mandatory rules of national, supranational and international law which, according to the relevant rules of private international law, are applicable irrespective of the law governing the contract.

[448] Article 1.4 (Mandatory rules)
Nothing in these Principles shall restrict the application of mandatory rules, whether of national, international or supranational origin, which are applicable in accordance with the relevant rules of private international law.

[449] 羅馬公約7(1)之法源見Giuliano and Lagarde Report, " the second paragraph of Article 13 of the non-entered-into-force Benelux Treaty of 1969 on uniform rules of private international law, which provides that 'where the contract is manifestly connected with a particular country, the intention of the parties shall not have the effect of excluding the provisions of the law of that country which, by reason of their special nature and subject-matter, exclude the application of any other law'.
The same attitude, at any event, underlies Article 16 of the Hague Convention of 14 March 1978 on the law applicable to agency, whereby, in the application of that convention, effect may be given to the mandatory rules of any State with which the situation has a significant connection, if and to the extent that, by the law of that State, those rules are applicable irrespective of the law indicated by its conflict rules."

[450] 陳隆修，《國際私法契約評論》，台北，五南圖書公司，民國75年2月，初版，80-85頁。

[451] 陳隆修，《2005年海牙法院選擇公約評析》，台北，五南圖書公司，2009年1月，初版1刷，92-95頁。

[452] 這或許亦印證了劉仁山教授所主張的國際私法應本於基礎法學而來之主張。

　　歐盟契約法原則中較後出來的10～17章[453]中第15：101條規定：「契約於違反歐盟會員國法律所認為屬於基本性原則之程度內是不生效力的。[454]」第15：102條1項規定契約違反1：103條強行法之規定，其效力依該強行法之規定。第2項規定若未明示，則該契約可能有效、部分生效、無效、或被加以修改。第3項規定：「依據第2項而來的決定必須對該侵犯之回應為合適且符合比例的，該決定必須考慮到所有之情況，包括(a)被侵犯法規之目的；(b)該法規之用以存在所欲保護的特定人；(c)該被侵犯法規所可能加予之處罰；(d)該侵犯之嚴重性；(e)該侵犯是否為有意的；及(f)該侵犯與契約之密切關連性。[455]」

　　第15：101條是個人所主張的實體法主流共同核心價值的代表。其註解如此論述：「對於違反公共政策或道德上的基本原則，所有歐洲的制度都有著使契約無效的條款。所用的名詞則不同。[456]」個人認為羅馬Ⅰ第9條2項「法院地的超越性強行法規」，應正大光明的與21條的「法院地公

---

[453] Principle of European Contract Law, Part Ⅲ, Prepare by The Commission on European Contract Law, Edited by Ole Lando, Eric Clive, André Prüm and Reinhard Zimmermann.

[454] Article 15:101: Contracts Contrary to Fundamental Principles
A contract is of no effect to the extent that it is contrary to principles recognised as fundamental in the laws of the Member States of the European Union.

[455] Article 15:102: Contracts Infringing Mandatory Rules
(1) Where a contract infringes a mandatory rule of law applicable under Article 1:103 of these Principles, the effects of that infringement upon the contract are the effects, if any, expressly prescribed by that mandatory rule.
(2) Where the mandatory rule does not expressly prescribe the effects of an infringement upon a contract, the contract may be declared to have full effect, to have some effect, to have no effect, or to be subject to modification.
(3) A decision reached under paragraph (2) must be an appropriate and proportional response to the infringement, having regard to all relevant circumstances, including:
(a) the purpose of the rule which has been infringed;
(b) the category of persons for whose protection the rule exists;
(c) any sanction that may be imposed under the rule infringed;
(d) the seriousness of the infringement;
(e) whether the infringement was intentional; and
(f) the closeness of the relationship between the infringement and the contract.

[456] Lando and Clive, p.212, "All European systems make provision for the ineffectiveness of contracts which are contrary to fundamental principles of morality or public policy. The terminology varies."例如p.213, "In ENGLISH, IRISH and SCOTTISH law the subject matter of Article 15:101 is often presented under such headings as 'illegality at common law', 'immoral contracts' or contracts 'contrary to public policy', While such a contract may be void, it is more often presented as 'unenforceable'."

共政策」結合，而不必增加困擾，亦即9條2項是不必要的累贅。歐盟契約法委員會於註釋B如此解釋：「於包括歐盟法在內之所有於歐盟內已存在之法律基本原則之寬廣概念之必須被引用，乃是15：101條之所以成立而被引用來避免各國於道德性、判例法之合法性、公共政策、公共秩序、及善良風俗之不同概念。[457]」於共同核心之已存在之法律基本原則之寬廣概念下，不同的法學名詞或選法技巧是不重要的。

但是違反15：101條之效力是絕對無效的[458]，違反根據1：103條而來之15：102條之強行法之後果於沒有規定下卻是不一定的。解釋報告認為15：102條所處理的是較15：101條不重要的侵犯法律之情況[459]。但解釋報告又小心翼翼的加上法院地的強行法規及公共政策（羅馬公約16條、規則9(2)及21條）自然應被加以適用的[460]。

如前述歐盟之羅馬公約及契約法原則將強行法（基本政策）分為二級，第一級為「基本的或普通的強行法」，亦即為15：102條所處理的較不重要的侵犯；第二級為「立法國家的強烈公共政策」或「直接適用法」，可能即為15：101條所規定的範圍。違反第二級強行法之契約或其條款是強制性不生效力的[461]，而違反第一級強行法之契約或其條款之效

---

[457] The formulation of Article 15:101 is intended to avoid the varying national concepts of immorality, illegality at common law, public policy, order public and bonos mores, by invoking a necessary broad idea of fundamental principles of law found across the European Union, including European Community law.

[458] Lando and Clive, p.212, "Unlike the position in Article 15:102, the judge or arbitrator is given no discretion to determine the effects of a contract which is contrary to European fundamental principles of law: such a contract is to be given no effect at all. The intentions and knowledge of the parties are irrelevant."

[459] 同上，p.214, "Article 15:102 deals with less important violations of the law than Article 15:101. Indeed, given the extent of statutory regulation in modern States, some infringements covered by Article 15:102 may be of a merely technical nature. This means that a flexible approach has to be taken to the effects of an infringement."

[460] 同上，p.241, "But nothing in the Convention restricts the application of the rules of the law of the forum in a situation where they are mandatory irrespective of the law otherwise applicable to the contract. It should also be noted that Article 16 of the Convention states that application of a rule of law of a country specified by the Convention may be refused only of such application is manifestly incompatible with the public policy (order public) of the forum."

[461] 同上，comment C, p.212, "C. of No Effect
The Principles here avoid the national concepts of nullity (absolute or relative), voidness, voidability and unenforceability, and use instead a concept of 'ineffectiveness'. Ineffectiveness extends to non-

力，於法律無明文下是不確定的。如前述歐盟契約法原則這種法律邏輯是
有著無法超越的障礙。首先如所一再重覆，所有被通過之法律都是該國應
被強制執行之基本政策。例如前面一再舉例的是誠信原則、合理性要求、
及比例原則皆為貫穿大部分文明國家整個契約法之強行基本政策。而又如
2004 UNIDROIT Principles將有關效力的第3章幾乎整個列為強行法，同
樣的歐盟契約法原則第15章合法性之強行規定亦與第4章有關效力之部分
連結[462]。**故而強行法最大的問題不是它不存在，而是它到處都存在。**

　　第二，如果首先對強行法範圍之認定就有困難，那麼對強行法加以種
類之區分自然是會有問題。第三，因為對強行法種類之區分有困難，故而
對於因種類之不同而給予不同效力之作法自然亦會有問題。歐盟契約法委
員會或許太健忘了，其於狹窄的4：110條中自己就認為「商業契約的多
樣性，使得表列是被一般認為不可能的」，「於職業人士間之契約，契約
條款的表列是其本身就是不公平的」。如果單就4：110條中是不可能、
不公平的，在整個契約法中應更是不可能、不公平的，故而違反強行法
（基本政策）之效果，應具體的依所牽連的個別實體法，就15：102條3
項的相關情況，合適而符合比例的認定其效力。大陸法的強行法概念應被
限定為學術上之議題，尤其更不應該將其應分為二級而賦予機械式截然不
同之效力[463]。

---

enforcement of the contract where enforcement (as distinct from the contract itself) would be contrary to principles regarded as fundamental in the laws of the Member States of the European Union."

[462] 同上，comment A, pp. 211, "A. Scope and placing of Chapter
This Chapter deals with the effects of illegality on contracts or contractual provisions. The topic is somewhat related to the matters dealt with in Chapter 4 (Validity) of the Principles, although it does not provide for the remedy of avoidance as such."

[463] 同上，comment B, pp.211, 212,對於15：101條之基本原則其解釋報告將層次提昇至最高境界，其作為參考之指引的為E C Treaty, the European Convention on Human Rights, and the European Union Charter on Fundamental Rights, "Guidance as to these fundamental principles may be obtained from such documents as the EC Treaty (e.g. in favour of free movement of goods, services and persons, protection of market competition), the European Convention on Human Rights (e.g. prohibition of slavery and forced labour (art. 3), and rights to liberty (art. 5), respect for private and family life (art. 8), freedom of thought (art. 9), freedom of expression (art. 10), freedom of association (art. 11), right to marry (art. 12) and peaceful enjoyment of possessions (First Protocol, art. 1)) and the European Union Charter on Fundamental Rights (which includes many of the rights already mentioned and adds such matters as respect for personal data (art. 8), freedom to choose an occupation and right to engage in work (art. 15),

　　無論對錯，羅馬公約與歐盟契約法原則將「強行法」分為2級，而羅馬公約第7條（相關國之強行法）又與16條（公共政策）被列為同一最具強度之級數[464]，故而現今之羅馬規則9(2)條法院地之強行法實應與21條之公共政策合併，如此一來或許可以大幅降低大陸法強行法概念於國際上適用之困擾。

　　強行法之大本營法國一向自豪於「直接適用法」是與公序良俗不同，其之特點是在其為不須透過選法規則而直接適用的法則。首先，於邏輯上這是個怪觀念。所有適用於跨國案件之法律皆為國際私法，怎麼會沒有適用選法規則？這是典型的「鞋帶困境」辯證[465]。但是個人信奉的是恩

---

freedom to conduct a business (art. 16), right to property (art.17), equality between men and women (art. 23), children's rights (art. 24), rights of collective bargaining and action (art. 28), protection in the event of unjustified dismissal (art. 30), and a high level of consumer protection (art. 38)." 個人近年來經常以聯合國人權法、歐盟人權法之大部分規定、及各國憲法之規定為所有法律（不只契約法）之主流共同核心價值。例如陳隆修、許兆慶、林恩瑋、李瑞生四人合著，《國際私法—管轄與選法理論之交錯》，台北，五南圖書公司，2009年3月，初版1刷，140-160頁中引用1989聯合國兒童權利公約。15:101條之引用歐盟人權公約，可見個人所主張之主流共同核心價值並非毫無見地。但如個人所一再強調，共同核心或強行法的確認經常不會有問題，但具體個案之適用程度上有時是會有爭執的。聯合國、歐盟、及各國憲法上所規定的平等權、訴訟權、財產權、及適當程序權（due process），為全世界所公認之主流共同核心之最超越強行法之基本政策。但個人去年指控美國之不方便法院原則、歐盟Brussels Convention (Regulation)art. 4之過度管轄、2005海牙法院選擇公約、及現在指控2008年鹿特丹規則67條，違反了上述公認的世界性強行法（陳隆修，《2005年海牙法院選擇公約評析》，台北，五南圖書公司，2009年1月，初版1刷，142-153頁），則完全不見美國及歐盟對此反躬自省的讓步。故而基本共同核心強行法之確認即使於完全一致而不構成問題下，其於具體個案的執行程度及範圍仍會造成問題。

個人於此再度慎重的提出另一個主流共同核心價值---階梯發展人權。任何先進國家對第3世界要求具有與他們同一位階之現狀，都是剝奪第3世界依1966聯合國經濟、社會、及文化人權公約第2(3)條之類似階梯權利。正如過去的第1世界，現今的第3世界有著遵從進化的階梯而循序漸進之權利。在中國「道法自然」順天應人之傳統哲學下，無論於人權、教育、政治、經濟、社會、環保、文化、及法律之問題上，第3世界有著遵循階梯而進化之權利。這個階梯權利是遵照大自然進化而來的權利，它的位階高過聯合國人權公約。西方國家如果抽掉第3世界進化之階梯，那麼就是侵犯了人類之平等權及生存權。

台灣有些年輕同僚詢問為何禮運大同篇是中國式法學之基礎？禮運大同就是中華民族他日爬上階梯上層後，不能舉著法律、人權、或環保的大纛，而藉此抽掉第3世界民族進化之階梯，應以本身之經濟力量扶助他們快速爬上階梯。故不方便法院、過度管轄、2005年海牙公約、及鹿特丹規則67條皆不是在中國式法學之範圍。

[464] Lando and Beale, p.102

[465] 見林恩瑋，強行法規的衝突，中華國際法與超國界評論第3卷第2期，346頁，其引述Lagarde如下：「法國學者Paul Lagarde教授在提及lois de police的概念不確定性時表示：『這有點像是我們放塊板子在沼澤上通行一樣，如果我們在板子上待太久，我們就會沈到流沙裡頭。但這種方法可以讓我們通過沼澤，達到目的，也是個不太差的方法。我們不需要去完美化被使用的不同的工具，只要把這些當成是單純可以讓我們達到目的的工具就行了。』(C'est un peu comme lorsqu'

師Prof. Graveson的有效正義理論[466]，故對此法律邏輯的困境並不十分在意。第二如前述，強行法最大的問題是它無所不在充斥著整個契約法，故而它的範圍難以界定。強行法是無法依據選法理論而解決，只能在所牽連的實體法之實質政策下，依個案之具體情形而決定其適用之範圍[467]。

　　無論是於國內法或國際法，強行法的問題不是在於其存在與否，而是在於其無所不在。強行法是個可疑的概念，如果它的確存在的話，它產生的問題只能於所牽連的實體政策下，依個案具體之情形合適而符合比例的解決[468]。個人以為U.C.C.1-301條之comment 6引用Cardozo法官之論

on pose une passerelle de bois pour traverser un marals: si on reste trop longtemps sur la passerelle, on va s'enfoncer et êtreenlisé dans les sables mouvants, mais cela permet de passer, d'arriver au resultat, ce qui n'est déjá pas mal. ll ne faut pas vouloir idéaliser les differents outils que nous utilisons, mais les accrpter comme de simples outlis qui permettent d'arriver á un certain résultat.)或許可以說明吾人對此一問題應採取功能性的態度，優於執著傳統名詞定義的爭辯。A. BUCHER, Vers l'adoption de la méthode interest? Réflexions á la lumiére des condifications récentes, TCFDIP, 1993-1995, éd. A Pédone, Paris 1996, p. 209, surtout á p. 230.」如果是因強行法太複雜而輕忽外國政策，這是其他國家所不能接受的。如果Lagarde強調的是強行法的功能性，那麼其應公開的以所牽連的實體法之實質政策為依據，如此才能達到保障個案正義的終極目的。

[466] R.H. Graveson, Conflict of Laws, p. 79 (7ed. 1974).

[467] 似乎有甚多法國同僚亦採同樣看法，見林恩瑋，大陸法系國際私法選理論，陳隆修、許兆慶、林恩瑋，《台灣財產法暨經濟法研究叢書（十三）—國際私法：選法理論之回顧與展望》，台灣財產法暨經濟法研究協會發行，2007年1月，初版，11頁，「如學者Loussouarn所批判的，『即刻適用法（lois de police）與其他的法律並無不同，在現代的國家中，我們可以說幾乎所有的法律實際上都是為了保障經濟與社會的利益。』仔細觀察，事實上即刻適用法的法源依據，主要在於法國民法第三條第一項的規定：『警察治安法規及保安法規對於居住於境內之人民全體，均有適用。（les lois de police et de sûreté obligent tous ceux qui habitent le territoire.）』其中不但包括了警察治安法規（lois de police），還包括了保安法規（lois de sûreté），而法國法院有時候更將公共秩序（L'ordre public）也納入為即刻適用法國法的理由之一，其內容與定義可謂極不確定。現時我國學者一般多將lois de poblic一詞同等於即刻適用法。但，正如Pierre Mayer指出的，我們雖然無法確定即刻適用法的意義，然而這種適用的情形的確存在，唯一能做的方式，就是依照個案去確定是否存在即刻適用法的情形。見Mayer et Heuzé, Droit international privé, p. 83.」故而法國同僚亦似乎認同兩點：一、強行法無所不在；二、強行法須依個案而處理。

[468] 個人認為「21世紀全球化法學的心與靈魂在個案正義」，如於評釋羅馬 II 時個人即主張強行法應以個案正義為依據，而不應以「公的利益」為基礎。見Jonathan Harris, Mandatory Rules and Public Policy under the Rome I Regulation p.296,
"one or both of the contracting parties against the imposition of unreasonable contractual terms. At one level, such rules of contract law can be considered to be part of the private law of obligations. At another level, however, they are not concerned with the protection of any one contracting party; but with the public at large insofar as they enter into contracts. Hence, a rule such as the Unfair Contract Terms Act 1977 protects parties in England against the insertion of unreasonable exclusion or limitation of liability clauses. A public interest in fair contractual dealings, and a social or economic public goal is fostered. But even then, there is scope for further complexity. Some provisions of that Act apply specifically to

述以為法院地拒絕適用外州法而引用自己本州基本政策之試金石，或許亦可作為全世界引用強行法之參考，「法院不得在法官的喜好下自由的去拒絕強制執行外國權利，以便迎合個別想法中的便利性及公平性。除非於協助這些外國權利會違反一些正義的基本原則，一些盛行的道德觀念，一些根深蒂固共同利益的傳統的情形下，法院是不可以關起他們的門。[469]」Cardozo法官這段擲地有聲之論述，亦被第2新編90條引為當外國訴因之執行會違反法院地之強烈公共政策時，該訴訟得不被審理之試金石[470]。如

---

consumers, rather than to the public at large. Although the protection of this group might still be considered to protect a public interest, it is true that the more specific protectionist legislation is to a particular class of persons, the less it might be said that it affects a section of the public. Indeed, if the term 'public interests' ' imports some sort of requirement that a sufficient section of the public benefits from the law, this will create further difficulties. There may, however, be a very strong public interest in protecting certain limited groups, such as, for instance, those with a rare form of disability. Hence, it may be better to ask in such circumstances whether the protection of a small group of persons is in the interests of the public at large, rather than whether a sufficient section of the public is directly affected by the legislation."

又另外法國最高法院於Huston案（Cour de cassation, lre Ch. civ., 28 May 1991）以「道德上的權利」作為強行法是用之依據，即為有些大陸法的同僚視為不符合羅馬Ⅰ第9(1)條保護公共利益之要件，見Yuko Nishitani, Contracts Concerning Intellectual Property Rights, 於Rome I Regulation: The Law Applicable to Contractual Obligations in Europe edited by Franco Ferrari, Stefan Leible, pp. 82, 83, In France, the Huston ruling of the Cour de cassaticm in 1991 constitutes a good test case. In this decision, the Cour de cassation did not make clear whether the initial ownership of copyright was subject to the lex loci originis, i.e., U.S. law in this case, or some other law. The Court simply condemned the colorization of the originally black-and-white film created in the U.S. by referring to the French provisions on moral rights-the right of integrit－as overriding mandatory rules ("lois d' application imperative".

This decision would contradict Article 9 (1) Rome I, as the rules on moral rights do not aim at protecting public interests, nor do they regulate contractual relations between the parties.

於Case C-167/00 Verein für Konsumentenformation v K H Henkel [2002] ECR I-8111中，歐盟法院認為消費者團體為防止商人對個別私人之不公平條款之契約之訴訟是符合布魯塞爾公約的第1條之民商事項：

"50 In the light of all the foregoing considerations, the answer to the question referred by the national court must be that the rules on jurisdiction laid down in the Brussels Convention must be interpreted as meaning that a preventive action brought by a consumer protection organisation for the purpose of preventing a trader from using terms considered to be unfair in contracts with private individuals is a matter relating to tort, delict or quasi-delict within the meaning of Article 5(3) of that convention."

[469] Loucks v. Standard Oil Co. of New York, 120 N.E. 198, 201, 202 (1918), "The courts are not free to refuse to enforce a foreign rights at the pleasure of the judges, to suit the individual notion of expediency or fairness. They do not close their doors, unless help would violate some fundamental principle of justice, some prevalent conception of good morals, some deep-rooted tradition of the common weal."

[470] s.90, comment C.

果近百年來Cardozo法官的論述，皆一直被引用為美國有關法院地基本政策的基礎，並且同時為第2新編及U.C.C於法院地基本政策之試金石一個人想不出這個論述為何不能成為全世界於強行法（如果存在的話）、基本政策、及超越性考量之基礎及試金石。

　　坦白說個人看不出Cardozo法官的論述與利益說[471]、最重要關連說、及羅馬公約與規則的選法技巧有何直接關連。或許於經過近百年後，我們可以更進一步的試圖闡明Cardozo法官之論述如下：**無論於國際或國內法上，所有的強行法（如果存在的話）、基本政策、或超越性考量，皆應於所牽連的實體法範圍內之實質政策，以誠信原則、合理性要求、及比例原則為基礎，依個案之具體情形做出符合正義的決定**[472]。

---

[471] 但許多英國同僚認為公約7(1)條是將為英國人所視為過份主觀的美國「利益說」帶入歐洲。Peter Kaye, The New Private International Law of Contract of the European Community, p.249, "effectively provides for the introduction of the United States governmental interests doctrine, whereby examinations are required of courts into the comparative importance to different law districts in having the policies contained in their laws upheld in an inter-state situation"。英格蘭及蘇格蘭法律委員會皆曾於侵權上拒絕利益說，Law Commission Working Paper No 87; Scottish Law Commission Consultative Memorandum No 62, Private International Law: Choice of Law in Tort and Delict (HMSO, 1984), paras 4.35-4.54.
另外早期對公約7(1)條加以保留之六個國家中，除了反對第三國家強行法之利益的適用外，亦有基於強行法之適用會造成契約之分割而加以反對。見Note-Article 7(1) of the European Contracts Convention: Codifying the Practice of Applying Foreign Mandatory Rules, 114 Harvard Law Review 2001, 2462, 2466, 2467. "Notwithstanding these motivations, the countries that have reserved the right not to apply article 7(1) contend that the article's provisions sanction the use of depecage-the severance of issues in order to apply different laws to the same factual situation n25 - and thus constitute a dramatic departure from traditional European theory and practice. n26 These states refuse to condone what they view as a move toward a more American approach, by which courts weigh the interests of various countries in regulating each issue being decided. In addition to a general apprehension about initiating such a paradigm shift, opponents of article 7(1) raise the concern that depecage will necessarily result in increased uncertainty regarding the law applicable to a contract. Commentators buttress these objections with convincing and rhetorically familiar arguments that emphasize the need for certainty and predictability in the realm of contract law in order to foster interstate commerce, especially between private parties within the European Union."
[472] 誠信原則或許早已源自希臘Stoics學派的正義與恆平概念（以下引自European Contract Law－Materials for a Common Frame of Reference: Terminology, Guiding Principles, Model Rules, Edited by Bénédicte Fauvarque-Cosson and Denis Mazeaud, pp.151, 152, 154, 155, 158, 159, 161, 164, 202, 141）：The introduction of the notion of good faith in Roman contract law would undoubtedly have been impossible without inspiration from the Greeks. Among others, the Stoics PYTHAGORAS and ZENO produced works that were at the origin of notions of justice and equity. "This new concept opens the contractual system to the ethics of what is just and equitable, the latter, according to CICERO's dream, linking all men, citizens or pagans, in a universal society of boni viri, of good men".
而於羅馬時期西賽羅更是早已對誠信原則給予甚為完整的定義："These words, good faith, have

a very broad meaning. They express all the honest sentiments of a good conscience, without requiring a scrupulousness which would turn selflessness into sacrifice; the law banishes from contracts ruses and clever manoeuvres, dishonest dealings, fraudulent calculations, dissimulations and perfidious simulations, and malice, which under the guise of prudence and skill, takes advantage of credulity, simplicity and ignorance."（R.-M. RAMPELBERG, Repères romains pour le droit européen des contrats, L.G.D.J., Systèmes, Droit, 2005, pp. 44, 45）後來查士丁尼時期甚至將衡平法作為法律之至高來源："Constantine even went so far as to proclaim this theory as being an essential principle of the entire Roman legal system. Later, Justinian made the jus aequuum into the supreme source of law.

誠信原則的自然法概念於19世紀前是經常被認為源自上帝：

Indeed, until the XIxth century, God was considered to be the origin of all things including good faith, which could not be altered by man. It is in this spirit that DOMAT distinguishes between immutable laws and arbitrary laws. Within immutable laws, there is a further distinction between those which can be derogated from and those which cannot. "Thus, the laws, which prescribe good faith, fidelity, sincerity and which forbid deceit, fraud and any surprise, are laws from which there cannot be any derogation" (J. DOMAT, Traité des lois, 1689, edited and commented by J. Remy, Paris 1835, chap. XI, De la nature et de l'esprit des lois, et de leurs différentes espèces, n° 1。然而亦可能因此而較少被深入的加以研究及給予定義："referring to God to legitimize the existence of good faith leads to the automatic deferral to God regarding the content of the rule. Perhaps this explains the absence of discussion regarding good faith in preparation work, in addition to the absence of any definition and in depth study of good faith".

但是法國1804年民法典之誠信原則本著自然法而來之概念卻為KANT及SAVIGNY等歷史及實證學派（the historical school and the Positivist doctrine）所反對；COMTE認為："a theory according to which social sciences should be experimental sciences, and the law was thus treated as a science of social relationships in which experience had an essential role"。（B. JALUZOT, La bonne foi dans les contracts, Etude comparative de droit français, allemand et japonais, Dalloz, 2001, n° 127, 130, p.39）但是德國1900年的民法（BGB）還是有著誠信原則。

而令人驚訝的是美國判例法早於一百多年前即要求保險人有著誠信之義務，Armstrong v Agricultural Ins. Co, [1890] 29 N. E. 991 (N.Y.)。而1981年的the Second Restatement of Contracts, section 205亦規定："Every contract imposes upon each party a duty of good faith and fait clearing in its performance Professor SUMMERS 認為下列行為不符合契約上之誠信："evasion of the spirit of the deal, lack of diligence and slacking off, willful rendering of only substantial performance, abuse of power to determine compliance, and interference with or failure to cooperate in the other party's performance". (R.S. SUMMERS, "Good faith in general contract law and the sales provisions of the Uniform Commercial Code", [1969] 54 Va. L. Rev. 195; "The general duty of good faith－Its recognition and conceptualization", [1981-1982] 67 Cornell L. Rev. 810。)

於國際公法誠信原則亦為基礎之原則，1969年的Vienna Convention on the Law of Treaties之第26條規定：

Article 26

"Pacta sunt servanda"

Every treaty in force is binding upon the parties to it and must be performed by them in good faith.

第31(1)條規定：

Article 31

General rule of interpretation

1. A treaty shall be interpreted in good faith in accordance with the ordinary meaning to be given to the terms of the treaty in their context and in the light of its object and purpose.

第46(2)條規定：

Article 46

Provisions of internal law regarding competence to conclude treaties

十七、契約違反履行地法

(一)國內法及國際法之共同法則

羅馬 I 雖然取消羅馬公約7(1)條強行法之規定，但羅馬 I 卻增加9(3)

---

2. A violation is manifest if it would be objectively evident to any State conducting itself in the matter in accordance with normal practice and in good faith.

另外一般又認為the European Union Treaty 的第10條是要求會員國有著作為與不作為之誠信義務：

Article 10

Member States shall take all appropriate measures, whether general or particular, to ensure fulfilment of the obligations arising out of this Treaty or resulting from action taken by the institutions of the Community. They shall facilitate the achievement of the Community's tasks.

They shall abstain from any measure which could jeopardise the attainment of the objectives of this Treaty.

雖然強行法與誠信原則是大陸法之概念，但一般比較法的同僚經常會同意英國法制時常會以具體的個案例子而達成這兩個模糊概念之目的。於Interfoto Picture Library Ltd v Stiletto Visual Programs Ltd, [1988] 1 All ER 348 at. 353 (CA), Sir Thomas Bingham說："English law has, characteristically, committed itself to no such overriding principle but has developed piecemeal solutions in response to demonstrated problems of unfairness. Many examples could be given. Thus equity has intervened to strike down unconscionable bargains. Parliament has stepped in to regulate the imposition of exemption clauses and the form of certain hire purchase agreements. The common law also has made its contribution by holding that certain classes of contract require the utmost good faith, by treating as irrecoverable what purport to be agreed estimates of damage but are in truth a disguised penalty for breach, and in many other ways."

由於誠信原則（善良道德）與強行法是淵源於大陸法，故英國法會有將他們與公共政策及合法性混和之情形，而有趣的是法國民法1133條亦是如此。提議之修正條文1126條不但將合法性建築於公共秩序、誠信原則（善良道德）與強行法上，更認為強行法之範圍大於公共政策：

In fact, on the whole, English law favours the notion of illegality, which goes beyond and includes the notion of public policy. French law is not far from this solution, as can be seen from the definition of illegal cause ("cause illicite", article 1133 of the Civil Code: "The cause is illegal, when it is prohibited by the law, when it is contrary to good morals or public policy"). The French Reform Proposals headed by Pierre CATALA follows this direction; it maintains the generic meaning of the notion of illegality and extends the meaning to cover public policy, good morals and "mandatory rules". The result is a proposed article 1126 drafted as follows: "An undertaking is without justification, and lacks a legal cause, when it is made, by at least one of the parties, with a purpose which is contrary to public policy, good morals or more generally contrary to a mandatory rule". Illegality is defined through a triple relationship with public policy, good morals and mandatory rules, notion which is now preferred to that of "laws". (see article 1133 above: "when it is prohibited by the law"). Furthermore, the text clearly endorses the idea that the notion of "mandatory rule" is wider than that of public policy ("more generally").

對於性善從事邏輯分析的大陸法同僚，個人不得不回應於於Castanho v. Brown& Root (U.K.) Ltd., [1981] A.C. 557, 573 (H.L.) (appeal taken Rom Eng.) 中，Lord Scarman膾炙人口的金剛咒："the width and flexibility of equity are not to be undermined by categorization."

如恩師Prof. Graveson所說的，「法律邏輯一致性的要求，應受限於判例法達成正義的基本目的限制」。對脫韁野馬的公序良俗、強行法、誠信原則的概念之行使，應以達成個案正義為基本目的─21世紀全球化法學的心與靈魂就是在個案正義。

條如下之規定：「如果契約義務應被或已被履行地之超越性強行法規規定契約之履行為非法，該超越性強行法得被給予效力。於考慮是否給予這些規定效力時，應注意到他們之性質與目的，及他們被適用或不被適用之後果。[473]」契約之履行不得違反履行地法於英國教科書之權威案例為Ralli Bros. v. Compania Naviera Sota y Aznar[474]，於該案中一船東與一託運人約定載貨從加爾各答到巴塞隆納，價格為一噸五〇鎊，運費於巴塞隆納交付。在契約訂定後，但在船尚未到達巴塞隆納，西班牙政府規定運費超過每噸一〇鎊以上為非法，英國法院判船東不得請求超過每噸一〇鎊以上的運費。英國上訴法院於本案中並未試圖定性該西班牙法是否為強行法。因為本案之準據法為英國法，法院並未採用英國國際私法，而直接適用英國國內法，依英國契約法不能履行理論（「doctrine of frustration」），一個原欲履行之協議於後來其履行變得不合法，是不能被執行的[475]。於該案中Scrutton L.J.做了以下著名的結論：「當一個契約要求於外國履行一個行為時，於沒有特殊之情形下，它包含著條文的持續有效性的一個默示條款，亦即於外國履行的行為依據該外國法不會是非法的。[476]」英國法不會強制執行違反履行地之履行行為，隨後又於Vita Food Products v. Unus Shipping Co.中為大英國協最高法院（the Privy Council）所認可[477]。

---

[473] 3. Effect may be given to the overriding mandatory provisions of the law of the country where the obligations arising out of the contract have to be or have been performed, in so far as those overriding mandatory provisions render the performance of the contract unlawful. In considering whether to give effect to those provisions, regard shall be had to their nature and purpose and to the consequences of their application or non-application.

[474] [1920] 2 K. B. 287 (C.A.).見陳隆修，《國際私法契約評論》，台北，五南圖書公司，民國75年2月，初版，82頁。

[475] Cheshire, Fifoot and Furmston's Law of Contract (13th ed.), p,583.如果契約履行地於外國，則不能履行理論被外國履行地法不合法之名詞取代，Bangladesh Export Import Co Ltd v Sucden Kerry SA [1995] 2 Lloyd's Rep 1 at 5-6, CA.見Cheshire and North, p. 601.

[476] [1920] 2 KB 287, 304, "Where a contract requires an act to be done in a foreign country, it is, in the absence of very special circumstances, an implied term of the continuing validity of such a provision that the act to be done in the foreign country shall not be illegal by the law of that State." See also Zivnostenska Banka National Corporation v. Frankman [1950] A.C. 57.

[477] [1939]A.C. 277; Cases, 299; "English law will not enforce a performance contrary to the law of the place of performance", per Lord Wright p, 291. 較近Millett LJ於Bangladesh Export Import Co Ltd v Sucden Kerry SA [1995] 2 Lloyd's Rep 1, 5-6 中，說 "Where a contract is governed by English law, the mere fact that its performance has become illegal under the law of a foreign country does not of

　　美國第2新編202條第1項規定契約之合法性依187、188所決定之準據法為依據。第2項規定：「當依履行地法該履行是不合法時，該契約通常會被拒絕執行。[478]」但其解釋報告卻圍繞著187、188條相關具有利益州之基本政策打轉，對契約履行地則認為依188條3項與契約洽商地為同一州，該州法才能於大多數情形下具有著主要利益[479]。於206條有關契約履

itself amount to a frustration of the contract unless the contract requires performance in that county.... The fact that performance in that country was within the contemplation of both parties is not enough; such performance must be required by a term of the contract express or implied."

而Walker LJ於Ispahani v Bank Melli Iran [1997] EWCA Civ 3047中，亦說"[T]he carrying out of prohibited acts within the territory in question is an essential and necessary element of the principle stated by Sankey LJ in Foster v Driscoll [1929] 1 KB 470, 521, and approved by the House of Lords in Regazzoni v Sethia [1958] AC 301. Apart from the formidable weight of judicial opinion behind that formulation of the principle, there are to my mind two compelling reasons against regarding as irrelevant the place where the prohibited acts are carried out. One reason is that international comity is naturally much readier to accept that a country's laws ought to be obeyed within its own territory, than to recognise them as having exorbitant effect. The other reason is that the Ralli Brothers principle, although now regarded as a distinct principle, grows from the same rootstock. In the Ralli Brothers line of authority it is clear beyond argument that it must be the law of the place of performance that prohibits the act of performance."

Ministry of Justice, Rome I-Should the UK Opt in? Response to Consultation CP05/08CP(R), January 2009, para 74，中說明基於下列兩個理由而認同第9(3)條：first, the only aspect of Article 9(3) which differs from English law is the level of discretion that can be given by courts to contractual obligations that have been, but did not have to be, performed in a place where performance was unlawful. For example, if a payment was made in a place where either the payment or the fact of the payment was illegal, this could be resolved by ensuring that performance in relation to financial obligations was made in a country where they were legal. If the obligation was to make a payment, then the place of payment could in most cases be changed to one where the payment was lawful. Analysis suggests that even this in itself is unlikely to have any significant impact on the UK. Indeed it is possible that the effect on contracts may even be less than existing English law; and

second... some respondents have made reference to Article 9(3) suggesting that it is less than ideal. Nevertheless, they agree that overall it appears less problematic than the Convention particularly in the context of litigation in the English courts. Others have stated that there may be some limited uncertainty as a result of the wording of the provision, whilst others suggest that although reservations in legal opinions on contract may need some adjustment, overall the substance would not be much different. The respondents making these views have clearly stated that these concerns are not sufficient reason in themselves for remaining outside the Regulation."

[478] s. 202 Illegality

(1) The effect of illegality upon a contract is determined by the law selected by application of the rules of ss. 187-188.

(2) When performance is illegal in the place of performance, the contract will usually be denied enforcement.

[479] Comment e, "As stated in Subsection (3) of the rule of s.188, if the place of negotiating the contract and the place of performance are in the same state, the local law of this state will usually be applied. This is because this state in the majority of instances will have the dominant interest in the determination of issues arising under the contract."另外註釋(f)為有關短暫之不合法。

行之細節依履行地法，其結尾之註釋(d)如此評述：「當行為應被執行地之當地州法律拒絕給予其效力時，當事人之選擇法律是否會被認定有效是尚未確定之事情。[480]」契約不得違反履行地法是於國際禮誼（「international comity」）下，對其他國家主權、公共政策、法律治安、社會經濟、及風俗人情之一種尊重，亦是維護國際秩序所必須。除了受限於「人類文明的公理[481]」外，履行地之法律是應受到尊重的。美國法於這個法則上似乎信心、經驗、及學理皆有待加強。

　　於英國如Dicey and Morris所謂：「於判例法[482]上已經見到一個法則是被認為存在的，亦即契約（無論依其準據法是否為合法）之履行如果依其履行地法（「lex loci solutionis」）是不合法，則通常該契約為無效[483]。」這個觀念於其第2版就已被提出[484]。但是Ralli Bros是履行地於外國而準據法為英國法之案件，英國判例法上尚未發生履行地於外國而準據法為另一國家法之案件。雖然法院有著甚多的附帶意見（dicta）是尊重

---

[480] Comment d, "It is uncertain whether such a choice would be held effective if it would be denied effect by the local law of the state where the act is to be done." 188條的註釋雖較為明示的引用202條，但其又認為若雙方當事人之履行地為同一州時，才會較有密切關連。個人以為如此論述則喪失了於國際禮誼（comity）下尊重其他國家法律之意義。Comment e將對履行地主權、政策之尊重，誤導為最重要關連法則之運用，這是概念上之混淆。

　　Comment e, "The place of performance. The state where performance is to occur under a contract has an obvious interest in the nature of the performance and in the party who is to perform. So the state where performance is to occur has an obvious interest in the question whether this performance would be illegal; (see s. 202). When both parties are to perform in the state, this state will have so close a relationship to the transaction and the parties that it will often be the state of the applicable law even with respect to issues that do not relate strictly to performance. And this is even more likely to be so if, in addition, both parties are domiciled in the state."

[481] 陳隆修，《國際私法契約評論》，台北，五南圖書公司，民國75年2月，初版，81頁。

[482] Ralli Bros v Compania Naviera Sota y Aznar [1920] 1 K.B. 614; [1920] 2 K.B. 287, 291, 300 (CA); Foster v Driscoll [1929] 1 K.B. 470, 520 (CA); R. v International Trustee, etc. [1937] A.C. 500, 519 (CA); Kleinwoet, Sons & Co v Ungarische Baumwolle Industrie AG [1939] 2 K.B. 678 (CA), See also Ford v Cotesworth (1870) L.R. 5 Q.B. 544 (Exch Ch); Cunningham v Dunn (1878) 3 C.P.D. 443; Trinidad Shipping abd Trading Co Ltd v Alston [1920] A.C. 888 (PC); Klatzer v Caselberg & Co (1909) 28 N.Z.L.R. 994; Dampskibsaktieselskapet Aurdal v Compania de Navegaction La Estrella 1916 S.C. 882; Montreal Trust Co v Stranrock Uranium Mines Ltd (1965) 53 D.L.R. (2d) 594 (Ont).

[483] Dicey and Morris, the conflict of Laws, 14th ed., p. 1594, "It has already been seen that at common law there was thought to be a principle that a contract (whether lawful by its governing law or not) was, in general, invalid in so far as the performance of it was unlawful by the law of the country where the contract was to be performed (*lex loci solutionis*)."

[484] 2nd ed. 1908, p.553. See also 1st ed. 1896, p. 560.

履行地法[485]，但Cheshire and North認為這與Ralli Bros不合，不應具有判例法之拘束力[486]。故而違反履行地法之契約不得被執行之法則，到底只限於國內契約法或於國際私法亦可適用，長久以來困擾著謹慎的英國法界。

於Kahler v Midland bank Ltd中Lord Reid說：「如果行為發生地國家之法律認為該行為是非法……英國法並不要求該英國契約之履行行為應被執行。[487]」但於Zivnostenska Banka v Frankman中，Lord Reid又認為這個原則：「無論契約準據法為何，已是一個確定的法律，當行為地之當地法規定契約之履行是非法時，英國法院不會要求該契約之履行被執行。[488]」Dicey and Morris認為：「學術界大部分認為，除非契約準據法為英國法，否則履行地法事後使得契約為違法，並不能阻止英國法院去執行該契約。依據這個觀點，Ralli Bros的原則根本都不是國際私法原則，而只是英國國內法有關事後不合法使得契約義務被停止或解除之法規之適用，因此履行地法使得履行之不合法，只不過是英國法院於決定履行是否變得不可能所考慮的事實因素而已。[489]」故而當外國準據法與履行地不

---

[485] Toprak v Finagrain [1979] 2 Lloyd's Rep 98 at 114; United City Merchants (Investments) Ltd v Rpyal Bank of Canada [1982] QB 208 at 228; revsd by the House of Lords on other point [1983] 1 AC 168, [1982] 2 All ER 720; XAG v A Bank [1983] 2 Lloyd's Rep 535 at 543; Euro-Diam Ltd v Bathurst [1990] 1 QB a at 15; affd by CA at 30; Libyan Arab Foreign Bank v Bankers Trust Co [1989] QB 728, [1989] 3 All ER 252; Apple Corpn Ltd v Apple Computer Ltd [1992] FSR 431 at 442.

[486] PM North, JJ Fawcett, Cheshire and North's Private International Law, 13th ed., p. 602, "There have been frequent dicta attributing decisive effect to illegality by the law of the place of performance, although it has been consistently argued in this book that such an approach is contrary to principle, and not dictated by the authorities."同樣的論述又於14thed., p.760中再次被確認。但現今英國已加入羅馬Ⅰ規則，故對於規則9(3)條其又於p.761中認為該9(3)條是與英國判例法不同，因而會造成不一樣的結果："The position would be very different if the provisional conclusion of the Ministry of justice is followed and the United Kingdom opts in to the Rome I Regulation. Under the Rome I Regulation, Article 9(3) allows a court of a Member State to give effect to the overriding mandatory provisions of the place of performance in so far as those provisions render performance of the contract unlawful."

[487] [1950] A.C. 24, 48, "the law of England will not require an act to be done in performance of an English contract if such act ... would be unlawful by the law of the country in which the act has to be done."

[488] [1950] A.C. 57, 78, "settled law that, whatever be the proper law of the contract, an English court will not require a party to do an act in performance of a contract which would be an offence under the law in force at the place where the act is to be done."

[489] Dicey and Morris, 14th ed., p.1596, "The prevailing academic view was that supervening illegality according to the law of the place of performance did not as such prevent an English court from enforcing the contract, unless it were governed by English law. The principle in Ralli Bros, on this view, was not a principle of the conflict of laws at all, but merely an application of the English domestic rules with re-

是同一個法律，並且於履行地認為該履行是非法仍要求該契約之履行情況下，Dicey and Morris做了如此結論：「如果它真的發生，那麼較好的建議應是這是個國內契約法的規則。[490]」

　　本著大陸法注重法律邏輯演繹之方法，個人年輕時即大膽的建議：「根據作者之實務經驗與研究英、美之判例，作者認為『只要契約履行地的法律不是違反世界上大部分文明國家所共同接受的公共政策，則違反契約履行地法律的契約應為無效（或者至少不應被強制執行）』，如此國際間的和諧（comity）方能維持，國際貿易也才能順利進行。作者之主張跟美國與英國學者不同之處，乃在於明白的反面強調契約履行地法若是違反了人類文明的公理（如種族歧視）則契約當事人可以不尊重之。作者所以如此主張乃是由於判例上與實務上作者曾見到第三世界國家立下不合乎公平正義之法律，如強制剝奪外國人之財產之法律，這些法律不應被尊重之。[491]」至於這個法則應只限於國內契約法或擴及國際私法之問題，個人去年更再度表示：「至於Ralli Bros規則應為國內契約法或國際私法規則之問題，既然八十多年來判例法未能給予答案，通常表示兩個選項應該皆有適當之理由。依實體法論之觀點，於大部分之案件中解決國內案件之標準亦通常可用來解決同類型之國際案件，故而契約違反履行地法不可被強制執行這個法規，應可構成國內契約法及國際私法之共通規則，而同時適用於國際及國內案件。只是該履行地法必須合乎『文明的公理』方可被加以尊重，亦即該履行地法不可違背聯合國人權宣言、歐盟人權及基本自由

---

gard to the discharge or suspension of contractual obligations by supervening illegality, and the illegality of performance under the *les loci solutionis* was no more than a fact to be taken into account by an English court in judging whether performance had become impossible."

[490] Dicey and Morris, p.1597, "Such a combination of factors would undoubtedly be very rare, and is no doubt the reason why the issue whether the rule in *Ralli Bros* is a rule of domestic law or a rule of the conflict of laws has not arisen for deicision in more than 80 years since it was decided and in more than 60 years since the issue was raised in academic writing. If it does arise, it is suggested that the better view is that it is a rule of the domestic law of contract."於Ispahani v Bank Melli Iran, The Times, December 29, 1997, [1998] Lloyd's Rep. Bank. 133 (CA)中，對這一點並未加以決定。

[491] 陳隆修，《國際私法契約評論》，台北，五南圖書公司，民國75年2月，初版，81、81頁。

公約、及較近的歐盟契約法強行法規。[492]」

　　現今個人主張誠信原則、合理性、及比例原則，應為所有國際及國內契約法之基本法理及警察法理。無論是於訂約時即已知悉或事後法律才變更，於履行地法禁止履行之情形下，權利人欲強迫義務人去履行法律所禁止之事情，為一既不合理又不符合誠信之要求。故而無論於國際或國內契約法上，「違反履行地法之契約不能被強制執行」之原則，既符合誠信原則及合理性之要求，本身亦是一個對抗契約準據法（或甚至法院地法）以維持個案正義之警察原則。無論是有意或無意，這個將實體契約法與國際私法融合之作法，於2004 UNIDROIT Principles 7.2.2條中充分被顯示出來：「除了給付金錢之債務外，當一個債務人負擔義務而未履行其義務時，他方當事人得要求該義務之履行，除非(a)於法律上或事實上該履行是不可能；(b)履行或，於相關執行時，構成不合理之負擔或過份昂貴；(c)有權利要求履行之一方得合理的由其他地方獲得該履行；(d)該履行是完全私人性質；或(e)於知悉，或應知悉，該不履行後，有權利要求履行之一方並未於一段合理之期間內要求該履行。[493]」因為2004 UNIDROIT Principles序言的第一句話便開宗明義的揭櫫：「這些原則是規範國際商業契約的一般規則。[494]」故而很明顯的，7.2.2條(a)款的契約「於法律上不能被履行」時權利人不能要求該履行，自然亦應於國際契約中被適用，故這個規則不但是實體法，亦是國際私法（當事人亦可指定該原則為準據法）。另外由廣義而言，個人認為7.1.7條1項的當事人不可控制的障

---

[492] 陳隆修，《2005年海牙法院選擇公約評析》，台北，五南圖書公司，2009年1月，初版1刷，95頁。

[493] Article 7.2.2 (Performance of non-monetary obligation) Where a party who owes an obligation other than one to pay money does not perform, the other party may require performance, unless
(a) performance is impossible in law or in fact;
(b) performance or, where relevant, enforcement is unreasonably burdensome or expensive;
(c) the party entitled to performance may reasonably obtain performance from another source;
(d) performance is of an exclusively personal character; or
(e) the party entitled to performance does not require performance within a reasonable time after it has, or ought to have, become aware of the non-performance.

[494] "These Principle set forth general rules for international commercial contracts. They shall be applied when the parties have agreed that their contract be governed by them."

礙,亦可將契約之履行視為事實上之不可能在內[495]。甚而6.2.2條履行之費用之增加或履行之價值之減少,這種履行的困難於某些情形下,或許亦可類推適用契約之履行於事實上不可能之法理的極度廣義類別[496]。2004 UNIDROIT Principles雖然將實體契約法與國際私法結合(無論有無採納實體法方法論之故意),但其只是標示「法律上履行之不可能」,至於何種「法律」並未明示。所謂「法律」應至少包含準據法與履行地法之實體法,及法院地之強烈公共政策(即強行法)在內。這種複雜之情況,可能為該7.2.2條避談「應適用法律」之主要原因。其6.1.17條規定政府許可之拒絕而影響到契約之效力,會使得契約無效[497]。在7.2.2條之註釋3(a)只是

---

[495] Article 7.1.7 (Force majeure)

(1) Non-performance by a party is excused if that party proves that the non-performance was due to an impediment beyond its control and that it could not reasonably be expected to have taken the impediment into account at the time of the conclusion of the contract or to have avoided or overcome it or its consequences.

(2) When the impediment is only temporary, the excuse shall have effect for such period as is reasonable having regard to the effect of the impediment on the performance of the contract.

(3) The party who fails to perform must give notice to the other party of the impediment and its effect on its ability to perform. If the notice is not received by the other party within a reasonable time after the party who fails to perform knew or ought to have known of the impediment, it is liable for damages resulting from such non-receipt.

(4) Nothing in this article prevents a party from exercising a right to terminate the contract or to withhold performance or request interest on money due.

[496] Article 6.2.2 (Definition of hardship) There is hardship where the occurrence of events fundamentally alters the equilibrium of the contract either because the cost of a party's performance has increased or because the value of the performance a party receives has diminished, and

(a) the events occur or become known to the disadvantaged party after the conclusion of the contract;

(b) the events could not reasonably have been taken into account by the disadvantaged party at the time of the conclusion of the contract;

(c) the events are beyond the control of the disadvantaged party; and

(d) the risk of the events was not assumed by the disadvantaged party.

事實上這並非是個極端的建議,第2新編205條有關契約義務之性質及程度,即認為不可預見的事情,即使契約仍可履行,可能造成當事人所未意圖之結果。見comment f, "Impossibility and frustration. The local law of the state selected by application of the rule of this Section determines whether a party is excused from performance by impossibility ... or by frustration, which means that, on account of unanticipated events, performance of the contract, although not impossible, cannot lead to the results the parties intended ...."

[497] Article 6.1.17 (Permission refused)

(1) The refusal of a permission affecting the validity of the contract renders the contract void. If the refusal affects the validity of some terms only, only such terms are void if, having regard to the circumstances, it is reasonable to uphold the remaining contract.

(2) Where the refusal of a permission renders the performance of the contract impossible in whole or in

規定6.1.17(1)條之「應適用國內法」[498]，而未論及何者為應適用之法律。個人一貫主張於國際私法選法規則之混亂下，與其談虎色變避之唯恐不及，倒不如化繁為簡的回歸實體契約法的規則。而於此處，很明顯的「契約違反履行地法不得被執行」之法規，應同時被視為國內法及國際法。

　　而且如7.2.2條所規定，不但於法律上不能被履行，於事實上不能（或有困難）被履行，該契約即不能被強制執行。這是符合誠信原則與合理性之作法。

　　歐盟契約法原則15：103條規定：「(1)如果根據15：101或15：102條只有契約之一部分是為無效，那麼剩餘部分仍然繼續有效，除非於適當的考慮案件的所有情形下，維持其效力是不合理的。(2)於部分無效之情形下，15：104及15：105條在適當之修改下，得被加以適用。[499]」第15：104條是有關恢復原狀之請求[500]，而15：105條是有關損害賠償之請求[501]。15：103條、15：104條、及15：105條之適用皆須本著合理性及比

---

part, the rules on non-performance apply.

[498] "The refusal of a public permission which is required under the applicable domestic law and which affects the validity of the contract renders the contract void (see Art. 6.1.17(1)), with the consequence that the problem of enforceability of the performance cannot arise."

[499] Article 15:103: Partial Ineffectiveness

(1) If only part of a contract is rendered ineffective under Article 15:101 or 15:102, the remaining part continues in effect unless, giving due consideration to all the circumstances of the case, it is unreasonable to uphold it.

(2) Article 15:104 and 15:105 apply, with appropriate adaptations, to a case of partial ineffectiveness.

[500] Article 15:104: Restitution

(1) When a contract is rendered ineffective under Articles 15:101 or 15:102, either party may claim restitution of whatever that party has supplied under the contract, provided that, where appropriate, concurrent restitution is made of whatever has been received.

(2) When considering whether to grant restitution under paragraph (1), and what concurrent restitution, if any, would be appropriate, regard must be had to the factors referred to in Article 15:102(3).

(3) An award of restitution may be refused to a party who knew or ought to have known of the reason for the ineffectiveness.

(4) If restitution cannot be made in kind for any reason, a reasonable sum must be paid for what has been received.

[501] Article 15:105: Damages

(1) A party to a contract which is rendered ineffective under Article 15:101 or 15:102 may recover from the other party damages putting the first party as nearly as possible into the same position as if the contract had not been concluded, provided that the other party knew or ought to have known of the reason for the ineffectiveness.

(2) When considering whether to award damages under paragraph (1), regard must be had to the factors

例原則（特別是15：102(3)之規則）之規定而進行，這是符合人情義理之常態性要求，故個人認為這3個條文不只是合適於國內契約，亦適用於國際契約。

於二十多年前大膽的提出契約違反履行地法不能被執行後，個人於此再次大膽的建議以下的規則應同時為國內法及國際私法：契約之履行於事實上及依履行地法為不可能或有困難或非法之情形下，契約不應被履行，但15：103條、15：104條、及15：105條有關部分有效、恢復原狀、及損害賠償之規定應被加以適用；而以上規則皆應本著合理性及比例原則為適用之基礎。

(二)違反履行地法之案例

另外個人年輕時又如此論述：「作者之主張跟美國與英國學者不同之處，乃在於明白的反面強調契約履行地法若違反了人類文明的公理（如種族歧視）則契約當事人可以不尊重之。作者所以如此主張乃是由於判例上與實務上作者曾見到第三世界國家立下不合乎公平正義之法律，如強制剝奪外國人之財產之法律，這些法律不應被尊重之。[502]」而於去年個人更加信心滿滿的對「人類文明的公理」闡明如下：「經過二十多年後，個人認為『文明的公理』應理所當然的包含聯合國人權宣言、European Rome Convention for the Protection of Human Rights and Fundamental Freedoms 1950，及歐盟契約法規則內之強行規定。這個論述或許應包含幾乎所有契約上一切之問題，而不只侷限於契約之效力（validity）或合法性（legality）。而且個人並不認同2005年海牙公約，管轄條款之效力並非如聖牛般不可侵犯，自然亦應受制於Ralli Bros法則。[503]」

---

referred to in Article 15:102 (3).

(3) An award of damages may be refused where the first party knew or ought to have known of the reason for the ineffectiveness.

[502] 陳隆修，《國際私法契約評論》，台北，五南圖書公司，民國75年2月，初版，81頁。

[503] 陳隆修，《2005年海牙法院選擇公約評析》，台北，五南圖書公司，2009年1月，初版1刷，94、95頁。另外個人又如此敘述：「事實上於前述The Hollandia中，管轄條款之適用只是觸犯了法院地的海商強行法規而已，即被英國法院視為無效（null and void）。於此再一次重申---英國法院於該案所欲保護的並非弱勢之當事人，而是有經驗之商人之商業行為；而該被引用之

　　有趣的是個人年輕時接受英美訓練，不由自主的認為只有第三世界才會立下不合乎公平正義之法律，但後來時間證明於國際私法界此方面最引人爭議的法律，經常是第一世界的美國所引起。於其時引起全世界注目的荷蘭法院Sensor案[504]中，美國政府對蘇聯下禁運令（embargo），禁止美國公司（包含歐洲之子公司在內）輸出建造跨西伯利亞之油管。一美國公司之荷蘭子公司原已答應賣油管給一法國公司，但基於美國外銷禁令而拒絕供給法國公司油管。由於荷蘭賣方之義務是契約之特徵，故於沒有選定準據法之情形下，荷蘭與該買賣有著最密切關連，故荷蘭法應為準據法。雖然契約並未於美國履行，但如果契約與相關之外國有著充分之關連，荷蘭法院還是應會給予該外國強行法超越荷蘭法之效力。但荷蘭法院認為該條件並未符合，故契約應被履行。

　　如前述強行法是個可疑的觀念，如果強行法存在的話其重點應是在其之適用範圍。用該外國與案件之地域性關連點來決定其強行法之適用範圍，只是最重要關連說為求得表面上之合理的直覺性運用而已，經常與案件之真正公平正義無關[505]。於對實體法之真正爭執無法解決時，訴之「地域性關連點」之集結，是人類規避實體法上真正難題之最便宜之藉口。如前述第2新編90條之註解中亦引述甚多早期之聯邦判例，其規定法院地必須與案件有合理關連時，才能引用法院之強烈政策而拒絕外國法之適用[506]。

Hague-Visby Rules強行規定並非為聯合國基本人權宣言、歐盟人權公約、或歐盟契約法規則之強行規定，而僅為世界上數個並行之海商公約之一而已，是否可構成世界主流核心共同價值仍有待海商法界同僚之協議。」The Hollandia [1983] 1 A.C. 565, 見陳隆修，《2005年海牙法院選擇公約評析》，台北，五南圖書公司，2009年1月，初版1刷，92頁，但英國已加入歐盟，根據2000年歐盟管轄規則可能會不一樣。另外由於2(2)(g)條之排除規定，本案可能不適用2005年海牙法院選擇公約。

[504] Cie européenne des petroles SA v Sensor Nederland BV, 1982 (1983) 23 Int. Legal Mat. 66.

[505] 陳隆修、許兆慶、林恩瑋，《台灣財產法暨經濟法研究叢書（十三）—國際私法：選法理論之回顧與展望》，台灣財產法暨經濟法研究協會發行，2007年1月，初版，177、178頁。

[506] "The rule of this Section does not justify striking down a defense good under the foreign law if the State of the forum has no reasonable relationship to the transaction or the parties. Home Insurance Co. v. Dick, 281 U.S. 397 (1930); Holzer v. Deutsche Reichsbahn-Gesellschaft, 277 N.Y. 474, 144 N.E. 2d 798 (1938). Contra: Fox v. Postal Tel. Cable Co., 138 Wis 648, 120 N.W. 399 (1909). Cf. Aboitzy v. Price, 99 F.Supp. 602 (D. Utah 1951)."

　　羅馬 I 9(3)要求履行地法必須為「超越性強行法」，而個人認為無論「強行法」或應被適用之「履行地法」，其被適用之範圍或程度皆應以「合理性」為基礎。無論是荷蘭法院或美國聯邦法院，將「合理性」之標準適用於地域性關連點上，而不是於真正實體上之實質內容，是個錯誤的方法論。於Sensor案中就算是美國並非為直接履行地（這僅是荷蘭觀點），但無可置疑的是其效力（effect）是直接於美國發生效果的。美國新編202條的註釋(e)講得非常清楚，「不合法的效力，對所牽連的州很可能代表著被強烈感受到的政策。[507]」本案中「真正」合理的個案因素或許為：於冷戰中對抗蘇聯是美國與其盟友荷蘭的重要政策，但對荷蘭而言石油之供給可能是更直接相關之政策。

　　類似案件亦發生於英國法院，於Libyan Arab Foreign Bank v. Bankers Trust Co.中，一利比亞銀行於一紐約銀行之倫敦分行存有大筆美金存款，而美國政府發布命令禁止美國銀行及其外國分行給予利比亞銀行提款。因為契約準據法為英國法，並且美國並非契約之履行地，故該美國禁令並不適用，英國法院准予利比亞銀行提款[508]。

　　同樣的道理，美國雖不是直接履行地，但卻是法律效力的發生地之一。本案中個案之合理考慮因素或許應為：美國與其盟邦英國皆有著對抗利比亞之政策，但英國作為一個金融重鎮，對其於國際金融上之信譽有著超越性之政策。於上述兩個著名之案件中，個人認為美國縱使為法律效力發生地，並有著不容置疑的強烈政策與決心（強行法），但其所頒佈之法律違反聯合國人權宣言與公約、歐盟的兩個人權公約、各國憲法上之平等

---

[507] "There is the further fact that rules on illegality, and on the effect of illegality, are likely to represent strongly-felt policies of the states involved. A court will be reluctant to subordinate such a policy of the state having the dominant interest in the issue to be decided to the choice-of-law policy favoring the protection of the justified expectations of the parties. For all of these reasons, a court, in determining which law determines the effect of illegality upon the validity of a contract and the rights created thereby, will give less weight to the protection of the justified expectations of the parties than it gives to the choice-of-law principle, also mentioned in s. 6, which seeks the effectuation of the relevant policies of the state with the dominant interest in the issue to be determined."

[508] [1989] Q.B. 728.見陳隆修，《2005年海牙法院選擇公約評析》，台北，五南圖書公司，2009年1月，初版1刷，93、94頁。

權、財產權、與適當程序權、歐盟契約法原則、及2004 UNIDROIT Principles等「人類共同核心之文明公理」，故相關美國法自然不應受尊重。但個人相信荷蘭及英國法院所注重的為其國家之利益，而與人類文明的公理無關。

　　Ralli Bros是有關訂約後履行地法使得該履行為不合法之情形。傳統上如果契約一開始訂立「當事人間使有意造成違反外國法之冒險[509]」，英國判例法上便可能會認定該契約違反英國公共政策及國際友誼，而不能被加以執行[510]。英國法界向來就傾向對法律邏輯加以鉅細靡遺的分門別類，無論是以公序良俗或違反履行地法之原則，個人認為只要能於合理性之基本原則上，在符合人類的文明公理下尊重履行地之法律，學術上之分類並沒有掌握實體法之共同核心價值重要。不幸的是英國法於此方面之技術性分類，困擾了歐盟，羅馬公約的解釋報告如此敘述：「由另一方面而言，雖有一些學者提出意見，我們必須明白的承認於這些英國案件中，似乎並沒有清楚的指示對目前所討論之原則有利的顯現。[511]」其所舉的3個判例中Ralli Bros的確是為訂約事後違反履行地法之案例，而Regazzoni[512]案及

---

[509] Foster v Driscoll [1929] 1 K.B. 470, 518 (CA), "made between parties to further an adventure to break the laws of a foreign state."有關該案及其他違反英國公共政策之案件，見陳隆修，《國際私法契約評論》，台北，五南圖書公司，民國75年2月，初版，66-77頁，該案為契約當事人訂立一合夥契約，合夥之目的乃欲違反美國法而將酒偷運入美國。英國法院判該契約違反友好國家之法律而無效。很有可能即使該契約之當事人皆為外國人，該契約於外國訂定，並且準據法為外國法，該契約仍為無效。

[510] Cheshire and North, p. 600, "At common law such an agreement, even though subject to a foreign law, was probably against the English doctrine of public policy and the comity of nations, and was not enfoeceable."又見較近之14thed.,pp.758,759。

[511] Giuliano and Lagarde Report, "On the other hand, despite the opinion of some jurists, it must be frankly recognized that no clear indication in favour of the principle in question seems discernible in the English cases (Ralli Bros v. Sota y Aznar; Regazzoni v. Sethia; Rossano v. Manufacturers Life Insurance Co.)" [1920] 2 K.B. 287; [1958] A.C. 301; [1963] 2 Q.B. 352.

[512] 陳隆修，《國際私法契約評論》，台北，五南圖書公司，民國75年2月，初版，71頁。「Regazzoni v. K.C. Sethia Ltd. X為於英經商之商人，其與A訂約，將麻布袋賣與A，C.I.F.幾內亞（義大利），亦即交貨地為義大利，A為於瑞士經商之商人，雙方知道麻袋之來源為印度而且A要將袋子轉賣到南非。依印度法將麻袋賣到南非是違法的，並且該交易行為必須欺騙印度官方方才可進行。雖然該買賣契約本身為只將貨從印度轉賣到義大利，故單就契約本身而言為一合法契約，但英法院仍判雙方當事人有意違反友好國家之法律，因而該契約無效。研究此案應知法院基本的態度乃深受國際社會排斥南非，不與南非貿易之政策所影響。」

Rossano[513]案為一開始便違反友好國家之法律[514]，或在英國法院拒絕直接或間接的執行外國稅法時債務人得否據此為抗辯之問題。這些案件個人於年輕時皆先後曾加以討論，個人並不以為有矛盾之處。Rossano案看似矛盾，事實上不然。因為不執行外國之公法並不表示不承認外國公法，更不會因為不執行外國公法而便允許當事人以訂約之方式去違反外國法[515]。歐

---

[513] Dicey and Morris, pp. 104, 576;又見陳隆修，《比較國際私法》，台北，五南圖書公司，78年10月，初版，13頁，「於Rossano v. Manufacturer's Life Insurance Co,中，被告於埃及因欠埃及政府稅款，故而埃及政府當局下達扣押命令給被告。而被告又於埃及對原告負有債務，當原告於英國法院提起訴訟，要求被告返還債務時，英法院判被告不得以埃及政府之扣押命令做為抗辯而不清償債款，蓋若英法院承認該扣押命令即等於間接地強制執行埃及稅法。」

[514] 英國上訴法院於Foster v. Driscoll [1929] 1 KB 470, 510 (CA) 中，Lawrence LJ說："On principle however I am clearly of opinion that a partnership formed for the main purpose of deriving profit from the commission of a criminal offence in a foreign and friendly country is illegal, even though the parties have not succeeded in carrying out their enterprise, and no such criminal offence has in fact been committed; and none the less so because the parties may have contemplated that if they could not successfully arrange to commit the offence themselves they would instigate or aid and abct some other person to commit it. The ground upon which I rest my judgment that such a partnership is illegal is that its recognition by our Courts would furnish a just cause for complaint by the United States Government against our Government (of which the partners are subjects), and would be contrary to our obligation of international comity as now understood and recognized, and therefore would offend against our notions of public morality."
雖然許多教科書認為這個規則是屬於公共政策部門，但恩師，T. C. Hartley, The Modern Approach to Private International Law: International Litigation and Transactions from a Common-Law Perspective: General Course on Private International Law, 319 Recueil des Cours 2006, 9, 241, 242, 卻認為這個規則應屬於公約7(2)條（即規則9(2)條）法院地國際強行法：
"In other words, a contract to commit a criminal offence in a foreign country is (in at least some cases) illegal under English (common) law. The question of choice of law did not arise in Foster v. Driscoll - it was accepted on all sides that English law applied but it cannot be doubted that the result would have been the same if the parties had chosen a foreign system of law to govern the contract, even if, under that law, the contract had been valid. Thus, (though this was not said in the case) the rule of English law (that a contract to commit a criminal offence in a foreign county is illegal) is internationally mandatory in terms of Article 7(2) of the Rome Convention."故而個人認為如果採後述的「效力」理論，是屬於「公共政策」或「強行法」的區別就不重要。
事實上這種違反外國履行地法（即使不違反法院地法）之案例，早期於大陸法亦經常以違反「公共道德」（德）或公共政策（法）而認為無效。
Juristische Wochenschrift [JW] 1927, 2288 (F.R.G.); Entscheidungen des Bundesgerichtshofes in Zivilsachen [BGHZ] 59, 82 (F.R.G.); Die deutsche Rechtsprechung auf dem Gebiet des internationalen Privatrechts [IPRspr] 1928, 20 (F.R.G.); Cour d'Alger, Feb. 20, 1925, 53 Clunet 1926, 701; Cour d'Appel de Douai, Nov. 11, 1907, D.P. II [1908] 15; Tribunal civil de la Seine, Jul. 2, 1932, 60 Clunet 1933, 73. （以上引自114 Harv. L. Rev. 2462, 2477）

[515] 陳隆修，《比較國際私法》，台北，五南圖書公司，78年10月，初版，130頁，「與刑罰法規一般，英美法之國際私法亦認為稅法為各國應自己處理及執行之法規，其他國家之法院不必去執行之。英國法官甚早以前即認定英國法院不必替外國政府收稅。於Government of India v. Taylor中，一家英國公司於印度經營業務，清算後尚欠印度政府稅，但英國最高法院卻拒絕替印度政府強制執行該欠稅。於Brokaw v. Seatrain U.K. Ltd.中，兩位美國人欠美國政府稅款，並將其傢

盟的忽視實體法價值，使得羅馬 I 的9(3)條整整晚了近三十年，而且直至現今9(3)條仍甚為不完整。

　　於Euro-Diam v. Bathurst[516]中，英國商人將鑽石賣與一德國人，並依德國買主之請求，低報發票價額，但該批鑽石卻以實價而被保險。於鑽石被偷後，英國法院認為英國商人之行為是應受譴責，並且違反德國稅法，但與鑽石之被偷無關，而且並未欺騙保險公司，因此保險契約之執行並未違反英國公共政策。這個案件是歐盟契約法原則15：102及15：103條之最佳代言。實體法政策之引用，不但可以釐清法律邏輯，更可以保證公平正義之達成。於Howard v. Shirlstar Ltd.[517]中，一英國公司之兩架飛機置於奈及利亞，於當地軍事政變後，該公司與原告訂約，請求原告將飛機帶離奈及利亞。原告於冒生命危險後將一架飛機開至象牙海岸，但象牙海岸政府仍將飛機送回奈及利亞，原告主張其已依約將飛機帶離奈及利亞，但英國公司主張原告飛離奈及利亞之方式違反奈及利亞法律。雙方於訂約時是假設契約應被合法的履行。但上訴法院認為原告及其同事之生命有危險，故不得不非法的偷跑，公眾的良心（「public conscience」）並未被侵犯，契約仍應被履行，原告應獲得其報酬。個人一再強調履行地法應受到尊重之先決要件是其必須符合「文明的公理」，亦即不能違反聯合國人

俱由一美國船載往英國。當船仍在海上時，美國政府將扣押傢俱之通知送達船東。當船到達英國後，船東要求必須有英國法院之命令，否則不願將傢俱交與受貨人。英國上訴法院判決，無論直接或間接地，英國法院不會幫助外國稅法之執行。但與刑罰法規一般，外國稅法法規仍會被英國法院所承認，並且非法地逃避外國稅法之行為將不會為英國法院所強制執行。」[1955] 1 All E.R. 292; [1971] 2 Q.B. 476; Re Visser [1928] 1 ch. 877. 又見早期案例Holman v. Johnson (1775) 1 Cowp. 341.
　另外有趣的是於United States of America v. Inkley, [1988] 3 WLR 304 (CA)中，一英國公民於佛羅里達因犯法而被起訴，在訂立應繳納出庭之債券後便被釋放，然其棄保逃回英國。於要求償還債券之訴訟中（於美國此被視為民事案件），英國上訴法院拒絕請求，認為這樣是在促使被告出席外國刑事法庭，等於是在執行美國公法。但是有趣的是於National Surety Co. v. Larsen, [1929] 4 DLR 918 (British Columbia Court of Appeal)中，加拿大哥倫比亞上訴法院，對於一個位於哥倫比亞之不動產被用為美國華盛頓州保釋之抵押，卻允許該抵押之執行，理由為該抵押契約並非不道德而且哥倫比亞並無公共利益存在。見Trevor C. Hartley, Mandatory Rules in International Contracts: The Common Law Approach, (1997) 266 Hague Recueil 341, 397, 398.
[516] [1990] QB 1; [1988] 2 WLR 517; [1988] 2 All ER 23;[1988] 1 Lloyd's Rep. 228 (CA).見Hartley, p. 392.
[517] [1990] 1 WLR 1292 (CA),見Hartley, p. 393.

權宣言與公約、歐盟的兩個人權公約的大部分規定、各國憲法的規定、歐盟契約法原則、及2004 UNIDROIT Principles。而奈及利亞軍政府之行為並不符合人類文明的公理，故原告之行為並不構成違法。本案應回歸契約法之一般實體法原則，直接認定該契約之履行合乎誠信原則及合理性要求即可，不必提昇至「公眾良心」的地步。

在Lemenda Trading Co. v. African Middle East Petroleum Co.[518]中，一英國石油公司欲繼續取得卡達國營公司供油之續約，便與一巴哈馬公司訂一遊說契約，希望透過巴哈馬公司的主要股東之影響力而繼續取得供油契約。英國公司於取得供油契約後並未付款。依卡達法，遊說契約並未違反其實際之法律，但卻違反其內部之公共政策。依英國法遊說國營企業是違反英國內部之公共政策，但未違反刑法或其他法律。英國法院認為該契約違反履行地之公共政策，因此契約不能被執行。這個契約之履行很明顯的違反友好國家之政策，因此於法律上是不可能履行[519]，該契約亦是違反歐盟契約法1：201條之誠信原則。本案之重點不在卡達官員是否於境外接見巴哈馬公司之股東，而是在於受影響之國家[520]，亦即美國第2新編所謂「效果」（effect）之發生地。近年台灣有領導人於國外洗錢而被起訴收押，承辦檢察官苦惱於該洗錢是透過跨國銀行，經由專業律師、會計師

---

[518] [1988] 3 WLR 735.見Hartley, pp. 394, 395.

[519] [1988] QB 448, 456,461, "There is a clear distinction between acts which infringe public policy and acts which violate provisions of law. I have been referred to no decided case that supports the proposition that the English courts should, as a matter of comity, refuse to enforce an English law contract on the sole ground that performance would be contrary to the public policy of the country of performance. The public policy of Qatar cannot, of itself, constitute any bar to the enforcement of the agreement in this case. It may, however, be a relevant factor when considering whether the court ought to refuse to enforce the agreement in this case under principles of English public policy."

"The English courts should not enforce an English law contract which falls to be performed abroad where: (i) it relates to an adventure which is contrary to a head of English public policy which is founded on general principles of morality, and (ii) the same public policy applied to the country of performance so that the agreement would not be enforceable under the law of that country."

"'In such a situation international comity combines with English domestic public poi icy to militate against enforcement."

[520] Hartley, p. 395, "It was argued that Mr. Yassin might have met the Qatar Minister outside Qatar and exercised his influence there. The court rejected this on the facts; however, it ought to be irrelevant where the meeting takes place: what is important is what Government is to be influenced."

所做之合法行為。無論透過幾十次之「合法」行為，只要其目的是在違反
台灣法，「或」已違反台灣的「基本公共政策」，該表面上於行為地完全
合法之「合法行為」，因為違反履行地台灣法或政策，「或」其「效果或
影響」發生於台灣[521]，該些「合法行為」皆於契約法上不應具有被執行的

---

[521] 此種以「效果或影響」作為法律對於外國行為所適用之標準，見陳隆修、劉仁山、許兆慶，
《國際私法-程序正義與實體正義》，台北，五南圖書公司，2011年9月，初版1刷，73～116
頁。於反托辣斯法上早已為許多國家所適用，見Restatement of the Law, Third, Foreign Relations
Law of the United States, §415
Jurisdiction to Regulate Anti-Competitive Activities
(3) Any agreement in restraint of United States trade that is made in the United States, and any conduct
　　or agreement in restraint of such trade that is carried out in significant measure in the United States,
　　are subject to the jurisdiction to prescribe of the United States, regardless of the nationality or place
　　of business of the parties to the agreement or of the participants in the conduct.
(4) Any agreement in restraint of United States trade that is made outside of the United States, and any
　　conduct or agreement in restraint of such trade that is carried out predominantly outside of the Unit-
　　ed States, are subject to the jurisdiction to prescribe of the United States, if a principal purpose of
　　the conduct or agreement is to interfere with the commerce of the United States, and the agreement
　　or conduct has some effect on that commerce.
(5) Other agreements or conduct in restraint of United States trade are subject to the jurisdiction to pre-
　　scribe of the United States if such agreements or conduct have substantial effect on the commerce of
　　the United States and the exercise of jurisdiction is not unreasonable.
又見FTAIA
§ 6a. Conduct involving trade or commerce with foreign nations
Sections 1 to 7 of this title shall not apply to conduct involving trade or commerce (other than import
trade or import commerce) with foreign nations unless—
(1) such conduct has a direct, substantial, and reasonably foreseeable effect—
　　(A) on trade or commerce which is not trade or commerce with foreign nations, or on import trade
　　　　or import commerce with foreign nations; or
　　(B) on export trade or export commerce with foreign nations, of a person engaged in such trade or
　　　　commerce in the United States; and
(2) such effect gives rise to a claim under the provisions of sections 1 to 7 of this title, other than this
section.
If sections 1 to 7 of this title apply to such conduct only because of the operation of paragraph (1)(B),
then sections 1 to 7 of this title shall apply to such conduct only for injury to export business in the
United States.
另於對人之司法管轄權上，見美國法律協會
(the American Law Institute)之Restatement (Second) of Conflict of Laws § 27 (1971)
(1) A state has power to exercise judicial jurisdiction over an individual on one or more of the following
bases:
(a) causing an effect in the state by an act done elsewhere。
另外對人或對物之司法管轄權上，見Restatement (Third) of Foreign Relations Law of the United
States(1987)
§ 421 Jurisdiction To Adjudicate
(1) A state may exercise jurisdiction through its courts to adjudicate with respect to a person or thing if
　　the relationship of the state to the person or thing is such as to make the exercise of jurisdiction rea-
　　sonable.

效力。

　　另外早期個人基於實務經驗而如此寫著：「此外作者於實務上有時遇見契約之一方當事人（通常為台灣廠方）於契約訂定後，欲以違反台灣外匯管制法為理由而不履行契約上之義務（實際上當然另有商業上之理由）。於此情形台灣尚無判例，但英國學者一般認為除非該被違反之外匯管制條例為契約準據法或履行地法之一部分外，不能構成契約不履行之正當原因。但是國際上有一例外，亦即契約違反了任何IMF之會員國所訂立與Bretton Woods Agreement相同之法律時，該契約不得在任何會員國被強制執行。[522]」依英國上訴法院於Wilson, Smithett & Cope v. Terruzzi[523]中之認定，所謂「exchange contracts」（匯兌契約）指的只是一種貨幣兌換另一種貨幣之契約。於案中原告為一倫敦金屬買賣公司，被告為一義大利人，其於原告處有著一個買賣戶頭。當其與原告之一交易導致重大損失時，其拒絕付款之理由為不能違反義大利外匯管制辦法。因為契約準據法為英國法，而付款履行地又是英國，故被告不能於傳統國際私法上有任何抗辯。而上訴法院又認為該金屬買賣不符合Brettom Woods Agreement, Art. VIII (2)(b)所規定的匯兌契約，故抗辯亦無效。除了必須遵守the IMF

---

(2) In general, a state's exercise of jurisdiction to adjudicate with respect to a person or thing is reasonable if, at the time jurisdiction is asserted:

(i) the person, whether natural or juridical, had carried on outside the state an activity having a substantial, direct, and foreseeable effect within the state, but only in respect of such activity。

有關立法管轄權規定於Restatement of the Law, Third, Foreign Relations Law of the United states § 402 Bases of Jurisdiction to Prescribe

Subject to § 403, a state has jurisdiction to prescribe law with respect to

(1) (a) conduct that, wholly or in substantial part, takes place within its territory;

(b) the status of persons, or interests in things, present within its territory;

(c) conduct outside its territory that has or is intended to have substantial effect within its territory;

(2) the activities, interests, status, or relations of its nationals outside as well as within its territory; and

(3) certain conduct outside its territory by persons not its nationals that is directed against the security of the state or against a limited class of other state interests.

[522] 陳隆修，《國際私法契約評論》，台北，五南圖書公司，民國75年2月，初版，81頁，the International Monetary Fund Agreement 1945. Article VIII(2) (b), "Exchange contracts which involve the currency of any member and which are contrary to the exchange control regulations of any member maintained or imposed consistently with this agreement shall be unenforceable in the territories of any member."

[523] [1976] QB 703; [1976] 2 WLR 418; [1976] 1 All ER 818; [1976] 1 Lloyd's Rep. 509 (CA). Hartley, p. 423.

Agreement外，當事人違反義大利外匯管制辦法亦是事實。英國法界向來以付款履行地為英國之理由而規避外國外匯管制辦法之適用[524]，這樣似乎對規避外國法之違法行為故意視而不見。

事實上如果依照羅馬公約及規則第4條所強調的「特徵性履行」，付款行為並非為商業契約之重點，故付款地法通常並非決定契約效力之法律。英國判例法上經常以付款地法（經常為英國國協之法律）來決定契約重大爭點之效力，於法律邏輯上似乎不甚順暢，至少其明顯的與歐盟的「特徵性履行」概念唱反調。於金融全球化之今日國際貿易上，付款地是可以隨時被改在全球任何地方之銀行戶頭的。而且英國法院這種作法是公開的藐視履行地或效果發生地國家（亦即匯出款項之國家之強行法），對國際貿易或國際禮誼是有傷害的。為了促進當事人間訂定契約之正當期待，個人認為傳統國際私法這種扭曲履行地法之作法應被拋棄。於光明正大的承認契約違反其他國家（亦即金額被匯出去之國家或效果發生地之國家）法律之情形下，法院應依歐盟契約法15：102及15：103條之規定，認定契約是否仍有效或部分有效。實體契約法之運用，不但能保障真正合法之貿易，尊重履行地或效果發生地國家之法律，更能釐清法律邏輯上無謂之困擾。

於UCM v. Royal Bank of Canada[525]中，一英國公司賣貨給一秘魯公司，付款地為英國。於秘魯公司之請求下，英國公司答應將發票報價為真實價格之兩倍，而將剩下的錢存於秘魯公司之人員於邁阿密之戶頭。後契

---

[524] 於Kleinwort, Sons & Co. v. Ungarische Baunwolle A/G, [1939] 2 K.B. 678 (C.A.)中，一英國銀行接受一個匈牙利公司的信用貸款，當債權期限到時該匈牙利公司以匈牙利法禁止其購買外匯或匯款到國外或處理在外國之財產為理由拒絕付款。英國法院判因付款地在英國，故既然匈牙利不是契約準據法或履行地法，該契約自然合法，匈牙利公司仍應付款。同樣的邏輯亦被用在非外匯管制辦法上。於Trinidad Shipping and Trading Co. Ltd. v. Alston [1920] A.C. 888 (P.C.)中，一船公司總行於倫敦，但有分行於紐約與格納達（Trinidad），其與A訂契約，替A載貨從Trinidad到美國，契約準據法為Trinidad的法律。契約中有規定在某情形應減低運費，但依美國法該減低運費為非法，英法院判既然該應減低之運費是應於Trinidad還給A，故美國法既非契約準據法，亦非履行地法，故船公司沒有理由不返還應減少之運費。見陳隆修，《國際私法契約評論》，台北，五南圖書公司，民國75年2月，初版，82、83頁。個人認為歐盟契約法原則15：102及15：103條於此情況下應被適用。

[525] [1983] AC 168; [1982] 2 WLR 1039; [1982] 2 All ER 720 (HL).

約發生糾紛並且於英國法院被提起訴訟。英國最高法院認定契約只能於其真實價格下被執行，至於超過之另一半則是一個隱藏的匯兌契約，因此違反the IMF Agreement Art. VⅢ (2)(b)而不能被執行。英國最高法院這個決定是個令人讚賞之判決[526]，既維持真正交易之效力，又能遵守IMF的公約。但是如果能常態性的以契約實體法為依據，則這種既維持真正交易之效力，又尊重履行地及效果發生地國法律之創造性判決，可能不需要IMF的公約即可造成符合法律邏輯的常態性正義結果，而且更重要的是很多國家被侵犯的法律是與IMF的公約無關的。本案可成為歐盟契約法原則15：102及15：103條之另一代言。

　　美國第2新編203條規定：「於面對高利貸之指控時，如果與契約有重大關連之州允許該利息之利率，並且並未重大的超過依188條本應適用之州之一般高利貸法所允許的利率時，該契約效力應被維持。[527]」如其註釋e所說：「高利貸法是被設計來保護個人以對抗較優勢議價能力一方的壓迫性使用，因此是立法之州的重要政策[528]」。註釋b又說：「為了保護債務人以對抗勒索，許多州已立下高利貸法以限制法律上可以合法取得的利息之利率。[529]」個人於三十年前已對這個議題提出論述，於許多基本理論仍大致上維持原議，但個人對自由經濟理論現今則產生甚大之懷疑。

　　利率是反映金錢於自由市場上之價值，這基本上是一個經濟問題，而非法律問題。個人年輕時於美國當時是有著廢除「過時高利貸法的趨

---

[526] Hartley, p. 425, "This decision shows how English courts try to balance the needs of legitimate commerce against the interests of foreign Governments. The narrow interpretation given to 'exchange contract' favours the former, while their willingness to look behind legal forms ... the action was actually brought by the assignee of the seller against the confirming bank under a letter of credit ... benefits the latter."

[527] s. 203 Usury

The validity of a contract will be sustained against the charge of usury if it provides for a rate of interest that is permissible in a state to which the contract has a substantial relationship and is not greatly in excess of the rate permitted by the general usury law of the state of the otherwise applicable law under the rule of s 188.

[528] "Usury laws are designed to protect a person against the oppressive use of superior bargaining power and thus represent an important policy of the enacting state."

[529] "To protect debtors against extortion, many states have enacted usury laws which limit the rate of interest that can legally be charged."

勢」[530]，而個人躬逢其盛。如註釋b所說的，除了於極少的例外下，契約
法及選法規則的主要目的是在保護當事人的正常期待。因此除非使得契約
無效法律之州之利益，於個案中是超過保護當事人正當期待之價值，法院
不會適用該無效之法律而使得契約不生效力。而「高利貸法是這種有效政
策特別明顯的一個範圍。[531]」60、70年代於擎著自由經濟的大纛下，甚多
法界及經濟界之專家堅信利率是反映市場的標準。但在經歷2008及2009
年之金融海嘯後，控制經濟又再度回籠為主流，這個信念是否仍應為全
球金融市場不可動移之教條？這是我們法界對經濟學界所應鄭重提出的質
疑。所幸對法界而言，高利貸法於國際商界上是個虛擬的問題。於金融市
場全球化之下，貸款履行地可發生於跨國銀行的任何一個戶頭之所在。故
而於國際商務上，違反履行地之高利貸法是個虛擬之問題。既然於國際商
務上這只是一個虛擬的議題，為何不尊重各國之法律以求得表面之國際禮
誼？

　　個人早期即將商務借款與其他借款區分[532]。事實上「大多數的法律
體系均有不同的法律規定，來防止陷於困境的借款人成為斂財的犧牲
品。[533]」另外個人亦陳述小額貸款「往往所需的行政管理成本，較大宗貸
款所需者高」，故「假如法院決定以附合契約的爭點來解決這類案件，它
必須非常慎重的決定[534]」。

---

[530] 陳隆修，《美國國際私法新理論》，台北，五南圖書公司，民國76年1月，初版，253-255頁。

[531] b. Rationale. A prime objective of both choice of law (see s 6) and of contract law is to protect the justified expectation of the parties. Subject only to rare exceptions, the parties will expect on entering a contract that the provisions of the contract will be binding upon them. For this reason, the courts will not apply an invalidating rule to strike down the contract unless the value of protecting the justified expectations of the parties is outweighed in the particular case by the interest of the state with the invalidating rule in having this rule applied. Usury is a field where this policy of validation is particularly apparent.

[532] 陳隆修，《美國國際私法新理論》，台北，五南圖書公司，民國76年1月，初版，254、255頁。

[533] 同上，255、256頁。

[534] 同上，256、257頁。第2新編203條comment f, " f. Special usury statutes. Many states have enacted special legislation relating to small loans, building and loan associations, credit unions and pawnbrokers. Frequently these statutes permit the charging of a higher rate of interest. In the alternative, or sometimes in addition, they may exclude from consideration certain items, such as the initial payment, which would be treated as interest under the general usury law. A contract will be upheld if it complies with a special usury statute of the state of the otherwise applicable law under the rules of ss. 188 and 195."

故而對高利貸契約違反履行地法之問題，個人仍認為應以實體法之內容而加以解決。於國際商務借貸之問題上，因為履行地可以遍及全球，故而是個虛擬問題。於其他之借貸上，各國皆有著真實性的重大社會政策，而且這些政策的世界性「共同核心主流價值」皆是在保護弱勢，全世界於此方面事實上並無政策上之衝突存在，故而尊重履行地之高利貸法是順應各國實體法基本政策的作法。無論是於國際商務契約或其他契約上，尊重履行地之高利貸法，既然於實務上或法學政策上通常不會造成困擾，故而以歐盟契約法原則15：102及15：103為這方面問題之解決依據自然似乎亦不應有困難。

個人主張契約之履行於法律上[535]或事實上（包括履行有困難之情形）為不可能時，契約不可能之部分不應被執行─這個規則應同時為國內法及國際法。所謂履行地應不限於直接行為地，而應包括行為效力（效果；「effect」）之發生地在內[536]。歐盟契約法原則第15章有關契約無效、部分有效、恢復原狀、及損害賠償等規定，應就個案於誠信原則、合理性、及比例原則等契約法基本原則下而被引為實體上之準據法。另外對履行地法尊重之原則必須受限於人類文明的公理，亦即該履行地法不得違反聯合

---

[535] 2004 UNIDROIT Principles art. 7.2.2是將金錢債務排除，但對高利貸及IMF公約的規定個人已加以詳述，故不覺得有必要排除金錢債務。

[536] 或許如果採用「效力理論」則可以避開「契約履行地」於適用上之困擾。見Jonathan Harris, Mandatory Rules and Public Policy under the Rome I Regulation, p.319, "Clearly, the contract in the Ralli case required performance in Spain. But in Regazzoni, the contract was for delivery to Genoa, not to South Africa. It was simply that there was a common understanding between the parties that the goods would be shipped on by the buyer to South Africa. South Africa was not, however, the place of performance under the contract of sale. It could not be said, under Article 9(3) of the Regulation, to be the place where the obligations arising out of the contract were to be performed. Similarly, although the intention in Foster v Driscoll was to smuggle alcohol into the USA, there was no contractual obligation to deliver in that country. It is very tempting to try and read into Article 9(3) a provision to the effect that if it is the common understanding of the parties that one of the parties will ultimate perform elsewhere, then the overriding mandatory rules of the place of ultimate performance might be applied. Otherwise, there is even a possibility of the parties conspiring to evade the law of another country for which goods are ultimately destined. But once again, the ECJ is likely to take a very literal approach to the wording of the Rome I Regulation; and it seems that unless the state in question is actually the place of performance under the contract, its overriding mandatory rules may not be considered under Article 9(3). This would mean that the Foster and Regazzoni line of cases would not be preserved under Article 9(3)."

國所有之人權宣言及公約、歐盟兩個人權公約之大部分規定、各國憲法上基本人權條款、歐盟契約法原則、及2004 UNIDROIT Principles。

羅馬 I 9(3)條離這個結論可能尚有一段距離，對於個人二十多年即已信誓旦旦的主張，個人衷心期盼全世界能儘速公開的承認、引用。羅馬 I 9(3)條雖較公約7(1)條明確，但仍不是非常穩定的條文。首先9(3)條應跳脫大陸法所謂「超越性強行法」之觀念；第二契約履行地及效力發生地之法律，於文明的公理之範圍內通常應受尊重；第三這個國內及國際法則之行使，應於誠信原則、合理性、及比例原則之基礎上，以實體契約法之實質原則為依據。

至於公約及規則I 3(3)條規避法律之規定，因為條文是規定所有案件事實的發生地，自然包括最重要的履行地在內，因此大陸法風味的3(3)條規避法律，事實上可由英美法風味的9(3)條履行地規則所取代。而且3(3)條太過機械性的被強硬適用，不如9(3)條得依實體法原則而具有裁量空間。無論如何公約16條規則21條有關法院地公共政策（即超越性強行政策）之行使權，是為英美法及大陸法截至目前為止所共同接受的最後萬應靈藥。

十八、契約之成立及效力依實體法規則

羅馬公約第8條被規則I引用於第10條如下：「1.契約或契約中之任何條款之存在及效力，應由如若契約或該條款有效時，依本規則應為適用之法律而決定。2.但是若由案件之情形顯示，於第1項所規定之法律去決定其行為之效力並不合理時，當事人得依其慣居地法去證明其並未同意契約之訂立。[537]」公約8條及規則10條又被重申於公約3(4)條及規則4(5)條中。

---

[537] Article 10 consent and material validity
1. The existence and validity of a contract, or of any term of a contract, shall be determined by the law which would govern it under this Regulation if the contract or term were valid.
2. Nevertheless, a party, in order to establish that he did not consent, may rely upon the law of the country in which he has his habitual residence if it appears from the circumstances that it would not be reasonable to determine the effect of his conduct in accordance with the law specified in paragraph 1.

於Egon Oldendorff v. Libera Corporation （No. 2）中[538]，一德國原告與一日本被告訂定一個傭船契約，契約中有規定應至倫敦仲裁之仲裁條款。因為當事人是以英文而且含有標準條款的著名的英國傭船契約之形式，去約定於倫敦仲裁之條款，故而可以默認當事人有意以英國法為準據法。英國法院認為日本被告主張應依日本法而去決定其行為之效力是不對的，應依假定契約成立時契約之準據法英國法為依據。英國法院之所以如此認定，乃是根據羅馬公約之解釋報告，第2項之規定只是有關同意（「consent」）之存在（「existence」），而非有關同意之效力（「validity」）[539]，故而本案並不合適主張羅馬公約第8條2項。解釋報告又認為本條款是為了解決「一方當事人之沈默對契約成立之影響所產生之問題。[540]」依英國法被要約人之沈默並不能被推定為接受要約[541]，但羅馬公約之解釋報告則認為應考慮到當事人間之行為及他們之前的商業關係[542]。本條款之「行為」包含作為及不作為，因此不應只限於當事人之沈默。

歐盟契約法原則1：104條第1項規定「當事人採用或引用本原則之協議之存在及效力依本原則而定」。而有趣的是其第2項亦採納羅馬公約8條2項（規則10條2項）[543]。這固然是實體法與國際私法融合的另一證據，但個人認為有關同意之存在與效力之合理性問題，歐盟契約法原則所規定

---

[538] [1996] 1 Lloyd's Rep. 380.見陳隆修，《2005年海牙法院選擇公約評析》，台北，五南圖書公司，2009年1月，初版1刷，72-74頁。

[539] Giuliano and Lagarde Report, "Notwithstanding the general rule in paragraph 1, paragraph 2 provides a special rule which relates only to the existence and not to the validity of consent."

[540] "The solution alopted by the Group in this respect is designed inter alia to solve the problem of the implications of silence by one party as to the formation of the contract.
The word 'conduct' must be taken to cover both action and failure to act by the party in question; it does not, therefore, relate solely to silence."

[541] Felthouse v Bindley (1862) 11 C.B. (N.S.) 869.

[542] "The Court will give particular consideration to the practice followed by the parties inter se as well as their previous business relationships."

[543] Article 1:104: Application To Questions Of Consent
(1) The existence and validity of the agreement of the parties to adopt or incorporate these Principles shall be determined by these Principles.
(2) Nevertheless, a party may rely upon the law of the country in which it has its habitual residence to establish that it did not consent if it appears from the circumstances that it would not be reasonable to determine the effect of the party's conduct in accordance with these Principles.

的條文之完備是遠超過羅馬公約8(2)條，故應如104條第1項所規定，有關協議存在及效力之合理性亦應由歐盟契約法本身作決定，而不必依8(1)條或慣居地所引用之法律。歐盟契約法原則無論於合理性或保護當事人上，應不會較8(1)條之法律或慣居地法遜色。

　　無論當事人是否依1：104條1項採用歐盟契約法原則為準據法，於Egon Oldendorff案中，個人認為2：210條有關專業人士之訂約或許應可適用：「如果專業人士訂定一個契約，但並未記錄於一個最後之文件中，其中一方沒有遲延的立即送給他方一個書面文件，該文件號稱是確認該契約，但卻包含附加或不同的條款，這些條款可以成為契約之一部分，除非(a)這些條款重大的改變了契約的條款，或(b)被送件人沒有遲延的立即反對他們。[544]」如同歐盟契約法委員會對於書面確認之解釋如下：「於大部分之情形接收人會以沈默之方式來同意該書面之確認。其並無理由去再次同意已經被達成協議之事。其沈默因此會被認為是同意。如果其不同意契約條款，其應沒有遲延的即刻反對。[545]」英國法亦認為即使於當事人間無習慣下，除非為不合理，沈默於這種溝通上得被視為同意[546]。另外當事人

---

[544] Article 2:210: Professional's Written Confirmation

If professionals have concluded a contract but have not embodied it in a final document, and one without delay sends the other a writing which purports to be a confirmation of the contract but which contains additional or different terms, such terms will become part of the contract unless:

(a) the terms materially alter the terms of the contract, or

(b) the addressee objects to them without delay.

[545] Comment, A "Between professionals, i.e. persons engaged in business transactions, who have made a contract, it may not be entirely clear on what terms their contract has been concluded, A party may then send the other party a written confirmation containing the terms which it believes were agreed upon, and the terms which it believes to be implied. It needs to send this confirmation in order to be sure of the terms of the contract before it starts performance. In most cases the recipient will assent to the written confirmation by its silence. It will have no reason to reconfirm what has already been agreed upon and confirmed by the other party. Its silence will, therefore, be considered as assent. If it disagrees with the terms, it must object without delay."

[546] Notes, 3, "It is argued that also under the COMMON LAW, usages and practices between the parties may mean that if a party receives a letter of confirmation or similar document modifying the terms of the contract, and does not object, he may nevertheless be bound. Although the principles of good faith and fair dealing are not generally adopted in ENGLISH law, some cases seem to show that even when there are no usages and practices between the parties, silence to such a communication may be regarded as acceptance when it would be unreasonable to hold otherwise, such as when the recipient had initiated the negotiations ...Rust v. Abbey Life Ins. Co. [1979] 2 Lloyd's Rep 355."

間如果存有慣例，則1：105條規定如下：「(1)當事人間所同意之習慣及它們之間所建立之任何慣例，對當事人有拘束力。(2)對所有的人於相同情形下若為當事人時通常皆應適用之慣例，對當事人有拘束力，但於適用該慣例時是為不合理之情形時則為例外。[547]」

　　故而Egon Oldendorff案，英國法院高明的以羅馬公約第8條的法律邏輯所達成的判決，事實上依歐盟契約法原則中的實體規定可能會更貼近案件中之爭點，更會於實質上對於爭點能造成符合商業習慣之公平正義的觀念之解決方案。**無論是羅馬公約第8條、規則I第10條、及歐盟契約法1：104、1：105、及2：210條於條文本文或注解中，皆仰賴「合理性」做為決定之標準，因此一個很簡單的問題是—為什麼要迂迴的用「合理性」的標準去鑑定應適用之準據法，而不直接的用「合理性」的標準直接去適用在所牽連的實體契約法上？**

　　公約第8條及規則第10條所採用的「假設契約成立時之準據法理論」（「putative proper law」），為個人早期所述英國案例法之觀念[548]。有關契約存在或效力之準據法有各種提案：法院地法（美國判例法上似乎大部分採此）、當事人宣稱所選擇之法（羅馬公約及規則採此）及於當事人沒有明示選法時應為準據法之法（英國Mackender v. Feldia案[549]並未明白的拒絕這個方法）。

　　去年個人對羅馬公約第8條、4條所作的評述仍可適用於羅馬規則第10、4條：「羅馬公約第8條第1項適用之結果通常準據法即為當事人宣稱所選擇之法，這種作法被英美稱為「bootstraps doctrine」（抓自己鞋帶出泥沼）。如果加以嚴苛之批評，這種作法之缺點是賦予當事人權利，使得原本不成立之契約變得有效。但對商業界而言，這種理論能促進貿易

---

[547] Article 1:105: Usages and Practice
　　(1) The parties are bound by any usage to which they have agreed and by any practice they have established between themselves.
　　(2) The parties are bound by a usage which would be considered generally applicable by persons in the same situation as the parties, except where the application of such usage would be unreasonable.
[548] 陳隆修，《國際私法契約評論》，台北，五南圖書公司，民國75年2月，初版，97-100頁。
[549] [1967] 2 Q.B. 590 (CA).

之發展與穩定性，自然為一可被接受之理論。若於當事人沒有約定準據法
（包括默示準據法）時，putative proper law（推定準據法）則依羅馬公
約第4條應為最親近關連之法。[550]」

於英國判例法 Mackender v. Feldia[551]中，一英國保險公司替一比利時
鑽石商人保險其貨物。契約之一條款規定準據法為比利時法，而比利時法
院又有專屬管轄權。要是沒有該條款之規定，英國法應為契約之準據法。
後鑽石於義大利遺失，比利時商人要求保險公司賠償。保險公司辯稱該
專屬管轄條款無效，英法院有管轄權，因為該比利時商人經常偷運鑽石入
義大利，故其在契約之隱瞞行為已使契約無效。英國法院判依英國法該隱
瞞行為只使契約得撤銷，而並非無效，故既然契約有效，則保險公司之抗
辯無效。英國高等法院（上訴法院，Court of Appeal）做此決定或許是本
案只是有關是否送達訴訟之通知至境外之階段而已（管轄階段）。審判
長 Lord Denning M.R. 及 Diplock L.J. 認為如果問題是有關契約是否曾存在
（當事人是否同意 consensus ad idem），則管轄條款可能不適用。Dip-
lock L.J. 認為假如「問題是有關當事人間是否有真正的同意，則應由英國
法來決定，而非由如果當事人有達成協議時，當事人所同意之契約準據法
來決定。[552]」這個案件自年輕時即如惡夢般的困擾個人，英國法之被適用
自然是因為法院地法之故，但是於沒有管轄及準據法指定條款下，其亦應
成為契約準據法，或許亦是法院考慮的重點之一。

無論 Mackender 之法律邏輯是什麼，因為英國的加入羅馬公約，故
而因為公約8(1)條之關係，這個法律邏輯的益智遊戲已經結束。Diplock
L.J. 之論述並不為英國最高法院所接受，個人認為或許是羅馬公約第8條
第1項對這個案子之影響所致。於 Dimskal Shipping Co., SA v. Interna-

---

[550] 陳隆修，《2005年海牙法院選擇公約評析》，台北，五南圖書公司，2009年1月，初版1刷，70頁。

[551] [1967] 2 Q.B. 590 (CA). 見陳隆修，《2005年海牙法院選擇公約評析》，台北，五南圖書公司，2009年1月，初版1刷，79、80頁。

[552] 同上，p. 603. "the question is whether there was any real consensus ad idem, it may well be that this question has to be determined by English law and not by the law which would have been agreed by them as the proper law of the contract if they had reached an agreement."

tional Transport Workers Federation[553]中，一賴比瑞亞船公司之船停於瑞典港口時，船員工會威脅除非船公司多付船員薪資及捐贈大筆捐款予工會之福利基金，否則會將船公司列入黑名單中。船公司同意這些條件，並且明定該「契約」以英國法為準據法，雖然依瑞典法該工會之經濟脅迫（economic duress）並非為非法行為，但英國法為若契約成立時契約之準據法，故契約之存在與否及脅迫之效果應依英國法而定。英國最高法院判經濟上之脅迫，構成契約得被撤銷之後果（voidable）。

　　契約之存在或效力有問題，應以當事人所約定之準據法為依據，或還是以如若沒有約定準據法或管轄法院時應為準據法之法律為依據？前者陷入「鞋帶理論」之困境，後者如Diplock L.J.於Mackender v. Feldia AG中所說的，客觀上契約會成立時之準據法是個「令人困惑」個觀念[554]。故而個人認為雖然putative proper law doctrine是或許除了美國以外，現今國際社會於契約及其條款之成立及效力所最能共同接受之國際私法規則，但個人認為其時代性之任務已結束，應由更為先進、更為具體之歐盟契約法原則及2004 UNIDROIT Principles來取代其過去之功能─而可預見的將來可能歐洲民法或UNIDROIT之其他新法亦會取代這兩個契約法之原則。

　　如在管轄條款之成立（formation）存在（existence）效力（validity）之問題上，對有關當事人之沈默、契約無對價、錯誤、詐欺、脅迫、標準格式契約、合併條款、相衝突條款、額外附加條款、其他有關當事人間之同意、及合法性等問題上，個人是直接以相關之歐盟契約法原則為解決案件爭點之依據[555]。而且個人認為在以實體法原則解決國際契約糾紛時，不但個案之正義能充分被保障，選法規則在法律邏輯上之困擾亦突然消失。故而羅馬公約8(2)條及規則10(2)條的警察規則於實體法方法論中

---

[553] [1992] 2 A.C. 152. 陳隆修，《2005年海牙法院選擇公約評析》，台北，五南圖書公司，2009年1月，初版1刷，80頁。

[554] [1967] 2 Q.B. 590 (CA), p. 603.

[555] 陳隆修，《2005年海牙法院選擇公約評析》，台北，五南圖書公司，2009年1月，初版1刷，70-102頁。

變得累贅而不必要,因為歐盟契約法及2004 UNIDROIT Principles本身就是以合理性及誠信原則為條文之基礎,並且更以他們作為條文中之警察條款。故而歐盟契約法原則的1:104(1)條既然以本身之原則取代了putative proper law doctrine,其1:104(2)條以慣居地法來做為其本身原則不合理性的警察條款是個奇怪的作法[556]。

2004 UNIDROIT Principles第3章是有關契約之效力,而其3.19條幾乎將整章皆列為強行法,該註釋如此論述:「本條文宣佈本章有關詐欺、脅迫、及過度之不平等之條文皆屬於強行性之性質。當事人於訂約時如果排除或修改這些條款,則構成違反誠信原則。但是於當事人知悉真正之事實後,或能自由的作為後,其得放棄撤銷該契約之權利。[557]」對英國判例法及羅馬公約8條規則10條以「假設推定準據法」為依據之作法,個人去年主張應以實體契約法原則取代之以符合時代之需求[558]。基於學術理想,個人之理由有兩個;第1依實體契約法較能貼切的維持個案之正義;第2

---

[556] 見the Commission of European Contract Law, Principles of European Contract Law, edited by Ole Lando and Hugh Beale (2000), p. 103,於1:104條中之comment,其所舉的例子在雙方有著指定不同準據法之相衝突的標準條款時,根據2:204條雙方之條款彼此抵銷後,卻根據羅馬公約4(2)條去尋找特徵性履行之準據法荷蘭法。個人認為歐盟契約法委員會對實體法方法論太沒有信心,此時應直接以歐盟契約法原則為契約之準據法,因為如其序言(2)(D)所說,該歐盟契約法原則為契約法之"common core"(歐洲契約法之共同核心),自然遠比荷蘭法更合適去處理此歐洲契約法上於個案之爭點。
"Illustration: A Dutch lessor sends an offer to lease a container to the German lessee on a standard form contract providing for arbitration and for the application of the Principles. The lessee accepts and refers to its standard form conditions which provides that disputes are to be settled by arbitration but which also contains a clause under which German law is to govern the contract.
After the parties have performed the contract a dispute arises relating to the quality of the container. The lessor claims that the Principles must govern, the lessee that German law must govern. Applying Article 2:209 of the Principles, the arbitrator will come to the conclusion that the two choice of law clauses 'neutralise' each other, that the Rome Convention, in force in Germany and Holland, will apply to decide which law governs in the absence of an effective choice of law by the parties, and that the law of the lessor, Dutch law, will govern the contract, see article 4(2) of the Convention."
[557] Official Comment
This article declares the provisions of this Chapter relating to fraud, threat and gross disparity to be of a mandatory character. It would be contrary to good faith for the parties to exclude or modify these provisions when concluding their contract. However, nothing prevents the party entitled to avoidance to waive that right once it learns of the true facts or is able to act freely.
[558] 陳隆修,《2005年海牙法院選擇公約評析》,台北,五南圖書公司,2009年1月,初版1刷,95-98頁。

避免「鞋帶困境」法律邏輯之困擾或於尋找應適用準據法上難以決定之
困惑。但是上述兩個學術理由相較於2004 Principles 3.19條皆黯然失色。
3.19條白紙黑字的命令著：有關契約效力之問題（經常包含存在之問題）
經常是屬於強行法、基本政策、或超越性考量的，任何選法規則的適用
（包括公約8條規則10條）如果違反他們，即構成違反誠信原則。故而反
對「假設推定準據法」理論之第3個理由，也是最重要的實際考量為：契
約於存在及效力之問題，經常是有關強行法、基本政策、及超越性考量之
問題，選法規則是不能違反他們或甚至無適用之餘地，相關連之實體契約
政策（通常是法院地法）應會被給予優先適用。

　　如前所述強行法是個可疑的觀念。如果其存在的話，那麼可能是充斥
於每一個被通過的法律中。如果強行法真正存在的話，那麼特別於有關契
約之成立、存在、及效力上，英美法與大陸法是有著共同核心的。無論是
在英美法或大陸法，當事人之協議或應適用之準據法皆於契約之成立、存
在、及效力上，通常是不能違反相關實體規則、誠信原則、及合理性之要
求。

　　如前述即使於英美法的美國U.C.C.1-304條對誠信原則亦有著強制
性之規定，其注釋(1)說明：「本條文是貫穿統一商法的基本原則。這個
原則是於商業行為中，所有協議及責任之履行與執行皆必須遵守誠信原
則……並且如本條文之規定，應普遍的適用於本商法的每個契約及責任之
履行或執行。[559]」而2-302條規定契約或其條款不得違背良心，其註釋(1)
認為本條款是個警察條款，包含要約與承諾及契約之目的皆在其範圍內。
本原則是為避免契約造成壓迫或不公平的驚奇之結果，及抑制一方過強之
議價能力[560]。另外1-302條規定誠信原則、勤勞、合理性、及注意之義務

---

[559] 1. This section sets forth a basic principle running throughout the Uniform Commercial Code. The principle is that in commercial transactions good faith is required in the performance and enforcement of all
agreements or duties. While this duty is explicitly stated in some provisions of the Uniform Commercial
Code, the applicability of the duty is broader than merely these situations and applies generally, as states
in this section, to the performance or enforcement of every contract or duty within this Act."

[560] "1. This section makes it possible for a court to police explicitly against the contracts or terms which the
court finds to be unconscionable instead of attempting to achieve the result by an adverse construction

不能被以協議而違反，這是個基本原則之規定。其注釋(1)認為契約自由
之例外於統一商法之其他條文中亦有規定，只是其明示之程度不一致[561]。

第2新編187(2)(b)條亦規定其他更有重大利益州之基本政策（強行
法）不得被違背，而如前述其註釋中充滿著有關契約成立、存在、及效力
之問題為基本政策（強行法）之論述。註釋(b)說明：「正如其他之契約
條款，如果是經由詐欺、脅迫、不當影響、或錯誤等不適當之方法而於訂
約時取得一方當事人之同意，則該選法條款不會被給予效力。這種同意是
否於事實上經由錯誤或不當之方法取得，是由法院依其自己之法律原則而
決定。[562]」另外於註釋(d)中又認為能力、形式要件、及實質效力（契約之
非法性）等問題，並非當事人能以明示協議而決定[563]。注釋(g)說明基本政
策可能是包含於使得契約無效之法規，或用以保護弱勢而對抗議價能力較
強一方之壓迫性作法之法規[564]。

---

[561] of language, by manipulation of the rules of offer and acceptance, or by a determination that the term is contrary to public policy or to the dominant purpose of the contract. ….. The principle is one of prevention of oppression and unfair surprise and not of disturbance of allocation of risks because of superior bargaining power."

[561] "This principle of freedom of contract is subject to specific exceptions found elsewhere in the Uniform Commercial Code and to the general exception stated here. The specific exceptions vary in explicitness: the statute of frauds found in Section 2-201, for example, does not explicitly preclude oral waiver of the requirement of a writing, but a fair reading denies enforcement to such a waiver as part of the 'contract' made unenforceable; Section 9-602, on the other hand, is a quite explicit limitation on freedom of contract."

[562] "b. Impropriety or mistake. A choice-of-law provision, like any other contractual provision, will not be given effect if the consent of one of the parties to its inclusion in the contract was obtained by improper means, such as by misrepresentation, duress, or undue influence, or by mistake. Whether such consent was in fact obtained by improper means or by mistake will be determined by the forum in accordance with its own legal principles."個人於此必須不客氣的向已故恩師Prof. von Mehren提出一個經典的問題---如果第2新編對選法條款的成立與效力認為是個法院地的強烈基本政策（強行法）而不得被違背，那麼很奇怪的是2005年海牙公約對法院選擇條款及該條款效力之準據法，為何皆機械式的以被指定法院地為唯一管轄法院及以該地法為準據法？

[563] "Subject to this qualification, the rule of this Subsection applies when it is sought to have the chosen law determine issues which the parties could not have determined by explicit agreement directed to the particular issue. Example of such questions are those involving capacity, formalities and substantial validity. A person cannot vest himself with contractual capacity by stating in the contract that he has such capacity. He cannot dispense with formal requirements, such as that of a writing, by agreeing with the other party that the contract shall be binding without them. Nor can he by a similar device avoid issues of substantial validity, such as whether the contract is illegal."

[564] "a fundamental policy may be embodied in a statute which makes one or more kinds of contracts illegal or which is designed to protect a person against the oppressive use of superior bargaining power."

　　無論是U.C.C.或第2新編的187條於基本政策（或強行法）的概念，與2004 UNIDROIT Principles的概念是相去不遠的。而且如前所述，他們皆是以合理性及誠信原則為條文之基礎及警察原則。2004 UNIDROIT Principles 3.19條有關契約效力為強行規定之法則，於U.C.C.及第2新編187條有關契約之存在及效力之規定上亦皆大致上將其包含在內。故而有關契約之存在及效力之法規皆以誠信原則及合理性為基礎，應是英美法與大陸法之共同核心主流價值。因此羅馬公約8條規則10條之適用性及其存在之必要性是令人質疑的。

　　英國判例法所採用之「假設推定準據法」理論[565]或許有著時代上之歷史意義，但是現代法學已遠較早期進步，為擺脫法律邏輯上及運作上之困擾，及充分尊重相關國家之強行法、基本政策、及超越性考量，歐盟應擺脫羅馬公約8條規則10條。而於契約之成立、存在、及效力上如2004 UNIDROIT Principles 3.19條般的，直接視為強行法而引用自己的歐盟契約法原則。個人希望這個實體法論述能為兩岸年輕同僚所引為中國式國際私法之一部分。[566]

---

[565] 陳隆修，《國際私法契約評論》，台北，五南圖書公司，民國75年2月，初版，97-100頁。
[566] 事實上UN1DR0IT Principles (2004) 之序言說明其目的如下：
PREAMMBLE
(Purpose of the Princinciples)
These Principles set forth general rules for international commercial contracts.
They shall be applied when the parties have agreed that their contract be governed by them.
They may be applied when the parties have agreed that their contract be governed by general principles of law, the lex mercatoria or the like.
They may be applied when the parties have not chosen any law to govern their contract.
They may be used to interpret or supplement international uniform law instruments.
They may be used to interpret or supplement domestic law.
They may serve as a model for national and international legislators.
故UNIDROIT Principles (2004)可做為國際商業契約法之基本原則、當事人所約定契約之依據、當事人沒有約訂契約準據法時之依據、用來解釋或補充國際統一法則(包含CISG在內)、用來解釋或補充國內法、及用來做為國際法及國內法之規範。因此個人認為the UN1DR0IT Principles (2004)是21世紀全球化法學於商業契約法上主流共同核心基本價值之實現。
故至少在商業契約法上，尊敬的Pro. Resse與個人三十年前在主流價值的爭辯上，時間不但站在個人這邊，而且「時間已經到來」。見陳隆修、許兆慶、林恩瑋、李瑞生四人合著，《國際私法-管轄與選法理論之交錯》，台北，五南圖書公司，2009年3月，初版1刷，254、255頁。更或許在CISG(1980)到來時，「時間已隨著到來。」
Willis Reese, The Second Restatement of Conflict of Laws Revisited, 34 Mercer L. Rev.

　　如前述個人之理由有3，第1避免法律邏輯於「鞋帶困境」之問題[567]（公約8條規則10條）；或英國傳統判例法上辨認應適用之準據法之困惑。第2以實體契約法原則去解決有關當事人重大權益之爭點較能確保個案之正義。「假設推定準據法」理論是個區域選擇法律規則，若被選定之法律為落伍之法律則對當事人會造成不公正之結果。第3於實際上契約存在及效力問題於許多或所有的國家都屬於當事人或應適用準據法無法超越之強行基本政策，選法規則之適用只是會增加不必要之困擾。但是個人最強而有力之證據來自美國。美國似乎並未引用這種繞口令式的英國益智法律邏輯，「假設推定準據法」理論似乎不存在於美國。但美國的「內部市場」仍高居世界第一，而全世界有許多人仍「飛蛾撲火」般想於美國提起訴訟。拒絕「假設推定準據法」理論會對市場經濟及司法名譽有妨礙[568]？歐盟應該問問美國人就知道答案。

501, at 518 (1983)

A criticism made of the Restatement Second by a number of writers dose not give proper emphasis to what, in their opinion, is the only-or at least the principal-value in choice of law. This is that the court should look to the policies underlying the potentially applicable local law rules of the state having contacts with the case... If these writers are correct, the Restatement Second is plainly wrong. It takes the position that this value, although important, dose not stand alone and that there are other values to be considered. This insistence that there are a number of relevant ralues is a primary reason for what can be justly termed the vagueness of some of the Restatement Second formulations. In defense,it can be said that a balancing of values inevitably will be an uncertain process until it is finally determined which of the values should carry the greatest weight in a given situation. In many instances, such a time has not yet come.

大陸法制既然於國內及國際買賣合同上皆採以CISG為依據之方法論，以進階版的the UNIDROIT Principles(2004)為國際及國內合同之依據、解釋或補充似乎是一種合乎「自然道法」之進化階段。大陸法學之採實體法論或全球化法學之程度，似乎遠比大陸同僚所願意承認的較為快速或徹底。做為一個有著同樣血緣、文化的台灣法學生，個人認為這種快速法學全球化的進展是直得驕傲之處，或許這是中國法學革命的開始。或許「法學全球化」(實體法論)的道路會引導再次崛起的中國，將2500年的傳統文化與全球化法學結合，並可望於近期內(50年)或許可以領導全世界人類文明於王道法學上之發展。

[567] 事實上個人遵守恩師Prof. Graveson的教誨，對法律邏輯一致性之要求並非十分在意。所真正在意的乃是以當事人所約定之法律做為契約或其條款之存在與效力之準據法，可能會給予強勢之一方濫用壓迫性權力之機會。這是第2新編、U.C.C.、歐盟契約法原則、及2004 UNIDROIT Principles所公認不可被超越之共同核心強行法，亦是個人反對2005年海牙法院選擇公約之主要原因。事實上公約8條規則10條亦違反羅馬規則要點23保護弱勢之政策。

[568] Rome I, recital (1), The Community has set itself the objective of maintaining and developing an area of freedom, security and justice, For the progressive establishment of such an area, the Community is to adopt measures relating to judicial cooperation in civil matters with a cross-border impact to the extent necessary for the proper functioning of the internal market.

　　有趣的是第2新編187(2)(b)條於註釋（9）中說明「法院應引用自己的法律原則以決定一個既存的政策是否為本條款範圍內之基本政策[569]」而U.C.C.1-301條是為有關選法規則適用之條款，其註釋(g)說明第1，法院地之基本政策有時會於即使當事人沒有指定準據法時應適用之法律之基本政策沒有被違反時，仍會超越當事人所選定之準據法。第2，於決定是否適用當事人所選定之準據法時，法院不可避免的必須決定契約基本效力之問題，例如能力及脅迫等問題[570]。故而U.C.C及第2新編似乎認為：第1，法院地之有些基本政策是不能被當事人之約定及應適用之準據法所超越；第2，契約或其條款之「效力」（於美國通常包含契約之「存在」在內）問題，是經常屬於基本政策之範圍內。**故而如果個人之推論是正確的，那麼這個美式作法不但與硬性規定契約效力問題屬於強行法的2004 UNIDROIT Principles 3.19條一致，美國式作法所更要表達的是一於契約及其條款之存在與效力之問題上，選法規則並不是重心，實體契約法之規則才是超越性之考量。個人以為這個美國人自己所實施的實體法方法論，是一個目前國際私法學中超越利益說及最重要關連說之最先進理論。只是可惜美國同僚似乎沒有注意到他們領先全球之處。這種實體法方法論於決定管轄條款之存在及效力上，個人去年已經由數個聯邦案例之探討而充分加以證明[571]。如果在最棘手的管轄條款上聯邦法院都能（或必須）**

---

[569] "The forum will apply its own legal principles in determining whether a given policy is a fundamental one within the meaning of the present rule and whether the other state has a materially greater interest than the state of the chosen law in the determination of the particular issue."

[570] "9. Matters not addressed by this section. As noted in comment 1, this section is not a complete statement of conflict of laws doctrines applicable in commercial cases. Among the issues this section does not address, and leaves to other law, three in particular deserve mention. First, a forum will occasionally decline to apply the law of a different jurisdiction selected by the parties when application of that law would be contrary to a fundamental policy of the forum jurisdiction, even if it would not be contrary to a fundamental policy of the State or country whose law would govern in the absence of contractual designation. Standards for application of this doctrine relate primarily to concepts of sovereignty rather than commercial law and are thus left to the courts. Second, in determining whether to give effect to the parties' agreement that the law of a particular State or country will govern their relationship, courts must, of necessity, address some issues as to the basic validity of that agreement. These issues might relate, for example, to capacity to contract and absence of duress." 其comment 6認為必須超越現代商業法的穩定性及預測性，及司法的經濟性，該基本政策才能被加以適用。

[571] 陳隆修，《2005年海牙法院選擇公約評析》，台北，五南圖書公司，2009年1月，初版1刷，18-55頁。

以實體法為依據，而放棄選法規則之操弄，契約或其他條款之存在與效力問題亦似乎沒有理由不能依實體法而解決。

如同U.C.C.1-304條、1-302條、及2：302條規定誠信、勤勞、合理、注意、及良心之標準為決定性之要求，2004 UNIDROIT Principles亦有甚多基本政策上之要求。例如1.7條誠信原則、2.1.20條避免驚奇條款、5.1.4最盡力條款、5.1.7價格決定條款、7.1.6免責條款之限制、及7.4.13條違約金之限制等。事實上如前所述，整個2004 UNIDROIT Principles幾乎都是有關商業契約上之世界性共同核心基本政策，其中有許多是有關契約之存在與效力之問題。而整個歐盟契約法原則亦充斥著一般契約法基本政策，及有關契約存在及效力基本政策之規定，這些都是所謂的強行法、基本政策、及超越性考量。如1：105條慣例條款、1：106條契約之解釋、1：201條誠信原則、1：202條合作義務、1：302條合理性、1：305條默示責任之推定、2：301及2：302條訂約前之責任，尤其是整個第2章有關契約之成立及第4章有關契約之效力（包括錯誤、詐欺、及脅迫在內），這些不但是一般契約法之基本政策，更是直接有關契約成立、存在、及效力之基本政策。如前所述，事實上整部契約法都是強行法與基本政策，只是於個案上其適用之程度與範圍不同而已。例如第6章有關內容及效力（效果）之規定，整章皆可能與契約之存在與效力有關，而且毫無疑問的皆屬於共同核心基本政策。例如6：105條規定即使當事人有相反的約定，單方決定之價格或條款不得違反合理性之規定，否則合理之價格應取代之[572]。像這種有關契約條款之存在與效力之基本強行政策，自然是全世界契約法上之共同核心價值，包含羅馬公約8條規則10條在內之所有選法規則之適用，皆會被6：105條所代表之價值所超越。

故而有關契約或其條款之成立、存在、與效力之問題，經常是屬於

---

[572] Article 6:105: Unilateral Determination by a Party

Where the price or any other contractual term is to be determined by one party and that party's determination is grossly unreasonable, then notwishstanding any provision to the contrary, a reasonable price or other term shall be substituted.

一般所認為的強行法、基本政策、及超越性考量之範圍，而且通常更是強行法、基本政策、及超越性考量中之最核心問題。由第2新編187條、U.C.C.、2004 UNIDROIT Principles、及歐盟契約法原則而論，於契約之存在與效力之問題上，世界性的共同核心基本強行政策是存在的。而於這些強行政策之運行下，「假設推定準據法」之運作空間有限，而且徒增法律邏輯上之困擾。更重要的是即使偏重市場自由資本主義的英國判例法，於「假設推定準據法」上並未明確的採納以當事人所選定法律為依據之作法[573]，歐盟卻自作聰明的採納以當事人所選定之法律為依據之作法。這種作法自然給予強勢一方有著濫用壓迫性權力之機會，而會在契約之存在及效力上與全世界契約法之共同核心基本政策相抵觸的。更有趣的是羅馬公約8條規則10條與規則自己本身的要點23完全相抵觸，要點23規定：「有關與被視為較弱勢之當事人所訂之契約，那些當事人應受到較一般性規則對他們的利益有幫助的國際私法的規則之保護。[574]」歐盟知道自己在作什麼嗎？

十九、主觀說與客觀說

　　羅馬公約及規則第4條是於當事人未明示或默示準據時，採「推定」法則（「presumption」）及最密切關連法則去認定準據法，這有些類似英國判例法長久以來之作法。有關英國之「適當法主義」（「proper law doctrine」）或許甚早就出現於Lord Mansfield在Robinson v. Bland中著名之附帶意見（「dictum」）：「當於交易時，當事人已明示其他國家之法律應為依據時，行為地法是不會被適用的[575]。」相較於其他法學，國際私法於英國之發展是較為遲緩的，歷經14至17世紀英國判例法院才

---

[573] 陳隆修，《國際私法契約評論》，台北，五南圖書公司，民國75年2月，初版，97-100頁。

[574] "(23) As regards contracts concluded with parties regarded as being weaker, those parties should be protected by conflict-of-law rules that are more favourable to their interests than the general rules."

[575] "The law of the Place can never be the Rule, where the Transaction is entered with an express View to the Law of Another Country, as the Rule by which it is to be governed." (1760) 2 Burr. 1078.但此意見於該案中並未受到充分之支持。

認為於外國商業契約中外國法是有關連的。於17及18世紀英國法院通常假定，於英國起訴之原告必須適用英國法。而一直至19世紀為止，適當法是與適當的管轄權沒有區分的。選法規則與管轄權的確認是混在一起的[576]。

Lord Atkin於R.v. International Trustee for the Protection of Bond-holders A.G.中對適當法原則作了如下著名之論述：「在契約適當法之問題上引導英國法院之法律原則現在已經確定。這個法律就是當事人意圖適用之法。他們的意思應由契約中之明示意思而被加以確認，如果的確是有這個意思，那麼這意思應為最後之結論。[577]」緊接著Lord Wright於Mount Albert Borough Council v. Australasian Temperance, etc. Scoiety中又更一步的論述：「契約之適當法指英國法院用以決定契約義務之法律。英國法律於決定這些問題時，拒絕引用這些終結性、死硬性、及獨斷性之標準，例如契約訂定地或履行地等，並且這些問題是根據於考慮契約之條款、當事人之情形、及案件所有之一般事實下，於個案中去確認當事人之意思。[578]」而Lord Reid又於Whitworth Street Estates （Manchester Ltd. v. James Miller & Partners Ltd.中更明白的表示：「一般的大原則是沒有疑問的。當事人是有權利去協議他們契約中之適當法，並且於如若他們沒有訂立此種協議時，法律會決定什麼是適當法。[579]」以上當事人明示自主準據法，及由契約條款及案件事實來認定當事人之意思，這些英國判例法

---

[576] R.H. Graveson, Conflict of Laws, 7th ed., p. 407.

[577] "The legal principles which are to guide an English court on the question of the proper law of a contract are now well settled. It is the law which the parties intended to apply. Their intention will be ascertained by the intention expressed in the contract, if any, which will be conclusive." [1937] A.C. 500, 529.

[578] "The proper law of the contract means that law which the English court is to apply in determining the obligations under the contact. English law in deciding these matters has refused to treat as conclusive, rigid or arbitrary criteria such as lex loci contractus or lex loci solutionis and has treated the matter as depending on the intention of parties to be ascertained in each case on a consideration of the terms of the contract, the situation of the parties, and generally on all the surrounding facts." [1938] A.C. 224, 240.

[579] "The general principle is not in doubt. Parties are entitled to agree what is to be the proper law of their contract, and if they do not make any such agreement then the law will determine what is the proper law." [1970] A.C. 587, 603

長久以來進化之結果，似乎大致上為近三十年來之羅馬公約及規則所認可。

　　但是英國之適當法理論較近之特徵為，於法院認定適當法時有兩種主要之理論於近70年中持續競爭著。Westlake之客觀說（objective theory）主張「最真實的關連」（「the most real connection」[580]），而Dicey的主觀說（「subjective theory」）主張探求當事人之「意思」（「intention」[581]）。Westlake認為法院應以「最真實的關連」來認定適當法：「於這些情形下應可說英國之選定決定契約內部之效力及效果之法律是基於實質之考量，對於與交易有著最真實關連的國家應給予優先考量，而不是這些契約的訂定地法。[582]」而Dicey則認為適當法之確認，重點應是於當事人之意思，而非在適當法地區的與契約有著最真實關連的關連點：「『契約適當法』的名詞指的是，當事人意圖，或得被相當的推定為有著意圖，做為契約依據的法律，或一些法律；或（用其他表達之方式）當事人有意思或得被相當的推定為有意思去接受其效力之法律或一些法律。[583]」

　　於這兩種理論之激盪中，探求當事人之真意顯然對法院是會造成困難的。Lord Normand在Kahler v. Midland Bank Ltd.中說：「為了確認契約之適當法，我們的法院必須去解決當事人意思之問題。[584]」而於依契約

---

[580] John Westlake, A Treatise on Private International Law 237 (London, William Maxwell & Son 2d ed. 1880) (1858).許多英美法的同僚認為現在於美國及歐洲（包括羅馬公約、規則Ⅰ、及規則Ⅱ）最盛行的 "the most significant relationship"（最重要關連）即源自於其理論。這似乎是個極合理的說法。

[581] A.V. Dicey, A Digest of the Law of England with Reference to the Conflict of Laws,（London, Stevens & Sons, Ltd. 1896）

[582] "In these circumstances it may be said that the law by which to determine the intrinsic validity and effects of a contract will be selected in England on substantial considerations, the preference being given to the country with which the transaction has the most real connection, and not to the law of the place of contract as such." Private International Law, 7th ed., 1925, p. 302.

[583] Dicey and Morris, the Conflict of Laws, 9th ed., Rule 148, "The term, 'proper law of a contract' means the law , or laws, by which the parties intended, or may fairly be presumed to have intended, the contract to be governed; or (in other words) the law or laws to which the parties intended or may fairly be presumed to have intended, to submit themselves."

[584] "In ascertaining what is the proper law of a contract our courts have to solve a question of the parties' intention." [1950] A.C. 24, 35.

條款、當事人之情形、及案件之一般事實去認定當事人之真正或被推定之意思時，Birkett L.J.於The Assunzione中坦白的承認這會有「不真實的感覺」[585]。因為當事人於訂約時很可能從未預想過契約被違背時之準據法。

無怪乎客觀說於後來似乎較為被接受。Lord Wright於Vita Food Products v. Unus Shipping Co.中說：「英國法現在已經確定（而加拿大Nova Scotia亦是同樣）契約之適當法為『當事人意圖適用之法律。』而這個意思是客觀的被確認，並且於沒有明示下，應由契約之條款及案件周遭之相關情形而被推定。[586]」Denning L.J.於Boissevain v. Weil中更是明白的認為適當法應：「非如此的依據契約訂立之地，甚至亦非依據當事人之意思或契約會被履行之地，而是依據其有著最重要關連之地。[587]」於當事人沒有明示準據法時，Megaw L.J.於Coast Lines Ltd. v. Hudig and Veder Chartering N.V.中如此說明：「於英國國際私法早期的發展，推定（當事人意思），是非常流行的，但現在無論好壞，是不再流行並且被拒絕的。這實在是採納『最密切且最真實關連』標準的必然結果。[588]」

---

[585] "sense of unreality", [1954] p. 150, 185.

[586] "It is now well settled that by English law (and the law of Nova Scotia is the same) the proper law of the contract 'is the law which the parties intended to apply.' That intention is objectively ascertained, and, if not expressed, will be presumed from the terms of the contract and the relevant surrounding circumstances." [1939] A.C. 277, 289

[587] "depends not so much on the place where it is made, nor even on the intention of the parties or on the place where it is to be performed, but on the place with which it has the most substantial connection." [1949] 1 K.B. 482, 490.但是Lord Denning M.R.在Tzortzis v. Monark Line A/B中修正自己之意見，而尊重當事人自己之選擇如下："It is clear that, if there is an express clause in a contract providing what the proper law is to be, that is conclusive in the absence of some public policy to the contrary. But where there is no express clause, it is a matter of inference from the circumstances of the case." [1968] 1 W.L.R. 406, 411.

[588] "Presumptions, once fashionable during the earlier development of English private international law, are now, whether for good or ill, out of fashion and rejected. That, indeed, is a necessary result of the adoption of the 'closest and most real connection' test." [1927] 2 Q.B. 34, 47.
個人早期於陳隆修，《國際私法契約評論》，台北，五南圖書公司，民國75年2月，初版，24-26頁中又如此寫著：「又於選擇準據法，英國傳統上有一說法，亦即應選擇與契約較有牽連的法律制度，而不是國家（the search should not be for the country but for local system which the contract has the closest links）。於Re United Railways ([1961] A.C. 1007, 1068, 1081.中Lord Denning採用後者，而Lord Morris採用前者。在代表案子Rossano v. Manufactuers, Life Insurance Co ([1963] 2Q.B. 352)中，一個埃及人於埃及跟加拿大安大略的一家保險公司在埃及簽訂一個保險契約，埃及為契約最有牽連的國家，但安大略省之法律為契約最有牽連之法律。因為契約是根據安大略法而訂成的McNair法官認為準據法為安大略法。此或許是由於英國國際私法與世界

　　現今於當事人沒有約定準據法時，不但英國偏向客觀說，連美國及歐盟亦偏向客觀說。但如最尊敬的恩師Prof. Graveson一針見血的說明：「正如一些衝突中的理論在許多情形對一個問題上一般，答案並非是一個是正確而另一個是錯誤，而是兩個皆不是該問題完整的說明。在Westlake正確的對英國法於程序、證據、及管轄方面歷史發展的強調時，而Dicey，在沒有忽略這些問題時，將其重點放在個人訂約自由的主要法律原則上。[589]」如個人早期之論述[590]，主觀說較能維護契約之本質，但於訴訟程序上法官較難認定，客觀說之優缺點則恰好相反。個人又論述：「現在當事人既已可以指定準據法，故上述二說之重要性當然降低，但於當事人訂定契約時未定準據法之狀況下，仍可做為法官推定準據法之依據。……事實上作者以為此種爭論於實務上並無多大益處，因為法官於推定準據法時常以契約客觀之事實來推定當事人主觀之意識」[591]。事實上Prof. Graveson對二百五十年前Lord Mansfield於Robinson v. Bland中之論述，即認為是「對客觀的關連點給予主觀的解釋」[592]。Lord Mansfield之論述如下：「於解釋及執行契約時，所已建立的國際禮誼及萬國公法的一般原則是，契約訂定之地，而非訴訟被提起之地，應被加以考慮。但是這個原則是承認一個例外，亦即於當事人（在訂約之時）看上另一不同之

各國出發點不同的地方---特別是與美國，蓋英國為一老牌殖民地國兼貿易王國，故其國際私法之發展性往往純粹是基於國際眼光。英國自古以來即為保險王國，其保險公司業務遍及世界，同一保險公司之契約可能在世界各地被簽訂，故為求契約之穩定，英國法院一般皆以保險公司所在地為保險契約之準據法，此亦為一般之商業習慣。Hodson大法官於Whitworth Street Estats (Manchester) Ltd. v. Fames and Partners Ltd([1969] 1 W.L.R. 337, 380 (C.A.)中所說的『這個文字上的變化實在不重要，但在某些情況下一種說法有可能比另一種重要』。事實上國際私法上的文字遊戲實在是不勝枚舉，這些文字遊戲如美國眾多之新理論一樣，只是徒增困擾，正本清源之道還是在於認清每類案件之基本價值（fundamental values）。」羅馬公約解釋報告中對此點似乎並未加以區分。

[589] R.H. Graveson, Conflict of Laws, 7th ed., p. 406, "As in many cases of conflicting theories on a single issue, the answer is not that one is right and the other wrong, but that neither is a complete exposition of the matter. Where Westlake was correctly stressing the historical development of English law in its procedural, evidentiary, and jurisdictional aspects, Dicey, while not neglecting these matters, laid his emphasis on the prevalent philosophical principle of individual liberty of contracting."

[590] 陳隆修，《國際私法契約評論》，台北，五南圖書公司，民國75年2月，初版，21-24頁。

[591] 陳隆修，《國際私法契約評論》，台北，五南圖書公司，民國75年2月，初版，23、24頁。

[592] R.H. Graveson, p. 405, "in which Lord Mansfield had given a subjective interpretation to an objective connection."

國家時。[593]」

　　早期Bowen L.J.於Jacobs v. Crédit Lyonnais中，即認為於事實上用以推定準據法的好證據為：「根據常識、商業便利性、及國際間之禮誼。[594]」又因尋找當事人「真正意思」（「actual intentions」）之困難，故Lord Wright於Mount Albert Borough Council v. Australasian Temperance and General Mutual Life Assurance Society中如此論述：「去替當事人決定什麼是適當法，亦即是做為正當及合理的人，他們應會有意思的如果當他們於訂約時他們曾經去想過這個問題的話。[595]」如恩師Prof. Graveson所述，Bowen L.J.早於Jacobs v. Crédit Lyonnais中已確認法院的第一責任，就是由案件的情形與主體去辨別當事人於契約中之意思。而當事人沒有明示選法時，法院必須替他們決定準據法。「一世紀前我們的法官於此種情形，是基於當事人之協議所引起的事實的推論來尋找當事人之意思。在較近的時間這個程序是以合理性這個傳統判例法名詞而被表達—在這種情形下合理的商人會選擇什麼法律？—而重心亦某些程度上由偏向一個或其他法律的個別推定而走向基於所有事實而來合理性的一般考量。於當事人沒有明示其意思時，最近的方法是，該交易與那個法律制度有著最密切與真實的關連？[596]」

---

[593] "The general Rule established ex comitate, and Jure Gentium is, that the Place where the Contract is made, and not where the Action is brought, is to be considered, in expounding and enforcing the Contract. But this Rule admits of an Exception, where the Parties (at the time of making the Contract) had a View to a different Kingdom." 1 W.Bl. 234, 257, 258, 259.

[594] "based upon common sense, business convenience, and upon the comity of nations". (1884) 12 Q.B.D. 589; Cases, 274.

[595] "to determine for the parties what is the proper law which, as just and reasonable persons, they ought to have intended if they had thought about the question when they made the contract" [1938] A.C. 224, 240; The Assunzione [1974] P. 150, 175, 179, Singleton L.J..

[596] R.H. Graveson, Conflict of Laws, 7th ed., p. 413, "In Jacobs v. Crédit Lyonnais Bowen L.J. affirmed the principle that the first duty of the court was to try to ascertain from the contract itself the intention of the parties, read by the light of the subject-matter and the surrounding circumstances. Where the parties fail to express their choice of the law to govern their contract, the court must try to determine the proper law for them. A century ago our judges in such circumstances were searching for the intention of the parties on the basis of presumptions raised by the facts of their agreement. In more recent times the process has been expressed in traditional common law terms of reasonableness – what law would reasonable business men have chosen in the circumstances? – and the emphasis has moved to some extent away from particular presumptions in favour of one law or another towards a general consideration of reasonable-

　　所謂「常識與商業便利性」、「正當及合理的人」、及「基於所有事實而來合理性的一般考量」，這與個人前述契約法應以合理性及誠信原則為基礎似乎一致。選法條款或應適用準據法之問題，本就為契約問題之一部分，故於混亂而無穩定之方法下，以契約法的共同核心基本原則合理性及誠信原則為基礎是很自然而「合理」的作法。無論是否透過「最密切且真實關連」或以關連點為依據之「推定」程序，合理性及誠信原則自然是尋找準據法之基礎。而且更有趣的是如前述合理性是一種偏向客觀的標準，而誠信原則是一種較偏向主觀的標準，如果於一般契約法上英美法之合理性及大陸法之誠信原則可以水乳交融般的互為引用相互支援[597]，個人實在想像不出主觀說與客觀說不能於選法規則上相互扶持彼此互補？

　　合理性及誠信原則不但是整個契約法引以為基礎之基本原則，更是所有契約法於適用上用以對抗程序上及實體上之不公平而以維持個案正義的警察原則。於如果不能直接適用實體契約法原則以作為所有契約上爭點之依據之情形下，沒有理由選法規則之適用（包括主觀及客觀說）不能以合理性及誠信原則為最根本的基礎之基本原則及警察原則。

二十、實體政策之全球化

　　有趣的是美國ALI Complex Litigation Proposal的6.01條（侵權）及6.02與6.03條（契約）於選法規則強調法律適用上之重大衝突及相關連州政策之促進，及大陸法的羅馬公約及規則的強調強行法規，這些都是強調所牽連國家的實體法之規則。如果美國法律協會（ALI）的較近建議及歐盟的羅馬公約及規則I皆不約而同的強調實體法之適用及其政策內容，那麼或許很明顯的結論便應該是一於近代人類文明的發展上，國際私法科學目前的進化階段是以實體法之政策為中心。

---

ness on the basis of all the facts. The latest formulation in the absence of expression of intention by the parties is, with which system of law did the transaction have its closest and most real connection?"

[597] 如歐盟契約法原則1:302條以誠信原則來解釋合理性，而U.C.C.1-302條將誠信與合理並列，1-201(b)(20)條以合理性來解釋誠信原則。

　　更有趣的是於ALI 6.01條（侵權）及6.02與6.03條（契約）之建議中，有關確認法律適用之重大衝突及某一州政策的促進的程序，於其規定中經常這種確認的程序是優先於其他選法規則的適用程序—亦即實體法政策的確認順序是往往優先於其他選法規則適用之順序。而法國人所謂的「即刻適用法」或羅馬公約與規則的強行法，亦通常是超越當事人之協議或應適用準據法之規定的。故而大陸法之即刻適用法或強行法於確認及適用之順序上，亦是往往超越其他選法規則之適用順序。故而有趣的巧合是不但美國ALI與歐盟皆「極度」的強調所牽連國家的實體法政策，並且不約而同的皆認為實體法政策經常是超越其他選法規則之適用順序的。這種方法論難道不是全世界目前國際私法科學的主流共同核心價值法學方法論？更具體的說—難道實體法方法論不是目前全世界國際私法的主流核心方法論？

　　如果ALI於政策分析的建議與大陸法的「直接適用法」及「強行法」有何重大不同之處，那麼應是ALI的「政策」與大陸法的「直接適用法」及「強行法」於強度上之不同。「直接適用法」及「強行法」是通常與英美法的「超越性考量」及「基本政策」相對，而非與一般性之政策相提並論的。通常必須為「重大的」、「基本的」政策，才能構成「直接適用法」與「強行法」，亦必須具備這種要件才能超越當事人之協議及應適用準據法之規定。ALI只是規定法律適用之「重大衝突」與州「政策」的被促進，並未規定或強調該些法律或政策必須為「重大的」或「基本的」，這是與大陸法的歐盟不同之處。

　　ALI Complex Litigation Proposal 6.01、6.02、及6.03條之「政策」與其原有第2新編187(2)(b)條之「基本政策」不同，其指的應是一般實體法上之政策。而如前所述個人認為「強行法」是個可疑的觀念，每個被通過的法律都是該國之基本政策，都是應被執行的「強行法」。故而強行法如果存在的話，它幾乎是無所不在。重點並非在確認該法律是否為「強行法」或「基本政策」，而是在確認該法律於個案中被適用的程度及範圍。個人認為ALI Complex Litigation Proposal似乎證實了個人的觀點，而羅

馬公約與規則似乎應對其於「強行法」的態度加以修正。

　　ALI Complex Litigation Proposal於契約之選法規則上一開始即擺明完全以契約法之實體政策為核心考量，6.02(a)規定：「於依3.01條被集中或依5.01條被移轉之訴訟中，當事人所主張適用之法律是有著重大衝突時，當事人有關契約請求之權利、義務、及抗辯，應依當事人於契約中所指定之法律，除非法院認定：(1)依6.03條本應適用之州法之規定，由於詐欺、脅迫、不當影響、或錯誤，該選法條款為無效，或(2)依6.03條本應適用之州法律，當事人所選定之法律是與其基本規定的目的有著重大的衝突。[598]」故而與羅馬公約與規則不同的，於錯誤、詐欺、及脅迫等有關選法條款之存在與效力上，其並不以當事人所選定之法律為依據。有關錯誤、詐欺、及脅迫等與條款之存在與效力上之問題，如2004 UNIDROIT Principles 3.19條一般，是通常被視為強行法規而不能被當事人所違背，這都是個人於本文所一再重複強調之重點—亦即或許於今日法學之注重實體法政策下（強行法、基本政策、及超越性考量），州利益、最重要關連、及傳統的區域選擇法規（或他們的混合適用）的適用性已經嚴重而有效的被限制。

　　另外有趣的是6.02(a)條中強調的是應適用法律之政策，而於第2新編187(2)(b)條及U.C.C.1-301(f)條中亦規定原應適用法律之基本政策不得被違背。但是第2新編187條之commentg卻說明：「法院應適用自己之法律原則，以決定一個既存之政策是否符合本規則之範圍而屬於基本政策。」而U.C.C. 1-301條之comment 9亦說法院地之基本政策不但可以決定契約

---

[598] § 6.02 Mass Contracts: Law Chosen by the Parties

　　(a) In actions consolidated under § 3.01 or removed under § 5.01, in which the parties assert the application of laws that are in material conflict, the rights, liabilities, and defenses of the parties with respect to a contract claim shall be governed by the law designated by the parties in the contract, unless the court finds either

　　　(1) that the clause is invalid for reasons of misinterpretation, duress, undue influence or mistake, as defined under state law that otherwise would be applicable under § 6.03, or

　　　(2) that the law chosen by the parties is in material conflict with fundamental regulatory objectives of the state law that otherwise would be applicable under § 6.03.

之效力上之一些問題，並且有時可以超越當事人所指定之法律及原應適用之法律。羅馬公約7(1)條規定密切關連國家之強行法得被遵守，而公約7(2)條及規則 I 9(2)條規定法院地之強行法得為超越性之適用。故而雖然毫無疑問的美國與歐盟皆再三的強調實體法政策的重要性，但是這個「新領域」似乎仍充滿不確定之因素。究竟應以那一個國家之實體法為依據？一定需要「基本政策」或「強行法」才能被具有超越性考量，一般的法律或政策不行嗎？什麼是「基本政策」或「強行法」？於「基本政策」或「強行法」的適用上法院是否具有裁量權？正如法國於「即刻適用法」上之爭執，個人相信美國及歐盟對「基本政策」及「強行法」亦無法給予明確的答案。正如「強行法」本身就是個可疑的觀念，以上的問題都是不存在的假議題。無論贊同或反對，現今歐盟契約法原則及2004 UNIDROIT Principles的存在，代表著我們人類文明於契約法或商業契約法共同核心基本政策存在之事實。歐盟契約法委員闡述：「本聯盟之特點是有許多不同的法律制度存在，欲適用於整個聯盟之一般性原則必須被建立在一個具有創造性之過程，其目的便是盡可能的在確認所有會員國契約法的共同核心，及於這個共同核心的基礎上去創造一個可行的制度。」[599]「本原則主要益處之一便是透過設計來協調他們不同的法律哲學的規定，以提供大陸法及英美法之間的橋樑。」[600]

　　與其嘗試著解開上述大陸法「強行法」及美國法「基本政策」上無解之謎題，倒不如開門見山的以這些國際性的契約法原則為依據。因為這些國際性的契約法（或商業契約法）原則於許多方面是事實上英美法與大陸

---

[599] 見the Commission of European Contract Law, Principles of European Contract Law, edited by Ole lando and Hugh Beale (2000), Introduction (5), "In the Union, which is characterized by the existence of a number of divergent legal system, general principles applicable across the Union as a whole must be established by a more creative process whose purpose is to identify, so far as possible, the common core of the contract law of all the Member States of the Union and on the basis of this common core to create a workable system."

[600] 同上，Introduction (1)(E), "one of the major benefits offered by the Principles is to provide a bridge between the civil law and the common law by providing rules designed to reconcile their differing legal philosophies."

法之共同核心，亦是共同的政策。「強行法」與「基本政策」不但他們本身就已創造出甚多無解之問題，更雪上加霜的是這些可疑的「強行法」及「基本政策」經常必須透過各國不同之選法規則才會被加以適用，故而近年來國際私法於這方面的發展或許可以如此的綜合描述：令人迷惑的「強行法」及「基本政策」，加上令人迷惑的選法規則。羅馬公約第7條的命運應就是上述說法的最佳證明。個人於此再次重申─既然「基本政策」及「強行法」的基本目的都是在執行實體法之政策，那麼就應該拋棄「利益說」、「最重要關連說」、及「傳統的區域選法規則」（如假設推定準據法）等選法規則，正本清源的以所牽連的實體法共同核心為依據。事實上大陸之採納CISG就是採納全球化法學之實體法共同核心之表徵。

　　但是如個人年輕時所說：「很不幸的是，法律發展總是尾隨社會發展，以緩慢腳步前進，並且常常慢一拍。而社會發展並非永遠能給我們，對其他態樣中的主要價值強烈且充分的信心。[601]」然而時間透過歐盟契約法委員會給予個人一個答案：「本委員會因此抗拒嘗試去涵蓋每個個別情形最後定案之誘惑，因為這會造成過份的特定及細節，並且會限制歐盟契約法將來的發展。因此1：106條規定本原則應依他們的目的而被解釋，並且未被明白規定的爭點應儘量依他們引為基礎的想法去解決，這對本原則開創性的功能而言是有著基本上的重要性。[602]」這個1：106條之規定亦為CISG（1980）7條及2004 UNIDROIT Principles1.6條所規定，故而這個規定為舉世契約法（或商業契約法）之主流共同核心價值應該是很難反駁的。而歐盟契約法原則1：106(1)條歸定「誠信及公平交易」應被引

---

[601] 陳隆修，《美國國際私法新理論》，台北，五南圖書公司，民國76年1月，初版，117頁。

[602] Lando and Beale, Introduction (6), The principles of European Contract Law are a set of general rules which are designed to provide maximum flexibility and thus to accommodate future developments in legal thinking in the field of contract law. The Commission therefore resisted the temptation to seek to cover every particular eventuality, which would lead to excessive detail and specificity and inhibit the future development of European contract law. Thus Article 1:106, which provides that the Principles are to be interpreted in accordance with their purposes and that issues not expressly settled by them are so far as possible to be settled in accordance with the ideas underlying them, is of fundamental importance to the creative function of the Principles.

為該原則之解釋基礎，CISG 7(1)條亦同樣規定「誠信原則」應被引為公約之解釋基礎，2004 UNIDROIT Principles的相對條款1.6雖未規定，但其緊接條款1.7條則亦規定「誠信及公平交易」於國際貿易上的必須被遵守。故而「誠信原則」為全世界契約法之主流共同核心價值亦應該是無法被反駁的。同樣的如前述個人主張這些1：106(2)條、7(2)條、及1.6(2)條的所謂該些原則及公約「引以為基礎的基本原則」即為「誠信原則」及「合理性」，亦由於「誠信原則」及「合理性」充斥在這些公約及原則自己之條款中，故應是很難加以反駁的。

故而在美國ALI Complex Litigation Proposal的政策分析及歐盟強行法之帶領下，國際私法以所牽連實體法政策為超越性之考量已是一個沒有被正名的事實。於這個現代法學進展的潮流中，州利益、最重要關連、及傳統的區域選法規則仍然莫名其妙的被供奉著，但是他們的實際功能已被陽奉陰違的限制著，則是個於美國及歐盟皆不爭的事實。故而英國於契約法上在傳統區域選法理論上主觀說及客觀說之世紀爭論或許已不是那麼的重要。

如前述英國之適當法理論於傳統理論上是應有三步驟的，而這個明示、默示、及推定準據法之三步驟亦為羅馬公約及規則3、4條所採納。Dicey and Morris如此說明[603]：「於第2個測試中為了確認當事人真正的意思，案件周遭之事實會被加以考慮，亦即如若於其時他們若有被問及時他們所會給予的答案；於第3步驟，周遭的事實是被考慮來客觀的決定，該交易與那個法律制度有著最密切及最真實的關連，而且並不是在決定當事人之意思，這個過程是有關法律的適用，而非法律的解釋過程。[604]」

---

[603] Dicey and Morris, the Conflict of laws, 14th ed., p. 1540, "In the second test the surrounding circumstances were considered in order to ascertain the parties' actual intention, in the sense of what they would have said if asked at the time; at the third stage, the surrounding circumstances were considered to determine, objectively and irrespective of the parties' intention, with which system of law the transaction had its closest and most real connection, and that process involved the application of a rule of law, not a process of construction."

[604] *The Komminos S* [1991] 1 Lloyd's Rep. 370, 374 (CA), per Bingham L.J.

客觀說不但早期被引為推定當事人之意思[605]（「objective presumed intention」），於當事人沒有默示意思時較近亦被引為第3步驟中確認最密切及真實關連準據法之依據[606]。故如前述Dicey and Morris即一針見血的說出國王新衣的真相：「但於實際上相同的結果可經由第2及第3步驟之適用而被達成，而且法院經常由第1步驟直接跳到第3步驟。這個最主要是因為默示意思之標準與密切關連之標準彼此相互融合之故，亦是因為於客觀密切關連標準被完全的建立之前，默示意思之標準於事實上是一種客觀之標準，它並不是被設計來引出真正之意思而是附加一種從未形成的意思。[607]」故而個人於前文即主張應如許多美國判例法一般，將第2與第3步驟合為一個步驟。

　　個人之所以主張於當事人未有明示意思時，即應將第2步驟的確認默示之意思與第3步驟的尋找最密切且真實關連的第3步驟合而為一，以確認應適用之法律，主要並非基於第2與第3步驟於法律邏輯上之模糊與混亂，亦非完全仿效美國之許多判例法。最主要是在於美國注重政策之衝突及基本政策，與歐盟的強調強行法之適用下，人類文明於現代國際私法的趨勢是逐漸縮小選法規則的適用範圍，而偏向實體政策上之強行適用。有關契約成立、存在、效力、履行、及其他一些基本契約上之事項，經常被

---

[605] *Lloyd v Guibert* (1865) L.R. 1 Q.B. 115; *PO & SS Co v Shand* (1865) 3 Moo. P.C. (NS) 272; *Re Missouri Steamship Co* (1889) 42 Ch.D. 321; *R. v International Trustee, etc.* [1937] A.C. 500; *Mount Albert Borough Council v Australasian, etc., Assurance Building society Ltd* [1938] A.C. 224 (PC); *Kahler v Midland Bank* [1950] A.C. 24; *The Metamorphosis* [1953] 1 W.l.R. 543; *The Assunzione* [1954] P. 150 (CA).

[606] *Amin Rasheed Shipping Corp v Kuwait Insurance Co* [1984] A.C. 50, 61, *per Lord Diplock; Whitworth Street Estates (Manchester) Ltd v James Miller and Partners Ltd* [1970] A.C. 583, 611, *per Viscount Dihorne; Coast Lines Ltd v Hudig & Veder Chartering NV* [1972] 2 Q.B. 34, 46, *per Megaw L.J.; Akai Pty Ltd v People's Insurance Co Ltd* (1996) 188 C.L.R. 418, 440-442.

[607] Dicey and Morris, p. 1540, "But in practice the same result could be reached by the application of the second or third tests, and frequently the courts moved straight from the first stage to the third stage. This was largely because the tests of inferred intention and close connection merged into each other, and because before the objective close connection test became fully established the test of inferred intention was in truth an objective test designed not to elicit actual intention but to impute an intention which had not been formed." 另外又述說第2及第3步驟之界限經常是模糊的："But the line between the search for the inferred intention and the search for the system of law with which the contract had its closest and most real connection was a fine one which was frequently blurred." p. 1539.

2004 UNIDROIT Principles、歐盟契約法原則、及各國之契約法視為基本政策或強行法。即使當事人自主條款亦必須於符合這些契約法之基本政策範圍內才能被加以適用，故而當事人默示意思及最密切及真實關連法律之確認程序，自然更應受限於這些基本政策。而又如前述契約法上所謂強行法及基本政策是幾乎無所不在的，近年來歐盟契約法原則及2004 UNIDROIT Principles的出現，或許代表著人類文明於此些方面共同核心基本政策的產生。

　　英國自18世紀以來判例法於國際私法之發展，或許曾經睥睨全球，有著莫大貢獻，對羅馬公約與規則亦有著重大的影響，但如Dicey and Morris所說：「正如其他國際私法的制度，英國衝突法的規則應配合國際貿易於技術上之改變。[608]」三十年前個人如此寫著：「所有的人都開豐田汽車，搭乘波音飛機，戴著瑞士手錶，穿著韓國襯衫，作者南非的黃金夢，關心中東石油的價格。[609]」如果真正有什麼重大的改變，可能現在要加上：大家都吃美國麥當勞。

　　人類科技文明的進展，使得法律全球化已變為一個既已存在之事

---

[608] "The law prior to the 1990 Act had undergone a process of continuous development and refinement since the 18th century, influenced at first by Huber and Story and subsequently Westlake, and then in the 20th century by Dicey, and latterly by Cheshire. Like other systems of the conflict of laws, the English rules of the conflict of laws had to respond to changes in the techniques of international trade." 而較為權威的判例法為 *Robinson v Bland* (1760) 2 Burr. 1077; *Allen v Kemble* (1848) 6 Moo. P.C. 314; *Lloyd v Guibert* (1865) L.R. 1 Q.B. 115; *PO & SS Co v Shand* (1865) 3 Moo. P.C. (N.S.) 272; *Chartered Mercantile Bank of India v Netherlands Co* (1883) 10 Q.B.D. 521 (CA); *Jacobs v Crédit Lyonnais* (1884) 12 Q.B.D. 589 (CA); *Re Missouri Steamship Co* (1889) 42 Ch.D. 321 (CA); *Chatenay v Brazilian Submarine Telegraph Co* [1891] 1 Q.B. 79 (CA); *Hamlyn v Talisker Distillery* [1894] A.C. 202; *The Industrie* [1894] P. 58 (CA); *Supurier v La Cloche* [1902] A.C. 446 (PC); *NV Kwik Hoo Tong Handel Maatschappij v james Finlay & Co* [1927] A.C. 604; *R.v International Trustee, etc.* [1937] A.C. 500; *Mount Albert Borough Council v Australasian, etc., Assurance Building Society Ltd* [1938] A.C. 224 (PC); *Vita Food Products Inc v Unus Shipping Co Ltd* [1939] A.C. 277 (PC); *Kahler v Midland Bank Ltd* [1950] A.C. 24; *Bonython v Commonwealth of Australia* [1951] A.C. 201 (PC); *The Assunzione* [1954] P. 150 (CA); *Re Helbert Wagg & Co Ltd* [1956] Ch. 323; *Re United Railways of Havana, etc. Warehouses Ltd* [1960] Ch. 52(CA), affirmed [1961] A.C. 1007; *Whitworth Street Estates (Manchester) Ltd v James Miller and Partners Ltd* [1970] A.C. 583; *Compagnie Tunisienne de Navigation SA v Compagnie d'Armement Maritime SA* [1971] A.C. 572; *Coast Linces Ltd v Hudig & Veder Chartering NV* [1972] 2 Q.B. 34 (CA); *Amin Rasheed Shipping Corp v Kuwait Insurance Co* [1984] A.C. 50. Dicey and Morris, p. 1538.

[609] 陳隆修，《美國國際私法新理論》，台北，五南圖書公司，民國76年1月，初版，28頁。

實。現代國際私法的現實是一在本著法律全球化的事實上，去確認最合適
全球化的法律。傳統的國際私法的重點是在調和不同法律制度間的衝突，
但是於法律全球化的潮流下，所應注重的是去確認引領全世界全球化的法
律。於全球化的現實世界中，仍舊本著傳統衝突法選法規則的作風企圖去
協調不同法制間的衝突，是落伍而不切實際的作法。英國判例法在契約選
法規則所創的主觀說、客觀說、及準據法確認的三步驟，對人類文明的進
展有著輝煌的貢獻，但已是落伍的區域選法規則，更重要的是他們與法律
全球化的需求不合。正如羅馬公約與規則對強行法的不知所措，他們面
對ALI Complex Litigation Proposal的強調實體政策之衝突與促進及歐盟
的強行法概念亦不知所措。面對新時代鋪天蓋地席捲而來的國際私法實
體法化新浪潮，只能墨守成規的遵從舊時代的法律邏輯。當美國及歐盟
跌跌撞撞的各自瞎子摸像般的探索著實體法的新方法論時，英國這些傳
統技巧不但不能跟上潮流，更糟糕的是他們面對歐盟契約法原則及2004
UNIDROIT Principles等已崛起的世界性契約法共同核心政策的既成事
實，仍固執的抱殘守缺與這些新崛起的人類文明的共同核心劃清界線。

　　全球化的趨勢既已充斥在全世界生活中的每一層次，法律的全球化
自然是順理成章的現象。契約法會率先成為法律全球化的標竿自然是因
為商業利益的驅動使然。但事實上早再三十多年前個人便已體認全世界
法律於許多方面早已有著「共同核心」之存在[610]，於人類文明走向全球化
之趨勢中，親屬、繼承、侵權、訴訟程序、刑法、憲法、及人權法等亦有
著全球化的共同核心基本政策及強行法之存在。**歐盟契約法原則及2004
UNIDROIT Principles的正式產生（無論他們尚有多大的改進空間），
或許代表著一個時代的正式揭幕：偏向協調、整合法律制度間之衝突的國
際私法選法理論應走入歷史的時光隧道，新時代的國際私法應偏向確認、
引領法律實體上之全球化**[611]。

---

[610] 陳隆修，《美國國際私法新理論》，台北，五南圖書公司，民國76年1月，初版，17-20頁。
[611] 實體法的全球化固然於講求快速、便捷的現代化社會中，能達成法律穩定性、判決一致性、及
　　個案正義較大的保障性，但個人三十年前就如此寫著：「從作者開始在英國及美國法學院研讀

　　羅馬公約及規則 I 之解讀及評價，皆必須以全球化下之實體法共同核心的標準為依據。非常遺憾的，他們大致上是本著英國傳統上適當法的規則，而未達到這個實體政策全球化之標準。公約第4條第1項規定「於沒有依第3條之規定而選法之情形下，契約應依關係最密切國家之法律。但於例外之情形下，契約可分割部分與其他國家有著更密切關連，得以該其他國家之法律為依據。」第2項規定「於本條第5項之規定下，與契約有著最密切關連的國家應被推定為，執行契約特徵之履行之一方當事人於訂約時其慣居地，或於法人或非法人團體之情形，其總公司所在地。但是若契約是該當事人在其營業或專業下而訂，則該國應為其主要營業地所在地國或，依契約之條款該履行是被執行於非主要營業地之營業地，該營業地之所在即為該國之所在。」第3項規定，即使於本條第2項之規定下，如若契約之標的（主體）為不動產之權利或使用不動產之權利，與契約有著最密切關連之國家應被推定為不動產所在地國。第4項規定，貨物運送契約應不屬於第2項推定之範圍。於此種契約如若於契約訂定時，運送人之主要營業地國家同時是裝載地或卸貨地或託運人主要營業地之國家，契約應被推定為與該國有最密切關連。於適用本項時，單一航次之傭船契約及主要目的為運送貨物之其他契約，應被視為貨物運送契約。第5項規定「如果特徵性履行不能被決定，第2項即不能適用，並且如果看起來契約整體之情形是與其他國家有著密切之關連，第2、3、及4項之推定應不被遵守。[612]」

具有彈性且不斷改變的習慣法制度起，就經常懷疑為什麼傳統的中國法律制度，在近兩千前年間並沒有非常重大的改變。最後才明瞭，是因為該項制度對當時農業社會而言，已達到近乎完美的地步。整個社會和儒家的價值觀，兩千年來並沒有太大的出入，法律制度自然不須有太大的改變。……現代工業社會中，總有一些新的社會問題不斷發生。我們不應該和其他美國現代法律衝突理論家一樣，有相同的美妙夢想，而認為法律衝突法有一天能完全確定。一個社會變得過於完善致使法律毋庸改變，一如兩千年來中國的經驗所顯示，並不是一件可喜的事。」陳隆修，《美國國際私法新理論》，台北，五南圖書公司，民國76年1月，初版，265～268頁。我們的後代子孫或許應該謹記，喪失法律多元化的社會，對整個社會長久的發展是絕對不利的。

[612] Article 4

Applicable law in the absence of choice

1. To the extent that the law applicable to the contract has not been chosen in accordance with Article 3, the contract shall be governed by the law of the country with which it is most closely connected.

　　這個第4條的規定是本著傳統客觀說的基礎而發展的，自然是屬於過時的區域選法規則的屬性。在近10年來契約法於實體政策上之全球化趨於公開化、明朗化後，這些傳統的區域選法規則之適用範圍可能在個案上依法院之偏好，隨時隨地皆可能被以基本政策或強行法之超越性考量而被縮限。我們現在所討論的是夕陽法學方法論中的夕陽法規，我們的注意力事實上是應放在改進及擴大歐盟契約法原則及2004 UNIDROIT Principles的國際適用範圍上。而如前述大陸早已在國際及國內買賣契約上採用CISG。

　　但若純粹依傳統的區域選法規則而言，第4條的客觀推定（「presumtion」）準據法是屬於英國法上之第3步驟。但如前述傳統英國判例法上對第2步驟（默示準據法）與第3步驟（客觀上推定準據法）並不加以清楚的切割—這是即使美國法院亦無法掌握的高超判例法之運用。亦即英國判例法上主觀或客觀上認定默示準據法之第2步驟是經常與客觀推定準

Nevertheless, a severable part of the contract which has a closer connection with another country may by way of exception be governed by the law of that other country.

2. Subject to the provisions of paragraph 5 of this Article, it shall be presumed that the contract is most closely connected with the country where the party who is to effect the performance which is characteristic of the contract has, at the time of conclusion of the contract, his habitual residence, or, in the case of a body corporate or unincorporate, its central administration. However, if the contract is entered into in the course of that party's trade or profession, that country shall be the country in which the principal place of business is situated or, where under the terms of the contract the performance is to be effected through a place of business other than the principal place of business, the country in which that other place of business is situated.

3. Notwithstanding the provisions of paragraph 2 of this Article, to the extent that the subject matter of the contract is a right in immovable property or a right to use immovable property it shall be presumed that the contract is most closely connected with the country where the immovable property is situated.

4. A contract for the carriage of goods shall not be subject to the presumption in paragraph 2. In such a contract if the country in which , at the time the contract is concluded, the carrier has his principal place of business is also the country in which the place of loading or the place of discharge or principal place of business of the consignor is situated, it shall be presumed that the contract is most closely connected with that country. In applying this paragraph single voyage charter-parties and other contracts the main purpose of which is the carriage of goods shall be treated as contracts for the carriage of goods.

5. Paragraph 2 shall not apply if the characteristic performance cannot be determined, and the presumptions in paragraph 2. 3 and 4 shall be disregarded if it appears from the circumstances as a whole that the contract is more closely connected with another country.

據法之第3步驟是混合在一起的。羅馬公約及規則I[613]的第4條明顯的違反英國判例法自18世紀以來歷經時間淬鍊的貿易法實務規則，這是歐盟自大與疏忽的一大錯誤。這是僵硬的大陸法仿效靈活的英美法的過程中，東施效顰的一個典型狀況。

　　Cheshire and North注意到第4條於邏輯上之困擾：「但是第4條之方法引起了一個剛開始就有的困難，而截至目前皆尚未被解決。目前並不清楚它是意圖三、二或甚至是一個步驟的過程。第4條之規定所展現的次序是指向三個步驟的程序。但是於Giuliano and Lagarde的報告中，至少於

---

[613] Article 4

Applicable law in the absence of choice

1. To the extent that the law applicable to the contract has not been chosen in accordance with Article 3 and without prejudice to Article 5 to 8, the law governing the contract shall be determined as follows:
   (a) a contract for the sale of goods shall be governed by the law of the country where the seller has his habitual residence;
   (b) a contract for the provision of services shall be governed by the law of the country where the service provider has his habitual residence;
   (c) a contract relating to a right in rem in immovable property or to a tenancy of immovable property shall be governed by the law of the country where the property is situated;
   (d) notwithstanding point (c), a tenancy of immovable property concluded for temporary private use for a period of no more than six consecutive months shall governed by the law of the country where the landlord has his habitual residence, provided that the tenant is a natural person and has his habitual residence in the same country;
   (e) a franchise contract shall be governed by the law of the country where the franchisee has his habitual residence;
   (f) a distribution contract shall be governed by the law of the country where the distributor has his habitual residence;
   (g) a contract for the sale of goods by auction shall be governed by the law of the country where the auction takes place, if such a place can be determined;
   (h) a contract concluded within a multilateral system which brings together or facilitates the bringing together of multiple third-party buying and selling interests in financial instruments, as defined by Article 4(1), point (17) of Directive 2004/39/EC, in accordance with non-discretionary rules and governed by a single law, shall be governed by that law.
2. Where the contract is not covered by paragraph 1 or where the elements of the contract would be covered by more than one of points (a) to (h) of paragraph 1, the contract shall be governed by the law of the country where the party required to effect the characteristic performance of the contract has his habitual residence.
3. Where it is clear from all the circumstances of the case that the contract is manifestly more closely connected with a country other than that indicated in paragraph 1 or 2, the law of that other country shall apply.
4. Where the law applicable cannot be determined pursuant to paragraph 1 or 2, the contract shall be governed by the law of the country with which it is most closely connected.

許多案件中，是預見只有一個步驟之程序，亦即皆以推定為開始及結束。這個看法是受到大陸法之判例所支持。但對這點可加以反對的是，除非首先採用最密切關連標準，否則很難見到法院如何可以決定是否合適去否定這個推定。這即是建議兩個步驟之程序，首先由推定開始，但是接著必須去考慮最密切關連標準，以便決定是否應對推定加以否認。這是英國判例法所支持的看法。當考慮到是否容易去取代這種一般推定的問題時，通常是一個或兩個步驟的程序的問題變得特別重要。[614]」但是荷蘭最高法院於Société Nouvelle des Papeteries de l'Aa[615]案中決定，即使契約特徵性履行之人之履行地及契約之很多關連點皆位於法國，而荷蘭與契約之關連點只是契約特徵性履行之人之營業地為荷蘭，荷蘭法仍被推定為準據法，而拒絕適用4(5)條。相對的於英國在Bank of Baroda v Vysya Bank[616]中Mance J.卻於一個關於信用狀之案件中採用4(5)條。如果根據4(2)條，原告確認銀行與受益人間之契約應依英國法，而被告發行銀行與受益人間之契約應依印度法。適用4(5)條之結果為後者契約亦適用英國法。Mance J認為這幾個獨立契約不應以不同之法律為依據，否則準據法會依受益人決定請求之銀行而不同。荷蘭法院與英國法院不同之處為Cheshire and North說明如下：「當契約中應履行特徵性履行之人之營業地與契約履行

---

[614] PM North, JJ Fawcett, Cheshire and North's Private International Law, 13th ed., p. 565, " Nonetheless, the scheme of Article 4 raise an initial dilemma, which is as yet unresolved. It is not clear whether what is intended is a three, two or even one stage process. The sequence in which the provisions are set out in Article 4 points to a three stage processs. However, the Giuliano and Lagarde Report envisages, at least in many cases, a one stage process which starts and finishes with the presumptions. This view is supported by Continental case law. Against this, it is hard to see how a court can decide whether it is appropriate to rebut a presumption unless it has first applied closest connection test. This would suggest a two stage process, which starts with a presumption, but then moves on necessarily to consider the closet connection test in order to see whether this presumption can be rebutted. This view is supported by English case law. The question of whether it is normally a one stage or two stage process becomes particularly important when it comes to the question of how easy it is to displace the general presumption." 同樣的論述又於14thed.,p.708中再次被確認。

[615] Société Nouvelle des Papeteries de l'Aa v Machinefabriek BOA 25 September, NJ (1992) No 750, RvdW (1992) No 207. 又見T.H.D. Struycken, Some Dutsh Judicial Reflections on the Rome Convention, Art. 4(5), 6 L.M.C.L.Q. 18 (1996).

[616] [1994] 2 Lloyd's Rep 87.

地不同時，兩個案件所採的方法是非常不同的。[617]」於Crédit Lyonnais v New Hampshire Insurance Co中，英國法院認為4(5)條：「使得推定的效果正式的變得非常薄弱[618]」，這與大陸法的荷蘭法院的態度是不同的[619]。英國法院認為於任何案件之情形中，如果推定是不合適的即應被取代，因此支持第4條應有兩步驟之適用。法院必須先適用最密切關連標準，然後才能衡量這些關連是否得以取代推定。相對的荷蘭法院認為推定是很重要的，僅能於例外案件中才能被否定。第4(2)條才是主條文，而不是4(1)條，除非其關連點並無真正的意義否則被推定程序所確認之法律應被適用。這種方法是支持第4條應是為一個步驟的程序[620]。

---

[617] Cheshire and North, p. 574, "the two cases adopt a very different approach towards the situation where the place of performance differs from the place of business of the party whose performance is characteristic of the contract." 類似的意見又重述於14[th] ed., p.722。

[618] "formally makes the presumption very weak", [1997] 2 Lloyd's Rep 1, 5, CA.

[619] 但是有趣的是歐洲同僚似乎忽略了Giuliano and Lagarde Report中之調查，除了義大利偏向死硬的連繫因素外，所有的國家皆希望能繼續有著一個彈性的制度，以便法官得於個案中依契約之各種因素及案件之情形，去選擇決定性之連繫因素以確認應適用之法律。"The foregoing survey has shown that, with the sole exception of Italy, where the subsidiary law applicable to the contract is determined once and for all by hard-and-fast connecting factors, all the other Community countries have preferred and continue to prefer a more flexible approach, leaving the judge to select the preponderant and decisive connecting factor for determining the law applicable to the contract in each specific case among the various elements of the contract and the circumstances of the case."

[620] Cheshire and North, p. 574, "the presumption is displaced if the court considers that it is not appropriate to apply it in the circumstances of any given case. This supports the two stage view of the process under Article 4. It is hard to see how the judge is to determine whether the presumption is displaced unless, as a matter of course, he has first applied the closest connection test, and weighed the connections so identified against the presumption. In contrast, the Dutch attitude is that the presumption is of great weight and should only be rebutted in exceptional cases, that Article 4(2) is the main rule not Article 4(1), and that the law identified by the presumption prevails unless it has no real significance as a connecting factor. This supports the one stage view of the process under Article 4." 於14thed., p.722，其評述下列蘇格蘭案件如下："The Dutch approach has been rejected by the Court of Appeal in England as being too rigid. However, it has been approved by a majority (Lords CAMERON and MARNOCH) in the First Division of the Court of Session in Scotland in Caledonia Subsea Ltd v Micoperi SRL. The presumption in Article 4(2) was said to be a strong one, which could only be displaced in exceptional cases. Lord President CULLEN disagreed with the Dicey and Morris proposition that the presumption may most easily be rebutted in those cases where the place of performance differs from the place of business of the party whose performance is characteristic of the contract and made the point that, whilst relevant, the place of performance may be only one of a number of factors to be assessed in the exercise of Article 4(5). The place of performance was regarded as playing a subordinate role as a circumstance in fixing the applicable law. Although the contract was performed in Egypt by a characteristic performer with its principal place of business in Scotland, there were distinct connections with Scotland both prior to the conclusion of the contract and during its currency. This was not considered to be an exceptional

英國適當法的原則就是必須具有彈性，故而荷蘭法院這種限制性的觀點是被英國法院所明示拒絕的[621]。但大陸法的蘇格蘭法院卻認同荷蘭法院之作法，於Caledonia Subsea Ltd. V. Micoperi Srl中Lord Marnoch主張第4條的一般性原則：「只有於應執行特徵性履行之當事人之營業地並非為具有真實性意義的關連點之特殊情形之案件中，才應不被適用。[622]」Prof. Fentiman如此陳述：「這個限制性的觀點的理由是，如此可以促成判決之統一，這是1980羅馬公約之公開目標。裁量權是統一性不可避免的敵人。如此的解釋第4條以保障一般性原則的被遵守可以促成這種統一性。[623]」而Lord Marnoch又坦白的陳述：「只有採納這種荷蘭的方法論，上述第4條的目的才能被給予真正與實際的效果，這個目的即為澄清及簡化法律。[624]」Prof. Fentiman對這種限制性的觀點，不以為然的加以評論如下：「這是個令人印象深刻的觀察。法律的穩定性及簡單性須要嚴格的規定去被加以遵守。但這並不表示政策或正義的利益會被達成。它不表示商業的功效會被達成或當事人的期望會被尊重。但這代表著法律會更簡單。[625]」

大陸法與英美法對羅馬公約同一個法條中「最密切關連」的運用與解釋上的不同，自然仍會延續到羅馬規則I第4條上[626]。如同Prof. Feintman

---

case and the presumption in favour of Scotland could not be displaced."

[621] Samcrete Egypt Eng'r & Contractors SAE. V. Eng. Land Rover Exp. Ltd., [2001] EWCA (Civ) 2019, [40]-[43]; Ennstone Prods. Ltd. v. Stanger Ltd., [2002] EWCA (Civ) 916, [13]-[14],[2002] 1 W.L.R. 3059, 3070 (A.C.)(Eng.).

[622] "should be disregarded only if, in the special circumstances of the case, the place of business of the party who is to effect the characteristic performance has no real significance as a connecting factor." [2003] S.C. 70, 79 (Scot.).

[623] "A justification for this restrictive view is that it encourages uniformity to decision, a stated objective of the 1980 Rome Convention. Discretion is the inevitable enemy of uniformity. To interpret article 4 so as to ensure adherence to the general rule promotes such uniformity." Richard Fentiman, Choice of Law in Europe: Uniformity and Integration, 82 Tul. L. Rev. 2021, 2048 (2008).

[624] "It is only by adopting the Dutch approach that real and practical effect can be given to the objective of art[.] 4 referred to above, namely that of clarifying and simplifying the law." [2003] S.C. p. 87.

[625] "This is a striking observation. Legal certainty and simplicity require adherence to strict rules. This does not mean that the interests of policy or justice will be served. It does not mean that commercial efficacy will be served or the expectations of the parties served. But it means that the law will be simpler." Fentiman, 82 Tul. L. Rev. 2021, 2048.

[626] "In the light of Owusu, how might the Court of Justice approach such issues? How would it interpret

所認為國際私法—正如同所有的其他法律部門一般—的基本目的在達成正義的結果。而於契約法部門過去的「政策的利益」，是在促進商業的功效及尊重當事人的期望。但是荷蘭及蘇格蘭法院的重點卻是在法律的統一性及簡化性，這是與所有法律部門（包括國際私法）的基本目的不合的，亦與契約法過去的政策不合的。但是這個基本問題應不只侷限於羅馬公約與規則Ⅰ第4條的運用而已[627]，亦應不是單純的英美法與大陸法之不同而已—個案正義與實體政策的達成會與法律的一致性相衝突，這是區域選法理論

---

in particular article 4 of the Rome I Regulation? Presumably, it has become irrelevant to ask what the objectives of the Regulation are. Certainly, it may be irrelevant to say that the goal of the Regulation should be to ensure commercial efficacy and the expectations of contracting parties. The question is what serves the goal of integration. The answer is uniformity. And if uniformity and certainty are the benchmarks, this favours the strict view that the rule can be displaced only if the presumptively applicable law has no significant connection with the contract." Fentiman, 同上。但是羅馬規則Ⅰ之4(3)條卻不同於公約第4(1)及(5)條及規則Ⅰ之4(4)條，於「最密切關連」之適用上要求需有著「明顯的」密切關連，或許歐盟法院將來會一如往常的更加嚴格限制英國法院彈性裁量權之適用。Cheshire and North's Private International Law, 14thed.,p725,認為需靜待歐盟法院之認定："It is not enough to show that the contract is more closely connected, it has to be 'manifestly' more closely connected. The addition of the word 'manifestly' is doubtless designed to underscore the exceptional nature of this let-out, which appears to be intended to be a narrower one than that under Article 4(5) of the Rome Convention. This could be regarded as being an acceptable compromise which reconciles the needs of certainty and flexibility. Whether the English courts would, in practice, interpret this new let-out more narrowly than the old let-out would remain to be seen. With any flexible let-out, a lack of uniform interpretation in different Member States is likely in the absence of a decision of the Court of Justice.

[627] Peter Hay, From Rule-Orientation to "Approach" in German Conflicts Law The Effect of the 1986 and 1999 Codifications, Fall, 1999 47 Am. J. Comp. L. 633,對德國使用最重要關連標準似乎過度推崇。個人以前於陳隆修、許兆慶、林恩瑋，《台灣財產法暨經濟法研究叢書（十三）—國際私法：選法理論之回顧與展望》，台灣財產法暨經濟法研究協會發行，2007年1月，初版，167、168頁評述如下：「德國1986年新法於契約法上引用羅馬公約，其第28條第5項亦是採納最重要關連說。故而比較法學者Peter Hay認為於契約法上近十年的經驗顯示，德國法院對使用最重要關連說是有節制的。故其認為德國法院於侵權行為上使用第41條最重要關連說應該是有所限制，而不同於美國第二新編的第145條的被使用狀況。德國第41條的使用，應是一種『法規式的取向』（rule-orientation），而不是一種『法學方法的取向』（approach）。德國新法無論第28條(5)項、第41條、及第46條於物權上對最重要關連說的引用，都不是做為一般性通用原則，而是做為特殊例外原則。但與Peter Hay之觀點不同，作者認為立法技術的取向，不見得能完全表達該國對最重要關連說的認同程度，還是應以法院的實務作法為準。英國因為長久以來採納『適當法』理論，故作者認為其有將最重要關連說契約法化，適當法化之趨勢，相對於世界上其他國家，其穩定性是可以適度預期的。個人雖對德國法之精神完全不了解，但基本上仍願相信德國新侵權行為法應會遵循其一貫之穩健、紮實傳統。Peter Hay 號稱德國新法會由『法規式取向』而導致『有原則的彈性』（principled flexibility），故而可預測性及穩定性可增加，作者對此則稍微有所保留。國際契約法為促進世界貿易的發展，故而在尊重當事人訂定契約的意願下，其穩定性是可以預期。相對的在現代科技社會的快速發展下，侵權行為的不可預測性及不穩定性是公認的。將過去十年引用羅馬公約的經驗放在侵權行為上，似乎過份牽強。事實上個人認為英國過去百年來發展適當法的經驗，實為羅馬公約穩定發展的一大助力。」

的原罪。英國同僚之可以大肆撻伐大陸法的適用公約及規則第4條，個人
以為主要是因為二百五十年來判例法的累積，使得適當法理論過去可以兼
顧個案正義與法律之穩定性。但是現今在法律急速的於實體法全球化的浪
潮下，有那個國家（包括英國在內）可以有二百五十年去發展判例法？

　　坦白的說個人以為上述英美法與大陸法於最密切關連適用上之衝
突，都是區域選法規則過去式的茶壺風暴[628]。不限於國際私法的區域選法
規則，個人以為在實體法全球化的趨勢下，事實上包含程序法、刑法、憲
法、及人權法等幾乎所有法學在內，重點應是在確認及引導法律於實體上
全球化之合適性。例如英國契約法上過去的政策是在尊重當事人的期望及
促進商業的功效，這些政策是需要再被檢視的。如前述，於相關契約的成
立、存在、效力、及履行等許多問題是被視為強行政策而超越當事人之期
望[629]與協議的；另外基於資本主義而來的自由放任市場思潮於人類文明到

---

[628] 事實上有些美國與歐洲同僚亦早已體會到羅馬Ⅰ規則所採用的區域選法規則之基本缺點。見
George A. Bermann, Rome I: A Comparative View: it may happen that a legal instrument, in its quest
for certainty and predictability, becomes "over-determined" in content. Of this risk, I would offer two
examples. Article 5(2) of the Rome I Regulation provides that the parties to a contract of carriage may
choose only among five named bodies of law as the law applicable to that contract. This is said to be in
the interest of passenger protection. Yet, as has been pointed out, the Regulation can offer no guarantee
that these bodies of law will, in any give case, actually afford passengers a high level of protection.
又見Francesca Ragno, The Law Applicable to Consumer Contracts under the Rome I Regulation:
As has been pointed in relation to the Rome Convention making applicable only the law of the consumer's country of habitual residence, even though it may provide the consumer with the advantage of being able to rely on the law he is more familiar with, may compromise consumers who live in countries
that do not provide satisfactory consumer protection; all the more so because a judge may not necessarily apply pro-consumer provisions of the law of the forum as per Article 9(2) of the Rome I Regulation,
or of another legal system as per Article 9(3). Doing so would require counting those provisions among
the overriding mandatory provisions, an assumption that cannot be made on the sole basis that their purpose is to protect consumers.載於Rome I Regulation: The Law Applicable to Contractual Obligations
in Europe edited by Franco Ferrari, Stefan Leible, pp. 357及154.
[629] 早期個人亦以「保護當事人的正當期待」為契約之主流價值，並強調所謂「正當」性應排除詐
欺、弱勢交易能力、及附合契約不符誠信原則之情形。陳隆修，《美國國際私法新理論》，
台北，五南圖書公司，民國76年1月，初版7，223、224頁。第2新編187條之comment e亦認為契
約法之主要目的是於保護當事人之正當期待，以便取得穩定性即可預測之結果。
"e. Rationale. Prime objectives of contract law are to protect the justified expectations of the parties and
to make it possible for them to foretell with accuracy what will be their rights and liabilities under the
contract. These objectives may best be attained in multistate transactions by letting the parties choose
the law to govern the validity of the contract and the rights created thereby. In this way, certainty and
predictability of result are most likely to be secured. Giving parties this power of choice is also consistent with the fact that, in contrast to other areas of the law, persons are free within broad limits to deter-

達一個地步後，應被嚴正的加以修正，「商業的功效」應不是21世紀全球化法學的重點，重點應是在抑制及監督商業的貪婪。21世紀法學全球化的重點應是在促進弱勢的正義及監督工業化國家盡力幫助第3世界早日爬上經濟及環保高科技的階梯[630]。

　　個人對羅馬公約及規則I真正良心的建議是：放棄羅馬公約及規則I的區域選法規則，而直接以歐盟契約法原則為依據，並以合理性及誠信原則為該些原則之基礎及警察原則。退一步務實的建議為：如ALI Complex Litigation Proposal一般，於適用選法規則之前先確認所牽連的實體政策是否有重大衝突；另外於適用最密切關連標準時應對實體政策加以考量，而非僅注重於地域性之關連。個人於此再次重述：大陸已經於國際及國內買賣契約上採用CISG。

　　另外有趣的是公約及規則的3(1)條皆允許當事人於契約不同之部分選定不同之準據法（「severability」），公約4(1)條亦於例外情形下允許分割準據法之適用，但規則第4條中或許因為不再重複公約4(1)條之規定，而沒有明示分割準據法之適用。如若拒絕分割之適用，則規則I於此不但與公約不一致，亦與規則I自己的3(1)條不一致。大陸法對英美法習以為

---

mine the nature of their contractual obligations."

[630] 見聯合國2002年高峰會Johannesburg Declaration on Sustainable Development

18. We welcome the focus of the Johannesburg Summit on the indivisibility of human dignity and are resolved, through decisions on targets, timetables and partnerships, to speedily increase access to such basic requirements as clean water, sanitation, adequate shelter, energy, health care, food security and the protection of biodiversity. At the same time, we will work together to help one another gain access to financial resources, benefit from the opening of markets, ensure capacity-building, use modern technology to bring about development and make sure that there is technology transfer, human resource development, education and training to banish underdevelopment forever.

19. We reaffirm our pledge to place particular focus on, and give priority attention. to, the fight against the worldwide conditions that pose severe threats to the sustainable development of our people, which include: chronic hunger; malnutrition; foreign occupation; armed conflict; illicit drug problems; organized crime; corruption; natural disasters; illicit arms trafficking; trafficking in persons; terrorism; intolerance and incitement to racial, ethnic, religious and other hatreds: xenophobia; and endemic, communicable and chronic diseases, in particular HIV/AIDS, malaria and tuberculosis.

故而聯合國宣言已表達第一世界是有著將必要之技術轉至第三世界之義務。歐美現在於智慧財產權及反托辣斯法上對中國人的追殺（見拙作智財法院97重附民1號，收錄於陳隆修、劉仁山、許兆慶合著，《國際私法-程序正義與實體正義》，台北，五南圖書公司，2011年9月，初版1刷。是很嚴重的違反聯合國宣言的強行超越性基本政策與規定。

國際私法所不可分割一部分之分割理論可能還不是十分適應。於英國判例法上契約訂立之準據法不見得皆為契約履行之準據法[631]，但通常單一準據法會處理與其相關之契約上所有問題，如Lord MacDermott所說：「我國之法院不會於沒有理由之下或輕易的於這方面去分割契約。[632]」Giuliano and Lagarde Report如此陳述：「委員會間於此問題之討論，顯示沒有代表團願意鼓勵分割之想法。但大部分之專家認同經由例外之方式，在有關契約而非爭點之方面，契約可分割且獨立之部分，若與其他國家有著更密切之關連（例如，共同投資契約或複數契約），則允許法院去加以分割。[633]」從事國際業務的事務所相信大部分會認同解釋報告在共同投資契約或複數契約之論述。但解釋報告之分割是以本就應為獨立之契約為主，而非以契約中之爭點或個別條款為主，這是奇怪的論述。如前述，有關契約之形式要件、當事人之能力及地位、合法性、及履行等問題，經常不是當事人所合議之準據法所能決定。無論羅馬公約或規則第4條對契約爭點的分割適用是如何的反對，契約爭點（「issue；dispute」）的分割適用是一個無法否認的事實[634]。於實體法全球化之趨勢下，一個契約中不同的爭點去適用不同的實體法規定，更是各國國內實體法已行之多年之事實，例如於有關契約的形式要件、同意、詐欺、脅迫、效力、履行、瑕疵擔

---

[631] Asquith L.J., Frankman v. Anglo-Prague Credit Bank [1949] 1 K.B. 199 p. 206 (reversed sub nom. Zivnostenska Banka National Corporation v. Frankman [1950] A.C. 57).又見陳隆修，《國際私法契約評論》，台北，五南圖書公司，民國75年2月，初版M11-20頁，契約不同部分之不同準據法。

[632] "the courts of this country will not split the contract in this sense readily or without good reason." Kahler v. Midland Bank Ltd. [1950] A.C. 24, 42.

[633] "Discussion of the matter within the Group revealed that no delegation wished to encourage the idea of severability (de'pec,age). However, most of the experts were in favour of allowing the court to effect a severance, by way of exception, for a part of the contract which is independent and separable, in terms of the contract and not of the dispute, where that part has a closer connection with another country (for example, contracts for joint venture, complex contracts)."

[634] 最明顯的例子就是2005年海牙法院選擇公約的管轄條款效力的獨立認定，及有些國家的認定仲裁條款效力的獨立認定。2005年海牙公約3(d)條規定不能以契約無效為理由而主張專屬管轄條款為無效。歐盟已正式簽訂2005年海牙公約，請問歐盟3(d)條難道不是「爭點」或「條款」的可分割性？
又見陳隆修，《國際私法契約評論》，台北，五南圖書公司，民國75年2月，初版，11-20頁有關形式要件、能力、程序（消滅時效、損害金額）、及履行等構成獨立爭點之問題。

保、及撤銷等爭點。

Giuliano and Lagarde Report又說：「為決定與契約有最密切關連之國家，契約訂立後所發生的因素亦是可能被加以考慮。[635]」英國最高法院於Whitworth Street Estates（Manchester）Ltd v James Miller and Partners Ltd中，欲決定於一個標準格式契約中當事人是否有默示準據法（被認為契約之解釋問題），Lord Reid認為於契約訂立後任何當事人所說或所作的事情，不應該被作為解釋契約之依據[636]。判例法之會與公約及規則不同，可能是公約及規則第4條只採用客觀說，而英國判例法上經常是第2與第3步驟混淆不清之故[637]。

另外Prof. Ehrenzweig主張「契約有效原則」（rule of validation）[638]，亦即法官於有糾紛之契約案件中，應選擇一個準據法來維持契約之效力。英國判例法上亦認定當事人通常是期望契約是會有效的[639]，故

---

[635] "In order to determine the country with which the contract is most closely connected, it is also possible to take account of factors which supervened after the conclusion of the contract."

[636] [1970]A.C. 583, 603.但英國最高法院認為事後（subsequent）之行為可以構成estoppel或一個新契約。又見Compagnie d'Armement Maritime SA v Cie Tunisienne de Navigation SA [1971] AC 572, [1970] 3 All ER 71; Amin Rasheed Shipping Corpn v Kuwait Insurance Co [1984] AC 50, [1983] 2 All ER 884.

[637] Cheshire and North, p. 566, "However, in contrast to the proper law of the contract approach, it is now possible to take account of factors which have supervened after the conclusion of the contract. Article 4 applies a purely objective test, so it is therefore inappropriate to talk about the intentions of the parties. "於14thed.,p.709又再次被重申。 "It follows that the fact that the contract would be valid under one country's law but not under another's cannot be considered under Article 4, since this factor is only relevant to the determination of the parties' intentions (ie the parties would expect the contract to be valid). Furthermore, although terms of the contract, such as a choice of jurisdiction or arbitration clause, should presumably be considered in the context of Article 4 in the situation where no clear inference can be drawn from them as to intention of the parties under Article 3(1), their relevance when operating the objective test is limited to showing an objective connection with a country, and not as evidence of the parties' intentions."

[638] A. A. Ehrenzweig, Contracts in the Conflict of Laws, 59 Colum. L. Rev. 973 (1959).

[639] Monterosso Shipping Co Ltd v International Transport Workers' Federation. The Rosso [1982] 2 Lloyd's Rep 120 at 131.這個見解亦為第2新編187條comment e所支持，當事人所選之準據法若使得契約無效，會被推定為錯誤而不被適用。但若該法為188條應適用之法律，則會被加以適用。"On occasion, the parties may choose a law that would declare the contract invalid. In such situations, the chosen law will not be applied by reason of the parties' choice. To do so would defeat the expectations of the parties which it is the purpose of the present rule to protect. The parties can be assumed to have intended that the provisions of the contract would be binding upon them (cf. s 188, Comment b). If the parties have chosen a law that would invalidate the contract, it can be assumed that they did so by mistake. If, however, the chosen law is that of the state of the otherwise applicable law under the rule of s

而無論是於確認當事人之默示準據法或推定準據法時，通常法院是不會去尋找一個使契約無效之法律。

二十一、一般基本及特別推定與契約基本政策

　　公約4(2)條及規則4(2)條的執行契約之特徵性履行當事人之慣居地或營業地法則[640]，是另一個使得英美法同僚眉毛挑高之法則（基本的推定）。特徵性履行法則是於不能適用特殊的推定規則之後才能被加以適用（公約4(3)、(4)條及規則4(1)條優先適用），但其之適用又可能會受到最密切關連法則之取代（公約4(5)條及規則4(3)條）。故而特徵性履行法則不但名稱怪異，它在法律邏輯的適用上亦有些奇怪，是個三明治法律邏輯。

　　契約履行地本就是推定契約準據法的重要連繫因素之一[641]，但問題是於一般契約（特別是商務上）中雙方皆負有履行之義務，故公約企圖以集中注意於一方之履行為主要之履行之方式來避免雙方皆履行之困擾。通常契約都是有對價的，而且大多數的對價都通常是相當的，故而公約與規則這種法律邏輯不但是異想天開，而且於根本法律邏輯之基礎上是對一方絕對不公平（尤其是對付款人）的，或許諷刺性的說它最大的功能是讓法律系教授的邏輯思考變得很簡單、容易。

188, this law will be applied even when it invalidates the contract. Such application will be by reason of the rule of s 188, and not by reason of the fact that this was the law chosen by the parties."

[640] Cheshire and North, 14thed., p.710,認為於保證及相關信用狀之情形，保證人及銀行之付款地為特徵性履行地。With a contract of guarantee, the characteristic performance is that of payment of money by the guarantor. In Bank of Baroda v Vysya Bank MANCE J regarded the position of a bank confirming a letter of credit as being analogous to that of a guarantor. The characteristic performance of the contract between the confirming bank and the issuing bank was the honouring by the confirming bank of its confirmation of credit in favour of the beneficiary. The characteristic performance of the contract between the issuing bank and the beneficiary was the issue of the letter of credit and that between the confirming bank and the beneficiary was that of the bank providing the banking service of payment under the letter of credit. In ascertaining the characteristic performance, one is not confined to the terms of the contract. The global picture must be assessed and the background to the contract may be of particular importance. [1994] 2 Lloyd's Rep 87.

[641] 陳隆修，《國際私法契約評論》，台北，五南圖書公司，民國75年2月，初版，37、38頁。

　　Giuliano and Lagarde Report認為：「於當事人沒有選定準據法時，契約的依據合適的特徵性履行之法律，可以由內部去定性契約的連繫因素，而不是由例如訂約當事人之國籍或契約訂定地等與契約義務之主旨無關的外部因素來定性。另外，可能可以將特徵性履行之觀念與一個甚至更基本的想法連結，該想法亦即為其履行可說是該法律關係之功能牽連到任何國家之經濟與社會生活之實現。特徵性履行之概念基本上連結契約與其所形成為部分之社會與經濟環境。……於雙務契約中當事人皆負起互相對等履行責任，於現代經濟中一方當事人之相對履行通常是以金錢給付之方式。這當然不是契約的特徵性履行。[642]」所謂特徵性履行通常構成該交易之社會經濟功能及重心[643]，是該付款行為所要求之履行，例如交付貨品、財產之使用權、供給服務、交通、保險、銀行業務、及擔保等。故於銀行契約是銀行所在地，於買賣契約是賣方之營業地，及於代理契約是代理人之營業地。

　　Cheshire and North很清楚的列舉這個特徵性履行之問題如下[644]。第1

---

[642] The submission of the contract, in the absence of a choice by the parties, to the law appropriate to the characteristic performance defines the connecting factor of the contract from the inside, and not from the outside by elements unrelated to the essence of the obligation such as the nationality of the contracting parties or the place where the contract was concluded.

In addition it is possible to relate the concept of characteristic performance to an even more general idea, namely the idea that his performance refers to the function which the legal relationship involved fulfils in the economic and social life of any country. The concept of characteristic performance essentially links the contract to the social and economic environment of which it will from a part.

Identifying the characteristic performance of a contract obviously presents no difficulty in the case of unilateral contracts. By contrast, in bilateral (reciprocal) contracts whereby the parties undertake mutual reciprocal performance, the counter-performance by one of the parties in a modern economy usually takes the form of money. This is not, of course, the characteristic performance of the contract. It is the performance for which the payment is due, i.e. depending on the type of contract, the delivery of goods, the granting of the right to make use of an item of property, the provision of a service, transport, insurance, banking operations, security, etc., which usually constitutes the centre of gravity and the socio-economic function of the contractual transaction.

[643] 於羅馬Ⅰ之Recital 19中亦認為特徵性之履行應依契約之重心而被加以考慮："In the case of a contract consisting of a bundle of rights and obligations capable of being categorised as falling within more than one of the specified types of contract, the characteristic performance of the contract should be determined having regard to its centre of gravity."

[644] PM North, JJ Fawcett, Cheshire and North's Private International Law, 13th ed., pp. 570, 571; 14th ed., pp. 713～715.

有些契約並不合適這個概念，例如以貨易貨之契約[645]及有關智慧財產權使用之複數契約。此時必須依公約4(5)條及規則4(4)條無法推定時依最重要關連處理[646]。第2付款行為雖是許多契約的共同點因而不是特色，但是於質押、分期付款買賣、及償還貨款等契約中仍有可能是契約之主要點。因為解釋報告只是說「通常」，故或許付款亦於此些例外情形可能構成特徵性履行[647]。第3於買賣契約中其假定賣方之履行較為複雜，但於大部分情形中買方之履行亦不應被忽略[648]7。第4「於有關經濟能力上，大企業，如產品製造商、提供服務之一方（如銀行及保險公司）、及專業人士，是比可能為經濟弱勢之他方而受到較為有利之對待。而公約是非常的關心弱勢之一方以致對受僱人及消費者有著特別的規定，其之採取有利製造商之

---

[645] Case 266/85 Shenavai v Kreischer [1987] ECR 239, 255.

[646] Cheshire and North's Private International Law, 14thed., pp. 713, 714, "First, there are some contracts which cannot be fitted easily within the concept, as the Print Concept case illustrates. Letters of credit are another example. Article 4(2) assumes the ability to identify a single party charged with the single performance characteristic of the contract. But with a letter of credit there are a number of autonomous bilateral contracts and it is desirable that each contractual relationship arising in the course of the transaction has the same governing law. With a contract of loan the characteristic performer could equally be regarded as being the borrower or the lender. Even worse, there are some contracts that cannot be fitted at all within the concept. With a contract of barter it is difficult, if not impossible, to say that one party's performance is more characteristic of the contract than the other's. The same is true with complex contracts for the commercial exploitation of intellectual property rights. It was not possible to identify the characteristic performance of a trade mark agreement under which each party had to do (or refrain from doing) the same acts vis à vis the other (ie using their marks in their respective defined fields of use). However, the Convention allows for this by providing in Article 4(5) that, if the characteristic performance cannot be determined, the presumption does not apply." Print Concept GmbH v GEW (EC) Ltd [2001] EWCA Civ 352,[2002]CLC 352.

[647] "Secondly, the definition of characteristic performance in terms of the performance for which payment is due does not stand up well to close scrutiny. The payment of money was presumably rejected as the characteristic is performance because this is a common feature of many contracts and therefore fails to distinguish between different types of contract. Nonetheless, there are some contracts where the payment of money is arguably the essence of the obligation, for example contracts of pledge or hire-purchase, or repayment of a loan. The Working Group qualified their statement about the payment of money by saying that this is not usually the essence of the obligation. The payment of money can, in unusual cases, constitute the characteristic performance. For example, the characteristic performance of a reinsurance contract has been described as being the making of payment in the event of a claim." 14th ed., pp. 714.

[648] "Thirdly, the effect of generally denying that the payment of money constitutes the essence of contract is to favour the seller of goods over the buyer. This has been justified on the basis that the seller's performance is generally more complicated and to a greater extent regulated by rules of law than that of the buyer. However, it is questionable whether this is sufficient to justify completely ignoring the buyer's performance in most cases." 14thed., pp. 714, 715.

立場是很奇怪的。[649]」有趣的是傳統上英國判例法上為維護英國之商業利益，於未指定準據法時，代理契約經常由代理關係的形成地法（常為本人之經商地[650]），而保險契約則經常以保險人之營業地法[651]為準據法。批評其他制度的不公平或許是可以比較客觀。

另外特徵性履行又與慣居地合在一起。英國判例法認為於有關銀行戶頭之契約，若債款是透過分行之戶頭，則該戶頭所在地英國法應為依據[652]；若契約為有關一銀行發行信用狀，而另一銀行確認該信用狀，則該確認銀行之倫敦營業處因為履行契約故英國法為準據法[653]。Cheshire and North不客氣的指出：「除非該推定很容易適用，否則於決定客觀準據法上其立法理由所欲產生的穩定性不會被達成。很不幸的，4(2)條的規定是個複雜的程序，牽連了甚多定義上之問題。尤其是經由推定程序，一個連繫因素之重要地位是被提升至超越其他。特徵性履行與慣居地的聯合是否值得這個地位是值得懷疑的。[654]」

機械式的特徵性履行雖然以最重要關連做為其警察條款（公約4(5)條規則4(3)條），但兩者都是區域性選擇法規，皆帶有忽視實體法政策的天生原罪，不見得能保障個案正義。尤其特徵性履行幾乎是個人少見的偏頗性法則—即使於傳統的區域選法規則個人亦很少見到如此偏祖生產者、銀行、保險公司、及其他強勢之一方。除了奉行資本主義及自由經濟的英國

---

[649] "Fourthly, in terms of economic strength, the large enterprises, the manufacture of goods, the provider of services (such as banks and insurance companies) and the professional is favoured against the other party who may well be in a weaker economic position. It is curious to find a pro-manufacturer stance being taken in a Convention which sufficiently concerned about protecting weaker parties to have special rules for consumers and employees." Cheshire and North, pp. 570, 571. 14th ed., pp. 715.

[650] 陳隆修，《國際私法契約評論》，台北，五南圖書公司，民國75年2月，初版，40-42頁。

[651] 同上，46、47頁。

[652] Sierra Leone Telecommunications Co Ltd v Barclays Bank Plc [1998] 2 All ER 821.

[653] Bank of Baroda v Vysya Bank [1994] 2 Lloyd's Rep 87, 92.

[654] "Unless a presumption is easy to apply it will not produce the certainty in determining the objective applicable law that is its raison d'etre. Unfortunately, the presumption in Article 4(2) is a complex one, involving considerable definitional problems. Moreover, with a presumption, one connection is elevated to a position of importance above all others. It is doubtful whether the combination of habitual residence and characteristic performance merits this." Cheshire and North, pp. 571, 572; 14thed., pp. 716，又再次加以重述。

傳統判例法外，這種漠視弱勢之作風是與近代法學之共同核心價值不合的。

於判例法上如拍賣場所[655]規則I 4(1)(g)條、律師之代理行為地[656]、股票經紀人及房地產經紀人之營業地[657]，或許因為市場穩定性之需求及政府執照之發給與監督之必要性，該些履行地的確是應被加以特徵性之考量，但即是如此仍並不能包括所有契約之一切必要之考量在內。例如於全球化之下，可能台灣人聘美國律師（或事務所）於台灣處理智慧財產權或公平交易之糾紛，則此時美國律師之抽成制度並非依特徵性履行之推定即可完全解決，或許應對此點於全球化之下加以實體上之考量。於法律全球化下，正如美國懲罰性應在被告人權與受害者要求正義間做一實質考量[658]；美國律師的抽成制度亦應在維護弱勢之訴訟權與不鼓勵訴訟間做一實質考量。而這些實質考量皆與特徵性履行及最重要關聯的區域選擇法規無關。特徵性履行與最重要關連的特徵或許可以陳述如下：因為完全忽視實體法政策的存在，故與個案正義的保障沒有關連[659]。再次崛起的中國因為於國際及國內買賣契約上採用全球化之CISG實體契約規則，故對特徵性履行與最重要關連等區域選法規則或許應交付時光隧道去處理。

---

[655] 陳隆修，《國際私法契約評論》，台北，五南圖書公司，民國75年2月，初版，37頁。

[656] 陳隆修，《國際私法契約評論》，台北，五南圖書公司，民國75年2月，初版，41頁，Re Maugham (1885) ZT.L.R 115 (C.A.).

[657] 同上，Ross v. McMullen (1971) 21 D.L.R. (3d) 228.

[658] 陳隆修，《2005年海牙法院選擇公約評析》，台北，五南圖書公司，2009年1月，初版1刷，299-304頁。

[659] 對瑞士1987年國際私法117條的引用特徵性履行，Dicey and Morris以判例說明不認同之意見。例如經銷契約中出賣人雖具有特徵性履行之特點，但是除了付款之相對義務外，經銷商亦經常有著以廣告來開拓市場及盡力促銷之義務。「這種案件證明了特徵性履行的脆弱性，及給予一個它可能無法決定，或應被忽視之一個例子。」Dicey and Morris, p.1585, "Swiss case-law provides more examples, including the case of a distribution agreement, where the characteristic performance has been held to be that of the vendor. But distribution agreement commonly involve reciprocal obligations other than the payment of money: the distributor of the goods may have an obligation to build up the market by advertising the goods, and using its best endeavours to market them. Such a case demonstrates the fragility of the concept of characteristic performance, and provides an example of a case where it may not be possible to determine it, or where it may be disregarded." Evans Marshall & Co Ltd v Bertola SA [1973] 1 W.L.R. 349 (CA); Optelec SA v Soc Midtronics BV (France, Case civ I, May 15, 2001), 2002 Rev. Crit. 86, note Lagarde; [2003] I.L.Pr. 57; Ammann v Soc Zwaans BVA (France, Cass. Civ. I. Novermber 25, 2003), 2004 Rev. Crit. 102, note Lagarde.現今這個不合理之推定於規則I 4(1)(f)條已更改為推定經銷商之慣居地為準據法。

　　或許為了避免最重要關連於公約4(1)條及4(5)條於法律邏輯上重覆性之困擾，規則Ⅰ將公約4(1)條取消，規則Ⅰ的4(1)條直接規定8個特殊的推定。公約及規則應為三、二、或一個步驟之問題，關係到最重要關連標準是否可以較容易否定推定之問題。除非歐盟法院加以強力介入，這個問題應會繼續存在於大陸法與英國法系間。但是如Cheshire and North所陳述：「但是，判例法規則並非如剛開始所看到般的開放及有彈性。為了促進法律的穩定性，法院於相關的某些契約中為了決定最重要關連，會去辨認某些特別的因素有著重大的影響。例如，於保險契約客觀的適當法通常會是保險人營業地之法院。[660]」

　　對於某些特定的連結因素的重大影響，英國判例早已有論述，於R. v. International Trustee for the Protection of Bondholders A.G.中Lord Atkin說：「於作成結論時，法院經常會被表示指向通常的推論的特別事實或情況，於有些情形是幾乎決定性的推論的法則所引導為當事人去適用特定法律的意思：例如契約訂定地國，契約履行地國，如果契約有關不動產不動產所在地國，契約所訂定欲裝載貨物之船旗國。[661]」雖然英國判例法對推定準據法早有論述，但如前述判例法並不贊同死硬的推定程序，並且甚至認為「推定」是過時的[662]。對於Giuliano and Lagarde Report的簡化4(2)條[663]，Cheshire and North認為是將判例法進化過程的倒轉：「公約的

---

[660] Cheshire and North, p. 568, "Nonetheless, the common law rule was not as open ended and flexible as might at first appear. In order to promote certainty in the law the courts identified specific factors as having great weight in identifying the closest connection in relation to certain contracts. For example, for insurance contracts the objective proper law would normally be the law of the state where the insurer carried on business." 於14[th] ed., pp. 711,中此論述再次被重申。

[661] "In coming to its conclusion the court will be guided by rules which indicate that particular facts or conditions lead to a prima facie inference, in some cases an almost conclusive inference, as to the intention of the parties to apply a particular law: e.g. the country where the contract is made, the country where the contract is to be performed, if the contract relates to immovables the country where they are situate, the country under whose flag the ship sails in which goods are contracted to be carried."[1937]A. C.500,529.

[662] Coast Lines Ltd v Hudig and Veder Chartering NV [1972] 2 QB 34, 50.

[663] "In conclusion, Article 4(2) gives specific form and objectivity to the, in itself, too vague concept of 'closest connection'. At the same time it greatly simplifies the problem of determining the law applicable to the contract in default of choice by the parties. The place where the act was done become unimportant. There is not longer any need to determine where the contract was concluded, with all the

解釋報告認為可以只單獨依據這些推定，而不必尋找最密切關連之國家，即可決定準據法。至少就英國法而言，推定程序之被引進是將時鐘倒轉。雖然於過去曾經有些時間裡推定是常被引用，但它已過時並且已被拒絕，批評它的理由之一就是，它們自己本身將注意力由依客觀標準應有必要被加以考慮的每個因素引開。[664]」

　　歐盟大陸法可能會百般不解，公約及規則I不但引用默示準據法、客觀推定準據法、及甚至個別情形中之特別推定準據法，這些於英國判例法上並非沒有，為何英國同僚會有如此異議。個人以前曾以此做為論文之結語：「個人認為全世界國際私法學上沒有理論之不同，只有進化腳步之不同。這是實體法方法論的真正精髓，亦是個人與Currie、Reese、Leflar及其他美國實體法論同僚基本立足點不同之處；亦是個人踽踽獨行三十年，一生懸念之堅持。[665]」**羅馬公約及規則之許多規定大致上仍為英國判例法今日還在引用，但是如英國資深同僚所說這是將「時鐘倒轉」。個人以為公約及規則I的法規並未完全被拋棄，更正確的說法個人以為應如下：英國已從「推定」的區域選法規則進化到注重實質政策的階段。英國判例法的法規與羅馬公約及規則的法規相去並不遠，但實際上於法規上之運用已脫胎換骨成政策導向。當公約及規則仍舊東施效顰的學習適當法的表面區域選法規則時，英國判例法所注重的不是法規，而是商業的有效性及當事人的期望之實質政策。**

---

difficulties and the problems of classification that arise in practice. Seeking the place of performance or the different places of performance and classifying them becomes superfluous. For each category of contract it is the characteristic performance that is in principle the relevant factor in applying the presumption for determining the applicable law, even in situations peculiar to certain contracts, as for example in the contract of guarantee where the characteristic performance is always that of the guarantor, whether in relation to the principal debtor or the creditor."

[664] "The Giuliano and Lagarde Report contemplates that the applicable law can be determined solely by applying the presumptions, without searching for the country with the closest connection. The introduction of presumptions turns the clock back as far as English law is concerned, Although popular at one time, presumptions went out of fashion and were rejected, one criticism being the very point that they diverted attention from the necessity to consider every single factor under the objective test." Cheshire and North, p. 568. 這個論述又於14th ed., pp. 711,中再次被確認。

[665] 陳隆修、許兆慶、林恩瑋、李瑞生四人合著，《國際私法-管轄與選法理論之交錯》，台北，五南圖書公司，2009年3月，初版1刷，260頁。

　　如Cheshire and North所說：「無疑的當英國法院於開始去確認契約客觀上之適當法時，它們企圖去達成一些基本政策上的目標，例如對契約給予商業上之有效性。於公約下英國法院將會發現達成這些目標會更加困難，這些推定的存在及法律被成文法化的事實降低了靈活性，並因此減少操縱的空間，使得法院想達成一定的結果較無法達成。[666]」事實上羅馬公約及規則之大致架構，與早期個人所敘述之英國判例法[667]於大架構上並無大區別。英國同僚所抱怨的是公約及規則於確認準據法上，不能如英國法院般的以達成基本政策上之目標為主—亦即公約及規則的選定準據法過份的偏向區域選法規則，而不能達成契約法上之基本政策。事實上英國的適當法則本身亦是個區域選法規則，只不過二百五十年的進化使得英國判例法文明到公開的透過適當法則去達成契約法的基本政策而已。相信歐盟的公約及規則亦會於將來公開的要求法院去達成契約法的基本政策，這是文明進化的必然過程。事實上羅馬規則I已於其要點中公開的陳述一些政策上之目標及對實體法強行法規加以要求，這與英國法對契約法基本政策上之目標，是有著同樣契約法實質政策化之一致進化過程，只是英國判例法之過程遠較為早而已。

　　「過去」英國判例法於契約法基本政策上之較早進化，並不表示其判例法合適於現代21世紀之文明。如前述「當事人的期望」及「商業的功效」，並非合適21世紀全球化契約法的基本政策。人類文明、財富、科技、及愛心到達一個階段後，契約法上的基本政策應是在監督及抑制商業的貪婪無厭，確保全世界體制上之安全及正義。故而21世紀全球化法學（不只於契約法）之重點政策應是在確保社會秩序之安全、促進弱勢之正義、及監督工業化國家盡力幫助第3世界早日爬上經濟及環保高科技之階

---

[666] Cheshire and North, p.566, "There can be little doubt that when the English courts set out to ascertain the objective proper law of the contract they sought to achieve certain underlying policy objectives, such as giving business efficacy to the contract. English courts are going to find it harder to achieve such objectives under the Convention. The presence of the presumptions and the fact that the law is codified reduces the flexibility, and thus the room for manoeuvre, for a court that wants to achieve a particular result." 這個論述又於14thed., pp. 709,中再次被確認。

[667] 陳隆修，《國際私法契約評論》，台北，五南圖書公司，民國75年2月，初版，第2章。

梯。

　　雖然藉著強行法去摸索契約法之實體政策，但公約及規則之基本架構上仍是本著區域性選法規則。於適用特徵性履行標準之前，公約及規則皆有一些特別的推定，但這些特別的推定是以最重要關連標準做為規避法則（公約4(5)條及規則4(3)條）。公約4(3)條規定契約之主體（標的）為有關不動產的權利或使用之權利，則不動產所在地為最密切關連所在地。解釋報告舉例認為若兩比利時人訂立一於義大利度假屋之租賃契約時，最重要關連不應於義大利，而應於雙方比利時之居所地[668]。另外4(3)條亦應不適用於不動產之修繕，因為契約之主體（標的）為該修繕或工程，而非不動產本身[669]。4(4)條規定於貨物運送時，運送人之主要營業地若亦是裝、卸貨物地、或託運人之主要營業地，則該地為最密切關連地。一次航程之傭船契約如果其實質上為貨物運送，亦適用本項之規定。但旅客運送則適用4(2)條一般之推定[670]。規則I則將貨物運送規定於5(1)條，旅客運送則增加規定於5(2)條[671]。於旅客運送中當事人之選法是有受到須有適當關連之

---

[668] Giuliano and Lagarde, "For example, this presumption could be rebutted if two persons resident in Belgium were to make a contract for renting a holiday home on the island of Elba (Italy). It might be thought in such a case that the contract was most closely connected with the country of the contracting parties' residence, not with Italy."

[669] 同上，"finally it should be stressed that paragraph 3 does not extend to contracts for the construction or repair of immovable property. This is because the main subject-matter of these contracts is the construction or repair rather than the immovable property itself."
此點或許參考英國判例法而來，於該案Whitworth Street Estates (Manchester) Ltd. v. James Miller and Partners Ltd., [1970] A.C. 583中，一家蘇格蘭公司答應替一家英格蘭公司在蘇格蘭的工廠修改建築物。契約是在蘇格蘭簽訂，所用的形式為英國建築師公會所發的範本，該公會的成員包括蘇格蘭及英格蘭會員，但該範本有暗示用英國法為準據法之記載，雖然契約訂定地與履行地皆在蘇格蘭，標的物亦在蘇格蘭，法院仍多以大數表決準據法為英國法。見陳隆修，《國際私法契約評論》，台北，五南圖書公司，民國75年2月，初版，65頁。

[670] Giuliano and Lagarde Report, "Contracts for the carriage of passengers remain subject to the general presumption, i.e. that provided for in Article 4 (2)."

[671] Article 5 Contracts of carriage
1. To the extent that the law applicable to a contract for the carriage of goods has not been chosen in accordance with Article 3, the law applicable shall be the law of the country of habitual residence of the carrier, provided that the place of receipt or the place of delivery or the habitual residence of the consignor is also situated in that country. If those requirements are not met, the law of the country where the place of delivery as agreed by the parties is situated shall apply.
2. To the extent that the law applicable to a contract for the carriage of passengers has not been chosen by the parties in accordance with the second subparagraph, the law applicable shall be the law of the

限制，而於沒有選法時若旅客之慣居地同時亦為啟航或終點地，則依該地法；若沒有，則依運送人之慣居地法。事實上運送契約為法律全球實體化之先驅，國際公約甚多，而且公約之內容儘量實體化，並且這些實體法規定經常具有強制性[672]。羅馬公約及規則事實上應避免區域選法之規定，而只作政策性之宣示。

有關規則4(1)條的特別推定為，規則4(1)(a)規定買賣契約以賣方之慣居地；4(1)(b)條規定服務契約以供及服務之人之慣居地[673]；4(1)(c)條規定不動產權或其租賃以不動產所在地；4(1)(d)條規定不動產之租賃不超過連續6個月，以地主之慣居地為依據，但承租人必須為自然人且慣居於同地；4(1)(e)條規定加盟契約以加盟人之慣居地；4(1)(f)條規定經銷契約以經銷人之慣居地；4(1)(g)條規定拍賣契約以賣場所在地（如果能確定）；4(1)(h)條規定有關Art. 4(1), point （17） of Directive 2004/39/EC之多次第3人金融交易[674]。(a)、(b)款之特別推定仍舊是依傳統判例法偏向

---

country where the passenger has his habitual residence, provided that either the place of departure or the place of destination is situated in that country. If these requirements are not met, the law of the country where the carrier has his habitual residence shall apply.

The parities may choose as the law applicable to a contract for the carriage of passengers in accordance with Article 3 only the law of the country where:

(a) the passenger has his habitual residence; or

(b) the carrier has his habitual residence; or

(c) the carrier has his place of central administration; or

(d) the place of departure is satiated; or

(e) the place of destination is situated.

3. Where it is clear from all the circumstance of the case that the contract, in the absence of a choice of law, is manifestly more closely connected with a country other than that indicated in paragraph 1 or 2, the law of that other country shall apply.

[672] 陳隆修，《國際私法契約評論》，台北，五南圖書公司，民國75年2月，初版，42-46頁。

[673] 貨物之買賣與服務之提供之概念應配合布魯塞爾規則第5條之範圍，見Recital 17:

Recital 17

"As far as the applicable law in the absence of choice is concerned, the concept of 'Provision of services' and 'sale of goods' should be interpreted in the same way as when applying Article 5 of Regulation (EC) No 44/2001 in so far as sale of goods and provision of services are covered by that Regulation. Although franchise and distribution contracts are contracts for services, they are the subject of specific rules. " 但除了這兩個條款之定義性概念外，羅馬I於此之選法規則並無配合布魯塞爾規則的管轄規則之意圖。

另外除了於經銷、加盟、及拍賣外，羅馬I之4(1)條與羅馬公約之4(2)及(3)條所達成之結果通常應會是一致的，但卻不必去辨認特徵性履行而可更直接達成結果。

[674] 對於羅馬I之第4(1)(h)，第6(4)(d)及(e)條，幾乎所有的國際私法同僚都覺得太過技術性。對於Di-

rective 2004/39/EC (Markets in Financial Instruments Directive)第4(1)(14)及(15)中所解釋的 "regulated markets "及 "multilateral trading facilities " , 一般亦認太過技術性（有趣的是這種技術性的
言詞違反了MiFID自己第44條要求資訊必須使用合理的商業名詞透明性之要求）

Matthias Lehmann, Financial Instruments, 於Rome I Regulation: The Law Applicable to Contractual
Obligations in Europe edited by Franco Ferrari, Stefan Leible, p88中解釋如下：Its Article 4 indeed
gives definitions of both expressions, but in a rather technical way. To put out it easily, a regulated
market is a specially authorized and supervised part of a stock exchange. A multilateral trading facilities, or "MTF", in essence is a platform for the electronic trade of financial instruments. It follows that
a typical example of the kind of contracts meant in Article 4(1)(h) Rome I Regulation are those that are
concluded on a stock exchange or on an electronic platform. The peculiarity of these contracts is that
they are entered into between special dealers who have the permission to trade on the exchange. Normal
customers will hardly ever conclude such contracts. For other, non-professional transactions on financial instruments, the Rome I Regulation does not contain a special provision. Rather, they fall under its
general rules.

另外根據the MiFID 第36(4)條，該市場之所在地法之公法應被加以適用：

4. Without prejudice to any relevant provisions of Directive 2003/6/EC, the public law governing the
   trading conducted under the systems of the regulated market shall be that of the home Member State
   of the regulated market.

而羅馬Ⅰ第4(1)(h)則進一步規定有關該市場所訂定之契約依市場所在地法，但一般是認為該種
契約皆有準據法。或許於此種情形下第36(4)條之公法可能會被視為強行法。

美國較有關連之類似規定請參閱U.C.C第8條：

§ 8-110. APPLICABILITY; CHOICE OF LAW.

(A) The local law of the issuer's jurisdiction, as specified in subsection (d), governs:

    (1) the validity of a security;

    (2) the rights and duties of the issuer with respect to registration of transfer;

    (3) the effectiveness of registration of transfer by the issuer;

    (4) whether the issuer owes any duties to an adverse claimant to a security; and

    (5) whether an adverse claim can be asserted against a person to whom transfer of a certificated or
uncertificated security is registered or a person who obtains control of an uncertificated security.

(B) The local law of the securities intermediary's jurisdiction, as specified in subsection (e), governs:

    (1) acquisition of a security entitlement from the securities intermediary;

    (2) the rights and duties of the securities intermediary and entitlement holder arising out of a secu-
rity entitlement;

    (3) whether the securities intermediary owes any duties to an adverse claimant to a security entitle-
ment; and

    (4) whether an adverse claim can be asserted asserted against a person who acquires a security en-
titlement from the securities intermediary or a person who purchases a security entitlement or
interest therein from an entitlement holder.

(C) The local law of the jurisdiction in which a security certificate is located at the time of delivery governs whether an adverse claim can be asserted against a person to whom the security certificate is
delivered.

(D) "Issuer's jurisdiction" means the jurisdiction under which the issuer of the security is organized or,
if permitted by the law of that jurisdiction, the law of another jurisdiction specified by the issuer. An
issuer organized under the law of this State may specify the law of another jurisdiction as the law
governing the matters specified in subsection (A)(2) through (5)

(E) The following rules determine a "securities intermediary's jurisdiction" for purposes of this section:

    (1) If an agreement between the securities intermediary and its entitlement holder governing the
securities account expressly provides that a particular jurisdiction is the securities intermediary'

強勢；但(e)、(f)款則為新時代之現象故較偏向弱勢；(c)、(g)款則與傳統英國判例法相似；(d)款則很明顯的是配合Council Regulation 44/2001 art. 22(1)專屬管轄之規定，但羅馬(1)是以慣居地而布魯塞爾規則是住所為依據。

　　如Cheshire and North所說：「任何企圖以關連點來地域化契約之客觀標準之困難就是不穩定性。公約以運用推定（包含一般及特別推定）之方式企圖解決不穩定之問題。[675]」公約及規則無論是三、二、或一步驟，其模式首先是推定（包括一般及特別推定），再來是最重要關連標準做為推定之規避法則或於無法推定時適用，最後是強行法（法院地、唯一關連地、及履行地之強行法）。

　　如Cheshire and North於評論特徵性履行時說：「除了強行法規之概念外，這是公約所引用中最為困難的概念。而公約對這個概念的缺乏定義，則沒有減輕它的困難性，即使其來源可以追訴至瑞士國際私法亦沒有助益。[676]」同樣的prof. Fentiman對羅馬公約及規則的第4條亦提出許多英

---

s jurisdiction for purposes of this part, this article, or this act, that jurisdiction is the securities intermediary's jurisdiction.

(2) If paragraph (1) does not apply and an agreement between the securities intermediary and its entitlement holder expressly provides that the agreement is governed by the law of a particular jurisdiction, that jurisdiction is the securities intermediary's jurisdiction.

(3) If neither paragraph (1) nor paragraph (2) applies and an agreement between the securities intermediary and its entitlement holder governing the securities account expressly provides that the securities account is maintained at an office in a particular jurisdiction, that jurisdiction is the securities intermediary's jurisdiction.

(4) If none of the preceding paragraphs applies, the securities intermediary's jurisdiction is the jurisdiction in which the office identified in an account statement as the office serving the entitlement holder's account is located.

(5) If none of the preceding paragraphs applies, the securities intermediary's jurisdiction is the jurisdiction in which the jurisdiction in which the chief executive office of the securities intermediary is located.

(F) A securities intermediary's jurisdiction is not determined by the physical location of certificates representing financial assets, or by the jurisdiction in which is organized the issuer of the financial asset with respect to which an entitlement holder has a security entitlement, or by the location of facilities for data processing or other record keeping concerning the account.

[675] Cheshire and North, p. 568, "The difficulty with any objective test that seeks to localise the contracts is that of uncertainty. The Convention tries to resolve this uncertainty by the use of presumptions." 又見 14thed., pp. 711.

[676] Cheshire and North, p. 569, "Apart from the concept of mandatory rules, this is the most difficult con-

國同僚共有的心聲[677]：「公約第4條的解釋已經引起相當多的辯論。特別是，何時及依什麼理由例外將會取代規則？英國法院企圖依此種例外而保有既有的彈性，它們傾向當其他法律是明顯的有較好的關連時即隨時取代推定的規則[678]。他們拒絕說這個規則只是於假如規則所認定的法律與契約沒有實質關連時才會被取代。證據顯示他們對密切關連所被評定的標準採取一種寬廣的評價方法。（例如標的所在、被使用物之所在、服務被提供地、及當事人之總事務所之所在地等。）他們拒絕對評價關連的標準以明列標準之方式來限制他們的裁量權。但於權威案例Bank of Baroda v. Vysya Bank Ltd.[679]中，法院並非以將事實關連點置於契約與競爭的法律中來解決問題，而是經由參考商業的功效及當事人之期望而來解決這個問題。[680]」

羅馬公約及規則I於第4條及許多其他條文所採的固定模式之程序首先為推定規則（包括特別及一般推定），在其次以最重要關連為規避法規[681]

---

cept used in the Convention. It does not help that the concept is not defined under the Convention nor that its origin is to be found in Swiss private international law." 又見14thed., pp. 712.

[677] Richard Fentiman, Choice of Law in Europe: Uniformity and Integration 82 Tul. L. Rev. 2021, 2047, 2048 (2008), "But he interpretation of article 4 of Convention has given rise to considerable debate. In particular, when and for what reasons will the exception displace the rule? English courts have attempted to preserve the flexibility inherent in such an exception. They have tended to say that it displaces whenever another law is clearly better connected. They have resisted saying that the rule is displaced only if the law identified by the rule has no material connection with the contract. There is also evidence that they have adopted a broad, evaluative approach to the criteria whereby close connection is judged. They have resisted fettering their discretion by specifying the criteria for judging connection. But in the leading case of Bank of Baroda v. Vysya Bank Ltd., the court approached the matter not by adumbrating the factual connections between the contract and the competing laws, but by reference to commercial efficacy and the expectations of the parties.
This approach stands in opposition to the more restrictive approach adopted by other courts. In the Netherlands, for example, it has been held that a contract will only be more closely connected with a law other than that identified by the general rule if that rule identifies a law lacking any significant connection with the contract. This restrictive view has been expressly rejected by the English courts."

[678] Ennstone Blog. Prod. Ltd. v. Stanger Ltd., [2002] 1 W.L.R. 3059, 3070 (A.C.).

[679] [1994] 2 Lloyd's Rep. 87, 90-94 (Q.B).

[680] 見最尊敬的恩師C.G.J. Morse於此案之論述，Letters of Credit and the Rome Convention, (1994) L.M.C.L.Q. 560 (U.K.).

[681] 以最密切關連為規避法規，見其序言中之要點20如下："Where the contract is manifestly more closely connected with a country other than that indicated in Article 4(1) or (2), an escape clause should provide that the law of that other country is to apply. In order to determine that country, account should be taken, *inter alia*, a whether the contract in question has a very close relationship with another con-

（或於無法推定時適用），最後則為所牽連的強行法規（羅馬 I 為法院地、案件事實唯一發生地、及履行地強行法）。這三個步驟中之每一個所牽連的法學概念無一不是國際私法之爭議風暴中心。第一階段所謂特別推定及一般推定（即特徵性履行之規定），即為英國客觀說長久以來的爭議點或甚至已為判例法所拒絕，尤其是近來大陸法的特徵性履行更是為英美法界普遍所懷疑的概念。而第2階段的最重要關連更是自Westlake主張「the most real connection」以來已經歷超過一百五十年的爭議。美國第2新編一面倒全力使用這概念只是使得池水更加混濁而已，沒有任何有理智的人會說美國選法規則很「平靜」。至於第3階段的強行法概念更是英美法所沒有，而於大陸法之國內法亦為屢有爭議之概念。它的爭議性延續至國際法上自然更加不可控制，羅馬公約7(1)條之經驗即為鐵證。羅馬公約及規則將這三個非常無法控制的概念混在一起使用，而自吹自擂認為可以達到判決的可預測性及法律適用的穩定性[682]，任何有常識的人都會對此加以懷疑。

如果真正的要達成這個目的，唯一的辦法便是完全忽視所牽連的實體法政策，而對個案正義的需求放在法律統一的最高目的下。然而這是歐盟全體同僚的意思，還是只是歐盟羅馬公約及規則之意思？歐盟契約法委員會於論述契約法原則4：110條非個別討論之不公平條款時，對於EC Council Directive 93/13 on Unfair Terms in Consumer Contracts（1993）的列表，認為專業人士間之商業契約是種類繁多，「契約條款的表列本身就是不公平的」，故而是不可能的[683]。如果僅就4：110條非個別討論不公平條款的表列「本身即為不公平」，那麼對「所有契約」的推

---

tract or contracts."
[682] 見羅馬I序言要點6，"The proper functioning of the internal market creates a need, in order to improve the predictability of the outcome of litigation, certainty as to the law applicable and the free movement of judgments, for the conflict-of-law rules in the Member States to designate the same national law irrespective of the country of the court in which an action is brought."
[683] Lando and Beale, p. 266, "Unlike the Directive, the Principle contain no list of clauses deemed to be unfair. In contracts between professional, a listing of contract terms as being per se unfair, because of the diversity of commercial contracts, is generally held to be all but impossible."

定給予硬性規定可能本身「即為更不公平」。**歐盟應如有經驗的英國判例法一般，以契約法之實質政策為解決案件之重心─但所謂的契約法實體政策應明顯的被給予新時代之定義，重點應在扶持弱勢而不在扶持企業的商業功效。這亦是歐盟發展所謂「強行法」概念所應走的新時代路線。亦即必須於契約法維持當事人間之平衡性及訴訟法確保當事人立足點平等及武器對等684之符合個案公平正義之情形下，方能促進商業之功效。**

　　而新時代契約法的實體政策如前述應在監督、控制商業的貪婪、維持社會安全與秩序、及扶持第3世界早日進昇經濟及環保的階梯。歐盟許多的法律應可做為全球化的標竿，故而於運送契約（規則5條）、消費契約（公約5條規則6條）、保險契約（規則7條）、及僱傭契約（公約6條規則8條），歐盟應可以繼續發展其已有之既存實體法規則，而於羅馬公約及規則I中只規定宣示性之政策性原則，放棄現有之區域選法規則所帶來之不穩定及無謂之爭議685。

---

684 英國1998年的Civil Procedure Rules, Rule 1及規定當事人間之「立足點平等」為「超越性之目的」。
　(1) These Rules are a new procedural code with the overriding objective of enabling the court to deal with cases justly.
　(2) Dealing with cases justly includes, so far as practicable –
　　(a) ensuring that the parties are on an equal footing;
　　(b) saving expense;
　　(c) dealing with the case in ways which are proportionate –
　　　(i) to the amount of money involved;
　　　(ii) to the importance of the case;
　　　(iii) to the complexity of the issues; and
　　　(iv) to the financial position of each party;
　　(d) ensuring that it is dealt with expeditiously and fairly; and
　　(e) allotting to it an appropriate share of the court's resources, while taking into account the need to allot resources
　歐盟人權法院於Dombo Beheer v. Netherlands ECtHR Ser. A.274 at para.33(1993)中，對當事人間之「武器對等」亦如此規定："equality of arms implies that each party must be afforded a reasonable opportunity to present his case-including his evidence-under conditions which do not place him at substantial disadvantage vis-à-vis his opponent".
685 有關14條債權轉讓，對於受讓人或其他債權人間之次序並未規定，或許應依the UNIDROIT Principles(2001)第9章的實體規則較為妥適。又見*Francisco J. Garcimartin Alférez, Assignment of claims in the Rome I Regulation: Article 14*, 載於Rome I Regulation: The Law Applicable Contractual Obligations in Europe edited by Franco Ferrari, Stefan Leible, pp.235, 246, "Under the current text, neither

　　另外公約10條規則12條[686]所規定契約準據法之適用範圍為：解釋、履行、責任之消滅及時效、違約之後果及賠償、履行之方式、及無效之後果。公約10(1)(e)條有關契約無效時返還已給付之金錢，於英國是屬於衡平法中之恢復原狀（restitution）及準契約法故英國沒有加入。另一個理由是於10(1)(e)條之準據法若為當事人所指定時，可能會與案件之事實無關，故可能不合適，但英國已加入羅馬 II 規則，故這已不是爭點。其他有關此條之規定，除了時效外，大致上與早期個人所述英國判例法上準據法之功能相似[687]。時效問題已如前述為the Foreign Limitation Periods Act 1984所視為實體法而不成問題。

　　規則12(1)(c)條規定：「於法院地之程序法所給予權力之範圍內，違反全部或部分契約義務之效果，此包含法律所規定的損害之估計。」這應是指有關損害賠償額度之限制規定及契約中預先估計損害賠償之規定等有

---

the conflict between the assignee and the creditors or insolvency administrator of the assignor, nor the conflict between two or more assignees of the same claim are within the scope of the Regulation; both aspects are left to the Private International Law rule (or rules) of each Member State."
"In spite of the differences, there was general consensus on two points:
a)That the third approach-i.e. the law of the assigned claim-was the most appropriate for a particular set of claims: bank deposits, receivables arising from securities, letters of credits, independent guarantees, derivatives, foreign exchange transactions and so forth, i.e. the claims enumerated in Article 4(2) of the UNCITRAL Convention. Many Member States also agreed on the idea that, if the law of the habitual residence of the assignor was eventually adopted as a general rule, this list should probably be expanded.
b)That the second approach-i.e. the law of the assignor-was most appropriate for operations such as factoring, invoice-discounting and other transactions based on the assigment of a mixed portfolio of receivables, specially if that law has established a system of registration or publicity. Third parties have a place and a law where to look for information about the assignor's entitlement and the legal risk assignees take by acquring these entitlements or by perfecting a security interest over them."
[686] Article 12 Scope of the law applicable
1. The law applicable to a contract by virtue of this Regulation shall govern in particular:
(a) interpretation;
(b) performance;
(c) within the limits of the powers conferred on the court by its procedural law, the consequences of a total or partial breach of obligations, including the assessment of damages in so far as it is governed by rules of law;
(d) the various ways of extinguishing obligations, and prescription and limitation of actions;
(e) the consequences of nullity of the contract.
2. In relation to the manner of performance and the steps to be taken in the event of defective performance, regard shall be had to the law of the country in which performance takes place.
[687] 陳隆修，《國際私法契約評論》，台北，五南圖書公司，民國75年2月，初版，7-11頁。

關損害賠償估計之法律。如Dicey and Morris所說：「於英國法有關因果關係及得請求損害賠償之項目之規則，是為實體問題由契約準據法決定，而有關損害賠償之計算或數量之規則，是為程序問題由法院地法決定，這是應有區別的。於契約義務之範圍內，有可能這種區別仍就適用於1990年法案（羅馬公約）。[688]」另外於傳統上衡平法上之救濟，例如禁止命令（injunction）或特別履行之命令（specific performance）通常是被認為屬於程序上之問題，自然是依法院地法而決定[689]。因此違背準據法為外國法之契約之衡平上之救濟，完全是依英國法院地法而決定[690]。於加入羅馬公約後，假處分（interlocutory relief）自然通常仍屬於程序法而由法院地法決定。但10(1)(c)條及12(1)(c)條中所規定「違反契約全部或部分義務之效果」，使得最後的禁止命令或處分的命令亦得由實體準據法而決定。但應注意的是其又規定「於法院地之程序法所給予之權力範圍」，亦

---

[688] Dicey and Morris, pp. 1613, 1614, "In English law a distinction is drawn between rules relating to remoteness and recoverable heads of damage, which are questions of substance governed by the *lex causae*, and rules relating to the measure or quantification of damage, which are questions of procedure governed by the *lex fori*. It is probable that in the field of contractual obligations, this distinction survives the 1990 Act."

個人早期於陳隆修，《國際私法契約評論》，台北，五南圖書公司，民國75年2月，初版，8、9頁中如此寫著：「契約一方當事人所受到的損害是否由於他當事人契約不履行所造成的（remoteness）。英國以前有關此方面（remoteness）的規定皆視為程序法（procedural law），而由法院地之法律規定，近來則視為實體法（substantive law），而由準據法做決定。至於實際上的損害賠償金額（quantity or measure of damages）則仍視為程序法，而由法院地來決定。有關此點大陸法系之學生應加以注意，至於有關損害賠償請求的項目（head of damages）則與成文法系統國家相同，是以準據法為依據。」

Cheshire and North, pp. 598,於損害賠償之估計上，公約第10(1)(c)條之後果應是認為事實問題依法院地法，法律問題則依準據法。"This draw a distinction between circumstances when assessment of damage raises questions of fact and those when it raises questions of law. If the question in relation to assessment is only one of fact (for example, a jury is to calculate the amount of damages) this is a matter purely for the court hearing the action and the applicable law under the Convention will not govern the issue. On the other hand, if the question raised is one of law (the Giulano and Lagarde Report gives as examples cases where the contract prescribes the amount of damages in cases of non-performance or there is an international convention fixing a limit to the right to compensation) then Article 10 (1)(c) will apply." 又見14[th] ed., pp. 756.

[689] Baschet v London Illustrated Standard Co [1900] 1 Ch. 73; Boys v Chaplin [1971] A.C. 356, 394 (Obiter).

[690] *Warner Brothers Pictures Inc v Nelson* [1937] 1 K.B. 209; Evans Marshall 7 Co Ltd v Bertola SA [1973] 1 W.L.R. 349 (CA).

即必須法院地之程序法規所允許的才能被加以執行[691]。故例如其執行須法院經常加以監督，而此為法院所無法執行，則此契約準據法之規定則無法被加以執行。

荷蘭法院於Buenaventura v Ocean Trade Company中，認為「契約被違背之效果」必須被加以寬廣的解釋，因此包含罷工在內[692]。該案中契約之準據法被明示選為菲律賓法，而於鹿特丹境內之沙烏地船之員工實施罷工。荷蘭法院認為依菲律賓法該罷工為非法，故命令他們返回工作職位。1948年聯合國人權宣言29(2)條每個人之自由及權力只應受限於尊重他人之權利及民主社會中道德、公共秩序、及公眾利益之需求[693]。1966年聯合國經濟、社會、及文化權利公約第8條1(d)規定於符合該國法律下，訂約國應保障罷工的權利[694]。歐盟1950年基本權利及人權保護公約17條規定任

---

[691] 羅馬 I 第17條規定抵銷當事人之自主選法，否則依被主張抵銷之債權之準據法，這是為了保護面對被主張抵銷之人。見Michael Hellner, Set-off, 於Rome I Regulation: The Law Applicable to Contractual Obligations in Europe edited by Franco Ferrari, Stefan Leible, pp. 256, 257: "The rationale behind applying the law of the claim against which set-off is declared is that the (main) creditor cannot defend himself against the extinction of his claim and therefore should have the benefit of the protective rules of the law applicable to his own claim. The rule protects the party facing set-off."

大陸法之所以迴避英美法將抵銷務實的視為程序法，（陳隆修，《比較國際私法》，台北，五南圖書公司，78年10月，初版，頁154,155。）乃是為避免當事人選購法院："The problems inherent in the application of the law of the forum are obvious. First of all the law of the forum need not have any connection whatsoever to the contractual obligations involved in the set-off. Applying the lex fori could therefore be quite inequitable. What is more, applying the law of the forum encourages forum shopping and the possibility of forum shopping in its turn leads to a race to the courts." p.254但是大陸法反躬自省的是他們為什麼沒有「不方便方便」的管轄裁量權。選購法院是管轄問題，不是選法問題。

但是至少在抵銷上，不能妨礙當事人生活所必須之費用是個既存的全球化法學規則："In many legal orders there is a prohibition to set off against a claim for, by way of example, salary or mainte-nance. In this context it should be noted that such a prohibition could be internationally mandatory and find application through Article 9 of the Regulation." P258。

[692] [1984] ECC 183, 186.

[693] 2. In the exercise of his rights and freedoms, everyone shall be subject only to such limitations as are determined by law solely for the purpose of securing due recognition and respect for the rights and free-doms of others and meeting the just requirements of morality, public order and the general welfare in a democratic society.

[694] Article 8

1. the States Parties to the present Convenant undertake to ensure:

......

(d) The right to strike, provided that it is exercised in conformity with the laws of the particular country.

何人、組織、或國家不得限制或破壞本公約所保障之權利及自由[695]。歐盟2000年的基本權利憲章15(3)條規定，「被允許於會員國境內工作之第3國之國民，應享有與聯盟公民相同之工作條件」[696]。2000年基本權利憲章28條又規定，「根據聯盟法律、國家法律、及習慣，工人與受僱者，或他們的個別組織，於適當的程度有著洽商及訂定集體協議的權利，並且於利益衝突時，得行使保障他們利益的集體權利，這包括罷工行動。[697]」如前述歐盟契約法原則15：101條規定任何契約違反歐盟會員國法律所認許的基本原則是無效的。其解釋報告B特別舉歐盟公約、歐盟人權公約、及歐盟基本權利憲章為不可違背之基本原則。尤其基本權利憲章的15及28條更是為解釋報告所指出為不可被違背的基本原則。而且如前述，其解釋報告D還特別強調：「不同於15：102條之地位，於決定違反歐盟基本法律原則的契約之效力時，法官與仲裁者並未被給與裁量權：這種契約是根本上就不能給予效力。當事人之意思或知道與否是沒有關連的。[698]」羅馬公約與規則的強行法之概念是其之適用不但超越當事人之協議，於本案例中甚至是超越應適用之準據法的。荷蘭法院這個決定不但違反了羅馬公約及規則，亦違反了包括歐盟契約原則在內之所有契約法基本原則，更糟糕的是其違反了歐盟自己的人權法。

另外公約10(1)(d)條及規則12(1)(d)條有關義務之解除依準據法之規

---

[695] Article 17 – Prohibition of abuse of rights
Nothing in this Convention may be interpreted as implying for any State, group or person any right to engage in any activity or perform any act aimed at the destruction of any of the rights and freedoms set forth herein or at their limitation to a greater extent than is provided for in the Convention.

[696] 3. Nationals of third countries who are authorised to work in the territories of the Member States are entitles to working conditions equivalent to those of citizens of the Union.

[697] Article 28 Right of collective bargaining and action
Workers and employers, or their respective organizations, have, in accordance with Community law and national laws and practices, the right to negotiate and conclude collective agreements at the appropriate levels and, in cases of conflicts of interest, to take collective action to defend their interests, including strike action.

[698] Lando and Clive, p. 212, D. No Discretion
Unlike the position in Article 15:102, the judge or arbitrator is given no discretion to determine the effects of a contract which is contrary to European fundamental principles of law: such a contract is to be given no effect at all. The intentions and knowledge of the parties are irrelevant.

定，亦適用於當事人以新契約之義務取代舊契約義務之情形。但是於公司之合併[699]或合夥章程變更因而合夥人有變化之情形[700]，公約1(2)(e)及規則1(2)(f)條排除這些情況之適用。Dicey and Morris認為於這些情況下應適用原債務人之屬人法[701]。個人早期於National Bank of Greece and Athens S.A. v. Metliss[702]中如此寫著：「一希臘公司A發行債券，債券之準據法為英國法，付款地由債券持有人之選擇得為英國或希臘。A依希臘法律得停止支付債務，後依另一希臘法A與另一希臘公司Y合併為X公司，X公司繼承A及Y之一切權利與義務。因債券之準據法為英國法，故依英國法X不得停止支付債券之持有人。（Graveson教授常常引用此案例為公平正義之代表。）須注意的是公司合併後或合夥發生變化，對外之權利義務不是根據契約關係而來，而是一種繼承關係，根據原債務人之屬人法而來。[703]」這種公司或合夥繼承之問題，基本上是有關公司或合夥之「地位」（status），故自然應依其屬人法較為合理。但個人以為法律邏輯之適用，不若最尊敬的Prof. Graveson以公平正義的理念加以詮釋來得貼切。個人早期於解釋準據法不一定能決定之情況未將其列入是一個遺憾[704]，後來證明於實務上經常有人詢問此問題。

　　另外對海牙會議的創造「慣居地」的概念，個人已於前文質疑其對

---

[699] 見英國the Companies Act 1985, s. 427.

[700] 英國Partnership Act 1890, s. 17.

[701] Dicey and Morris, p. 1617, "Where the substitution of one debtor for another results not from a transaction or from governmental action referring to a particular debt, but from *a succession in universum* jus, as, e.g. in the case of a merger of companies or in connection with the liability of incoming or outgoing partners in the event of a change in the constitution of a partnership, this issue would be outside the scope of the Rome Convention and will be governed by the personal law of the original debtor."

[702] [1958] A.C. 509.

[703] 陳隆修，《國際私法契約評論》，台北，五南圖書公司，民國75年2月，初版，93頁。

[704] 陳隆修，《國際私法契約評論》，台北，五南圖書公司，民國75年2月，初版，11-20頁。例如有大陸仲裁者以契約準據法為大陸法，故拒絕已解散之台灣公司之申請仲裁。依國際法及台灣法，尚有財產之法人應仍被視為清算中之公司。另外更有趣的一法國公司承包台灣一都市之地鐵，該公司被法國政府以違反托辣斯而被分為4個公司。繼承台灣部分之新公司卻被台灣律師主張契約準據法為台灣法，而其時台灣公司法沒有公司分割之規定，而被拒絕請求。此時新公司之地位應依屬人法法國法才是，而且如此主張亦違反合理性及誠信原則，是Prof. Graveson所謂的違反公平正義。該法國新公司無論時效，個人主張仍可請求其權利。

「品質」與「時間長久」的平衡無法拿捏[705]。另外對當事人離棄舊居地而未取的新居地的空檔亦提出質疑[706]。另外更重要的是慣居地對於尊重當事人之意願並未加以充分之尊重，這是泯滅人性的一個做法[707]。個人還如此寫著：「個人雖無法對歐盟其他國家之管轄基礎及行政法規做詳細之研究，但個人相信『一個人於同一時間，為了不同之目的，可以有不同之慣居地』，即使現在還未被正式提出來探討，將來必是歐盟各國及海牙公約不可避免之趨勢。[708]」有趣的是羅馬I 19條[709]及羅馬II 23條除了規定分公司或代理人之職業上行為，其所在地可視為慣居地，尤其又規定自然人之職業行為所在地亦為慣居地[710]。隨著人類文明進展的加快，個人近年來感覺個人之預測實現之速度亦是加快非常多。但如個人先前之建議，個人認為美式住所之定義應是較為符合現代人類社會之需求[711]，個人認為東方

<hr/>

[705] 陳隆修、許兆慶、林恩瑋、李瑞生四人合著，《國際私法—管轄與選法理論之交錯》，台北，五南圖書公司，2009年3月，初版1刷，166、167頁。
[706] 同上，167-172頁。
[707] 同上，172-174頁。
[708] 同上，176頁。
[709] Article 19 Habitual residence
1. For the purposes of this Regulation, the habitual residence of companies and other bodies, corporate or unincorporated, shall be the place of central administration.
The habitual residence of a natural person acting in the course of his business activity shall be his principal place of business.
2. Where the contract is concluded in the course of the operations of a branch, agency or other establishment, or it under the contract, performance is the responsibility of such a branch, agency or establishment, the place where the branch, agency or any other establishment is located shall be treated as the place of habitual residence.
3. For the purposes of determining the habitual residence, the relevant point in time shall be time of the conclusion of the contract.
[710] 有趣的是Rome I 的Recifal 39說明不同於布魯塞爾規則I 第60(1)條對團體之住所可以在管轄權之認定有3個標準，選法規則在慣居地之認定標定只能有一個標準，以達法律適用之可預測性。(39)
For the sake of legal certainty there should be a clear definition of habitual residence, in particular for companies and other bodies, corporate or unincorporated. Unlike Article 60(1) of Regulation (EC) No 44/2001, which establishes three criteria, the conflict-of-law rule should proceed on the basis of a single criterion; otherwise, the parties would be unable to foresee the law applicable to their situation.
另外在Council Regulation (EC) No 2201/2003（布魯塞爾II）第3(1)(a)(5)條規定一年之慣居地期限："the applicant is habitually resident if he or she resided there for at least a year immediately before the application was made"。故而「為了不同目的可以有著不同慣居地」之概念事實上是個已發生的現象。
[711] 陳隆修、許兆慶、林恩瑋、李瑞生四人合著，《國際私法—管轄與選法理論之交錯》，台北，五南圖書公司，2009年3月，初版1刷，180-182頁。

安土重遷之社會應以美式住所為基礎概念。然而為了配合海牙會議，個人建議「以經常居住（ordinary residence；常居地）這個事實上之概念為慣居地之基準。但為尊重當事人之意願及避免慣居地之空檔期，於移民之情形，應特別考慮其是否有長久居住之意願。若其有久住之意願，則於抵達時身體在於該地即應視為慣居於該地。」[712]

羅馬公約及規則 I 的選法方法論是首先以傳統的推定法則為依據，而這個推定程序又以特別推定先於一般推定（亦即特徵性履行）。然後再以最密切關連標準於推定程序不適用時為後備或為規避之法則。最後再以強行法規為基本政策的保障法規（規則 I 為事實唯一關連地、法院地、或履行地之強行法）。推定程序是於英國判例法經歷二百五十年之時空在選法理論上之洗鍊後，被認為「時鐘倒轉」之作法，更遑論大陸法所謂「特徵性履行」之對弱勢所造成之侵犯及不合乎保障社會安全之現代社會之需求。而最密切（重要）關連標準更是戰功輝煌，幾乎其一出生就與主觀說纏鬥近八十年，較近於上世紀之六〇年代更是為美國選法革命風暴核心之一。及至尊敬的 Prof. Reese 逝世前幾年，他還必須以第 2 新編模糊的第 6 條來掩飾最重要關連忽略實體政策的區域選法規則的致命性弱點[713]。而最後所謂強行法的概念，如果其存在的話那麼應是無所不在的。這個偏重實體政策的概念卻莫名其妙的被大陸法以區域選法規則來表達，自然造成全世界包括英美法與大陸法在內皆對其談虎色變。強行法於英國法判例法並無相對的概念，而個人不認為大陸法至今有完全體認到「每個法律於不同的情況下皆是為於不同程度上應被執行的基本政策」之概念。

任何有理智的人都知道把這三個不穩定的概念放在一起是不可能會有穩定而可預測的結果與規則，然而歐盟的財大氣粗卻經常給予其機會去造成隻手遮天之假象—於這三個不穩定之組合下，惟有罔顧個案正義才能達

[712] 陳隆修、許兆慶、林恩瑋、李瑞生四人合著，《國際私法—管轄與選法理論之交錯》，台北，五南圖書公司，2009年3月，初版1刷，239頁。

[713] Will Reese, The Second Restatement of Conflict of Laws Revisited, 34 Mercer L. Rev., 501, 518 (1983)；陳隆修、許兆慶、林恩瑋、李瑞生四人合著，《國際私法—管轄與選法理論之交錯》，台北，五南圖書公司，2009年3月，初版1刷，252-256頁。

成穩定的鐵血規則。Prof. F.A. Mann回覆Prof. P. North對公約的期盼如下：「但是更重要的是以一個宣稱『清楚、穩定的立法架構』，來取代一個已被良好的建立，但是又具彈性且盛行於英國及許多其他國家間相似的判例法，意味著以立法解釋的危險來取代一個健全而可信的制度。正如幾乎公約中的每一行字所已可能證實的，這包含了許多危險及不穩定性，雖然它有些支持者傾向去模糊這些困難。而有些什麼利益是Dr. North所主張的？『整個歐洲共同體重要的和諧性。』直接講白了，為了幫助有些共同體國家去改進他們的法律，英國與有些國家，是被期望去犧牲他們固有而最令人滿意的法律制度中之一。[714]」

二十二、中國思想下的全球化實體規則

　　美國ALI Complex Litigation Proposal的6.01條（侵權行為）及6.02、6.03條（契約行為）對於選法規則之建議為，在其他選法規則之被適用前，應先確認相關連州之法律於適用上是否會有重大衝突，如若於有重大衝突時，再確認相關連州之政策的是否會被促進。故而個人對羅馬公約、規則I、及大中華地區於契約法選法規則之務實建議為：**於適用其選法規則之前先確認所牽連之實體政策是否有重大衝突；另外於適用最密切關連標準時應對實體政策加以考量，而非僅注重於地域性之關連**。事實上第2新編無論於適用契約、侵權、或其他選法規則之前，第6條的基本政策是應被先加以考量的。而更令人欣慰的是崛起中的中國早已氣勢如虹的

---

[714] "Many are likely to have considerable doubts about some parts of this judgment: the basis will be neither clear nor firm; harmonization throughout the EEC leaves the rest of the world out of account; and how the Convention could contribute to 'the free provision of goods and services within the Community' is a mystery. It is, however, much more significant that the substitution of an allegedly 'clear, firm, statutory basis' for the well-established, yet flexible and largely identical judge-made rules prevailing in English as well as in most other countries means the replacement of a sound and trusted instrument by the hazards of statutory interpretation. It involves many dangers and uncertainties, as almost every line of the Convention is likely to prove, though some of the enthusiasts tend to blur the difficulties. And what is the benefit that Dr. North holds out? 'Substantial harmonization throughout the EEC.' To put it more bluntly, in order to enable certain EEC countries to improve their law, Britain, among others, is expected to sacrifice one of the most satisfactory indigenous bodies of law." F.A. Mann, Book Reviews, Vol. 32 I.C.L.Q. 265, 266 (1983).

於國際及國內買賣契約法上，採用全球化實體規則及政策的CISG，而將區域選法規則的「最重要關連」及「特徵性履行」留在時光隧道中。

　　CISG（1980）7(2)條有關公約所未規定之問題，應以其引以為基礎的一般原則為依據之規定[715]，為2004 UNIDROIT Principles的1.6條及歐盟契約法原則1：106條所採納[716]，而U.C.C的s.1-102(1)亦規定該商法應於促進其基本目的及政策下而被解釋及適用[717]，故而個人認為這個規則應是世界契約法全球化之共同核心理念。而CISG的7(1)條又規定「誠信原則」於國際貿易中必須被遵守，相同的規定亦被明示於2004 UNIDROIT Principles之1.7條、歐盟契約法原則1：106條、及美國U.C.C 1-304條。如歐盟契約法原則1：201條[718]亦規定誠信原則應被遵守及不可加以限制，

---

[715] (2) Questions concerning matters governed by this Convention which are not expressly settled in it are to be settled in conformity with the general principles on which it is based or, in the absence of such principles, in conformity with the law applicable by virtue of the rules of private international law.

[716] 其註釋(1)(a)及(b)對英美法與大陸法於此條款之運用上如此評述：

"(a) It is in harmony with the canons of interpretation in the CIVIL LAW countries that statutory provisions are interpreted in accordance with the purposes of the statute and the general principles underlying it. In the civil law countries the courts often extract general principles of law from statutes. This idea was alien to the ENGLISH tradition which was to interpret the statutes narrowly and to find the general principles in the unwritten common law, though now the English courts regularly interpret legislation in the light of its purpose…….

In the UNITED STATES, however, the civil law approach is adopted under the UCC, see §1.102(1): 'This Act should be liberally construed and applied to promote its underlying purposes and policies',

(b) Likewise the idea of supplementation is accepted in the CIVIL LAW countries where the general principles laid down in the statutes may be applied to situations not covered by the language of the statutory provisions. This, however, is not in accordance with the ENGLISH, IRISH and SCOTTISH tradition. English, Irish and Scottish courts will generally not extend statutory provisions by analogy to deal with situations not covered by the words of the statute."

[717] §1-102. Purposes; Rules of Construction; Variation by Agreement.

(1) This Act shall be liberally construed and applied to promote its underlying purposes and policies.

(2) Underlying purposes and policies of this Act are

(a) to simplify, clarify and modernize the law governing commercial transactions;

(b) to permit the continued expansion of commercial practices through custom, usage and agreement of the parties;

(c) to make uniform the law among the various jurisdictions.

(3) The effect of provisions of this Act may be varied by agreement, except as otherwise provided in this Act and except that the obligations of good faith, diligence, reasonableness and care prescribed by this Act may not be disclaimed by agreement but the parties may by agreement determine the standards by which the performance of such obligations is to be measured if such standards are not manifestly unreasonable.

[718] Article 1:201: Good Faith and Fair Dealing

(1) Each party must act in accordance with good faith and fair dealing.

其解釋報告A說：「本條文規定一個貫穿本契約法原則的基本原則。[719]」故而以大陸法主觀之誠信原則，做為全球化實體契約法上「引為基礎的一般原則」之共同核心概念，個人以為應該有相當之依據。而相對的客觀上之合理性之標準，不但為英美法於判例法上所常用之標準，亦如前述為2004 UNIDROIT Principles及歐盟契約法原則所遠較誠信原則所更為被大量引用之標準[720]。並如前述，一般亦經常以客觀之合理性來解釋主觀誠信原則之規定。**故而相較於大陸法之誠信原則，判例法之合理性標準無論是於被引用之數量及品質上亦或許應為契約法之共同核心。亦即誠信原則及合理性標準不但應為全球化實體契約法（包含國際契約法及國際私法）上「引為基礎之一般原則」，亦應為全球化實體契約法（包含國際契約法及國際私法）上之警察原則，以對抗實體法及程序法上之可能於個案上之不公平正義[721]。**

---

(2) The parties may not exclude or limit this duty.

[719] "This Article sets forth a basic principle running through the Principles. Good faith and fair dealing are required in the formation, performance and enforcement of the parties' duties under a contract, and equally in the exercise of a party's rights under the contract."

[720] U.C.C. s.1-102(3)規定誠信、勤勞、及合理性之不可被違背。

[721] 事實上個人認為「合理性」及「誠信原則」亦為21世紀「所有的」全球化法學之「引為基礎之一般原則」及警察原則。例如於司法及立法管轄基礎上，「合理性」原則就一再被引為基礎。見Restatement (Second) of Conflict of Laws §24（1988 Revision）

(1) A stare has power to exercise judicial Jurisdiction over a person if the person's relationship to the State is such as to make the exercise of such jurisdiction reasonable.

(2) The relationships which are sufficient to support an exercise of judicial jurisdiction over a person are stated in §§27-52.

其comment b 則認為「合理性」貫穿整個管轄規則。

b. The basic principle. One basic principle underlies all rules of jurisdiction. This principle is that a state does not have jurisdiction in the absence of some reasonable basis for exercising it. With respect to judicial jurisdiction, this principle was laid down by the Supreme Court of the United States in Interactional Shoe Co. v. State of Washington, 326 U.S. 310 (1945). In that case, the Court stated that for jurisdiction to exist the exercise of jurisdiction by the State must be "reasonable, in the context of our federal system of government" and also that there must be "such minimum contacts" with the State as not to offend "traditional notions of fair play and substantial justice."

又見Restatement of the Law, Third, Foreign Relations Law of the United States, §403 (1987)

§403 Limitations on Jurisdiction to Prescribe

(1) Even when one of the bases for jurisdiction under §402 is present, a state may not exercise jurisdiction to prescribe law with respect to a person or activity having connections with another state when the exercise of such jurisdiction is unreasonable.

其comment a 又認為於不合理之情況下，法院不會去適用管轄規則：

a. Reasonableness in international law and practice. The principle that an exercise of jurisdiction on one

　　上個世紀六〇年代美國前輩同僚為了爭取個案正義，不惜掀起選法革命而企圖推翻機械式法則。2008年11月個人於西安兩岸研討會上主張中華民族應帶領第3世界，要求第一世界依聯合國人權宣言及歐盟人權公約公平的給予弱勢民族訴訟權、財產權、平等權、及適當程序權等應有之基本人權[722]。個人認為無論美國選法革命的要求個案正義，或各民族間要求公平對待，於現代化之社會最好或唯一的辦法就是法律於實質政策上之全球化。無論於那一部門之法律，法律於實質上之全球化不但可消極的避免第一世界於國際私法上令人迷惑的操縱及混淆是非，並且一視同仁的可以探測於個案上真正屬於公平正義的共同核心概念，以確保各種族人民間於個案上之真正公平正義，並而更進一步的維護大同世界之理想。

　　於實質政策全球化之趨勢及思潮下，英國判例法上當事人明示選法、默示選法、及客觀推定選法之適當法三步驟已不是非常重要。如前述傳統上英國判例法對第二級第三步驟之區分並不明顯，羅馬公約及規則Ⅰ對此兩步驟採涇渭分明的作法似乎不十分恰當，但若重點是放在實體法之

---

of the bases indicated in § 402 is nonetheless unlawful if it is unreasonable is established in United States law, and has emerged as a principle of international law as well. There is wide international consensus that the links of territoriality or nationality, § 402, while generally necessary, are not in all instances sufficient conditions for the exercise of such jurisdiction. Legislatures and administrative agencies, in the United States and in other states, have generally refrained from exercising jurisdiction where it would be unreasonable to do so, and courts have usually interpreted general language in a statute as not intended to exercise or authorize the exercise of jurisdiction in circumstances where application of the statute would be unreasonable.

而Restatement (Third) of Foreign Relations Law § 421 (1987).亦規定對人或對物司法管轄權之行使，必須受到合理性之限制。

§ 421 Jurisdiction To Adjudicate

(1) A state may exercise jurisdiction through its courts to adjudicate with respect to a person or thing if the relationship of the state to the person or thing is such as to make the exercise of jurisdiction reasonable.

而更有趣的是ALI/UNIDROIT Principles of Transnational Civil Procedure (2004)的comment P-3A不但認為合理性貫穿整個2004年的管轄規則，並且認為合理性的概念應排除過份技術性的法律論述。The term "reasonable" is used throughout the Principles and signifies "proportional," "significant," "not excessive," or "fair," according to the context. It can also mean the opposite of arbitrary. The concept of reasonableness also precludes hyper-technical legal argument and leaves a range of discretion to the court to avoid severe, excessive, or unreasonable application of procedural norms.所謂排除過份技術性的法律論述，或許就是Cardozo J.所謂的法律邏輯的推演通常應受到常識之限制，及Prof. Graveson 所說的法律邏輯一致性的要求應受限於判例法實現正義的概括目的。而這些21世紀全球化的基本核心法學概念，就是2500年來中國文化「道法自然」之傳統。

[722] 陳隆修，2005年海牙選擇法院協議—是福還是禍？，中國國際私法與比較法年刊，2009，3頁。

全球化上則這個錯誤就不十分重要。尤其是於有關契約或其條款之成立與效力上，因為經常牽涉到契約法之基本政策，故如2004 UNIDROIT Principles art. 3.19一般，許多制度的契約法會將有關這方面之法規視為強行法。故而英國判例法（美國似乎沒有）及羅馬公約及規則所採納的「假設推定準據法」理論（putative proper law doctrine）似乎已面臨被淘汰而成為過眼雲煙之理論依據。而實體法全球化在國際私法的影響上一個非常明顯的例子，即為羅馬規則I 9(3)條的契約履行地法得被遵守之規定。2004 UNIDROIT Principles art. 7.2.2(b)規定，於非金錢債務之履行「於事實上或法律上無法被履行時」，他方不得要求履行。而個人以前早期即主張只要履行地法符合人類文明的公理，契約之履行（包含金錢債務之履行）不得違反履行地法（現今又主張所謂履行包括效果發生地）。後來又闡釋文明的公理為聯合國所有的人權公約、歐盟絕大部分之人權公約、各國憲法之規定（如Due Process Clause）、及契約法（2004 UNIDROIT Principles、歐盟契約法原則、及各國契約法）之基本政策。而本文更進一步主張不限於法律上之無法履行，於事實上如果有合理的困難（例如費用之增加或價值之減少[723]）亦得不履行。無法履行之後果（effects）應如

---

[723] 例如2004 UNIDROIT Principles art. 6.2.2之情形。

Article 6.2.2 (Definition of hardship)

There is hardship where the occurrence of events fundamentally alters the equilibrium of the contract either because the cost of a party's performance has increased or because the value of the performance a party receives has diminished, and

(a) the events occur or become known to the disadvantaged party after the conclusion of the contract;

(b) the events could not reasonably have been taken into account by disadvantaged party at the time of the conclusion of the contract;

(c) the events are beyond the control of the disadvantaged party; and

(d) the risk of the events was not as assumed by the disadvantaged party.

Article 6.2.3 (Effects of hardship)

(1) In case of hardship the disadvantaged party is entitled to entitled to request renegotiations. The request shall be made without undue delay and shall indicate the grounds on which it is based.

(2) The request for renegotiation does not in itself entitle the disadvantaged party to withhold performance.

(3) Upon failure to reach agreement within a reasonable time either party may resort to the court.

(4) If the court finds hardship it may, if reasonable,

(a) terminate the contract at a date and on terms to be fixed, or

(b) adapt the contract with a view to restoring its equilibrium.

歐盟契約法原則15章所規定於個案上依合理性及比例原則而決定是否全部或部分無效、恢復原狀、及損害賠償等問題。

　　20世紀60年代美國選法革命是我們人類文明史上非常輝煌的一頁，美國的前輩同僚們以行動向人類宣示我們的文明已經進展到拋棄死硬、統一的規則，而達到注重個案正義的階段[724]**。隨著中華民族的再次崛起，個人認為21世紀的文明應進一步將個案正義拓展至民族間的正義。第一世界認為理所當然的掠奪式新殖民主義法學，隨著中華民族的再次崛起應壽終正寢。個人認為虛無飄渺的美國選法理論及傳統的區域選法規則（包括最密切關連），不但不能達成個案正義，亦無法維護第3世界的人權。無論是於人權法、憲法、刑法、訴訟法、契約法、公司法、海商法、票據法、親屬繼承法、及破產法等一切法規，法律實質政策全球化之趨勢是不可避免的。於全球化之潮流下，國際私法之重點不再是如過去幾百年來（包括美國新理論在內）以協調各法律制度間之衝突為主，而是在於確認並引導最合適全球化之實體政策。個人又期望階梯式經濟、社會、及法律發展理論的能為兩岸年輕同僚所注意，王道精神更能成為全球化法學之主軸，以期達到禮運大同之祖傳理念，個人認為這亦就是中國法學革命（Chinese legal revolution）的核心價值。不過個人承認中國式法學之最後詮釋權是落在兩岸年輕同僚之手中。**

　　個人以為與其於國際私法的濁水中繼續混亂下去，倒不如正視人類文明已發展到實質政策全球化之既有事實。去年個人即數度舉例說明，例如於Iveco Fiat SpA v. Van Hool NV中歐盟法院判決：「當一書面契約中有包含一管轄條款，並且規定契約只能以書面被更新，該契約在已過期後，

---

[724] 於加拿大最高法院的Pro Swing Inc. v. Elta Golf Inc., 2006 Can, Sup, Ct, LEXIS 52; 2006 SCC 52; [2006] S.C.J, No. 52, para. 1, Deschamps J.認為商業的全球化及人口的流動，使得判例法被要求去改變，「法律與司法正義應是社會的僕人，而並非相反」：
Modern-day commercial transactions require prompt reactions and effective remedies. The advent of the Internet has heightened the need for appropriate tools. On the one hand, frontiers remain relevant to national identlty and jurisdietion, but on the other hand, the globalization of commerce and mobility of both people and assets make them less so. The law and the justice system are servents of society, not the reverse. The Court has been asked to change the common law.

仍繼續被執行，而該契約仍做為當事人契約關係之法律基礎，該管轄條款應可以滿足第17條形式要件之要求，但必須依應適用之準據法，當事人除了以書面外能夠有效的更新契約，或如果相反的，對管轄條款或已被默示更新的整組條款，而管轄條款是其中之一部分，當事人之一已經以書面證實，而他方當事人已受到這個證實的通知並且沒有提出任何異議。[725]」事實上當一個契約已到期，但雖然沒有以書面延期，卻繼續於實際上持續二十年，任何正常有理智（reasonable）之人都會認為契約已被默示延期[726]。

　　歐盟法院於該案中為了維持個案正義，不惜違背布魯塞爾公約17條有關形式要件上之自主性強行法規，對於個案正義與法律一致性終極對立之假象，個人以歐盟契約法原則2：106條之實體規則去打破這個既定的假象。2：106條規定：「(1)一個書面契約中之一條款要求任何修改或終止的協議必須以書面為之，只是建立一個推定，亦即推定除非是以書面，

---

[725] Case 313/85 [1986] E.C.R. 3337, "Article 17 of the Convention of 27 September 1968 on Jurisdiction and the Enforcement of Judgments in Civil and Commercial Matters must be interpreted as meaning that where a written agreement containing a jurisdiction clause and stipulating that an agreement can be renewed only in writing has expired but has continued to serve as the legal basis for the contractual relations between the parties, the jurisdiction clause satisfies the formal requirements in Article 17 if, under the law applicable, the parties could validly renew the original agreement otherwise than in writing, or it, conversely, one of the parties has confirmed in writing either the jurisdiction clause or the set of terms which has been tacitly renewed and of which the jurisdiction clause forms part, without any objection from the other party to whom such confirmation has been notified."

[726] 對該案個人於陳隆修，《2005年海牙法院選擇公約評析》，台北，五南圖書公司，2009年1月，初版1刷，114頁中如此評述：「本案既不符合(a)款書面、(b)款當事人間習慣及(c)款國際商業習慣之要求，但如眾所周知當事人間事實上應有默示契約繼續存在之意圖，歐盟法院於此案上為了維持個案公平正義之判決，不惜違背布魯塞爾公約第17條有關形式要件的自主性強行規定，而以應適用之準據法為依據。如前述歐盟法院一向自豪於管轄條款形式要件之規定，一向對此方面有著自主性的解釋並有著強行法規之意涵，通常並不給予會員國之法律有適用之空間。歐盟法院於第17條近乎完美之規則有了缺失後，只好違背第17條之明示強行規定，而回歸選法規則的『應適用之法律』。所謂應適用之法律到底指的是契約準據法、管轄條款準據法、繫屬法院地法、被指定法院地法（如2005年海牙公約所規定）、契約準據法之putative proper law或管轄條款之putative proper law？而上述有可能之『應適用之法律』是否包含其國際私法之選法規則在內？或putative proper law之確認是否應包含選法條款或管轄條款在內？上面所提之問題相信都有不同的判例及不同之學說之支持，本案所能確定的只是歐盟法院明顯的違背第17條之強行規定及其自主性之主張。」對布魯塞爾公約17條歐盟於形式要件上之強行法自主性規定，見陳隆修，《2005年海牙法院選擇公約評析》，台北，五南圖書公司，2009年1月，初版1刷，111-115頁，又見Mainschiffahrts-Genossenschaft eG (MSG) v. Les Gravieres Rhenanes SARL. Case C-106/95 [1997] E.C.R. I-911, [1997] Q.B. 731.

否則修改或終止契約的協議不是意圖於法律上有拘束力。(2)在他方當事人合理的信賴其言詞或行為之程度下，一方當事人得以其言詞或行為去排除這個條款的主張。[727]」歐盟法院違背（或至少明顯的迴避）第17條形式要件的強行規則，及留下「應適用法律」之難題，看起來似乎令人困惑。但如以歐盟契約法則則第2：106條再加以解釋，則一切問題迎刃而解，法律邏輯清晰可見。故第2：106條之規則至少於歐盟中，不折不扣是個主流核心共同價值。

　　但是事實上類似之概念應不限於歐盟中，2004 UNIDROIT Principles 1.8條規定當事人之不一致使得他方合理的依據其行為應有效力[728]；2.1.4(2)(b)條規定有關受要約人合理的依賴要約[729]；特別是2.1.18條更是幾乎直接與歐盟契約法原則2：106條相對，可能是其大致上之翻版[730]。更為有趣的是U.C.C. s. 2-209[731]有關契約之修改、撤銷、及棄權，於4及5項

---

[727] Article 2:106: Written Modification Only

(1) A clause in a written contract requiring any modification or ending by agreement to be made in writing establishes only a presumption that an agreement to modify or end the contract is not intended to be legally binding unless it is in writing.

(2) A party may by its statements or conduct be precluded from asserting such a clause to the extent that the other party has reasonably relied on them.

[728] Article 1.8 (Inconsistent Behaviour)

A party cannot act inconsistently with an understanding it has caused the other party to have and upon which that other party reasonably has acted in reliance to its detriment.

[729] Article 2.1.4 (Revocation of offer)

(1) Until a contract is concluded an offer may be revoked if the revocation reaches the offeree before it has dispatched an acceptance.

(2) However, an offer cannot be revoked.

(a) if it indicates, whether by stating a fixed time for acceptance or otherwise, that it is irrevocable; or

(b) if it was reasonable for the offeree to rely on the offer as being irrevocable and the offeree has acted in reliance on the offer.

[730] Article 2.1.18 (Modification in a particular from)

A contract in writing which contains a clause requiring any modification or termination by agreement to be in a particular from may not be otherwise modified or terminated. However, a party may be precluded by its conduct from asserting such a clause to the extent that the other party has reasonably acted in reliance on that conduct.

[731] SECTION 2-209. MODIFICATION; RESCISSION AND WAIVER

(1) An agreement modifying a contract within this Article needs no consideration to be binding.

(2) An agreement in a signed record which excludes modification or rescission except by a signed record may not be otherwise modified or rescinded, but except as between merchants such a requirement in a form supplied by the merchant must be separately signed by the other party.

上亦有類似規定。其解釋報告(4)如此評述：「雖然有著2及3項之規定，第4項適用來避免那些只允許有著簽名的書面才可以修改契約的條款，免得當事人於後來真實的行為之法律效果會於其他方面被限制。這種行為於棄權上之效果是再被規定於第5項。[732]」

　　故而個人於此再次重申三十五年來個人一生懸命之論述—「唯有於與案件相關的實體法領域內，國際上能對符合個案公平正義的解決方案達成一致的見解，法律邏輯的一致性才能真正達到。[733]」雖然文化的多元性才是確保人類文明持續的大拇指原則，但個案正義與法律邏輯一致性的迫切需求，於目前唯有實體政策全球化的法學方法論才能兼顧這兩個需求。亦唯有實體政策之全球化，第3世界才能避免第1世界岳不群法則之操弄，以爭取應有之法律人權（例如要求國際公約的規定必須與其國內法一致）。法學多元化之重責可能須由後輩同僚多所擔負。

　　於經歷亞洲金融風暴及2008、2009之世界金融風暴後，全世界之共識（主流共同核心價值）為商業市場（特別是金融市場）必須加以監督及控制[734]，自由市場理論突然於造成禍國殃民之世界性災害後便成過街老

---

(3) The requirements of Section 2-201 must be satisfied if the contract as modified is within its provisions.

(4) Although an attempt at modification or rescission does not satisfy the requirements of subsection (2) or (3), it may operate as a waiver.

(5) A party that has made a waiver affecting an executory portion of a contract may retract the waiver by reasonable notification received by the other party that strict performance will be required of any term waived, unless the retraction would be unjust in view of a material change of position in reliance on the waiver.

[732] 4. Subsection (4) is intended, despite the provisions of subsections (2) and (3), to prevent contractual provisions excluding modification except by a signed writing from limiting in other respects the legal effect of the parties' actual later conduct. The effect of such conduct as a waiver is further regulated in subsection (5).此為舊註釋，但仍被加以保留。

NOTES:

In this amended Section in 2003, the original Official Comments have not been amended and continue to be an effective discussion of the Section as amended. The original official comment has not been amended to reflect the change from "writing" to "record".

[733] 陳隆修，《2005年海牙法院選擇公約評析》，台北，五南圖書公司，2009年1月，初版1刷，115頁。

[734] 事實上歐盟早於金融風暴之前，便明確的要求投資公司必須誠實、公正、及專業的促進市場的完整。見DIRECTIVE 2004/39/EC OF THE EUROPEAN PARLLAMENT AND OF THE COUNCIL of 21 April 2004 on markets in financial instruments,

鼠。相對於大陸法系，英國為資本市場之發源帝國，英國判例法上向來較為傾向奉自由市場放任主義為圭臬。相較之下比起大陸法，英國判例法傳統上較為尊重當事人訂立契約之自由，而較不願介入當事人之所定訂契約之內容[735]。如前述英國判例法於契約法上是注重「商業功效」（com-

---

Article 25

Obligation to uphold integrity of markets, report transactions and maintain records.

1. Without prejudice to the allocation of responsibilities for enforcing the provisions of Directive 2003/6/EC of the European Parliament and of the Council of 28 January 2003 on insider dealing and market manipulation (market abuse) (1), Member States shall ensure that appropriate measures are in place to enable the competent authority to monitor the activities of investment firms to ensure that they act honestly, fairly and professionally and in a manner which promotes the integrity of the Market.

並且亦規定資訊必須以合理的術語而對大眾達成透明化。

Article 44

Pre-trade transparency requirements for regulated markets

1. Member Stares shall, at least, require regulated markets to make public current bid and offer prices and the depth of trading interests at those prices which are advertised through their systems for shares admitted to trading. Member States shall require this information to be made available to the public on reasonable commercial terms and on a continuous basis during normal trading hours.

而第9條及37條更要求投資公司管理人必須有著好聲譽及經驗以確保健全及謹慎之管理。

Article 9

Persons who effusively direct the business

1. Member States shall require the persons who effectively direct the business of an investment firm to be of sufficiently good repute and sufficiently experienced as to ensure the sound and prudent management of the investment firm.

Article 37

Requirements for the management of the regulated market

1. Member States shall require the persons who effectively direct the business and the operations of the regulated market to be of sufficiently good repute and sufficiently experience as to ensure the sound and prudent management and operation of the regulated market. Member States shall also require the operator of the regulated market to inform the competent authority of the identity and any other subsequent changes of the persons who effectively direct the business and the operations of the regulated market.

故而21世紀的全球化法學已有充分的法學科技去防止金融風暴的發生，只是人性對於資本主義所帶來的財富假象之渴望，遠大於追求司法正義的決心。個人真誠的認為我們祖先二千多年來的「不患寡患不均」之王道精神，應為21世紀全球化法學最核心的共同基本政策——而這或許就是黃道教授所主張的「中國法學革命」之真正特色。

[735] 例如歐盟契約法委員會於解釋4:110條有關非個別討論之不公平條款時，即引述英國判例法而認為於不公平條款時，英國判例法之司法監督較大陸法受到限制，即使下級法院認為於契約受到基本上的重大違背時，契約中不公平的免責及限制責任條款應不適用，英國最高法院卻仍為並無此種法律之得可以如此引用（但最高法院對該種契約條款加以嚴格之解釋）。Lando and Beale, p. 270, "In other countries the judicial controls were more limited. For example, in the U.K. there were attempts by the courts to prevent the use of unfair exemption and limitation of liability clauses by holding that they could not apply when there had been a fundamental breach of contract, but the House of Lords held that there was no rule to this effect, though the courts will interpret such clauses narrowly: Suisse Atlantique Société d'Armement Maritime SA v. Rotterdamsche Kolen Centrale NV [1967] 1 A.C.

mercial efficacy；business efficacy），並且於加入歐盟後對大陸法之死
硬作風並不能十分融入。法國同僚Prof. Muir Watt亦舉例說明此方面之不
同[736]。英國法與大陸法對在資訊不對等之情形下所訂之協議的拘束力是有
不同之規定。依英國法除非於有著明顯的詐欺之情形下，否則一個藝術品
交易商得利用其優越的專業知識，以遠低於市場之價格由一不知情之賣方
處買得一有價值的畫。依法國法該交易為無效。「英國法允許有著較好
資訊的當事人為著去得更有利的契約，可以沒有限制的利用其資訊。相
對的，法國法於利用不對稱之資訊以透過契約而取得利益上，對於專業知
識在這種情形之使用是有程度上之限制。[737]」對於這種差異，Prof. Muir
Watt認為在沒有彈性的制度被發現前，就只能以硬性的規定來解決這個衝
突，而可能的方法是「共同參考架構」，或各國契約法最終之統一[738]。

361; Photo Production Ltd v. Securicor Transport Ltd [1980] A.C. 827.”
另外歐盟契約法委員會又於解釋1:201條誠信原則條款時，於Note 1及3一再重申英國及愛爾蘭雖
然不承認誠信原則之義務，但卻以更詳細之法律達成其他法律制度依誠信原則而達成之結果。
故而某種程度上1:201條只是表達英國法律上既有之趨勢。「但英國本著解釋契約而來的方法
論是一種較弱之方法論，因為這種解釋不能超越契約中明確的相反的條款（限制或排除責任條
款），或甚至不能超越案件事實中明確的後果（契約被違背時可能不產生任何嚴重後果之契約
中止權）。因此1:201條代表著英國與愛爾蘭法之一個進步。」Lando and Beale, pp. 116-118, “But
the English approach based on construction of the agreement is a weak one as it cannot prevail against
clear contrary provisions in the agreement (see Photo Production Ltd. v. Securicor Transport Ltd. [1980]
A.C. 827 (H.L.), clauses excluding or limiting liability) or even clear implication from the circumstances (Bunge Corporation v. Tradax SA [1981] 1 W.L.R. 711 (H.L.): right to terminate for breach which
might not have any serious consequences). Thus Article 1:201 represents an advance on English and
Irish law.”

[736] Horatia Muir Watt, Experiences from Europe: Legal Diversity and the Internal Market, 39 Tex. Int'l
L.J. 429. 446 (2004),該案例及內容其引自Hugh Collins, Regulating Contracts for Fairness in Europe 1
(2003).

[737] Muir Watt, p. 446. “An excellent example from general contract law, given by Hugh Collins, concerns
the different rules relating to the effects of information asymmetries on the binding nature of a promise.
Under English law, an art dealer may take advantage of his superior expertise when buying a valuable
painting from an uninformed seller at much less than its market value unless there is a clear case of
fraud. In French law the transaction will be invalid. Thus, “the English rule permits those with better
information to take advantage of it without restriction in order to obtain more favourable contracts. In
contrast, the French rule inhibits the extent to which expertise can be used in situations of information
asymmetry in order to obtain advantages through contract.’”

[738] 同上，“Unless more flexible processes are explored, the only solution to such conflicts is the strait-
jacket, whether in the form of a ‘common frame of reference’ or, ultimately, wholesale unification of
national contract law to ensure proper fit.”

二十三、王道與聯合國人權公約

坦白說做為一個講究人「情」[739]文化的中國人，個人於英國大學時代即震撼於英國制度及判例法的無情。個人不得不讚佩其制度及法律的無情，因為法院及國家不是上帝，一個人如果不保護自己，以法院及國家之能力是無法對所有的人加以全面性之保護，故寧使一家哭，不使一路哭，無情亦是有情。但過去的兩次金融風暴徹底的證明「商業功能」的自私、貪婪、沒有節制。大陸經濟的崛起充分的證明市場功能神話的破滅，控制市場的必要性，今天歐盟於此問題上會有疑慮，乃是由於歐盟之建立基礎是本於「內部市場」利益而來。事實上有關錯誤、詐欺，共同參考架構、歐盟契約法原則、2004 UNIDROIT Principles、及各國內部實體契約法皆有詳細規定，而且通常是屬於基本政策上之強行法規。亦是通常被羅馬公約及規則I列為得超越當事人之協議，或應適用準據法，之強行法規之適用範圍。

個人承認英國判法於此之作法可能於表面上較能促進「商業功效」[740]，但有著13億人口及二千多年持續文化的中華民族須要接受這種促

---

[739] 35年前個人寫中國刑法的碩士論文時，即苦於西方似乎對「情」字沒有完全相對之概念，當時將其翻為"human sentiments"，至今仍無法找出更好的字，西方中國法專家將其認為"compassion"。西方法學認為"justice is blind"，固然表面上是公平。講人情之中國古代法治或許的確有不公平之處，但反面而言，盲目的正義怎會是正義？無情對中國人而言就是無義。全中國的法律學生必須謹記---中國古代法律「情」自是經常出現於正式法典的。自年輕至今個人堅信—無論那一種族—無情無義則不符合構成法律正義之要件。中國式的正義從來就不是求表面平等的天秤式正義，而要求圓滿、不絕對的太極陰陽式正義。實質內容裡陰中有陽，陽中有陰，並求得表面之圓滿。一些（或幾乎全部）中國法制史的西方同僚認為中國古代量刑沒有依據「罪」（"guilt"），故而是侵犯人權。個人35年前即認為西方刑法學量刑「完全」依照被告是否有罪，是可笑的制度。所有的中國人都知道清官不能斷家務事，而事實上許多事情亦不是黑白分明。中國古代刑法是極度發達，個人曾研究極少數之英文中國判例，驚駭莫名的發現中國古代是依「事實量刑」。經過35年這個發現仍然對個人產生極度之震撼。個人至今仍然深信「量刑完全依據被告有罪與否」是個極度簡化而幼稚的法學。對恩師Prof. Jerome Cohen等研究現代中國法，而不先以中國古代法制之「情」、「依事實量刑」、及人本思想為依據，個人於此表達遺憾。但個人亦承認現代文明之進展，使我們研究中國法學時必須更注重我們祖先較為缺乏之個案正義。例如為求得社會秩序之圓滿，是否個案正義會被忽略；而不探究被告之真正犯「罪」，是否人權會被侵犯。相信我們的祖先亦希望中國法學能隨著人類文明而有進展。

[740] Muir Watt, p. 466, "These two positions obviously give rise to very different incentives for investing in the creation of information."另外於p. 459,有同僚以經濟分析來證明有關錯誤之判例法在法國是於經濟上對生產力是不利的，Bernard Rudden, Le Juste et l'Inefficace Pour un Non-Devoir de Renseignements, 84 Revue Trimestrielle de Proit Civil 91, 102-03 (1985).

進「商業功效」的幼稚說法嗎？所有的中國人都知道商人無祖國，更長久
流傳著「人為財死，鳥為食亡」的基本常識。「商業的功效」是需要控
制，而不是促進。個人亦完全承認短期的促進「商業功效」能增進社會經
濟。但是罔顧個案正義或社會正義，一昧追求「商業功效」，除了經濟成
長外，貧富不均亦會加劇。二千多年來我們的祖先一直告誡「不患寡患不
均」，禮運大同篇數千年來一直都是中華民族的根基。奉行自由放任市場
法學的英國有二百年的盛世嗎？美國有一百年的盛世嗎？我們奉行「大
同」理想的民族綿延二千多年，那一種經濟法律哲學才是千年顛撲不破的
基本政策強行主流共同核心價值？以不符合正義的手段刺激市場的病態成
長，潮起潮落，只是促成後代子孫的加速毀滅—中國有二千年的見證。個
人不認同完全的市場經濟或控制經濟，個人追隨我們祖先二千多年來一貫
的「中庸」哲學—無論法律、經濟、或法律經濟學都應採「中庸」哲學，
並隨著情況而適度的調整「中庸」路線。

　　個人以為全球化的契約實體法應摒棄英美法注重市場功效的迷思，
禮運大同的王道精神不但或許應是中國式法學的基礎哲學，更應或許在現
代文明的發展下做為全球化法學之基礎。而階梯式經濟、法律理論，因為
保障第3世界去遵循第1世界過去既有之發展過程中經濟、環保、科技、
及社會之階梯[741]，而循序按步就班發展之生存權，故應是超越聯合國人權
公約及歐盟人權公約之最基本核心之強行法則。個人以為階梯式法律、經
濟、社會、科技、及環保理論，只是公開的承認落後國家務實的追隨先進
國家的發展過程以求得發展、進化的基本生存權而已。基本生存權[742]一無

---

[741] 個人認為聯合國1966之International Covenant on Economic, Social and Cultural Rights之第2 (3)條
規定發展中國家得依據其經濟狀況而決定給予外國人經濟人權之程度，即為階梯人權之承認。
"3. Developing countries, with due regard to human rights and their national economy, may determine
to what extent they would guarantee the economic rights recognized in the present Covenant to non-
nationals." 「階梯理論」（ladder theory）於實際上並非為一個理論，它只是一種對人類現實生活
經驗的敘述。

[742] 聯合國1966之兩個人權公約，International Covenant on Civil and Political Rights及International
Covenant on Economic, Social and Cultural Rights之第1(2)條皆規定各國得在國際法、互利下，不
妨礙國際經濟合作之義務而自由處分其資產，故而美國及歐盟透過不方便法院或過度管轄之高
度法律技術以剝奪第三世界之司法權、財產權、或生存權是違反這個規定的。甚至於2009年為

論第1世界承認與否—自然是超越所有的聯合國及歐盟的人權公約，而為所有法律中最強行的基本政策。或許21世紀的中國式法學應是本著禮運大同的王道祖訓，率領第3世界去逼迫第1世界承認弱小民族的階梯發展生存權。於階梯發展生存權的理論下，即使WTO引為基礎的比較利益經濟哲學亦應適度的讓步，畢竟生存權是最超越性的強行基本政策。或許21世紀可以見證不患寡患不均禮運大同王道式的中國法學[743]，與西方本著

了解決世界金融風暴之問題，美國大量發行美鈔造成第三世界通貨膨脹社會動盪，亦是違反第1(2)條之規定。另外最值得注意的是該第1(2)條規定：「無論如何任何人皆不得被剝奪其生存之依據。」個人認為這即是個人所強調之生存權。"2. All peoples may, for their own ends, freely dispose of their natural wealth and resources without prejudice to any obligations arising out of international economic co-operation, based upon the principle of mutual benefit, and international law. In no case may a people be deprived of its own means of subsistence."
第一世界經常以不方便法院、過度管轄、反托辣斯法、智財法等許多高科技法學而侵犯第三世界人民之生存權，故而個人稱之「掠奪性新殖民地法學」。第一世界所主張的自由貿易、比較經濟利益事實上皆是以這種高技術性掠奪性法學為掩護之後盾，而光明正大的踐踏第三世界人民之生存權及環境權。高舉自由貿易及人權價值的WTO及諾貝爾和平獎卻對第一世界大肆侵害第三世界之生存權及環境權視若未睹，故是21世紀中高技術性的岳不羣機構。

[743] 個人認為聯合國1948的Universal Declaration of Human Rights之序言(Preamble)及第25(1)條是我們2500年來「禮運大同」「王道」文化於21世紀之見證："have determined to promote social progress and better standards of life in larger freedom"；"Everyone has the right to a standard of living adequate for the health and well-being of himself and of his family, including food, clothing, housing and medical care and necessary social services, and the right to security in the event of unemployment, sickness, disability, widowhood, old age or other lack of livelihood in circumstances beyond his control."
事實上我們數千年來歷經不同時空千錘百鍊所凝聚而成之「不患寡患不均」「禮運大同」之「王道」哲學是一再被聯合國高峰會之宣言所揭櫫。1992年之Rio Declaration on Environment and Development規定：
Principle 5.
All States and all people shall cooperate in the essential task of eradicating poverty as an indispensable requirement for sustainable development, in order to decrease the disparities in standards of living and better meet the needs of the majority of the people of the world.
Principle6
The special situation and needs of developing countries, particularly the least developed and those most environmentally vulnerable, shall be given special priority. International actions in the field of environment and development should also address the interests and needs of all countries. .
Principle 7
States shall cooperate in a spirit of global partnership to conserve, protect and restore the health and integrity of the Earth's ecosystem. In view of the different contributions to global environmental degradation, States have common but differentiated responsibilities. The developed countries acknowledge the responsibility that they bear in the international pursuit of sustainable development in view of the pressures their societies place on the global environment and of the technologies and financial resources they command.
而2002年之Johannesburg Declaration on Sustainable Development 亦一再強調全球化所造成貧富不均之問題：
12. The deep fault line that divides human society between the rich and the poor and the ever-increasing

促進利益為基礎的法學之不同處。不過中國式法學最後之詮釋權仍是操之
於兩岸年輕同僚之手中。

gap between the developed and developing worlds pose a major threat to global prosperity, security and stability.

13. The global environment continues to suffer. Loss of biodiversity continues, fish stocks continue to be depleted, desertification claims more and more fertile land, the adverse effects of climate change are already evident, natural disasters are more frequent and more devastating, and developing countries more vulnerable, and air, water and marine pollution continue to rob millions of a decent life.

14. Globalization has added a new dimension to these challenges. The rapid integration of markets, mobility of capital and significant increases in investment flows around the world have opened new challenges and opportunities for the pursuit of sustainable development. But the benefits and costs of globalization are unevenly distributed, with developing countries facing special difficulties in meeting this challenge.

15. We risk the entrenchment of these global disparities and unless we act in a manner that fundamentally changes their lives the poor of the world may lose confidence in their representatives and the democratic systems to which we remain committed, seeing their representatives as nothing more than sounding brass or tinkling cymbals.

於2010年黃進教授與個人皆同意或許21世紀的中國式法學大致上應以「王道」為共同核心基礎。21世紀的全球化法學是應以上述數個聯合國宣言作為法學上引為最基礎之基本原則及於個案上對抗程序法或實體法上所可能產生之不公平之警察原則。而上述的聯合國宣言又與我們2500年來之「禮運大同」「不患寡患不均」之「王道」思想一致，故21世紀之全球化法學以中國「王道」思想為共同核心基本政策，似乎是一種符合正義及人類生活常識的「自然道法」。

國家圖書館出版品預行編目資料

中國思想下的全球化選法規則／陳隆修著.
 ――初版. ――臺北市：五南，2012.07
　面；　公分
　ISBN 978-957-11-6667-4（平裝）
1.國際私法　2.論述分析
579.9　　　　　　　　101007924

1T79

中國思想下的全球化選法規則

作　　者 ― 陳隆修

發 行 人 ― 楊榮川

總 編 輯 ― 王翠華

主　　編 ― 林振煌

責任編輯 ― 李奇蓁

封面設計 ― P. Design視覺企劃

出 版 者 ― 五南圖書出版股份有限公司

地　　址：106台北市大安區和平東路二段339號4樓

電　　話：(02)2705-5066　傳　　真：(02)2706-6100

網　　址：http://www.wunan.com.tw

電子郵件：wunan@wunan.com.tw

劃撥帳號：01068953

戶　　名：五南圖書出版股份有限公司

台中市駐區辦公室/台中市中區中山路6號

電　　話：(04)2223-0891　傳　　真：(04)2223-3549

高雄市駐區辦公室/高雄市新興區中山一路290號

電　　話：(07)2358-702　傳　　真：(07)2350-236

法律顧問　元貞聯合法律事務所　張澤平律師

出版日期　2012年7月初版一刷

定　　價　新臺幣480元